Philosophy Matters

Anthony J. Lisska
Denison University

Charles E. Merrill Publishing Company
A Bell & Howell Company
Columbus   Toronto   London   Sydney

Published by
Charles E. Merrill Publishing Company
A Bell & Howell Company
Columbus, Ohio 43216

This book was set in Century Light and Helios.
The Production Editor was Linda Lowell.
The cover was designed by Will Chenoweth.

Library of Congress Catalog Card Number: 76-27994

ISBN: 0-675-08592-6

1 2 3 4 5 6 7 — 82 81 80 79 78 77

Printed in the United States of America

In Memory of

SHARON C. MACMILLAN

(1941–1976)

whose all too short life admirably
exemplified the characteristics of
Aristotle's magnanimous person

Acknowledgments

This book has been a long time in the making, perhaps too long. The author owes a special word of thanks to many people who were extremely helpful in the writing of the text and the preparation of the final manuscript for publication. A word of thanks goes to Roger Ratliff, formerly of Charles E. Merrill Publishing Company, who generously supported the original proposal for this book from a fledgling young philosopher. A special note of thanks goes to Fred Kinne, Administrative Editor for Philosophy at Charles E. Merrill, whose patience and understanding certainly exceeds that of Job. Mrs. Miriam Blake and Mrs. Flic Marshall, the two nicest secretaries in the world, graciously undertook the tedious task of typing the final manuscript. Ron Clark was extremely helpful in proofreading and making editorial suggestions for the first four chapters. Linda Lowell, production editor at Charles E. Merrill, made many very helpful and useful editorial suggestions. And finally, Marianne Lisska, who proofread, edited, reread, and generally worried with the author over what an introductory book in philosophy ought to be, deserves a public word of thanks and gratitude.

Contents

chapter 3   Descartes and the Rationalist Tradition   111

chapter 4   The Empiricists: Establishing a Methodology   179

Preface

This book grew out of the author's desire to see a beginning book in philosophy which provided the reader with exposure to the written work of both classical and contemporary philosophers and yet contained instructive commentary suitable to a reader coming to philosophy for the first time. This book hovers in that middle ground between an ordinary anthology and a straightforward textbook. A standard book of readings certainly provides the beginning reader with ample opportunity to confront philosophical texts directly. Nonetheless, without the aid of detailed commentary, readers unfamiliar with the general thrust of philosophical problems often become bewildered in a bundle of learning problems.

Obviously, a clear and lucid textbook can solve this problem. However, a standard textbook of itself precludes the possibility for the reader to experience first-hand extended passages from the writings of significant philosophers, be it selections from Plato's *Republic,* Descartes' *Meditations,* or Sartre's *Existentialism.* This book attempts to find a middle ground pedagogically appropriate for beginning students in philosophy. The present volume incorporates lengthy passages from the writings of both classical and contemporary philosophers together with extended commentary by the author explicating the nature of the philosophical problems under discussion. In this way, the beginning reader will have the educational experience of working through some significant philosophical texts and the additional advantage of having in the same volume extended commentary providing information and analysis useful in facilitating the process of philosophical understanding.

An additional feature of this volume should be noted. Each chapter begins with ordinary and elemental discussions and proceeds to somewhat more complicated and involved analysis near the end of the chapter. The final pages of each chapter contain selections and discussions indicating how philosophers today analyze the issues encountered in the body of the chapter. Hence, the instructor has the opportunity and advantage of choosing the level and the amount of detail and complexity desired for meeting the pedagogical needs of individual classes.

one

Philosophy as an Activity

The Nature of Philosophical Inquiry

Philosophy is derived from two Greek words, *philos* (love) and *sophia* (wisdom). Philosophy etymologically means the "love of wisdom." The Greeks had a unique notion of wisdom. The wise person—the person who possessed the habit of wisdom—not only had knowledge but, rather, possessed a special kind of knowledge. Wisdom was defined as a knowledge of things through their proper and appropriate causes. A proper cause was equal to an ultimate explanation or ultimate justification. An explanation of this kind occurred when a person knew the "reasons why" regarding any event or thing. For example, in matters pertaining to morality, the wise person not only knew *that* stealing was wrong, but he or she also knew *why* it was wrong. In other words, the wise person could give clearly reasoned grounds why stealing was an immoral action. For the Greek philosophers, therefore, the "why" question was the matter for philosophical activity.

The basis for the philosophical enterprise as envisaged by the Greeks is found in the first sentence of Aristotle's philosophical treatise, the *Metaphysics:* "All persons, by nature, desire to know." Aristotle further claimed that when we *really knew,* then we possessed wisdom. That there were solutions to the problems confronting philosophers—problems about the conditions of knowledge, the basic categories of reality, the notion of God, and the nature of right and wrong actions—was granted by Aristotle. As we shall soon see, not all philosophers have shared his optimism. Nevertheless philosophers have continued to seriously confront the many issues to which we ask "why?" The conditions both necessary and sufficient toward establishing the resolution of these

1

questions pertain to the activity of philosophy. Philosophy, then, is not so much a handbook of ready-made answers as it is a serious intellectual attempt to "come to terms" with some of the many puzzles which confound the human mind both about human existence and the outside world. As Socrates put it, "The unexamined life is not worth living."

We might look at the matter in another way. Not all philosophers will agree with the following account about the nature of philosophical activity. Nonetheless it will provide a basis for beginning our inquiry into matters philosophical. A philosopher, it might be said, provides an analysis of the "truths" of common sense. The basic starting point of philosophical reflection is our "common sense" awareness of both ourselves and the world around us. The medieval philosopher, Thomas Aquinas, stated the matter as *primum vivere, deinde philosophari*, which, roughly translated, means "First you must have many experiences and only afterwards are you ready to philosophize." It is only after we have had many experiences encountering ourselves, others, the world around us, and the relations of all of these to our modes of awareness that each of us is ready to reflect on these experiences. To be meaningful, therefore, philosophy demands as a necessary condition a rich experience of ourselves, of other persons, and of objects found in the world around us.

When philosophy is looked upon in this manner, it becomes an attempt to make our common sense experience "hang together" in some sort of unified whole. For example, in reflecting upon the manner in which we acquire knowledge, it is obvious that much of what we know is gained by means of our five external senses. Yet we may rightly wonder—do we have any other means of knowledge besides direct sense experience? This question concerning the nature and limits of knowledge is an important philosophical question. Of course, we need not concern ourselves about the details of this controversy now. Our concern now is to gain a primitive awareness of the type of intellectual activity philosophy is. Yet unless one has experienced different types of knowledge— e.g., knowing that an acid and a base yield a soluble salt and water; that the square of the hypotenuse is equal to the square of the sum of the two sides; that murder is wrong; that sometimes our senses deceive us, and so on—then philosophy will not be an interesting inquiry. Throughout the time spent pondering the texts in this book, it is important that the student always try to relate the questions under discussion to personal experiences. Keep in mind that philosophy is basically a reflective activity about other experiences. Without these other experiences, the activity of philosophy cannot proceed in any meaningful way.

The twentieth-century British philosopher, C.D. Broad, characterizes the activity of philosophy in a twofold manner—critical philosophy and speculative philosophy. Consider carefully the following account from Broad's *Scientific Thought*, which is a famous passage describing the nature of philosophical activity.

I shall devote this introductory chapter to stating what I think Philosophy is about, and why the other sciences are important to it and it is important to the other sciences. A very large number of scientists will begin such a book as this with the strong conviction that Philosophy is mainly moonshine, and with the gravest doubts as to whether it has anything of the slightest importance to tell them. I do not think that this view of Philosophy is true, or I should not waste my time and cheat my students by trying to teach it. But I do think that such a view is highly plausible, and that the proceedings of many philosophers have given the general public some excuse for its unfavourable opinion of Philosophy. I shall therefore begin by stating the case against Philosophy as strongly as I can, and shall then try to show that, in spite of all objections, it really is a definite science with a distinct subject-matter. I shall try to show that it really does advance and that it is related to the special sciences in such a way that the co-operation of philosophers and scientists is of the utmost benefit to the studies of both.

I think that an intelligent scientist would put his case against Philosophy somewhat as follows. He would say: "Philosophers discuss such subjects as the existence of God, the immortality of the soul, and the freedom of the will. They spin out of their minds fanciful theories, which can neither be supported nor refuted by experiment. No two philosophers agree, and no progress is made. Philosophers are still discussing with great heat the same questions that they discussed in Greece thousands of years ago. What a poor show does this make when compared with mathematics or any of the natural sciences! Here there is continual steady progress; the discoveries of one age are accepted by the next, and become the basis for further advances in knowledge. There is controversy indeed, but it is fruitful controversy which advances the science and ends in definite agreement; it is not the aimless wandering in a circle to which Philosophy is condemned. Does this not very strongly suggest that Philosophy is either a mere playing with words, or that, if it has a genuine subject-matter, this is beyond the reach of human intelligence?"

Our scientist might still further strengthen his case by reflecting on the past history of Philosophy and on the method by which it is commonly taught to students. He will remind us that most of the present sciences started by being mixed up with Philosophy, that so long as they kept this connexion they remained misty and vague, and that as soon as their fundamental principles began to be discovered they cut their disreputable associate, wedded the experimental method, and settled down to the steady production of a strapping family of established truths. Mechanics is a case in point. So long as it was mixed up with Philosophy it made no progress; when the true laws of motion were discovered by the experiments and reasoning of Galileo it ceased to be part of Philosophy and began to develop into a separate science. Does this not suggest that the subject-matter of Philosophy is just that ever-diminishing fragment of the universe in which the scientist has not yet discovered laws,

From C.D. Broad, *Scientific Thought* (London: Routledge and Kegan Paul, Ltd.; Atlantic Highlands, N.J.: Humanities Press, 1927), pp. 11–22. Reprinted by permission of both publishers.

and where we have therefore to put up with guesses? Are not such guesses the best that Philosophy has to offer; and will they not be swept aside as soon as some man of genius, like Galileo or Dalton or Faraday, sets the subject on the sure path of science?

Should our scientist talk to students of Philosophy and ask what happens at their lectures, his objections will most likely be strengthened. The answer may take the classical form: "He tells us what everyone knows in language that no one can understand." But, even if the answer be not so unfavourable as this, it is not unlikely to take the form: "We hear about the views of Plato and Kant and Berkeley on such subjects as the reality of the external world and the immortality of the soul." Now the scientist will at once contrast this with the method of teaching in his own subject, and will be inclined to say, if *e.g.* he be a chemist: "We learn what *are* the laws of chemical combination and the structure of the Benzene nucleus, we do not worry our heads as to what exactly Dalton thought or Kekule said. If philosophers really know anything about the reality of the external world why do they not say straightforwardly that it is real or unreal, and prove it? The fact that they apparently prefer to discuss the divergent views of a collection of eminent 'back-numbers' on the question strongly suggests that they know that there is no means of answering it, and that nothing better than groundless personal opinions can be offered."

I have put these objections as strongly as I can, and I now propose to see just how much there is in them. First, as to the alleged unprogressive character of Philosophy. This is, I think, an illusion; but it is a very natural one. Let us take the question of the reality of the external world as an example. Commonsense says that chairs and tables exist independently of whether anyone happens to perceive them or not. We study Berkeley and find him claiming to prove that such things can only exist so long as they are perceived by someone. Later on we read some modern realist, like Alexander, and we are told that Berkeley was wrong, and that chairs and tables can and do exist unperceived. We seem merely to have got back to where we started from, and to have wasted our time. But this is not really so, for two reasons. (i) What we believe at the end of the process and what we believed at the beginning are by no means the same, although we express the two beliefs by the same form of words. The original belief of common-sense was vague, crude and unanalysed. Berkeley's arguments have forced us to recognize a number of distinctions and to define much more clearly what we mean by the statement that chairs and tables exist unperceived. What we find is that the original crude belief of common-sense consisted of a number of different beliefs, mixed up with each other. Some of these may be true and others false. Berkeley's arguments really do refute or throw grave doubt on some of them, but they leave others standing. Now it may be that those which are left are enough to constitute a belief in the independent reality of external objects. If so this final belief in the reality of the external world is much clearer and subtler than the *verbally* similar belief with which we began. It has been purified of irrelevant factors, and is no longer a vague mass of different beliefs mixed up with each other.

(ii) Not only will our final belief differ in content from our original one, it will also differ in certainty. Our original belief was merely instinctive, and was at the mercy of any sceptical critic who chose to cast doubts on it. Berkeley has played this part. Our final belief is that part or that modification of our original one that has managed to survive his criticisms. This does not of course *prove* that it is true; there may be other objections to it. But, at any rate, a belief that has stood the criticisms of an acute and subtle thinker, like Berkeley, is much more likely to be true than a merely instinctive belief which has never been criticised by ourselves or anyone else. Thus the process which at first sight seemed to be merely circular has not really been so. And it has certainly not been useless; for it has enabled us to replace a vague belief by a clear and analysed one, and a merely instinctive belief by one that has passed through the fire of criticism.

The above example will suggest to us a part at least of what Philosophy is really about. Common-sense constantly makes use of a number of concepts, in terms of which it interprets its experience. It talks of *things* of various kinds; it says that they have *places* and *dates,* that they *change,* and that changes in one *cause* changes in others, and so on. Thus it makes constant use of such concepts or categories as thinghood, space, time, change, cause, etc. Science takes over these concepts from common-sense with but slight modification, and uses them in its work. Now we can and do *use* concepts without having any very clear idea of their meaning or their mutual relations. I do not of course suggest that to the ordinary man the words *substance, cause, change,* etc., are mere meaningless noises, like *Jabberwock* or *Snark.* It is clear that we mean something, and something different in each case, by such words. If we did not we could not use them consistently, and it is obvious that on the whole we do consistently apply and withhold such names. But it is possible to apply concepts more or less successfully when one has only a very confused idea as to their meaning. No man confuses place with date, and for practical purposes any two men agree as a rule in the places that they assign to a given object. Nevertheless, if you ask them what exactly they mean by *place* and *date,* they will be puzzled to tell you.

Now the most fundamental task of Philosophy is to take the concepts that we daily use in common life and science, to analyse them, and thus to determine their precise meanings and their mutual relations. Evidently this is an important duty. In the first place, clear and accurate knowledge of anything is an advance on a mere hazy general familiarity with it. Moreover, in the absence of clear knowledge of the meanings and relations of the concepts that we use, we are certain sooner or later to apply them wrongly or to meet with exceptional cases where we are puzzled as to how to apply them at all. For instance, we all agree pretty well as to the place of a certain pin which we are looking at. But suppose we go on to ask: "Where is the image of than pin in a certain mirror; and is it in this place (whatever it may be) in precisely the sense in which the pin itself is in *its* place?" We shall find the question a very puzzling one, and there will be no hope of answering it until we have carefully analysed what we mean by *being in a place.*

Again, this task of clearing up the meanings and determining the relations of fundamental concepts is not performed to any extent by any other science. Chemistry *uses* the notion of substance, geometry that of space, and mechanics that of motion. But they assume that you already know what is meant by *substance* and *space* and *motion.* So you do in a vague way; and it is not their business to enter, more than is necessary for their own special purposes, into the meaning and relations of these concepts as such. Of course the special sciences do in some measure clear up the meanings of the concepts that they use. A chemist, with his distinction between elements and compounds and his laws of combination, has a clearer idea of substance than an ordinary layman. But the special sciences only discuss the meanings of their concepts so far as this is needful for their own special purposes. Such discussion is incidental to them, whilst it is of the essence of Philosophy, which deals with such questions for their own sake. Whenever a scientist begins to discuss the concepts of his science in this thorough and disinterested way we begin to say that he is studying, not so much Chemistry or Physics, as the *Philosophy* of Chemistry or Physics. It will therefore perhaps be agreed that, in the above sense of Philosophy, there is both room and need for such a study, and that there is no special reason to fear that it will be beyond the compass of human faculties.

At this point a criticism may be made which had better be met at once. It may be said: "By your own admission the task of Philosophy is purely verbal; it consists entirely of discussions about the meanings of words." This criticism is of course absolutely wide of the mark. When we say that Philosophy tries to clear up the meanings of concepts we do not mean that it is simply concerned to substitute some long phrase for some familiar word. Any analysis, when once it has been made, is naturally *expressed* in words; but so too is any other discovery. When Cantor gave his definition of Continuity, the final result of his work was expressed by saying that you can substitute for the word "continuous" such and such a verbal phrase. But the essential part of the work was to find out exactly what properties are present in objects when we predicate continuity of them, and what properties are absent when we refuse to predicate continuity. This was evidently not a question of words but of things and their properties.

Philosophy has another and closely connected task. We not only make continual use of vague and unanalysed concepts. We have also a number of uncriticized beliefs, which we constantly assume in ordinary life and in the sciences. We constantly assume, *e.g.* that every event has a cause, that nature obeys uniform laws, and that we live in a world of objects whose existence and behaviour are independent of our knowledge of them, and so on. Now science takes over these beliefs without criticism from common-sense, and simply works with them. We know by experience, however, that beliefs which are very strongly held may be mere prejudices. . . . Is it not possible that we believe that nature as a whole will always act uniformly simply because the part of nature in which the human race has lived has happened to act so up to the present? All such beliefs, then, however deeply rooted, call for criticism. The first duty of Philosophy is to state them clearly; and this can only be done when we have analysed and defined the concepts that they involve. Until you know exactly what you mean by *change* and *cause* you cannot know what is meant by the statement that *every change has a cause.* And not much weight can be attached to a person's most passionate beliefs if he does not know what precisely he is passionately believing. The next duty of Philosophy is to test such beliefs; and this can only be done by resolutely and honestly exposing them to every objection that one can think of oneself or find in the writings of others. We ought only to go on believing a proposition if, at the end of this process, we still find it impossible to doubt it. Even then of course it may not be true, but we have at least done our best.

These two branches of Philosophy—the analysis and definition of our fundamental concepts, and the clear statement and resolute criticism of our fundamental beliefs—I call *Critical Philosophy*. It is obviously a necessary and a possible task, and it is not performed by any other science. The other sciences *use* the concepts and *assume* the beliefs; Critical Philosophy tries to analyse the former and to criticise the latter. Thus, so long as science and Critical Philosophy keep to their own spheres, there is no possibility of conflict between them, since their subject-matter is quite different. Philosophy claims to analyze the general concepts of substance and cause, *e.g.* it does not claim to tell us about particular substances, like gold, or about particular laws of causation, as that *aqua regia* dissolves gold. Chemistry, on the other hand, tells us a great deal about the various kinds of substances in the world, and how changes in one cause changes in another. But it does not profess to analyse the general concepts of substance or causation, or to consider what right we have to assume that every event has a cause.

It should now be clear why the method of Philosophy is so different from that of the natural sciences. Experiments are not made, because they would be utterly useless. If you want to find out how one substance behaves in presence of another you naturally put the two together, vary the conditions, and note the results. But no experiment will clear up your ideas as to the meaning of *cause* in general or of *substance* in general. Again, all conclusions from experiments rest on some of those very assumptions which it is the business of Philosophy to state clearly and to criticise. The experimenter assumes that nature obeys uniform laws, and that similar results will follow always and everywhere from sufficiently similar conditions. This is one of the assumptions that Philosophy wants to consider critically. The method of Philosophy thus resembles that of pure mathematics, at least in the respect that neither has any use for experiment.

There is, however, a very important difference. In pure mathematics we start either from axioms which no one questions, or from premises which are quite explicitly assumed merely as hypotheses; and our main interest is to deduce remote consequences. Now most of the tacit assumptions of ordinary life and of natural science claim to be true and not merely to be hypotheses, and at the same time they are found to be neither clear nor self-evident when critically reflected upon. Most mathematical axioms are very simple and clear, whilst most other propositions which men strongly believe are highly complex and confused. Philosophy is mainly concerned, not with remote conclusions, but with the analysis and appraisement of the original premises. For this purpose analytical power and a certain kind of insight are necessary, and the mathematical method is not of much use.

Now there is another kind of Philosophy; and, as this is more exciting, it is what laymen generally understand by the name. This is what I call *Speculative Philosophy*. It has a different object, is pursued by a different method, and leads to results of a different degree of certainty from Critical Philosophy. Its object is to take over the results of the various sciences, to add to them the results of the religious and ethical experiences of mankind, and then to reflect upon the whole. The hope is that, by this means, we may be able to reach some general conclusions as to the nature of the Universe, and as to our position and prospects in it.

There are several points to be noted about Speculative Philosophy. (i) If it is to be of the slightest use it must presuppose Critical Philosophy. It is useless to take over masses of uncriticised detail from the sciences and from the ethical and religious experiences of men. We do not know what they mean, or what degree of certainty they possess till they have been clarified and appraised by Critical Philosophy. It is thus quite possible that the time for Speculative Philosophy has not yet come; for Critical Philosophy may not have advanced far enough to supply it with a firm basis. In the past people have tended to rush on to Speculative Philosophy, because of its greater practical interest. The result has been the production of elaborate systems which may quite fairly be described as moonshine. The discredit which the general public quite rightly attaches to these hasty attempts at Speculative Philosophy is reflected back on Critical Philosophy, and Philosophy as a whole thus falls into undeserved disrepute.

(ii) At the best Speculative Philosophy can only consist of more or less happy guesses, made on a very slender basis. There is no hope of its reaching the certainty which some parts of Critical Philosophy might quite well attain. Now speculative philosophers as a class have been the most dogmatic of men. They have been more certain of everything than they had a right to be of anything.

(iii) A man's final view of the Universe as a whole, and of the position and prospects of himself and his fellows, is peculiarly liable to be biased by his hopes and fears, his likes and dislikes, and his judgments of value. One's Speculative Philosophy tends to be influenced to an altogether undue extent by the state of one's liver and the amount of one's bank-balance. No doubt livers and bank-balances have their place in the Universe, and no view of it which fails to give them their due weight is ultimately satisfactory. But their due weight is considerably less than their influence on Speculative Philosophy might lead one to suspect. But, if we bear this in mind and try our hardest to be "ethically neutral," we are rather liable to go to the other extreme and entertain a theory of the Universe which renders the existence of our judgments of value unintelligible.

A large part of Critical Philosophy is almost exempt from this source of error. Our analysis of truth and falsehood, or of the nature of judgment, is not very likely to be influenced by our hopes and fears. Yet even here there is a slight danger of intellectual dishonesty. We sometimes do our Critical Philosophy, with half an eye on our Speculative Philosophy, and accept or reject beliefs, or analyse concepts in a certain way, because we feel that this will fit in better than any alternative with the view of Reality as a whole that we happen to like.

(iv) Nevertheless, if Speculative Philosophy remembers its limitations, it is of value to scientists, in its methods, if not in its results. The reason is this. In all the sciences except Philosophy we deal with objects and their changes, and leave out of account as far as possible the mind which observes them. In Psychology, on the other hand, we deal with minds and their processes, and leave out of account as far as possible the objects that we get to know by means of them. A man who confines himself to either of these subjects is likely therefore to get a very one-sided view of the world. The pure natural scientist is liable to forget that minds exist, and that if it were not for them he could neither know nor act on physical objects. The pure psychologist is inclined to forget that the main business of minds is to know and act upon objects; that they are most intimately connected with certain portions of matter; and that they have apparently arisen gradually in a world which at one time contained nothing but matter. Materialism is the characteristic speculative philosophy of the pure natural scientist, and subjective idealism that of the pure psychologist. To the scientist subjective idealism seems a fairy tale, and to the psychologist materialism seems sheer lunacy. Both are right in their criticisms, but neither sees the weakness of his own position. The truth is that both these doctrines commit the fallacy of over-simplification; and we can hardly avoid falling into some form of this unless at some time we make a resolute attempt to think *synoptically* of all the facts. Our *results* may be trivial; but the *process* will at least remind us of the extreme complexity of the world, and teach us to reject any cheap and easy philosophical theory. . . .

———————————

In the preceding passage Broad delineates two functions for philosophers: (a) the *critical* function and (b) the *speculative* function. From the text it is obvious that Broad thinks more highly of critical philosophy than he does of speculative philosophy. As we shall soon see, not all philosophers have held speculative philosophy in disdain.

Even though we shall consider both types of philosophy in our inquiry into the philosophical enterprise, it is important that one immerse oneself in critical philosophy from the beginning. The activity of philosophy is best exemplified when one does a good job at critical philosophy. And critical philosophy, as Broad has suggested, is best described as the activity of examining the fundamental presuppositions and assumptions of every facet of human experience. Keep in mind Broad's suggestion about the nature of critical philosophy: " . . . the analysis and definition of our fundamental concepts, and the clear statement and resolute criticism of our fundamental beliefs. . . ."

The student beginning his/her inquiry into philosophical problems should note the following suggestion: one of the best ways to acquire this critical attitude so important in analyzing presuppositions of experiences is to seriously and attentively read the texts of past philosophers who have already confronted these questions so central to human existence. We must take the writers seriously. We must become absorbed with their problems and solutions. Of course this never means that we adopt a particular position just because a famous philosopher has argued it. Rather, it means that we see how they operate, how they function. To be absorbed means to ask "Why does this philosopher make this claim?" After seeing for ourselves why a philosopher makes a claim, we must *critically evaluate* the claim. Is the philosopher adequately posing the problem? Does the purported solution fit the bill for the problem considered? By actively engaging oneself in this way, the student will learn the "tools of the philosophical trade," and will gain the skills necessary to success-fully practice the activity of critical philosophy.

When beginning our encounter with the philosophical texts contained in this book, we constantly must be aware of the following three questions:

1. What does the philosopher *mean* by the claims made?
2. What kind of *rational support* does the philosopher provide for these claims?
3. Do these claims *satisfy me* as a person engaged in the activity of philos-ophy—i.e., are the claims clearly and sufficiently reasoned.

Through active participation with the philosopher, by asking oneself these questions, one will acquire the skills necessary to successfully practice critical philosophy. If, however, one remains passive in this inquiry and reads the philo-sophical texts in a matter-of-fact way, then philosophy will become nothing more than a string of inert facts which have little or no relation to one's sense of human existence.

While discussing the activity of philosophy, the distinction made by a con-temporary philosopher, Gilbert Ryle, between "knowing that" and "knowing how" will shed light on this active process so central to the successful practice of critical philosophy. In the following passage pay close attention to the rea-sons Ryle provides in justifying his distinction.

. . . A familiar and indispensable part or sort of teaching consists in teaching by rote lists of truths or facts, for example the proposition that 7 X 7 is 49, etc., the proposition that Waterloo was fought in 1815, etc., and the proposition that Madrid is the capital of Spain, etc. That the pupil has learned a lesson of this propositional sort is shown, in the first instance, by his being able and reasonably ready to reproduce word-perfectly these pieces of information. He gets them by heart, and he can come out with them on demand. Now every teacher knows that only a vanishingly small fraction of his teaching-day really consists in simply reciting lists of such snippets of information to pupils, but very unfortunately, it happens to be the solitary part which unschooled parents, Sergeant Majors, some silly publicists and some educationalists always think of when they think of teaching and learning. They think or half-think that the request "Recite what you have learned in school today, Tommy" is a natural and proper one, as if all that Tommy could or should have learned is a number of memorizable propositions; or as if to have learned anything consisted simply in being able to echo it, like a gramophone. As you all know, most teaching has nothing whatsoever in common with this crude, semi-surgical picture of teaching as the forcible insertion into the pupil's memory of strings of officially approved propositions; and I hope to show before long that even that small and of course indispensable part of instruction which is the imparting of factual information is grossly mis-

From Gilbert Ryle, "Teaching and Training," in R.S. Peters, ed., *The Concept of Educa-tion* (London: Routledge and Kegan Paul, Ltd.; Atlantic Highlands, N.J.: Humanities Press, 1967), pp. 107–12. Reprinted by permission of both publishers.

pictured when pictured as literal cramming. Yet, bad as the picture is, it has a powerful hold over people's general theorizings about teaching and learning. Even Tommy's father, after spending the morning in teaching Tommy to swim, to dribble the football or to diagnose and repair what is wrong with the kitchen clock, in the afternoon cheerfully writes to the newspapers letters which take it for granted that all lessons are strings of memorizable propositions. His practice is perfectly sensible, yet still his theory is as silly as it could be.

Perhaps the prevalence of this very thin and partial notion of teaching and learning inherits something from the teaching and learning that are done in the nursery, where things such as "Hickory Dickory Dock" and simple tunes are learned by heart from that mere vocal repetition which enables the parrot to pick them up too.

Well, in opposition to this shibboleth, I want to switch the centre of gravity of the whole topic on to the notions of Teaching-to so and so, and Learning-to so and so, that is, on to the notion of the development of abilities and competences. Let us forget for a while the memorization of truths, and, of course, of rhymes and tunes, and attend, instead, to the acquisition of skills, knacks and efficiencies. Consider, for example, lessons in drawing, arithmetic and cricket—and, if you like, in philosophy. These lessons cannot consist of and cannot even contain much of dictated propositions. However many true propositions the child had got by heart, he has not begun to learn to draw or play cricket until he has been given a pencil or a bat and a ball and has practised doing things with them; and even if he progresses magnificently in these arts, he will have little or nothing to reply to his parents if they ask him in the evening to recite to them the propositions that he has learned. He can exhibit what he has begun to master, but he cannot *quote* it. To avoid the ambiguity between "teach" in the sense of "teach that" and "teach" in the sense of "teach to" or "teach now to" I shall now sometimes use the word "train." The drawing-master, the language-teacher or the cricket-coach *trains* his pupils in drawing or in French pronunciation or in batting or bowling, and this training incorporates only a few items of quotable information. The same is true of philosophy.

Part, but only part of this notion of training is the notion of drilling, i.e., putting the pupil through stereotyped exercises which he masters by sheer repetition. Thus the recruit learns to slope arms just by going through the same sequence of motions time after time, until he can, so to speak, perform them in his sleep. Circus-dogs and circus-seals are trained in the same way. At the start piano-playing, counting and gear-changing are also taught by simple habituation. But disciplines do not reduce to such sheer drills. Sheer drill, though it is the indispensable beginning of training, is, for most abilities, only their very beginning. Having become able to do certain low-level things automatically and without thinking, the pupil is expected to advance beyond this point and to employ his inculcated automatisms in higher level tasks which are not automatic, and cannot be done without thinking. Skills, tastes and scruples are more than mere habits, and the disciplines and the self-disciplines which develop them are more than mere rote-exercises.

His translators and commentators have been very unjust to Aristotle on this matter. Though he was the first thinker and is still the best, systematically to study the notions of ability, skill, training, character, learning, discipline, self-discipline, etc., the translators of his works nearly always render his key-ideas by such terms as "habit" and "habituation"—as if, for example, a person who has been trained and self-trained to play the violin, or to behave scrupulously in his dealings with other people acts from sheer habit, in the way in which I do tie up my shoelaces quite automatically and without thinking what I am doing or how to do it. Of course Aristotle knew better than this, and the Greek words that he used are quite grossly mistranslated when rendered merely by such words as "habit" and "habituation." The well-disciplined soldier, who does indeed slope arms automatically, does not also shoot automatically or scout by blind habit or read maps like a marionette.

Nor is Tommy's control of his bicycle merely a rote-performance, though he cannot begin to control his bicycle until he has got some movements by rote. Having learned through sheer habit-formation to keep his balance on his bicycle with both hands on the handlebars, Tommy can now try to ride with one hand off, and later still with both hands in his pockets and his feet off the pedals. He now progresses by experimentation. Or, having got by heart the run of the alphabet from ABC through to XYZ, he can now, but not without thinking, tell you what three letters run *backwards* from RQP, though he has never learned by heart this reversed sequence.

I suggest that our initial seeming paradox, that a learner can sometimes of himself, after a bit of instruction, better his instructions, is beginning to seem less formidable. The possibility of it is of the same pattern as the familiar fact that the toddler who has this morning taken a few aided steps, tries this afternoon with or without success to take some unaided steps. The swimmer who can now keep himself up in salt water, comes by himself, at first with a bit of extra splashing, to keep himself up in fresh water. How do any formerly difficult things change into now easy things? Or any once untried things into now feasible ones? The answer is just in terms of the familiar notions of the development of abilities by practice, that is trying and failing and then trying again and not failing so often or so badly, and so on.

Notoriously a very few pupils are, over some tasks, so stupid, idle, scared, hostile, bored or defective, that they make no efforts of their own beyond those imposed on them as drill by their trainer. But to be non-stupid, vigorous and interested *is* to be inclined to make, if only as a game, moves beyond the drilled moves, and to practise of oneself, e.g., to multiply beyond 12 X 12, to run through the alphabet backwards, to bicycle with one hand off the handlebar, or to slope arms in the dark with a walking-stick when no drill-sergeant is there. As Aristotle says "the things that we have got to do when we have learned to do them, we learn to do by doing them." What I can do today I could not do easily or well or successfully yesterday; and the day before I could not even try to do them; and if I had not tried unsuccessfully yesterday, I should not be succeeding today.

Before returning to go further into some of these key notions of ability, practice, trying, learning to, teaching to, and so on, I want to look back for a moment to the two over-influential notions of teaching *that* so and so, i.e., telling or informing, and of learning *that* so and so, i.e., the old notion of propositional cramming. In a number of nursery, school and university subjects, there are necessarily some or many true propositions to be accumulated by the student. He must, for example, learn that Oslo is the capital of Norway, Stockholm is the capital of Sweden and Copenhagen is the capital of Denmark. Or he must learn that the Battle of Trafalgar was fought in 1805 and that of Waterloo in 1815. Or that $7 + 5 = 12$, $7 + 6 = 13, 7 + 7 = 14$, etc.

At the very start, maybe, the child just memorizes these strings of propositions as he memorizes "Hickory Dickory Dock," the alphabet or "Thirty days hath September." But so long as parroting is all he can do, he does not yet know the geographical fact, say, that Stockholm is the capital of Sweden, since if you ask him what Stockholm is the capital of, or whether Madrid is the capital of Sweden, he has no idea how to move. He can repeat, but he cannot yet use, the memorized dictum. All he can do is to go through the memorized sequence of European capitals from start through to the required one. He does not qualify as knowing that Stockholm is the capital of Sweden until he can detach this proposition from the memorized rigmarole; and can, for example, answer new-type questions like "of which country out of the three, Italy, Spain and Sweden is Stockholm the capital?" or "Here is Stockholm on the globe—whereabouts is Sweden?" and so on. To know the geographical fact requires having taken it in, i.e., being able and ready to operate with it, from it, around it and upon it. To possess a piece of information is to be able to mobilize it apart from its rote-neighbours and out of its rote-formulation in unhackneyed and *ad hoc* tasks. Nor does the pupil know that $7 + 7 = 14$ while this is for him only a still undetachable bit of a memorized sing-song, but only when, for example, he can find fault with someone's assertion that $7 + 8 = 14$, or can answer the new-type question, How many 7s are there in 14?, or the new-type question "If there are seven boys and seven girls in a room, how many children are in the room?" etc. Only then has he taken it in.

In other words, even to have learned the piece of information *that something is so* is more than merely to be able to parrot the original telling of it— somewhat as to have digested a biscuit is more than merely to have had it popped into one's mouth. Can he or can he not infer from the information that Madrid is the capital of Spain that Madrid is not in Sweden? Can he or can he not tell us what sea-battle occurred ten years before Waterloo?

Notice that I am not in the least deprecating the inculcation of rotes like the alphabet, the figures of the syllogism, "Hickory Dickory Dock," the dates of the Kings of England, or sloping arms. A person who has not acquired such rotes cannot progress from and beyond them. All that I am arguing is that he does not qualify as knowing even that Waterloo was fought in 1815 if all that he can do is to sing out this sentence inside the sing-song of a memorized string of such sentences. If he can only echo the syllables that he has heard, he has not yet taken in the information meant to be conveyed by them. He has not grasped it if he cannot handle it. But if he could not even echo things told to him, *a fortiori* he could not operate with, from or upon their informative content. One cannot digest a biscuit unless it is first popped into one's mouth. So we see that even to have learned a true proposition is to have learned *to do* things other than repeating the words in which the truth had been dictated. To have learned even a simple geographical fact is to have become able to cope with some unhabitual geographical tasks, however elementary.

Think seriously about the nature of learning as presented in the preceding article by Gilbert Ryle. From our earlier discussions, it should be obvious that the "learning how" is the important active role in which each of us must participate if our encounter with philosophy is to be meaningful and worthwhile. "Knowing or learning that" could be merely a memorized bit of information, and it is a waste of time to try memorizing one's way through philosophy. "Knowing and learning how," on the other hand, is the possession of a *skill*. The activity of philosophy is a skill that can be acquired. The wisdom Aristotle considered so essential to the philosophical enterprise is an example of Ryle's "learning how." For wisdom is a skill as "learning how" is a skill. Accordingly, the conditions necessary for successfully practicing the activity of critical philosophy are skills to be acquired and not facts to be memorized. It is toward the successful acquisition of these skills that this book is directed. Furthermore, if one acquires these skills necessary to evaluate critically the structure of philosophical arguments, this ability of critical thinking will be immensely beneficial when confronting other academic methods and disciplines.

The Divisions of Philosophy: Some Examples of Philosophical Questions

In this book, we shall consider several perennial problems philosophers have confronted. Both historically and contemporarily, there have been sets of closely related problems which philosophers have pondered and analyzed. Even though philosophy is an activity in which we participate, rather than a handbook of ready-made answers, it will be important and helpful for our understanding of philosophy to be aware of these sets of philosophical problems. As an introduction to some of these problems, we shall discuss briefly six of the more important areas of philosophy. This discussion is not a detailed and thorough analysis. Rather, it is an exposition designed to introduce the beginning student to the major areas of philosophical inquiry and to the kinds of questions philosophers ask. Although it would be asking too much to comprehend thoroughly all of what will immediately follow, nonetheless we should familiarize ourselves with the terminology describing the various divisions and branches of philosophy. We shall refer to these areas of philosophical inquiry frequently during our study in the remainder of the book. Generally, these six areas or divisions of philosophy are as follows:

1. The problems of knowledge (usually called *Epistemology*).
2. The problems of the categories of reality (usually called *Metaphysics* or *Ontology*).
3. The problem of God (usually called *The Philosophy of Religion* or *Natural Theology*).

4. The problems of morality (usually called *Ethics* or *Moral Philosophy*).
5. The problem of meaning and reference (usually called the *Philosophy of Language*).
6. The problem of the human condition (usually called *Existentialism*).

During our encounter with the activity of philosophy throughout this book, we shall become aware of the significant problems and questions found in each of these areas of philosophical inquiry. We shall do this from both a historical and a contemporary perspective. One must realize that the above categories are *not* strict limiting definitions agreed upon by all philosophers. However these broad categories, even though loosely defined, will serve as working divisions in our first encounter with the philosophical enterprise.

The following discussion will illustrate and develop more fully each of these six general divisions of philosophical activity. It also will utilize the method made famous by one of the principal figures in contemporary British philosophy, Ludwig Wittgenstein (1889-1951). This method capitalizes on using examples as a means of becoming familiar with types of knowledge rather than attempting to provide an all-exclusive and exhaustive definition. The function of this section is to introduce the student to the types of questions and problems confronted in each of the six general areas of philosophy.

Epistemology. The issues philosophers confront in the area of knowledge are usually called epistemological problems. The term *epistemology*—which is etymologically derived from the Greek term, *episteme*, meaning "scientific knowledge"—usually covers that branch of philosophy concerned with the nature, conditions, and limits of human knowledge. For example, one very important question considered in epistemology is the relation of sense experience to knowledge. Some epistemologists have argued that all we can know is what we can learn by our direct sense experience. Those philosophers who depend upon the five external senses as the sufficient conditions for knowledge are normally called *empiricists.* In the history of philosophy, George Berkeley (1685-1753), David Hume (1711-1776), John Stuart Mill (1806-1873) and the twentieth-century logical positivist, A.J. Ayer (1910-   ), are important empiricists. Upon critical analysis of empiricism, one important question which an empiricist must face is: "What about the status of mathematical knowledge?" Can a person "prove" mathematical axioms and theorems, such as the Pythagorean Theorem, simply by using the five external senses? If we remember plane geometry, we will soon realize that the basic axioms and derived theorems in that type of geometry are never claimed to be directly verified through sense experience. Accordingly, if empiricism is to be an adequate theory of knowledge, then it must take into account the special status of geometrical knowledge. As we shall see, various empiricists offered alternative accounts, ranging from the vastly confirmed empirical general statements of John Stuart Mill to the purely definitional approach of A.J. Ayer.

One epistemological problem which has been extremely vexing to philosophers is the problem of criterion. Simply put, how do we distinguish a piece of "correct" knowledge from a piece of "incorrect" knowledge? In chapter 3, we shall consider this problem as discussed by the "Father of Modern Philosophy," Rene Descartes (1596-1650).

Another important epistemological question is the attempt at establishing the nature and criterion of *truth*. Is there such a thing as "truth"? Is the characteristic of "being true" something found in the external world? Or is it a relation or connection between a thought in a mind and an object in the external world? If this latter theory is correct, then if there were no minds—e.g., before human beings as we know them evolved on the earth—would there still be "truth"? The influential medieval philosopher, Thomas Aquinas (1224–1274), defined truth as a relation between a mind and the world, *"Veritas est adequatio rei et intellectus."* In other words, an idea or proposition is true if it corresponds to the way the world is. This kind of analysis of truth is usually called the *Correspondence Theory of Truth*.

Perhaps "truth" is simply a property or characteristic of our language. Is "true" a characteristic—what some philosophers call a "predicate"—applied only to some propositions in a language?

Other philosophers, on the contrary, have suggested that a proper analysis of truth consists of sets of statements or propositions which fit together in a consistent conceptual scheme. This is usually called the *Coherence Theory of Truth*. In essence, this theory asserts that a given statement is true if it fits in consistently with all the other statements in a given system or conceptual scheme. Euclidean geometry would be an example of the coherence theory of truth. Many mathematicians agree that a theorem is true in Euclidean geometry, not because it refers to some particular facet of the world, but rather because it "cohers" or "fits in with" all the other propositions in the Euclidean system. On this model of truth, the Pythagorean Theorem is true only because it is correctly and validly derived from preceding theorems and postulates, according to the proper rules of inference. Accordingly, the coherence theory of truth differs from the correspondence theory of truth because the latter asserts that a proposition is true only if it refers to some object in the world, while the former asserts that a proposition is true because it "cohers" with the rest of the propositions in the given system.

Another analysis of truth made popular by some late nineteenth-century American philosophers is the *Pragmatic Theory of Truth*. Charles Sanders Peirce (1839–1914) argued that truth is a "habit of action." In this view, a statement or proposition is true if it can be acted upon or scientifically verified. Simply put, a statement is "true" if it has some "cash value," i.e., if it "works." As might be expected, Pragmatism has been influential among philosophers of science.

The above discussion is admittedly brief. However it should indicate to the student that many important and difficult problems are categorized under the umbrella of epistemology.

Metaphysics.　　Another vexing problem faced by philosophers concerns the categories of reality or categories of existents. This aspect of the philosophical inquiry is usually called "metaphysics" or "ontology." W.V. Quine (1908–   ), perhaps the most influential American logician of the twentieth century, entitled one of his philosophical articles, "On What There Is." Any attempt to answer Quine's question is to provide a metaphysical response.

Ontology comes from the Greek word, *ons*, which is translated as "being." A "being" is something which exists in some way or other. Let us think for a moment about the grammatical function of a participle. As we will remember from our English classes, a participle is a verb form denoting the "state of possession" of an activity by an object. "Being" is the participle of the verb "to be." "To be," in one sense, can mean "to exist." Accordingly, the participle of the verb "to be" denotes the state of "existing." Therefore a "being" is an object which has "existence." Ontology then is the study of existents or the categories of objects which have existence.

Metaphysics is etymologically derived from two Greek terms: *meta,* meaning "beyond," and *physis,* meaning the account of the physical things of the world. Using this etymological derivation, metaphysics is that branch of philosophy which concerns itself with the aspects of reality which are beyond the evidence of direct sense experience.

One of the many fundamental questions encountered in ontology is the mind-body problem. Are there two fundamental categories in the world—minds and bodies? If this is correct—as the seventeenth-century philosopher, Descartes, thought—then one must account for the connection between the two. In other words, how does a spiritual mind causally interact with a physical body? Other philosophers have argued that the only category of reality is material bodies. This position, obviously, is called *materialism.* The early modern philosopher, Thomas Hobbes (1588-1679), and the influential twentieth-century Harvard psychologist, B.F. Skinner (1904-), can be classified as materialists. Simply put, materialists reduce all human mental activity to interactions among the material components of the brain cells. Thus an act of mental awareness is reducible to a mechanical, physiological reaction. In the following passage from his *Leviathan,* Hobbes argues for materialism:

> All which qualities, called *sensible,* are in the object that causeth them, but so many several motions of the matter, by which it presseth our organs diversely. Neither in us that are pressed, are they any thing else, but diverse motions; For motion produceth nothing but motion. [1]

In opposition to the materialists, some philosophers have argued that everything is a manifestation of and derivation from *Absolute Spirit.* This is usually called *Absolute Idealism.* The mechanics of this speculative philosophical system are difficult, but suffice it for now to indicate that an idealist is diametrically opposed to a materialist. G.W.F. Hegel (1770-1831) is probably the most famous *absolute idealist,* although the late nineteenth-century Harvard philosopher, Josiah Royce (1855-1916), and the third-century mystic, Plotinus (205-270), also provided absolute idealist accounts of reality. Parenthetically, any pantheistic system—in which God becomes all things—is an example of an absolute idealist system of ontology.

Another important problem facing metaphysicians is the *free will-determinism* issue. Are we human beings scientifically determined in everything we do— programmed like computers—or are we actually capable of freely choosing what we want and what we do? Is the analysis of human choice essentially different from a chemical reaction? The analysis of the precise nature of human freedom is an important philosophical question which necessarily complements many psychological investigations, especially behaviorism. Anyone who has read Skinner's *Walden Two,* is aware of the importance of this question.

One other aspect of reality bothering philosophers is the exact nature of the basic categories themselves. This is usually called the *problem of universals.* The following questions illustrate the basis for this problem. Why are all human beings alike? It is true that all of us can be put in the same category called "human beings." Yet what is the basis in reality for this classification? Do each of us "share" in some common characteristic which makes us essentially the same? Plato (427–347 B.C.) thought so, and, as we shall see in chapter 2, his influential *Theory of the Forms* attempts to resolve this problem. Plato's position is called *extreme realism.* Plato argued that the category of human nature itself is an existing entity in addition to individual instances of human beings—e.g., Ron, Megan, and Elin.

Diametrically opposed to extreme realism is *nominalism.* This position, held by many empiricists—e.g., George Berkeley and David Hume—affirms that the categories of reality called universals are nothing more than mere verbal signs by means of which we conveniently pigeonhole different types of things and events in our language.

Even this short account of metaphysical questions should indicate the depth, subtlety, and difficulty of this aspect of the matters of philosophy. In our study of philosophy, we shall analyze in detail some of these problems with special emphasis given to the differing theories accounting for the status of universals.

The Philosophy of Religion.   Traditionally, the principal problem faced in the philosophy of religion is evaluating the evidence used to assert the existence of a divine being. Put differently, the question is: Can I rationally demonstrate the existence of a god? Various arguments have been proposed to establish the claim that God exists. Some depend upon an analysis of the external world, some demand an intricate metaphysical system, others depend upon the uniqueness of religious experience. One fundamental question concerns the status of the evidence required to demonstrate the existence of a divine being. Must this evidence be rooted in sense experience? If so, then what is the nature of the connection between the sense experience and the existence of a nonsensible divine being? On the other hand, is there something about the very concept of God— an all-perfect being—which entails that this unique being must necessarily exist independently of any evidence from sense experience?

Some philosophers have argued that it is impossible to say anything meaningful about either the existence or the nature of God. God becomes an object of "faith alone." God is an entity beyond any rational comprehension. The third-century theologian, Tertullian (165–220), emphasized this position in his claim: "I believe because it is absurd." (*Credo, quia absurdum est.*) Tertullian claimed that the "absurd" was beyond the capability of any rational demonstration. The nineteenth-century existentialist, Soren Kierkegaard (1813–1855), argued in the same way, as we shall see in chapter 7 on existentialism.

Yet is this "blind faith" approach compatible with philosophy? Is the assertion that a divine being exists such that philosophy can say nothing about it? Does this result in mysticism? In this same vein, another important question concerns how we attribute characteristics to this divine being. For example, does God have human characteristics? If so, which ones? What criterion do we use to make this judgment? A further question concerns the reconciliation of the existence of God with the fact that evil exists in the world. Is the existence of an all-good and an all-powerful being compatible with the fact that evil exists in the world? What is a consistent analysis of "evil"? The Scottish empiricist, David Hume, treats many of these issues extensively in his *Dialogues on Natural Religion.*

Contemporary philosophers of religion have been very interested in ascertaining the claims for the significance of religious language. Are statements found in religious discourse structurally similar to statements about matters of fact? If not, then what are they? Expressions of preference? On what grounds is religious language verifiable?

It should be noted that much traditional philosophy of religion has been referred to as *natural religion, philosophical theology,* and *theodicy.* In our discussions, we shall consider the nature and structure of three examples of purported demonstrations for the existence of God.

Ethics.   The branch of philosophy whose task it is to determine criteria enabling us to make reasonable judgments about right and wrong actions is called *ethics* or *moral philosophy.* Obviously this branch of philosophy has tremendous practical importance for the kinds of lives we can and should lead. Ethics is concerned with human agents and the actions they perform.

One division of moral philosophy is called *normative ethics.* The problem confronted in this area of moral philosophy is establishing a viable philosophy of value. Essentially this is the inquiry which attempts to determine criteria necessary to classify right and wrong actions. Should this criterion, for instance, be solely in terms of effects or consequences of actions? Some philosophers, like John Stuart Mill, have provided complete normative theories in terms of the effects of an action. This position has a common-sense basis. For example, we all have probably asked ourselves at one time or another the following question, when attempting to determine the morality of a particular course of action: "Should I do this action—well, will it hurt anybody?" This is an example of making consequences the criterion for judging right and wrong actions. In order to become aware of the difficulty involved in providing an analysis of moral theories, let's examine this position for a moment. What if one claims, like the classical utilitarians, that an act is wrong if it produces more pain for more people than not doing the action or doing the opposite of the action? This is an obvious example of a moral theory asserting that the criterion for moral judgments rests with the consequences of an action. The converse of this proposition is that an act is right if it produces the greatest amount of happiness for the greatest number of people. In his classic text, *Utilitarianism,* John Stuart Mill actually made this claim. Note his words in the following passage:

> The creed which accepts as the foundation of morals Utility, or the Greatest Happiness Principle, holds that actions are right in proportion as they tend to promote happiness, wrong as they tend to produce the reverse of happiness. By "happiness" is intended pleasure, and the absence of pain; by "unhappiness," pain, and the privation of pleasure.[2]

Is the utilitarian criterion an adequate one for determining the basis for morality? Can we make all of our ethical judgments using this criterion? Let's examine this position for a moment. How would we determine if an action is indeed a right action? If we count all of the people affected by the action in question, all we really have is a list of people who are either receiving pleasure or enduring pain. Yet does this numbering of people tell us anything about morality itself? What would happen if the action were to hurt just a few people? Would this alone make it a right action? If we push this position a little further, what would happen if a certain portion of any given society would be forced to endure pain at the expense of a greater majority who might be made happy by some particular action. Is this enough to justify the rightness of an action? Although we shall treat utilitarianism in detail in chapter 6, it is well for us to become somewhat familiar with the types of critical, probing questions philosophers ask about propositions expressed in moral theories.

Is the effect alone the sole criterion for determining the morality of an action? Is there any other facet of moral experience which ought to be considered? In opposition to utilitarianism, philosophers like Immanuel Kant (1724–1804) have placed great emphasis on the "proper motive" or "intention" which a person has when deciding what to do in a moral situation. In other words, a correct or proper intention is the criterion necessary for determining the morality of an action. Of course, the important question here concerns establishing the adequate philosophical machinery enabling us to know what counts as a "proper" or "correct" intention.

Still other philosophers have been quite concerned with the role particular situations play in affecting the outcome of a moral deliberation. The proponents of this type of theory—which is sometimes called *situationist ethics*—question the very possibility of ever having a set of moral rules which could apply for all situations. Situational ethics claims that every moral judgment is relative to an individual person, at a particular time, and dependent upon a unique set of circumstances. Some American theologians have held this position and it has been argued that some contemporary existentialists fit into this category.

Studies in anthropology have contributed to the development of another aspect of moral philosophy sometimes referred to as *ethical relativism*. Ethical relativism asserts that each culture or society determines what is ethically justifiable for its members. Not only is this a descriptive claim about what different cultures in fact have held for their normative theories, but the ethical relativist argues that each culture is philosophically—and thus morally—justified in its own unique set of moral principles. Needless to say, ethical relativism is a complicated problem.

Another question faced by moral philosophers concerns the status of moral qualities or properties. In other words, is "goodness" a characteristic or quality found in the external world? If so, is it a property we can discover empirically? Or is it a quality which depends upon human knowers? Simply put, is goodness an objective facet of the world or is it purely dependent upon the subjective state of a knower? If objective, how is it known? By intuition? By inference from a set of empirical properties? If by inference, does a moral argument have the same structure as a scientific demonstration? Or is it different? Many twentieth-century philosophers have been very concerned about the status of moral language and the structure of moral arguments. Some contemporary philosophers, like A.J. Ayer and C.L. Stevenson (1908–), have failed to see any warrant for asserting empirical evidence for moral properties. On the contrary, they have argued that moral terms refer to the expression of emotional states of persons who find themselves in moral situations. This position has been called *emotivism*.

Other philosophers have argued that human values are found in the development of a human being's potentialities or capacities. The contemporary psychologist, Carl Rogers (1902–), and the ancient Greek philosopher, Aristotle (384–322 B.C.), have held such a position. Value is defined as the actualization of the self—one's capacities being developed and fulfilled.

These are a few of the many complicated and involved questions each of us—as rational beings—must confront if we are to live a truly human life. Probably more appropriate to moral philosophy than the other divisions of philosophy is the maxim of Socrates: "The unexamined life is not worth living." The considerations of moral philosophy in chapter 6 should force each of us to reevaluate the foundations upon which we make our moral decisions. And this must be relevant to each of us, for none of us can live without making moral decisions.

Philosophy of Language. A principal concern of many twentieth-century English speaking philosophers has been the analysis of meaning. Historians of philosophy have characterized this as the *philosophy of language*. This concern about meaning has been directed both toward ordinary language and toward the specific language used at times by philosophers. During this century, the language and methodology of science and mathematics in particular have been subjected to much critical analysis. Moreover, in one case the claim was put forward that all philosophical questions arise because of mistakes in ordinary language. In other words, if philosophers had paid closer attention to the way ordinary people speak, then most, if not all, philosophical problems would dissolve. That this is a controversial claim should be obvious.

The English philosopher, G.E. Moore (1873–1958), emphasized the distinction between the "truth" of a statement and the "analysis" of that statement. The analysis of a philosophical statement is primarily concerned with the question, "What does this mean?" In one sense, analysis of philosophical propositions is linked to C.D. Broad's notion of critical philosophy, which we discussed above. It should be noted that often various aspects of the analysis of philosophical language merge with ontological theories. In the case of some twentieth-century philosophers, it is a difficult question to separate ontology from analysis.

Since the analysis of language primarily revolves around the question concerning meaning, an important analysis is to determine the exact status of "meaning" itself. Is the meaning of a term principally obtained by reference? In other words, does meaning come to terms chiefly because of the fact in the world to which a term or statement refers? Yet if this is so, then how do we account for false statements? Is a false statement just nonreference? Or is there some entity called a "false fact"? The same questions can be asked about negative statements. The position that language acquires meaning by referring to objects is called the *Reference Theory of Meaning*.

On the other hand, many philosophers, following the insights of Ludwig Wittgenstein's *Philosophical Investigations*, have argued that meaning is determined by the use of a single term or combination of terms in particular contexts and circumstances. According to this theory, usually called the *Use*

Theory of Meaning, a term or group of terms acquire meaning by the "use" of the linguistic expressions in specific contexts. According to this theory, meaning does not occur only because of reference to objects. In other words, meaning is not determined solely by reference.

These questions of meaning have had a central place in much twentieth-century philosophy. As we proceed with our inquiry into the matters of philosophy, the significance of these linguistic questions will become apparent.

Existentialism and the Human Condition.   In opposition to the general direction and scope of much contemporary Anglo-American philosophy, especially the attention paid to the problems of meaning and reference just discussed, many continental philosophers (i.e., philosophers from the continent of western Europe, excluding the British Isles) have become greatly concerned with the questions involving human existence. "How are we to exist so that we can lead meaningful lives?" is the fundamental philosophical question posed by the existentialists. The Danish philosopher, Soren Kierkegaard, is usually considered the first existentialist. Kierkegaard was aghast at the total passivity characteristic of nearly every mid-nineteenth-century Danish Christian. To counter this passivity and its accompanying noninvolvement, Kierkegaard urged the Danes to live passionately and thus become committed and involved with their existence as human beings.

Students may have read the plays and novels of the leading French existentialists, Jean-Paul Sartre (1905-   ) and Albert Camus (1913-1958). Philosophers like Sartre and Camus are interested in accounting for meaningful human existence given the rigors and alienation of twentieth-century life. Sartre explicitly claims that the heart of his existentialism is the absolute character of the free commitment by which an individual realizes himself or herself. Sartre and Camus talk about action, commitment, and involvement from free choice as the only way to provide meaning for our existence. Some historians of philosophy have argued that Sartre and Camus are desperately trying to account for meaning in human life for the twentieth century, given that the traditional grounds of meaning in theism are no longer generally accepted and followed. Sartre has explicitly argued that his existentialism is nothing but an attempt to draw the full conclusions from a consistently atheistic position.

Existentialism has been interpreted by some historians of philosophy to be a repudiation of the classical way of doing philosophy. Too much classical philosophy, they say, has been devoted to abstract generalizations and universal truths. In this search for generalities, the existence of the concrete individual has been ignored and neglected. However, the existentialists argue, what are we but individuals? The motive of existentialism, therefore, has been to return the thrust of philosophy to the concrete concerns of human existence. For example, some of the existentialists are interested in coming to grips with the anguish and abandonment experienced by so many of us in the twentieth century. That the questions raised by the existentialists are important no one will deny; that their method and proposals are totally different from, and repudiations of, traditional philosophy can be questioned. In chapter 7, we shall consider in detail the writings of three of the most important and influential existentialists.

Additional Areas of Philosophy

The divisions of philosophy and the brief explications just completed are those whose issues we shall treat in some detail later in this book. There are other areas of philosophical inquiry, however, about which students of philosophy should have at least a rudimentary awareness.

Logic.   Logic is that part of philosophy whose task it is to provide an analysis of valid argument forms. The correct methods of reasoning, both deductive and inductive, together with a consideration of the various formal and informal fallacies form the material for discussions in logic.

Aesthetics.   Aesthetics is that branch of philosophy which analyzes concepts presupposed in the discussion of the fine arts. It is chiefly concerned with the nature of aesthetic objects, the qualities of aesthetic experiences and the norms for judgments in the fine arts. Often aesthetics is referred to as the *philosophy of the arts.*

Jurisprudence.   This is the area of philosophical analysis directed towards the concepts presupposed in any system of law. Concepts, such as justice, foundation of law, human right, and so forth, are critically evaluated in jurisprudence. Often jurisprudence is called the *philosophy of law.* One important issue concerns the relation of moral theories to the structure of the legal system. Also, there is the problem concerning how much of any given ethical theory should be legislated into the legal system.

Philosophy of Science.   This area is probably the best known of the branches of philosophy. Its concern is to analyze the basic concepts and presuppositions of another discipline. Much twentieth-century British and American philosophy has been directed toward adequately elucidating the structure of scientific methodology and scientific terminology. Philosophy of science is a good example of critical philosophy, as C.D. Broad used this term previously. The philosopher of science subjects the methodology and the concepts presupposed by the natural sciences to critical analysis.

Philosophy of the Social Sciences.   Like the philosophy of science from which it is derived, the philosophy of the social sciences has for its province the methodology and concepts of another discipline. One important methodological question in this division of philosophy concerns the difference in procedure between the natural sciences and the social sciences.

Philosophy of Education.   This area of philosophy, like moral philosophy, has a two-fold task. First of all, philosophy of education attempts to elucidate the grounds of value in educational theory. This is usually stated in terms of the goals and purposes for education. The American philosopher, John Dewey (1859–1952), spent much of his life theorizing about the concept of value and its relation to education. Second, following contemporary philosophy of language, some philosophers of education have spent their time analyzing the structure of the concepts presupposed in educational theory.

Philosophy of History.   The structure of this branch of philosophy is partially derived from the philosophy of science. Traditionally, the philosophy of history has had two functions. First, some philosophers of history—usually referred to as the "speculative" philosophers of history—have attempted to develop and elucidate grand themes which explain the historical process. For example, some philosophers of history have held that the historical process is basically cyclical in nature, history fundamentally repeating itself over and over again, while others have postulated that history has a straight-line character, directed towards a specific goal. Second, some philosophers, somewhat sceptical at the possibility of ever discovering a pattern in history, argue that the nature and limits of the philosophy of history are bound by the analysis of historical arguments, concepts, and evidence. These philosophers disdain the project of discovering a "purpose" for the historical process. As an example, much debate has centered around the differing claims regarding the nature of historical explanation—is it unique or is in conceptually similar to a scientific explanation?

Philosophy of Mathematics.   This study, like the philosophy of science, discusses the underlying assumptions of mathematical theory. Much discussion has centered around the nature of number theory. Some questions considered in the philosophy of mathematics merge with ontological issues. Problems of consistency and completeness for mathematical systems are quite important in this branch of philosophy.

Phenomenology.   This is a type of philosophy practiced by many contemporary European philosophers. At times phenomenology and existentialism are exemplified in the same philosopher.

Following the lead of the German philosopher, Edmund Husserl (1859–1938), phenomenology has developed as a descriptive methodology used in analyzing subjective processes, especially the knowing processes. The beginning point of phenomenology is the human subject and his or her consciousness. One important aspect of phenomenology has been the discussion of *intentionality*. This is usually described as the inquiry attempting to determine the fundamental and rudimentary characteristic distinguishing knowers from nonknowers. In chapter 3, when discussing the philosophy of Rene Descartes, we shall have the opportunity to analyze intentionality theories, and, in chapter 7, we shall briefly discuss phenomenology as a dimension of recent continental philosophy.

Studies in the History of Philosophy.   Many philosophers, especially contemporary American philosophers, have spent much time and effort attempting to clearly elucidate the exact nature and structure of a given problem treated by a historical figure in the philosophical tradition. This is often referred to as the *structural history* of philosophy. The point of these inquiries is not to merely repeat what a figure in the history of philosophy has uttered but rather to critically elucidate and "unpack" the structure of the problem and its purported solution. Quite often, the methods and skills of the philosophy of language are utilized on the writings of important philosophers from other eras. Some of the critical questions we shall ask of the various historical philosophers encountered in this book will be attempts at engaging in the structural history of philosophy.

NOTES

1. *Leviathan,* Part I, chapter 1, 1863.
2. John Stuart Mill, *Utilitarianism* (New York: World Publishing).

two

Plato:
The First
Systematic Philosopher

Breaking Away From Mythology

From the available historical evidence, the study of philosophy began in the sixth century B.C. The first philosopher, Thales (624–550 B.C.), lived on the islands of Ionia off the coast of Greece. Thales is regarded as the first philosopher because he was the first person to separate Greek mysticism and orphic religion from rational inquiry. Thales placed mystical accounts and rational accounts into separate and distinct categories. For us it is not important to consider the precise details of the theory Thales postulated in response to his inquiry into the ultimate nature of the material world. What is important, however, is Thales's broad and wide-ranging search utilizing reason alone and avoiding the prevailing mythological accounts as he sought a solution to the basic causal questions of the world around him. The following passage from Aristotle's *Metaphysics* (third century) describes for us the essential nature and result of Thales's inquiry:

> Most of the earliest philosophers conceived only of material principles as underlying all things. That of which all things consist, from which they first come and into which on their destruction they are ultimately resolved, of which the essence persists although modified by its affections—this, they say, is an element and principle of existing things. Hence they believe that nothing is either generated or destroyed, since this kind of primary entity always persists. . . . Thales, the founder of this school of philosophy, says the permanent entity is water (which is why he also propounded that the earth floats on water). Presumably he derived this assumption from seeing that the nutriment of everything is moist, and that heat itself is generated from moisture and depends upon it for its existence (and that from

which a thing is generated is always its first principle). He derived his assumption, then, from this; and also from the fact that the seeds of everything have a moist nature, whereas water is the first principle of the nature of moist things.[1]

If we analyze this passage, we soon realize that Thales regarded a philosophical response to be a natural, causal, materialist theory of explanation as opposed to an explanation based solely in terms of the "whims" of the gods so central to Greek mythology. It is true that to us as modern readers not only do Thales's conclusions appear odd and quite naive—for as Aristotle's description indicated, Thales did claim that the basic substance of all things was water—but it is fair to say that the general tone of Thales's work is what we would today call a scientific inquiry rather than a philosophical inquiry. As we shall see later, it was not until rather recent times that a straightforward and precise distinction was drawn between philosophy and science. Thales is important in this history of philosophy, however, because he was the first one to face squarely the problem of providing solutions to philosophical and scientific questions without reference to mythical beings and supernatural fantasies. Thales's insistence on arriving at material causes in the natural order warrants his place as the founder of western philosophy. It is interesting to note that in his history of philosophy, *Thales to Dewey*, G.H. Clark argues that philosophy began on May 28, 585 B.C., at 6:13 P.M.[2] This was the time that an eclipse predicted by Thales occurred. Some historians note that Thales's prediction was a bit in error, as he said the eclipse was to have occurred at 6:00 P.M.!

Following Thales, there were many interesting and intriguing figures in what is generally known as pre-Socratic philosophy. Names like Anaxamander, Heraclitus, Parmenides, Phythagoras, and Democritus are listed among the creative minds who, following Thales, attempted to provide rational answers to questions concerning the basic constitution of the material world and man's place in that world. What we might refer to today as speculative metaphysical questions occupied most of the time of these pre-Socratic philosophers.

With each philosopher espousing his own distinct and unique philosophical position in attempting to answer these questions, a serious problem emerged. Because of the wide divergency of philosophical schools and their opposing theories, the enlightened layman soon became terribly confused. Not only did the theories of the pre-Socratic philosophers differ, but they often categorically contradicted one another. For example, Heraclitus claimed that everything was in constant change and flux. On the other hand, Parmenides and his disciple, Zeno, argued that everything was stable and that the apparent fact of motion in the world was nothing but an illusion. Zeno popularized the tenets of his master, Parmenides, by his famous paradoxes. One paradox concludes that the fact of motion is inherently contradictory and thus impossible. One example of Zeno's paradoxes is the following:

> Argument of the stadium: Before a moving object can reach a given goal, it must first traverse half the distance of the race course. Now what is true of the total distance is true also of half of that distance; the body must first arrive at the quarter mark, and so on. Hence, to cross the stadium, it would have to traverse an infinite number of points. Moreover, if it is ever to reach its goal, it would have to travel the distance in finite time. But an object cannot traverse an infinite number of points in a finite time. On the basis of this dichotomy, no object can cross the stadium.[3]

Consider for a moment the force of Zeno's claim. Zeno argues that our experience of motion is indeed an illusion and cannot be rationally explained. What is the student's reaction to these paradoxes? Remember, the conclusion of the paradox denies a common-sense datum from our experience of the world. One might first claim that, if Zeno is correct, what's the use of having philosophical theories? This is exactly what happened in ancient Greece. From the vast assortment of philosophical doctrines, many of which were diametrically opposed to one another, and from the effect of Parmenides and Zeno who argued that our basic experience of the world was an illusion, there eventually emerged a radical quandary about the value of philosophy itself. A profound distrust emerged concerning the ability of reason to ever discover, confront, and resolve any definitive claims about either the human person or the external world. This distrust brought about an intense scepticism. In turn, this scepticism fostered an exaggerated relativism in metaphysical, epistemological, and ethical claims. This spirit of relativism was seen as the only viable solution to the myriad opinions offered to the problems confronted by the pre-Socratic philosophers. Such relativism was expressed forcefully in the teachings and writings of a group of philosophers called the *sophists*.

It is important to confront the tenets of the sophists in the beginning of the study of philosophy. In a very real sense, this position is akin to statements often expressed by some college students today:

    a. "No one ever really knows an absolute truth!"

    b. "Every moral question is just a matter of preference."

    c. "There is no such thing as truth—everything is just a matter of opinion."

If all students have not uttered one of the above claims, they have at least heard classmates firmly expound on the soundness of these opinions.

Since all of us have experienced relativism in one form or another, it is fitting that we begin our investigation of philosophical matters with a consideration of the sophists. As a group, the sophists vigorously defended the tenets of metaphysical, epistemological, and ethical relativism. Following our discussion of the sophists, we shall discover the imaginative responses to this extreme relativism provided by Socrates and his illustrious student, Plato. Plato's importance in the development of Western philosophy cannot be overestimated. In addition, if one does not see the problems of relativism against which Socrates and Plato reacted, then he/she will not understand the general direction of Platonic philosophy. Therefore a serious consideration of the sophistic philosophy is crucial both for ourselves and for learning about Plato and his important and influential metaphysical system.

The Sophists

Theoretically, the sophists were the first group of philosophers to ask the hard, critical questions about the use of reason itself as a means toward establishing correct and viable solutions for philosophical problems. Until the time of the sophists, most of the pre-Socratic philosophers assumed that reason was a sound guide toward finding correct answers about the nature of the world. It is important to note from the start that not all sophists were charlatans practicing "sophistry." However the sophists did engage in metaphysical, epistemological, and ethical relativism. Our present interest is to examine some of the claims of the sophists in order that we might more readily understand the structure of their relativism. This understanding will enable us to appreciate the philosophical statements uttered by Socrates and Plato in response to the sophists. Socrates and Plato can best be understood in their roles as philosophers who provided a counterargument to the claims of philosophical relativism espoused by the sophists.

Etymologically, the term *sophist* is derived from the Greek term, *sophia*. As we saw earlier, the word philosophy is a derivative of sophia, which means "wisdom." The sophists were itinerant teachers who travelled about from Greek city to city, offering to instruct the local citizens in the ways of wisdom. Quite often, however, in the hands of the lesser sophists this instruction readily descended to nothing more than practical instruction on how to become wise to the ways of the world. It is true that the sophists differed from nearly all of their predecessors in philosophy in that they were more interested in the questions pertaining to the development of human beings and less interested in a philosophical-scientific inquiry about ultimate principles or causes of the material world. This, obviously, is an important development in the history of philosophy. This concern about human beings as the object of philosophical inquiry instead of the material world as the sole focus of the activity of philosophy is indeed laudable. However this concern about human beings too quickly and sadly evolved into an activity of developing methods showing how one person could politically and socially exert mastery over another person. With no philosophical standards in either epistemology or ethics, the purpose of the sophists became extremely relative and quite practical. In essence, the entire philosophical purview of the sophists was definitely pragmatic. An early twentieth-century version of the sophist manifesto could easily be the theme of Dale Carnegie's *How To Win Friends and Influence People.*

Primarily, the sophists taught rhetoric. This concerned the methods of argumentation used to effectively persuade others. Rhetoric can easily be defined as the art of skillful persuasion. Rhetoric became very important for many of the citizens of the Greek city-states during the fifth century B.C. During this time, many of the citizens were acquiring great wealth. In turn, they were willing to pay expensive fees in order that their sons might be educated in the arts of skillful persuasion. Being proficient in matters of rhetoric was especially important in light of the Greek democracies in whose public assemblies each citizen had the right and opportunity to speak freely. As often happens in any mass meeting, people are persuaded by the forcefulness of an argument rather than by the truth claims of the situation. In order to be effective at swaying his fellow citizens, the young Greek citizen needed to acquire the skills enabling him to master the art of rhetorical persuasion. The sophists met this need. They travelled among the Greek city-states as paid teachers of rhetoric. Some historians of philosophy note that the rise of the sophists was merely symptomatic of the general attitudes and tenor of this age of Greek development. For example, in the Greek democracy a quick way to become wealthy was to win a lawsuit. A jury is sometimes persuaded by the facility and rhetoric of the defendant's lawyer, rather than the objective merits of the case, and the juries of the Greek city-states were no different. The demand for acquiring proficiency in rhetorical skills was handsomely met by the sophists, the self-proclaimed masters of rhetoric. In fact, some of the lesser sophists even professed to be able to teach the correct way to win lawsuits.

A little reflection will indicate the connection between relativism and rhetoric. If there are no objective claims to be expressed by means of true propositions, then "the truth alone" is totally unable to convince another person because there is no such thing as "the truth alone." The only way left to convince another person without using force is by *effective persuasion.* Hence, once objectivity is denied, then effective persuasion becomes a very important tool used to convince another person about the merits of any given argument.

Of course rhetoric is a useful skill. However it should be noted that, in the hands of the lesser sophists, rhetoric quite often tragically descended to mere "eristic," which is nothing more than specious reasoning. Some sophists even suggested that winning an argument at any cost was an ideal to be pursued. Soon philosophy became almost coextensive with sophism.

The early sophist, Protagoras (480—410 B.C.), best exemplifies some of the extreme relativism characteristic of the sophists. Protagoras was a serious sceptic in matters of knowledge. Consequently, in his view, all knowledge is radically subjective. What has historically been called the dictum of Protagoras is as follows:

> Man is the measure of all things, of things that are that they are and of things that are not that they are not. How something seems to me, so it is for me; how it appears to you, so it is for you, because you and I are similarly men.

In this same manner, Protagoras has also written the following:

> Two mutually contradictory propositions can be advanced about any state of affairs.

This statement of Protagoras's dictum indicates clearly that each person's subjective judgment is the ultimate criterion of knowledge. Moreover, this maxim holds in metaphysical and ethical matters. For the sophists, radical scepticism was rampant in all avenues of philosophical inquiry.

This extreme scepticism, when applied to matters of morality, quickly leads to the dire consequence that "might makes right." With no objective foundation for moral judgments, it is a very quick and easy move for a sophist to claim that the individual who has the most power can legitimately lord it over all the rest. Historically, this is exactly what happened. Consider for a moment the following passage in which one of the younger sophists, Thrasymachus—who was a well-known teacher in ancient Greece—propounds the thesis that justice is found in those who have the most power.

> Consider further, most foolish Socrates, that the just is always a loser in comparison with the unjust. First of all in their private dealings: wherever the unjust is the partner of the just the conclusion of the affair always is that the unjust man has more and the just less. Next, in their dealings with the State: when there is an income-tax, the just man will pay more and the unjust less on the same amount of income; and when there is anything to be received the one gains nothing and the other much. Observe also that when they come into office, there is the just man neglecting his affairs and perhaps suffering other losses, but he will not compensate himself out of the public purse because he is just; moreover he is hated by his friends and relations for refusing to serve them in unlawful ways. Now all this is reversed in the case of the unjust man. I am speaking of injustice on a large scale in

which the advantage of the unjust is most apparent, and my meaning will be most clearly seen in that highest form of injustice the perpetrator of which is the happiest of men, as the sufferers or those who refuse to do injustice are the most miserable— I mean tyranny, which by fraud and force takes away the property of others, not retail but wholesale; comprehending in one, things sacred as well as profane, private and public; for any one of which acts of wrong, if he were detected perpetrating them singly, he would be punished and incur great dishonor; for they who are guilty of any of these crimes in single instances are called robbers of temples, and man-stealers and burglars and swindlers and theives. But when a man has taken away the money of the citizens and made slaves of them, then, instead of these dishonorable names, he is called happy and blessed, not only by the citizens but by all who hear of his having achieved the consummation of injustice. For injustice is censured because the censurers are afraid of suffering, and not from any fear which they have of doing injustice. And thus, as I have shown, Socrates, injustice, when on a sufficient scale, has more strength and freedom and mastery than justice; and, as I said at first, justice is the interest of the stronger, whereas injustice is a man's own profit and interest.

One of the sophists argued explicitly that "there is no objective or absolutely valid criterion or norm of morality, but only a subjective and relative one." With no objective moral norms, what is to stop someone like Thrasymachus from asserting that injustice is a person's own profit and interest while justice is the interest of the stronger?

In line with Thrasymachus, another young sophist, Callicles, argued that the traditional Greek virtues of moderation, discipline, and temperance were completely baseless. Not only were they devoid of rational foundation, but they were a positive hinderance to man's full development. Thus we can see how radical scepticism in regard to moral matters led the sophists into denying that anything but self-assertive power is virtuous. Could the sophists say anything less? Possibly there is a role for standards of some sort after all. Consider the following passage illustrating Callicles's views taken from the Platonic dialogue, *Gorgias*:

. . . the makers of laws are the many weak; and they make laws and distribute praises and censures with a view to themselves and to their own interests; and they terrify the mightier sort of men, and those who are able to get the better of them, in order that they may not get the better of them; and they say, that dishonesty is shameful and unjust; meaning, when they speak of injustice, the desire to have more than their neighbors, for knowing their own inferiority they are only too glad of equality. And therefore this seeking to have more than the many, is conventionally said to be shameful and unjust, and is called injustice, whereas nature herself intimates that it is just for the better to have more than the worse, the more powerful than the weaker; and in many ways she shows, among men as well as among animals, and indeed among whole cities and races, that justice consists in the superior ruling over and having more than the inferior. For on what principle of justice did Xerxes invade Hellas, or his father the Scythians (not to speak of numberless other examples)? They, I conceive, act according to nature; yes, and according to the law of nature: not, perhaps, according to that artificial law, which we frame and fashion, taking the best and strongest of us from their youth upwards, and taming them like young lions, and charming them with the sound of the voice, saying to them, that with equality they must be content, and that this is the honorable and the just. But if there were a man who had sufficient force, he would shake off and break through, and escape from all this he would trample under foot all our formulas and spells and charms, and all our laws, sinning against nature: the slave would rise in rebellion and be lord over us, and the light of natural justice would shine forth.

Socrates

Whenever a brand of philosophical extremism is rampant, another creative philosophical mind usually comes to the forefront in order to contest and confront the prevalent extremism. The rise in popularity of the sophists and their corresponding radical scepticism was not an exception to this general norm found in the history of philosophy. The emerging counterforce—indeed one who established a counterculture—was Socrates (470–399 B.C.).

In order to understand the philosophical insights proposed by Socrates, it is important to have a feeling for the consequences of the extreme scepticism taught and practised by the sophists. By grasping what happens to a philosophical system which contains no standards whatsoever, we will be able to realize the basic "static" which arose between Socrates and the sophists. In essence, this static arose because Socrates witnessed sophism at its worst. We have just seen that sophism can be viewed as a philosophical trend which forced philosophers to scrutinize more critically certain epistemological and moral assumptions. However too many of the more popular sophists were totally uninterested in these more subtle and tremendously important philosophical questions. On the contrary, they used their doctrines for merely pragmatic and quite often selfish ends. The evil of it all, as Socrates so deeply felt, was that the sophist was purporting to be a "wise person" when, in effect, he was equating wisdom with mere rhetoric if not specious reasoning. Philosophy, as the love of wisdom, no longer stood for a deep and meaningful inquiry into the ultimate causes and explanations of the cosmos and man's place in that cosmos. Rather, philosophy became known as an acquired ability which used rhetoric if not eristic to win law suits for the acquisition of personal wealth and fame. Socrates viewed sophism as an evil in that it reduced the "love of wisdom" to a mere grasp for power. To Socrates, this was an atrocious descent from the once lofty though difficult pinnacle of philosophical speculation. The disdain with which Socrates held the sophists forced him to critically evaluate their positions. The result of this Socratic evaluation is a serious philosophical theory which will use an elaborate ontology and a sophisticated epistemology as a foundation for a moral theory.

Eduard Zeller, perhaps one of the foremost historians of ancient Greek philosophy, describes the character of Socrates in the following memorable passage:

> A model of self-sufficiency, purity, integrity and virtue, yet full of human kindliness and social charm, cultured and witty, of unfailing good humor and imperturbable serenity, he became an object of veneration to men of the most diverse rank and character. A son of his people, he performed his duty fearlessly in war as in peace and took part in three campaigns. . . . On the other hand his principles kept him apart from politics. But when he was drawn against his will into the turmoil of public affairs, he did not flinch. . . . His criticism of the democratic constitution, his

habitual cross examination of the people with whom he came into contact, and the strong and self-conscious contrast which his whole nature presented with that of the average athenian made him many enemies. . . .

His character shows a remarkable combination of critical shrewdness and a deep religious sense, of sober rationalism and mystical belief. Both these sides, however diametrically opposed they might have been, had their roots in one and the same thing—in a passionate longing which drove him in search of something absolute and unconditioned, which could be apprehended by the intellect and serve as a norm for moral conduct and which he believed to be also the wise and just power that governs universal events.[4]

As Zeller notes, Socrates was indeed a moral hero.

In a very real sense, Socrates was at one with the sophists over the general object of philosophical inquiry. We have seen that the sophists, because of the incompatible philosophical opinions of the early pre-Socratic philosophers of nature, urged that epistemological, metaphysical, and ethical scepticism was the only way for a human to confront philosophy. Socrates agreed that the principal object of philosophical inquiry ought to be the human person and the value questions based upon the development of that person. However Socrates was not so distrustful of reason that he would give up on the merits of speculative philosophy as the sophists had. In other words, Socrates merged the speculative propensity of the pre-Socratic philosophers with the accent on questions of human beings raised by the sophists. The result was the production of a new set of provisional solutions to the basic questions of human existence. With this in mind, Socrates saw as his philosophical mission the establishment of stable and certain truths regarding the possible moral development and perfection of human beings. Obviously this accent on stable truths was opposed to the extreme relativism of the sophists. Insofar as he questioned the sophists on the nature of goodness and virtue, Socrates was confronting and contesting the basic issues of his time. He was thoroughly appalled that virtuous living should be equated with mere rhetorical persuasion and, ultimately, control over one's fellow citizens. In effect, Socrates was advocating freedom and dignity for each individual. Socrates was metaphysician enough, however, to realize that an advocation of dignity alone was a mere will-of-the-wisp in face of the critical scepticism of the sophists. In order to justify his claims of human dignity based upon standards of value, Socrates had to provide an ontology within which he would justify his moral claims. This ontology became very important in the history of philosophy, especially as developed by the most famous student of Socrates, Plato. Plato (428–347 B.C.) emphasized the metaphysical insights of his prodigious tutor and eventually constructed an all-encompassing metaphysical system which proved to be a most influential theory in the development of western philosophy.

Because he was deeply concerned with the nature of a human person and the dignity of that person, Socrates started to question severely the prevailing opinions fostered by the sophists. Socrates conceived the search for the true meaning of virtue to be coextensive with the nature of philosophy. As the Greek commentator, Xenaphon, notes, Socrates had the following qualities:

(Socrates) . . . always disputed about human things, making inquiries about what piety was, what impiety, what beauty, what ugliness, what was the just, the unjust, what bravery, what cowardice, what wisdom, what foolishness.

Predictably enough, this severe questioning produced many bitter enemies for Socrates. To make matters worse, Socrates himself was becoming a quite popular teacher among the young people. He encouraged them to freely and severely question the basic assumptions and convictions of virtue and human morality which were tenaciously held by most of the Greek citizens, and *a fortiori*, of the sophists themselves. As usually happens, persons in power seldom like their first principles and basic moral axioms questioned. Athens of the fifth century was no different. Socrates was eventually brought to trial on a charge of "corrupting the youth" and finally sentenced to die by drinking hemlock. The account of Socrates' life is vividly portrayed in the Platonic dialogue, the *Apology*. This work is a magnificent defense of the free philosophic spirit. The *Apology* is indeed a dramatic statement of what the activity of philosophy is all about. An "apology" is not meant to "apologize" for some fault committed; rather, it is a "defense" of what is sacred and meaningful to a person. In effect, the *Apology* is a defense of the philosophic spirit as Socrates himself practiced it through the activity of serious dialectical questioning.

The Socratic Notion of Virtue

In the *Apology*, a frequently repeated exhortation from this quite personal statement of the philosophic life is Socrates' urging his fellow men to become virtuous. "Know thyself!" became the crucial precept of Socrates. This exhortation to seek virtue above all else is eloquently contained in the Socratic maxim, "The unexamined life is not worth living." It is by knowing oneself that we lead examined lives. Socrates kept insisting that someone is needed to guide and train the young people according to virtuous maxims. Socrates used an interesting analogy—just as a trainer is needed for animals, and as this training is not left to just anyone who happens to drop by, so too is a skilled trainer needed to foster and guide the young in the ways of virtue.

In proposing a model for the acquisition of moral virtue, Socrates made at least three claims:
  1. Virtue can be taught.
  2. Young people will better be able to cope with life if they are taught virtuous maxims.
  3. Not just anybody is to be entrusted with the teaching of virtue.
These are important philosophical claims, especially the first one concerning the teachability of virtue. Is there a difficulty with this claim? A moment's reflection will indicate that it is extremely difficult to teach "morality." Yet Socrates thought it was indeed possible and argued that it needed to be performed by a philosopher. We must analyze the reasons Socrates provided in order to justify this connection between education and the acquisition of virtue.

In order to come to terms with this fundamental tenet of Socratic philosophy, the first question which we must deal with concerns the meaning Socrates attributed to virtue. When first considering the acquisition or the practice of virtue, we might immediately imagine a very straight-laced, narrow concept of "rule-following." In effect, this connection with virtue is quite probably due to the excessive puritanism inherent in American norms of morality. Quite often we tend to view virtue as the exclusive possession of narrow-minded, straight-laced people. This approach to virtue certainly commands neither the immediate interest nor respect of most of us. For us, virtue is too often associated with an extremely repressive, inhibiting set of rules which denies any zest, forcefulness or spice to that precious event called living.

Upon consideration of the Socratic notion of the concept of virtue, we must totally eliminate from our minds all of the repressive and inhibiting uses of the concept of virtue. We simply must forget all pietistic notions of virtue. The Greek mind would be totally unfamiliar with and unsympathetic to the linking of repressiveness with the concept of virtue. The Greek notion of virtue depends upon a translation of *arete*, which means excellence or perfection. It is important to grasp this notion of excellence or perfection—what later philosophers will call *self-actualization*—as the rudimentary meaning for the Greek concept of virtue. There is nothing at all repressive or pietistic about this notion of virtue.

The Greeks were very impressed with the idea of completeness. In the case of all living beings, there was a proper "completeness" which was to be attained. A horse trainer trains the race horse so that it may excel at horse racing. In the case of human beings, perfection or completeness is attained when all human capacities are fulfilled. When one "functions well" as a human being, he or she has attained human perfection or excellence; this excellence is "virtue" for the Greeks. For example, as human beings we all have the capacity to read. If we do not perfect this capacity, the perfection or the capacity, which in this case would be actually being *able* to read, would not be fulfilled or satisfied. To function well is to have the skill of living as a human is supposed to live. *Arete* is connected with the fine performance of a skill. In fact, for the Greeks, an art is never equated with the fine arts. Art is any practical accomplishment of skill. Accordingly, a cabinetmaker has an "art" if he makes cabinets. In addition, he possesses the "arete" (virtue) of cabinetmaking if he really is a fine cabinetmaker. The "virtue" is the excellent performance of a skill. The same holds true in the realm of human affairs and moral actions. A human being has virtue when he or she "lives well" or "functions well" as a human being. Accordingly, virtue for Socrates was quite removed from any repressive aspect. To have virtue is to have attained the excellence proper to a human being. A virtuous action is one which always serves the true end of satisfaction and fulfillment of a human nature. As we shall soon see, not any end will be a satisfied end. Socrates argued for what he considered to be *the* true end and true good for human beings. Obviously this will require an adequate ontological system in order to establish the foundation for a true end. This ontological system will become more clear as we explicitly discuss more of the Platonic dialogues later in this chapter. Immediately we should notice that, if Socrates is to establish a true end for human beings, his position will be diametrically opposed to the radical relativism characteristic of the sophists. We must rigorously analyze this position in order to see if it indeed can surmount the sophist scepticism.

Virtue and Knowledge

We must now consider the connection between virtue and knowledge. In the Socratic scheme, knowledge is the correct means to attaining moral virtue. In other words, there is an intrinsic connection between knowledge and moral action. Knowledge is not to be separated from the moral commitments a person makes regarding either his or her life or the norms for a society. In order to understand the Socratic position about virtue, it is necessary to understand the Socratic epistemology. As we shall see, Socrates built his scheme of moral perfection around an extremely intricate epistemological position.

Socrates claimed that virtue and knowledge are one. The wise person, i.e., the person who knows what is the right action to do, will always do what is right. In other words, if one knows the right action to do, then one will perform that action. The converse to the claim that virtue is knowledge is that immorality is ignorance. Therefore an immoral action occurs when one acts from ignorance. This Socratic analysis is one of the first attempts to formulate a rational ethic. An implied principle here is: knowledge is that which will promote a human's true completion or "well being." This concept of well being (*eudaimonia*) is connected with the notion of moral excellence discussed above. The Socratic claim that true virtue is connected with knowledge in turn depends upon a worked-out epistemology.

The Platonic Dialogue

Before beginning our discussion of Platonic epistemology, a few words are in order concerning the nature of the Platonic dialogues. Plato is a magnificent writer. As a master of language he is aware of many literary moves. Keeping this in mind when reading the dialogues, the reader must be constantly on the alert to avoid missing insights or suggestions. However, never lose sight of the literary genre of the dialogue. A philosophic-literary interpretation will work best of all in our attempt to analyze Plato's philosophical insights. This literary interpretation has some historical precedent in that the greatness of Plato was rediscovered during the Renaissance, a period well known for its devotion to the fine arts.

Most of the extant Platonic writings are in the form of dialogues. Although some historians claim that Plato did in fact write other detailed philosophical treatises, none of these has survived. The dialogues themselves are popular presentations devoted to stimulating questioning over a wide range of issues. Usually a dialogue has Socrates as the pivotal figure. By asking many incisive questions in a dialectical manner, Socrates leads the discussion toward a designated end. In a dialogue, the dramatic setting is also important. The philosophical thought and the setting go together in making a complete whole. It would be well to keep the following thoughts in mind while reading the dialogues.

1. A dialogue is a genuine dramatic work of literature. In that it has a dramatic character, one must pay attention to the setting of the dialogue, the characters involved in the discussions, their backgrounds, the metaphors used, who is speaking and why, and so forth. As in any good novel, watch for clues and hints as to the direction that the thrust of the argument will take. Plato is a writer who wastes few words.

2. The primary object of a dialogue is to engage the whole and undivided attention of each reader. Plato is out to arouse our curiosity and to force us to extend our cognitive awareness. In extending this awareness, we too become a part of the dialogue as it gropes along searching for a hint towards establishing a resolution of the problem under discussion. Accordingly, in his dialogues

Plato looks upon his reader as an unidentified character. It is important that we realize this. Too often, students look upon the dialogue as an uninspired monograph which is to be read passively. This attitude will do nothing but make the reading of Plato terribly unexciting. Moreover, it will evoke precious little interest for the matters of philosophy in us as readers. Plato can stimulate some very creative thinking if we face the dialogue with the proper frame of mind and are adequately disposed to take all we can from the wellspring of the dialogue. On the other hand, if we expect Plato to stimulate us without a questioning participation on our part, then there is no way we will appreciate the insights, the new awarenesses, and the creative probing of Plato at his best.

3. Plato, like many twentieth-century philosophers, regards philosophy as an activity. Each of us must partake in this activity of coming to terms with certain fundamental questions which are brought to bear on the readers of the dialogue. Plato never considers philosophy as a complete system which is to be taught like Euclidean geometry or organic chemistry. In his dialogue, the *Meno*, Socrates describes the role of the philosopher as analogous to a midwife rather than as an instructor. The philosopher as midwife is one who educates. Education is an etymological derivation from the Latin term *educare*, which means "to bring forth." The midwife brings forth what is already present latently in the knower. However this "birth" will not occur successfully unless the reader is actively involved in the Socratic discussions.

4. Finally, the dialogue has, as a pivotal factor, the role of reason. The affirmation of rational ascent is crucial. Reason serves as the judge which determines what is important and what is unimportant in the dialogues. Reason also serves as an overriding force which guides the disputants of the dialogue along in their hunt for a philosophic solution to a specific problem. This produces a paradoxical result in that, in every dialogue, each person is both a winner and a loser. A person wins in that he or she now has a better understanding of the subject under discussion. Yet he or she also loses in that each participant must change to some degree. The most obvious change is that the confidence of each participant regarding the acceptance of one truth or another is somewhat shaken. New vistas and new insights are presented to each member of the discussion—and to the reader—so that one goes away from a dialogue less complacent in his/her opinions than before. Hopefully, the reader will have his or her confidence shaken. If this happens, Plato will have fulfilled his role as "gadfly." In essence, a dialogue prevents any opinion from being inextricably frozen. There is always a certain openness toward each philosophical position. Yet each opinion must pass through the test of fire brought about by the Socratic dialectic. In the *Apology*, Socrates often characterized himself as a "gadfly," one who went around stinging other people in order to prod them so that they might confront their existence by intellectually probing the foundations of their views of life. Socrates never considered himself an "imparter" of wisdom. He was not a provider of a traditional system which was to be accepted as the bona fide set of answers to every problem which one might face during life. Socrates never looked upon philosophy as a "cookbook" or "giant index" in which an adequate solution to any given philosophical problem might be found. Quite the contrary, philosophy for Socrates was an existing and exacting activity probing the depths of human existence.

There are certain obstacles which any newcomer to the Platonic dialogue must overcome. First of all, there is an unfamiliarity with the dialogue form, a form which is rarely used in contemporary literature. A greater problem, however, is the lack in most of the dialogues of a set, intractable conclusion. Most of the dialogues are rather incomplete in that a conclusive answer is seldom provided. This is difficult for most of us to accept. Sometimes there is no pat solution to the long and difficult questionings which transpire in a dialogue. Another minor problem is that a dialogue is a genuine discussion and not a one-sided expression of rhetorical skill. Men of diverse opinions, prejudices, judgments, feelings, and so forth come together to seriously confront some topic of common interest. There is much give and take in which a reader must participate if the dialogue is to be appreciated.

A very good example of an early Platonic dialogue is the *Euthyphro*. In this dialogue, Plato provides a masterful example of Socratic dialectic. Socrates asks Euthyphro a series of serious and pointed questions in search of an adequate definition of "piety." It would be well to keep in mind the previous discussion concerning the nature of a dialogue and try to apply these hints while reading the *Euthyphro*.

Before reading the *Euthyphro*, however, there is one historical note which should be mentioned. Socrates either left nothing in writing or his written pieces have been lost over the centuries. Much of our knowledge of Socrates is attributed to Plato. In fact, as we shall soon see, Socrates is the principal figure in many of the early and middle dialogues of Plato. This fact has caused much scholarly debate over how much of the Platonic dialogues in which Socrates is the main character are really descriptive reports of the Socratic positions or, rather, interpretations and elaborations of Plato's own philosophical doctrines. This debate, while important, should not hinder our beginning awareness of the philosophical insights of Platonism. For our purposes, we shall consider early and middle Platonism to be coextensive with the mind of Socrates. In other words, what Plato writes in the early and middle dialogues shall be considered as equivalent to the teachings of the historical Socrates.

EUTHYPHRO

Plato

PERSONS OF THE DIALOGUE
Socrates   Euthyphro

Scene: The Porch of the King Archon

Euth. Why have you left the Lyceum, Socrates? and what are you doing in the porch of the King Archon? Surely you cannot be engaged in an action before the king, as I am.

Socrates. Not in an action, Euthyphro; impeachment is the word which the Athenians use.

Reprinted from B. Jowett, trans., *The Dialogues of Plato* (New York: Charles Scribner's Sons, 1895).

Euth. What! I suppose that some one has been prosecuting you, for I cannot believe that you are the prosecutor of another.

Soc. Certainly not.

Euth. Then some one else has been prosecuting you.

Soc. Yes.

Euth. And who is he?

Soc. A young man who is little known, Euthyphro; and I hardly know him: his name is Meletus, and he is of the deme of Pitthis. Perhaps you may remember his appearance; he has a beak, and long straight hair, and a beard which is ill grown.

Euth. No, I do not remember him, Socrates. And what is the charge which he brings against you?

Soc. What is the charge? Well, a very serious charge, which shows a good deal of character in the young man, and for which he is certainly not to be despised. He says he knows how the youth are corrupted and who are their corrupters. I fancy that he must be a wise man, and seeing that I am anything but a wise man, he has found me out, and is going to accuse me of corrupting his young friends. And of this our mother the state is to be the judge. Of all our political men he is the only one who seems to me to begin in the right way, with the cultivation of virtue in youth; he is a good husbandman, and takes care of the shoots first, and clears away us who are the destroyers of them. That is the first step; he will afterwards attend to the elder branches; and if he goes on as he has begun, he will be a very great public benefactor.

Euth. I hope that he may; but I rather fear, Socrates, that the reverse will turn out to be the truth. My opinion is that in attacking you he is simply aiming a blow at the state in a sacred place. But in what way does he say that you corrupt the young?

Soc. He brings a wonderful accusation against me, which at first hearing excites surprise: he says that I am a poet or maker of gods, and that I make new gods and deny the existence of old ones; this is the ground of his indictment.

Euth. I understand, Socrates; he means to attack you about the familiar sign which occasionally, as you say, comes to you. He thinks that you are a neologian, and he is going to have you up before the court for this. He knows that such a charge is readily received, for the world is always jealous of novelties in religion. And I know that when I myself speak in the assembly about divine things, and foretell the future to them, they laugh at me as a madman; and yet every word that I say is true. But they are jealous of all of us. I suppose that we must be brave and not mind them.

Soc. Their laughter, friend Euthyphro, is not a matter of much consequence. For a man may be thought wise; but the Athenians, I suspect, do not care much about this, until he begins to make other men wise; and then for some reason or other, perhaps, as you say, from jealousy, they are angry.

Euth. I have no desire to try conclusions with them about this.

Soc. I dare say that you don't make yourself common, and are not apt to impart your wisdom. But I have a benevolent habit of pouring out myself to everybody, and would even pay for a listener, and I am afraid that the

Athenians know this; and therefore, as I was saying, if the Athenians would only laugh at me as you say that they laugh at you, the time might pass gayly enough in the court; but perhaps they may be in earnest, and then what the end will be you soothsayers only can predict.

Euth. I dare say that the affair will end in nothing, Socrates, and that you will win your cause; and I think that I shall win mine.

Soc. And what is your suit? and are you the pursuer or defendant, Euthyphro?

Euth. I am pursuer.

Soc. Of whom?

Euth. You will think me mad when I tell you whom I am pursuing.

Soc. Why, has the fugitive wings?

Euth. Nay, he is not very volatile at his time of life.

Soc. Who is he?

Euth. My father.

Soc. Your father! good heavens, you don't mean that?

Euth. Yes.

Soc. And of what is he accused?

Euth. Murder, Socrates.

Soc. By the powers, Euthyphro! how little does the common herd know of the nature of right and truth. A man must be an extraordinary man and have made great strides in wisdom, before he could have seen his way to this.

Euth. Indeed, Socrates, he must have made great strides.

Soc. I suppose that the man whom your father murdered was one of your relatives; if he had been a stranger you would never have thought of prosecuting him.

Euth. I am amused, Socrates, at your making a distinction between one who is a relation and one who is not a relation; for surely the pollution is the same in either case, if you knowingly associate with the murderer when you ought to clear yourself by proceeding against him. The real question is whether the murdered man has been justly slain. If justly, then your duty is to let the matter alone; but if unjustly, then even if the murderer is under the same roof with you and eats at the same table, proceed against him. Now the man who is dead was a poor dependant of mine who worked for us as a field laborer at Naxos, and one day in a fit of drunken passion he got into a quarrel with one of our domestic servants and slew him. My father bound him hand and foot and threw him into a ditch, and then sent to Athens to ask of a diviner what he should do with him. Meantime he had no care or thought of him, being under the impression that he was a murderer; and that even if he did die there would be no great harm. And this was just what happened. For such was the effect of cold and hunger and chains upon him, that before the messenger returned from the diviner, he was dead. And my father and family are angry with me for taking the part of the murderer and prosecuting my father. They say that he did not kill him, and if he did, the dead man was but a murderer, and I ought not to take any notice, for that a son is impious who prosecutes a father. That shows, Socrates, how little they know of the opinions of the gods about piety and impiety.

Soc. Good heavens, Euthyphro! and have you such a precise knowledge of piety and impiety, and of divine things in general, that, supposing the circumstances to be as you state, you are not afraid that you too may be doing an impious thing in bringing an action against your father?

Euth. The best of Euthyphro, and that which distinguishes him, Socrates, from other men, is his exact knowledge of all these matters. What should I be good for without that?

Soc. Rare friend! I think that I cannot do better than be your disciple, before the trial with Meletus comes on. Then I shall challenge him, and say that I have always had a great interest in religious questions, and now, as he charges me with rash imaginations and innovations in religion, I have become your disciple. Now you, Meletus, as I shall say to him, acknowledge Euthyphro to be a great theologian, and sound in his opinions; and if you think that of him you ought to think the same of me, and not have me into court; you should begin by indicting him who is my teacher, and who is the real corrupter, not of the young, but of the old; that is to say, of myself whom he instructs, and of his old father whom he admonishes and chastises. And if Meletus refuses to listen to me, but will go on, and will not shift the indictment from me to you, I cannot do better than say in the court that I challenged him in this way.

Euth. Yes, Socrates; and if he attempts to indict me I am mistaken if I don't find a flaw in him; the court shall have a great deal more to say to him than to me.

Soc. I know that, dear friend; and that is the reason why I desire to be your disciple. For I observe that no one, not even Meletus, appears to notice you; but his sharp eyes have found me out at once, and he has indicted me for impiety. And therefore, I adjure you to tell me the nature of piety and impiety, which you said that you knew so well, and of murder, and the rest of them. What are they? Is not piety in every action always the same? and impiety, again, is not that always the opposite of piety, and also the same with itself, having, as impiety, one notion which includes whatever is impious?

Euth. To be sure, Socrates.

Soc. And what is piety, and what is impiety?

Euth. Piety is doing as I am doing; that is to say, prosecuting any one who is guilty of murder, sacrilege, or of any other similar crime—whether he be your father or mother, or some other person, that makes no difference—and not prosecuting them is impiety. And please to consider, Socrates, what a notable proof I will give you of the truth of what I am saying, which I have already given to others,—of the truth, I mean, of the principle that the impious whoever he may be, ought not to go unpunished. For do not men regard Zeus as the best and most righteous of the gods?—and even they admit that he bound his father (Cronos) because he wickedly devoured his sons, and that he too had punished his own father (Uranus) for a similar reason, in a nameless manner. And yet when I proceed against my father, they are angry with me. This is their inconsistent way of talking when the gods are concerned, and when I am concerned.

Soc. May not this be the reason, Euthyphro, why I am charged with impiety—that I cannot away with these stories about the gods? and therefore I suppose that people think me wrong. But, as you who are well informed about them approve of them, I cannot do better than assent to your superior wisdom. For what else can I say, confessing as I do, that I know nothing of them. I wish you would tell me whether you really believe that they are true?

Euth. Yes, Socrates; and things more wonderful still, of which the world is in ignorance.

Soc. And do you really believe that the gods fought with one another, and had dire quarrels, battles, and the like, as the poets say, and as you may see represented in the works of great artists? The temples are full of them; and notably the robe of Athene, which is carried up to the Acropolis at the great Panathenaea, is embroidered with them. Are all these tales of the gods true, Euthyphro?

Euth. Yes, Socrates; and, as I was saying, I can tell you, if you would like to hear them, many other things about the gods which would quite amaze you.

Soc. I dare say; and you shall tell me them at some other time when I have leisure. But just at present I would rather hear from you a more precise answer, which you have not as yet given, my friend, to the question, What is "piety?" In reply, you only say that piety is, Doing as you do, charging your father with murder.

Euth. And that is true, Socrates.

Soc. I dare say, Euthyphro, but there are many other pious acts.

Euth. There are.

Soc. Remember that I did not ask you to give me two or three examples of piety, but to explain the general idea which makes all pious things to be pious. Do you not recollect that there was one idea which made the impious impious, and the pious pious?

Euth. I remember.

Soc. Tell me what this is, and then I shall have a standard to which I may look, and by which I may measure the nature of actions, whether yours or any one's else, and say that this action is pious, and that impious?

Euth. I will tell you, if you like.

Soc. I should very much like.

Euth. Piety, then, is that which is dear to the gods, and impiety is that which is not dear to them.

Soc. Very good, Euthyphro; you have now given me just the sort of answer which I wanted. But whether it is true or not I cannot as yet tell, although I make no doubt that you will prove the truth of your words.

Euth. Of course.

Soc. Come, then, and let us examine what we are saying. That thing or person which is dear to the gods is pious, and that thing or person which is hateful to the gods is impious. Was not that said?

Euth. Yes, that was said.

Soc. And that seems to have been very well said too?

Euth. Yes, Socrates, I think that; it was certainly said.

Soc. And further, Euthyphro, the gods were admitted to have enmities and hatreds and differences—that was also said?

Euth. Yes, that was said.

Soc. And what sort of difference creates enmity and anger? Suppose for example that you and I, my good friend, differ about a number; do differences of this sort make us enemies and set us at variance with one another? Do we not go at once to calculation, and end them by a sum?

Euth. True.

Soc. Or suppose that we differ about magnitudes, do we not quickly put an end to that difference by measuring?

Euth. That is true.

Soc. And we end a controversy about heavy and light by resorting to a weighing-machine?

Euth. To be sure.

Soc. But what differences are those which, because they cannot be thus decided, make us angry and set us at enmity with one another? I dare say the answer does not occur to you at the moment, and therefore I will suggest that this happens when the matters of difference are the just and unjust, good and evil, honorable and dishonorable. Are not these the points about which, when differing, and unable satisfactorily to decide our differences, we quarrel, when we do quarrel, as you and I and all men experience?

Euth. Yes, Socrates, that is the nature of the differences about which we quarrel.

Soc. And the quarrels of the gods, noble Euthyphro, when they occur, are of a like nature?

Euth. They are.

Soc. They have differences of opinion, as you say, about good and evil, just and unjust, honorable and dishonorable: there would have been no quarrels among them, if there had been no such differences—would there now?

Euth. You are quite right.

Soc. Does not every man love that which he deems noble and just and good, and hate the opposite of them?

Euth. Very true.

Soc. But then, as you say, people regard the same things, some as just and others as unjust; and they dispute about this, and there arise wars and fightings among them.

Euth. Yes, that is true.

Soc. Then the same things, as appears, are hated by the gods and loved by the gods, are both hateful and dear to them?

Euth. True.

Soc. Then upon this view the same things, Euthyphro, will be pious and also impious?

Euth. That, I suppose, is true.

Soc. Then, my friend, I remark with surprise that you have not answered what I asked. For I certainly did not ask what was that which is at once pious and impious: and that which is loved by the gods appears to be hated by them. And therefore, Euthyphro, in thus chastising your father you may very likely be doing what is agreeable to Zeus but disagreeable to Cronos or Uranus, and what is acceptable to Hephaestus but unacceptable to Here, and there may be other gods who have similar differences of opinion.

Euth. But I believe, Socrates, that all the gods would be agreed as to the propriety of punishing a murderer: there would be no difference of opinion about that.

Soc. Well, but speaking of men, Euthyphro, did you ever hear any one arguing that a murderer or any sort of evil-doer ought to be let off?

Euth. I should rather say that they are always arguing this, especially in courts of law; they commit all sorts of crimes, and there is nothing that they will not do or say in order to escape punishment.

Soc. But do they admit their guilt, Euthyphro, and yet say that they ought not to be punished?

Euth. No; they do not.

Soc. Then there are some things which they do not venture to say and do: for they do not venture to argue that the guilty are to be unpunished, but they deny their guilt, do they not?

Euth. Yes.

Soc. Then they do not argue that the evil-doer should not be punished, but they argue about the fact of who the evil-doer is, and what he did and when?

Euth. True.

Soc. And the gods are in the same case, if as you imply they quarrel about just and unjust, and some of them say that they wrong one another, and others of them deny this. For surely neither God nor man will ever venture to say that the doer of evil is not to be punished: you don't mean to tell me that?

Euth. That is true, Socrates, in the main.

Soc. But they join issue about particulars; and this applies not only to men but to the gods; if they dispute at all they dispute about some act which is called in question, and which some affirm to be just, others to be unjust. Is not that true?

Euth. Quite true.

Soc. Well then, my dear friend Euthyphro, do tell me, for my better instruction and information, what proof have you that in the opinion of all the gods a servant who is guilty of murder, and is put in chains by the master of the dead man, and dies because he is put in chains before his corrector can learn from the interpreters what he ought to do with him, dies unjustly; and that on behalf of such a one a son ought to proceed against his father and accuse him of murder. How would you show that all the gods absolutely agree in approving of his act? Prove to me that, and I will applaud your wisdom as long as you live.

Euth. That would not be an easy task, although I could make the matter very clear indeed to you.

Soc. I understand; you mean to say that I am not so quick of apprehension as the judges: for to them you will be sure to prove that the act is unjust, and hateful to the gods.

Euth. Yes indeed, Socrates; at least if they will listen to me.

Soc. But they will be sure to listen if they find that you are a good speaker. There was a notion that came into my mind while you were speaking; I said to myself: "Well, and what if Euthyphro does prove to me that all the gods regarded the death of the serf as unjust, how do I know anything more of the nature of piety and impiety? for granting that this action may be hateful to the gods, still these distinctions have no bearing on the definition of piety and impiety, for that which is hateful to the gods has been shown to be also pleasing and dear to them." And therefore, Euthyphro, I don't ask you to prove this; I will suppose, if you like, that all the gods condemn and abominate such an action. But I will amend the definition so far as to say that what all the gods hate is impious, and what they love pious or holy; and what some of them love and others hate is both or neither. Shall this be our definition of piety and impiety?

Euth. Why not, Socrates?

Soc. Why not! certainly, as far as I am concerned, Euthyphro. But whether this admission will greatly assist you in the task of instructing me as you promised, is a matter for you to consider.

Euth. Yes, I should say that what all the gods love is pious and holy, and the opposite which they all hate, impious.

Soc. Ought we to inquire into the truth of this, Euthyphro, or simply to accept the mere statement on our own authority and that of others?

Euth. We should inquire; and I believe that the statement will stand the test of inquiry.

Soc. That, my good friend, we shall know better in a little while. The point which I should first wish to understand is whether the pious or holy is beloved by the gods because it is holy, or holy because it is beloved of the gods.

Euth. I don't understand your meaning, Socrates.

Soc. I will endeavor to explain: we speak of carrying and we speak of being carried, of leading and being led, seeing and being seen. And here is a difference the nature of which you understand.

Euth. I think that I understand.

Soc. And is not that which is beloved distinct from that which loves?

Euth. Certainly.

Soc. Well; and now tell me, is that which is carried in this state of carrying because it is carried, or for some other reason?

Euth. No; that is the reason.

Soc. And the same is true of that which is led and of that which is seen?

Euth. True.

Soc. And a thing is not seen because it is visible, but conversely, visible because it is seen; nor is a thing in the state of being led because it is led, or in the state of being carried because it is carried, but the converse of this. And now I think, Euthyphro, that my meaning will be intelligible; and my meaning is, that any state of action or passion implies previous action or passion. It does not become because it is becoming, but it is becoming because it comes; neither does it suffer because it is in a state of suffering, but it is in a state of suffering because it suffers. Do you admit that?

Euth. Yes.

Soc. Is not that which is loved in some state either of becoming or suffering?

Euth. Yes.

Soc. And the same holds as in the previous instances; the state of being loved follows the act of being loved, and not the act the state.

Euth. That is certain.

Soc. And what do you say of piety, Euthyphro: is not piety according to your definition, loved by all the gods?

Euth. Yes.

Soc. Because it is pious or holy, or for some other reason?

Euth. No, that is the reason.

Soc. It is loved because it is holy, not holy because it is loved?

Euth. Yes.

Soc. And that which is in a state to be loved of the gods, and is dear to them, is in a state to be loved of them because it is loved of them?

Euth. Certainly.

Soc. Then that which is loved of God, Euthyphro, is not holy, nor is that which is holy loved of God, as you affirm; but they are two different things.

Euth. How do you mean, Socrates?

Soc. I mean to say that the holy has been acknowledged by us to be loved of God because it is holy, not to be holy because it is loved.

Euth. Yes.

Soc. But that which is dear to the gods is dear to them because it is loved by them, not loved by them because it is dear to them.

Euth. True.

Soc. But, friend Euthyphro, if that which is holy is the same as that which is dear to God, and that which is holy is loved as being holy, then that which is dear to God would have been loved as being dear to God; but if that which is dear to God is dear to him because loved by him, then that which is holy would have been holy because loved by him. But now you see that the reverse is the case, and that they are quite different from one another. For one ($\theta\epsilon o\phi\iota\lambda\grave{\epsilon}s$) is of a kind to be loved because it is loved, and the other ($\mathring{o}\sigma\iota o\nu$) is loved because it is of a kind to be loved. Thus you appear to me, Euthyphro, when I ask you what is the essence of holiness, to offer an attribute only, and not the essence—the attribute of being loved by all the gods. But you still refuse to explain to me the nature of piety. And therefore, if you please, I will ask you not to hide your treasure, but to tell me once more what piety or holiness really is, whether dear to the gods or not (for that is a matter about which we will not quarrel). And what is impiety?

Euth. I really do not know, Socrates, how to say what I mean. For somehow or other our arguments, on whatever ground we rest them, seem to turn round and walk away.

Soc. Your words, Euthyphro, are like the handiwork of my ancestor Daedalus; and if I were the sayer or propounder of them, you might say that this comes of my being his relation and that this is the reason why my arguments walk away and won't remain fixed where they are placed. But now, as the notions are your own, you must find some other gibe, for they certainly, as you yourself allow, show an inclination to be on the move.

Euth. Nay, Socrates, I shall still say that you are the Daedalus who sets arguments in motion; not I, certainly, make them move or go round, for they would never have stirred, as far as I am concerned.

Soc. Then I must be a greater than Daedalus; for whereas he only made his own inventions to move, I move those of other people as well. And the beauty of it is, that I would rather not. For I would give the wisdom of Daedalus, and the wealth of Tantalus, to be able to detain them and keep them fixed. But enough of this. As I perceive that you are indolent, I will myself endeavor to show you how you might instruct me in the nature of piety; and I hope that you will not grudge your labor. Tell me, then,—Is not that which is pious necessarily just?

Euth. Yes.

Soc. And is, then, all which is just pious? or, is that which is pious all just, but that which is just only in part and not all pious?

Euth. I don't understand you, Socrates.

Soc. And yet I know that you are as much wiser than I am, as you are younger. But, as I was saying, revered friend, the abundance of your wisdom makes you indolent. Please to exert yourself, for there is no real difficulty in understanding me. What I mean I may explain by an illustration of what I do not mean. The poet (Stasinus) sings:—

Of Zeus, the author and creator of all these things,
You will not tell: for where there is fear there is also reverence.

And I disagree with this poet. Shall I tell you in what I disagree?

Euth. By all means.

Soc. I should not say that where there is fear there is also reverence; for I am sure that many persons fear poverty and disease, and the like evils, but I do not perceive that they reverence the objects of their fear.

Euth. Very true.

Soc. But where reverence is, there is fear; for he who has a feeling of reverence and shame about the commission of any action, fears and is afraid of an ill reputation.

Euth. No doubt.

Soc. Then we are wrong in saying that where there is fear there is also reverence; and we should say, where there is reverence there is also fear. But there is not always reverence where there is fear; for fear is a more extended notion, and reverence is a part of fear, just as the odd is a part of number, and number is a more extended notion than the odd. I suppose that you follow me now?

Euth. Quite well.

Soc. That was the sort of question which I meant to raise when asking whether the just is the pious, or the pious the just; and whether there may not be justice where there is not always piety; for justice is the more extended notion of which piety is only a part. Do you agree in that?

Euth. Yes; that, I think, is correct.

Soc. Then, now, if piety is a part of justice, I suppose that we inquire what part? If you had pursued the inquiry in the previous cases; for instance, if you had asked me what is an even number, and what part of number the even is, I should have had no difficulty in replying, a number which represents a figure having two equal sides. Do you agree?

Euth. Yes.

Soc. In like manner, I want you to tell me what part of justice is piety or holiness; that I may be able to tell Meletus not to do me injustice, or indict me for impiety; as I am now adequately instructed by you in the nature of piety or holiness, and their opposites.

Euth. Piety or holiness, Socrates, appears to me to be that part of justice which attends to the gods, as there is the other part of justice which attends to men.

Soc. That is good, Euthyphro; yet still there is a little point about which I should like to have further information, What is the meaning of "attention?" For attention can hardly be used in the same sense when applied to the gods as when applied to other things. For instance, horses are said to require attention, and not every person is able to attend to them, but only a person skilled in horsemanship. Is not that true?

Euth. Quite true.

Soc. I should suppose that the art of horsemanship is the art of attending to horses?

Euth. Yes.

Soc. Nor is every one qualified to attend to dogs, but only the huntsman.

Euth. True.

Soc. And I should also conceive that the art of the huntsman is the art of attending to dogs?

Euth. Yes.

Soc. As the art of the oxherd is the art of attending to oxen?

Euth. Very true.

Soc. And as holiness or piety is the art of attending to the gods?—that would be your meaning, Euthyphro?

Euth. Yes.

Soc. And is not attention always designed for the good or benefit of that to which the attention is given? As in the case of horses, you may observe that when attended to by the horseman's art they are benefited and improved, are they not?

Euth. True.

Soc. As the dogs are benefited by the huntsman's art, and the oxen by the art of the oxherd, and all other things are tended or attended for their good and not for their hurt?

Euth. Certainly, not for their hurt.

Soc. But for their good?

Euth. Of course.

Soc. And does piety or holiness, which has been defined as the art of attending to the gods, benefit or improve them? Would you say that when you do a holy act you make any of the gods better?

Euth. No, no; that is certainly not my meaning.

Soc. Indeed, Euthyphro, I did not suppose that this was your meaning; far otherwise. And that was the reason why I asked you the nature of this attention, because I thought that this was not your meaning.

Euth. You do me justice, Socrates; for that is not my meaning.

Soc. Good: but I must still ask what is this attention to the gods which is called piety?

Euth. It is such, Socrates, as servants show to their masters.

Soc. I understand—a sort of ministration to the gods.

Euth. Exactly.

Soc. Medicine is also a sort of ministration or service, tending to the attainment of some object,—would you say health?

Euth. Yes.

Soc. Again, there is an art which ministers to the shipbuilder with a view to the attainment of some result?

Euth. Yes, Socrates, with a view to the building of a ship.

Soc. As there is an art which ministers to the house-builder with a view to the building of a house?

Euth. Yes.

Soc. And now tell me, my good friend, about this art which ministers to the gods: what work does that help to accomplish? For you must surely know if, as you say, you are of all men living the one who is best instructed in religion.

Euth. And that is true, Socrates.

Soc. Tell me then, O tell me,—what is that fair work which the gods do by the help of us as their ministers?

Euth. Many and fair, Socrates, are the works which they do.

Soc. Why, my friend, and so are those of a general. But the chief of them is easily told. Would you not say that victory in war is the chief of them?

Euth. Certainly.

Soc. Many and fair, too, are the works of the husbandman, if I am not mistaken; but his chief work is the production of food from the earth?

Euth. Exactly.

Soc. And of the many and fair things which the gods do, which is the chief and principal one?

Euth. I have told you already, Socrates, that to learn all these things accurately will be very tiresome. Let me simply say that piety is learning how to please the gods in word and deed, by prayers and sacrifices. That is piety, which is the salvation of families and states, just as the impious, which is unpleasing to the gods, is their ruin and destruction.

Soc. I think that you could have answered in much fewer words the chief question which I asked, Euthyphro, if you had chosen. But I see plainly that you are not disposed to instruct me : else why, when we had reached the point, did you turn aside? Had you only answered me, I should have learned of you by this time the nature of piety. Now, as the asker of a question is necessarily dependent on the answerer, whither he leads I must follow; and can only ask again, what is the pious, and what is piety? Do you mean that they are a sort of science of praying and sacrificing?

Euth. Yes, I do.

Soc. And sacrificing is giving to the gods, and prayer is asking of the gods?

Euth. Yes, Socrates.

Soc. Upon this view, then, piety is a science of asking and giving?

Euth. You understand me capitally, Socrates.

Soc. Yes, my friend; the reason is that I am a votary of your science, and give my mind to it, and therefore nothing which you say will be thrown away upon me. Please then to tell me, what is the nature of this service to the gods? Do you mean that we prefer requests and give gifts to them?

Euth. Yes, I do.

Soc. Is not the right way of asking to ask of them what we want?

Euth. Certainly.

Soc. And the right way of giving is to give them in return what they want of us. There would be no meaning in an art which gives to any one that which he does not want.

Euth. Very true, Socrates.

Soc. Then piety, Euthyphro, is an art which gods and men have of doing business with one another?

Euth. That is an expression which you may use, if you like.

Soc. But I have no particular liking for anything but the truth. I wish, however, that you would tell me what benefit accrues to the gods from our gifts. That they are the givers of every good to us is clear; but how we can give any good thing to them in return is far from being equally clear. If they give everything and we give nothing, that must be an affair of business in which we have very greatly the advantage of them.

Euth. And do you imagine, Socrates, that any benefit accrues to the gods from what they receive of us?

Soc. But if not, Euthyphro, what sort of gifts do we confer upon the gods?

Euth. What should we confer upon them, but tributes of honor; and, as I was just now saying, what is pleasing to them?

Soc. Piety, then, is pleasing to the gods, but not beneficial or dear to them?

Euth. I should say that nothing could be dearer.

Soc. Then once more the assertion is repeated that piety is dear to the gods?

Euth. No doubt.

Soc. And when you say this, can you wonder at your words not standing firm, but walking away? Will you accuse me of being the Daedalus who makes them walk away, not perceiving that there is another and far greater artist than Daedalus who makes them go round in a circle; and that is yourself: for the argument, as you will perceive, comes round to the same point. I think that you must remember our saying that the holy or pious was not the same as that which is loved of the gods. Do you remember that?

Euth. I do.

Soc. And do you not see that what is loved of the gods is holy, and this is the same as what is dear to them?

Euth. True.

Soc. Then either we were wrong in that admission; or, if we were right then, we are wrong now.

Euth. I suppose that is the case.

Soc. Then we must begin again and ask, What is piety? That is an inquiry which I shall never be weary of pursuing as far as in me lies; and I entreat you not to scorn me, but to apply your mind to the utmost, and tell me the truth. For, if any man knows, you are he; and therefore I shall detain you, like Proteus, until you tell. For if you had not certainly known the nature of piety and impiety, I am confident that you would never, on behalf of a serf, have charged your aged father with murder. You would not have run such a risk of doing wrong in the sight of the gods, and you would have had too much respect for the opinions of men. I am sure, therefore, that you know the nature of piety and impiety. Speak out then, my dear Euthyphro, and do not hide your knowledge.

Euth. Another time, Socrates; for I am in a hurry, and must go now.

Soc. Alas! my companion, and will you leave me in despair? I was hoping that you would instruct me in the nature of piety and impiety, so that I might have cleared myself of Meletus and his indictment. Then I might have proved to him that I had been converted by Euthyphro, and had done with rash innovations and speculations, in which I had indulged through ignorance, and was about to lead a better life.

The *Euthyphro* is an appropriate dialogue with which to begin our study of Platonism. The background for the dialogue is important. In the *Apology* Socrates had been indicted by the Athenians on the charge of impiety (for worshiping false gods) and of corrupting the young. Euthyphro's plight is similar to Socrates' own concerns. Euthyphro himself has been charged with impiety because he brought charges against his father. In addition to being interested in the socratic mission of attending after virtue, Euthyphro is a theologian; hence, he should know something about the nature of piety and impiety. Given this background, an important philosophical discussion should occur.

Because both Socrates and Euthyphro have been charged with impiety, it is a natural question for them to ponder together the question concerning the nature of piety and impiety. In the dialogue, different proposals for an adequate definition of piety are brought forward and analyzed. The discussion itself is a very good example of Platonic dialectic. Questions are raised concerning each definition and counterexamples are put forward in order to test the adequacy of the proposal. Euthyphro puts forward his first definition of piety; it is to prosecute anyone guilty of murder, sacrilege, or similar crimes. Right away, Socrates notes that this is not a definition but a listing of examples. For Socrates only a definition which spells out the necessary and sufficient conditions for a concept will be acceptable. Euthyphro then suggests a second definition: piety is doing that which is dear to the gods. Socrates immediately notes that the gods might differ regarding what they considered as dear. Given this definition, the same things might be both pious and impious depending upon which god was considered.

Another proposal is put forward. Piety is what all the gods love and impiety is what all the gods hate. Socrates raises an important question. Is an act or event pious because it is loved by the gods? Or is it loved by the gods because it is pious? Does the mere act of being loved by the gods constitute piety or do the gods love certain things because they indeed are pious? If the second case holds, then Socrates still needs to know what characteristic or property things possess which makes the gods love them. Socrates seeks an internal, constitutive property which defines the essence of piety. Another definition is suggested: piety is that part of justice which attends to the gods. Socrates asks about the process of attending—will this benefit the gods? But do the gods need to be benefited by humans? Euthyphro responds by claiming that piety is the art of doing business with the gods. The gods receive honor, and this is very dear to them. But isn't this where we started? Socrates suggests that Euthyphro begin anew—what is the nature of piety? But Euthyphro walks away. This dialogue suggests the extreme difficulty encountered in attempting to discover the defining properties of things.

The *Euthyphro* illustrates very well the nature of platonic dialectic. Plato, through Socrates, continually sought after the nature or essences of things, events, and actions. The essence contains the defining property of a specific kind of thing, event, or action. This project led Plato to postulate his Theory of the Forms, which is the next aspect of Platonism which we must consider.

The Theory of the Forms

Plato was the first philosopher to work out a thorough analysis of the problems of knowledge. He was convinced that human knowledge is not exhausted in terms of mere sense perceptions alone. Quite probably influenced by the Pythagoreans, a mystical-religious sect interested in mathematics, Plato argued strenuously for a strict division of human knowledge into sense perception and intellectual knowledge. By sense perception, Plato meant the mental acts of direct awareness of objects by means of our external senses. Examples of sense perception would be: the red color we see with our faculty of sight; the sound of C-sharp heard with our faculty of hearing; any direct awareness of a specific individual, as when we see a particular snow-flake, a certain building, or a particular individual. This category of knowledge was called "opinion" by Plato.

The second general category of knowledge was intellectual knowledge. By intellectual knowledge, Plato considered the processes by which we have a conceptual awareness of absolutes, like justice, piety, horseness, triangularity, goodness, and so forth. As we shall see, in the history of philosophy this awareness of absolutes has been termed the problem of universals. Plato stresses this division of knowledge into the two categories of opinion and intellectual knowledge in the following passages taken from one of his better known dialogues, *The Republic*. These pages (beginning in *Book VI* of *The Republic*) illustrate Plato's famous "divided line example" and the Analogy of the Cave.

. . . And this is he whom I call the child of the good, whom the good begat in his own likeness, to be in the visible world, in relation to sight and the things of sight, what the good is in the intellectual world in relation to mind and the things of mind?

Will you be a little more explicit? he said.

Why, you know, I said, that the eyes, when a person no longer directs them towards those objects on the colors of which the light of day is

Reprinted from B. Jowett, trans., *The Dialogues of Plato* (New York: Charles Scribner's Sons, 1895).

shining, but the moon and stars only, see dimly, and are nearly blind; they seem to have no clearness of vision in them?

Very true.

But when they are directed towards objects on which the sun shines, they see clearly and there is sight in them?

Certainly.

And the soul is like the eye: when resting upon that on which truth and being shine, the soul perceives and understands, and is radiant with intelligence; but when turning towards the twilight of generation and destruction, then she has opinion only, and goes blinking about, and is first of one opinion and then of another, and seems to have no intelligence?

Yes.

Now, that which imparts truth to the object and knowledge to the subject is what I would have you term the idea of good, and that you will regard as the cause of science and of truth, as known by us; beautiful too, as are both truth and knowledge, you will be right in esteeming this other nature as more beautiful than either; and, as in the previous instance, light and sight may be truly said to be like the sun, and yet not to be the sun, so in this other sphere, science and truth may be deemed like the good, but not the good: the good has a place of honor yet higher.

What a wonder of beauty that must be, he said, which is the author of science and truth, and yet surpasses them in beauty; for you surely cannot mean to say that the good is pleasure?

Speak not of that, I said; but please to consider the image in another point of view.

What is that?

Why, you would say that the sun is not only the author of visibility in all visible things, but of generation and nourishment and growth, though not himself a generation?

Certainly.

In like manner the good may be said to be not only the author of knowledge in all things known, but of their being and essence, and yet the good is not essence, but far exceeds essence in dignity and power.

Glaucon said, with a ludicrous earnestness: By the light of heaven, how amazing!

Yes, I said, and that all comes of you, for you made me utter my fancies.

Nay, he said, but do not leave off; at any rate let us hear if there is anything more to be said about the similitude of the sun.

Yes, I said, there is a great deal more.

Then omit nothing, however slight.

I will do my best; but I fancy, I said, that a great deal will have to be omitted.

I hope not, he said.

You have to imagine, then, that there are two ruling powers, and that one of them is set over the intellectual world, the other over the visible. I do not say heaven, lest you should fancy that I was refining about the name. May I suppose that you have this distinction of the visible and intelligible fixed in your mind?

I have.

Now take a line which has been cut into two unequal parts, and divide each of them again in the same proportion, and suppose the two main divisions to answer, one to the visible and the other to the intelligible, and then compare the subdivisions as to their relative clearness and want of clearness, and you will find that the first section in the sphere of the visible consists of images. And by images I mean, in the first place, shadows, and in the second place, reflections in water and in solid, smooth and polished bodies, and all that sort of thing, as you understand.

Yes, I understand.

Imagine, now, the other section, of which this is only the resemblance, to include ourselves and the animals, and everything in nature and everything in art.

Very good.

Would you not admit that this latter section has a different degree of truth, and that the copy is to the object which is copied as the sphere of opinion is to the sphere of knowledge?

Most undoubtedly.

Next proceed to consider the manner in which the sphere of the intellectual is to be divided.

In what manner?

As thus: there are two subdivisions, in the lower of which the soul uses the figures given by the former division as images; the inquiry can only be hypothetical, and instead of going upwards to a principle descends to the other end; in the higher of the two, the soul passes out of hypotheses, and goes up to a principle which is above hypotheses, making no use of images as in the former case, but proceeding only in and by the ideas themselves.

I do not quite understand your meaning, he said.

I will try again, I said; for you will understand me better now that I have made these preliminary remarks. You are aware that students of geometry, arithmetic, and the kindred sciences assume the odd and the even and the figures and three kinds of angles and the like in their several branches of science; these are their hypotheses, which everybody is supposed to know, and of which therefore they do not deign to give any account either to themselves or others; but they begin with these, and go on until they arrive at last, and in a consistent manner, at their conclusion?

Yes, he said, I know that.

And do you not know also that although they use and reason about the visible forms, they are thinking not of these, but of the ideals which they resemble; not of the figures which they draw, but of the absolute square and the absolute diameter, and so on: and, while using as images these very forms which they draw or make, and which in turn have their shadows and reflections in the water, they are really seeking for the things themselves, which can only be seen with the eye of the mind?

That is true.

And of this kind I still spoke as intelligible, although in inquiries of this sort the soul is compelled to use hypotheses; not proceeding to a first principle because unable to ascend above hypotheses, but using as images the objects of which the shadows are resemblances in a still lower sphere, they having in relation to the shadows a higher value and distinctness.

I understand, he said, that you are speaking of geometry and the sister arts.

And when I speak of the other division of the intellectual, you will also understand me to speak of that knowledge which reason herself attains by the power of dialectic, using the hypotheses not as first principles, but only as hypotheses—that is to say, as steps and points of departure into a region which is above hypotheses, in order that she may soar beyond them to the first principle of the whole; and clinging to this and then to that which depends on this, by successive steps she descends again without the aid of any sensible object, beginning and ending in ideas.

I understand you, he replied; not perfectly, for the matter of which you speak is too great for that; but, at any rate, I understand you to say that knowledge and being, which the science of dialectic contemplates, are clearer than the notions of the arts, as they are termed, which proceed from hypotheses only: these are also contemplated by the understanding, and not by the senses: yet, because they start from hypotheses and do not ascend to a principle, those who contemplate them appear to you not to exercise the higher reason upon them, although when a first principle is added to them they are cognizable by the higher reason. And the habit which is concerned with geometry and the cognate sciences I suppose that you would term understanding and not reason, as being intermediate between opinion and reason.

You have quite conceived me, I said; and now, corresponding to these four sections, let there be four faculties in the soul—reason answering to the highest, understanding to the second, faith or persuasion to the third, and knowledge of shadows to the last—and let there be a scale of them, and let us suppose that the several faculties have clearness in the same degree that their objects have truth.

I understand, he replied, and give my assent, and will arrange them as you say.

BOOK VII

After this, I said, imagine the enlightenment or ignorance of our nature in a figure: Behold! human beings living in a sort of underground den, which has a mouth open towards the light and reaching all across the den; they have been here from their childhood, and have their legs and necks chained so that they cannot move, and can only see before them; for the chains are arranged in such a manner as to prevent them from turning round their heads. At a distance above and behind them the light of a fire is blazing, and between the fire and the prisoners there is a raised way; and you will see, if you look, a low wall built along the way, like the screen which marionette players have before them, over which they show the puppets.

I see, he said.

And do you see, I said, men passing along the wall carrying vessels, which appear over the wall; also figures of men and animals, made of wood and stone and various materials; and some of the passengers, as you would expect, are talking, and some of them are silent?

That is a strange image, he said, and they are strange prisoners.

Like ourselves, I replied; and they see only their own shadows, or the shadows of one another, which the fire throws on the opposite wall of the cave?

True, he said; how could they see anything but the shadows if they were never allowed to move their heads?

And of the objects which are being carried in like manner they would only see the shadows?

Yes, he said.

And if they were able to talk with one another, would they not suppose that they were naming what was actually before them?

Very true.

And suppose further that the prison had an echo which came from the other side, would they not be sure to fancy that the voice which they heard was that of a passing shadow?

No question, he replied.

There can be no question, I said, that the truth would be to them just nothing but the shadows of the images.

That is certain.

And now look again, and see how they are released and cured of their folly. At first, when any one of them is liberated and compelled suddenly to go up and turn his neck round and walk and look at the light, he will suffer sharp pains; the glare will distress him, and he will be unable to see the realities of which in his former state he had seen the shadows; and then imagine some one saying to him, that what he saw before was an illusion, but that now he is approaching real being and has a truer sight and vision of more real things,—what will be his reply? And you may further imagine that his instructor is pointing to the objects as they pass and requiring him to name them,—will he not be in a difficulty? Will he not fancy that the shadows which he formerly saw are truer than the objects which are now shown to him?

Far truer.

And if he is compelled to look at the light, will he not have a pain in his eyes which will make him turn away to take refuge in the object of vision which he can see, and which he will conceive to be clearer than the things which are now being shown to him?

True, he said.

And suppose once more, that he is reluctantly dragged up a steep and rugged ascent, and held fast and forced into the presence of the sun himself, do you not think that he will be pained and irritated, and when he approaches the light he will have his eyes dazzled, and will not be able to see any of the realities which are now affirmed to be the truth?

Not all in a moment, he said.

He will require to get accustomed to the sight of the upper world. And first he will see the shadows best, next the reflections of men and other objects in the water, and then the objects themselves; next he will gaze upon the light of the moon and the stars; and he will see the sky and the stars by night, better than the sun, or the light of the sun, by day?

Certainly.

And at last he will be able to see the sun, and not mere reflections of him in the water, but he will see him as he is in his own proper place, and not in another, and he will contemplate his nature.

Certainly.

And after this he will reason that the sun is he who gives the seasons and the years, and is the guardian of all that is in the visible world, and in a certain way the cause of all things which he and his fellows have been accustomed to behold?

Clearly, he said, he would come to the other first and to this afterwards.

And when he remembered his old habitation, and the wisdom of the den and his fellow-prisoners, do you not suppose that he would felicitate himself on the change, and pity them?

Certainly, he would.

And if they were in the habit of conferring honors on those who were quickest to observe and remember and foretell which of the shadows went before, and which followed after, and which were together, do you think that he would care for such honors and glories, or envy the possessors of them? Would he not say with Homer, "Better to be a poor man, and have a poor master," and endure anything, rather than to think and live after their manner?

Yes, he said, I think that he would rather suffer anything than live after their manner.

Imagine once more, I said, that such a one coming suddenly out of the sun were to be replaced in his old situation, is he not certain to have his eyes full of darkness?

Very true, he said.

And if there were a contest, and he had to compete in measuring the shadows with the prisoners who have never moved out of the den, during the time that his sight is weak, and before his eyes are steady (and the time which would be needed to acquire this new habit of sight might be very considerable), would he not be ridiculous? Men would say of him that up he went and down he comes without his eyes; and that there was no use in even thinking of ascending: and if any one tried to loose another and lead him up to the light, let them only catch the offender in the act, and they would put him to death.

No question, he said.

This allegory, I said, you may now append to the previous argument; the prison is the world of sight, the light of the fire is the sun, the ascent and vision of the things above you may truly regard as the upward progress of the soul into the intellectual world; that is my poor belief, to which, at your desire, I have given expression. Whether I am right or not God only knows; but, whether true or false, my opinion is that in the world of knowledge the idea of good appears last of all, and is seen only with an effort; and, when seen, is also inferred to be the universal author of all things beautiful and right, parent of light and the lord of light in this world, and the source of truth and reason in the other: this is the first great cause which he who would act rationally either in public or private life must behold.

I agree, he said, as far as I am able to understand you.

I should like to have your agreement in another matter, I said. For I would not have you marvel that those who attain to this beatific vision are unwilling to descend to human affairs; but their souls are ever hastening into the upper world in which they desire to dwell; and this is very natural, if our allegory may be trusted.

Certainly, that is quite natural.

And is there anything surprising in one who passes from divine contemplations to human things, misbehaving himself in a ridiculous manner; if, while his eyes are blinking and before he has become accustomed to the darkness visible, he is compelled to fight in courts of law, or in other places, about the images or shadows of images of justice, and is endeavoring to meet the conceptions of those who have never yet seen the absolute justice?

There is nothing surprising in that, he replied.

Any one who has common sense will remember that the bewilderments of the eyes are of two kinds, and arise from two causes, either from coming out of the light or from going into the light, which is true of the mind's eye, quite as much as of the bodily eye; and he who remembers this when he sees the soul of any one whose vision is perplexed and weak, will not be too ready to laugh; he will first ask whether that soul has come out of the brighter life, and is unable to see because unaccustomed to the dark, or having turned from darkness to the day is dazzled by excess of light. And then he will count the one happy in his condition and state of being, and he will pity the other; or, if he have a mind to laugh at the soul which comes from below into the light, there will be more reason in this than in the laugh which greets the other from the den.

That, he said, is a very just remark.

But if this is true, then certain professors of education must be mistaken in saying that they can put a knowledge into the soul which was not there before, like giving eyes to the blind.

Yes, that is what they say, he replied.

Whereas, I said, our argument shows that the power is already in the soul; and that as the eye cannot turn from darkness to light without the whole body, so too, when the eye of the soul is turned round, the whole soul must be turned from the world of generation into that of being, and become able to endure the sight of being, and of the brightest and best of being—that is to say, of the good.

Very true.

And this is conversion; and the art will be how to accomplish this as, easily and completely as possible; not implanting eyes, for they exist already, but giving them a right direction, which they have not.

Yes, he said, that may be assumed.

And hence while the other qualities seem to be akin to the body, being infused by habit and exercise and not originally innate, the virtue of wisdom is part of a divine essence, and has a power which is everlasting, and by this conversion is rendered useful and profitable, and is also capable of becoming hurtful and useless. Did you never observe the narrow intelligence flashing from the keen eye of a clever rogue—how eager he is, how clearly his paltry soul sees the way to his end; he is the reverse of blind, but his keen eyesight is taken into the service of evil, and he is dangerous in proportion to his intelligence?

Very true, he said.

But what if there had been a circumcision of such natures in the days of their youth; and they had been severed from the leaden weights, as I may call them, with which they are born into the world, which hang on to sensual pleasures, such as those of eating and drinking, and drag them down and turn the vision of their souls about the things that are below,—if, I say, they had been released from them and turned round to the truth, the very same faculty in these very same persons would have seen the other as keenly as they now see that on which their eye is fixed.

That is very likely.

Yes, I said; and there is another thing which is likely, or rather a necessary inference from what has preceded, that neither the uneducated and uninformed of the truth, nor yet those who never make an end of their education, will be able ministers of State: not the former, because they have no single aim of duty which is the rule of their actions, private as well as public; nor the latter, because they will not act at all except upon compulsion, fancying that they are already in the islands of the blest.

Very true, he replied.

Then, I said, the business of us who are the founders of the State will be to compel the best minds to attain that knowledge which has been already declared by us to be the greatest of all,—to that eminence they must ascend and arrive at the good, and when they have ascended and seen enough we must not allow them to do as they do now.

What do you mean?

I mean that they remain in the upper world: but this must not be allowed; they must be made to descend again among the prisoners in the den, and partake of their labors and honors, whether they are worth having or not.

But is not this unjust? he said; ought we to give them an inferior life, when they might have a superior one?

You have again forgotten, my friend, I said, the intention of the legislator; he did not aim at making any one class in the State happy above the rest; the happiness was to be in the whole State, and he held the citizens together by persuasion and necessity, making them benefactors of the State, and therefore benefactors of one another; to this end he created them, not that they should please themselves, but they were to be his instruments in binding up the State.

True, he said, I had forgotten that.

Observe them, I said, Glaucon, that there will be no injustice in compelling our philosophers to have a care and providence of others; we shall explain to them that in other States, men of their class are not obliged to share in the toils of politics: and this is reasonable, for they grow up at their own sweet will, and the government would rather not have them. Now the wild plant which owes culture to nobody, has nothing to pay for culture; but we have brought you into the world expressly for this end, that you may be rulers of the hive, kings of yourselves and of the other citizens. And you have been educated far better and more perfectly than they have, and are better able to share in the double duty. And therefore each of you, when his turn comes, must go down to the general underground abode, and get the habit of seeing in the dark; for all is habit; and when you are accustomed you will see ten thousand times better than those in the den, and you will know what the images are, and of what they are images, because you have seen the beautiful and just and good in their truth. And thus the order of our State will be a waking reality, and not a dream, as is commonly the manner of States; in most of them men are fighting with one another about shadows and are distracted in the struggle for power, which in their eyes is a great good. But the truth is, that the State in which the rulers are most reluctant to govern is best and most quietly governed, and that in which they are most willing, the worst.

Quite true, he replied.

And will our pupils, when they hear this, refuse to share in turn the toils of State, when they are allowed to spend the greater part of their time with one another in the heaven of ideas?

Impossible, he answered; for they are just men, and the commands which we impose upon them are just; there can be no doubt that every one of them will take office as a stern necessity and not like our present ministers of State.

Yes, my friend, I said; and that is just the truth of the case. If you contrive for your future rulers another and a better life than that of a ruler, then you may have a well-ordered State; for only in the State which offers this will they rule who are truly rich, not in silver and gold, but in virtue and wisdom, which are the true blessings of life. Whereas if they go to the administration of public affairs, poor and hungering after their own private advantage, thinking that hence they are to snatch the good of life, order there can never be. . . .

In the tradition of western philosophy, the preceding passages from *The Republic* are probably the cornerstone selections in epistemology. The distinction between opinion and knowledge has influenced, either positively or negatively, almost every philosopher who has engaged in a serious pursuit of the problems of knowledge. As we shall see in our further investigations of philosophers and their epistemological and ontological theories, this distinction will be affirmed or denied repeatedly.

The passages just read do not indicate merely an epistemological problem. Plato's theory of knowledge implies a radical dualism about objects which exist. Plato discusses knowledge because he is convinced that there are different types or categories of objects which really do exist. This is an important ontological claim. Both categories illustrated in the divided line example and cave analogy have existence. Plato is not just talking about the ideas in his own mind. We shall see that many metaphysicians, including some twentieth-century philosophers, will make use of this distinction and incorporate its consequences into their ontologies.

The ontological scheme devised by Plato is profoundly dualistic. The cave analogy and the divided line example indicate explicitly the dimensions of this dualism. There is, first of all, the world of ordinary, everyday sense experience.

This is the empirical world of sense perception. Plato calls this the realm of "opinion." Second, there is the world of forms. The world of the forms—which is variously called the world of essences or the world of ideas—provides the explanation for the ordinary world of sense perceptions. Plato is quite serious about this dualism. The following diagram illustrates the relationships between the analogy of the divided line and the myth of the cave:

Comparison of Analogy of the Divided Line with the Myth of the Cave

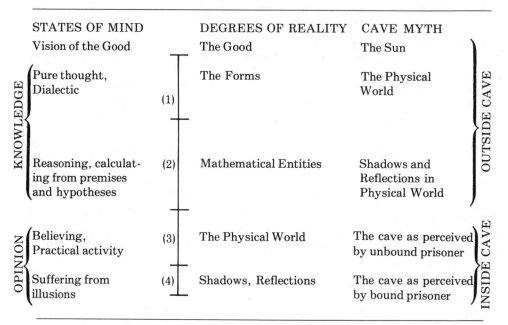

STATES OF MIND		DEGREES OF REALITY	CAVE MYTH	
Vision of the Good		The Good	The Sun	
Pure thought, Dialectic	(1)	The Forms	The Physical World	OUTSIDE CAVE
KNOWLEDGE Reasoning, calculating from premises and hypotheses	(2)	Mathematical Entities	Shadows and Reflections in Physical World	OUTSIDE CAVE
OPINION Believing, Practical activity	(3)	The Physical World	The cave as perceived by unbound prisoner	INSIDE CAVE
Suffering from illusions	(4)	Shadows, Reflections	The cave as perceived by bound prisoner	INSIDE CAVE

Historically, Plato's ontology is quite important in that it was the first explicit rational attempt to provide a system of ethical and epistemological absolutes. In effect, the world of the forms is Plato's way around the claims of relativity expounded by the sophists. Plato's scheme will be absorbed into the early attempts by the Judeo-Christian tradition to formulate theological positions. From these sources, the medieval philosophers spent much time elucidating different positions to account for the problem of universals. And, as we shall see later, some twentieth-century philosophers will also hark back to Plato as the foremost exponent of ontological dualism.

Obviously this radical dualism poses two problems for a philosopher. First, what are these forms, ideas, or essences and why are they needed? This is a metaphysical question demanding that an advocate of universals sufficiently explain what they are and why they are philosophically necessary. Second, there is an epistemological problem demanding an explanation as to how we know these forms. The epistemological question is important in that we certainly cannot find universals on a supermarket shelf. In this analysis of the nature of a platonic form, our first consideration will be to analyze the metaphysical questions bound up in Plato's dualism. This will be followed by an inquiry into the nature of our knowledge of these essences or forms. Our analysis will indicate problems germane to each position.

To assure that each student is aware of Plato's meaning when the theory of forms is discussed, we will consider some additional passages in which Plato argues explicitly for the existence and the nature of the forms.

Nature of the Forms

1. *One over Many*

a. Whenever a number of individuals have a common name, we assume them to have a corresponding idea or form. . . .   (*The Republic,* 596).

b. The old story, that there is a many beautiful and a many good, and so of other things which we describe and define; to all of them the term "many" is applied.

True, he said.

And there is an absolute beauty and an absolute good, and so of other things to which the term "many" is applied; they may be brought under a single idea, which is called the essence of each.

That is true.

The many, as we say, are seen but not known, and the ideas are known but not seen.

Exactly.   (*The Republic,* 507)

2. *The Absolute; the Essence; True Existence*

a. And what do you say of another question, my friend, about which I should like to have your opinion, and the answer to which will probably throw light on our present inquiry: Do you think that the philosopher ought to care about the pleasures—if they are to be called pleasures—of eating and drinking?

Certainly not, answered Simmias.

And what do you say of the pleasures of love—should he care about them?

By no means.

And will he think much of the other ways of indulging the body, for example, the acquisition of costly raiment, or sandals, or other adornments of the body? Instead of caring about them, does he not rather despise anything more than nature needs? What do you say?

I should say that the true philosopher would despise them.

Would you not say that he is entirely concerned with the soul and not with the body? He would like, as far as he can, to be quit of the body and turn to the soul.

That is true.

In matters of this sort philosophers, above all other men, may be observed in every sort of way to dissever the soul from the body.

That is true.

Whereas, Simmias, the rest of the world are of opinion that a life which has no bodily pleasures and no part in them is not worth having; but that he who thinks nothing of bodily pleasures is almost as though he were dead.

That is quite true.

What again shall we say of the actual acquirement of knowledge?—is the body, if invited to share in the inquiry, a hinderer or a helper? I mean to say, have sight and hearing any truth in them? Are they not, as the poets are always telling us, inaccurate witnesses? and yet, if even they are inaccurate and indistinct, what is to be said of the other senses?—for you will allow that they are the best of them?

Certainly, he replied.

Then when does the soul attain truth?—for in attempting to consider anything in company with the body she is obviously deceived.

Yes, that is true.

Then must not existence be revealed to her in thought, if at all?

Yes.

And thought is best when the mind is gathered into herself and none of these things trouble her—neither sounds nor sights nor pain nor any pleasure,—when she has as little as possible to do with the body, and has no bodily sense or feeling, but is aspiring after being?

That is true.

And in this the philosopher dishonors the body; his soul runs away from the body and desires to be alone and by herself?

That is true.

Well, but there is another thing, Simmias: Is there or is there not an absolute justice?

Assuredly there is.

And an absolute beauty and absolute good?

Of course.

But did you ever behold any of them with your eyes?

Certainly not.

Or did you ever reach them with any other bodily sense? (and I speak not of these alone, but of absolute greatness, and health, and strength, and of the essence or true nature of everything). Has the reality of them ever been perceived by you through the bodily organs? or rather, is not the nearest approach to the knowledge of their several natures made by him who so orders his intellectual vision as to have the most exact conception of the essence of that which he considers?

Certainly.

And he attains to the knowledge of them in their highest purity who goes to each of them with the mind alone, not allowing when in the act of thought the intrusion or introduction of sight or any other sense in the company of reason, but with the very light of truth in each; he has got rid, as far as he can, of eyes and ears and of the whole body, which he conceives of only as a disturbing element, hindering the soul from the acquisition of knowledge when in company with her—is not this the sort of man who, if ever man did, is likely to attain the knowledge of existence?

There is admirable truth in that, Socrates, replied Simmias.

And when they consider all this, must not true philosophers make a reflection, of which they will speak to one another in such words as these: We have found, they will say, a path of speculation which seems to bring us and the argument to the conclusion, that while we are in the body, and while the soul is mingled with this mass of evil, our desire will not be satisfied, and our desire is of the truth. For the body is a source of endless trouble to us by reason of the mere requirement of food; and also is liable to diseases which overtake and impede us in the search after truth: and by filling us so full of loves, and lusts, and fears, and fancies, and idols, and every sort of folly, prevents our ever having, as people say, so much as a thought. For whence come wars, and fightings, and factions? whence but from the body and the lusts of the body? For wars are occasioned by the love of money, and money has to be acquired for the sake and in the service of the body; and in consequence of all these things the time which ought to be given to philosophy is lost. Moreover, if there is time and an inclination toward philosophy, yet the body introduces a turmoil and confusion and fear into the course of speculation, and hinders us from seeing the truth; and all experience shows that if we would have pure knowledge of anything we must be quit of the body, and the soul in herself must behold all things in themselves: then I suppose that we shall attain that which we desire, and of which we say that we are lovers, and that is wisdom; not while we live, but after death, as the argument shows; for if while in company with the body, the soul cannot have pure knowledge, one of two things seems to follow — either knowledge is not to be attained at all, or, if at all, after death. For then, and not till then, the soul will be in herself alone and without the body. In this present life, I reckon that we make the nearest approach to knowledge when we have the least possible concern or interest in the body, and are not saturated with the bodily nature, but remain pure until the hour when God himself is pleased to release us. And then the foolishness of the body will be cleared away and we shall be pure and hold converse with other pure souls, and know of ourselves the clear light everywhere; and this is surely the light of truth. For no impure thing is allowed to approach the pure. These are the sort of words, Simmias, which the true lovers of wisdom cannot help saying to one another, and thinking. . . .   (*Phaedo,* 65–76)

b. . . . Now of the heaven which is above the heavens, no earthly poet has sung or ever will sing in a worthy manner. But I must tell, for I am bound to speak truly when speaking of the truth. The colorless and formless and intangible essence is visible to the mind, which is the only lord of the soul. Circling around this in the region above the heavens is the place of true knowledge. And as the divine intelligence, and that of every other soul which is rightly nourished, is fed upon mind and pure knowledge, such an intelligent soul is glad at once more beholding being; and feeding on the sight of truth is replenished, until the revolution of the worlds brings her round again to the same place. During the revolution she beholds justice, temperance, and knowledge absolute, not in the form of generation or of relation, which men call existence, but knowledge absolute in existence absolute; and beholding other existences in like manner, and feeding upon them, she passes down into the interior of the heavens and returns home, and there the charioteer putting up his horses at the stall, gives them ambrosia to eat and nectar to drink.   (*Phaedrus,* 247)

c. Socrates proceeded: I thought that as I had failed in the contemplation of true existence, I ought to be careful that I did not lose the eye of my soul; as people may injure their bodily eye by observing and gazing on the sun during an eclipse, unless they take the precaution of only looking at the image reflected in the water, or in some similar medium. That occurred to me, and I was afraid that my soul might be blinded altogether if I looked at things with my eyes or tried by the help of the senses to apprehend them. And I thought that I had better have recourse to ideas, and seek in them the truth of existence. I dare say that the simile is not perfect—for I am very far from admitting that he who contemplates existences through the medium of ideas, sees them only "through a glass darkly," any more than he who sees them in their working and effects. However, this was the method which I adopted: I first assumed some principle which I judged to be the strongest, and then I affirmed as true whatever seemed to agree with this, whether relating to the cause or to anything else; and that which disagreed I regarded as untrue. But I should like to explain my meaning clearly, as I do not think that you understand me.

No indeed, replied Cebes, not very well.

There is nothing new, he said, in what I am about to tell you; but only what I have been always and everywhere repeating in the previous discussion and on other occasions: I want to show you the nature of that cause which has occupied my thoughts, and I shall have to go back to those familiar words which are in the mouth of every one, and first of all assume that there is an absolute beauty and goodness, and greatness, and the like; grant me this, and I hope to be able to show you the nature of the cause, and to prove the immortality of the soul.

Cebes said: You may proceed at once with the proof, as I readily grant you this.

Well, he said, then I should like to know whether you agree with me in the next step; for I cannot help thinking that if there be anything beautiful other than absolute beauty, that can only be beautiful in as far as it partakes of absolute beauty—and this I should say of everything. Do you agree in this notion of the cause?

Yes, he said, I agree.

He proceeded: I know nothing and can understand nothing of any other of those wise causes which are alleged; and if a person says to me that the bloom of color, or form, or anything else of that sort is a source of beauty, I leave all that, which is only confusing to me, and simply and singly, and perhaps foolishly, hold and am assured in my own mind that nothing makes a thing beautiful but the presence and participation of beauty in whatever way or manner obtained; for as to the manner I am uncertain, but I stoutly contend that by beauty all beautiful things become beautiful. That appears to me to be the only safe answer that I can give, either to myself or to any other, and to that I cling, in the persuasion that I shall never be overthrown, and that I may safely answer to myself or any other, that by beauty beautiful things become beautiful.   (*Phaedo,* 100)

3. *Unchangeable Patterns*

And do you not agree with me also as to the cause of the harsh feeling which the many have towards philosophy? This originates in the pretenders, who enter in, like a band of revelers, where they have no business, and are always abusing and quarreling with them, who make persons instead of things the theme of their conversation; and this is most unbecoming in philosophers.

Most unbecoming.

For he, Adeimantus, whose mind is fixed upon true being has no time to look down upon the affairs of men, or to be filled with jealousy and enmity in the struggle against them; his eye is ever directed towards fixed and immutable principles, which he sees neither injuring nor injured by one another, but all in order moving according to reason; these he imitates, and to these he would, as far as he can, conform himself. Can a man help imitating that with which he holds reverential converse?

Impossible.

And the philosopher also, conversing with the divine and immutable, becomes a part of that divine and immutable order, as far as nature allows; but all things are liable to detraction.

Certainly.

And if a necessity be laid upon him of fashioning, not only himself but human nature generally, whether in States or individuals, into that which he there beholds, think you that he will be an unskilled artificer of justice, temperance, and every civil virtue?

Anything but unskillful.

And if the world perceives that we are speaking the truth about him, will they be angry with philosophy? Will they disbelieve us, when we tell them that the State can only be happy which is planned by artists who make use of the heavenly pattern?

They will not be angry if they only understand, he replied. But what do you mean about the plan?

I mean, I replied, that they will take a State and human nature for their tablet and begin by making a clean surface. Now this is not an easy thing to do; and this is the mark which at once distinguishes them from every other legislator,—they will have nothing to do, either with individual or State, and will inscribe no laws, until they have either found, or themselves made, a clean surface.

They will be very right, he said.

Having effected this, they will proceed to make an outline of the constitution.

No doubt.

And in the course of the work, as I conceive, they will often turn their eyes first towards one, then towards the other. I mean that they will look at justice and beauty and temperance as they are in nature, and again at the corresponding quality in mankind, and they will inlay the true human image, moulding and selecting out of the various forms of life; and this they will conceive according to that other image, which, when existing among men, Homer calls the form and likeness of God.

That is true, he said.   (*The Republic,* 500–501)

The One-Many Problem

Now that we have studied some of Plato's philosophical texts, think for a moment about what Plato is emphasizing. Throughout the preceding passages Plato argues for an ontology which is radically dualistic. The following diagram illustrates the fundamental dualism which runs through Plato's entire philosophy:

Relationships between mind, knowledge, and reality in the Platonic System:

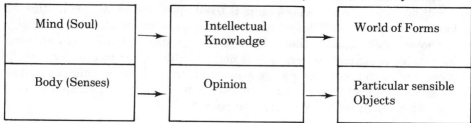

Why would Plato assert this fundamental dualism? First of all, Plato was deeply concerned about the possibility of providing a metaphysical explanation of the external world. Plato was impressed with the search for the causes and explanations of things. Remember that this question faced the early pre-Socratic philosophers. Philosophy, as the love of wisdom, was the search for the ultimate causes and explanations of the things around us. For Plato, philosophy became the relentless search for absolute standards to be used both in judgments about the world and judgments about values.

The starting point for Plato, as well as the pre-Socratics, is what western philosophy has called the *one-many problem*. The origins of the one-many problem lie in the overwhelming Greek worry about providing an explanation for the fact of change. Probably more than any other group of philosophers, the Greeks were extremely fascinated about the ever-present datum of change. What fascinated them can easily be understood by thinking about the world for a moment. Change is everywhere. The leaf goes from green in summer to orange in autumn; snow goes from a solid at 20 degrees Fahrenheit to a liquid at 40 degrees Fahrenheit to a gas at 212 degrees Fahrenheit; a human being goes from baby to adolescent to young adult to maturity to senility. Change is a basic datum to even our most primitive awareness of the world around us. With change, however, comes a fundamental philosophical problem demanding an explanation. Even though the human goes through various stages from embryo to baby to youngster to adolescent to young adult to middle age to senior citizen, the same person remains—the same "entity" undergoes the many changes. We may take a chunk of clay and sculpt it into a statue. The clay was used to make the statue yet it still is clay. This is the basis of the one-many problem. The concern is over what constitutes the stabilizing element or factor which permits change to be orderly and not chaotic. In other words, what is the "stable" amid the "flux."

We might look at the one-many problem from a different perspective. We observe that there are many different cats existing in the external world: there are Boots and Felix and Samantha. Each of these three cats, though a specific individual, is still a cat and not a dog, horse, or hippopotamus. There is a fundamental similarity among the members of the group. Plato wondered why all cats are alike and yet each one is a specific individual, different from the rest. However, what we might call zoological classification was not Plato's only worry. He asked the same type of question regarding moral values and the standards used to make moral judgments, as well as regarding the foundation of mathematical truths. For example, there are many different acts of justice—paying one's debts, keeping one's promises, granting to another one's human rights; yet, Plato wondered, is there some common property or characteristic which these individual acts of justice share? Plato sought a definition of a unique property not only separating acts of justice from acts of injustice but also from the other classes of virtuous actions. He was concerned about the defining character found in every act of justice.

Plato employed the same reasoning in regard to mathematical questions. In fact, in the philosophy of mathematics, questions of universals are earnestly debated in contemporary philosophy. Examples are numerous in mathematics. For instance, there are many collections of objects which add up to the number two. Yet why is it the case that it is a necessary truth that every time we add one plus one, we arrive at the sum of two? This cannot be just a fact of sense experience, as we do not perceive necessary truths with our senses. The same can be asked about plane figures used in Euclidean geometry. There are many kinds and shapes of triangles, yet there are certain theorems which will apply to each and every triangle. This nonsensitive universal characteristic of mathematical truths is fundamental to Plato's worry concerning the one-many problem. How do we account for the necessity of mathematical truths when every material, physical manifestation of a mathematical truth is something less than the necessary truth itself? Remember studying plane geometry, when the teacher went to great pains to get students to realize that a mathematical figure was indeed independent of and incapable of being represented by sense experience. Could we ever find a "mathematical point" in the physical realm? Of course not. Plato too noted this fact of mathematical knowledge. How could mathematical propositions be true if they cannot be exhausted in terms of sense experience? What makes them true? Since they're true for everyone, they cannot be just subjective experiences.

In all the above cases, Plato demands that, for an adequate solution to the one-many problem, there must be *something beyond* the particular instances of cats, just acts, collections of "twos," and individual triangles. To use the Platonic gambit, the question is: is "catness" different from individual cats; "justice" different from specific just acts; "twoness" different from all instantiations of two, and "triangularity" different from individual triangles? Since we have already read the passages from *The Republic,* we will not be surprised that the Platonic answer is a definite and unequivocal "yes!" Plato postulates an essence for every group of similar things existing in the sensible world. The essence is that property or characteristic or group of properties or characteristics which will ultimately differentiate one "kind" of thing from another "kind" of thing. Therefore, to continue with our examples, there will be an essence of cat, of justice, of two, and of triangularity. The individuals of a group are what we perceive in our everyday experience—the objects of Platonic "opinion"—while the essences or ideas are the objects of knowledge, which we must grasp by means of reason alone using the Platonic dialectic.

With his conception of forms, which possess the essential properties or characteristics of any given group, Plato distinguishes an essential property from an accidental or incidental property. To common-sensically grasp this distinction, consider the usual way in which we use the term "accident." In the case of an auto accident, for example, we use accident to distinguish an event which "just happens" from one which was planned. This common-sense meaning of the term "accident" is an indication of how Plato uses it in his *Dialogues.* An accidental property is a quality or characteristic which an individual object

possesses but which is not essentially linked to that object. This is in contrast
to an essential property. An essential property is a "defining characteristic."
The essential property determines a thing to be the very type of thing it is. For
example, a cat may be brown, gray, or white and still be a cat; a cat can be
long, short, or squatty and still be a cat; a cat can be male or female and still be
a cat. Accordingly, neither color, size, shape, nor sex is an essential characteristic of a cat. These are accidental or incidental characteristics which "happen"
to a specific individual object or a particular group. On the other hand, the
essential property is that property which specifically determines an individual
to be a member of a distinctive group.

The same can be said regarding human beings. Think about the following
problem. You could invite Peter, Paul, and Marianne to a party but you could
not invite "human nature" to the party. Yet according to Plato, Peter, Paul,
and Marianne are human precisely insofar as they possess the essential property of human nature. Human nature—the essence of all human beings—is
common to all the individual human beings which exist, have existed, or will
exist. Again we have an illustration of the one-many problem. Human nature
subsists as a *form* which provides a solution for the one-many problem. By way
of summary, we might look at the one-many problem in the following two ways:

1. Change in an individual
2. Group classification

In order to account for both of these cases, Plato demands the existence of an
essential property. In the first case, Plato asks us to consider the distinction
between essential properties and incidental properties. In regard to changes in
an individual, the individual may change incidentally but still remain essentially the same. A piece of oak is fabricated into a chair while still remaining
essentially oak. A baby hippopotamus grows to be a mature and complete
hippo, yet it is still a hippo and neither an elephant nor a kangaroo. Such essential persistence demands a metaphysical foundation, and this Plato calls a
form. The form, therefore, is a *subsistent* essential property.

In the case of group classification, the accent is still placed upon determining
an essential property. Plato suggests that, even though members of a natural
kind may differ in regard to incidental properties, they nonetheless possess the
same essential property. Remember our above discussion of the incidental
properties. The ontological ground for group classification is the essential property. This essential property is the defining characteristic which distinguishes
members of a class. Each group demands an essential property so that the classification can be properly made and not be based on merely an arbitrary
decision.

Throughout his discussion, Plato is insistent that there is a rational foundation for explaining the cosmos. This is a fundamental Platonic presupposition.
The cosmos is fundamentally rational and thus capable of being understood.
The twentieth-century assertion of some existentialists that "the world is absurd" is a radical denial of this Platonic presupposition. It is by means of the
world of the forms that Plato explained the order and regularity of the sensible
world. That this order existed Plato knew; how it was to be explained was in
terms of the world of the forms.

The Platonic form determines the essential characteristics of a specific group.
In the Platonic *Dialogues,* Plato continually seeks the "whatness" or "essential
property" by which a group of things is to be radically distinguished from any
other group. Yet it is important to realize that Plato considered these forms to

be *realities* which actually had existence. Each form is a "subsistent reality." It is not merely a mental construct or fabrication. At times, philosophers have chosen to use the term *subsistence* when referring to a transcendental entity. "Existence" is reserved for the things which pertain to our everyday world of experience—tables, chairs, and beer cans. Accordingly, the Platonic forms can be said to subsist. However, to repeat, we must realize that a subsisting entity is a *real* entity. It is not just a concept or figment of one's intellect or imagination. In Plato's ontology, the world of the forms is a bona fide subsisting realm. This realm of essences accounts for the "sameness" predicated of any group of individuals. The individuals themselves can differ according to various accidental or incidental characteristics. The world of the forms was Plato's method of accounting for certain regularities and universal characteristics which he observed in his everyday experience of the world. Plato emphasized this relationship between individuals existing in the sensible world and the transcendental world of the forms when he wrote the following passage in *The Republic:* "Whenever a number of individuals have a common name, we assume them to have a corresponding idea or form." The individual member belonged to a group because it in some way participated with the form. The form itself guaranteed the essential characteristic to each member of the group. Accordingly, this participation of an individual with its appropriate form was a crucial feature of the Platonic ontology.

The Theory of Reference

At this time it is appropriate to ask if any philosophical presupposition prompted Plato to postulate the world of the forms as a subsisting realm. Some contemporary philosophers, in applying a linguistic criterion to Plato's ontology, have discovered an interesting presupposition. In order to account for the meaningfulness of our language, Plato assumed what we might call an *Exaggerated Theory of Reference.* Quite simply, this theory of meaning states that, if a name is to have any meaning or significance, it must *refer* to some existing or subsisting entity. This linguistic axiom is in accord with the passage quoted, in the preceding paragraph, from *The Republic.*

Schematically put, an object is necessary as a referent if a name is to have meaning:

NAME ⟶ OBJECT (REFERENT)

RELATION OF REFERRING

In order to realize the import of the presupposition for Plato's ontology, let's return for a moment to our previous example of the cats. It is quite easy to have a referent for most individualized proper names. Thus Boots would have meaning because it referred to a particular cat:

"BOOTS" ⟶ CAT₁

And Felix would have meaning because it referred to another individual, particular cat:

"FELIX" ⟶ CAT₂

The objects which determine the meaning of proper names would be the individuals of sense experience. As we know, Plato referred to this as "opinion."

However what about common names? In accord with the Exaggerated Theory of Reference, if Felix and Boots have meaning because they refer to some particular object, then a common name also can receive its meaning only because it refers to a subsisting entity. The essential properties mentioned above—cat, triangle, justice, human nature—are all common names. Given the Exaggerated Theory of Reference, common names too must refer. Do they refer to anything within the realm of sense experience? Think again of our discussion above. We could invite Peter, Paul, and Marianne to our party, but we couldn't invite human nature. The same goes with all the other essential properties. Plato emphatically considers this problem when, in the *Phaedo,* he remarks that when we know equality we must be aware of something above and beyond our sense experiences; the only things we perceive in the world are two equal sticks or two equal ice-cream cones or two equal sacks of apples. All of the essential properties acquire their meaning from some referent. This referent cannot be found in sense experience. Accordingly, there must be some entity above and beyond the realm of sensible entities to which the common names refer. Schematically, let's again refer to the instance of the cats.

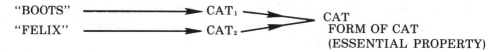

The entity which determines the meaning of a common name is what Plato considered form. Therefore a basic linguistic presupposition in favor of a reference theory of meaning forced Plato into opting for the world of the forms in order to account for the significance of common names.

As we shall see later, the reference theory of meaning has not been generally accepted by many contemporary philosophers. Since the time of Ludwig Wittgenstein's *Philosophical Investigations,* many philosophers accept Wittgenstein's hint that meaning comes about by the "use" of a term in particular contexts. This, quite obviously, has become known as the *Use Theory of Meaning.* We shall consider the Use Theory of Meaning later in this chapter.

It is by means of the world of the forms that Plato introduced into western philosophy the first worked-out ontological system of metaphysical dualism. It was a classic attempt to establish a system of *ontological dependence* for the individual things of sense experience. The individuals were what they were only because they participated in a form. Take away the subsisting forms and the individuals of the world would no longer exist. Accordingly, the relationship of participation is crucial for Plato. In the later Platonic dialogue, *Parmenides,* this relationship of participation is explicitly stated:

> In my opinion, the forms are, as it were, patterns fixed in nature, and other things are like them, and resemblances of them—what is meant by the participation of other things in the Forms is really assimilation to them.

With the relationship of "participation," Plato purports to establish a connection between the world of the forms and the world of sense experience. Schematically put, these two distinct ontological realms constitute the core of Platonic dualism.

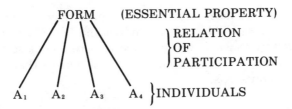

In the end, this relationship of participation is the core of Platonic ontological dependence of individual on form. This radical dualism connected through the relation of participation accounts for Plato's solution for the one-many problem. Plato thought this solution, which demands an ontological realm of subsisting essences, is necessary if our language is to be significant. Therefore, the Exaggerated Theory of Reference is an extremely important presupposition necessary for understanding the Platonic ontology.

By way of schematic summary, we might consider Plato's world of the forms in the following manner:

I.   *Qualities of the World of the Forms:*
     They exist in no space.
     They exist in no time.
     They are eternal.
     They subsist in a metaphysical realm.

II. *Function of the Forms:*
     They are the essential properties of things.
     They are the absolute standards for judgment.
     They are "real" beings as opposed to the world of "becoming."
     They are the patterns for the individuals of the sensible world.

III. *Characteristics of the Forms:*
     Eternal
     Uncreated
     Immutable
     Purely intelligible

IV. *Kinds of Forms:*
     Mathematical
     Ethical
     Physical

A Contemporary Account of Universals

Although Plato was the first philosopher to work out a detailed metaphysical theory of universals, he certainly was not the only philosopher to hold such a radical dualism in his ontology. The questions Plato considered have been very influential in the formation and development of western philosophy. As Alfred North Whitehead once remarked, all of western philosophy is but a footnote to Plato. An early twentieth-century exponent of a dualistic theory of universals structurally similar to Plato's position was Bertrand Russell. Many historians of philosophy consider Russell to be a principal exponent of that branch of contemporary philosophy known as "Philosophical Analysis." In the following passage from his work, *Problems of Philosophy*, Russell emphatically argued for subsistence of universals. Russell will mention some figures in the history of

British empiricism—Berkeley and Hume—which may be unfamiliar to the reader. Nonetheless, we will be able to understand how Russell criticizes their theories denying universals. It will be important to pay close attention to the use of "relation" in Russell's argument. Russell will insist that relations are the prime example of universals.

The problem with which we are now concerned is a very old one, since it was brought into philosophy by Plato. Plato's "theory of ideas" is an attempt to solve this very problem, and in my opinion it is one of the most successful attempts hitherto made. The theory to be advocated in what follows is largely Plato's, with merely such modifications as time has shown to be necessary.

The way the problem arose for Plato was more or less as follows. Let us consider, say, such a notion as *justice*. If we ask ourselves what justice is, it is natural to proceed by considering this, that, and the other just act, with a view to discovering what they have in common. They must all, in some sense, partake of a common nature, which will be found in whatever is just and in nothing else. This common nature, in virtue of which they are all just, will be justice itself, the pure essence the admixture of which with facts of ordinary life produces the multiplicity of just acts. Similarly with any other word which may be applicable to common facts, such as "whiteness" for example. The word will be applicable to a number of particular things because they all participate in a common nature or essence. This pure essence is what Plato calls an "idea" or "form." (It must not be supposed that "ideas," in his sense, exist in minds, though they may be apprehended by minds.) The "idea" *justice* is not identical with anything that is just: it is something other than particular things, which particular things partake of. Not being particular, it cannot itself exist in the world of sense. Moreover it is not fleeting or changeable like the things of sense: it is eternally itself, immutable and indestructible.

Thus Plato is led to a supra-sensible world, more real than the common world of sense, the unchangeable world of ideas, which alone gives to the world of sense whatever pale reflection of reality may belong to it. The truly real world, for Plato, is the world of ideas; for whatever we may attempt to say about things in the world of sense, we can only succeed in saying that they participate in such and such ideas, which, therefore, constitute all their character. Hence it is easy to pass on into a mysticism. We may hope, in a mystic illumination, to *see* the ideas as we see objects of sense; and we may imagine that the ideas exist in heaven. These mystical developments are very natural, but the basis of the theory is in logic, and it is as based in logic that we have to consider it.

The word "idea" has acquired, in the course of time, many associations which are quite misleading when applied to Plato's "ideas." We shall therefore use the word "universal" instead of the word "idea," to describe what Plato meant. The essence of the sort of entity that Plato meant is that it is opposed to the particular things that are given in sensation. We speak of whatever is given in sensation, or is of the same nature as things given in sensation, as a *particular*; by opposition to this, a *universal* will be anything which may be shared by many particulars, and has those characteristics which, as we saw, distinguish justice and whiteness from just acts and white things.

When we examine common words, we find that, broadly speaking, proper names stand for particulars, while other substantives, adjectives, prepositions, and verbs stand for universals. Pronouns stand for particulars, but are ambiguous: it is only by the context or the circumstances that we know what particulars they stand for. The word "now" stands for a particular, namely the present moment; but like pronouns, it stands for an ambiguous particular, because the present is always changing.

It will be seen that no sentence can be made up without at least one word which denotes a universal. The nearest approach would be some such statement as "I like this." But even here the word "like" denotes a universal, for I may like other things, and other people may like things. Thus all truths involve universals, and all knowledge of truths involves acquaintance with universals.

Seeing that nearly all the words to be found in the dictionary stand for universals, it is strange that hardly anybody except students of philosophy ever realizes that there are such entities as universals. We do not naturally dwell upon those words in a sentence which do not stand for particulars; and if we are forced to dwell upon a word which stands for a universal, we naturally think of it as standing for some one of the particulars that come under the universal. When, for example, we hear the sentence, "Charles I's head was cut off," we may naturally enough think of Charles I, of Charles I's head, and of the operation of cutting off *his* head, which are all particulars; but we do not naturally dwell upon what is meant by the word "head" or the word "cut," which is a universal. We feel such words to be incomplete and insubstantial; they seem to demand a context before anything can be done with them. Hence we succeed in avoiding all notice of universals as such, until the study of philosophy forces them upon our attention.

Even among philosophers, we may say, broadly, that only those universals which are named by adjectives or substantives have been much or often recognized, while those named by verbs and prepositions have been usually overlooked. This omission has had a very great effect upon philosophy; it is hardly too much to say that most metaphysics, since Spinoza, has been largely determined by it. The way this has occurred is, in outline, as follows: Speaking generally, adjectives and common nouns express qualities or properties of single things, whereas prepositions and verbs tend to express relations between two or more things. Thus the neglect of prepositions and verbs led to the belief that every proposition can be regarded as attributing a property to a single thing, rather than as expressing a relation between two or more things. Hence it was supposed that, ultimately, there can be no such entities as relations between things. Hence either there can be only one thing in the universe, or, if there are many things, they cannot possibly interact in any way, since any interaction would be a relation, and relations are impossible.

The first of these views, advocated by Spinoza and held in our own day by Bradley and many other philosophers, is called *monism;* the second, advocated by Leibniz but not very common nowadays, is called *monadism,* because each of the isolated things is called a *monad.* Both these opposing philosophies, interesting as they are, result, in my opinion, from an undue attention to one sort of universals, namely the sort represented by adjectives and substantives rather than by verbs and prepositions.

As a matter of fact, if any one were anxious to deny altogether that there are such things as universals, we should find that we cannot strictly prove that there are such entities as *qualities,* i.e. the universals represented by adjectives and substantives, whereas we can prove that there must be *relations,* i.e., the sort of universals generally represented by verbs and prepositions. Let us take in illustration the universal *whiteness.* If we believe that there is such a universal, we shall say that things are white because they have the quality of whiteness. This view, however, was strenuously denied by Berkeley and Hume, who have been followed in this by later empiricists. The form which their denial took was to deny that there are such things as "abstract ideas." When we want to think of whiteness, they said, we form an image of some particular white thing, and reason concerning this particular, taking care not to deduce anything concerning it which we cannot see to be equally true of any other white thing. As an account of our actual mental processes, this is no doubt largely true. In geometry, for example, when we wish to prove something about all triangles, we draw a particular triangle and reason about it, taking care not to use any characteristic which it does not share with other triangles. The beginner, in order to avoid error, often finds it useful to draw several triangles, as unlike each other as possible, in order to make sure that his reasoning is equally applicable to all of them. But a difficulty emerges as soon as we ask ourselves how we know that a thing is white or a triangle. If we wish to avoid the universals *whiteness* and *triangularity,* we shall choose some particular patch of white or some particular triangle, and say that anything is white or a triangle if it has the right sort of resemblance to our chosen particular. But then the resemblance required will have to be a universal. Since there are many white things, the resemblance must hold between many pairs of particular white things; and this is the characteristic of a universal. It will be useless to say that there is a different resemblance for each pair, for then we shall have to say that these resemblances resemble each other, and thus at last we shall be forced to admit resemblance as a universal. The relation of resemblance, therefore, must be a true universal. And having been forced to admit this universal, we find that it is no longer worthwhile to invent difficult and unplausible theories to avoid the admission of such universals as whiteness and triangularity.

Berkeley and Hume failed to perceive this refutation of their rejection of "abstract ideas," because, like their adversaries, they only thought of *qualities,* and altogether ignored *relations* as universals. We have therefore here another respect in which the rationalists appear to have been in the right as against the empiricists, although, owing to the neglect or denial of relations, the deductions made by rationalists were, if anything, more apt to be mistaken than those made by empiricists.

Having now seen that there must be such entities as universals, the next point to be proved is that their being is not merely mental. By this is meant that whatever being belongs to them is independent of their being thought of or in any way apprehended by minds. We have already touched on this subject at the end of the preceding chapter, but we must now consider more fully what sort of being it is that belongs to universals.

Consider such a proposition as "Edinburgh is north of London." Here we have a relation between two places, and it seems plain that the relation subsists independently of our knowledge of it. When we come to know that Edinburgh is north of London, we come to know something which has to do only with Edinburgh and London: we do not cause the truth of the proposition by coming to know it, on the contrary we merely apprehend a fact which was there before we knew it. The part of the earth's surface where Edinburgh stands would be north of the part where London stands, even if there were no human being to know about north and south, and even if there were no minds at all in the universe. This is, of course, denied by many philosophers, either for Berkeley's reasons or for Kant's. But we have already considered these reasons, and decided that they are inadequate. We may therefore now assume it to be true that nothing mental is presupposed in the fact that Edinburgh is north of London. But this fact involves the relation "north of," which is a universal; and it would be impossible for the whole fact to involve nothing mental if the relation "north of," which is a constituent part of the fact, did involve anything mental. Hence we must admit that the relation, like the terms it relates, is not dependent upon thought, but belongs to the independent world which thought apprehends but does not create.

This conclusion, however, is met by the difficulty that the relation "north of" does not seem to *exist* in the same sense in which Edinburgh and London exist. If we ask "Where and when does this relation exist?" the answer must be "Nowhere and nowhen." There is no place or time where we can find the relation "north of." It does not exist in Edinburgh any more than in London, for it relates the two and is neutral as between them. Nor can we say that it exists at any particular time.

Now everything that can be apprehended by the senses or by introspection exists at some particular time. Hence the relation "north of" is radically different from such things. It is neither in space nor in time, neither material nor mental; yet it is something.

It is largely the very peculiar kind of being that belongs to universals which has led many people to suppose that they are really mental. We can think *of* a universal, and our thinking then exists in a perfectly ordinary sense, like any other mental act. Suppose, for example, that we are thinking of whiteness. Then *in one sense* it may be said that whiteness is "in our mind." We have here the same ambiguity as we noted in discussing Berkeley in Chapter IV. In the strict sense, it is not whiteness that is in our mind, but the act of thinking of whiteness. The connected ambiguity in the word "idea," which we noted at the same time, also causes confusion here. In one sense of this word, namely the sense in which it denotes the *object* of an act of thought, whiteness is an "idea." Hence, if the ambiguity is not guarded against, we may come to think that whiteness is an "idea" in the other sense, i.e. an act of thought; and thus we come to think that whiteness is mental. But in so thinking, we rob it of its essential quality of universality. One man's act of thought is necessarily a different thing from another man's; one man's act of thought at one time is necessarily a different thing from the same man's act of thought at another time. Hence, if whiteness were the thought as opposed to its object, no two different men could think of it, and no one man could think of it twice. That which many different thoughts of whiteness have in common is their *object,* and this object is different from all of them. Thus universals are not thoughts, though when known they are the objects of thoughts.

We shall find it convenient only to speak of things *existing* when they are in time, that is to say, when we can point to some time *at* which they exist (not excluding the possibility of their existing at all times). Thus thoughts and feelings, minds and physical objects *exist.* But universals do not exist in this sense; we shall say that they *subsist* or *have being,* where "being" is opposed to "existence" as being timeless. The world of universals, therefore, may also be described as the world of being. The world of being is unchangeable, rigid, exact, delightful to the mathematician, the logician, the builder of metaphysical systems, and all who love perfection more than life. The world of existence is fleeting, vague, without sharp boundaries, without any clear plan or arrangement, but it contains all thoughts and feelings, all the data of sense, and all physical objects, everything that can do either good or harm, everything that makes any difference to the value of life and the world. According to our temperaments, we shall prefer the contemplation of the one or of the other. The one we do not prefer will probably seem to us a pale shadow of the one we prefer, and hardly worthy to be regarded as in any sense real. But the truth is that both have the same claim on our impartial attention, both are real, and both are important to the metaphysician. Indeed no sooner have we distinguished the two worlds than it becomes necessary to consider their relations.[5]

Criticism of the Theory of the Forms

We have now considered two formulations of the theory of universals as subsistent entities, one ancient and another contemporary. As might be expected, an exaggerated account of speculative metaphysics like Plato's Theory of the Forms would encounter much philosophical criticism. In the history of philosophy, the theory of universals has come under attack quite often. Interestingly enough, the first intense criticism leveled against the forms as separated entities came from Plato himself. In one of his later dialogues, the *Parmenides,*

Plato presents an extremely honest intellectual appraisal of the Theory of the Forms. Consider carefully Plato's arguments provided in the following passages taken from the *Parmenides*. The philosopher, Parmenides, has Socrates very much on the defensive. Parmenides rigorously questions the young Socrates on issues relating to the ontological status of the forms and regarding the nature of the relation of participation between the forms and the individual instances under them.

. . . While Socrates was saying this, Pythodorus thought that Parmenides and Zeno were not altogether pleased at the successive steps of the argument; but still they gave the closest attention, and often looked at one another, and smiled as if in admiration of him. When he had finished, Parmenides expressed these feelings in the following words: —

Socrates, he said, I admire the bent of your mind towards philosophy; tell me now, was this your own distinction between abstract ideas and the things which partake of them? and do you think that there is an idea of likeness apart from the likeness which we possess, or of the one and many, or of the other notions of which Zeno has been speaking?

I think that there are such abstract ideas, said Socrates.

Parmenides proceeded. And would you also make abstract ideas of the just and the beautiful and the good, and of all that class of notions?

Yes, he said, I should.

And would you make an abstract idea of man distinct from us and from all other human creatures, or of fire and water?

I am often undecided, Parmenides, as to whether I ought to include them or not.

And would you feel equally undecided, Socrates, about things the mention of which may provoke a smile?—I mean such things as hair, mud, dirt, or anything else that is foul and base; would you suppose that each of these has an idea distinct from the phenomena with which we come into contact, or not?

Certainly not, said Socrates; visible things like these are such as they appear to us, and I am afraid that there would be an absurdity in assuming any idea of them, although I sometimes get disturbed, and begin to think that there is nothing without an idea; but then again, when I have taken up this position, I run away, because I am afraid that I may fall into a bottomless pit of nonsense, and perish; and I return to the ideas of which I was just now speaking, and busy myself with them.

Yes, Socrates, said Parmenides; that is because you are still young; the time will come when philosophy will have a firmer grasp of you, if I am not mistaken, and then you will not despise even the meanest things; at your age, you are too much disposed to look to the opinions of men. But I should like to know whether you mean that there are certain forms or ideas of which all other things partake, and from which they are named; that similars, for example, become similar, because they partake of similarity;

Reprinted from Plato, *Parmenides*, 131–35.

and great things become great, because they partake of greatness; and that just and beautiful things become just and beautiful, because they partake of justice and beauty?

Yes, certainly, said Socrates, that is my meaning.

And does not each individual partake either of the whole of the idea or of a part of the idea? Is any third way possible?

Impossible, he said.

Then do you think that the whole idea is one, and yet being one, exists in each one of many?

Why not, Parmenides? said Socrates.

Because one and the same existing as a whole in many separate individuals, will thus be in a state of separation from itself.

Nay, replied the other; the idea may be like the day, which is one and the same in many places, and yet continues with itself; in this way each idea may be one and the same in all.

I like your way, Socrates, of dividing one into many; and if I were to spread out a sail and cover a number of men, that, as I suppose, in your way of speaking, would be one and a whole in or on many—that will be the sort of thing which you mean?

I am not sure.

And would you say that the whole sail is over each man, or a part only?

A part only.

Then, Socrates, the ideas themselves will be divisible, and the individuals will have a part only and not the whole existing in them?

That seems to be true.

Then would you like to say, Socrates, that the one idea is really divisible and yet remains one?

Certainly not, he said.

Suppose that you divide greatness, and that of many great things each one is great by having a portion of greatness less than absolute greatness—is that conceivable?

No.

Or will each equal part, by taking some portion of equality less than absolute equality, be equal to some other?

Impossible.

Or suppose one of us to have a portion of smallness; this is but a part of the small, and therefore the small is greater; and while the absolute small is greater, that to which the part of the small is added, will be smaller and not greater than before.

That is impossible, he said.

Then in what way, Socrates, will all things participate in the ideas, if they are unable to participate in them either as parts or wholes?

Indeed, he said, that is a question which is not easily determined.

Well, said Parmenides, and what do you say of another question?

What is that?

I imagine that the way in which you are led to assume the existence of ideas is as follows: You see a number of great objects, and there seems to you to be one and the same idea of greatness pervading them all; and hence you conceive of a single greatness.

That is true, said Socrates.

And if you go on and allow your mind in like manner to contemplate the idea of greatness and these other greatnesses, and to compare them, will not another idea of greatness arise, which will appear to be the source of them all?

That is true.

Then another abstraction of greatness will appear over and above absolute greatness, and the individuals which partake of it; and then another, which will be the source of that, and then others, and so on; and there will be no longer a single idea of each kind, but an infinite number of them.

But may not the ideas, asked Socrates, be cognitions only, and have no proper existence except in our minds, Parmenides? For in that case there may be single ideas, which do not involve the consequences which were just now mentioned.

And can there be individual cognitions which are cognitions of nothing?

That is impossible, he said.

The cognition must be of something?

Yes.

Of something that is or is not?

Of something that is.

Must it not be of the unity, or single nature, which the cognition recognizes as attaching to all?

Yes.

And will not this unity, which is always the same in all, be the idea?

From that again, there is no escape.

Then, said Parmenides, if you say that other things participate in the ideas, must you not say that everything is made up of thoughts or cognitions, and that all things think; or will you say that being thoughts they are without thoughts?

But that, said Socrates, is irrational. The more probable view, Parmenides, of these ideas is, that they are patterns fixed in nature, and that other things are like them, and resemblances of them; and that what is meant by the participation of other things in the ideas, is really assimilation to them.

But if, said he, the individual is like the idea, must not the idea also be like the individual, in as far as the individual is a resemblance of the idea? That which is like, cannot be conceived of as other than the like of like.

Impossible.

And when two things are alike, must they not partake of the same idea?

They must.

And will not that of which the two partake, and which makes them alike, be the absolute idea [of likeness]?

Certainly.

Then the idea cannot be like the individual, or the individual like the idea; for if they are alike, some further idea of likeness will always arise, and if that be like anything else, another and another; and new ideas will never cease being created, if the idea resembles that which partakes of it?

Quite true.

The theory, then, that other things participate in the ideas by resemblance, has to be given up, and some other mode of participation devised?

That is true.

Do you see then, Socrates, how great is the difficulty of affirming self-existent ideas?

Yes, indeed.

And further, let me say that as yet you only understand a small part of the difficulty which is involved in your assumption, that there are ideas of all things, which are distinct from them.

What difficulty? he said.

There are many, but the greatest of all is this: If an opponent argues that these self-existent ideas, as we term them, cannot be known, no one can prove to him that he is wrong, unless he who is disputing their existence be a man of great genius and cultivation, and is willing to follow a long and laborious demonstration—he will remain unconvinced, and still insist that they cannot be known.

How is that, Parmenides? said Socrates.

In the first place, I think, Socrates, that you, or any one who maintains the existence of absolute ideas, will admit that they cannot exist in us.

Why then they would be no longer absolute, said Socrates.

That is true, he said; and any relation in the absolute ideas is a relation which is among themselves only, and has nothing to do with resemblances, or whatever they are to be termed, which are in our sphere, and the participation in which gives us this or that name. And the subjective notions in our mind, which have the same name with them, are likewise only relative to one another, and not to the ideas which have the same name with them, and belong to themselves and not to the ideas.

How do you mean? said Socrates.

I may illustrate my meaning in this way, said Parmenides: A master has a slave; now there is nothing absolute in the relation between them; they are both relations of some man to another man; but there is also an idea of mastership in the abstract, which is relative to the idea of slavery in the abstract; and this abstract nature has nothing to do with us, nor we with the abstract nature; abstract natures have to do with themselves alone, and we with ourselves. Do you see my meaning?

Yes, said Socrates, I quite see your meaning.

And does not knowledge, I mean absolute knowledge, he said, answer to very and absolute truth?

Certainly.

And each kind of absolute knowledge answers to each kind of absolute being?

Yes.

And the knowledge which we have, will answer to the truth which we have; and again, each kind of knowledge which we have, will be a knowledge of each kind of being which we have?

Certainly.

But the ideas themselves, as you admit, we have not, and cannot have?

No, we cannot.

And the absolute ideas or species, are known by the absolute idea of knowledge?

Yes.

And that is an idea which we have not got?

No.

Then none of the ideas are known to us, because we have no share in absolute knowledge?

They are not.

Then the ideas of the beautiful, and of the good, and the like, which we imagine to be absolute ideas, are unknown to us?

That appears to be the case.

I think that there is a worse consequence still.

What is that?

Would you, or would you not, say, that if there is such a thing as absolute knowledge, that must be a far more accurate knowledge than our knowledge, and the same of beauty and other things?

Yes.

And if there be anything that has absolute knowledge, there is nothing more likely than God to have this most exact knowledge?

Certainly.

But then, will God, having this absolute knowledge, have a knowledge of human things?

And why not?

Because, Socrates, said Parmenides, we have admitted that the ideas have no relation to human notions, nor human notions to them; the relations of either are in their respective spheres.

Yes, that has been admitted.

And if God has this truest authority, and this most exact knowledge, that authority cannot rule us, nor that knowledge know us, or any human thing; and in like manner, as our authority does not extend to the gods, nor our knowledge know anything which is divine, so by parity of reason they, being gods, are not our masters; neither do they know the things of men.

Yet, surely, said Socrates, to deprive God of knowledge is monstrous.

These, Socrates, said Parmenides, are a few, and only a few, of the difficulties which are necessarily involved in the hypothesis of the existence of ideas, and the attempt to prove the absoluteness of each of them; he who hears of them will doubt or deny their existence, and will maintain that even if they do exist, they must necessarily be known to man, and he will think that there is reason in what he says, and as we were remarking just now, will be wonderfully hard of being convinced; a man must be a man of real ability before he can understand that everything has a class and an absolute essence; and still more remarkable will he be who makes out all these things for himself, and can teach another to analyze them satisfactorily.

I agree with you, Parmenides, said Socrates; and what you say is very much to my mind.

And yet, Socrates, said Parmenides, if a man, fixing his mind on these and the like difficulties, refuses to acknowledge ideas or species of existences, and will not define particular species, he will be at his wit's end; in this way he will utterly destroy the power of reasoning; and that is what you seem to me to have particularly noted.

Very true, he said.

But, then, what is to become of philosophy? What resource is there, if the ideas are unknown?

I certainly do not see my way at present.

In the preceding passage from the *Parmenides*, it is obvious that Plato is extremely worried about the metaphysical consequences of his Theory of the Forms. In discussing the nature of the forms, the young Socrates appears quite uncertain about where to draw the line between what indeed needs a form and what does not. In the history of philosophy, some plausibility has been recognized for considering both mathematical and ethical absolutes. We saw that Russell asserted the subsistence of mathematical universals. Moreover, there might be some plausibility in considering forms for physical objects—human beings, cats, dogs, trees, and so forth. Yet there is a difficulty in providing an adequate account for the forms of physical things. It is extremely difficult to establish what exactly the essential characteristic of physical objects might be. With mathematical definitions it is not all that difficult. One can easily be persuaded to define a triangle as a three-sided plane figure all of whose sides intersect. We might refer to a triangle as a "closed concept." But what would be the essential characteristic of a collie dog as distinct from a German shepherd? And what becomes of the various mixed breeds—the common "mutt"? Plato faces a serious problem in attempting to provide content for the forms of physical objects. As a dialectical device, the one-many problem Plato uses might be convincing. However, the content of the forms, especially the forms for physical objects, leaves much to be desired. The problem becomes more acute when we consider human artifacts—tables, chairs, and beer cans. Is there a form for "beer can"? And what about stop signs, post holes, and barn siloes? Furthermore, what about the parts of these artifacts: the left side of a stop sign, the top half of a stop sign, and so forth? Each of these instances might meet the criterion of the one-many problem, and each might meet the demand of the Exaggerated Theory of Reference. But if all of the above mentioned items have a form, then the Platonic world of the forms will indeed become overpopulated. If it is so overpopulated, then it loses any explanatory function which a simpler theory might provide. The world of the forms becomes not, to paraphrase a contemporary philosopher, a "desert landscape," but rather a cluttered slum of ontological entities. Therefore a crucial problem for a metaphysical dualism like Plato's Theory of the Forms is to determine what needs a form and what does not. Plato seems not to have successfully resolved this problem.

In addition, an explanation of the relation of participation between the form and the individual instance under it is of utmost importance. Plato often reverted to metaphor when discussing this relation. Yet if one postulates the forms as separated entities, the connection between the forms and the individuals is necessary. In the *Parmenides,* the young Socrates cannot explain this relation satisfactorily to Parmenides.

Yet Plato remains convinced that universal characteristics must be accounted for if knowledge and language are to make sense. Recall the famous last words in the *Parmenides* selection.

An Ordinary Language Analysis of Universals

Some contemporary philosophers, especially the followers of Ludwig Wittgenstein, have utilized insights from Wittgenstein's important work, *Philosophical Investigations*, in order to reject any theory calling for the existence of universals. In writing *Philosophical Investigations*, Wittgenstein was troubled over the restrictive conditions of the reference theory of meaning. Strangely enough, in an earlier work, *Tractatus Logico-Philosophicus*, Wittgenstein himself had strongly defended a referential theory of meaning. If the Reference Theory of Meaning is false, and if Plato's world of the forms depends upon this theory, then there need not be any subsistent universals to account for the meaning of common names. Wittgenstein attacked the need for essential properties in *Philosophical Investigations*. This attack prompted the formulation of what has become known as the *Use Theory of Meaning*. The Use Theory of Meaning is opposed to the Reference Theory of Meaning, because it asserts that a term acquires its meaning, not by the relation of reference to an object, but by the manner in which it is used in a particular situation by speakers of a language. Wittgenstein continually asks us to "look and see" the actual uses of language. He does not want us to assume a theory of meaning and try to force it onto language. In the following article, Renford Bambrough suggests that Wittgensteinian insights are sufficient to render the search for universals insignificant. In addition to providing a clear elucidation of Wittgenstein's Use Theory of Meaning, Bambrough introduces us to some important philosophical concepts. in particular, the concepts of nominalism and realism. Realism is taken to refer to Plato's demand for universals as existent entities. Nominalism refers to the denial that any ontological counterpart exists to common names or universal terms in language.

UNIVERSALS AND FAMILY RESEMBLANCES

Renford Bambrough

I believe that Wittgenstein solved what is known as "the problem of universals", and I would say of his solution, as Hume said of Berkeley's treatment of the same topic, that it is "one of the greatest and most valuable discoveries that has been made of late years in the republic of letters."

I do not expect these claims to be accepted by many philosophers.

Since I claim that Wittgenstein solved the problem I naturally do not claim to be making an original contribution to the study of it. Since I recog-

---

From *Proceedings of the Aristotelian Society*, Vol. LX (1960–61). Copyright 1961, the Aristotelian Society. Reprinted by permission of the Editor of the Aristotelian Society.

nise that few philosophers will accept my claim that Wittgenstein solved it, I naturally regard it as worth while to continue to discuss the problem. My purpose is to try to make clear what Wittgenstein's solution is and to try to make clear that it is a solution.

Philosophers ought to be wary of claiming that philosophical problems have been finally solved. Aristotle and Descartes and Spinoza and Berkeley and Hume and the author of the *Tractatus Logico-Philosophicus* lie at the bottom of the sea not far from this rock, with the skeletons of many lesser men to keep them company. But nobody suggests that their journeys were vain, or that nothing can be saved from the wrecks.

In seeking for Wittgenstein's solution we must look mainly to his remarks about "family resemblances" and to his use of the example of games. In the *Blue Book* he speaks of "our craving for generality" and tries to trace this craving to its sources:

> This craving for generality is the resultant of a number of tendencies connected with particular philosophical confusions. There is—
>
> (a) The tendency to look for something in common to all the entities which we commonly subsume under a general term.—We are inclined to think that there must be something in common to all games, say, and that this common property is the justification for applying the general term "game" to the various games; whereas games form a *family* the members of which have family likenesses. Some of them have the same nose, others the same eyebrows and others again the same way of walking; and these likenesses overlap. The idea of a general concept being a common property of its particular instances connects up with other primitive, too simple, ideas of the structure of language. It is comparable to the idea that *properties* are *ingredients* of the things which have the properties; *e.g.,* that beauty is an ingredient of all beautiful things as alcohol is of beer and wine, and that we therefore could have pure beauty, unadulterated by anything that is beautiful.
>
> (b) There is a tendency rooted in our usual forms of expression, to think that the man who has learnt to understand a general term, say, the term "leaf", has thereby come to possess a kind of general picture of a leaf, as opposed to pictures of particular leaves. He was shown different leaves when he learnt the meaning of the word "leaf"; and showing him the particular leaves was only a means to the end of producing "in him" an idea which we imagine to be some kind of general image. We say that he sees what is in common to all these leaves; and this is true if we mean that he can on being asked tell us certain features or properties which they have in common. But we are inclined to think that the general idea of a leaf is something like a visual image, but one which only contains what is common to all leaves. (Galtonian composite photograph.) This again is connected with the idea that the meaning of a word is an image, or a thing correlated to the word. (This roughly means, we are looking at words as though they all were proper names, and we then confuse the bearer of a name with the meaning of the name.) (Pp. 17–18).

In the *Philosophical Investigations* Wittgenstein again speaks of family resemblances, and gives a more elaborate account of the similarities and differences between various games:

> 66. Consider for example the proceedings that we call "games". I mean board-games, card-games, ball-games, Olympic games, and so on. What is common to them all?—Don't say: "there *must* be something common, or they would not be called 'games' "—but *look and see* whether there is anything common to all.—For if you look at them you will not see something that is

common to *all,* but similarities, relationships, and a whole series of them at that. To repeat: don't think, but look!—Look for example at board-games, with their multifarious relationships. Now pass to card-games; here you find many correspondences with the first group, but many common features drop out, and others appear. When we pass next to ball-games, much that is common is retained, but much is lost.—Are they all "amusing"? Compare chess with noughts and crosses. Or is there always winning and losing, or competition between players? Think of patience. In ball-games there is winning and losing; but when a child throws his ball at the wall and catches it again, this feature has disappeared. Look at the parts played by skill and luck; and at the difference between skill in chess and skill in tennis. Think now of games like ring-a-ring-a-roses; here is the element of amusement, but how many other characteristic features have disappeared! And we can go through the many, many other groups of games in the same way; can see how similarities crop up and disappear.

   And the result of this examination is: we see a complicated network of similarities overlapping and criss-crossing: sometimes overall similarities, sometimes similarities of detail.

   67. I can think of no better expression to characterise these similarities than "family resemblances"; for the various resemblances between the members of a family: build, features, colour of eyes, gait, temperament, etc. etc. overlap and criss-cross in the same way.—And I shall say: "games" form a family.

Wittgenstein expounds his analogy informally, and with great economy. Its power can be displayed in an equally simple but more formal way by considering a situation that is familiar to botanical taxonomists.[1] We may classify a set of objects by reference to the presence or absence of features *ABCDE.* It may well happen that five objects *edcba* are such that each of them has four of these properties and lacks the fifth, and that the missing feature is different in each of the five cases. A simple diagram will illustrate this situation:

e	*d*	*c*	*b*	*a*
ABCD	*ABCE*	*ABDE*	*ACDE*	*BCDE*

Here we can already see how natural and how proper it might be to apply the same word to a number of objects between which there is no common feature. And if we confine our attention to any arbitrarily selected four of these objects, say *edca,* then although they all *happen* to have *B* in common, it is clear that it is not in virtue of the presence of *B* that they are all rightly called by the same name. Even if the actual instances were indefinitely numerous, and they all happened to have one or more of the features in common, it would not be in virtue of the presence of the common feature or features that they would all be rightly called by the same name, since the name also applies to *possible* instances that lack the feature or features.

   The richness of the possibilities of the family resemblances model becomes more striking still if we set it out more fully and formally in terms of a particular family than Wittgenstein himself ever did. Let us suppose that "the Churchill face" is strikingly and obviously present in each of ten members of the Churchill family, and that when a family group photograph is set before us it is unmistakable that these ten people all belong to the same family. It may be that there are ten features in terms of which we can describe "the family face" (high forehead, bushy eyebrows, blue eyes, Roman nose, high cheekbones, cleft chin, dark hair, dimpled cheeks, pointed ears and ruddy complexion). It is obvious that the unmistakable presence of the family face in every single one of the ten members of the family is compatible with the absence from each of the ten members of the family of one of the ten constituent features of the family face. It is also obvious that it does not matter if it happens that the feature which is absent from the face of each individual member of the family is present in every one of the others. The members of the family will then have no *feature* in common, and yet they will all unmistakably have *the Churchill face* in common.

This example is very artificial, and it may seem at first sight that its artificiality plays into my hands. But on the contrary, the more natural the example is made the more it suits my purpose. If we remember that a family face does not divide neatly into ten separate features, we widen rather than reduce the scope for large numbers of instances of the family face to lack a single common feature. And if we remember that what goes for faces goes for features too; that all cleft chins have nothing in common except that they are cleft chins, that the possible gradations from Roman nose to snub nose or from high to low cheekbones are continuous and infinite, we see that there could in principle be an infinite number of unmistakable Churchill faces which had no feature in common. In fact it now becomes clear that there is a good sense in which *no two* members of the Churchill family need have *any* feature in common in order for *all* the members of the Churchill family to have the Churchill face.

The passages that I have quoted contain the essence of Wittgenstein's solution of the problem of universals, but they are far from exhausting his account of the topic. Not only are there other places where he speaks of games and of family resemblances: what is more important is that most of his philosophical remarks in *The Blue and Brown Books* and in the *Philosophical Investigations* are concerned with such questions as "What is the meaning of a word?" "What is language?" "What is thinking?" "What is understanding?" And these questions are various forms of the question to which theories of universals, including Wittgenstein's theory of universals, are meant to be answers. There is a clear parallel between what Wittgenstein says about games and what he says about reading, expecting, languages, numbers, propositions; in all these cases we have the idea that there is a common element or ingredient, and Wittgenstein shows us that there is no such ingredient or element. The instances that fall under each of these concepts *form a family.*

It is already clear that the point Wittgenstein made with the example of games has a much wider range of application than that example itself. But exactly how wide is its application meant to be? Wittgenstein's own method of exposition makes it difficult to answer this question. In his striving to find a cure for "our craving for generality," in his polemic against "the contemptuous attitude towards the particular case," he was understandably wary of expressing his own conclusions in general terms. Readers and expositors of Wittgenstein are consequently impelled to make use of glosses and paraphrases and interpretations if they wish to relate his work to philosophical writings and doctrines that are expressed in another idiom; that is to say, to most other philosophical writings and doctrines.

I believe that this is why Wittgenstein's solution of the problem of universals has not been widely understood, and why, in consequence, it has not been widely seen to be a solution.[2] In avoiding the generalities that are characteristic of most philosophical discussion he also avoided reference to the standard "problems of philosophy" and to the "philosophical theories" which have repeatedly been offered as answers to them. He talks about games and families and colours, about reading, expecting and understanding, but not about "the problem of universals." He practised an activity which is "one of the heirs of the subject which used to be called 'philosophy'", but he did not relate the results of his activity to the results of the enquiries to which it was an heir. He did not, for example, plot the relation between his remarks on games and family resemblances and the doctrines of those philosophers who had been called Nominalists and Realists.

When I claim that Wittgenstein solved the problem of universals I am claiming that his remarks can be paraphrased into a doctrine which can be set out in general terms and can be related to the traditional theories, and which can then be shown to deserve to supersede the traditional theories. My purpose in this paper is to expound such a doctrine and to defend it.

But first I must return to my question about the range of application of the point that is made by the example of games, since it is at this crucial first stage that most readers of Wittgenstein go wrong. When we read what he says about games and family resemblances, we are naturally inclined to ask ourselves, "With what kinds of concepts is Wittgenstein *contrasting* the concepts of game, language, proposition, understanding?" I shall consider three possible answers to this question.

The first answer is suggested by Professor Ayer's remarks about games and family resemblances on pp. 10–12 of *The Problem of Knowledge.* Ayer contrasts the word "game" with the word "red", on the ground that the former does not, while the latter does, mark "a simple and straightforward resemblance" between the things to which the word is applied. He claims that, "The point which Wittgenstein's argument brings out is that the resemblance between the things to which the same word applies may be of different degrees. It is looser and less straightforward in some cases than in others." Now this contrast between simple and complicated concepts is important, and the games example is a convenient means of drawing attention to it, but I am sure that this is not the point that Wittgenstein was making with his example. In the *Brown Book* (p. 131) he asks, "Could you tell me what is in common between a light red and a dark red?" and in the *Philosophical Investigations* (Section 73) he asks, "Which shade is the 'sample in my mind' of the colour green—the sample of what is common to all shades of green?" Wittgenstein could as easily have used the example of red things as the example of games to illustrate "the tendency to look for something in common to all the entities which we commonly subsume under a general term." Just as cricket and chess and patience and ring-a-ring-a-roses have nothing in common *except that they are games,* so poppies and blood and pillar-boxes and hunting-coats have nothing in common *except that they are red.*

A second possible answer is implied by a sentence in Mr. P.F. Strawson's *Individuals:* "It is often admitted, in the analytical treatment of some fairly specific concept, that the wish to understand is less likely to be served by the search for a single strict statement of the necessary and sufficient conditions of its application than by seeing its applications—in Wittgenstein's simile—as forming a family, the members of which may, perhaps, be grouped around a central paradigm case and linked with the latter by various direct or indirect links of logical connexion and analogy." (p. 11). The contrast is not now between simple and complex concepts, but between two kinds of complex concepts: those which are definable by the statement of necessary and sufficient conditions and those which are not. But once again the contrast, although it is important, and is one which the family resemblances simile and the example of games are well able to draw, is not the point that Wittgenstein is concerned with. In the sense in which, according to Wittgenstein, games have nothing in common except that they are games, and red things have nothing in common except that they are red, *brothers have nothing in common except that they are brothers.* It is true that brothers have in common that they are male siblings, but their having in common that they are male siblings is their having in common that they are *brothers,* and not their having in common something in addition to their being brothers. Even a concept which can be explained in terms of necessary and sufficient conditions cannot be *ultimately* explained in such terms. To satisfy the craving for an ultimate explanation of "brother" in such terms it would be necessary to define "male" and "sibling", and the words in which "male" and "sibling" were defined, and so on *ad infinitum* and *ad impossibile.*

What then *is* the contrast that Wittgenstein meant to draw? I suggest that he did not mean to draw a *contrast* at all. Professor Wisdom has remarked that the peculiar difficulty of giving a philosophical account of universals lies in this: that philosophers are usually engaged in implicitly or explicitly comparing and contrasting one type of proposition with another type of proposition (propositions about minds with propositions about bodies, propositions of logic with propositions about matters of fact, propositions about the present and the past with propositions about the future, etc.) whereas propositions involving universals cannot be compared or contrasted with propositions that do not involve universals, since *all* propositions involve universals.[3] If we look at Wittgenstein's doctrine in the light of this remark we can understand it aright and can also see why it has been misunderstood in just those ways that I have mentioned. It is because of the very power of the ways of thought against which Wittgenstein was protesting that philosophers are led to offer accounts of his doctrine which restrict the range of its application. They recognise the importance of Wittgenstein's demonstration that *at least some* general terms can justifiably be applied to their instances although those instances have nothing in common. But they are so deeply attached to the idea that there must be something in common to the instances that fall under a general term that they treat Wittgenstein's examples as special cases, as rogues and vagabonds in the realm of concepts, to be contrasted with the general run of law-abiding concepts which *do* mark the presence of common elements in their instances.

Here we come across an ambiguity which is another obstacle to our gettng a clear view of the problem of universals and of Wittgenstein's solution of it. Ayer remarks, in the passage to which I have already referred, that, "It is correct, though not at all enlightening, to say that what games have in common is their being games." It is certainly correct, but I strongly deny that it is unenlightening. It is of course trivially and platitudinously true, but trivialities and platitudes deserve emphatic affirmation when, as often in philosophy, they are explicitly or implicitly denied, or forgotten, or overlooked. Now the platitude that all games have in common that they *are* games is denied by the nominalist, who says that all games have nothing in common except that they are *called* games. And it is not only the nominalist, but also his opponent, who misunderstands the central importance of the platitude that all games have in common that they are games. When he is provoked by the nominalist's claim that all games have nothing in common except that they are called games, and rightly wishes to insist that games have something more in common than simply that they are called games, he feels that he must look for something that games have in common apart from *being* games. This feeling is entirely misplaced. The very terms of the nominalist's challenge require only that the realist should point out something that games have in common apart from *being called* games, and this onus is fully discharged by saying that they *are* games.

Although the feeling is misplaced, it is a very natural feeling, as we can see by considering the kinds of case in which we most typically and ordinarily ask what is in common to a set of objects. If I ask you what these three books have in common, or what those four chairs have in common, you will look to see if the books are all on the same subject or by the same author or published by the same firm; to see if the chairs are all Chippendale or all three-legged or all marked "Not to be removed from this room." It will never occur to you to say that the books have in common that they are books or the chairs that they are chairs. And if you find after close inspection that the chairs or the books do not have in common any of the features I have mentioned, and if you cannot see any other specific feature that they have in common, you will say that as far as you can see they have nothing in common. You will perhaps add that you suppose from the form of my question that I must know of something that they have in common. I may then tell you that all the books once belonged to John Locke or that all the chairs came from Ten Rillington Place. But it would be a poor sort of joke for me to say that the chairs were all chairs or that the books were all books.

If I ask you what *all* chairs have in common, or what *all* books have in common, you may again try to find a feature like those you would look for in the case of *these three* books or *those four* chairs; and you may again think that it is a poor sort of joke for me to say that what all books have in common is that they are books and that what all chairs have in common is that they are chairs. And yet this time it is not a joke but an important philosophical truth.

Because the normal case where we ask "What have all *these* chairs, books or games in common?" is one in which we are not concerned with their all being chairs, books or games, we are liable to overlook the extreme peculiarity of the *philosophical* question that is asked with the words "What do *all* chairs, *all* books, *all* games have in common?" For of course games *do* have something in common. They *must* have something in common, and yet when we look for what they have in common we cannot find it. When we try to say what they have in common we always fail. And this is not because what we are looking for lies deeply hidden, but because it is too obvious to be seen; not because what we are trying to say is too subtle and complicated to be said, but because it is too easy and too simple to be worth saying: and so we say something more dramatic, but something false, instead. The simple truth is that what games have in common is that they are games. The nominalist is obscurely aware of this, and by rejecting the realist's talk of transcendent, immanent or subsistent forms or universals he shows his awareness. But by his own insistence that games have nothing in common except that they are called games he shows the obscurity of his awareness. The realist too is obscurely aware of it. By his talk of transcendent, immanent or subsistent forms or universals he shows the obscurity of his awareness. But by his hostility to the nominalist's insistence that games have nothing in common except that they are called games he shows his awareness.

All this can be more fully explained by the application of what I will call "Ramsey's Maxim." F.P. Ramsey, after mapping the course of an inconclusive dispute between Russell and W.E. Johnson, writes as follows:

> Evidently, however, none of these arguments are really decisive, and the position is extremely unsatisfactory to any one with real curiosity about such a fundamental question. In such cases it is a heuristic maxim that the truth lies not in one of the two disputed views but in some third possibility which has not yet been thought of, which we can only discover by rejecting something assumed as obvious by both the disputants. (*The Foundations of Mathematics,* pp. 115–16.)

It is assumed as obvious by both the nominalist and the realist that there can be no objective justification for the application of a general term to its instances unless its instances have something in common over and above their having in common that they *are* its instances. The nominalist rightly holds that there is no such additional common element, and he therefore wrongly concludes that there is no objective justification for the application of any general term. The realist rightly holds that there is an objective justification for the application of general terms, and he therefore wrongly concludes that there *must* be some additional common element.

Wittgenstein denied the assumption that is common to nominalism and realism, and that is why I say that he solved the problem of universals. For if we deny the mistaken premiss that is common to the realist's argument and the nominalist's argument then we can deny the realist's mistaken conclusion and deny the nominalist's mistaken conclusion; and that is another way of saying that we can affirm the true premiss of the nominal-ist's argument and can also affirm the true premiss of the realist's argument.

The nominalist says that games have nothing in common except that they are called games.

The realist says that games must have something is common, and he means by this that they must have something in common other than that they are games.

Wittgenstein says that games have nothing in common except that they are games.

Wittgenstein thus denies at one and the same time the nominalist's claim that games have nothing in common except that they are called games and the realist's claim that games have something in common other than that they are games. He asserts at one and the same time the realist's claim that there is an objective justification for the application of the word "game" to games and the nominalist's claim that there is no element that is common to all games. And he is able to do all this because he denies the joint claim of the nominalist and the realist that there cannot be an objec-tive justification for the application of the word "game" to games unless there is an element that is common to all games (*universalia in rebus*) or a common relation that all games bear to something that is not a game (*uni-versalia ante res*).

Wittgenstein is easily confused with the nominalist because he denies what the realist asserts: that games have something in common other than that they are games.

When we see that Wittgenstein is not a nominalist we may easily confuse him with the realist because he denies what the nominalist asserts: that games have nothing in common except that they are called games.

But we can now see that Wittgenstein is neither a realist nor a nominal-ist: he asserts the simple truth that they both deny and he also asserts the two simple truths of which each of them asserts one and denies the other.

I will now try to put some flesh on to these bare bones.

The value and the limitations of the nominalist's claim that things which are called by the same name have nothing in common except that they are called by the same name can be seen if we look at a case where a set of ob-jects literally and undeniably have nothing in common except that they are called by the same name. If I choose to give the name "alpha" to each of a number of miscellaneous objects (the star Sirius, my fountain-pen, the Parthenon, the colour red, the number five, and the letter Z) then I may well succeed in choosing the objects so *arbitrarily* that I shall succeed in pre-venting them from having any feature in common, other than that I call them by the name "alpha." But this imaginary case, to which the nominalist likens the use of all general words, has only to be described to be sharply contrasted with the typical case in which I apply a general word, say "chair", to a number of the instances to which it applies. In the first place, the *arbitrariness* of my selection of alphas is not paralleled in the case in which I apply the word "chair" successively to the chair in which I am now sitting, the Speaker's Chair in the House of Commons, the chair used at Bisley for carrying the winner of the Queen's Prize, and one of the deck chairs on the beach at Brighton. In giving a list of chairs I cannot just mention anything that happens to come into my head, while this is exactly what I do in giving my list of alphas. The second point is that the class of alphas is a *closed* class. Once I have given my list I have referred to every single alpha in the universe, actual and possible. Although I *might* have included or excluded any actual or possible object whatsoever when I was drawing up my list, once I have in fact made my arbitrary choice, no further application can be given to the word "alpha" according to the use that I have prescribed. For if I later add an object that I excluded from my list, or remove an object that I included in it, then I am making a different use of the word "alpha." With the word "chair" the position is quite different. There are an infinite number of actual and possible chairs. I cannot aspire to complete the enumeration of all chairs, as I can arbitrarily and at any point complete the enumeration of all alphas, and the word "chair," unlike the word "alpha", can be applied to an infinite number of instances without suffering any change of use.

These two points lead to a third and decisive point. I cannot teach the use of the word "alpha" except by specifically attaching it to each of the objects in my arbitrarily chosen list. No observer can conclude anything from watching me attach the label to this, that, or the other object, or to any number of objects however large, about the nature of the object or objects, if any, to which I shall later attach it. The use of the word "alpha" cannot be learned or taught as the use of a general word can be learned or taught. In teaching the use of a general word we may and must refer to characteristics of the objects to which it applies, and of the objects to which it does not apply, and indicate which of these characteristics count for the application of the word and which count against it. A pupil does not have to consult us on every separate occasion on which he encounters a new object, and if he did consult us every time we should have to say that he was not *learning* the use of the word. The reference that we make to a finite number of objects to which the word applies, and to a finite number of objects to which the word does not apply, is capable of equipping the pupil with a capacity for correctly applying or withholding the word to or from an infinite number of objects to which we have made no reference.

All this remains true in the case where it is not I alone, but a large number of people, or all of us, who use the word "alpha" in the way that I suggest. Even if everybody always called a particular set of objects by the same name, that would be insufficient to ensure that the name was a general name, and the claim of the name to be a general name would be defeated by just that necessity for reference to the arbitrary choices of the users of the name that the nominalist mistakenly claims to find in the case of a genuinely general name. For the nominalist is right in thinking that if we always had to make such a reference then there would be no general names as they are understood by the realist.

The nominalist is also right in the stress that he puts on the role of human interests and human purposes in determining our choice of principles of classification. How this insistence on the role of human purposes may be reconciled with the realist's proper insistence on the objectivity of the similarities and dissimilarities on which any genuine classification is based can be seen by considering an imaginary tribe of South Sea Islanders.

Let us suppose that trees are of great importance in the life and work of the South Sea Islanders, and that they have a rich and highly developed language in which they speak of the trees with which their island is thickly clad. But they do not have names for the species and genera of trees as they are recognised by our botanists. As we walk round the island with some of its inhabitants we can easily pick out orange-trees, date-palms and cedars. Our hosts are puzzled that we should call by the same name trees which appear to them to have nothing in common. They in turn surprise us by giving the same name to each of the trees in what is from our point of view a very mixed plantation. They point out to us what they called a mixed plantation, and we see that it is in our terms a clump of trees of the same species. Each party comes to recognise that its own classifications are as puzzling to the other as the other's are puzzling to itself.

This looks like the sort of situation that gives aid and comfort to the nominalist in his battle against the realist. But if we look at it more closely we see that it cannot help him. We know already that our own classification is based on similarities and differences between the trees, similarities and differences which we can point out to the islanders in an attempt to teach them our language. Of course we may fail, but if we do it will not be because we *must* fail.

Now *either* (a) The islanders have means of teaching us their classifications, by pointing out similarities and differences which we had not noticed, or in which we had not been interested, in which case *both* classifications are genuine, and no rivalry between them, of a kind that can help the nominalist, could ever arise;

or (b) Their classification is arbitrary in the sense in which my use of the word "alpha" was arbitrary, in which case it is not a genuine classification.

It may be that the islanders classify trees as "boat-building trees," "house-building trees," etc., and that they are more concerned with the height, thickness and maturity of the trees than they are with the distinctions of species that interest us.

In a particular case of *prima facie* conflict of classifications, we may not in fact be able to discover whether what appears to be a rival classification really *is* a classification. But we can be sure that *if* it is a classification *then* it is backed by objective similarities and differences, and that if it is *not* backed by objective similarities and differences then it is merely an arbitrary system of names. In no case will it appear that we must choose between rival systems of genuine classification of a set of objects in such a sense that one of them is to be recognised as *the* classification for all purposes.

There is no limit to the number of possible classifications of objects. (The nominalist is right about this.) [4]

There is no classification of any set of objects which is not objectively based on genuine similarities and differences. (The realist is right about this.)

The nominalist is so impressed by the infinite diversity of possible classifications that he is blinded to their objectivity.

The realist is so impressed by the objectivity of all genuine classifications that he underestimates their diversity.

Of course we may if we like say that there is one complete system of classification which marks all the similarities and all the differences. (This is the realist's summing up of what we can learn by giving critical attention to the realist and the nominalist in turn.)

Or we may say that there are only similarities and differences, from which we may choose according to our purposes and interests. (This is the nominalist's summing up.)

In talking of genuine or objective similarities and differences we must not forget that we are concerned with similarities and differences between *possible* cases as well as between actual cases, and indeed that we are concerned with the actual cases only because they are themselves a selection of the possible cases.

Because the nominalist and the realist are both right and both wrong, each is driven into the other's arms when he tries to be both consistent and faithful to our language, knowledge and experience. The nominalist talks of resemblances until he is pressed into a corner where he must acknowledge that resemblance is unintelligible except as resemblance *in a respect,* and to specify the respect in which objects resemble one another is to indicate a *quality* or *property.* The realist talks of properties and qualities until, when properties and qualities have been explained in terms of other properties and other qualities, he can at last do nothing but point to the *resemblances* between the objects that are said to be characterised by such and such a property or quality.

The question "Are resemblances ultimate or are properties ultimate?" is a perverse question if it is meant as one to which there must be a simple, *single* answer. They are both ultimate, or neither is ultimate. The craving for a single answer is the logically unsatisfiable craving for something that will be the ultimate terminus of explanation and will yet itself be explained.

NOTES

1. I have profited from several discussions with Dr. S.M. Walters on taxonomy and the problem of universals. On the more general topics treated in this paper I have had several helpful discussions with Mr. R.A. Becher. Miss G.E.M. Anscombe kindly lent me the proofs of her essay on Aristotle, which is to appear in *Three Philosophers* by Miss Anscombe and Mr. P.T. Geach.

2. Of recent writings on this topic I believe that only Professor Wisdom's *Metaphysics and Verification* (reprinted in *Philosophy and Psycho-analysis*) and Mr. D.F. Pears' *Universals* (reprinted in Flew, *Logic and Language,* Second Series) show a complete understanding of the nature and importance of Wittgenstein's contribution.

3. Professor Wisdom has pointed out to me that further discussion would be necessary to show that claims of the form "This is Jack" are not exceptions to this rule.

4. Here one may think of Wittgenstein's remark that "Every application of every word is arbitrary," which emphasises that we can always find *some* distinction between any pair of objects, however closely similar they may be. What might be called the principle of the diversity of discernibles guarantees that we can never be *forced* to apply the same word to two different things.

The use theory of meaning as expressed by Wittgenstein and interpreted by Bambrough has been accepted by many philosophers as sufficient for indicating that it is a meaningless question to search for essences and defining properties for things, events, or actions. To look for an essence is to be misguided. As Wittgenstein suggested, one must look for the use of a term and not predetermine the conditions for significance. Plato, in assuming a reference theory of meaning, would undoubtedly be regarded by Wittgenstein as one who determined the conditions for significance prior to considering how words are actually used in linguistic situations. Recall Wittgenstein's example of a game; there are no defining conditions which meet every use of the term *game*. Nonetheless, we know how to use the term significantly in ordinary language. The Wittgensteinian analysis of terms through their use has convinced many philosophers that Plato and Russell were indeed mistaken in their quest for universals.

The Theory of Recollection

Having discussed the Theory of the Forms and the ontological problems regarding that theory, it is now time to consider the epistemological questions relevant to that dualistic theory. One crucial problem for any philosopher who posits this type of metaphysical dualism is to account successfully for our knowledge of the forms. In other words, how is our human knowing capacity aware of the transcendental entities. As we shall see, Plato's epistemology ultimately will demand a corresponding dualism in the capacities for knowledge. This dualism in knowing capacities is necessary because Plato believes that our senses alone are unable to grasp the essential properties which comprise the content of the forms. The object of our sense knowledge—i.e., what we see with our eyes, hear with our ears, taste with our taste buds, and so forth—is what Plato refers to as opinion. This type of knowledge is limited to the perception of individuals found in the external world. Recall the analogy of the divided line and the myth of the cave discussed earlier in this chapter. Plato adamantly affirms that the senses never grasp the essences of things. The senses merely perceive the individual instances—i.e., the particular exemplifications—of the forms. Accordingly, in using just the senses, a human perceiver is aware of Peter, Paul, and Mary. However, through sense knowledge or opinion alone, the human perceiver is never directly aware of the form of human nature. In a similar vein, the human perceiver is aware of two equal lengths of a board but is never directly aware through sense knowledge of "equality" itself. The same holds for all of the sense perceptions of individuals in the external world. In the Platonic epistemology, therefore, the senses are strictly limited to an awareness of the individual instances of things and not of the essential properties which define the nature of the things perceived. We perceive Peter, Paul, and Mary with our external senses, but we never know the nature of the human essence by means of our external senses.

Insofar as the senses lack the ability to grasp the content of the forms, Plato concludes that there must be some other faculty of knowing by means of which a human knower can be directly aware of the forms themselves. Plato explicitly asserts that we do in fact have knowledge of the forms. But if we cannot grasp the forms through our senses, this type of knowledge must be attained by means of some other faculty. This depends upon Plato's distinction between opinion and knowledge. In the following passage from *The Republic*, Plato argues for a category difference between opinion (sense knowledge) and knowledge (intellectual knowledge). Each kind of knowledge requires its own faculty. The senses know the objects of opinion while the soul knows the objects of knowledge.

. . . And may we not say of the philosopher that he is a lover, not of a part of wisdom only, but of the whole?

True.

Then he who dislikes knowledge, especially in youth, when he has no power of judging what is good and what is not good, such an one we maintain not to be a philosopher or a lover of knowledge, just as he who refuses his food is not hungry, and may be said to have a bad appetite and not a good one?

And in that we are right, he said.

Whereas he who has a taste for every sort of knowledge and who is curious to learn and is never satisfied, may be justly termed a philosopher? Is not that true?

Glaucon said: If curiosity makes a philosopher, you will find many a strange being claiming the name. For all the lovers of sights have a delight in learning, and will therefore have to be included. Musical amateurs, too, are a folk wonderfully out of place among philosophers, as they are the last persons in the world who would come to anything like a philosophical discussion, if they could help, while they run about at the Dionysiac festivals as if their ears were under an engagement to hear every chorus; whether the performance is in town or country—that makes no difference—they are there. Now are we to maintain that all these and any who have similar tastes, as well as the professors of minor arts, are philosophers?

Certainly not, I replied, they are only an imitation.

He said: But who are the true philosophers?

Those, I said, who are lovers of the sight of truth.

That is also good, he said; but I should like to know what you mean?

To another, I replied, I might have a difficulty in explaining; but I am sure that you will admit a proposition which I am about to state.

What is that?

That beauty is the reverse of ugliness; they are two and not one?

Certainly.

And as they are two, each of them is one?

True again.

And the same holds of every class—just and unjust, good and evil: taken singly, each of them is one; but in all the various combinations of them with things and persons and with one another, they are seen in various lights and appear many?

Reprinted from Plato, *The Republic* 475–80.

That is true.

And this is the distinction which I draw between the sight-loving, art-loving, practical class, and those of whom I am speaking, and who are alone worthy of the name of philosophers.

How do you distinguish them? he said.

The lovers of sounds and sights, I replied, are, as I conceive, fond of fine tones and colors and forms, and all the artificial products that are made out of them, but their mind is incapable of seeing or loving absolute beauty.

That is true, he replied.

Few are they who are able to attain the sight of absolute beauty.

Very true.

And he who, having a sense of beautiful things, has no sense of absolute beauty, or who, if another lead him to a knowledge of that beauty is unable to follow—of such an one I ask, Is he awake or in a dream only? Reflect: is not the dreamer, either awake or asleep, one who puts the resemblance in the place of the real object?

I should certainly say that such an one was dreaming.

But take the case of the other, who recognizes the existence of absolute beauty and is able to distinguish the idea from the objects which participate in the idea, neither putting the objects in the place of the idea nor the idea in the place of the objects—is he a dreamer, or is he awake?

He is the reverse of a dreamer, he replied.

And may we not say that the mind of the one has knowledge, and that the mind of the other has opinion only?

Certainly.

But suppose that the latter quarrels with us and disputes our statement, can we administer any soothing cordial or advice to him, without revealing to him that there is sad disorder in his wits?

That is what is wanted, he replied.

Come, then, and let us think of something to tell him. Suppose we begin by assuring him that he is welcome to any knowledge he may have, and that we rejoice to see him in possession of such a blessing. But we should like to ask him a question: Does he who has knowledge know something or nothing? (You must answer for him.)

I answer that he knows something.

Something that is or is not?

Something that is; for how can that which is not ever be known?

And are we assured, after looking at the matter in every point of view, that perfect existence is or may be perfectly known, but that the absolutely non-existent is utterly unknown and unknowable?

Nothing can be more certain.

Good. But if there be anything which is of such a nature as to be and not be, that will have a place intermediate between pure being and the absolute negation of being?

Yes, between them.

And, as knowledge corresponded to being and ignorance to not-being, for that intermediate between being and not-being there has to be discovered a corresponding intermediate between ignorance and knowledge, if there be such?

Certainly.

Do we admit the existence of opinion?

Undoubtedly.

As being the same with knowledge, or another faculty?

Another faculty.

Then opinion and knowledge have to do with different kinds of matter corresponding to this difference of faculties?

Yes.

And knowledge is relative to existence and knows existence: but I will first make a division.

What division?

I will begin by placing faculties in a class by themselves: they are powers in us and in all things by which we do as we do. Sight and hearing, for example, I should call faculties. Have I clearly explained the class which I mean?

Yes, I quite understand.

Then let me tell you my view about them. I do not see them, and therefore the distinctions of figure, color, and the like, which enable me to discern the differences of some things, do not apply to them. In speaking of a faculty I think only of the end and working; and that which has the same end and the same operation I call the same faculty, but that which has another end and another operation I call different. Would that be your way of speaking?

Yes.

To return. Would you place knowledge among faculties, or in some other class?

Certainly knowledge is a faculty, and the most powerful of all faculties.

And is opinion also a faculty?

Certainly, he said; for opinion is that with which we are able to form an opinion.

And yet you were surely admitting a little while ago that knowledge is not the same as opinion?

Why, yes, said he: for how can any reasonable being ever identify that which is fallible with that which errs?

That is very good, I said, and clearly shows that there is a distinction between them which is admitted by us?

Yes.

Then knowledge and opinion, having distinct powers, have also distinct ends or subject-matters?

That is certain.

Being is the end or subject-matter of knowledge, and knowledge is the knowledge of being?

Yes.

And opinion is to have an opinion?

Yes.

And is the subject-matter of opinion the same as the subject-matter of knowledge?

Nay, he replied, that is already disproven; if difference in faculty implies difference in the end or subject-matter, and opinion and knowledge are equally faculties and also distinct faculties, the subject-matter of knowledge cannot be the same as the subject-matter of opinion.

Then if being is the subject-matter of knowledge, something else must be the subject-matter of opinion?

Yes, something else.

Well then, is not-being the subject-matter of opinion? or, rather, how can there be an opinion at all about not-being? Reflect: when a man has an opinion, has he not an opinion about something? Can he have an opinion which is an opinion about nothing?

Impossible.

He who has an opinion has an opinion about some one thing?

Yes.

And not-being is not one thing but, properly speaking, nothing?

True.

Of not-being, ignorance was assumed to be the necessary correlative; of being, knowledge?

True, he said.

Then opinion is not concerned either with being or with not-being?

Not with either.

And can therefore neither be ignorance nor knowledge?

That seems to be true.

Then is opinion to be sought without and beyond either of them in a greater clearness than knowledge, or in a greater darkness than ignorance?

Neither.

Then I suppose that opinion appears to you darker than knowledge, but lighter than ignorance?

Both; and in no small degree.

And also to be within and between them?

Yes.

Then you would infer that opinion is intermediate?

No question.

But were we not saying before, that if anything appeared to be a sort which is and is not at the same time, that sort of thing would appear also to lie in the interval between pure being and absolute not-being; and that the corresponding faculty is neither knowledge nor ignorance, but will also be discovered in the interval between them?

True.

And in that interval there has now been discovered a thing which we call opinion?

There has.

Then what remains to be discovered is the object which partakes equally of the nature of being and not-being, and cannot rightly be termed the pure form of either; this unknown term, when discovered, we may justly hail as the subject of opinion, and assign to each their due—to the extreme the faculty of the extreme, and to the mean the faculty of the mean.

True.

This being premised, I would ask the gentleman who is of opinion that there is no absolute or unchangeable idea of beauty—in whose opinion the beautiful is diverse—he, I say, your lover of beautiful sights, who cannot bear to be told that the just is one, or the beautiful is one, or that anything is one—to him I would appeal, saying, Best of men, of all these beautiful things is there one which will not also appear ugly; or of the just, which will not appear to be unjust; or of the holy, which will not also be unholy?

No, he replied; they must in some way appear both beautiful and ugly; and the same is true of the rest.

And may not the many which are doubles be also halves?—doubles, that is, of one thing, and halves of another?

Yes.

And things great and small, heavy and light, may equally be termed either in different points of view?

Yes; either name will always attach to all of them.

And can anything which is called by a particular name be said to be this rather than not to be this?

He replied: They are like the punning riddles which are asked at feasts, and the children's puzzle about the eunuch aiming at the bat, with what he hit him, as they say in the puzzle, and what the bat was sitting upon; for these things are a riddle also, and have a double sense: nor can you fix them in your mind, either as being or not-being, or both or neither.

Then what do you do with them? I said. Can they have a better place than between being and not-being? For they are clearly not in greater darkness or negation than not-being, or more full of light and existence than being.

That is quite true, he said.

Thus then we seem to have discovered that the diverse principles of beauty and the like, which are held by divers men, are tossing about in some region which is intermediate between pure existence and pure non-existence?

That has now been discovered by us.

Yes; and we have before agreed that anything of this kind which we might find was to be described as matter of opinion, and not as matter of knowledge; being the intermediate flux which is caught and detained by the intermediate faculty.

That was admitted.

Then those who see the many beautiful, and who yet neither see, nor can be taught to see, absolute beauty; who see the many just, and not absolute justice, and the like,—such persons may be said to have opinion but not knowledge?

That is certain.

But those who see the absolute and eternal and immutable may be said to know, and not to have opinion only?

Neither can that be denied.

The one love and embrace the subjects of knowledge, the other those of opinion? The latter are the same, as I dare say you will remember, who listened to sweet sounds and gazed upon fair colors, but would not tolerate the existence of absolute beauty?

Yes, I remember.

Shall we then be guilty of any impropriety in calling them lovers of opinion rather than lovers of wisdom, and will they be very angry with us for thus describing them?

I shall tell them that they ought not to be angry at a description of themselves which is true.

But those who embrace the absolute are to be called lovers of wisdom and not lovers of opinion?

Assuredly.

Plato's Notion of the Soul

Plato has shown the epistemological necessity of establishing another faculty by means of which the forms are known. Plato refers to this faculty as the *soul* or *intellect*. The faculty of the soul is able to come into contact with the forms and thus is the means by which a human knower is able to have knowledge of the essential properties of things. Accordingly, by arguing for a distinction of knowing powers, Plato is able to undercut the sophists' claim that all knowledge is exhausted by sense experience alone. When the soul is in contact with the forms, this contact produces true knowledge and not just opinion which is attained through the senses. Therefore Plato provides an analysis for knowledge which leads to what the Greeks referred to as "science." Science is knowledge of a thing through its causes. In the Platonic ontology, the cause of any individual—its reason for being—is the form of the thing itself. Accordingly, knowledge of the forms will be scientific knowledge.

The Platonic notion of the soul requires a bit more analysis. This theory enforces a radical dualism into Plato's theory of human nature. Plato considered a human being as composed of two primary principles—body and soul. In other words, there are two "things" or "entities" which comprise each human person. Plato went even further by asserting that the soul was a "prisoner" trapped in a body. In the *Phaedo*, Plato suggests that the purpose of philosophy is to free the soul from its entrapment in the body. This freedom is to be attained insofar as the soul attempts to realize its awareness of the forms, and this directly connects Plato with unifying knowledge and virtue. A human person attains his or her highest perfection insofar as the soul is in direct contact with the forms. When a human knower is directly aware of the forms, the human person has attained the zenith of moral perfection. Plato's ontology of the world of the forms coupled with his epistemology explains his equation of true virtue with knowledge. The knowledge which defines virtue is not the knowledge of the senses, however. Such sense knowledge is merely opinion. Rather, it is the knowledge of the forms which constitutes true knowledge.

For Plato, the soul is an entity which possesses certain characteristics. In the *Phaedo*, Plato aligns the soul with the forms. It is a simple entity containing no parts. Also, it is an immaterial entity, which means that it is independent of matter and thus a spirit. But probably the most important characteristic of the soul insofar as Plato is concerned is that it is an active principle. The soul is what activates the body. Etymologically, this facet of the soul is brought out in the Latin term for soul, *anima*. From anima is derived the English term, *animated*. This denotes the concept of movement. The soul, in Plato's ontology of the human person, is a principle of motion. It is intrinsically active. Furthermore it is analogous to the forms in that it is spiritual, simple, and immortal. For a further consideration of Plato's treatment of the soul, the text of the *Phaedo* should be read in its entirety. In fact, the *Phaedo* has often been considered as the first classical attempt to establish the immortality of the soul. The philosophical insights suggested by Plato were very influential in the early Christian Church when the theologians first attempted to justify rationally some of the theological tenets of the Christian faith.

We still need to discuss the actual acquaintance of the soul with the forms. Plato is aware that the soul is not in direct contact now with the world of the forms. Yet each person has some knowledge of the forms. Plato is confronted with a serious epistemological problem. We have an awareness of the essences, but our senses are conceptually unable to account for that kind of awareness. Plato's answer to the problem is the classic position that knowledge is recollection or *anamnesis*. This claim asserts that an awareness of a universal is a recollecting of what the soul had experienced during a previous existence. Plato elaborates this complex theory in at least two places. There is the celebrated account of the servant boy in the *Meno* and the following passage from the *Phaedo*.

. . . Cebes added: Your favorite doctrine, Socrates, that knowledge is simply recollection, if true, also necessarily implies a previous time in which we learned that which we now recollect. But this would be impossible unless our soul was in some place before existing in the human form; here then is another argument of the soul's immortality.

But tell me, Cebes, said Simmias interposing, what proofs are given of this doctrine of recollection? I am not very sure at this moment that I remember them.

One excellent proof, said Cebes, is afforded by questions. If you put a question to a person in a right way, he will give a true answer of himself, but how could he do this unless there were knowledge and right reason already in him? And this is most clearly shown when he is taken to a diagram or to anything of that sort.

But if, said Socrates, you are still incredulous, Simmias, I would ask you whether you may not agree with me when you look at the matter in another way; I mean, if you are still incredulous as to whether knowledge is recollection?

Incredulous, I am not, said Simmias; but I want to have this doctrine of recollection brought to my own recollection, and, from what Cebes has said, I am beginning to recollect and be convinced: but I should still like to hear what more you have to say.

This is what I should say, he replied: We should agree, if I am not mistaken, that what a man recollects he must have known at some previous time.

Reprinted from Plato, *Phaedo* 73–77.

Very true.

And what is the nature of this recollection? And, in asking this, I mean to ask, whether when a person has already seen or heard or in any way perceived anything, and he knows not only that, but something else of which he has not the same but another knowledge, we may not fairly say that he recollects that which comes into his mind. Are we agreed about that?

What do you mean?

I mean what I may illustrate by the following instance: The knowledge of a lyre is not the same as the knowledge of a man?

True.

And yet what is the feeling of lovers when they recognize a lyre, or a garment, or anything else which the beloved has been in the habit of using? Do not they, from knowing the lyre, form in the mind's eye an image of the youth to whom the lyre belongs? And this is recollection: and in the same way any one who sees Simmias may remember Cebes; and there are endless other things of the same nature.

Yes, indeed, there are—endless, replied Simmias.

And this sort of thing, he said, is recollection, and is most commonly a process of recovering that which has been forgotten through time and inattention.

Very true, he said.

Well; and may you not also from seeing the picture of a horse or a lyre remember a man? and from the picture of Simmias, you may be led to remember Cebes?

True.

Or you may also be led to the recollection of Simmias himself?

True, he said.

And in all these cases, the recollection may be derived from things either like or unlike?

That is true.

And when the recollection is derived from like things, then there is sure to be another question, which is, Whether the likeness of that which is recollected is in any way defective or not?

Very true, he said.

And shall we proceed a step further, and affirm that there is such a thing as equality, not of wood with wood, or of stone with stone, but that, over and above this, there is equality in the abstract? Shall we affirm this?

Affirm, yes, and swear to it, replied Simmias, with all the confidence in life.

And do we know the nature of this abstract essence?

To be sure, he said.

And whence did we obtain this knowledge? Did we not see equalities of material things, such as pieces of wood and stones, and gather from them the idea of an equality which is different from them?—you will admit that? Or look at the matter again in this way: Do not the same pieces of wood or stone appear at one time equal, and at another time unequal?

That is certain.

But are real equals ever unequal? or is the idea of equality ever inequality?

That surely was never yet known, Socrates.

Then these (so-called) equals are not the same with the idea of equality?

I should say, clearly not, Socrates.

And yet from these equals, although differing from the idea of equality, you conceived and attained that idea?

Very true, he said.

Which might be like, or might be unlike them?

Yes.

But that makes no difference: whenever from seeing one thing you conceived another, whether like or unlike, there must surely have been an act of recollection?

Very true.

But what would you say of equal portions of wood and stone, or other material equals? and what is the impression produced by them? Are they equals in the same sense as absolute equality? or do they fall short of this in a measure?

Yes, he said, in a very great measure too.

And must we not allow, that when I or any one look at any object, and perceive that the object aims at being some other thing, but falls short of, and cannot attain to it,—he who makes this observation must have had a previous knowledge of that to which, as he says, the other, although similar, was inferior?

Certainly.

And has not this been our own case in the matter of equals and of absolute equality?

Precisely.

Then we must have known absolute equality previously to the time when we first saw the material equals, and reflected that all these apparent equals aim at this absolute equality, but fall short of it?

That is true.

And we recognize also that this absolute equality has only been known, and can only be known, through the medium of sight or touch, or of some other sense. And this I would affirm of all such conceptions.

Yes, Socrates, as far as the argument is concerned, one of them is the same as the other.

And from the senses then is derived the knowledge that all sensible things aim at an idea of equality of which they fall short—is not that true?

Yes.

Then before we began to see or hear or perceive in any way, we must have had a knowledge of absolute equality, or we could not have referred to that the equals which are derived from the senses?—for to that they all aspire, and of that they fall short?

That, Socrates, is certainly to be inferred from the previous statements.

And did we not see and hear and acquire our other senses as soon as we were born?

Certainly.

Then we must have acquired the knowledge of the ideal equal at some time previous to this?

Yes.

That is to say, before we were born, I suppose?

True.

And if we acquired this knowledge before we were born, and were born having it, then we also knew before we were born and at the instant of birth not only the equal or the greater or the less, but all other ideas; for we are not speaking only of equality absolute, but of beauty, good, justice, holiness, and all which we stamp with the name of essence in the dialectical process, when we ask and answer questions. Of all this we may certainly affirm that we acquired the knowledge before birth?

That is true.

But if, after having acquired, we have not forgotten that which we acquired, then we must always have been born with knowledge, and shall always continue to know as long as life lasts—for knowing is the acquiring and retaining knowledge and not forgetting. Is not forgetting, Simmias, just the losing of knowledge?

Quite true, Socrates.

But if the knowledge which we acquired before birth was lost by us at birth, and if afterwards by the use of the senses we recovered that which we previously knew, will not that which we call learning be a process of recovering our knowledge, and may not this be rightly termed recollection by us?

Very true.

For this is clear, that when we perceived something, either by the help of sight, or hearing, or some other sense, there was no difficulty in receiving from this a conception of some other thing like or unlike which had been forgotten and which was associated with this; and therefore, as I was saying, one of two alternatives follows: either we had this knowledge at birth, and continued to know through life; or, after birth, those who are said to learn only remember, and learning is recollection only.

Yes, that is quite true, Socrates.

And which alternative, Simmias, do you prefer? Had we the knowledge at our birth, or did we remember afterwards the things which we knew previously to our birth?

I cannot decide at the moment.

At any rate you can decide whether he who has knowledge ought or ought not to be able to give a reason for what he knows.

Certainly, he ought.

But do you think that every man is able to give a reason about these very matters of which we are speaking?

I wish that they could, Socrates, but I greatly fear that tomorrow at this time there will be no one able to give a reason worth having.

Then you are not of opinion, Simmias that all men know these things?

Certainly not.

Then they are in process of recollecting that which they learned before?

Certainly.

But when did our souls acquire this knowledge?—not since we were born as men?

Certainly not.

And therefore, previously?

Yes.

Then, Simmias, our souls must have existed before they were in the form of man—without bodies, and must have had intelligence?

Unless indeed you suppose, Socrates, that these notions were given us at the moment of birth; for this is the only time that remains.

Yes, my friend, but when did we lose them? for they are not in us when we are born—that is admitted. Did we lose them at the moment of receiving them, or at some other time?

No, Socrates, I perceive that I was unconsciously talking nonsense.

Then may we not say, Simmias, that if, as we are always repeating, there is an absolute beauty, and goodness, and essence in general, and to this, which is now discovered to be a previous condition of our being, we refer all our sensations, and with this compare them—assuming this to have a prior existence, then our souls must have had a prior existence, but if not, there would be no force in the argument. There can be no doubt that if these absolute ideas existed before we were born, then our souls must have existed before we were born, and if not the ideas, then not the souls.

Yes, Socrates; I am convinced that there is precisely the same necessity for the existence of the soul before birth, and of the essence of which you are speaking: and the argument arrives at a result which happily agrees with my own notion. For there is nothing which to my mind is so evident as that beauty, good, and other notions of which you were just now speaking, have a most real and absolute existence; and I am satisfied with the proof.

Well, but is Cebes equally satisfied? for I must convince him too.

I think, said Simmias, that Cebes is satisfied: although he is the most incredulous of mortals, yet I believe that he is convinced of the existence of the soul before birth. But that after death the soul will continue to exist is not yet proven even to my own satisfaction. I cannot get rid of the feeling of the many to which Cebes was referring—the feeling that when the man dies the soul may be scattered, and that this may be the end of her. For admitting that she may be generated and created in some other place, and may have existed before entering the human body, why after having entered in and gone out again may she not herself be destroyed and come to an end?

Very true, Simmias, said Cebes; that our soul existed before we were born was the first half of the argument, and this appears to have been proven; that the soul will exist after death as well as before birth is the other half of which the proof is still wanting, and has to be supplied.

The preceding passage explicitly claims that our awareness of universal knowledge is due to a process of recollecting what the soul has previously experienced. Philosophically, Plato is working within the confines of a specific epistemological principle. This principle, which was also adopted by Bertrand Russell in the twentieth century, asserts that "knowledge is acquaintance." In other words, in order to account for the acquisition of any type of knowledge, the knower must be in direct contact or be directly acquainted with the object of knowledge. In the case of opinion, there is no problem as far as Plato is concerned. The senses are directly aware of the individual things in the external world. But the senses, as we have seen, are not directly aware of the world of the forms. Accordingly, insofar as Plato adopts the epistemological maxim that "knowledge is acquaintance," there must be a time when the soul is directly acquainted with the forms. This forces Plato to admit that the soul must pre-exist the body. During this state of preexistence it is directly acquainted with the forms. In this life, the human person, in order to have an understanding of essences, must recollect what the soul had previously known during its state of separation from the body. The soul is entrapped in the body. The practice of philosophy is the way to attain this recollected knowledge. Since the knowledge is within, Socrates characterized the activity of the philosopher as the "midwife," which is to help bring forth what is already there; and to recollect the essences is to attain virtue. Hence virtue, or human excellence, consists of recollecting the knowledge of the forms.

In a very real sense, the theory of recollection concentrates on the essentially intelligent character of the human being. Plato strongly affirms that the human mind knows independently of sense experience. This ability to "go beyond the data of sensation" impresses Plato very much. Yet Plato does not forget the senses. He admits that sense knowledge provides the initial stimulus leading to the theory of recollection. Simply put, Plato's claim that human knowledge is not exhausted by sense experience alone denies credence to any theory of strict empiricism. Plato emphasizes that terms like justice, good, beauty, and the various definitions of mathematics are indeed used every day. Yet they do not refer to objects presented in sense experience alone. A paradigm case is the concept of a mathematical point used in plane geometry. A point has no dimension. Accordingly, it is incapable of being perceived. Can we perceive any object which lacks extension? Yet we do know what a mathematical point in plane geometry is. Plato accounts for this knowledge through the recollection of forms.

Plato's whole epistemology hints at a theme which has dominated western philosophy. Plato assumes that the order of thought and the order of being or reality are parallel. In other words, the human reason is not private. The consequence is that reason is a reliable guide to knowledge of reality. Conversely, reality is rationally ordered. Plato was the first philosopher to develop a complete ontological system of a rationally ordered cosmos. This theme has remained entrenched in much of western philosophy. In the late nineteenth century, Friedrich Nietzsche suggested that a theme of irrationality was preferable. This theme of irrationality and its consequence of an "absurd" universe reaches its fruition in the writings of the twentieth-century existentialists, most notably Jean-Paul Sartre and Albert Camus. This problem will be discussed in great detail in chapter 7 of this book.

The Role of Reason

The function of reason is very important in the Platonic system. In the *Phaedo*, Plato argues against *misology,* which is the distrust of the function of reason itself. Reason is used by Plato through the process of dialectic. As we have seen, this consists in positing a hypothesis, which might serve as the definition of a thing, action, or event. Each hypothesis is forced through a process of refinement. This is accomplished, as we have seen, by attempting to find a counter instance to the hypothesis. If no counter instance is found, the hypothesis might indeed serve as a true and adequate definition, and this definition will correspond to the real form. As we also have seen, Plato is convinced that there are true definitions in the world which can be discovered. These true definitions are neither stipulative nor merely verbal. A true definition will correspond to a form, and each form determines the essential properties of a given group of individual things. Misology, however, is diametrically opposed to this process. It is a profound distrust of reason and reason's ability to discover the truth. Ultimately, it is a refusal to engage in the process of Platonic dialectic. In the *Phaedo,* moreover, Plato additionally argues that misology will ultimately lead to *misanthropy,* which is the hatred of human beings. Plato sees both misology and misanthropy as causally related. Plato claims that the possession of *logos,* i.e., the exercise of reason, is what constitutes a person as a human being. Accordingly, a consequence of such a theory is that if a human is denied his or her reason, that person is no longer human and, thus, devoid of value as such. Accordingly, a lack of reason implies a lack of value. Plato suggests that if a person has no moral principles, this implies that he or she is untrustworthy. And to be untrustworthy is to lack any value as a human. Thus a lack of reason implies misanthropy in that the irrational is that which is to be hated. Conversely, Plato affirms that the rational element in human beings is the primary ontological source of moral commitment. If a human is not rational, then he or she is not to be trusted. The assertion of misology leads to misanthropy.

Obviously Plato has the sophists in mind here. Not only did they deny the value of reason—and *a fortiori* of philosophy itself—but they refused to engage in the process of dialectic. Refer back to the *Apology* and consider why Socrates was condemned to drink the hemlock. He practiced dialectic with the young Athenians and encouraged them to confront the basic existential issues of the day. The sophists refused to acknowledge the value of this activity of philosophy. Plato suggests that in condemning Socrates, the sophists also condemned reason itself. The sophists were guilty of misology, and *a fortiori* of misanthropy.

As we shall discover later in our study of philosophy, the brilliant eighteenth-century philosopher, Immanuel Kant, will once again argue the point that reason is the necessary condition on which to build a theory of human value. In the area of moral philosophy, as in so many other philosophical fields, Plato laid the groundwork for much fruitful philosophy. Again we see the truth to Alfred North Whitehead's assertion that all western philosophy is nothing but a footnote to Plato.

NOTES

1. Aristotle, *Metaphysics,* Book I, chapter 3.

2. G.H. Clark, *Thales to Dewey* (Boston: Houghton Mifflin, 1957), p. 3.

3. George F. McLean and Patrick J. Aspell, *Ancient Western Philosophy* (New York: Appleton Century Crofts, 1971), p. 60.

4. Eduard Zeller, *Outlines of the History of Greek Philosophy,* 13th ed., revised by Wilhelm Nestle and translated by L.R. Palmer (New York: Meridian Books, 1955), pp. 115-16.

5. Bertrand Russell, *The Problems of Philosophy* (Oxford: At the University Press, 1912), pp. 91-100. Reprinted by permission of the Oxford University Press.

three

Descartes and the Rationalist Tradition

Descartes and the Rise of the New Science

The second major figure to be encountered in our discussion of philosophy and philosophers will be Rene Descartes (1596-1650). Historians of philosophy have designated Descartes as the "Father of Modern Philosophy." This appellation came about for two reasons. First, Descartes is considered to have "purified" philosophy from its dependence upon theological studies. In the Middle Ages, philosophy was often looked upon as the "handmaiden of theology." At any length, Descartes considered his philosophy as divorcing itself from any dependence upon the tenets of the theological systems handed down to him from his medieval predecessors. How well he succeeded in providing a new twist to philosophical activity is a debated question. We shall discuss some aspect of this debate later in this analysis of Cartesian philosophy. Descartes was hoping to make philosophy stand on its own feet and not be subservient to any other discipline, especially theology. Partially because of this radical breaking away from a dependence on theology, Descartes is considered to be the father of distinctly modern philosophy. It must be kept in mind that this approach of Descartes was in marked contrast to that of many medieval philosophers who thought that the only role that philosophy had was as an aid in clarifying the issues in theology.

The second reason is the more important because it is rooted in the very issues around which Descartes philosophized. Structurally, this reason is intricately connected with the rise of the new science. The new science refers to the scientific revolution in the seventeenth century. These new physical theories were expounded in the writings of Galileo, Copernicus, and Kepler and culminated in the physical theories of Sir Isaac Newton. The forcefulness of the change in thought patterns fostered by the scientific revolution should not be underestimated. A scientific revolution of this magnitude could do nothing but tremendously influence the philosophy of the time.

Metaphysically, the new science dismantled the ontological scheme which the medievals—following the neoplatonic heritage of Augustine—had constructed. This ontological structure had God at the apex of a metaphysical system called a "chain of being" scheme. Everything fitted under the apex by a series of relationships of causal dependence. A hierarchy of beings was postulated. All things fitted together in a giant network of planned activity under the watchful eye of an omnipresent and all-knowing supreme being. The proponents of new science, in opposition to this vast network of teleological (purposeful) dependency, resurrected the materialist principles of the Greek and Roman philosophers, especially Democritus and Lucretius. Basically, in opting for materialism, the new science denied the viability of any "chain of being" scheme. Galileo, for example, postulated that the world was made up of atoms and atoms alone. Each atom had certain properties like extension, weight, shape, motion/rest, size, and density. The atoms had no teleological or purposeful direction whatsoever. There was no divine plan to account for the motions of the atoms. Rather than being causally ordered on a cosmic level, the atoms were arranged because of chance occurrences. The atoms moving in the void and clustering in different arrangements accounted for the existence of physical objects. In thus adopting the principle that chance occurrences were the fundamental explanatory principles of the cosmos, the ontology of the new science was diametrically opposed to the causally ordered metaphysics of the "chain of being" philosophers. Accordingly, this adoption of materialism as the correct ontological view of bodies, together with its corresponding denial of a causally ordered ontological synthesis, ranks Descartes as the Father of Modern Philosophy in a much more radical sense than his mere separation of philosophy and theology into two distinct and unrelated areas of academic interest.

It is no understatement to claim that Descartes was immersed in the scientific revolution. To him, it was an exciting world view and one which was more philosophically satisfying than the systems of his medieval predecessors with their closed neoplatonic schemes. However Descartes was astute enough to realize that there still were serious philosophical problems caused by the rise of the new science, questions which could not be brushed aside but which had to be confronted with penetrating philosophical analysis. In one sense, we might regard Descartes as a philosopher who was committed to the notion that philosophical inquiry was indeed compatible with the advances made in the new science. It was up to Descartes to provide a new direction to philosophy so that this compatibility might be made known and appreciated.

In general, in Descartes' attempt to make philosophy compatible with the new science, there were two sorts of problems with which he concerned himself. First, Descartes was an epistemologist. Because of the scientific revolution, a new set of philosophical problems arose concerning the scope, foundation, and ultimate veracity of knowledge. Descartes would spend, as we shall soon see, much time providing an analysis of these epistemological issues. Second, Descartes was clever enough to realize that the tenets of the new science radically undercut the world view of the medieval neoplatonists. With this undercutting, the need for a supreme being occupying the apex position in a teleologically ordered cosmos was obviously dismissed. Descartes, however, was convinced about the necessity of postulating a transcendental realm for the existence of God. In addition, he believed in the possibility of demonstrating the existence of a spiritual soul or mind. Insofar as materialism was fundamentally mechanistic, it was thought that this theory could do without any type of God or spiritual soul. Accordingly, together with his purely epistemological concerns, Descartes was interested in the metaphysical problems connected with demonstrating the existence of God and a spiritual human soul. That these two latter problems were part of the Cartesian program is obvious if one but reads the dedicatory letter at the beginning of the *Meditations*:

> I have always been of the opinion that the two questions respecting God and the soul were the chief of those that ought to be determined by help of philosophy rather than of theology.

Descartes can be looked upon as a philosopher who was determined to show that the claims of the new science were not a priori or, by definition, incompatible with the metaphysical demonstrations of the existence of God and of the spiritual soul. In fact, we can regard Descartes' philosophy as a demonstration of the existence of God and of the human soul starting from the claims of the new science. Thus, while granting the propositions of the new science, Descartes argued that these propositions need both God and human souls in order to be a complete metaphysical system.

It is true that there has been much scholarly debate over the merits of Descartes' assertion that his real interest lay in the ontological issues of God and souls. The debate, simply stated, concerns whether or not Descartes was an epistemologist and a materialist who cared little or nothing about the metaphysical claims about God and the spiritual soul. Copernicus and Galileo had suffered verbal abuse and condemnation from the ecclesiastical authorities following the dissemination of their ideas. Some historians of philosophy maintain that Descartes was well aware of what happened to scientists like Copernicus and Galileo and, moreover, he dreaded any such condemnation. Accordingly, as this theory goes, he couched his new philosophical approach to epistemology and materialism with a metaphysical image—especially one of philosophical theology—in order that his *Meditations* might successfully pass the criterion of the ecclesiastical censors. In other words, Descartes makes reference to the demonstrations of the existence of God and of the nature of the human soul, not because he was convinced of the merit of these ontological discussions but rather in order not to have his works condemned. However this theory is debatable. Therefore each student must analyze the structure of the *Meditations* as we read and discuss them in this chapter. It will be seen that the notions of God and a spiritual soul act as unifying factors throughout the entire six *Meditations* of Descartes. These structurally important steps shall be indicated as we proceed. At any length, Descartes shall be considered as a philosopher interested in both metaphysical and epistemological problems. In one very real sense, this interest will mirror the same worries which bothered Plato. These similarities should become apparent as we proceed in our analysis of Descartes' philosophy as espoused in the *Meditations*.

First, we shall consider the epistemological problems which Descartes confronted. These are important problems and Descartes' contribution has been tremendous when viewed historically. The questions which Descartes raised concerning the status of knowledge have remained as fundamental philosophical problems.

Descartes accepted the ontological scheme of the new science. On the scientific level this acceptance entailed adopting mechanism. The basic particle of the ontological scheme for bodies was material. This basic particle had certain properties or characteristics. These properties—extension, size, shape, motion/rest, and weight—were to become known in philosophical parlance as the "primary qualities." Thinking about the relation of these qualities to the structure of materialism should indicate that the philosophers were linguistically consistent in calling these properties "primary." Any particle is a rudimentary "chunk" of matter. In so far as it is matter, it must be extended. To be extended, it must occupy some portion of space. A piece of matter cannot be a nondimensive mathemathical point. Insofar as the basic particle is extended, it will have a certain shape, a particular size, some weight, and it will be either moving or at rest. Consequently, the primary qualities are those characteristics which primarily or fundamentally belong to matter.

We have observed that the ontological scheme provided by the new science took into account only the primary qualities of matter. The question we must ask is: Are primary qualities enough to provide an account of the world which we experience? If matter only possesses primary qualities, then part of the world which we experience is not accounted for by the ontology of the new science. Let's examine this point. In addition to size, shape, motion, and the other primary qualities, human perceivers—we ordinary perceivers who are aware of the world around us—perceive colors, sounds, tastes, objects of touch, and odors or fragrances. Yet, given the principles of materialism, the bits of matter themselves do not possess any of these qualities. In accord with this scheme of materialism, part of the content of our ideas appears to have no corresponding pattern in the external world.

The experience of these qualities is usually referred to as "secondary qualities." In line with our present discussion, the secondary qualities are the perceptual objects of sight, taste, hearing, touch, and smell. With its ontological commitment to primary qualities alone, the new science presented extreme sceptical difficulties for an epistemologist. The consequence of this ontological scheme is that the secondary qualities or characteristics depend or exist *only* in the presence of a human perceiver actually engaging in an act of perception. Thus the secondary qualities are in some way "mind dependent." This means that if there were no minds around—the situation which some philosophers have called the "truncated world"—then the secondary qualities could never have a complete existence. In other words, since matter possesses only the primary qualities, by definition it fundamentally lacks the characteristics associated with the secondary qualities. However it is certainly a fact of our everyday experience that we do have an explicit awareness of the secondary qualities. All we must do is look around. The immediate datum we see is color— reds, greens, blues, and so forth. Yet the materialist scheme has no ontological position for these secondary qualities. Note the following passage from Sextus Empiricus (circa 200 A.D.) delineating the ontological force of his materialistic atomism:

Democritus has said: It is only by convention that sweet is sweet and that bitter is bitter and that hot is hot and that cold is cold and that color is color. But in reality, there are atoms and the void. Therefore, the objects of sense, which it is customary to call real, in truth are not real. Only atoms and the void are real.[1]

The Roman atomist, Lucretius (98-54 B.C.), discusses the issue in the following passage:

Do not think that color is the only quality which the atoms lack. They also lack warmth and cold and piercing heat; they have no sound and lack any semblance of taste, and they give forth no odor from their substance.[2]

The materialism espoused by some proponents of the new science accepted this ontological consequence. Given this problem, Descartes was forced to explain how the perception of reality is possible and still be faithful to the propositions contained in the materialist ontology of the new science.

Because of the assertions made by the new science and its corresponding materialism, Descartes had to confront both metaphysical and epistemological problems. Metaphysically, Descartes had to analyze the claim that material particles comprise the only ontological category of reality. To the question, "On what there is?" the new science adamantly responds, "Matter with primary qualities." Consequently it is a materialist metaphysics. If materialism is true, then what becomes of the human "mind"? Is the mind nothing more than certain types of material particles? The following text indicates that Lucretius responded affirmatively to the material constitution of the mind: ". . . mind and spirit are both composed of matter . . . (and mind) . . . is of very fine texture and composed of exceptionally small particles which are very smooth and round." We shall see that Descartes would not accept this solution. Descartes will answer the question concerning the existence of a nonmaterial human mind in the affirmative. However we must follow his arguments leading up to this claim.

If matter contains only the primary qualities, the secondary qualities must be mind dependent. This ontological system, however, creates a tremendous epistemological problem. If a human perceiver is aware of the secondary qualities, and if these secondary qualities lack a causally *identical* counterpart in the external world, how can human perceivers ever be sure that they have *veridical* knowledge. By veridical knowledge philosophers mean that mental state in which what is known truly conforms to what is real. This is the basic problem involved in the theory of perception called "representative realism." As we shall see, Descartes adopts representative realism as a theory of perception.

Direct and Representative Realism

Before continuing with Descartes' analysis of perception, it will be well to first briefly sketch two main divisions in theories of perception as devised by philosophers. These two divisions are usually called (1) *direct realism,* or presentative realism, and (2) *representative realism,* or indirect realism.

Direct realism is the theory which holds that the mind perceives the world as the world really is. The mind is directly aware of the condition of the world. Whatever is perceived has a causally efficacious identical counterpart in the external world. The following illustration indicates schematically the nature of direct realism:

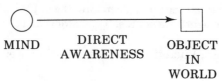

MIND   DIRECT   OBJECT
          AWARENESS   IN
                          WORLD

Most of us are direct realists. When we first encountered the world on our philosophical grandmother's knee, we suspected that in some way or other our knowledge reached out and directly grasped the world. We became convinced that the content of our mental awareness about the world was as the world really is. Very few of us are natural sceptics. The assumption in direct realism is that the mind is in direct contact with the world.

Direct realism, however, traditionally has been beset with various structural problems. The first and probably the most serious problem concerns how, with this theory, one is to account for perceptual error. If we are directly aware of the world, doesn't it follow that the world is as we perceive it? Only a little reflection is required to see that sometimes the world is not as we perceive it. In order to appreciate the gravity of this difficulty, consider the following problem. Get a beaker of water; place a thin stick in the water so that part of the stick is submerged and part is sticking out of the water. Now since the stick is in the water, what does the stick look like—does it appear to be straight or bent? Think about this example for a moment. Although it *appears* to be bent, is the stick really bent when it is put in the water? We don't want to say that. Yet it does appear bent. What can the direct realist do to account for this apparent inconsistency between what constitutes the qualities of the objects in this world—in this case, the water, beaker, and stick—and the way these things appear to us? Certainly the objects appear to be different than they actually are. The case of the bent stick in water is not the only example of an inconsistency between what we perceive and what we take the world to be.

Consider the following examples. Stand at a railroad crossing and look down the tracks—what happens to the tracks in the distance? They appear to converge. However do the tracks *really* converge in the distance? Of course not, or certainly a train couldn't negotiate the tracks. Yet they *appear* to converge. Again, if direct realism is correct, then this *appearance* is certainly distinct from the *reality* of the tracks. For another case, let us look directly at a half dollar held directly in front of us. Then look at the same half dollar from a distance of ten feet and at a forty-five degree angle from where it was first observed. Does the half dollar still look circular? It will probably appear elliptical. Again, there is a difference between the reality of the half dollar, which certainly is circular, and the appearance to us, which from the forty-five degree angle seems to be elliptical. Another example may occur when driving down a highway on a hot, muggy August afternoon. Looking ahead, we will see what appears to be water—this is the phenomenon called a mirage. Is the water really there? Certainly not. Yet it is something which appears to us.

For an additional example of the difference between what is real and what appears to us, consider the following brief passage from Arthur O. Lovejoy's *The Revolt Against Dualism*. Lovejoy is one of the foremost American philosophers of the early twentieth century:

The doctrine of the finite velocity of light meant that the sense from which most of our information about the world beyond our epidermal surfaces is derived never discloses anything which (in Francis Bacon's phrase) "really exists" in that world, at the instant at which it indubitably exists in perception. It is with a certain phase in the history of a distant star that the astronomer, gazing through his telescope at a given moment, is supposed to become acquainted. But that phase, and perhaps the star itself, have, ages since, ceased to be. And the astronomer's present sense data—it has therefore seemed inevitable to say—whatever else they may be, are not identical with the realities they are believed to reveal.[3]

Given the preceding examples, the direct realist is forced to account for this discrepancy between what "appears" to us and what is "real" in the world. These examples should convince us that on occasion we do perceive the world in a nonveridical fashion. Accordingly, the problem of perceptual error is a fundamental difficulty confronting a philosopher who has adopted direct realism.

This consideration of perceptual error has forced many epistemologists into the position of representative realism. Representative realism claims that the mind is directly aware of an idea or image—i.e., some mental entity—which is somehow related by a causal relation to the objects in the external world. The mental entity exists as an intermediary between the mind and the world. The mind is never in direct contact with the things in the world; rather, it is always directly acquainted with a mental entity corresponding in some way or other to the things in the world. With most representative realists, the ideas or images are caused by the material objects by means of a causal relation. Schematically, we can express representative realism in the following way:

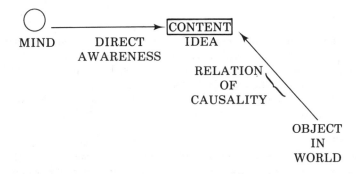

By thinking about this model for perception, we should soon realize that it has the structural possibility for explaining perceptual error. On the occasions of perceptual error, the representative realist would claim that the idea does not correspond to the thing in the world. The theory of representative realism is the basis for the theory of truth called the *Correspondence Theory of Truth*. We will consider this point later. Because the mind is directly aware of an idea and not of the thing—as the direct realist claims—the representative realist has a move open enabling him to account for perceptual error. Again, this is in terms of the representational content of the image not corresponding to the things of the world. A crude example illustrating the structure of representative realism is to consider what happens during a television broadcast. There is a camera picking up the objects in the studio. Yet what is represented on the screen and perceived by the viewer is an *image* of what is taking place in the studio. The image is, in some sense, a "copy" of what is happening in the studio. The mental entity in representative realism is just like the picture on the TV screen. It is a *copy* representing something else.

Because the problem of perceptual error has been solved in principle, however, it does not follow that representative realism is a viable theory of perception. Representative realism has an additional problem which should be apparent after considering the structure of this perceptual theory. We need not think too long before we realize that an important question now demands an answer. How is the perceiver to know that his or her idea or mental entity truly matches up with the world as it is. If the mind is always and only aware of the mental entities, the ideas, then how can a perceiver ever be certain that the ideas are veridical copies of the world itself? Consider again the schematic drawing of representative realism (see page 117).

There is always a "wedge" driven between the idea which is known by direct awareness and the object in the world. Accordingly, the crucial problem for representative realism is to provide a criterion justifying veridical knowledge. This is difficult, given that there is always a gap between the objects in the world and what is known. In representative realism, the idea by definition is a *tertium quid*—a third thing—existing between a knowing mind and the objects in the world. From what we have said, students who can intuit the difficulties encountered by representative realism are well on their way toward understanding the problems which Descartes attempted to overcome in the *Meditations*. Concerning the ontological scheme of the new science, it should be apparent that representative realism would be the theory of perception that the materialists would be forced to accept. Note the following passage from Galileo's treatise entitled *The Assayer:*

> I think that tastes, odors, colors, and so on are no more than mere names so far as the object in which we place them is concerned, and that they reside only in the consciousness. Hence, if the living creature were removed, all these qualities would be wiped away and annihilated. But since we have imposed upon them special names, distinct from those of the other and real qualities mentioned previously (i.e., the primary qualities), we wish to believe that they really exist as actually different from those. . . .
>
> To excite in us tastes, odors and sounds I believe that nothing is required in external bodies except shapes, numbers and slow or rapid movements. I think that if ears, tongues and noses were removed, shapes and numbers and motions would remain, but not odors or tastes or sounds. The latter, I believe, are nothing more than names when separated from living beings. . . .

In accepting the new science, Descartes also accepts representative realism. However his acceptance is not dogmatic. He is terribly vexed by the crucial weakness of this theory. This weakness, as we mentioned earlier, consists of connecting the idea perceived with the object in the world. Stated differently, must a representative realist be forever locked up in his/her own mind? Descartes' principal worry is to account for the fact that our ideas do correspond to the external world. Thus Descartes' epistemological problem is over establishing the possibility of veridical knowledge given representative realism. To do this, Descartes utilizes a unique method in philosophy, one which will help determine his claim as the Father of Modern Philosophy.

As we shall soon see, Descartes uses what has been called *methodological doubt* in order to resolve his philosophical difficulties. This method is exemplified in *Meditations I* and *II*. Descartes uses this method in order to get the reader to confront the problem concerning representative realism. Descartes' question is, "How do I know when a veridical perception is had?"

The Cartesian Method

Before going into the text of the *Meditations*, it will be best to consider briefly Descartes' use of the concept, *method*. Descartes was an accomplished mathematician. In fact, he discovered analytic geometry. Furthermore, Descartes was very impressed with the remarkable advances made in the natural sciences by the new scientists utilizing mathematics as the key to their new knowledge. With this extremely fruitful application of the mathematical method by the new scientists, Descartes wondered why the same success could not be attained in philosophy if the mathematical method were used to solve some difficult philosphical problems. Accordingly, Descartes sought to utilize the method of mathematics for solving philosophical problems.

In accepting the mathematical method as a useful tool for philosophers to use in searching for true philosophical propositions, Descartes settled upon a new criterion for truth in philosophy. This criterion for truth stated that only a clear and distinct idea will be true. The following passage indicates this criterion together with Descartes' method of procedure in doing philosophy.

> And as a multitude of laws often only hampers justice, so that a state is best governed when, with few laws, these are rigidly administered; in like manner, instead of the great number of precepts of which Logic is composed, I believed that the four following would prove perfectly sufficient for me, provided I took the firm and unwavering resolution never in a single instance to fail in observing them.
>
> The *first* was never to accept anything for true which I did not clearly know to be such; that is to say, carefully to avoid precipitancy and prejudice, and to comprise nothing more in my judgement than what was presented to my mind so clearly and distinctly as to exclude all ground of doubt.
>
> The *second*, to divide each of the difficulties under examination into as many parts as possible, and as might be necessary for its adequate solution.
>
> The *third*, to conduct my thoughts in such order that, by commencing with objects the simplest and easiest to know, I might ascend by little and little, and, as it were, step by step, to the knowledge of the more complex; assigning in thought a certain order even to those objects which in their own nature do not stand in a relation of antecedence and sequence.
>
> And the *last*, in every case to make enumerations so complete, and review so general, that I might be assured that nothing was omitted.
>
> The long chains of simple and easy reasonings by means of which geometers are accustomed to reach the conclusions of their most difficult demonstrations, had led me to imagine that all things, to the knowledge of which man is competent, are mutually connected in the same way, and that there is nothing so far removed from us as to be beyond our reach, or so hidden that we cannot discover it, provided only we abstain from accepting the false for the true, and always preserve in our thoughts the order necessary for the deduction of one truth from another.[4]

The criterion and method are modeled after mathematics. For example, in Euclidean geometry, that a triangle has three sides is self-evident to an observer the moment one considers what a triangle is. What is self-evident is a clear and distinct idea. Let us consider a moment the way we proceeded in learning plane geometry. First, we established a set of postulates. Were these postulates proven to us? No, we accepted them because they were intuitively obvious. Descartes wants to utilize this same procedure in his philosophical analyses. He is searching for a set of clear and distinct philosophical ideas from which he can deduce an entire philosophical system. In plane geometry once our postulates were intuited, we made use of them in order to demonstrate new theorems. A theorem was judged to be correct if it was deduced from the postulates and if no extraneous statements were used in the proof. Descartes utilizes this same procedure. He is searching for a clear and distinct idea which is self-evident and from which, by means of deduction, he can deduce every other true philosophical proposition. Accordingly, by this methodological device, Descartes will construct an entire ontological system deduced from only clear and distinct ideas. If such a system could be devised, so Descartes thought, then this philosophical synthesis would be one based upon indubitable principles which could not be dismissed. These principles would be clear and distinct and thus beyond doubt. How do we know them? In his *Rules for the Direction of the Mind,* Descartes speaks of intuition in the following manner:

> By *intuition* I understand not the fluctuating testimony of the senses, nor the misleading judgment that proceeds from the blundering constructions of imagination, but the conception which an unclouded and attentive mind gives us so readily and distinctly that we are wholly freed from doubt about that which we understand.

In addition, by using the mathematical method, Descartes would build a philosophical system which would be in harmony with the new science. As can be seen, Descartes was immensely influenced by the mathematical method. This indicated to him the prospect of deducing a rationally consistent system from a small set of indubitable first principles.

We must not mistake Descartes' mathematical method—which is essentially a deductive process—with his method of doubt. Admittedly, in the Cartesian writings there is a blur concerning method. The method of doubt, sometimes referred to as methodological doubt, is what Descartes refers to in *Meditation I.* Descartes uses the method of doubt in order to discover the indubitable first principles. The methodological doubt consists in the actual process of withholding rational assent to any proposition until it is observed to be a self-evident, clear, and distinct proposition. In effect, as Descartes argues, very few propositions will pass the test—what we might call the necessary and sufficient conditions—of being self-evident because they are clearly and distinctly perceived. Keeping this in mind, the blur on the use of method in Cartesian philosophy might be resolved in the following manner: (1) Descartes follows the mathematical method; this is essentially a deductive methodology from self-evident principles which have been clearly and distinctly perceived. (2) In order to discover the clear and distinct propositions, Descartes must use the method of doubt. Thus the method of doubt is used in order to attain a grasp of the clear and distinct ideas; once the set of clear and distinct ideas is known, they in turn will serve as the postulates from which Descartes will, by means of a strictly deductive system, make known the rest of this philosophical system.

It is now time to consider directly the texts of Descartes. The following passages comprise the complete text of *Meditation I*. Descartes' use of methodological doubt should be immediately obvious, even on a first reading.

MEDITATION I: OF THE THINGS OF WHICH WE MAY DOUBT

René Descartes

Several years have now elapsed since I first became aware that I had accepted, even from my youth, many false opinions for true, and that consequently what I afterwards based on such principles was highly doubtful; and from that time I was convinced of the necessity of undertaking once in my life to rid myself of the opinions I had adopted, and of commencing anew the work of building from the foundation, if I desired to establish a firm and abiding superstructure in the sciences. But as this enterprise appeared to me to be one of great magnitude, I waited until I had attained an age so mature as to leave me no hope that at any stage of life more advanced I should be better able to execute my design. On this account, I have delayed so long that I should henceforth consider I was doing wrong were I still to consume in deliberation any of the time that now remains for action. To-day, then, since I have opportunely freed my mind from all cares, [and am happily disturbed by no passions], and since I am in the secure possession of leisure in a peaceable retirement, I will at length apply myself earnestly and freely to the general overthrow of all my former opinions. But, to this end, it will not be necessary for me to show that the whole of these are false—a point, perhaps, which I shall never reach; but as even now my reason convinces me that I ought not the less carefully to withhold belief from what is not entirely certain and indubitable, than from what is manifestly false, it will be sufficient to justify the rejection of the whole if I shall find in each some ground for doubt. Nor for this purpose will it be necessary even to deal with each belief individually, which would be truly an endless labour; but, as the removal from below of the foundation necessarily involves the downfall of the whole edifice, I will at once approach the criticism of the principles on which all my former beliefs rested.

All that I have, up to this moment, accepted as possessed of the highest truth and certainty, I received either from or through the senses. I observed, however, that these sometimes misled us; and it is the part of prudence not to place absolute confidence in that by which we have even once been deceived.

But it may be said, perhaps, that, although the senses occasionally mislead us respecting minute objects, and such as are so far removed from us

Reprinted from John Veitch, trans., *The Method, Meditations and Philosophy of Descartes* (Washington: M. Walter Dunne, 1901).

as to be beyond the reach of close observation, there are yet many other of their informations (presentations), of the truth of which it is manifestly impossible to doubt; as for example, that I am in this place, seated by the fire, clothed in a winter dressing-gown, that I hold in my hands this piece of paper, with other intimations of the same nature. But how could I deny that I possess these hands and this body, and withal escape being classed with persons in a state of insanity, whose brains are so disordered and clouded by dark bilious vapours as to cause them pertinaciously to assert that they are monarchs when they are in the greatest poverty; or clothed [in gold] and purple when destitute of any covering; or that their head is made of clay, their body of glass, or that they are gourds? I should certainly be not less insane than they, were I to regulate my procedure according to examples so extravagant.

Though this be true, I must nevertheless here consider that I am a man, and that, consequently, I am in the habit of sleeping, and representing to myself in dreams those same things, or even sometimes others less probable, which the insane think are presented to them in their waking moments. How often have I dreamt that I was in these familiar circumstances—that I was dressed, and occupied this place by the fire, when I was lying undressed in bed? At the present moment, however, I certainly look upon this paper with eyes wide awake; the head which I now move is not asleep; I extend this hand consciously and with express purpose, and I perceive it; the occurrences in sleep are not so distinct as all this. But I cannot forget that, at other times, I have been deceived in sleep by similar illusions; and, attentively considering those cases, I perceive so clearly that there exist no certain marks by which the state of waking can ever be distinguished from sleep, that I feel greatly astonished; and in amazement I almost persuade myself that I am now dreaming.

Let us suppose, then, that we are dreaming, and that all these particulars —namely, the opening of the eyes, the motion of the head, the forth-putting of the hands—are merely illusions; and even that we really possess neither an entire body nor hands such as we see. Nevertheless, it must be admitted at least that the objects which appear to us in sleep are, as it were, painted representations which could not have been formed unless in the likeness of realities; and, therefore, that those general objects, at all events—namely, eyes, a head, hands, and an entire body—are not simply imaginary, but really existent. For, in truth, painters themselves, even when they study to represent sirens and satyrs by forms the most fantastic and extraordinary, cannot bestow upon them natures absolutely new, but can only make a certain medley of the members of different animals; or if they chance to imagine something so novel that nothing at all similar has ever been seen before, and such as is, therefore, purely fictitious and absolutely false, it is at least certain that the colours of which this is composed are real.

And on the same principle, although these general objects, viz. [a body], eyes, a head, hands, and the like, be imaginary, we are nevertheless absolutely necessitated to admit the reality at least of some other objects still more simple and universal than these, of which, just as of certain real colours, all those images of things, whether true and real, or false and fantastic, that are found in our consciousness (*cogitatio*), are formed.

To this class of objects seem to belong corporeal nature in general and its extension; the figure of extended things, their quantity or magnitude, and their number, as also the place in, and the time during, which they exist, and other things of the same sort. We will not, therefore, perhaps reason illegitimately if we conclude from this that Physics, Astronomy, Medicine, and all the other sciences that have for their end the consideration of composite objects, are indeed of a doubtful character; but that Arithmetic, Geometry, and the other sciences of the same class, which regard merely the simplest and most general objects, and scarcely inquire whether or not these are really existent, contain somewhat that is certain and indubitable: for whether I am awake or dreaming, it remains true that two and three make five, and that a square has but four sides; nor does it seem possible that truths so apparent can ever fall under a suspicion of falsity [or incertitude].

Nevertheless, the belief that there is a God who is all-powerful, and who created me, such as I am, has, for a long time, obtained steady possession of my mind. How, then, do I know that he has not arranged that there should be neither earth, nor sky, nor any extended thing, nor figure, nor magnitude, nor place, providing at the same time, however, for [the rise in me of the perceptions of all these objects, and] the persuasion that these do not exist otherwise than as I perceive them? And further, as I sometimes think that others are in error respecting matters of which they believe themselves to possess a perfect knowledge, how do I know that I am not also deceived each time I add together two and three, or number the sides of a square, or form some judgment still more simple, if more simple indeed can be imagined? But perhaps Deity has not been willing that I should be thus deceived, for He is said to be supremely good. If, however, it were repugnant to the goodness of Deity to have created me subject to constant deception, it would seem likewise to be contrary to his goodness to allow me to be occasionally deceived; and yet it is clear that this is permitted. Some, indeed, might perhaps be found who would be disposed rather to deny the existence of a Being so powerful than to believe that there is nothing certain. But let us for the present refrain from opposing this opinion, and grant that all which is here said of a Deity is fabulous: nevertheless in whatever way it be supposed that I reached the state in which I exist, whether by fate, or chance, or by an endless series of antecedents and consequents, or by any other means, it is clear (since to be deceived and to err is a certain defect) that the probability of my being so imperfect as to be the constant victim of deception, will be increased exactly in proportion as the power possessed by the cause, to which they assign my origin, is lessened. To these reasonings I have assuredly nothing to reply, but am constrained at last to avow that there is nothing of all that I formerly believed to be true of which it is impossible to doubt, and that not through thoughtlessness or levity, but from cogent and maturely considered reasons; so that henceforward, if I desire to discover anything certain, I ought not the less carefully to refrain from assenting to those same opinions than to what might be shown to be manifestly false.

But it is not sufficient to have made these observations; care must be taken likewise to keep them in remembrance. For those old and customary opinions perpetually recur—long and familiar usage giving them the right of occupying my mind, even almost against my will, and subduing my belief; nor will I lose the habit of deferring to them and confiding in them so long as I shall consider them to be what in truth they are, viz., opinions to some extent doubtful, as I have already shown, but still highly probable, and such as it is much more reasonable to believe than deny. It is for this reason I am persuaded that I shall not be doing wrong, if, taking an opposite judgment of deliberate design, I become my own deceiver, by supposing, for a time, that all those opinions are entirely false and imaginary, until at length, having thus balanced my old by my new prejudices, my judgment shall no longer be turned aside by perverted usage from the path that may conduct to the perception of truth. For I am assured that, meanwhile, there will arise neither peril nor error from this course, and that I cannot for the present yield too much to distrust, since the end I now seek is not action but knowledge.

I will suppose, then, not that Deity, who is sovereignly good and the fountain of truth, but that some malignant demon, who is at once exceedingly potent and deceitful, has employed all his artifice to deceive me: I will suppose that the sky, the air, the earth, colours, figures, sounds, and all external things, are nothing better than the illusions of dreams, by means of which this being has laid snares for my credulity; I will consider myself as without hands, eyes, flesh, blood, or any of the senses, and as falsely believing that I am possessed of these; I will continue resolutely fixed in this belief, and if indeed by this means it be not in my power to arrive at the knowledge of truth, I shall at least do what is in my power, viz., [suspend my judgment], and guard with settled purpose against giving my assent to what is false, and being imposed upon by this deceiver, whatever be his power and artifice.

But this undertaking is arduous, and a certain indolence insensibly leads me back to my ordinary course of life; and just as the captive, who, perchance, was enjoying in his dreams an imaginary liberty, when he begins to suspect that it is but a vision, dreads awakening, and conspires with the agreeable illusions that the deception may be prolonged; so I, of my own accord, fall back into the train of my former beliefs, and fear to arouse myself from my slumber, lest the time of laborious wakefulness that would succeed this quiet rest, in place of bringing any light of day, should prove inadequate to dispel the darkness that will arise from the difficulties that have now been raised.

Descartes' Quest for Certainty

In order to properly appreciate the *Meditation I,* keep in mind that representative realism is occupying a principal spot in the back of Descartes' mind. With this criterion, Descartes wonders if the content of the ideas he possesses truly represent the things in the external world. Descartes' concerns about the representational function of his ideas can be placed in the following two categories:

(1) the ideas of perception, and (2) the ideas of dreaming. In the *Meditation* just read, Descartes is puzzled over the veridical character of the images which are had during both sensing and dreaming.

We shall consider the category of the ideas of perception first. Descartes tries, in the first part of the *Meditation,* to get the reader to realize that the content of some of our ideas from sense perception—i.e., the ideas perceived during the processes of seeing, hearing, feeling, tasting, and smelling—are in fact on occasion nonveridical perceptions. Of course, nonveridical here means that the content of the image does not truly represent the objects in the world. Following our earlier discussion, remember that occasions of nonveridical perception are many—the bent stick in water, the converging railroad tracks, and so forth. Remembering that he is searching for an *indubitable* first principle, Descartes realizes that, because we do in fact have nonveridical perceptions, the indubitable first principle cannot be found in sense knowledge. The crucial point of the problem of error is that it is used in order to cast doubt on the representative character of images caused during sense perception. In other words, Descartes is concerned about the connection between the idea which is supposedly representative and that which is represented—i.e., the object in the external world. We can refer to the problem of perceptual error as the *qualitative* problem. This means that perceptual error stresses the fact that the qualities represented in an idea may not truly correspond to the qualities as found in the object outside the mind. The qualitative problem is a restatement of the basic worry with representative realism. Descartes was aware of this problem, yet he was convinced that representative realism was the only position compatible with the tenets of the new science. Accordingly, he was searching for some way in which he could bring veracity to representative realism as the theory of perception compatible with the new science.

Following his worry about perceptual error, Descartes next considers what may be termed the dream problem. This is Descartes' famous example of his dreaming that he is sitting by the fireplace. His dream image, he claims, is as vivid and lucid as his direct perception of the same event when he is awake. Most of us have had a similar experience while dreaming. A sequence of dream images is so vivid and lifelike that later we wonder if it really didn't happen after all. It is occasions like this that Descartes is asking us to think about now. Descartes is in a quandary about how he may ever tell that he is not, in fact, dreaming. In pursuit of an indubitable principle, the dream problem is the final blow to the possibility that sense knowledge could serve as a basis for that principle. The question Descartes ponders can always be asked: "Do I, as a perceiver, ever know that I am really perceiving and not dreaming?"

Descartes focuses on a very serious epistemological problem. He wants us to realize that, if one adopts representative realism as a theory of perception, then there is no clear indication on the side of the representational image itself which would distinguish an image of one's waking life from an image of one's dreaming life. If we were to take a perceptual slice from our knowing faculties, there would be no unique property or characteristic which the perception image had and the dream image lacked. With no such unique property, Descartes seriously entertains the possibility that it is epistemologically impossible to discover an indubitable criterion by which to distinguish dreaming from perceiving. In essence, the dream problem can be called the *causative* problem. What this means is that Descartes is focusing on the fact that at times when a human knower is aware of images, these images lack a direct causal foundation in the external world of which the images are supposed to be mental copies. The causative problem is used to cast doubt on whether ideas do in fact represent anything at all in the external world. The same type of representational image comes from two sources: (a) the external senses, and (b) the imagination and dreaming. The dream problem undermines the claim that images are always caused by an external object in the real world. A consequence of the dream problem is that the whole world of images may indeed be a delusion. A human perceiver may be locked within his own mind, having a mind full of images which do not represent anything at all. Descartes ends his discussion of sense perception by postulating a state of total schizophrenia of perception.

An example of the causative problem regarding dreams might be as follows. I fall asleep one evening. During the night, I dream that I am drinking a can of Dutch beer while sunning myself on the beautiful sand beaches of Nassau. There is a causative problem here because there is no objective cause in the world which is here and now reacting with my sense organs and producing the images. I am not saying that there is no cause for my dream image. But the cause, whatever it might be, is not the sand and sea and Dutch beer about which I have images in my dream. The causative problem differs from the qualitative problem. In the latter case, there is an object here and now causing my image, but the qualities represented in the image are different from the qualities of the object. Remember the example of looking down the railroad tracks. In the dream case—the causative problem—there is no object which in any way corresponds to the image of which I am directly aware. Accordingly, this possibility of the lack of any causative factor in the world together with the actual possession of an image entails the final blow to the veridical functioning of, or ideas of, sense knowledge. Therefore, whatever might be Descartes' indubitable criterion, it will not be found in the realm of sense knowledge.

Note the following example to better understand what Descartes is driving at in this *Meditation*. Descartes seems to be utilizing something like a "movie projector" view of perception. An image is like a frame in a movie film. The frame passes through the light of the projector. In our analogy, the light is an act of "direct awareness." The question Descartes raises is: "Is there any mark or defining characteristic found on each frame which would distinguish a perceptual frame from a dream frame?" Relying on his own introspective experience, Descartes is forced to say "No!, there is no such defining characteristic." Therefore any given image could be either from perception or from dreaming. If the former case holds, it would either have qualitative correspondence or lack qualitative correspondence. Thus Descartes is bound up in this "movie projector" view of perception. His search for defining characteristics, which would sort dream images from perceptual images, has proven futile. He thus withdraws any claims of indubitability from the realm of sense knowledge.

As a quick summary, we have seen that in regard to sense knowledge Descartes discusses two problems: (a) the qualitative problem and (b) the causative problem. The qualitative problem can be said to be asking if the representational qualities—the content—of an idea are structurally similar to the real qualities of the things in the world of which the ideas are supposed to be representative copies. The causative problem can be stated as asking whether the object in the external world indeed caused the idea represented in the mind. Introspective facts of which we all are aware, like imagining, daydreaming, hallucinating, dreaming, and so forth, establish the causative problem. Descartes, who began with representative realism, ends with a doubt that representations of sense actually represent any object at all. Therefore the propositions of sense are, in principle, dubitable. Thus we must search further with Descartes in order to find an indubitable first principle. In order to better appreciate the forcefulness of Descartes' dream problem and its relation to metaphysics and epistemology, it will be helpful to consider the following account written by Jerome Shaffer in his book, *Reality, Knowledge and Value.*

HOW DO I KNOW I AM NOT NOW DREAMING?

Jerome Shaffer

Let us start our investigation into metaphysics and epistemology by raising a specific question: How do I know I am not now dreaming? This question was posed by Plato and, later, by the father of modern philosophy, Descartes, who published his *Meditations on First Philosophy* in 1641. How do I know I am not now dreaming? Well, everything certainly *seems* perfectly normal. The book that I am looking at now *seems* clear and sharp to me. The room I am in *seems* perfectly normal and real. There is nothing particularly strange or unusual going on right now. It certainly *seems* that I am wide awake. But still we must remember that people frequently have very realistic *dreams*—dreams in which everything *seems* to be quite normal. If dreams didn't seem so real to us, then things that happen in dreams would never frighten us. But as we know, we sometimes get quite frightened by a dream because it does seem to be so real. Perhaps I am at this very minute in bed having a most realistic dream, dreaming that I am sitting at my desk, reading a philosophy book. It is certainly possible that there might be a dream just like this. How do I know that *this* is not such a dream?

If I seriously raised the question, How do I know I am not now dreaming? —I might feel that there are things I could do to determine whether it is a dream or not. For example, I could try pinching myself, slapping myself in the face, getting up and stretching, or reciting "Abou Ben Adhem." Yet what would this show? For is it not quite possible that I should *dream* that I am pinching myself, slapping my face, getting up and stretching, or reciting "Abou Ben Adham"? One can imagine that kind of dream occurring. How do I know that this is not that kind of dream? Suppose I try to do a little experiment. I seem to remember writing my name in the front of this book, and I predict that it will still be there. So, if I look in the front of the book and find it there, this will confirm my seeming to remember that I did write it there, and perhaps that will show that I am now awake. But suppose I look and I see my name in the front of the book. What does this show? Surely I can dream that I put my name there, surely I can dream that I am now checking, and surely I can dream that I am now finding my name there. We have still not broken out of the dream world. Suppose I try to remember something difficult—the names of all the states, for example. Can I not also dream that I am remembering them? Suppose that I try doing a mathematical problem in my head. Can I not dream that I am trying to do a mathematical problem in my head? Can I not dream that I have solved it successfully? It does not seem that any test that I try to perform will prove anything, because I can never be sure whether I am actually performing the test or merely dreaming that I am performing it; and I can never be sure whether the outcome of the test is successful or whether I am only dreaming that the outcome of the test is successful. So, in general, it looks as though there is no way of showing that I am now awake and not dreaming.

The following thought may occur to you: I grant that I cannot be *sure,* cannot *prove* that I am now awake, but I can at least make it *probable* that I am awake. But this thought would miss the fundamental point of our problem. It is not that I cannot *prove* that I am awake; it is that there does not seem to be even *the slightest reason* for thinking that I am now awake. All of the apparent evidence that I have—the way things appear to be now—have no weight at all if I am only dreaming them. No matter how much like waking life all of this seems to me to be, the fact remains that I may well be dreaming that everything is going on normally. So the fact that everything seems to be going on normally gives not the slightest weight to the supposition that I am awake. For all I know, this may be a very realistic dream, and I cannot infer from the realistic appearances that it is *not* a realistic dream.

"Well," you might say, "what does it matter? If it is a very realistic dream, then that is just the same as being awake, so who cares whether it is a dream or waking life?" But it obviously does matter. If this is all a dream, then, for example, you are not awake and studying now, so that you are not getting your philosophy assignment done. You may find yourself waking up in the next five minutes to discover that you have overslept and missed your class. Here the importance of deciding whether it is a dream or not is based on the importance of having some reasonable expectations about what is going to happen next. Of course, it is true that even if this is a dream, it is a pleasant enough dream—let us hope even an interesting dream. But suppose that in the next few minutes things begin to get more unpleasant. Suppose your roommate rushes in with some bad news. Suppose you suddenly notice a person creeping toward you with a knife. Then it will be quite important whether it is a dream or not—whether you are really in danger or not. Of course, we can't go through our lives constantly asking ourselves, Is this a dream or not? But this does not mean that we should *never* raise the question. Here is one comparatively convenient time to raise this question, and we have seen that once it is raised, it does not seem very easy to answer.

The problem we have been discussing so far is a problem in epistemology. That is to say, it is a problem concerned with what can be known and how it is to be known, if it can be known. We can see connected with this epistemological problem a metaphysical problem, that is, a problem concerned with the nature of reality. The metaphysical problem would be this: How are the things that happen in dreams different in their basic nature from the things that happen in "real life"? We have already seen that the difference cannot lie in whether what happens is normal or ordinary or "realistic," since dreams may be exactly like real life in their content. In fact, that is what makes us believe during the dream that these things are really happening. So the difference between dreams and real life cannot be in the content of each. It must be something else. But what is the difference, then, between something that happens in a dream and something that happens in real life? Might the difference consist only in this: What we call "real life" is simply an elaborate, consistent, prolonged dream; and what we call "a dream" is a comparatively short sequence that does not fit in with the longer part? Here is another possibility. Perhaps each person in the world is having his own dream, but all the dreams are in phase, so that when you dream you are speaking with your roommate, he at the same time is dreaming that he is speaking with you. Here would be a case where there was a common world to some degree, although each of us existed only in his dream world.

There are a number of different possibilities here. All of these would be somewhat different metaphysical schemes. Each would give us a somewhat different account of the ultimate nature of things. We see how intertwined epistemology and metaphysics are when we notice that each of these metaphysical schemes is possible and that the epistemological question of whether we have any reason for believing that our world is one way rather than another is always pertinent.

Having dismissed the category of sense knowledge as a possible candidate for the indubitable first principle, Descartes next considers the realm of mathematical propositions. Remember that Descartes was a fine mathematician. He discovered *analytical geometry,* which proved to be a most fruitful tool for later proponents of the new science. Analytical geometry presupposes an exact one-to-one correspondence between the world of numbers and the world of geometry. Descartes' discovery laid out the conceptual correspondence between arithmetic and algebra to the realm of Euclidean space. This indicates, of course, that a scientist might use mathematical formulae to discuss the structure of the world. Note the assumption for analytical geometry. The realm of algebra and arithmetic corresponds to the realm of Euclidean space. The world, so Descartes supposed, is in Euclidean space. Thus the rules of mathematics will be useful in talking about the structure of the world which is found in space. With this firm background in mathematics, it is obvious that Descartes would recommend that mathematical propositions might indeed be the locus of the indubitable first principle.

A moment's reflection will show us what Descartes had in mind. Intuitively, no set of propositions appears more certain and devoid of doubt than the propositions of mathematics. For instance, a triangle always has three sides and three angles of a sum of 180 degrees. If we doubt this definition of a triangle, then we do not know what a triangle is. Further reflection will help grasp the insights Descartes suggests here. Remember how we treated certain theorems in plane geometry. Starting with the suggestion, "Consider any triangle," the implication was that the demonstrative force and content of the theorem will apply univocally to any triangle we might happen to consider. There is a certain universal applicability of the theorem. On these grounds of universal applicability, Descartes' suggestion about mathematical propositions being the place of an indubitable first principle has a strong plausibility.

Descartes, however, will first subject the realm of mathematical propositions to the force of the methodological doubt. In pushing this consideration to the limits of doubt, Descartes postulates the existence of an "evil genius," the "malignant demon." In introducing this odd entity, we must remember that Descartes is searching for a principle about which he can entertain no possible doubt, no matter what the circumstances or how remote the possibility. It is also important to realize that Descartes is not asserting that an evil genius exists. He is merely pushing the methodological doubt as far as he can. His claim is that the notion of an evil genius is not a contradictory notion. Therefore it could be a possible existent. Insofar as it is possible, the ramifications of its existence on the indubitable status of mathematical propositions must be analyzed. The evil genius is able to misrepresent any truthful proposition. Accordingly, even though $(2 + 2 = 4)$ is a true mathematical proposition as it appears to us, possibly the sum is not four. Perhaps the evil genius is deceiving us into thinking that it is four. Thus the possibility of an evil genius forces us to question the necessary veracity of mathematical propositions. As a result of this postulation, the entire category of mathematical propositions cannot be the seat of indubitability which Descartes needs in order to construct his deductive system. The crucial worry is that if the evil genius is always misleading us regarding the truth of mathematical propositions, then these propositions are likewise subject to the rigors of methodological doubt. Therefore mathematics cannot serve as the ground of indubitability.

Meditation I ends with Descartes not having resolved his dilemma. He is still faced with the question with which he began: Is there any proposition at all which can successfully pass the scathing attack of methodological doubt? That this question has been unresolved provides the background for *Meditation II*.

MEDITATION II: OF THE NATURE OF THE HUMAN MIND; AND THAT IT IS MORE EASILY KNOWN THAN THE BODY

René Descartes

The Meditation of yesterday has filled my mind with so many doubts, that it is no longer in my power to forget them. Nor do I see, meanwhile, any principle on which they can be resolved; and, just as if I had fallen all of a sudden into very deep water, I am so greatly disconcerted as to be unable either to plant my feet firmly on the bottom or sustain myself by swimming on the surface. I will, nevertheless, make an effort, and try anew the same path on which I had entered yesterday, that is, proceed by casting aside all that admits of the slightest doubt, not less than if I had discovered it to be absolutely false; and I will continue always in this track until I shall find something that is certain, or at least, if I can do nothing more, until I shall know with certainty that there is nothing certain. Archimedes, that he might transport the entire globe from the place it occupied to another, demanded only a point that was firm and immovable; so also, I shall be entitled to entertain the highest expectations, if I am fortunate enough to discover only one thing that is certain and indubitable.

I suppose, accordingly, that all the things which I see are false (fictitious); I believe that none of those objects which my fallacious memory represents ever existed; I suppose that I possess no senses; I believe that body, figure, extension, motion, and place are merely fictions of my mind. What is there, then, that can be esteemed true? Perhaps this only, that there is absolutely nothing certain.

But how do I know that there is not something different altogether from the objects I have now enumerated, of which it is impossible to entertain the slightest doubt? Is there not a God, or some being, by whatever name I may designate him, who causes these thoughts to arise in my mind? But why suppose such a being, for it may be I myself am capable of producing them? Am I, then, at least not something? But I before denied that I possessed senses or a body; I hesitate, however, for what follows from that? Am I so dependent on the body and the senses that without these I cannot exist? But I had the persuasion that there was absolutely nothing in the world, that there was no sky and no earth, neither minds nor bodies; was I not, therefore, at the same time, persuaded that I did not exist? Far from it; I assuredly existed, since I was persuaded. But there is I know not what being, who is possessed at once of the highest power and the deepest cunning, who is constantly employing all his ingenuity in deceiving me. Doubtless, then, I exist, since I am deceived; and, let him deceive me as he may, he can never bring it about that I am nothing, so long as I shall be conscious that I am something. So that it must, in fine, be maintained, all things being maturely and carefully considered, that this proposition (*pronunciatum*) I am, I exist, is necessarily true each time it is expressed by me, or conceived in my mind.

Reprinted from John Veitch, trans., *The Method, Meditations and Philosophy of Descartes* (Washington: M. Walter Dunne, 1901).

But I do not yet know with sufficient clearness what I am, though assured that I am; and hence, in the next place, I must take care, lest perchance I inconsiderately substitute some other object in room of what is properly myself, and thus wander from truth, even in that knowledge (cognition) which I hold to be of all others the most certain and evident. For this reason, I will now consider anew what I formerly believed myself to be, before I entered on the present train of thought; and of my previous opinion I will retrench all that can in the least be invalidated by the grounds of doubt I have adduced, in order that there may at length remain nothing but what is certain and indubitable. What then did I formerly think I was? Undoubtedly I judged that I was a man. But what is a man? Shall I say a rational animal? Assuredly not; for it would be necessary forthwith to inquire into what is meant by animal, and what by rational, and thus, from a single question, I should insensibly glide into others, and these more difficult than the first; nor do I now possess enough of leisure to warrant me in wasting my time amid subtleties of this sort. I prefer here to attend to the thoughts that sprung up of themselves in my mind, and were inspired by my own nature alone, when I applied myself to the consideration of what I was. In the first place, then, I thought that I possessed a countenance, hands, arms, and all the fabric of members that appears in a corpse, and which I called by the name of body. It further occurred to me that I was nourished, that I walked, perceived, and thought, and all those actions I referred to the soul; but what the soul itself was I either did not stay to consider, or, if I did, I imagined that it was something extremely rare and subtile, like wind, or flame, or ether, spread through my grosser parts. As regarded the body, I did not even doubt of its nature, but thought I distinctly knew it, and if I had wished to describe it according to the notions I then entertained, I should have explained myself in this manner: By body I understand all that can be terminated by a certain figure; that can be comprised in a certain place, and so fill a certain space as therefrom to exclude every other body; that can be perceived either by touch, sight, hearing, taste, or smell; that can be moved in different ways, not indeed of itself, but by something foreign to it by which it is touched [and from which it receives the impression]; for the power of self-motion, as likewise that of perceiving and thinking, I held as by no means pertaining to the nature of body; on the contrary, I was somewhat astonished to find such faculties existing in some bodies.

But [as to myself, what can I now say that I am], since I suppose there exists an extremely powerful, and, if I may so speak, malignant being, whose whole endeavours are directed towards deceiving me? Can I affirm that I possess any one of all those attributes of which I have lately spoken as belonging to the nature of body? After attentively considering them in my own mind, I find none of them that can properly be said to belong to myself. To recount them were idle and tedious. Let us pass, then, to the attributes of the soul. The first mentioned were the powers of nutrition and walking; but, if it be true that I have no body, it is true likewise that I am capable neither of walking nor of being nourished. Perception is another attribute of the soul; but perception too is impossible without the body: besides, I have frequently, during sleep, believed that I perceived objects which I afterwards observed I did not in reality perceive. Thinking is another attribute of the soul; and here I discover what properly belongs to myself. This alone is inseparable from me. I am—I exist: this is certain; but how often? As often as I think; for perhaps it would even happen, if I should wholly cease to think, that I should at the same time altogether cease to be. I now admit nothing that is not necessarily true: I am therefore, precisely speaking, only a thinking thing, that is, a mind (*mens sive animus*), understanding, or reason—terms whose signification was before unknown to me. I am, however, a real thing, and really existent; but what thing? The answer was, a thinking thing. The question now arises, am I aught besides? I will stimulate my imagination with a view to discover whether I am not still something more than a thinking being. Now it is plain I am not the assemblage of members called the human body; I am not a thin and penetrating air diffused through all these members, or wind, or flame, or vapour, or breath, or any of all the things I can imagine; for I supposed that all these were not, and, without changing the supposition, I find that I still feel assured of my existence.

But it is true, perhaps, that those very things which I suppose to be nonexistent, because they are unknown to me, are not in truth different from myself whom I know. This is a point I cannot determine, and do not now enter into any dispute regarding it. I can only judge of things that are known to me: I am conscious that I exist, and I who know that I exist inquire into what I am. It is, however, perfectly certain that the knowledge of my existence, thus precisely taken, is not dependent on things, the existence of which is as yet unknown to me: and consequently it is not dependent on any of the things I can feign in imagination. Moreover, the phrase itself, I frame an image (*effingo*), reminds me of my error; for I should in truth frame one if I were to imagine myself to be anything, since to imagine is nothing more than to contemplate the figure or image of a corporeal thing; but I already know that I exist, and that it is possible at the same time that all those images, and in general all that relates to the nature of body, are merely dreams [or chimeras]. From this I discover that it is not more reasonable to say, I will excite my imagination that I may know more distinctly what I am, than to express myself as follows: I am now awake, and perceive something real; but because my perception is not sufficiently clear, I will of express purpose go to sleep that my dreams may represent to me the object of my perception with more truth and clearness. And, therefore, I know that nothing of all that I can embrace in imagination belongs to the knowledge which I have of myself, and that there is need to recall with the utmost care the mind from this mode of thinking, that it may be able to know its own nature with perfect distinctness.

But what, then, am I? A thinking thing, it has been said. But what is a thinking thing? It is a thing that doubts, understands, [conceives], affirms, denies, wills, refuses, that imagines also, and perceives. Assuredly it is not little, if all these properties belong to my nature. But why should they not belong to it? Am I not that very being who now doubts of almost everything; who, for all that, understands and conceives certain things; who affirms one alone as true, and denies the others; who desires to know more of them, and does not wish to be deceived; who imagines many things, sometimes even despite his will; and is likewise percipient of many, as if through the medium of the senses? Is there nothing of all this as true as that I am, even although I should be always dreaming, and although he who gave me being employed all his ingenuity to deceive me? Is there also any one of these attributes that can be properly distinguished from my thought, or that can be said to be separate from myself? For it is of itself so evident that it is I who doubt, I who understand, and I who desire, that it is here unnecessary to add anything by way of rendering it more clear. And I am as certainly the same being who imagines; for, although it may be (as I before supposed) that nothing I imagine is true, still the power of imagination does not cease really to exist in me and to form part of my thought. In fine, I am the same being who perceives, that is, who apprehends certain objects as by the organs of sense, since, in truth, I see light, hear a noise, and feel heat. But it will be said that these presentations are false, and that I am dreaming. Let it be so. At all events it is certain that I seem to see light, hear a noise, and feel heat; this cannot be false, and this is what in me is properly called perceiving (*sentire*), which is nothing else than thinking. From this I begin to know what I am with somewhat greater clearness and distinctness than heretofore.

But, nevertheless, it still seems to me, and I cannot help believing, that corporeal things, whose images are formed by thought, [which fall under the senses], and are examined by the same, are known with much greater distinctness than that I know not what part of myself which is not imaginable; although, in truth, it may seem strange to say that I know and comprehend with greater distinctness things whose existence appears to me doubtful, that are unknown, and do not belong to me, than others of whose reality I am persuaded, that are known to me, and appertain to my proper nature; in a word, than myself. But I see clearly what is the state of the case. My mind is apt to wander, and will not yet submit to be restrained within the limits of truth. Let us therefore leave the mind to itself once more, and, according to it every kind of liberty, [permit it to consider the objects that appear to it from without], in order that, having afterwards withdrawn it from these gently and opportunely, [and fixed it on the consideration of its being and the properties it finds in itself], it may then be the more easily controlled.

Let us now accordingly consider the objects that are commonly thought to be [the most easily, and likewise] the most distinctly known, viz., the bodies we touch and see; not, indeed, bodies in general, for these general notions are usually somewhat more confused, but one body in particular. Take, for example, this piece of wax; it is quite fresh, having been but recently taken from the bee-hive; it has not yet lost the sweetness of the honey it contained, it still retains somewhat of the odour of the flowers from which it was gathered; its colour, figure, size, are apparent (to the sight); it is hard, cold, easily handled; and sounds when struck upon with the finger. In fine, all that contributes to make a body as distinctly known as possible, is found in the one before us. But, while I am speaking, let it be placed near the fire—what remained of the taste exhales, the smell evaporates, the colour changes, its figure is destroyed, its size increases, it becomes liquid, it grows hot, it can hardly be handled, and, although struck upon, it emits no sound. Does the same wax still remain after this change? It must be admitted that it does remain; no one doubts it, or judges otherwise. What, then, was it I knew with so much distinctness in the piece of wax? Assuredly, it could be nothing of all that I observed by means of the senses, since all the things that fell under taste, smell, sight, touch, and hearing are changed, and yet the same wax remains. It was perhaps what I now think, viz., that this wax was neither the sweetness of honey, the pleasant odour of flowers, the whiteness, the figure, nor the sound, but only a body that a little before appeared to me conspicuous under these forms, and which is now perceived under others. But, to speak precisely, what is it that I imagine when I think of it in this way? Let it be attentively considered, and, retrenching all that does not belong to the wax, let us see what remains. There certainly remains nothing, except something extended, flexible, and movable. But what is meant by flexible and movable? Is it not that I imagine that the piece of wax, being round, is capable of becoming square, or of passing from a square into a triangular figure? Assuredly such is not the case, because I conceive that it admits of an infinity of similar changes; and I am, moreover, unable to compass this infinity by imagination, and consequently this conception which I have of the wax is not the product of the faculty of imagination. But what now is this extension? Is it not also unknown? for it becomes greater when the wax is melted, greater when it is boiled, and greater still when the heat increases; and I should not conceive [clearly and] according to truth, the wax as it is, if I did not suppose that the piece we are considering admitted even of a wider variety of extension than I ever imagined. I must, therefore, admit that I cannot even comprehend by imagination what the piece of wax is, and that it is the mind alone (*mens,* Lat., *entendement,* F.) which perceives it. I speak of one piece in particular; for, as to wax in general, this is still more evident. But what is the piece of wax that can be perceived only by the [understanding or] mind? It is certainly the same which I see, touch, imagine; and, in fine, it is the same which, from the beginning, I believed it to be. But (and this it is of moment to observe) the perception of it is neither an act of sight, of touch, nor of imagination, and never was either of these, though it might formerly seem so, but is simply an intuition (*inspectio*) of the mind, which may be imperfect and confused, as it formerly was, or very clear and distinct, as it is at present, according as the attention is more or less directed to the elements which it contains, and of which it is composed.

But, meanwhile, I feel greatly astonished when I observe [the weakness of my mind, and] its proneness to error. For although, without at all giving expression to what I think, I consider all this in my own mind, words yet occasionally impede my progress, and I am almost led into error by the terms of ordinary language. We say, for example, that we see the same wax when it is before us, and not that we judge it to be the same from its retaining the same colour and figure: whence I should forthwith be disposed to conclude that the wax is known by the act of sight, and not by the intuition of the mind alone, were it not for the analogous instance of human beings passing on in the street below, as observed from a window. In this case I do not fail to say that I see the men themselves, just as I say that I see the wax;

and yet what do I see from the window beyond hats and cloaks that might cover artificial machines, whose motions might be determined by springs? But I judge that there are human beings from these appearances, and thus I comprehend, by the faculty of judgment alone which is in the mind, what I believed I saw with my eyes.

The man who makes it his aim to rise to knowledge superior to the common, ought to be ashamed to seek occasions of doubting from the vulgar forms of speech: instead, therefore, of doing this, I shall proceed with the matter in hand, and inquire whether I had a clearer and more perfect perception of the piece of wax when I first saw it, and when I thought I knew it by means of the external sense itself, or, at all events, by the common sense (*sensus communis*), as it is called, that is, by the imaginative faculty; or whether I rather apprehend it more clearly at present, after having examined with greater care, both what it is, and in what way it can be known. It would certainly be ridiculous to entertain any doubt on this point. For what, in that first perception, was there distinct? What did I perceive which any animal might not have perceived? But when I distinguish the wax from its exterior forms, and when, as if I had stripped it of its vestments, I consider it quite naked, it is certain, although some error may still be found in my judgment, that I cannot, nevertheless, thus apprehend it without possessing a human mind.

But, finally, what shall I say of the mind itself, that is, myself? for as yet I do not admit that I am anything but mind. What, then! I who seem to possess so distinct an apprehension of the piece of wax—do I not know myself, both with greater truth and certitude, and also much more distinctly and clearly? For if I judge that the wax exists because I see it, it assuredly follows, much more evidently, that I myself am or exist, for the same reason: for it is possible that what I see may not in truth be wax, and that I do not even possess eyes with which to see anything; but it cannot be that when I see, or, which comes to the same thing, when I think I see, I myself who think am nothing. So likewise, if I judge that the wax exists because I touch it, it will still also follow that I am; and if I determine that my imagination, or any other cause, whatever it be, persuades me of the existence of the wax, I will still draw the same conclusion. And what is here remarked of the piece of wax, is applicable to all the other things that are external to me. And further, if the [notion or] perception of wax appeared to me more precise and distinct, after that not only sight and touch, but many other causes besides, rendered it manifest to my apprehension, with how much greater distinctness must I now know myself, since all the reasons that contribute to the knowledge of the nature of wax, or of any body whatever, manifest still better the nature of my mind? And there are besides so many other things in the mind itself that contribute to the illustration of its nature, that those dependent on the body, to which I have here referred, scarcely merit to be taken into account.

But, in conclusion, I find I have insensibly reverted to the point I desired: for, since it is now manifest to me that bodies themselves are not properly perceived by the senses nor by the faculty of imagination, but by the intellect alone; and since they are not perceived because they are seen and touched, but only because they are understood [or rightly comprehended by thought], I readily discover that there is nothing more easily or clearly apprehended than my own mind. But because it is difficult to rid one's self so promptly of an opinion to which one has been long accustomed, it will be desirable to tarry for some time at this stage, that, by long continued meditation, I may more deeply impress upon my memory this new knowledge.

Meditation I provides the dramatic setting for the philosophical reflections Descartes suggests throughout *Meditation II*. The principal claim set forth in *Meditation II* is that, even when we have successfully doubted every category of propositions, still there will be one proposition which we cannot doubt. This indubitable principle concerns one's very existence as a thinking being. Descartes is suggesting that the very activity of thinking guarantees that one is a thinking being. Even if we are doubting, the mental act of doubting entails that we must exist as a source of that act of doubting. This argument is Descartes' famous *cogito* argument. The argument runs as follows: "Cogito, ergo sum." This is translated as follows: "I think, therefore I am." The following statement is found in *Meditation II:* "I am, I exist is necessarily true each time it is expressed by me, or conceived in my mind." In *The Discourse on Method*, however, another formulation of this argument is found; this latter formulation, which follows, is the classical expression of the cogito argument.

WHAT IS INDUBITABLE

René Descartes

I am in doubt as to the propriety of making my first meditations, in the place above mentioned, matter of discourse; for these are so metaphysical, and so uncommon, as not, perhaps, to be acceptable to everyone. And yet, that it may be determined whether the foundations that I have laid are sufficiently secure, I find myself in a measure constrained to advert to them. I had long before remarked that, in relation to practice, it is sometimes necessary to adopt, as if above doubt, opinions which we discern to be highly uncertain, as has been already said; but as I then desired to give my attention solely to the search after truth, I thought that a procedure exactly the opposite was called for, and that I ought to reject as absolutely false all opinions in regard to which I could suppose the least ground for doubt, in order to ascertain whether after that there remained aught in my belief that

Reprinted from John Veitch, trans., "The Discourse on Method," Part IV, in *The Method, Meditations and Philosophy of Descartes* (Washington: M. Walter Dunne, 1901).

was wholly indubitable. Accordingly, seeing that our senses sometimes deceive us, I was willing to suppose that there existed nothing really such as they presented to us; and because some men err in reasoning, and fall into paralogisms, even on the simplest matters of Geometry, I, convinced that I was as open to error as any other, rejected as false all the reasonings I had hitherto taken for demonstrations; and finally, when I considered that the very same thoughts (presentations) which we experience when awake may also be experienced when we are asleep, while there is at that time not one of them true, I supposed that all the objects (presentations) that had ever entered into my mind when awake, had in them no more truth than the illusions of my dreams. But immediately upon this I observed that, whilst I thus wished to think that all was false, it was absolutely necessary that I, who thus thought, should be somewhat; and as I observed that this truth, I THINK, HENCE I AM, was so certain and of such evidence, that no ground of doubt, however extravagant, could be alleged by the Sceptics capable of shaking it, I concluded that I might, without scruple, accept it as the first principle of the philosophy of which I was in search.

In the next place, I attentively examined what I was, and as I observed that I could suppose that I had no body, and that there was no world nor any place in which I might be; but that I could not therefore suppose that I was not; and that, on the contrary, from the very circumstance that I thought to doubt of the truth of all things, it most clearly and certainly followed that I was; while, on the other hand, if I had only ceased to think, although all the other objects which I had ever imagined had been in reality existent, I would have had no reason to believe that I existed; I thence concluded that I was a substance whose whole essence or nature consists only in thinking, and which, that it may exist, has need of no place, nor is dependent on any material thing; so that "I", that is to say, the mind by which I am what I am, is wholly distinct from the body, and is even more easily known than the latter, and is such, that although the latter were not, it would still continue to be all that it is.

After this I inquired in general into what is essential to the truth and certainty of a proposition; for since I had discovered one which I knew to be true, I thought that I must likewise be able to discover the ground of this certitude. And as I observed that in the words I THINK, HENCE I AM, there is nothing at all which gives me assurance of their truth beyond this, that I see very clearly that in order to think it is necessary to exist. I concluded that I might take, as a general rule, the principle, that all the things which we very clearly and distinctly conceive are true, only observing, however, that there is some difficulty in rightly determining the objects which we distinctly conceive.

The Cogito Argument

It is important to realize a shift in meaning that Descartes has made in *Meditation II* and in the passage from *The Discourse on Method*. During the discussions found in *Meditation I,* Descartes continually refers to the contents of our ideas. He asks if the content of our sensible ideas or the contents of our mathematical ideas are indeed veridical. Yet in *Meditation II,* Descartes places the emphasis on the act of knowing. Descartes is making what later philosophers were to call the act-object distinction. This distinction stresses the difference between the act by which we know something and the object which is known. The twentieth-century philosopoher, G.E. Moore, perhaps best explained the act-object distinction in the following passage from his celebrated 1903 paper, "The Refutation of Idealism":

> We have then in every sensation two distinct elements, one which I call consciousness, and another which I call the object of consciousness. This must be so if the sensation of blue and the sensation of green, though different in one respect, are alike in another: blue is one object of sensation and green is another, and consciousness, which both sensations have in common, is different from either.

Schematically, the act-object distinction can be represented by the following illustration:

MIND   ACT OF   OBJECT OF
                            AWARENESS   AWARENESS
                                                            (CONTENT OF)
                                                             THE IDEA

Descartes is suggesting that no matter what the content of an act of awareness might be—i.e., whether or not the content of an idea is veridical—the perceiver is, nevertheless, aware of the act of awareness. Insofar as this act of awareness occurs, Descartes argues that we cannot doubt our existence. It is important to realize that now Descartes is placing emphasis on the act of awareness and not the object of awareness.

Cartesian scholars have differed regarding the precise structure of the argument contained within the above propositions taken from Descartes' writings. Our present discussion will consider two possible interpretations of the argument.

The first interpretation we shall consider might be called the *intuitionist view.* The claim of this intuitive analysis is that Descartes is calling attention to the experience of mental awareness. This immediate introspection is of a self-evident truth. The intuitionist interpretation asserts that when one apprehends the truth of "I think," he/she cannot but accept the truth of "I am." Put differently, the truth of "I am" is immediately intuited as soon as the truth of "I think" is apprehended. In effect, this interpretation reduces the cogito to an immediate intuition of a self-evident truth. However an intuition itself is not an argument form. An argument form must contain premises and a conclusion, and there must be a process of going from these premises to the conclusion. The strength of any conclusion rests completely upon the strength of the premises. A self-evident proposition which is intuited does not depend upon the rational movement from premise to conclusion. If we accept this first formulation, we really take away the structure of an argument per se from Descartes.

The second interpretation suggests that Descartes is using an argument, but one with an assumed premise. This assumed premise can be stated as, "Qualities must inhere in a substance." This statement indicates the philosophical claim that a property or characteristic is always rooted in or tied down to some form of substance. Consider for a moment the etymological derivation of the term *substance*. It comes from two Latin terms, *sub* and *stare*. This is translated as "to stand under." Accordingly, a substance is an entity which "stands under" the qualities. Descartes seems to be focusing on a common sense point here. He is suggesting that there are no such things as "free-floating" qualities. This claim asserts that every time a quality occurs, e.g., red, it is a quality which modifies some thing or object. For example, red is never found alone. It is always a modification of a box, leaf, sports car, or some other object in the world. We do not refer to a "red" but rather to a "red object." This assumed premise forces us to think about this characteristic of adjectival terms: they always modify another thing. Another way of analyzing this assumed premise is to suggest that it is indicating that a participle needs a subject. We might also say that any adjectival modification or activity demands a subject which is so modified or is doing the activity. The assumed premise asserts that if there is an activity, then there must be a corresponding subject which is the "doer" of that activity. In other words, there is no such thing as an activity which occurs by itself independently of a subject. Think for a moment of the common sense implications of this assumed premise. A "running" which occurs without a "runner" is absurd. So, too, Descartes is suggesting, is a "thinking" without a "thinker."

Utilizing the function of the assumed premise, the structure of the "cogito argument" can be presented as follows:

1. Qualities must belong to a subject.
2. Thinking is a quality.
3. Therefore, thinking must belong to a subject.

The awareness of thinking as an activity pertains to the "I think." If thinking is a quality, and if qualities must belong to a subject, then there must be an existing subject to which the qualities belong. Accordingly, from the "I think," Descartes concludes that the "I" (i.e., the "ego") must exist as a thing.

The structure of the above interpretation will apply to any of the mental qualities considered. Accordingly, insofar as thinking is a quality and thus entails a thinker, so too is doubting a quality which implies a doubter and perceiving a quality which implies a perceiver. The same can be said of any mental activity. With the presupposed premise, Descartes claims that it would in essence be an invalid argument for us to argue that, even though we are thinking, we still do not exist. As we know from *Meditation II*, Descartes considers many kinds of thinking:

> But what is a thinking thing? It is a thing that doubts, understands, (conceives), affirms, denies, wills, refuses, that imagines also, and perceives.

Let us reflect for a moment about what Descartes has done during the first two *Meditations*. He has asked us to engage in a process of methodological doubt. This doubting has forced us to remain uncommitted to any category of propositions. Then Descartes has sprung the cogito argument on us. All along, we have been actively engaged in critical thinking. Granted, we have been using the process of methodological doubt. Nevertheless, this method of doubt is still a form of thinking. Descartes has forced us, by doubting, to overcome any skepticism which we might have had. Descartes also has asked us to actively engage in thought. In so doing, we have proven our own existence. The structure of *Meditations I* and *II* has forced us to think actively, and this activity entails our existence. Think about it for a moment.

Having discussed the structure of the cogito argument, we will now subject the Cartesian arguement to critical analysis. Let's consider the following problem. The Scottish empiricist, David Hume, brings the following objection to Descartes' cogito argument. The objection of Hume centers around Descartes' claim that he introspects or intuits that he is an existing thing. To paraphrase Hume: "Lucky Descartes! He gets to his soul; I just get an experience." The point Hume asks us to consider is that the totality of the content attained in any introspection is an awareness of the immediate experience itself. Hume demands that Descartes spell out how the intuition indeed grasps at the notion of an existing thing which is having the introspective experience. Of course, the point Hume emphasizes is that the intuition or awareness of a "substance"— the thinking thing—is beyond the intuitive act of awareness itself. Let's analyze our own introspective awarenesses for a moment. Do we intuit a substance beyond the experience itself? We probably will discover that Hume is correct. Also, we probably will be aware that we are aware; that is, we are aware that we are having an awareness, but are we aware of the "self"? Think about it.

Now consider what follows from the acceptance of Hume's criticism. Does one continue to exist when he/she is not actually thinking? If so, on what grounds can that assertion be made, given the structure of the Cartesian argument? Also, how would Descartes account for the fact that a succession of thoughts by the same person is in some way connected to that person? Certainly, one wants to say that the thoughts which were had before lunch yesterday afternoon occurred to the same "self" which was thinking after eating lunch. Yet can Descartes account for the problem of "personal identity"? If Hume is correct, then is there an identical referent for all our thoughts? If not, then how can we have any guarantee that our next thought will indeed be ours and not a thought floating around on its own, not tied down to a self? In effect, Hume points out Descartes' assumption that the mental substance (i.e., the mind) will indeed last through time. And Hume forces us to consider if that assumption will successfully pass Descartes' own methodological doubt. This inability to account for personal identity given the objection of Hume has forced many philosophers studying the *Meditations* to abandon the intuitionist interpretation of the cogito argument.

The second objection concerns Descartes' presupposed premise. If it is a correct interpretation of the cogito that Descartes has used as a presupposed premise, "qualities belong to a substance," then a very serious question emerges concerning the consistency of Descartes' methodological doubt. The point can be put this way. Is the presupposed premise itself a clear and distinct idea? Can it be doubted? Is it possible to consider that a quality might not demand the existence of a substance in order for the quality itself to exist? Descartes appears to assume that the necessity of a substance in order to "tie down" qualities cannot be doubted.

However we might extrapolate from Hume's objection. In essence, Hume's denial of personal identity implies the nonacceptance of Descartes' presupposed maxim. Later in our discussion we shall consider the philosophy of George Berkeley. Berkeley asserted that a quality of a material thing need not demand a material substance. He argued that a physical object is nothing more than a collection of all its sensible qualities. This collection has no need for a material substance. Therefore, given the fact that Berkeley did doubt this premise, it follows that this presupposed premise is indeed dubitable. Insofar as it is dubitable, then it is not part of a philosophically indubitable argument, which, of course, was Descartes' goal. In other words, it appears that Descartes should have subjected the presupposed premise to the process of methodological doubt. The history of philosophy indicates that later philosophers will not accept Descartes' premise as a clear and distinct indubitable idea.

Now that Descartes has convinced himself that he is an existing thing and that the argument establishing his existence is indubitably true, his next question concerns the nature or essence of this existing thing. Traditionally, the ancient and medieval philosophers before Descartes had concerned themselves with two principal metaphysical problems. First of all, they were concerned about the existence of different categories of objects; second, they sought to establish the essence or nature of those objects which existed. Descartes, influenced as he was by his philosophical predecessors, asked the very same series of questions. Now that he has established the existence of one human being—himself—he is concerned about knowing something about the nature of this human being. Descartes argued that the nature of a human being is fundamentally rooted in the ability of thinking. The essence of a human is to be a "thinking thing." Obviously, here Descartes is making explicit use of Plato's distinction between an essential property and an incidental property. Descartes asserts that the essential property of a human being—i.e., the property which distinguishes a human being from all the other categories of existents—is the ability to think. Crudely put, this essential property is "thinkability." Remember how Descartes described a thinking being:

> It is a thing that doubts, understands, (conceives), affirms, denies, wills, refuses, that imagines also, and perceives.

Descartes is using thinking as a generic term which has at least all of the above uses. Furthermore, he asserts that thinking alone is the essential property of human beings. This claim is justified for him in that he can clearly and distinctly conceive of no other essential property. In other words, thinking is the only property which Descartes cannot doubt when he conceives the nature of a human being. Accordingly, thinking is the essential property or defining characteristic separating humans from the rest of the categories of real things. Recall the passage in which Descartes argues that the definition of a human being is not "rational animal." Think for a moment why Descartes omits "animal" from the definition of a human being.

The above discussion has interesting consequences for Descartes' philosophical system. Descartes' ontology is not unlike Plato's. Descartes too will adopt a radical dualism between mind and body. The essence of a human, in the Cartesian ontology, is to be a spiritual mind. The essence of a human is exercised in the mind's activity. Simply put, the essence of each one of us is spiritual and not material. Our essence has nothing to do with our physical body. Accordingly, the essential property of a spiritual substance is thinking. The next part of our discussion will dwell on the ramifications of this radical metaphysical dualism.

An objection was raised against the cogito by one of Descartes' contemporaries. The content of this objection is as follows: If thinking can prove your existence, why can't walking? This has been called the *Ambulo, ergo sum* objection (I walk, therefore, I am).

Consider for a moment the force of the above objection. The objector forces Descartes to answer why "thinking" is the only activity which will unequivocally demonstrate one's existence. Stated differently, the gist of this objection is: Why won't any type of activity work in the structure of the argument? Why did Descartes insist that it be a "mental activity"? Note that the focus of the objector is on the activity of walking itself and not on the "awareness" of walking. Accordingly, if the above objection works, then walking does indeed imply a walker. Walking is an adjectival activity which demands an object—a walker. However, does walking establish the existence of a walker in the same fashion that thinking establishes the existence of a thinker? Think back to *Meditation I*.

The simple fact of the matter is that one could be imagining or dreaming to be walking. Certainly to dream of walking is not to exist as a walker. Accordingly, the notion of walking does not pass the dream problem which we discussed in *Meditation I*. In responding to this objection, Descartes forces us to consider the unique relation between the activity of thinking and the state of existing. This type of objection will not affect the cogito argument. We could not think without existing. We could imagine that we were thinking, but if we are imagining, then we are at least imaginers, and if we are dreaming then we are dreamers. The general thrust of the whole Cartesian argument is on mental activity and not on physical activity. Walking is a physical activity. Any physical activity could be subject to the dream problem. In other words, to be aware of a physical activity implies that one is aware of something beyond the very act of thinking itself; and Descartes is convinced that the only category of propositions about which he has absolutely certain knowledge concerns the mental activity itself.

We might consider the objection just mentioned in a different way. Note the following structure:

I am aware that I am walking,
Therefore, I am.

In this formulation, the accent is placed on the "act of awareness" and not on the physical activity itself. Insofar as there is a definite mental activity occurring, this argument is reducible in principle to the cogito argument. This formulation again forces us to consider the category difference between mental activity and physical activity. It is only with the former that Descartes will be successful in establishing his existence.

The Mind-Body Problem

We must now consider in detail the philosophical ramifications of the radical metaphysical dualism characteristic of the Cartesian ontology. The major issue western philosophy inherited from Descartes is the *mind-body problem*. This issue is also called the problem of interaction. Simply put, Descartes' radical dualism forces the philosopher to account for the interaction of mind and body. In order to see the philosophical import of the mind-body problem for Descartes, remember the structure of the Cartesian ontology. Descartes' ontology is composed of two fundamental categories: spiritual substances and material substances. A human appears to be a combination of two things: a mind and a body. Given Cartesian dualism, this combination demands that two substances be placed together. Spiritual substances have the property of thinking while physical substances, characterized as they are by materialistic mechanism, have their essential properties in extension. In the Cartesian metaphysical system, the problem of interaction can be characterized as how to explain the causal interdependence between two radically different entities. Recall that, in chapter 2, Plato faced a similar problem with his ontology.

In the Cartesian system it is obvious how two material things act upon each other. One billiard ball simply bangs into another billiard ball. But how is something which is spiritual—and thereby totally lacking extension—capable of causally affecting something which is extended. What is the area of contact between spirit and matter?

That interaction occurs is a facet of our common sense awareness of ourselves. It is obvious that the body affects the mind and vice-versa. For example, when we are tired, we are unable to exercise our mental powers to study effectively or when we are overstuffed from Thanksgiving dinner, we don't feel like working through theorems in non-Euclidean geometry. The effects of alcohol and drugs on our mental processes are obvious. And thought, on the other hand, can affect our physical well being. Without here dealing about the intricacies of psychosomatic medicine, it is obvious that a thought or wish can affect our physical actions. A desire for ice cream can cause us to go to the snack bar for a sundae and so forth.

However the problem comes to this: How can this apparent interaction that is so obvious to our common sense awareness be explained, granting the conclusions of the Cartesian ontology? Given this radical dualism, we have a substance whose essence is spiritual acting on a substance whose essence is extension. The philosophical concern is over how we are to account for the connection of causal efficacy given the radical dualism of Descartes' system.

Descartes provided a response to this problem. He claimed that the pineal gland was the point of interaction. Descartes referred to the pineal gland as the "most inward of all the parts of the brain." Here the mind becomes heavier and the body becomes lighter. Thus a proper medium for causal interaction is provided. Descartes hoped that the pineal gland could resolve the terrific implications of his radical dualism. That this response is woefully inadequate should be obvious. At best, it is an unsuccessful attempt to solve a fundamentally philosophical problem by means of a physiological account. The philosophical problem still remains. Even in the rarefied medium of the pineal gland, Descartes has not explained how a spirit can act upon something extended.

One might wonder why Descartes postulated the pineal gland as the explanation for mind-body interaction. It is possible to offer a conjecture for Descartes' purported solution. As we have seen, Descartes was greatly influenced by the mechanism of the early materialists. On this system, a push-pull type of interaction was the paradigm case for explaining causal interaction. Obviously the model is bits of matter banging into each other like billiard balls on a pool table. In order for one physical object to move another physical object, there must be a meeting of the two. Descartes applied this model to the mind-body interaction problem. By means of the rarefied atmosphere in the pineal gland, the mind was in a proper medium to be able to meet with the body and "give it a push." It was the pineal gland to which Descartes beckoned to accomplish this miraculous task. That this response has philosophical problems should be obvious. Descartes fails to inform us *how* the interaction really occurs—i.e., how the spirit really affects the matter. In effect, Descartes has thrown up an anatomical smoke screen which completely fails to confront the onotological issue at stake.

Is Cartesian dualism necessary in order to explain the human mind? Must the mind be essentially distinct from the body? Both of these formulations imply a metaphysical dualism arguing for the existence of two fundamental categories, mind and body.

One response to radical dualism of the Cartesian variety has been materialism. In the history of philosophy, materialism has been formulated in many ways. Yet all these formulations have in common the thesis that all that exists is exhausted in terms of material explanations. One of the more forceful attempts expressed in contemporary philosophy to undercut dualism, especially by psychologists, has been behaviorism. In essence, behaviorism attempts to explain all mental activity in terms of bodily responses. As of most academic categories, behaviorism has different nuances when employed by different theorists. Three types of behaviorism, all of which have been argued for in twentieth-century philosophy and psychology, are:

Metaphysical Behaviorism.   This position asserts that there is indeed no such thing as mental or spiritual existence. It is, in effect, the position of philosophical materialism. The American psychologists, J.B. Watson, and probably B.F. Skinner, can be classified as metaphysical behaviorists.

Methodological Behaviorism.   This is a weaker position than metaphysical behaviorism. As its name indicates, this position uses behaviorism as a method rather than as a fully developed ontological position. Methodological behaviorism argues that we should proceed in our investigations as if no purely mental events exist, while not committing ourselves to an answer to this question. In a sense, a methodological behaviorist is an agnostic regarding the existence of mental phenomena. He/she simply asks that we not worry about mental phenomena and, instead, spend our time researching human behavior. Many contemporary American psychologists fit into this category.

Logical Behaviorism (Linguistic Behaviorism).   This position has been espoused by some twentieth-century English and American philosophers, most notably Gilbert Ryle in his influential book, *The Concept of Mind.* Ryle focuses his efforts on considering the logical structure of mental language. He argues that mental concepts expressed in our language, e.g., thinking, understanding, and so on, are understood to function only in terms of actual or possible behavior. In other words, the criteria for successful application of mental language is always in terms of explicit bodily behavior. Ryle insists that he is not asserting a metaphysical claim. He is only asking us to consider the functioning and criteria for "mental language."

At this time, it would be beneficial for us to consider logical behaviorism as exemplified by Ryle. The following text is from Ryle's famous "Descartes' Myth" chapter in *The Concept of Mind.* In reading this passage, pay close attention to Ryle's criticism of the "official doctrine" and his use of the method of "category mistake" to resolve philosophical difficulties.

DESCARTES' MYTH

Gilbert Ryle

(I) *The Official Doctrine.*
There is a doctrine about the nature and place of minds which is so prevalent among theorists and even among laymen that it deserves to be described as the official theory. Most philosophers, psychologists and religious teachers subscribe, with minor reservations, to its main articles and, although they admit certain theoretical difficulties in it, they tend to assume that these can be overcome without serious modifications being made to the architecture of the theory. It will be argued here that the central principles of the doctrine are unsound and conflict with the whole body of what we know about minds when we are not speculating about them.

The official doctrine, which hails chiefly from Descartes, is something like this. With the doubtful exceptions of idiots and infants in arms every human being has both a body and a mind. Some would prefer to say that every human being is both a body and a mind. His body and his mind are ordinarily harnessed together, but after the death of the body his mind may continue to exist and function.

Human bodies are in space and are subject to the mechanical laws which govern all other bodies in space. Bodily processes and states can be inspected by external observers. So a man's bodily life is as much a public affair as are the lives of animals and reptiles and even as the careers of trees, crystals and planets.

But minds are not in space, nor are their operations subject to mechanical laws. The workings of one mind are not witnessable by other observers; its career is private. Only I can take direct cognisance of the states and processes of my own mind. A person therefore lives through two collateral histories, one consisting of what happens in and to his body, the other

----

Reprinted from Gilbert Ryle, *The Concept of Mind* (London: Hutchinson Publishing Group, 1949), by permission of the publisher.

consisting of what happens in and to his mind. The first is public, the second private. The events in the first history are events in the physical world, those in the second are events in the mental world.

It has been disputed whether a person does or can directly monitor all or only some of the episodes of his own private history; but, according to the official doctrine, of at least some of these episodes he has direct and un-challengeable cognisance. In consciousness, self-consciousness and introspection he is directly and authentically apprised of the present states and operations of his mind. He may have great or small uncertainties about concurrent and adjacent episodes in the physical world, but he can have none about at least part of what is momentarily occupying his mind.

It is customary to express this bifurcation of his two lives and of his two worlds by saying that the things and events which belong to the physical world, including his own body, are external, while the workings of his own mind are internal. This antithesis of outer and inner is of course meant to be construed as a metaphor, since minds, not being in space, could not be described as being spatially inside anything else, or as having things going on spatially inside themselves. But relapses from this good intention are common and theorists are found speculating how stimuli, the physical sources of which are yards or miles outside a person's skin, can generate mental responses inside his skull, or how decisions framed inside his cranium can set going movements of his extremities.

Even when 'inner' and 'outer' are construed as metaphors, the problem how a person's mind and body influence one another is notoriously charged with theoretical difficulties. What the mind will, the legs, arms and the tongue execute; what affects the ear and the eye has something to do with what the mind perceives; grimaces and smiles betray the mind's moods and bodily castigations lead, it is hoped, to moral improvement. But the actual transactions between the episodes of the private history and those of the public history remain mysterious, since by definition they can belong to neither series. They could not be reported among the happenings described in a person's autobiography of his inner life, but nor could they be reported among those described in some one else's biography of that person's overt career. They can be inspected neither by introspection nor by laboratory experiment. They are theoretical shuttlecocks which are for-ever being bandied from the physiologist back to the psychologist and from the psychologist back to the physiologist.

Underlying this partly metaphorical representation of the bifurcation of a person's two lives there is a seemingly more profound and philosophical assumption. It is assumed that there are two different kinds of existence or status. What exists or happens may have the status of physical existence, or it may have the status of mental existence. Somewhat as the faces of coins are either heads or tails, or somewhat as living creatures are either male or female, so, it is supposed, some existing is physical existing, other existing is mental existing. It is a necessary feature of what has physical existence that is is in space and time, it is a necessary feature of what has mental existence that it is in time but not in space. What has physical existence is composed of matter, or else is a function of matter; what has mental existence consists of consciousness, or else is a function of consciousness.

There is thus a polar opposition between mind and matter, an opposition which is often brought out as follows. Material objects are situated in a common field, known as 'space', and what happens to one body in one part of space is mechanically connected with what happens to other bodies in other parts of space. But mental happenings occur in insulated fields, known as 'minds', and there is, apart maybe from telepathy, no direct causal connection between what happens in one mind and what happens in another. Only through the medium of the public physical world can the mind of one person make a difference to the mind of another. The mind is its own place and in his inner life each of us lives the life of a ghostly Robinson Crusoe. People can see, hear and jolt one another's bodies, but they are irremediably blind and deaf to the workings of one another's minds and inoperative upon them.

What sort of knowledge can be secured of the workings of a mind? On the one side, according to the official theory, a person has direct knowledge of the best imaginable kind of the workings of his own mind. Mental states and processes are (or are normally) conscious states and processes, and the consciousness which irradiates them can engender no illusions and leaves the door open for no doubts. A person's present thinkings, feelings and willings, his perceivings, rememberings and imaginings are intrinsically 'phosphorescent'; their existence and their nature are inevitably betrayed to their owner. The inner life is a stream of consciousness of such a sort that it would be absurd to suggest that the mind whose life is that stream might be unaware of what is passing down it.

True, the evidence adduced recently by Freud seems to show that there exist channels tributary to this stream, which run hidden from their owner. People are actuated by impulses the existence of which they vigorously disavow; some of their thoughts differ from the thoughts which they acknowledge; and some of the actions which they think they will to perform they do not really will. They are thoroughly gulled by some of their own hypocrisies and they successfully ignore facts about their mental lives which on the official theory ought to be patent to them. Holders of the official theory tend, however, to maintain that anyhow in normal circumstances a person must be directly and authentically seized of the present state and workings of his own mind.

Besides being currently supplied with these alleged immediate data of consciousness, a person is also generally supposed to be able to exercise from time to time a special kind of perception, namely inner perception, or introspection. He can take a (non-optical) 'look' at what is passing in his mind. Not only can he view and scrutinize a flower through his sense of sight and listen to and discriminate the notes of a bell through his sense of hearing; he can also reflectively or introspectively watch, without any bodily organ of sense, the current episodes of his inner life. The self-observation is also commonly supposed to be immune from illusion, confusion or doubt. A mind's reports of its own affairs have a certainty superior to the best that is possessed by its reports of matters in the physical world. Sense-perceptions can, but consciousness and introspection cannot, be mistaken or confused.

On the other side, one person has no direct access of any sort to the events of the inner life of another. He cannot do better than make problematic inferences from the observed behaviour of the other person's body to the states of mind which, by analogy from his own conduct, he supposes to be signalised by that behaviour. Direct access to the workings of a mind is the privilege of that mind itself; in default of such privileged access, the workings of one mind are inevitably occult to everyone else. For the supposed arguments from bodily movements similar to their own to mental workings similar to their own would lack any possibility of observational corroboration. Not unnaturally, therefore, an adherent of the official theory finds it difficult to resist this consequence of his premises, that he has no good reason to believe that there do exist minds other than his own. Even if he prefers to believe that to other human bodies there are harnessed minds not unlike his own, he cannot claim to be able to discover their individual characteristics, or the particular things that they undergo and do. Absolute solitude is on this showing the ineluctable destiny of the soul. Only our bodies can meet.

As a necessary corollary of this general scheme there is implicitly prescribed a special way of construing our ordinary concepts of mental powers and operations. The verbs, nouns and adjectives, with which in ordinary life we describe the wits, characters and higher-grade performances of the people with whom we have do, are required to be construed as signifying special episodes in their secret histories, or else as signifying tendencies for such episodes to occur. When someone is described as knowing, believing or guessing something, as hoping, dreading, intending or shirking something, as designing this or being amused at that, these verbs are supposed to denote the occurrence of specific modifications in his (to us) occult stream of consciousness. Only his own privileged access to this stream in direct awareness and introspection could provide authentic testimony that these mental-conduct verbs were correctly or incorrectly applied. The onlooker, be he teacher, critic, biographer or friend, can never assure himself that his comments have any vestige of truth. Yet it was just because we do in fact all know how to make such comments, make them with general correctness and correct them when they turn out to be confused or mistaken, that philosophers found it necessary to construct their theories of the nature and place of minds. Finding mental-conduct concepts being regularly and effectively used, they properly sought to fix their logical geography. But the logical geography officially recommended would entail that there could be no regular or effective use of these mental-conduct concepts in our descriptions of, and prescriptions for, other people's minds.

(2) *The Absurdity of the Official Doctrine.*

Such in outline is the official theory. I shall often speak of it, with deliberate abusiveness, as 'the dogma of the Ghost in the Machine', I hope to prove that it is entirely false, and false not in detail but in principle. It is not merely an assemblage of particular mistakes. It is one big mistake and a mistake of a special kind. It is, namely, a category-mistake. It represents the facts of mental life as if they belonged to one logical type or category (or range of types or categories), when they actually belong to another. The dogma is therefore a philosopher's myth. In attempting to explode the myth I shall probably be taken to be denying well-known facts about the mental life of human beings, and my plea that I aim at doing nothing more than rectify the logic of mental-conduct concepts will probably be disallowed as mere subterfuge.

I must first indicate what is meant by the phrase 'Category-mistake'. This I do in a series of illustrations.

A foreigner visiting Oxford or Cambridge for the first time is shown a number of colleges, libraries, playing fields, museums, scientific departments and administrative offices. He then asks 'But where is the University? I have seen where the members of the Colleges live, where the Registrar works, where the scientists experiment and the rest. But I have not yet seen the University in which reside and work the members of your University.' It has then to be explained to him that the University is not another collateral institution, some ulterior counterpart to the colleges, laboratories and offices which he has seen. The University is just the way in which all that he has already seen is organized. When they are seen and when their co-ordination is understood, the University has been seen. His mistake lay in his innocent assumption that it was correct to speak of Christ Church, the Bodleian Library, the Ashmolean Museum *and* the University, to speak, that is, as if 'the University' stood for an extra member of the class of which these other units are members. He was mistakenly allocating the University to the same category as that to which the other institutions belong.

The same mistake would be made by a child witnessing the march-past of a division, who, having had pointed out to him such and such battalions, batteries, squadrons, etc., asked when the division was going to appear. He would be supposing that a division was a counterpart to the units already seen, partly similar to them and partly unlike them. He would be shown his mistake by being told that in watching the battalions, batteries and squadrons marching past he had been watching the division marching past. The march-past was not a parade of battalions, batteries, squadrons *and* a division; it was a parade of the battalions, batteries and squadrons *of* a division.

One more illustration. A foreigner watching his first game of cricket learns what are the functions of the bowlers, the batsmen, the fielders, the umpires and the scorers. He then says 'But there is no one left on the field to contribute the famous element of team-spirit. I see who does the bowling, the batting, and the wicket-keeping; but I do not see whose role it is to exercise *esprit de corps.*' Once more, it would have to be explained that he was looking for the wrong type of thing. Team-spirit is not another cricketing-operation supplementary to all of the other special tasks. It is, roughly, the keenness with which each of the special tasks is performed, and performing a task keenly is not performing two tasks. Certainly exhibiting team-spirit is not the same thing as bowling or catching, but nor is it a third thing such that we can say that the bowler first bowls *and* then exhibits team-spirit or that a fielder is at a given moment *either* catching *or* displaying *esprit de corps.*

These illustrations of category-mistakes have a common feature which must be noticed. The mistakes were made by people who did not know how to wield the concepts *University, division* and *team-spirit.* Their puzzles arose from inability to use certain items in the English vocabulary.

The theoretically interesting category-mistakes are those made by people who are perfectly competent to apply concepts, at least in the situations with which they are familiar, but are still liable in their abstract thinking to allocate those concepts to logical types to which they do not belong. An instance of a mistake of this sort would be the following story. A student of politics has learned the main differences between the British, the French and the American Constitutions, and has learned also the differences and connections between the Cabinet, Parliament, the various Ministries, the Judicature and the Church of England. But he still becomes embarrassed when asked questions about the connections between the Church of England, the Home Office and the British Constitution. For while the Church and the Home Office are institutions, the British Constitution is not another institution in the same sense of that noun. So inter-institutional relations which can be asserted or denied to hold between the Church and the Home Office cannot be asserted or denied to hold between either of them and the British Constitution. 'The British Constitution' is not a term of the same logical type as 'the Home Office' and 'the Church of England'. In a partially similar way, John Doe may be a relative, a friend, an enemy or a stranger to Richard Roe; but he cannot be any of these things to the Average Taxpayer. He knows how to talk sense in certain sorts of discussions about the Average Taxpayer, but he is baffled to say why he could not come across him in the street as he can come across Richard Roe.

It is pertinent to our main subject to notice that, so long as the student of politics continues to think of the British Constitution as a counterpart to the other institutions, he will tend to describe it as a mysteriously occult institution; and so long as John Doe continues to think of the Average Taxpayer as a fellow-citizen, he will tend to think of him as an elusive insubstantial man, a ghost who is everywhere yet nowhere.

My destructive purpose is to show that a family of radical category-mistakes is the source of the double-life theory. The representation of a person as a ghost mysteriously ensconced in a machine derives from this argument. Because, as is true, a person's thinking, feeling and purposive doing cannot be described solely in the idioms of physics, chemistry and physiology, therefore they must be described in counterpart idioms. As the human body is a complex organised unit, so the human mind must be another complex organised unit, though one made of a different sort of stuff and with a different sort of structure. Or, again, as the human body, like any other parcel of matter, is a field of causes and effects, so the mind must be another field of causes and effects, though not (Heaven be praised) mechanical causes and effects.

(3) *The Origin of the Category-mistake.*

One of the chief intellectual origins of what I have yet to prove to be the Cartesian category-mistake seems to be this. When Galileo showed that his methods of scientific discovery were competent to provide a mechanical theory which should cover every occupant of space, Descartes found in himself two conflicting motives. As a man of scientific genius he could not but endorse the claims of mechanics, yet as a religious and moral man he could not accept, as Hobbes accepted, the discouraging rider to those claims, namely that human nature differs only in degree of complexity from clockwork. The mental could not be just a variety of the mechanical.

He and subsequent philosophers naturally but erroneously availed themselves of the following escape-route. Since mental-conduct words are not to be construed as signifying the occurrence of mechanical processes, they must be construed as signifying the occurrence of non-mechanical processes; since mechanical laws explain movements in space as the effects of other movements in space, other laws must explain some of the non-spatial workings of minds as the effects of other non-spatial workings of minds. The difference between the human behaviours which we describe as intelligent and those which we describe as unintelligent must be a difference in their causation; so, while some movements of human tongues and limbs are the effects of mechanical causes, others must be the effects of non-mechanical causes, i.e. some issue from movements of particles of matter, others from workings of the mind.

The differences between the physical and the mental were thus represented as differences inside the common framework of the categories of 'thing', 'stuff', 'attribute', 'state', 'process', 'change', 'cause' and 'effect'. Minds are things, but different sorts of things from bodies; mental processes are causes and effects, but different sorts of causes and effects from bodily movements. And so on. Somewhat as the foreigner expected the University to be an extra edifice, rather like a college but also considerably different, so the repudiators of mechanism represented minds as extra centres of causal processes, rather like machines but also considerably different from them. Their theory was a para-mechanical hypothesis.

That this assumption was at the heart of the doctrine is shown by the fact that there was from the beginning felt to be a major theoretical difficulty in explaining how minds can influence and be influenced by bodies. How can a mental process, such as willing, cause spatial movements like the movements of the tongue? How can a physical change in the optic nerve have among its effects a mind's perception of a flash of light? This notorious crux by itself shows the logical mould into which Descartes pressed his theory of the mind. It was the self-same mould into which he and Galileo set their mechanics. Still unwittingly adhering to the grammar of mechanics, he tried to avert disaster by describing minds in what was merely an obverse vocabulary. The workings of minds had to be described by the mere negatives of the specific descriptions given to bodies; they are not in space, they are not motions, they are not modifications of matter, they are not accessible to public observation. Minds are not bits of clockwork, they are just bits of not-clockwork.

As thus represented, minds are not merely ghosts harnessed to machines, they are themselves just spectral machines. Though the human body is an engine, it is not quite an ordinary engine, since some of its workings are governed by another engine inside it—this interior governor-engine being one of a very special sort. It is invisible, inaudible and it has no size or weight. It cannot be taken to bits and the laws it obeys are not those known to ordinary engineers. Nothing is known of how it governs the bodily engine.

A second major crux points the same moral. Since, according to the doctrine, minds belong to the same category as bodies and since bodies are rigidly governed by mechanical laws, it seemed to many theorists to follow that minds must be similarly governed by rigid non-mechanical laws. The physical world is a deterministic system, so the mental world must be a deterministic system. Bodies cannot help the modifications that they undergo, so minds cannot help pursuing the careers fixed for them. *Responsibility, choice, merit* and *demerit* are therefore inapplicable concepts—unless the compromise solution is adopted of saying that the laws governing mental processes, unlike those governing physical processes, have the congenial attribute of being only rather rigid. The problem of the Freedom of the Will was the problem how to reconcile the hypothesis that minds are to be described in terms drawn from the categories of mechanics with the knowledge that higher-grade human conduct is not of a piece with the behaviour of machines.

It is an historical curiosity that it was not noticed that the entire argument was broken-backed. Theorists correctly assumed that any sane man could already recognise the differences between, say, rational and non-rational utterances or between purposive and automatic behaviour. Else there would have been nothing requiring to be salved from mechanism. Yet the explanation given presupposed that one person could in principle never recognise the difference between the rational and the irrational utterances issuing from other human bodies, since he could never get access to the postulated immaterial causes of some of their utterances. Save for the doubtful exception of himself, he could never tell the difference between a man and a Robot. It would have to be conceded, for example, that, for all that we can tell, the inner lives of persons who are classed as idiots or lunatics are as rational as those of anyone else. Perhaps only their overt behaviour is disappointing; that is to say, perhaps 'idiots' are not really idiotic, or 'lunatics' lunatic. Perhaps, too, some of those who are classed as sane are really idiots. According to the theory, external observers could never know how the overt behaviour of others is correlated with their mental powers and processes and so they could never know or even plausibly conjecture whether their applications of mental-conduct concepts to these other people were correct or incorrect. It would then be hazardous or impossible for a man to claim sanity or logical consistency even for himself, since he would be debarred from comparing his own performances with those of others. In short, our characterisations of persons and their performances as intelligent, prudent and virtuous or as stupid, hypocritical and cowardly could never have been made, so the problem of providing a special causal hypothesis to serve as the basis of such diagnoses would never have arisen. The question, 'How do persons differ from machines?' arose just because everyone already knew how to apply mental-conduct concepts before the new causal hypothesis was introduced. This causal hypothesis could not therefore be the source of the criteria used in those applications. Nor, of course, has the causal hypothesis in any degree improved our handling of those criteria. We still distinguish good from bad arithmetic, politic from impolitic conduct and fertile from infertile imaginations in the ways in which Descartes himself distinguished them before and after he speculated how the applicability of these criteria was compatible with the principle of mechanical causation.

He had mistaken the logic of his problem. Instead of asking by what criteria intelligent behaviour is actually distinguished from non-intelligent behaviour, he asked 'Given that the principle of mechanical causation does not tell us the difference, what other causal principle will tell it us?' He realised that the problem was not one of mechanics and assumed that it must therefore be one of some counterpart to mechanics. Not unnaturally psychology is often cast for just this role.

When two terms belong to the same category, it is proper to construct conjunctive propositions embodying them. Thus a purchaser may say that he bought a left-hand glove and a right-hand glove, but not that he bought a left-hand glove, a right-hand glove and a pair of gloves. 'She came home in a flood of tears and a sedan-chair' is a well-known joke based on the absurdity of conjoining terms of different types. It would have been equally ridiculous to construct the disjunction, 'She came home either in a flood of tears or else in a sedan-chair'. Now the dogma of the Ghost in the Machine does just this. It maintains that there exist both bodies and minds; that there occur physical processes and mental processes; that there are mechanical causes of corporeal movements and mental causes of corporeal movements. I shall argue that these and other analogous conjunctions are absurd; but, it must be noticed, the argument will not show that either of the illegitimately conjoined propositions is absurd in itself. I am not, for example, denying that there occur mental processes. Doing long division is a mental process and so is making a joke. But I am saying that the phrase 'there occur mental processes' does not mean the same sort of thing as 'there occur physical processes', and, therefore, that it makes no sense to conjoin or disjoin the two.

If my argument is successful, there will follow some interesting consequences. First, the hallowed contrast between Mind and Matter will be dissipated, but dissipated not by either of the equally hallowed absorptions of Mind by Matter or of Matter by Mind, but in quite a different way. For the seeming contrast of the two will be shown to be as illegitimate as would be the contrast of 'she came home in a flood of tears' and 'she came home in a sedan-chair'. The belief that there is a polar opposition between Mind and Matter is the belief that they are terms of the same logical type.

It will also follow that both idealism and Materialism are answers to an improper question. The 'reduction' of the material world to mental states and processes, as well as the 'reduction' of mental states and processes to physical states and processes, pre-suppose the legitimacy of the disjunction 'Either there exist minds or there exist bodies (but not both)'. It would be like saying, 'Either she bought a left-hand and a right-hand glove or she bought a pair of gloves (but not both)'.

It is perfectly proper to say, in one logical tone of voice, that there exist minds and to say, in another logical tone of voice, that there exist bodies. But these expressions do not indicate two different species of existence, for 'existence' is not a generic word like 'coloured' or 'sexed'. They indicate two different senses of 'exist', somewhat as 'rising' has different senses in 'the tide is rising', 'hopes are rising', and 'the average age of death is rising'. A man would be thought to be making a poor joke who said that three things are now rising, namely the tide, hopes and the average age of death. It would be just as good or bad a joke to say that there exist prime numbers and Wednesdays and public opinions and navies; or that there exist both minds and bodies. In the succeeding chapters I try to prove that the official theory does rest on a batch of category-mistakes by showing that logically absurd corollaries follow from it. The exhibition of these absurdities will have the constructive effect of bringing out part of the correct logic of mental-conduct concepts.

(4) *Historical Note.*

It would not be true to say that the official theory derives solely from Descartes' theories, or even from a more widespread anxiety about the implications of seventeenth century mechanics. Scholastic and Reformation theology had schooled the intellects of the scientists as well as of the laymen, philosophers and clerics of that age. Stoic-Augustinian theories of the will were embedded in the Calvinist doctrines of sin and grace; Platonic and Aristotelian theories of the intellect shaped the orthodox doctrines of the immortality of the soul. Descartes was reformulating already prevalent theological doctrines of the soul in the new syntax of Galileo. The theologian's privacy of conscience became the philosopher's privacy of consciousness, and what had been the bogy of Predestination reappeared as the bogy of Determinism.

It would also not be true to say that the two-worlds myth did no theoretical good. Myths often do a lot of theoretical good, while they are still new. One benefit bestowed by the para-mechanical myth was that it partly superannuated the then prevalent para-political myth. Minds and their Faculties had previously been described by analogies with political superiors and political subordinates. The idioms used were those of ruling, obeying, collaborating and rebelling. They survived and still survive in many ethical and some epistemological discussions. As, in physics, the new myth of occult Forces was a scientific improvement on the old myth of Final Causes, so, in anthropological and psychological theory, the new myth of hidden operations, impulses and agencies was an improvement on the old myth of dictations, deferences and disobediences.

Let us consider for a moment the claims Ryle has made concerning the inadequacy and untenability of Cartesian dualism. First, we must take Ryle's metaphor seriously, "The Ghost in the Machine." From our discussion of the Cartesian ontology and its dualism of spirit and mechanistic materialism, we should be able to grasp the meaning of Ryle's metaphor.

The "official theory" Ryle mentions is definitely Cartesian dualism. Descartes had claimed that each human being has a mind and a body. The mind and its activities are private to the individual while the body and its activities are public to outside observers. Thus there are two categories of existence here.

On the official theory, mental conduct language must refer to a nonmaterial entity—mind or soul—distinguishable from the body in virtue of being private, nonspatial, and knowable only by introspection.

Ryle introduces the notion of "category mistake" to force us to think about how unnecessary it is to postulate a spiritual mind in order to account for mental language. Remember Ryle's examples of category mistakes—the university, the army on parade, the notion of team spirit. In each of these cases Ryle suggests that it is "logically odd" for us to ask for an additional entity over and above the data we have already observed. Think back over his three examples.

Ryle then suggests that Descartes' postulation of a spiritual entity for mind is indeed the result of a category mistake. Ryle asks us to consider how we know the correct function of mental-concept language. In other words, what are the criteria we use when we realize that certain words like "understanding" are indeed significant. Ryle suggests that the criteria establishing the significance of mental language is indeed bodily behavior. Take his example of "knowing long division." Ryle asks on what grounds does the official theory demand that "knowing long division" refer to a private, spiritual, nonspatial phenomenon occurring in a spiritual entity called a mind? He asks us also to consider how we determine if someone indeed does know long division. We give one a pencil and paper and some problems in long division and see if the person can work them out. Therefore the criteria for the significant use and application of mental concepts like "understanding" is in terms of descriptions of appropriate bodily behavior. Thus a person indeed "understands" the process of long division if he or she "knows how" to work out the problems. If one could not work out any of the problems and yet still claimed to really understand the process of long division, we would have good grounds for believing that this person really did not know how to do long division. Ryle thus affirms that "understanding" has significance in our language because of certain bodily behavior which illustrates that the speaker does have a grasp of the concept in question. Again, the criteria we utilize in determining successful use of mental language is always in terms of bodily behavior and never in terms of reference to private mental phenomena.

Ryle, therefore, becomes an example of a logical behaviorist. He suggests that mental language need not refer to a realm of private, mental events at all but, rather, gains its significance in terms of manifest bodily behavior. Think, for a moment, as to how one knows if someone else really understands a solution to a given problem. Ryle's suggestion is that we become convinced that another person "understands" a concept only when that person can physically show you that he or she knows. Ryle insists that this "showing" is only possible in terms of bodily behavior. Furthermore Ryle insists that this is the total criterion for significance of mental-concept language like "understanding."

The exact status of the category mistake regarding Cartesian dualism, then, appears to be that the processes of the physical realm are transferred unnecessarily to the mental realm. Thus the "mind" in Cartesian ontology becomes an unnecessary postulation. All the activities of the mind which are expressed in mental language can be accounted for in terms of bodily behavior. Accordingly, Ryle uses ordinary language as an impetus to solve a philosophical problem. This has been a method quite common to many contemporary analytic philosophers.

Parenthetically, we might note that Ryle's claim that he is indeed only doing "logical behaviorism" and not "metaphysical behaviorism" has been the cause of much debate. For instance, note the following comments by G.J. Warnock:

> There are here and there in Ryle's book some traces of a more extreme, and in a way much simpler thesis. This thesis is that there *really exist* only bodies and other physical objects, that there *really occur* only physical events or processes, and that *all* statements ostensibly referring to minds are really categorical statements about current bodily behavior, or more commonly hypothetical statements about predicted bodily behavior; that, hence, there is really no such thing as a private, inner life at all, and that in principle everything about every individual could be known by sufficiently protracted observation of his bodily doings. . . . It cannot, I believe, be wholly an accident that many people have believed that Ryle's book presents this thesis.[5]

That Warnock's analysis implies metaphysical and not just methodological behaviorism for Ryle's theory is obvious from the above passage. Having read Ryle's work, what do you think?

Epiphenomenalism

In discussing the problem of mind-body interaction, we have placed emphasis on two alternative theories: mind-body dualism and materialism. In the history of philosophy, however, there have been other proposed solutions to this problem. These solutions have gone under many different names: idealism, double-aspect theory, epiphenominalism, parallelism, occasionalism and preestablished harmony. As some of these positions have only a historical interest for philosophers, we shall now consider only one of these positions, namely, epiphenominalism. This theory is important in that it recognizes some important problems with a strict materialism account of mental activity yet is not open to accept the full implications of Cartesian dualism.

Epiphenomenalism asserts that the "content" of a "thought" or a "mental event" is a "by-product" of the physical activities of the body, especially the brain cells and the central nervous system. Epiphenomenalism differs from dualism in that this theory asserts only a one-way causality and not equal causal interaction between mind and body. In Cartesian dualism, the mind could—at least in principle—causally interact with the body and the body with the mind. With epiphenominalism, however, the class of "mental events" is caused by the physical activities of the brain cells and the central nervous system. This by-product itself, however, has no ontological existence apart from the body. Therefore it is incapable of causally interacting with the body. The body is a necessary condition for the existence of thought. Epiphenominalism is a one-way street as far as causal efficacy is concerned.

Why would a philosopher of mind postulate epiphenominalism? What can this theory account for which straightforward materialism cannot account for?

Many contemporary epistemologists and philosophers of mind have been concerned about the unique status of mental events and the content of thought. This uniqueness has caused some philosophers to reject materialism as inadequate to explain the structure and process of mental events. The core of the dispute concerns the public-private distinction as applied to the nature of "brain event" and to the nature of "content of thought." A brain event is a public datum suitable for empirical investigation by sophisticated technological apparatus. Yet a thought is a private event not open to public empirical investigation.

Let's examine this claim for a moment. A brain event can be considered to consist of the set of biochemical reactions which occur in the brain cells during mental activity. In so far as this is a physical event, it is, at least in principle, open to empirical investigation. Yet is this biochemical reaction equivalent to the content of a thought? In other words, when an investigator, through empirical investigation, actually observes the biochemical reaction, is the investigator also at that time perceiving the content of the thought produced at that moment and perceived by the individual? If materialism is true, this equivalence must hold. Note the following schema indicating the structure of this problem:

(BIOCHEMICAL REACTION) = (CONTENT OF THOUGHT)

Consider the following example. I am participating in an experiment on dreams. By means of a sophisticated network of probes and measuring devices, the activity and biochemical reactions within my brain cells can be sufficiently measured. Suppose even, for the sake of argument, that the experimental apparatus is so sophisticated that every last physical reaction which is to occur during a dream state can be empirically measured and determined. The question which now arises is this: Is the result of the empirical investigation equivalent to the dream image? Suppose I was dreaming about my vacation last spring in Nassau. Could the mere determination of the physical reactions also permit the investigator to perceive the content of my dream image? If materialism is true, this consequence would appear to follow. Yet the unique "private" status of the content of thought—in this case, the dream image of a beach in Nassau—has caused some philosophers to question this conclusion. Therefore the difference between the status of the "brain event" and the status of the "content of a thought" has forced some philosophers to conclude that materialism is inadequate for solving the mind-body problem. This difference between the public brain-event and the private thought-content is one reason some philosophers have postulated the theory of epiphenominalism. Accordingly, the content of a thought, although it is a by-product of the physical activities of the brain cells and the central nervous system, is not equivalent to nor exhausted by those physically determined biochemical reactions.

Think about epiphenominalism for a moment. What might be some philosophical problems with this theory? For instance, what is the ontological status of "thought"? Is epiphenominalism compatible with Ryle's logical behaviorism?

The Wax Example

The last part of *Meditation II* contains Descartes' famous *wax example*. Descartes uses this illustration to aid in his discovery of the essential property of material things. Consider for a moment what Descartes is doing with this example. He is asking us to think about what happens when all of the sensible qualities of any given material object indeed change. Does something still remain even though all the sensible qualities are different? By using the wax example, Descartes will argue that even when all of the sensible qualities of any given thing have changed, we still think that the given thing is in some way still there. For example, the characteristics of a candle, before being burned, are hardness, a bright red color, a weight of ten ounces, a bayberry fragrance, and a cylindrical shape. This state we will call T_1. We light the candle and let it burn down. Now its characteristics are softness, a dull red color, a weight of four ounces, no fragrance, and an irregular shape. We will call this the T_3 state. As a result, all of the sensible characteristics at T_1 are different at T_3.

All of the sensible qualities have undergone some alteration between T_1 and T_3. However Descartes is convinced that something has remained the same. He claims that the substance, *wax*, has not disappeared but has perdured during the change. Obviously this is an explicit example of the maxim we considered earlier — "Qualities belong to a substance."

A chemist mixes hydrogen with oxygen and heats the combination with a spark of potassium chlorate. The result of the experiment is water. Yet even though the sensible appearances of the two gases have changed, it is still conceivable that the two elements are present in the new compound substance in some form. Another example is the growth of a human. A person progresses through the stages of embryo, baby, youngster, adolescent, maturity, and senility. Through all of these changes, we still believe that the same person essentially is there.

Descartes is concerned over the nature of the material substance. He will suggest that the extension has remained the same. Descartes is asking us to consider the hypothesis that what essentially determines any physical object is its extension. To be a physical object demands a "place in space." An essential characteristic of any physical object is that it be extended. Accordingly, extension becomes the essential property of physical objects.

Once extension is established as the essential characteristic determining physical objects, Descartes must analyze how it is that this type of nonperceptual knowledge is attained. Obviously it is not a type of sense knowledge. In the wax example, all of the sensible characteristics have changed. Take Descartes seriously here — every quality which is apparent to our external senses changes from T_1 to T_3. To solve this problem, Descartes suggests that there must be another means of attaining knowledge. Descartes will refer to this other means as *conception*. Conception is connected with the Cartesian notion of "innate ideas." An innate idea is part of the structure of the mind; it is built into the mind independently of any sense experiences. It is not acquired by sense experience in any way whatsoever. We shall discuss the structure of the innate idea later. At any length, Descartes utilizes the wax example to indicate that humans have an innate idea of extension. Extension (i.e., being spread out) is the essential property of a material substance. Obviously this is intricately connected with the claims of atomism. The atoms are the basic particles of the external world. Insofar as an atom is the basic particle, it occupies space. Whatever occupies space must be extended — i.e., it must be spread out over the amount of space in a definite area. Accordingly, Descartes is quite consistent when he claims that extension is the essential property of any material substance. Nonetheless, Descartes is not strictly speaking an atomist.

By way of summary, consider for a moment the ontological scheme Descartes has established. There are two categories of existents: (a) minds and (b) matter. A mind has the essential property of thinking, while a piece of matter has the essential property of being extended. This is an ontology of radical dualism. E.A. Burtt sums up this dualism nicely:

> Such, then, is Descartes' famous dualism—one world consisting of a huge, mathematical machine, extended in space; and another world consisting of unextended, thinking spirits. And whatever is not mathematical or depends at all on the activity of thinking substance, especially the so-called secondary qualities, belongs with the latter.[6]

That the Cartesian world view should have caused much philosophical criticism should be apparent. As we have seen, many philosophers have been disturbed greatly over some of the implications of this dualism.

So far in the *Meditations,* Descartes has established two propositions. He is convinced that the proposition asserting his existence is true and that the proposition describing his nature as essentially consisting of his ability to think is true. From these two propositions, Descartes will deduce the rest of his metaphysical system. Remember our discussion before *Meditation I.* Descartes, we realized, was very much influenced by the mathematical method. The central feature of this method is deductive demonstration. In *Meditation III,* Descartes will show how he intends to illustrate the use of deduction in his ontology. By a deductive machinery based on the two propositions he has already established, Descartes will prove the existence of an "all-perfect being."

MEDITATION III: OF GOD—THAT HE EXISTS

René Descartes

I will now close my eyes, I will stop my ears, I will turn away my senses from their objects, I will even efface from my consciousness all the images of corporeal things; or at least, because this can hardly be accomplished, I will consider them as empty and false; and thus, holding converse only with myself, and closely examining my nature, I will endeavor to obtain by degrees a more intimate and familiar knowledge of myself. I am a thinking (conscious) thing, that is, a being who doubts, affirms, denies, knows a few objects, and is ignorant of many,—[who loves, hates], wills, refuses, who imagines likewise, and perceives; for, as I before remarked, although the things which I perceive or imagine are perhaps nothing at all apart from me [and in themselves], I am nevertheless assured that those modes of consciousness which I call perceptions and imaginations, in as far only as they are modes of consciousness, exist in me. And in the little I have said I think I have summed up all that I really know, or at least all that up to this time I was aware I knew. Now, as I am endeavoring to extend my knowledge

Reprinted from John Veitch, trans., *The Method, Meditations and Philosophy of Descartes* (Washington: M. Walter Dunne, 1901).

more widely, I will use circumspection, and consider with care whether I can still discover in myself anything further which I have not yet hitherto observed. I am certain that I am a thinking thing; but do I not therefore likewise know what is required to render me certain of a truth? In this first knowledge, doubtless, there is nothing that gives me assurance of its truth except the clear and distinct perception of what I affirm, which would not indeed be sufficient to give me the assurance that what I say is true, if it could ever happen that anything I thus clearly and distinctly perceived should prove false; and accordingly it seems to me that I may now take as a general rule, that all that is very clearly and distinctly apprehended (conceived) is true.

Nevertheless, I before received and admitted many things as wholly certain and manifest, which yet I afterward found to be doubtful. What, then, were those? They were the earth, the sky, the stars, and all the other objects which I was in the habit of perceiving by the senses. But what was it that I clearly [and distinctly] perceived in them? Nothing more than that the ideas and the thoughts of those objects were presented to my mind. And even now I do not deny that these ideas are found in my mind. But there was yet another thing which I affirmed, and which, from having been accustomed to believe it; I thought I clearly perceived, although, in truth, I did not perceive it at all; I mean the existence of objects external to me, from which those ideas proceeded, and to which they had a perfect resemblance; and it was here I was mistaken, or if I judged correctly, this assuredly was not to be traced to any knowledge I possessed (the force of my perception, Lat.).

But when I considered any matter in arithmetic and geometry, that was very simple and easy, as, for example, that two and three added together make five, and things of this sort, did I not view them with at least sufficient clearness to warrant me in affirming their truth? Indeed, if I afterward judged that we ought to doubt of these things, it was for no other reason than because it occurred to me that a God might perhaps have given me such a nature as that I should be deceived, even respecting the matters that appeared to me the most evidently true. But as often as this preconceived opinion of the sovereign power of a God presents itself to my mind, I am constrained to admit that it is easy for him, if he wishes it, to cause me to err, even in matters where I think I possess the highest evidence; and, on the other hand, as often as I direct my attention to things which I think I apprehend with great clearness, I am so persuaded of their truth that I naturally break out into expressions such as these: Deceive me who may, no one will yet ever be able to bring it about that I am not, so long as I shall be conscious that I am, or at any future time cause it to be true that I have never been, it being now true that I am, or make two and three more or less than five, in supposing which, and other like absurdities, I discover a manifest contradiction.

And in truth, as I have no ground for believing that Deity is deceitful, and as, indeed, I have not even considered the reasons by which the existence of a Deity of any kind is established, the ground of doubt that rests only on this supposition is very slight, and, so to speak, metaphysical. But, that I may be able wholly to remove it, I must inquire whether there is a God, as soon as an opportunity of doing so shall present itself; and if I find that there is a God, I must examine likewise whether he can be a deceiver; for, without the knowledge of these two truths, I do not see that I can ever be certain of anything. And that I may be enabled to examine this without interrupting the order of meditation I have proposed to myself [which is, to pass by degrees from the notions that I shall find first in my mind to those I shall afterward discover in it], it is necessary at this stage to divide all my thoughts into certain classes, and to consider in which of these classes truth and error are, strictly speaking, to be found.

Of my thoughts some are, as it were, images of things, and to these alone properly belongs the name IDEA; as when I think [represent to my mind] a man, a chimera, the sky, an angel or God. Others, again, have certain other forms; as when I will, fear, affirm, or deny, I always, indeed, apprehend something as the object of my thought, but I also embrace in thought something more than the representation of the object; and of this class of thoughts some are called volitions or affections, and others judgments.

Now, with respect to idea, if these are considered only in themselves, and are not referred to any object beyond them, they cannot, properly speaking, be false; for, whether I imagine a goat or chimera, it is not less true that I imagine the one than the other. Nor need we fear that falsity may exist in the will or affections; for, although I may desire objects that are wrong, and even then never existed, it is still true that I desire them. There thus only remain our judgments, in which we must take diligent heed that we be not deceived. But the chief and most ordinary error that arises in them consists in judging that the ideas which are in us are like or conformed to the things that are external to us; for assuredly, if we but considered the ideas themselves as certain modes of our thought (consciousness), without referring them to anything beyond, they would hardly afford any occasion of error.

But among these ideas, some appear to me to be innate, others adventitious, and others to be made by myself (factitious); for, as I have the power of conceiving what is called a thing, or a truth, or a thought, it seems to me that I hold this power from no other source than my own nature; but if I now hear a noise, if I see the sun, or if I feel heat, I have all along judged that these sensations proceeded from certain objects existing out of myself; and, in fine, it appears to me that sirens, hippogryphs, and the like, are inventions of my own mind. But I may even perhaps come to be of opinion that all my ideas are of the class which I call adventitious, or that they are all innate, or that they are all factitious; for I have not yet clearly discovered their true origin; and what I have here principally to do is to consider, with reference to those that appear to come from certain objects without me, what grounds there are for thinking them like these objects.

The first of these grounds is that it seems to me I am so taught by nature; and the second that I am conscious that those ideas are not dependent on my will, and therefore not on myself, for they are frequently presented to me against my will, as at present, whether I will or not, I feel heat; and I am thus persuaded that this sensation or idea (*sensum vel ideam*) of heat is produced in me by something different from myself, viz., by the heat of the fire by which I sit. And it is very reasonable to suppose that this object impresses me with its own likeness rather than any other thing.

But I must consider whether these reasons are sufficiently strong and convincing. When I speak of being taught by nature in this matter, I understand by the word nature only a certain spontaneous impetus that impels me to believe in a resemblance between ideas and their objects, and not a natural light that affords a knowledge of its truth. But these two things are widely different; for what the natural light shows to be true can be in no degree doubtful, as, for example, that I am because I doubt, and other truths of the like kind; inasmuch as I possess no other faculty whereby to distinguish truth from error, which can teach me the falsity of what the natural light declares to be true, and which is equally trustworthy; but with respect to [seemingly] natural impulses, I have observed, when the question related to the choice of right or wrong in action, that they frequently led me to take the worse part; nor do I see that I have any better ground for following them in what relates to truth and errors. Then, with respect to the other reason, which is that because these ideas do not depend on my will, they must arise from objects existing without me, I do not find it more convincing than the former; for just as those natural impulses, of which I have lately spoken, are found in me, notwithstanding that they are not always in harmony with my will, so likewise it may be that I possess some power not sufficiently known to myself capable of producing ideas without the aid of external objects, and, indeed, it has always hitherto appeared to me that they are formed during sleep, by some power of this nature, without the aid of aught external. And, in fine, although I should grant that they proceeded from those objects, it is not a necessary consequence that they must be like them. On the contrary, I have observed, in a number of instances, that there was a great difference between the object and its idea. Thus, for example, I find in my mind two wholly diverse ideas of the sun; the one, by which it appears to me extremely small draws its origin from the senses, and should be placed in the class of adventitious ideas; the other, by which it seems to be many times larger than the whole earth, is taken up on astronomical grounds, that is, elicited from certain notions born with me, or is framed by myself in some other manner. These two ideas cannot certainly both resemble the same sun; and reason teaches me that the one which seems to have immediately emanated from it is the most unlike. And these things sufficiently prove that hitherto it has not been from a certain and deliberate judgment, but only from a sort of blind impulse, that I believed in the existence of certain things different from myself, which, by the organs of sense, or by whatever other means it might be, conveyed their ideas or images into my mind [and impressed it with their likenesses].

But there is still another way of inquiring whether, of the objects whose ideas are in my mind, there are any that exist out of me. If ideas are taken in so far only as they are certain modes of consciousness, I do not remark any difference or inequality among them, and all seem, in the same manner, to proceed from myself; but, considering them as images, of which one represents one thing and another a different, it is evident that a great diversity obtains among them. For, without doubt, those that represent substances are something more, and contain in themselves, so to speak, more objective reality [that is, participate by representation in higher degrees of being or perfection], than those that represent only modes or accidents; and again, the idea by which I conceive a God [sovereign], eternal, infinite, [immutable], all-knowing, all-powerful, and the creator of all things that are out of himself, this, I say, has certainly in it more objective reality than those ideas by which finite substances are represented.

Now, it is manifest by the natural light that there must at least be as much reality in the efficient and total cause as in its effect; for whence can the effect draw its reality if not from its cause? And how could the cause communicate to it this reality unless it possessed it in itself? And hence it follows, not only that what is cannot be produced by what is not, but likewise that the more perfect, in other words, that which contains in itself more reality, cannot be the effect of the less perfect; and this is not only evidently true of those effects, whose reality is actual or formal, but likewise of ideas, whose reality is only considered as objective. Thus, for example, the stone that is not yet in existence, not only cannot now commence to be, unless it be produced by that which possesses in itself, formally or eminently, all that enters into its composition, [in other words, by that which contains in itself the same properties that are in the stone, or others superior to them]; and heat can only be produced in a subject that was before devoid of it, by a cause that is of an order, [degree or kind], at least as perfect as heat; and so of the others. But further, even the idea of the heat, or of the stone, cannot exist in me unless it be put there by a cause that contains, at least, as much reality as I conceive existent in the heat or in the stone: for although that cause may not transmit into my idea anything of its actual or formal reality, we ought not on this account to imagine that it is less real; but we ought to consider that, [as every idea is a work of the mind], its nature is such as of itself to demand no other formal reality than that which it borrows from our consciousness, of which it is but a mode [that is, a manner or way of thinking]. But in order than an idea may contain this objective reality rather than that, it must doubtless derive it from some cause in which is found at least as much formal reality as the idea contains of objective; for, if we suppose that there is found in an idea anything which was not in its cause, it must of course derive this from nothing. But, however imperfect may be the mode of existence by which a thing is objectively [or by representation] in the understanding by its idea, we certainly cannot, for all that, allege that this mode of existence is nothing, nor, consequently, that the idea owes its origin to nothing. Nor must it be imagined that, since the reality which is considered in these ideas is only objective, the same reality need not be formally (actually) in the causes of these ideas, but only objectively: for, just as the mode of existing objectively belongs to ideas by their peculiar nature, so likewise the mode of existing formally appertains to the causes of these ideas (at least to the first and principal), by their peculiar nature. And although an idea may give rise to another idea, this regress cannot, nevertheless, be infinite; we must in the end reach a first idea, the cause of which is, as it were, the archetype in which all the reality [or perfection] that is found objectively [or by representation] in these ideas is contained formally [and in act]. I am thus clearly taught by the natural light that ideas exist in me as pictures or images, which may, in truth, readily fall short of the perfection of the objects from which they are taken, but can never contain anything greater or more perfect.

And in proportion to the time and care with which I examine all those matters, the conviction of their truth brightens and becomes distinct. But, to sum up, what conclusion shall I draw from it all? It is this: if the objective reality [or perfection] of any one of my ideas be such as clearly to convince me, that this same reality exists in me neither formally nor eminently, and if, as follows from this, I myself cannot be the cause of it, it is a necessary consequence that I am not alone in the world, but that there is besides myself some other being who exists as the cause of that idea; while, on the contrary, if no such idea be found in my mind, I shall have no sufficient ground of assurance of the existence of any other being besides myself; for, after a most careful search, I have, up to this moment, been unable to discover any other ground.

But, among these my ideas, besides that which represents myself, respecting which there can be here no difficulty, there is one that represents a God; others that represent corporeal and inanimate things; others angels; others animals; and, finally, there are some that represent men like myself. But with respect to the ideas that represent other men, or animals, or angels, I can easily suppose that they were formed by the mingling and composition of the other ideas which I have of myself, of corporeal things, and of God, although they were, apart from myself, neither men, animals, nor angels. And with regard to the ideas of corporeal objects, I never discovered in them anything so great or excellent which I myself did not appear capable of originating; for, by considering these ideas closely and scrutinizing them individually, in the same way that I yesterday examined the idea of wax, I find that there is but little in them that is clearly and distinctly perceived. As belonging to the class of things that are clearly apprehended, I recognize the following, viz, magnitude or extension in length, breadth, and depth; figure, which results from the termination of extension; situation, which bodies of diverse figures preserve with reference to each other; and motion or the change of situation; to which may be added substance, duration, and number. But with regard to light, colors, sounds, odors, tastes, heat, cold, and the other tactile qualities, they are thought with so much obscurity and confusion, that I cannot determine even whether they are true or false; in other words, whether or not the ideas I have of these qualities are in truth the ideas of real objects. For although I before remarked that it is only in judgments that formal falsity, or falsity properly so called, can be met with, there may nevertheless be found in ideas a certain material falsity, which arises when they represent what is nothing as if it were something. Thus, for example, the ideas I have of cold and heat are so far from being clear and distinct, that I am unable from them to discover whether cold is only the privation of heat, or heat the privation of cold; or whether they are or are not real qualities: and since, ideas being as it were images that can be none that does not seem to us to represent some object, the idea which represents cold as something real and positive will not improperly be called false, if it be correct to say that cold is nothing but a privation of heat; and so in other cases. To ideas of this kind, indeed, it is not necessary that I should assign any author besides myself: for if they are false, that is, represent objects that are unreal, the natural light teaches me that they proceed from nothing; in other words, that they are in me only because something is wanting to the perfection of my nature; but if these ideas are true, yet because they exhibit to me so little reality that I cannot even distinguish the object represented from non-being, I do not see why I should not be the author of them.

With reference to those ideas of corporeal things that are clear and distinct, there are some which, as appears to me, might have been taken from the idea I have of myself, as those of substance, duration, number, and the like. For when I think that a stone is a substance, or a thing capable of existing of itself, and that I am likewise a substance, although I conceive that I am a thinking and non-extended thing, and that the stone, on the contrary, is extended and unconscious, there being thus the greatest diversity between the two concepts, yet these two ideas seem to have this in common that they both represent substances. In the same way, when I think of myself as now existing, and recollect besides that I existed some time ago, and when I am conscious of various thoughts whose number I know, I then acquire the ideas of duration and number, which I can afterward transfer to as many objects as I please. With respect to the other qualities that go to make up the ideas of corporeal objects, viz, extension, figure, situation, and motion, it is true that they are not formally in me, since I am merely a thinking being; but because they are only certain modes of substance, and because I myself am a substance, it seems possible that they may be contained in me eminently.

There only remains, therefore, the idea of God, in which I must consider whether there is anything that cannot be supposed to originate with myself. By the name God, I understand a substance infinite, [eternal, immutable], independent, all-knowing, all-powerful, and by which I myself, and every other thing that exists, if any such there be, were created. But these properties are so great and excellent, that the more attentively I consider them the less I feel persuaded that the idea I have of them owes its origin to myself alone. And thus it is absolutely necessary to conclude, from all that I have before said, that God exists: for though the idea of substance be in my mind owing to this, that I myself am a substance, I should not, however, have the idea of an infinite substance, seeing I am a finite being, unless it were given me by some substance in reality infinite.

And I must not imagine that I do not apprehend the infinite by a true idea, but only by the negation of the finite, in the same way that I comprehend repose and darkness by the negation of motion and light: since, on the contrary, I clearly perceive that there is more reality in the infinite substance than in the finite, and therefore that in some way I possess the perception (notion) of the infinite before that of the finite, that is, the perception of God before that of myself, for how could I know that I doubt, desire, or that something is wanting to me, and that I am not wholly perfect, if I possessed no idea of a being more perfect than myself, by comparison of which I knew the deficiencies of my nature?

And it cannot be said that this idea of God is perhaps materially false, and consequently that it may have arisen from nothing [in other words, that it may exist in me from my imperfection], as I before said of the ideas of heat and cold, and the like; for, on the contrary, as this idea is very clear and distinct, and contains in itself more objective reality than any other, there can be no one of itself more true, or less open to the suspicion of falsity.

The idea, I say, of a being supremely perfect, and infinite, is in the highest degree true; for although, perhaps, we may imagine that such a being does not exist, we cannot, nevertheless, suppose that his idea represents nothing real, as I have already said of the idea of cold. It is likewise clear and distinct in the highest degree, since whatever the mind clearly and distinctly conceives as real or true, and as implying any perfection, is contained entire in this idea. And this is true, nevertheless, although I do not comprehend the infinite, and although there may be in God an infinity of things that I cannot comprehend, nor perhaps even compass by thought in any way; for it is of the nature of the infinite that it should not be comprehended by the finite; and it is enough that I rightly understand this, and judge that all which I clearly perceive, and in which I know there is some perfection, and perhaps also an infinity of properties of which I am ignorant, and formally or eminently in God, in order that the idea I have of him may become the most true, clear, and distinct of all the ideas in my mind. . . .

In order to understand this proof for the existence of God, it is important to remember that Descartes asserts that the concept of God is one of absolute perfection. Absolute perfection means a fully complete being. God, as the all-perfect being, is necessarily all good, all holy, omniscient, omnipotent, and so forth. Furthermore Descartes is convinced that he has an idea of this all-perfect being. Therefore his question is: From whence did this idea arise? Stated a little differently, Descartes has already established his own existence as a thinking being. He now examines the content of his mind. One of the ideas he discovers is that of an all-perfect being. Descartes then seeks to determine the source of this idea. As we noted in the proof, Descartes insists that only God can explain sufficiently the origin of the idea of an all-perfect being. Simply put, God is needed in order to explain the existence of the idea of the all-perfect being in Descartes' mind. However we must bear with Descartes for a moment. His proof is far more subtle than we probably believe it to be right now.

Formal and Intentional Existence

In order to better understand the machinery of Descartes' argument, it is necessary first to realize that fundamentally Descartes is using two senses of existence. The concept of existence is not univocal, i.e., it does not have a single meaning for Descartes. Descartes places existence into two categories: (a) formal existence, and (b) objective or intentional existence. By formal existence Descartes means what we might refer to as the "furniture of the world."

Another way of putting this is to say that the category of formally existing things contains all the things which exist in reality. This category contains both material substances and spiritual substances. Thus, in the Cartesian ontology, a table, a brick, a tree, God, and a human mind are all formally existing things. It is very important to realize that a formal existent is not equivalent to a material existent. In brief, what is formally existent is what exists independently of any knowing mind. Parenthetically, to assert a formal existence is to deny idealism.

Objective or intentional existence refers to the kind of existence the content of an idea has in the human mind. A formally existing brick, when it is the object of knowledge by a knower—i.e., when it is known by a knower—has an objective existence in the mind of the knower. The objective existence refers to the content of the idea of the brick, a brick which in turn has a formal existence outside of the mind. In other words, the content of a representation is an objective existence. The very thing in the external world is a formal existence. From this discussion, it should be apparent that in order for there to be any objective existents, there must be minds which have formal existence. In a truncated world, i.e., a world without minds, there would be no realities which possessed objective existence. The objective reality refers to the representative function of an idea which pictures something beyond or other than itself. The notion of intentional existence becomes clear here. For our purposes, intentional existence and objective existence will become univocal concepts. An idea is not an object or an end in itself. Its function is to represent some object other than itself.

While discussing the formal-objective reality distinction, it will be useful to consider the implications of this distinction on contemporary philosophy. Twentieth-century epistemologists have treated this distinction in their discussions of the problem of *intentionality*. The characteristic of intentionality is that property which generically distinguishes a knower from a nonknower. The contemporary American philosopher, Roderick Chisholm, describes the function of intentionality by claiming that it is ". . . a funny kind of characteristic that ordinary physical things don't have."[7]

Intentionality is thus the characteristic of a knower. Basically, the gist is that an idea "points to" or "intends" some object beyond itself. Intentionality signifies a certain "aboutness." An idea is about things other than itself. The characteristic of intentionality should bring out the basic representational function of ideas. Franz Brentano (1838-1917) reinstilled into philosophical discussions the use and significance of the concept of intentionality. Note the following passage from his "Psychologie vom empirischen Standpunkt," in which Brentano forces us to think about the differences between ideas and things.

> The data of our consciousness make up a world which, taken in its entirety, falls into two great classes, the class of *physical* and the class of *mental* phenomena. . . .
> Every mental phenomenon is characterized by what the scholastics of the middle ages called the intentional or mental inexistence of an object, and what we, although with not entirely unambiguous terms, would call the reference towards an object . . . or an immanent objectivity.[8]

The following illustration indicates the functions of formal and objective, or intentional, reality:

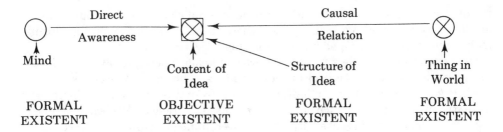

Before continuing, it is important to realize that, as the preceding scheme illustrates, an idea itself has both a formal and an objective existence. It has a formal existence in that it is really and actually present in the mind of a knower. In other words a person who actually has an idea has a different structure in his or her mind than a person who does not have the idea. The objective reality of the idea comes from the representative function of the idea itself. The objective or intentional reality consists of the "content" of the idea—what the idea represents. However, before it can represent, the idea must have a certain structure within the mind itself. This structure would be the formal reality of the idea. A useful analogy might be to consider a mirror. A mirror has a silvered-glass backing located within a wood or metal frame. This is the *formal* reality of the mirror. Beyond this ontological structure, the mirror also can depict or represent another object on it. The representation in the mirror of a person standing in front of the mirror would be the objective reality. Thus the "content" represented is different from the structure itself. Try to construct a similar analogy using the notion of a color television set. What would be the formal reality? The objective reality? From this discussion, we should see that it is not "double-talk" to insist that an idea has both an intentional and a formal existence. We must grasp the meaning of the objective-formal reality distinction if we are ever to understand the structure of Descartes' proof for God in *Meditation III*.

The Principle of Causality

In addition to the formal-objective existence distinction, Descartes accepts as a philosophical maxim the proposition that "there must be as much reality in the cause as in the effect." This is a basic statement of what philosophers in the Middle Ages understood to be the principle of causality. In essence, this principle asserts that an effect cannot occur without a corresponding proportional cause. Fundamentally, the proportional correspondence between effect and cause constitutes Descartes' understanding of this principle. By using common sense, we might say that a baby cannot lift a 100-pound lead weight because the baby does not have the causally efficacious power to get the weight off the ground. To lift the 100 pounds requires at least 101 pounds of opposite force. This is Descartes' meaning in positing the principle that "there must be as much reality in the cause as in the effect."

In addition to applying this principle to cases of physical causality, Descartes uses it to discuss the origin of ideas in the human mind. To use the Cartesian vocabulary, the objective content of an idea must be caused by a reality with as much formal reality as is represented in the objective reality. In other words, there must be a corresponding proportional cause for all of our ideas. If an idea has an objective reality, then there must be a corresponding formal reality which could serve as a cause for this objective content.

Descartes then considers three categories of ideas. There are (a) innate ideas, (b) adventitious ideas, and (c) fabricated ideas. The innate ideas are built-in structured ideas which each individual has from the moment of birth. An adventitious idea is one which comes from sense experience. A fabricated idea is one which has been invented by the knower himself. However Descartes is insistent that each of these categories of ideas must be subsumed under the principle of causality. In order to satisfy the Cartesian search for certainty, each objective reality must have an adequate causal explanation.

Before discussing Descartes' proof for God in detail, we must consider some important terminology. Philosophical proofs for the existence of God can be considered to be essentially of two kinds: (a) *a priori* proofs and (b) *a posteriori* proofs. An a priori proof is one whose structure is independent of sense experience, while an a posteriori proof depends upon sense experience. We shall discuss these distinctions in greater detail in chapter 5. Descartes' proof, in *Meditation III*, is an example of an a priori proof. By reflecting on our discussion of the structure of the Cartesian methodology so far, we will see that Descartes' use of an a priori argument is completely consistent with the methodological scepticism involved with representative realism. Insofar as Descartes has argued against the validity of sense knowledge and has concluded that the only indubitable proposition depends upon the cogito argument, then the possibility of an a posteriori argument is unavailable to him. Accordingly, if Descartes wants to discuss the possibility of a proof for God's existence at all, he is forced logically to consider an a priori argument. Any insistence on an a posteriori methodology would be inconsistent with the methodological doubt.

Think back to what we discussed concerning the structure of the *Meditations*. Descartes' intention is to demonstrate an entire metaphysical system starting from an indubitable set of propositions. He begins his discussion of the proof for God's existence by asking himself from whence came the idea of the all-perfect being he has within his mind. Using the philosophical terminology we have just learned, Descartes is concerned about what formal existent could have caused the objective representation he has in his mind. He begins with the notion that he introspectively is aware of the idea of an all-perfect being. Of course this is an awareness of the objective reality of an idea—the content of an all-perfect being. Assuming that he indeed has this objective reality, Descartes is searching for an adequate causal explanation for this objective reality. In other words, granted that the representative function of the idea is of an all-perfect being, what is causally efficacious as a formal reality capable of causing this corresponding objective content?

Descartes considers the possibility that he might have received the idea of the all-perfect being from the external world by means of his senses. Descartes immediately dismisses this. Obviously, he has already argued satisfactorily in *Meditation I* that sense knowledge is in principle open to scepticism. His reasons, however, for rejecting sense knowledge here are more sophisticated than those given in *Meditation I*. Descartes reiterates Plato's problem concerning the inability of the senses to grasp anything of an absolute or essential nature. Descartes modifies this claim and asserts that a human sense perceiver has never been directly aware of an all-perfect being by merely using his senses alone. As Plato claimed in the *Phaedo,* a sense perceiver is aware of equal sticks but never of equality itself. Accordingly, Descartes claims that it is in principle impossible for the senses to be aware of the source of all absolutes, which is what the all-perfect being is.

Think for a moment about the nature of Descartes' claim here. One might object that he or she has never been directly aware of a mermaid either, or a leprechaun, or a gremlin. Yet he or she can indeed have an idea of such "objects." The force of this objection is that we do at times have images of nonexistent objects—fictitious things like Mickey Mouse, Pegasus, and mermaids. Even though these "things" have no formal existence, nonetheless, they do have an objective existence. Descartes' response is that every perceiver has, at sometime or another, perceived the component parts of, for example, a mermaid. If we have the image of a mermaid, then we, at one time or another, were aware of a "woman" and of a "fish." The mind then combines these simple notions to form a composite image of a mermaid. The interesting point is that Descartes is assuming that all our ideas of nonformally existing things are compound images. Descartes suggests that from a group of formally existing things, we may fabricate a new object in our minds which has its own objective reality. With this distinction, the mermaid does not have to have a formal existence even though it may have an objective reality. Descartes will further suggest, however, that the qualities of the divine being are so perfect that they are beyond the comprehension of any sense knowledge. Accordingly, the objective reality of the all-perfect being transcends any possible component parts which might have been grasped through our external senses. Descartes then concludes that the idea of a mermaid and the idea of God—the all-perfect being— are in principle different in structure and character.

Descartes considers the possibility that he might have conjured up this idea of an all-perfect being from the confines or structure of his own mind. This too is rejected. Descartes argues that he himself is an imperfect being. The principle of causality is invoked to rule out the possibility that an imperfect being could ever be the source or cause of an idea of an all-perfect being. Next Descartes claims that, insofar as he is a doubting being, then he is an imperfect being. And a perfect being would have neither the ability nor the need to doubt. Accordingly, Descartes asserts that he could not have fashioned the idea of an all-perfect being from his own mind as a cause since he is a doubting, hence imperfect, being.

Think about the procedure Descartes has followed. Note that there is a philosophical blur here concerning the notion of a perfect idea. Descartes is quite unclear regarding the significance of this perfect intentional entity. Is he referring to the structure of the idea or to the objective content of the idea? This author suggests that he is referring to the content, but it is unclear from the texts what Descartes really means. What difference can be seen if one interpretation is compared to the other?

Having ruled out the other possibilities, Descartes concludes by claiming that the objective reality of the all-perfect being must have come from a formally existing all-perfect being. This formally existing all-perfect being is what persons in the Judeo-Christian tradition have referred to as God. The structure of the argument is philosophically interesting. Descartes proceeds from an analysis of intentionality linked together with his principle of causality to evoke an a priori proof for the existence of an all-perfect being. Schematically, we might reconstruct Descartes' argument in the following manner:

1. Every entity has a cause.
2. The cause must have as much reality as the effect.
3. Descartes has an idea of perfection.
4. Because he doubts, Descartes is not perfect.

5. Therefore God, the all-perfect being, exists.

In effect, Descartes has established that he is not God. Whatever the objective merits of the argument, it is still an interesting attempt at philosophical analysis involving a theory of intentionality and a principle of causality. Does this argument meet our standards of philosophical analysis?

In using critical philosophy upon this proof in *Meditation III,* at least three principal problems become evident. The first problem is the rather obvious point that Descartes may very well be wrong in claiming that everyone has an objective reality—an idea—in his or her mind of an all-perfect being. It must be remembered that Descartes did live in a particular religious milieu in which conversations about an all-perfect being were engaged in more or less universally. Obviously, in the twenieth century, this omnipresent religious climate is not prevalent.

Second, the above observation becomes philosophically interesting when it is linked with Descartes' view of the mind. Descartes is a rationalist. Philosophers of a rationalist persuasion have argued in favor of a structured mind. In other words, the mind has built-in features. Descartes calls these built-in features *innate ideas.* The rationalists use the innate ideas to interpret the world. Descartes argues that the idea of the all-perfect being is indeed an innate idea which every human person possesses in virtue of being a human being. As we shall see in the next chapter, the empiricist philosophers will claim that the mind is completely unstructured, a blank slate, as they claim. Descartes' argument hinges on the validity of a rationalist critique of mental acts. If rationalism fails, then so does Descartes' proof that God exists.

Third, an objection can be made concerning Descartes' thesis of intentionality. The notion that an objective reality must have as much reality as its corresponding formal reality is a very difficult proposition to scrutinize philosophically. In fact, some philosophers have claimed that it is an incomprehensible notion. This is probably the most difficult part of the proof to analyze adequately. What this maxim means is not lucidly explained by Descartes.

There is another minor proof in *Meditation III.* Descartes realizes that he is not the cause of his own existence. He did not cause himself because, as he has already noticed, he is an imperfect being in that he is a doubting being. If he had caused himself, he would not have created himself as an imperfect being. Since he is not the author of his own being, some other being is necessary in order to satisfy the principle of causality. Thus God exists. A crucial presupposition here is Descartes' notion that "perfection" denotes "completeness." Again this is probably a notion Descartes inherited from his medieval predecessors who were greatly influenced by Plotinus.

Finally, in *Meditation III,* two other unique Cartesian notions must be mentioned. The first concerns the "light of nature." Descartes seems to be referring to a truth which is self-evident. Accordingly, the light of nature would be similar to a direct intuition or intuitive awareness. Descartes is not completely lucid in considering the light of nature. However the notion of intuitive insight perhaps best exemplifies what he meant.

Second, Descartes also mentions that God, the all-perfect being, is not a deceiver. This is the case because deception would indeed imply a deficiency. God, however, is the all-perfect being. Therefore God could not be a formally existing evil deceiver. This claim is important because of Descartes' argument of establishing the existence of the external world in *Meditation VI.*

Descartes and the External World

There are a total of six *Meditations.* However we shall not discuss and analyze all six in our present inquiry. In *Meditation IV* Descartes presents his analysis of truth and falsity; in *Meditation V* another argument for God's existence is offered; and in *Meditation VI* Descartes establishes the existence of the external world as a formally existing reality. We shall now briefly consider Descartes' procedure for establishing the formal reality of the external world. Then we shall conclude our inquiry into Cartesian rationalism by considering some problems unique to Descartes' philosophy.

In order to adequately grasp Descartes' argument in *Meditation VI,* remember the structure of representative realism. On this model of perception, which Descartes had accepted because of his adherence to the tenets of the new science, the direct object of perception is always an *objective reality* separated from and causally distinct from the objects formally existing in the external world. We noted at the time representative realism was discussed that the principal problem with this theory is to connect the idea (the objective reality) with the world (the formal reality). Representative realism drives a wedge between that which is known and that which is. In *Meditation VI,* Descartes will attempt to bridge this gap between knowledge and the world. His argument accomplishing this feat depends upon the previous claims of his ontology. In effect, this *Meditation* is an attempt to establish the ultimate veracity of sense knowledge. This move is directly connected with the attempt to justify the formal existence of the external world, given Descartes' perceptual scheme of representative realism.

To accomplish this task, Descartes argues from an epistemological position. Two principles which underlie his argument are:

1. Sense and imagination are knowing powers or faculties which do not depend upon the mind.
2. God, the all-perfect being, is not a deceiver.

The claim that the sense faculties and the imagination are indeed distinct from the mind is crucial for Descartes' argument. To establish this distinction, Descartes uses the following example concerning the *chiligon*—the thousand-sided figure.

The point Descartes is driving at is that the functions of the imagination and the mind are distinct. In his example, both the imagination and the mind, or intellect, can be aware of a triangle. We can both imagine and conceive the nature of a triangle. In other words, we can picture to ourselves via our imaginations an image of a triangle, and we can also understand the function of a triangle as used in Euclidean geometry. Descartes' point is that having a concept is different from having an image. This is where the chiligon example applies. With a chiligon, although we may have a concept of it in our mind, we are unable to conjure up a thousand-sided figure with our imagination alone. Think for a moment about the force of Descartes' suggestion. Try to picture a figure with a thousand sides. Obviously, Descartes is stressing the similarity of a chiligon to a circle. Yet a chiligon is not a circle. Also, we may have a concept of, but not an image of, a chiligon. The concept of a chiligon is the geometric function that a thousand-sided figure might have in a possible theorem in plane geometry. At any length, the division of capabilities between having a concept and having an image, Descartes suggests, indicates a difference between the intellect and the imagination.

Descartes' next move is to claim that the imagination acquires images from extended things. But the question all along—the ultimate problem with representative realism—is how to connect the image with the formally existing thing in the external world. In order to establish this connection, Descartes appeals to the ultimate veracity of God, the all-perfect being. Descartes claims that the sense faculties of the external senses and the imagination are intrinsically veridical in that they are ultimately reducible to God as their efficient cause. In other words, God, as the all-perfect creator, is the cause of the sensory apparatus of a human being. Insofar as God is not a practical joker, these sense faculties are intrinsically veridical. Thus, if the sensory apparatus has come from God, who has already been established as a formally existing all-perfect being, and if these faculties are such that a human being instinctively believes that they do indeed represent the real world, then God would be a deceiver if he provided human knowers with this sensory apparatus which was inherently defective and always deceptive. But God cannot be a deceiver. Descartes concludes that material objects must exist for these sense faculties to be aware of. Otherwise God would be a deceiver and a practical joker, but the notion of a deceptive practical joker is contrary to the notion of the all-perfect being.

The structure of the entire six *Meditations* can now be seen. Descartes began with the problem of knowledge. He sought an indubitable first principle. He discovered the cogito argument. This established the existence of at least one formally existent object in the external world—his very own spiritual mind. From there, Descartes, using just the contents of his mind—the objectively existing ideas—established the formal existence of an all-perfect being. Once this all-perfect being had been established as the ultimate cause of all existing things, Descartes used this causal reaction as the explanatory force for the formal existence of the rest of the physical world. As God is not a deceiver and as he provided us with a sensory apparatus to be aware of the physical world, then there must exist an object which corresponds to the objective reality of human perceptions. It is for this reason, as argued earlier in this chapter, that Descartes was in earnest in establishing God as a pivotal part of his metaphysical system. If one takes away the all-perfect being, the whole Cartesian system falls asunder.

The following schema depicts the movements of Descartes' six *Meditations:*

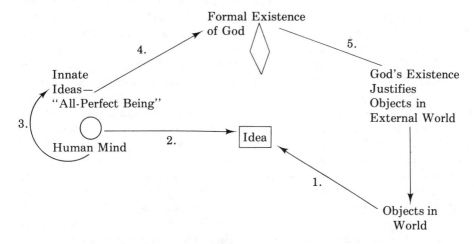

Do you think Descartes is consistent when he argues in *Meditation VI* that the sense and the imagination are not part of the mind? Remember how Descartes described a thinking being in *Meditation III:*

> But what is a thinking thing? It is a thing that doubts, understands, (conceives), affirms, denies, wills, refuses, that imagines also, and perceives.

Here Descartes explicitly mentions perceiving and imagining as processes which belong to the nature of a "thinking being." Is Descartes consistent with his claim in *Meditation VI,* establishing a distinction between imagination and mind?

Second, has Descartes really solved the problem of representative realism? Is the claim of *Meditation VI* a weaker claim than the problem posed by representative realism? In other words, has Descartes provided a criterion for distinguishing a "dream image" from a "perceived image"? This was the question posed in *Meditation I.* How strong is Descartes' criterion involving God as a nondeceiver in answering the problems he has raised at the beginning of the *Meditations?*

Innate Ideas

Before concluding our discussion of Descartes' philosophical system, there are two problems which should be treated: (1) Descartes' response to the problem of universals, and (2) the problem of circularity in the *Meditations.*

Descartes handles the problem of universals in a unique way. Recall from our discussion of universals in connection with the Platonic Theory of the Forms that there are two aspects to the question of universals: (1) the ontological question, and (2) the epistemological question. These two questions refer to the nature of the universals and to the process by which the universals are known.

Ontologically, Descartes is quite probably a nominalist, i.e., a philosopher who denies the metaphysical existence of universals. However Descartes, influenced as he was by mathematics, will attempt to account for our knowledge of universal and necessary truths, especially those of mathematics. Descartes' response to this problem is in terms of innate ideas. Descartes asserts that the mind, by its very own power independent of sense experience, can attain an awareness of universal knowledge. Structurally, Descartes is taking the Platonic world of the forms and placing it into the human mind as the structure for innate ideas. These innate ideas ultimately come about through the causal efficacy of God. Accordingly, the mind has of its very structure built-in concepts which are universal in nature and scope. As we discussed earlier, the position of the structured mind is what places Descartes into the category of "rationalist philosopher." Accordingly, Descartes argues that although there are no separately existing universals—except possibly the ideas in the mind of God—nevertheless a human knower can have universal knowledge because of the innate structures of the human mind itself. For Descartes these innate structures account especially for mathematical knowledge.

An exact analysis of innate ideas is rather difficult, to say the least. Descartes does not provide a very clear explication. There seem to be at least two possible alternative accounts. First, Descartes has been interpreted as claiming that a mind from its very beginning has the completed structure and content of the innate idea within its own confines. On this interpretation the objective content of an innate idea would be fully developed. This analysis is obviously quite problematic. For it seems odd to claim that a newborn baby has a developed objective reality of the Pythagorean Theorem.

A second more plausible interpretation is based upon a theory of dispositions. A disposition is a capacity or ability to be able to perform some particular action. This second interpretation of innate ideas asserts that the mind is so disposed that it can develop universal truths within itself. This development can occur by the human mind ruminating among its other ideas alone and without the need of any sense experience from the external world. In other words, sense experience is not a necessary condition for the development of an innate concept. A human being can develop and discover the content of these ideas within his or her mind by means of rational discourse alone. Therefore the disposition of an innate idea will be the ability of the mind, from its own structure, to know certain truths independently of sense experience. Stated another way, this will be a type of understanding of truths by means of reason alone without any empirical basis. An example would be progress in acquiring a mastery of the theorems of Euclidean geometry. Descartes claims that this mastery can be attained without any use of a human being's sensory apparatus. From this discussion, it should be rather clear why Descartes is considered to be a rationalist. As we shall see in the next chapter, the question concerning the possibility of innate ideas is the root difference between the rationalists and the empiricists. The empiricist philosophers will argue that the human mind is a *blank slate,* with all knowledge being acquired through, and because of, sense experience.

A contemporary exponent of an innate idea position is Noam Chomsky, a linguist at the Massachusetts Institute of Technology. Chomsky argues that an adequate and consistent explanation of the acquisition of language cannot be given unless innate structures of the mind are postulated. In regard to the acquisition of language, Chomsky explicitly denies the adequacy of a strictly empiricist view of the mind. In the following brief selection, Chomsky states his case for the innate structure of the mind.

As far as language learning is concerned, it seems to me that a rather convincing argument can be made for the view that certain principles intrinsic to the mind provide invariant structures that are a precondition for linguistic experience. . . .

The study of language, it seems to me, offers strong empirical evidence that empiricists theories of learning are quite inadequate. Serious efforts have been made in recent years to develop principles of induction, generalization, and data analysis that would account for knowledge of a language. These efforts have been a total failure. The methods and principles fail not for any superficial reason such as lack of time or data. They fail because they are intrinsically incapable of giving rise to the system of rules that underlies the normal use of language. What evidence is now available supports the view that all human languages share deep-seated properties of organization and structure. These properties—these linguistic universals —can be plausibly assumed to be *an innate mental endowment* rather than the result of learning. If this is true, then the study of language sheds light on certain long-standing issues in the theory of knowledge. Once again, I see little reason to doubt that what is true of language is true of other forms of human knowledge as well.

There is one further question that might be raised at this point. How does the human mind come to have the innate properties that underlie acquisition of knowledge. Here linguistic evidence obviously provides no information at all. The process by which the human mind has achieved its present state of complexity and its particular form of innate organization are a complete mystery, as much of a mystery as the analogous questions that can be asked about any other complex organism. It is perfectly safe to attribute this to evolution, so long as we bear in mind that there is no substance to this assertion—it amounts to nothing more than the belief that there is surely some naturalistic explanation for these phenomena.

There are, however, important aspects of the problem of language and mind that can be studied sensibly within the limitations of present understanding and technique. I think that, for the moment, the most productive investigations are those dealing with the nature of particular grammars and with the universal conditions met by all human languages. I have tried to suggest how one can move, in successive steps of increasing abstractness, from the study of percepts to the study of grammar and perceptual mechanisms, and from the study of grammar to the study of universal grammar and the mechanisms of learning.

In this area of convergence of linguistics, psychology, and philosophy, we can look forward to much exciting work in the coming years. (Italics added.) [9]

The rationalist overtones of Chomsky's claims about the necessary conditions for the acquisition of language should be obvious. Because of Chomsky's theories about linguistic structures and the "innate mental endowment," there is much current interest in the general philosophical themes common to rationalism.

One issue remains before terminating the discussion of Descartes' philosophical system. This concerns the implicit problem of circularity in the *Meditations*. A circular argument is one which presupposes, as a premise, something which it also claims to prove. What is to be proven is assumed in the premise. This fallacy is also called *begging the question*. Such an argument is called circular for the obvious reason that the hearer is being led around the circumference of a circle instead of on a straight line path to some new and distinct conclusion. The charge of circularity is brought against Descartes' *Meditations* in the following way. One might ask Descartes, "In virtue of what is a clear and distinct idea or intuition really *true*?" Remember that the qualities of being "clear and distinct" were those which established a necessarily true proposition. As we noted, some philosophers have indicated that this is the result of an intuition. Descartes seems to provide a justification for a clear and distinct idea, and this justification is that God is not a deceiver. Therefore the veracity of God is the criterion for the true character of a clear and distinct idea.

Now the crucial question of circularity comes to the forefront of the discussion. How does Descartes prove the existence of God? Recalling *Meditation III*, the structure of the proof depends upon the notion of a clear and distinct idea of an all-perfect being. However, if this is the case, then Descartes is using God as the ground for veracity of the very same idea which is being used to prove the existence of God. In other words, Descartes' proof depends upon a clear and distinct idea of the all-perfect being; yet the criterion for the veracity of a clear and distinct idea is God's truthfulness. Thus Descartes needs God to prove the existence of God. This is a circular argument. Therefore Descartes is charged with begging the question regarding the existence of God. Insofar as God is needed to ground the veracity of clear and distinct ideas, the *Meditations* become circular because God assumes a pivotal position in them.

NOTES

1. Sextus Empiricus, *Adversus Mathematicos* VII, 135.
2. Lucretius, *De Rerum Natura,* Book II.
3. Arthur O. Lovejoy, *The Revolt Against Dualism* (Chicago: Open Court Publishing, 1930), p. 18.
4. René Descartes, *Discourse on Method,* Part II.
5. G.J. Warnock, *English Philosophy since 1900,* 2nd ed. (Oxford: At the University Press, 1969), p. 72. Copyright © 1969, Oxford University Press. Reprinted by permission of the Oxford University Press.
6. E.A. Burtt, *The Metaphysical Foundations of Modern Science* (Garden City, N.Y.: Doubleday and Co., 1954), p. 121.
7. Roderick Chisholm, "Intentionality and the Mental," a correspondence with Wilfrid Sellars, in H. Feigl et al., eds., *Minnesota Studies in the Philosophy of Science,* vol. 2 (Minneapolis: University of Minnesota Press, 1958), p. 524.
8. Franz Brentano, "Psychologie vom empirischen Standpunkt," in Roderick Chisholm, ed., and D.B. Terrell, trans., *Realism and the Background to Phenomenology* (Glencoe, Ill.: Free Press, 1960), pp. 39 and 50.
9. Noam Chomsky, "Language and the Mind," in *Readings in Psychology Today* (Del Mar, Calif.: C.R.M. Books, 1969), pp. 282, 286. Reprinted by permission of Noam Chomsky.

four

The Empiricists: Establishing a Methodology

The Character of Empiricism

The previous chapter covered the scheme of rationalist philosophy as elucidated by Descartes, both in metaphysics and epistemology. The fundamental philosophical presupposition utilized by the rationalists is that knowledge is *not* exhausted in terms of sense experience alone. Given this assumption, both Descartes and Plato can be classified in the same philosophical category of rationalism. In the history of philosophy, the rationalist position has not gone unchallenged. The principal attack upon the rationalist school in philosophy, especially concerning issues in epistemology, has come from the British empiricists. There was a triumvirate of empiricists from the British Isles: John Locke (1632-1714), George Berkeley (1685-1753), and David Hume (1711-1776). As empiricists, they were adamant in their denial that any content to knowledge could exceed the data of sense experience. Largely, they firmly accepted the following epistemological maxim: "Nothing is to be found in the mind which was not first located in the senses." (*Nihil est in intellectu quod non prius fuerit in sensu.*) Given this maxim, it follows that the empiricists would outrightly deny any epistemology which postulated the Cartesian scheme of innate ideas. David Hume forcefully expresses this claim in the following passage from his *An Enquiry Concerning Human Understanding*:

> Here therefore we may divide all the perceptions of the mind into two classes or species, which are distinguished by their different degrees of force and vivacity. The less forcible and lively are commonly denominated as THOUGHTS or IDEAS. The other species lack a name in our language, and in most other languages. I

suppose, because it was not requisite for any, but philosophical purposes, to rank them under a general term or appellation. Let us, therefore, use a little freedom and call them IMPRESSIONS, employing that word in a sense somewhat different from the usual. By the term IMPRESSION I mean all our more lively perceptions, when we hear, or see, or feel, or love, or hate, or desire, or will. And impressions are distinguished from ideas, which are less lively perceptions—of which we are conscious —when we reflect on any of those sensations or movements above mentioned.

In the above passage, Hume explicitly asserts that all of our ideas are nothing but faint copies of our impressions, and all of our impressions are gained from our direct sense experiences. This is empiricism at its strongest.

The empiricists have been extremely important in the development of the philosophical tradition since the scientific revolution in the seventeenth century. This is especially true of English-speaking philosophers. As we shall see later, a strong empiricist influence has characterized much Anglo-American philosophy, and most of the radical empiricist heritage has its explicit origins in the philosophical writings of Locke, Berkeley, and Hume.

Two philosophical questions dominate the discussions of the early empiricists. The first has been previously mentioned. This concerns our knowledge of the external world as elucidated through the epistemology of perception. The empiricists disavow any type of innate structure to the mind or to knowledge in the manner postulated by Descartes or Plato. The second question concerns the ontological status of substance. Recalling our discussion of Descartes in the preceding chapter, the Cartesian ontology consisted of two categories of substance, spiritual substance and material substance. As we shall see, the empiricists will disagree among themselves concerning the ontological status of substance. In fact, as British empiricism unfolded in the seventeenth and eighteenth centuries, there was a progressive elimination of the need for the concept of substance. Locke argued for both material substance and spiritual substance. Berkeley argued against the ontological need for material substance but postulated the necessity for spiritual substances. Finally, Hume's philosophical methodology refuted the ontological status of both material and spiritual substance. These two philosophical concerns—(1) to account for our knowledge of the external world through an adequate assay of perception, and (2) what to do with the ontological category of substance—have been problems for philosophers up to the present time, especially Anglo-American philosophers.

Historically, it is interesting to note that the three principal figures of British empiricism philosophized around the same time as three philosophers who were to become famous in the development of rationalism: Descartes, Spinoza, and Leibniz. This historical relationship is depicted as follows:

Classical British Empiricists
John Locke: 1632–1714
George Berkeley: 1685–1753
Davis Hume: 1711–1776

Classical Continental Rationalists
René Descartes: 1596–1650
Benedict Spinoza: 1632–1677
Gottfried Leibniz: 1646–1716

The following point—perhaps a bit simplified—is interesting in light of the development of the history of philosophy in the twentieth century. From the tradition of British empiricism evolved Anglo-American analytic philosophy, and from continental rationalism emerged phenomenology and existentialism.

Thus it is not just out of historical concern that beginning students in philosophy are asked to consider the problems of knowledge and substance. In a very real sense, these are problems for contemporary philosophers.

Locke and Material Substance

The first problem of the empiricists which we will discuss is John Locke's analysis of the ontological necessity for the category of substance. Locke's position is important because, by understanding Locke, we will readily understand Berkeley and Berkeley's astute criticisms of materialism. The following is from Locke's *Essay Concerning Human Understanding*:

The mind being, as I have declared, furnished with a great number of the simple ideas, conveyed in by the senses, as they are found in exterior things, or by reflection on its own operations, takes notice also, that a certain number of these simple ideas go constantly together; which being presumed to belong to one thing, and words being suited to common apprehensions, and made use of for quick dispatch, are called, so united in one subject, by one name: which, by inadvertency, we are apt afterward to talk of, and consider as one simple idea, which indeed is a complication of many ideas together; because, as I have said, not imagining how these simple ideas can subsist by themselves, we accustom ourselves to suppose some substratum wherein they do subsist, and from which they do result; which therefore we call substance.

—So that if any one will examine himself concerning his notion of pure substance in general, he will find he has no other idea of it at all, but only a supposition of he knows not what support of such qualities, which are capable of producing simple ideas in us; which qualities are commonly called accidents. If any one should be asked, what is the subject wherein colour or weight inheres, he would have nothing to say, but the solid extended parts: and if he were demanded, what is it that solidity and extension adhere in, he would not be in a much better case than the Indian, who, saying that the world was supported by a great elephant, was asked what the elephant rested on; to which his answer was, a great tortoise. But being again pressed to know what gave support to the broad-backed tortoise, replied, something he knew not what. And thus here, as in all other cases where we use words without having clear and distinct ideas, we talk like children; who being questioned what such a thing is, which they know not, readily give this satisfactory answer, that it is something; which in truth signifies no more, when so used either by children or men, but that they know not what; and that the thing they pretend to know and talk of, is what they have no distinct idea of at all, and so are perfectly ignorant of it, and in the dark. The idea then we have, to which we give the general name substance, being nothing but the supposed, but unknown support of those qualities we find existing, which we imagine cannot subsist, *sine re substante*, without something to support them, we call that support *substantia;* which, according to the true import of the word, is in plain English, standing or upholding.

—An obscure and relative idea of substance in general being thus made, we come to have the ideas of particular sorts of substances, by collecting such combinations of simple ideas, as are by experience and observation of men's senses taken notice of to exist together, and are therefore supposed to flow from the particular internal constitution, or unknown essence of that substance. Thus we come to have the ideas of a man, horse, gold, water, etc., of which substances, whether any one has any other clear idea, farther than of certain simple ideas co-existent together, I appeal to every man's own experience. It is the ordinary qualities observable in iron, or a diamond, put together, that make the true complex idea of those substances, which a smith or a jeweller commonly knows better than a philosopher; who, whatever substantial forms he may talk of, has no other idea of those substances, than what is framed by a collection of those simple ideas which are to be found in them; only we must take notice, that our complex ideas of substances, besides all those simple ideas they are made up of, have always the confused idea of something to which they belong, and in which they subsist. And therefore, when we speak of any sort of substances, we say it is a thing having such or such qualities: as body is a thing that is extended, figured, and capable of motion; spirit, a thing capable of thinking; and so hardness, friability, and power to draw iron, we say, are qualities to be found in a loadstone. These, and the like fashions of speaking, intimate that the substance is supposed always something besides the extension, figure, solidity, motion, thinking, or other observable ideas, though we know not what it is.

—Hence, when we talk or think of any particular sort of corporeal substances, as horse, stone, etc., though the idea we have of either of them be but the complication or collection of those several simple ideas of sensible qualities, which we used to find united in the thing called horse or stone; yet because we cannot conceive how they should subsist alone, or one in another, we suppose them existing in and supported by some common subject; which support we denote by the name substance, though it be certain we have no clear or distinct idea of that thing we suppose a support. . . . [1]

To analyze this passage adequately forces us to consider Locke's ontology. For Locke, the external world has two generic types of categories, substance and accident. A substance is that which "stands under" or "supports" the accidents or qualities. Substance comes from the Latin term, *substare*, meaning "to stand under." A substance is that which can exist by itself. There is no dependence in being—i.e., for its existence—on anything else in the temporal scheme. This excludes a dependence on God, however. Stated differently, a substance exists in and of itself with no demand for any other ontological category as a necessary condition for its existence.

Substance and accident are correlative terms; the one is defined in relation to the other. In contrast to substance, an accident is an ontological category to which belong qualities which cannot exist by themselves but rather must "exist in" or "inhere" in a substance. An accident is also referred to as a quality, property, or characteristic. Recall our discussion of substance and accident from the preceding chapter. Accident comes from the Latin term, *accidens*, meaning "it happens." An accident is something which "happens" to a substance without radically affecting the nature of the substance. In contrast to a substance, an accident *does have* a dependence on the existence of another being. It cannot exist unless it is found in a substance. Thus, a necessary condition for the existence of an accident is that it inhere in a substance. For example, red is not found "floating" around by itself. Rather, it always qualifies or modifies something else. In Locke's ontology, an accident could only modify a substance. Obviously Locke accepts Descartes' maxim that "qualities must inhere in a substance." Locke's ontology contains both material and spiritual substances and accidents. The following discussion, however, will only deal with the *material* substances and accidents.

Similar to Descartes, Locke divides material accidents into primary and secondary qualities. A primary quality is that which a substance has independently of any mind actually perceiving that substance. Primary qualities for

Locke are bulk, extension, figure, motion, rest, and number. A substance will have the primary qualities even if no minds exist to perceive that substance. Therefore in the truncated world—remembering that a truncated world is the hypothetical condition in which there are no minds—both material substance and primary qualities will be found. Neither requires that minds be present for its existence. Locke also claims that the "powers" of the secondary qualities exist in the external world. The power can best be illustrated as a "causally efficacious disposition" able to react with a mental substance and produce an image. In different terms, a power is a disposition or capacity modifying a material substance so that it can cause certain sensations in knowing beings. For example, a material substance would be modified by the power to produce the sensation of red when that power causally reacts with a knowing being possessing the faculty of normal sight. Similarly, the sensation of sweet would be caused by the power in the substance to react with a knowing being possessing the faculty of normal taste. We should realize that, regarding the ontological status of secondary qualities, Locke is structurally similar to Descartes. In the truncated world, red does not exist in and of itself. Rather, for Locke, a certain atomic configuration so exists that it can react with a sense organ. The resulting interaction, or confrontation of power with sense faculty, is a sensation of "red." Redness as experienced by knowing beings is mind dependent. Take away the minds and the redness has no ontological status above the causally efficacious atomic structure. This atomic structure, considered as a dispositional property, has the ability to react with a sense faculty and produce the sensation of red. Yet the atomic structure is not red itself. Another example might help here. When we're healthy, an ice-cream bar tastes sweet. But when we're sick with a head cold, the ice-cream bar might very well taste terrible. Assuming that we have the same type of ice-cream bar on both occasions, it is clear that we—as perceivers—contribute something positive to the sensation of taste. This is the point of Locke's discussion. The perceiver actually contributes something in an awareness of secondary qualities. In other words, the secondary qualities are *mind dependent*. Accordingly, in Locke's ontology, there exist substances (both material and spiritual), primary qualities, and the powers of secondary qualities. The following schematic drawing might help in elucidating Locke's ontology.

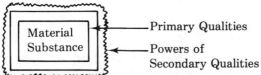

The primary qualities fundamentally modify the material substratum. Remember the list of the primary qualities: bulk, extension, figure, motion, rest, and number. Think for a moment what Locke is saying. A bit of matter, the basic "stuff" of the universe, is fundamentally modified by the primary qualities. A bit of matter, insofar as it is a bit of matter, must have some bulk or other, must occupy some place in space (i.e., be extended), have some shape or other, either be moving or be at rest, and—assuming that monism is false—there will be a number of bits of matter. Yet, we might ask, why is material substance necessary? Because, say Locke and Descartes, a "bulk" by itself is meaningless—a bulk is always a bulk *of* something. Likewise, a figure is a figure *of* something, and so on, for the rest of the primary qualities. What is the "something"? It is material substance. Material substance is what "stands under" the primary qualities.

Locke's Epistemology

The epistemology of John Locke is based upon his ontology. Locke's principal question concerns how things in the world are known. Like many seventeenth century philosophers, Locke is very much impressed with the new science and its prevalent atomism. Accordingly, Locke analyzes any type of causal reaction in terms of impulse, i.e., the push-pull mechanism. Locke applies this type of mechanism to sensation in the following manner. There are small, imperceptible bodies which come from the objects in the external world. These imperceptible bodies affect the sense organs. Therefore, it is because of these imperceptible bodies that we have sense knowledge. In effect, this is a basic restatement of the atomist position. Centuries earlier, Lucretius and Democritus asserted similar positions.

Granting an atomistic account of perception, a serious epistemological problem immediately becomes apparent. Which of these bodies produces a true resemblance in the knower? Is the resultant sensation or idea one which actually corresponds to the physical object in the external world? The problem of the distinction between primary and secondary qualities is immediately raised. Obviously this is the problem of representative realism faced by Descartes.

Like Descartes, in his epistemology of perception, Locke is a *representative realist*. Accordingly, the crucial philosophical problem—which is merely a restatement of representative realism—is: Does the idea or sensation resemble the thing in the world? Locke, however, does not appear to have been motivated by the scepticism which bothered Descartes. In the following passage, Locke provides his theory of perception.

Ideas in the mind, qualities in bodies: To discover the nature of our ideas the better, and to discourse of them intelligibly, it will be convenient to distinguish them, as they are ideas or perceptions in our minds, and as they are modifications of matter in the bodies that cause such perceptions in us; that so we may not think (as perhaps usually is done) that they are exactly the images and resemblances of something inherent in the subject; most of those of sensation being in the mind no more the likeness of something existing without us than the names that stand for them are the likeness of our ideas, which yet upon hearing they are apt to excite in us.

Whatsoever the mind perceives in itself, or is the immediate object of perception, thought, or understanding, that I call "idea;" and the power to produce any idea in our mind, I call "quality" of the subject wherein that

Reprinted from John Locke, *An Essay Concerning Human Understanding*, Book II, chapter 8, sections 7–19, 23, and 26.

power is. Thus a snowball having the power to produce in us the ideas of white, cold, and round, the powers to produce those ideas in us as they are in the snowball, I call "qualities;" and as they are sensations or perceptions in our understandings, I call them "ideas;" which ideas, if I speak of them sometimes as in the things themselves, I would be understood to mean those qualities in the objects which produce them in us.

Primary qualities of bodies: Qualities thus considered in bodies are, First, such as are utterly inseparable from the body, in what estate soever it be; such as, in all the alterations and changes it suffers, all the force can be used upon it, it constantly keeps; and such as sense constantly finds in every particle of matter which has bulk enough to be perceived, and the mind finds inseparable from every particle of matter, though less than to make itself singly be perceived by our senses: *v.g.*, take a grain of wheat, divide it into two parts, each part has still solidity, extension, figure, and mobility; divide it again, and it retains still the same qualities; and so divide it on till the parts become insensible, they must retain still each of them all those qualities. For, division (which is all that a mill or pestle or any other body does upon another, in reducing it to insensible parts) can never take away either solidity, extension, figure, or mobility from any body, but only makes two or more distinct separate masses of matter of that which was but one before; all which distinct masses, reckoned as so many distinct bodies, after division, make a certain number. These I call *original* or *primary* qualities of body, which I think we may observe to produce simple ideas in us, viz., solidity, extension, figure, motion or rest, and number.

Secondary qualities of bodies: Secondly, such qualities, which in truth are nothing in the objects themselves, but powers to produce various sensations in us by their primary qualities, *i.e.*, by the bulk, figure, texture, and motion of their insensible parts, as colours, sounds, tastes, etc., these I call *secondary* qualities. To these might be added a third sort, which are allowed to be barely powers, though they are as much real qualities in the subject as those which I, to comply with the common way of speaking, call qualities, but, for distinction, *secondary* qualities. For, the power in fire to produce a new colour or consistence in wax or clay by its primary qualities, is as much a quality in fire as the power it has to produce in me a new idea or sensation of warmth or burning, which I felt not before, by the same primary qualities, viz., the bulk, texture, and motion of its insensible parts.

How primary qualities produce ideas in us: The next thing to be considered is, how bodies produce ideas in us; and that is manifestly by impulse, the only way which we can conceive bodies operate in.

If, then, external objects be not united to our minds when they produce ideas in it, and yet we perceive these original qualities in such of them as singly fall under our senses, it is evident that some motion must be thence continued by our nerves or animal spirits, by some parts of our bodies, to the brain or the seat of sensation, there to produce in our minds the particular ideas we have of them. And since the extension, figure, number, and motion of bodies of an observable bigness, may be perceived at a distance by the sight, it is evident some singly imperceptible bodies must come from them to the eyes, and thereby convey to the brain some motion which produces these ideas which we have of them in us.

How secondary qualities produce ideas: After the same manner that the ideas of these original qualities are produced in us, we may conceive that the ideas of secondary qualities are also produced, viz., by the operation of insensible particles in our senses. For it being manifest that there are bodies, and good store of bodies, each whereof are so small that we cannot by any of our senses discover either their bulk, figure, or motion (as is evident in the particles of the air and water, and others extremely smaller than those, perhaps as much smaller than the particles of air or water as the particles of air or water are smaller than peas or hailstones): let us suppose at present that the different motions and figures, bulk and number, of such particles, affecting the several organs of our senses, produce in us those different sensations which we have from the colours and smells of bodies, *v.g.,* that a violet, by the impulse of such insensible particles of matter of peculiar figures and bulks, and in different degrees and modifications of their motions, causes the ideas of the blue colour and sweet scent of that flower to be produced in our minds; it being no more impossible to conceive that God should annex such ideas to such motions with which they have no similitude, than that he should annex the idea of pain to the motion of a piece of steel dividing our flesh, with which that idea hath no resemblance.

What I have said concerning colours and smells may be understood also of tastes and sounds, and other like sensible qualities; which, whatever reality we by mistake attribute to them, are in truth nothing in the objects themselves, but powers to produce various sensations in us, and depend on those primary qualities, viz., bulk, figure, texture, and motion of parts, as I have said.

Ideas of primary qualities are resemblances; of secondary, not. From whence I think it is easy to draw this observation, that the ideas of primary qualities of bodies are resemblances of them, and their patterns do really exist in the bodies themselves; but the ideas produced in us by these secondary qualities have no resemblance of them at all. There is nothing like our ideas existing in the bodies themselves. They are, in the bodies we denominate from them, only a power to produce those sensations in us; and what is sweet, blue, or warm in idea, is but the certain bulk figure, and motion of the insensible parts in the bodies themselves, which we call so.

Flame is denominated *hot* and *light;* snow, *white* and *cold;* and manna, *white* and *sweet,* from the ideas they produce in us which qualities are commonly thought to be the same in those bodies that those ideas are in us, the one the perfect resemblance of the other, as they are in a mirror; and it would by most men be judged very extravagant, if one should say otherwise. And yet he that will consider that the same fire that at one distance produces in us the sensation of warmth, does at a nearer approach produce in us the far different sensation of pain, ought to bethink himself what reason he has to say, that his idea of warmth which was produced in him by the fire, is actually in the fire, and his idea of pain which the same fire produced in him the same way is not the fire. Why is whiteness and coldness in snow and pain not, when it produces the one and the other idea is us, and can do neither by the bulk, figure, number and motion of its solid parts?

The particular bulk, number, figure, and motion of the parts of fire or snow are really in them, whether any one's senses perceive them or no; and therefore they may be called *real* qualities, because they really exist in those bodies. But light, heat, whiteness, or coldness, are no more really in them than sickness or pain is in manna. Take away the sensation of them; let not the eyes see light or colours, nor the ears hear sounds; let the palate not taste, nor the nose smell; and all colours, tastes, odours, and sounds, as they are such particular ideas, vanish and cease, and are reduced to their causes, *i.e.,* bulk, figure, and motion of parts.

A piece of manna of a sensible bulk is able to produce in us the idea of a round or square figure; and, by being removed from one place to another, the idea of motion. This idea of motion represents it as it really is in the manna moving; a circle or square are the same, whether in idea or existence, in the mind or in the manna; and this both motion and figure are really in the manna, whether we take notice of them or no: this every body is ready to agree to. Besides, manna, by the bulk, figure, texture, and motion of its parts, has a power to produce the sensations of sickness, and sometimes of acute pains or grippings, in us. That these ideas of sickness and pain are not in the manna, but effects of its operations on us, and are nowhere when we feel them not; this also every one readily agrees to. And yet men are hardly to be brought to think that sweetness and whiteness are not really in manna, which are but the effects of the operations of manna by the motion, size, and figure of its particles on the eyes and palate; as the pain and sickness caused by manna, are confessedly nothing but the effects of its operations on the stomach and guts by the size, motion, and figure of its insensible parts (for by nothing else can a body operate, as has been proved): as if it could not operate on the eyes and palate, and thereby produce in the mind particular distinct ideas which in itself it has not, as well as we allow it can operate on the guts and stomach, and thereby produce distinct ideas which in itself it has not. These ideas being all effects of the operations of manna on several parts of our bodies, by the size, figure, number, and motion of its parts, why those produced by the eyes and palate should rather be thought to be really in the manna than those produced by the stomach and guts: or why the pain and sickness, ideas that are the effects of manna, should be thought to be nowhere when they are not felt: and yet the sweetness and whiteness, effects of the same manna on other parts of the body, by ways equally as unknown, should be thought to exist in the manna, when they are not seen nor tasted; would need some reason to explain.

Let us consider the red and white colours in porphyry: hinder light but from striking on it, and its colours vanish; it no longer produces any such ideas in us. Upon the return of light, it produces these appearances on us again. Can any one think any real alterations are made in the porphyry by the presence or absence of light, and that those ideas of whiteness and redness are really in porphyry in the light, when it is plain it has no colour in the dark? It has indeed such a configuration of particles, both night and day, as are apt, by the rays of light rebounding from some parts of the hard stone, to produce in us the idea of redness, and from others the idea of whiteness. But whiteness or redness are not in it at any time, but such a texture that hath the power to produce such a sensation in us.

Three sorts of qualities in bodies: The qualities then that are in bodies, rightly considered, are of three sorts:

First. The bulk, figure, number, situation, and motion or rest of their solid parts; those are in them, whether we perceive them or no; and when they are of that size that we can discover them, we have by these an idea of the thing as it is in itself, as is plain in artificial things. These I call *primary* qualities.

Secondly. The power that is in any body, by reason of its insensible primary qualities, to operate after a peculiar manner on any of our senses, and thereby produce in us the different ideas of several colours, sounds, smells, tastes, etc. These are usually called *sensible* qualities.

Thirdly. The power that is in any body, by reason of the particular constitution of its primary qualities, to make such a change in the bulk, figure, texture, and motion of another body, as to make it operate on our senses differently from what it did before. Thus the sun has a power to make wax white, and fire, to make lead fluid. These are usually called "powers."

The first of these, as has been said, I think may be properly called real, original, or primary qualities, because they are in the things themselves, whether they are perceived or no; and upon their different modifications it is that the secondary qualities depend.

The other two are only powers to act differently upon other things, which powers result from the different modifications of these primary qualities. . . .

Secondary qualities (are) twofold: first, immediately perceivable; secondly, mediately perceivable. To conclude: Besides those before-mentioned primary qualities in bodies, viz., bulk, figure, extension, number, and motion of their solid parts, all the rest whereby we take notice of bodies, and distinguish them one from another, are nothing else but several powers in them depending on those primary qualities, whereby they are fitted, either by immediately operating on our bodies, to produce several different ideas in us; or else by operating on other bodies, so to change their primary qualities as to render them capable of producing ideas in us different from what before they did. The former of these, I think, may be called secondary qualities immediately perceivable; the latter, secondary qualities mediately perceivable.

Let's examine Locke's analysis as provided in the preceding passage. Concerning primary qualities, the content of the idea or image—the "objective reality," to use Cartesian terminology from the preceding chapter—is an exact image of what is in the real world. The image is, as contemporary philosophers would say, *isomorphic* with the object. In other words, the idea of shape, for example, is caused by the imperceptible bodies. The image which results is a "mirror image" of what is in the real world. By this Locke indicates that the primary qualities are independent of a perceiving mind. In arguing this way, Locke indicates that no matter how much one tries to alter any given material object, it will always have some shape, occupy a certain place in space, either be moving or be at rest, and so forth for the rest of the primary qualities.

The case is different for the secondary qualities. With secondary qualities, the content of the idea or image—again the "objective reality"—does not resemble the quality as found in the external world. Rather, a specific causal power or causative factor produces a sensation or a secondary quality—color, for instance—in conjunction with certain dispositions found in the sense organ itself. In Locke's epistemology, if there were no sense organs, there would be no secondary qualities. The sense organs, insofar as they possess the necessary conditions for sense perception, are indispensible factors for the existence of the secondary qualities. In a truncated world, there would be no full-blown, perfected, or completed secondary qualities. This is the cash value of the representative realist claim that secondary qualities are mind dependent. Therefore Locke's claim that the perceiver contributes a crucial component in the perception of secondary qualities grounds his representative realism. The causal factor does exist in the external world, even in a truncated world. Yet this causal factor only produces a secondary quality when it works in conjunction with the sense faculty. In effect, the content of a secondary quality—the image produced—is a result of the interaction between the powers in the thing and the sense organs. Accordingly, what is represented by the content of a secondary quality is mind-dependent. With no mind, there would be no perfected example of a secondary quality.

In his ontology, Locke's position is that certain specific movements of a certain given number and mass of the imperceptible bodies are what constitute the "power" or "causative factor" which, when reacting with the sense organ, produces the sensation of the secondary quality. Throughout this discussion, it is important that we keep in mind that the perceiver does not experience directly the power or causal factor as such. Rather, the experience of the sensation is a joint product of the causal factor together with the sense faculty. Accordingly, the perceiver experiences the sensation of red, C-sharp, or sweetness. These are full-blown, perfected secondary qualities. The power itself is a necessary condition for the experience of the secondary quality, but it is not a sufficient condition. Therefore the "image" of red and the "power" of red are neither identical as to content nor isomorphic with each other.

Locke admits the category of material substance into his ontology. Yet he also admits that we do not experience material substance. In fact, he once described material substance as "Je ne sais quoi"—the "I know not what." Locke is ontologically committed to the category of material substance because, if substance were not present, there would not be an adequate explanation for the metaphysical category of accidents. "Qualities must inhere in a substance."

Locke's analysis of material substance has been the impetus for much philosophical discussion. As we shall soon see, one of Locke's principal critics was George Berkeley. However, a theologian named Stillingfleet, a contemporary of Locke's, made some astute observations regarding Locke's epistemological analysis of substance. Stillingfleet was bothered over how Locke, while adhering to empiricism, could consistently argue for an idea of "material substance" and yet admit that it was an "I know not what." Stillingfleet's objection centered on the following point: If all our ideas are derived from sensation, then how can Locke account for the idea of material substance? This is a fundamental empiricist criticism of Locke's analysis of material substance.

Locke responded to Stillingfleet in the following way. The mind forms the correlative idea of a "support" or "substratum." The mind does this because it concludes that a substance is needed by forming the "relation of inherence." This is a reiteration of the Cartesian maxim that "Qualities inhere in a substance." This principle, when elucidated, claims that the mind forms the idea of two items: (1) the relation of inherence, and (2) the idea of a support or substratum, i.e., substance.

Stillingfleet, however, was not satisfied with this response. He answered by criticizing Locke's conception of the idea of "relation of inherence." How, Stillingfleet asked, can the mind form this relation? A relation is formed by a comparison of at least two objects. Philosophers call this a *dyadic* relation. But can Locke make such a comparison? According to Locke's epistemology, we lack one side of the comparative relation. We have an idea of "quality," but we do not have the idea of "substance." Accordingly, how can Locke claim we have the idea of the "relation of inherence" if he does not know what one of the terms of the relation is? Only one relata, i.e., the terms of the relation, is known. If a relation is a comparison between two relata, how can Locke argue for the relation if one of the relata is unknown? Stillingfleet, therefore, refuted Locke's attempt to justify the existence of substance by appealing to the relation of inherence. Was Locke a consistent empiricist when he argued for the idea of material substance?

In summary, Locke admits in his epistemology an awareness of both primary and secondary qualities but not of material substance. Of the accidental qualities, both primary and secondary, Locke claims that only the idea of a primary quality corresponds identically to the causal factor in the external world. Image of primary quality and cause are isomorphic. The secondary quality is a joint product of both mind and matter. Both are necessary yet individually insufficient conditions to produce an image of a secondary quality. The idea of "material substance" is an "I know not what," so it corresponds to nothing in our experience. However Locke was convinced material substance existed in the external world. This sets the stage for Berkeley's critique of materialism.

Berkeley's Critique of Materialism

Probably the most astute and clever critic of the corpuscular materialism espoused by Locke was George Berkeley. In addition to writing several important philosophical works, Berkeley was an Anglican bishop who had an illustrious ecclesiastical career. In fact, he was the first person important in the history of philosophy to set foot on mainland America. Berkeley landed at Newport, Rhode Island, in 1729 with the hope of eventually traveling to Bermuda in order to establish a missionary college. Despite a busy church-related career, Berkeley wrote several ingenious philosophical treatises, including *A New Theory of Vision, A Treatise Concerning the Principles of Human Understanding,* and *Three Dialogues Between Hylas and Philonous.* The *Principles* and the *Dialogues* are very good illustrations of the philosophical position called *subjective idealism.* Idealism, in general, refers to the philosophical theory that the nature of reality is essentially and fundamentally mind-dependent. There are two kinds of idealism: *absolute idealism* and *subjective idealism.* Absolute idealism asserts that all reality is a dependent progression from a primary principle which is spiritual. Granting this description, it is obvious that pantheism would exemplify one version of absolute idealism. Subjective idealism, on the other hand, asserts that the entire realm of existent reality is limited to that which a human mind perceives. Stated differently, no object—other than minds—has an existence apart from a relation to a mind. This relation to a mind is a necessary and sufficient condition for existence. Therefore, by taking away the mental relation, we take away reality. As we shall see, Berkeley makes the claim that "to be" is identified with "to be perceived." We shall analyze this ontological claim in detail soon. In order to establish the merits of subjective idealism, Berkeley will use a rather intricate dialectic.

A word of caution. Don't dismiss Berkeley's dialectic too quickly. He is not just using a semantical gambit in order to play games. Berkeley will raise some fundamental issues that still confront contemporary philosophers.

Berkeley advocates subjective idealism in order to undercut the corpuscular materialism of Locke. Materialism leads, according to Berkeley, to scepticism and atheism. And scepticism, Berkeley believes, can be refuted if representative realism can be refuted. Representative realism can be derived from atomistic materialism, as we know from our earlier discussions of the primary-secondary quality distinction. Accordingly, Berkeley sees materialism, scepticism, and atheism as all intricately connected with the corpuscular theories of the new science. The thrust of Berkeley's position is to refute philosophically both scepticism and atheism by arguing that materialism is false. This in turn will lead to a type of direct realism theory of perception.

Berkeley's philosophy is a critique of materialism. He pushes the empiricist criterion further than Locke. In effect, for Berkeley, materialism is coextensive with the acceptance of material substance. Above all, Berkeley's position purports to establish the nonviability of the notion of material substance. The thrust of Berkeley's argument showing that material substance will not withstand serious philosophical analysis hinges on a different elucidation of what "to exist" means. In other words, Berkeley provides a metaphysical analysis indicating what it means to claim that something exists. Berkeley's principal maxim is "Esse est percipi." This is translated as "to be is to be perceived." In order for something "to be," it must necessarily have a relation of "being perceived" by a mind. This is subjective idealism. With this maxim defining existence, Berkeley possesses the ontological machinery necessary to undercut material substance. Berkeley establishes the ontological maxim of "esse est percipi" by means of an analysis of primary and secondary qualities. In effect, it seems that ultimately Berkeley provides a rather subtle criterion of meaning. In other words, he offers an analysis of what it *means* for any one of us to perceive a primary and/or a secondary quality. Berkeley also shows that he can account for perception without any appeal to the necessity of material substance.

Berkeley is a radical empiricist; he works from a concept of a "sensible object" which is defined as "that which is immediately perceived." From this starting point, which is in effect the basic commitment of any empiricist philosophical position, Berkeley establishes philosophically that the materialism advocated by the acceptance of a material substance ontology is fundamentally inconsistent with the position of radical empiricism.

Critique of Primary/Secondary Quality Distinction

In his *First Dialogue* between Hylas and Philonous, Berkeley uses a variety of arguments to philosophically undercut material substance. The first category of arguments used might be called the *relativity argument*. Berkeley argues that there is a perceptual relativity to both primary and secondary qualities. It must be remembered that Locke and Descartes both argued that an idea of a secondary quality is mind-dependent and thus relative to the mental dispositions of the perceiver. The idea of a primary quality, on the contrary, is not relative to a perceiver. In other words, the idea of a primary quality does not depend upon the perceiver in the same way as the idea of a secondary quality. Remember Locke's position that the idea of a primary quality is isomorphic with the ontological referent of the primary quality in the external world. In opposition to Locke, Berkeley argues that there is an inherent relativity in the perception of both primary and secondary qualities. Both primary and secondary qualities are relative to the perceiver. Just as the secondary qualities of color and taste depend very much on the state of the perceiver and on the conditions of perception, so too does the awareness of primary qualities depend upon the variables of state and conditions. Berkeley asks us to consider the example of the "mite": what seems large to it would seem small to a human perceiver. Accordingly, Berkeley argues, the distinction between primary and secondary qualities based upon relativity is not as definite and precise as Locke and Descartes had supposed. Note the following passage from the *Principles*.

> 14. I shall add, that, after the same manner as modern philosophers prove certain sensible qualities (secondary qualities) to have no existence in matter, or without the mind, the same thing may be likewise proved of all other sensible qualities whatsoever. For example, it is said that heat and cold are affections only of the mind, and not at all patterns of real beings, existing in the corporeal substances which excite them, for that the same body which appears cold to one hand seems warm to another. Why may we not as well argue that figure and extension are not patterns or resemblances of qualities existing in matter, because to the same eye at different stations, or eyes of a different texture at the same station, they appear various, and cannot therefore be the images of anything settled and determinate without the mind? Again it is proved that sweetness is not really in the sapid thing, because the thing remaining unaltered the sweetness is changed into bitter, as in the case of a fever or otherwise vitiated palate. Is it not as reasonable to say that motion is not without the mind, since if the succession of ideas in the mind become swifter the motion, it is acknowledged, shall appear slower without any alteration in any external object.[2]

Berkeley uses an additional argument denying the purported distinction between primary and secondary qualities. This is the "dependence" argument. In this argument, Berkeley claims that it is impossible to abstract a primary quality from a secondary quality. A perceiver, according to Berkeley, only knows a shape insofar as it has some color. In other words, Berkeley focuses our attention on the common sense datum that we never experience a shape of something unless it has some color. Further, if it is a necessary condition that a shape have a color in order for it to be perceived, what, Berkeley asks, is the ground for making the absolute distinction between primary and secondary qualities? Berkeley provides a further example when he asks us to consider that motion is never perceived without a shape. In other words, we are never aware of a "mere" motion. We always see a "moving thing." According to the materialists, motion was another of the absolute, mind-independent primary qualities. Berkeley's argument should be obvious. If an awareness of a motion depends upon an awareness of shape, and if a shape depends upon a color, once again there seems to be no reason to claim the absolute difference between primary and secondary qualities. Berkeley radically denies that there is any foundation for making an abstraction of primary qualities from secondary qualities, and secondary qualities are indeed mind-dependent. Accordingly, the primary qualities, because they depend upon the secondary qualities and cannot be separated or abstracted from them, must also depend upon the mind. Therefore the primary qualities are also mind-dependent. In the following passage from the *Principles,* Berkeley makes this point abundantly clear:

> 10. They who assert that figure, motion, and the rest of the primary . . . qualities do exist without the mind in unthinking substances, do at the same time acknowledge that colours, sounds, heat, cold, and suchlike secondary qualities, do not; which they tell us are sensations existing in the mind alone, that depend on and are occasioned by the different size, texture, and motion of the minute particles of matter. This they take for an undoubted truth, which they can demonstrate beyond all exception. Now, if it be certain that those original qualities are inseparably united with the other sensible qualities, and not, even in thought, capable of being abstracted from them, it plainly follows that they exist only in the mind. But I desire any one to reflect and try whether he can, by any abstraction of thought, conceive the extension and motion of a body without all other sensible qualities. For my own part, I see evidently that it is not in my power to frame an idea of a body extended and moving but that I must give it some colour or other sensible quality which is acknowledged to exist only in the mind. In short, extension, figure, and motion, abstracted from all other qualities, are *inconceivable.* Where therefore the other sensible qualities are, there must these be so also, i.e., in the mind and nowhere else [i.e., as perceived].[3]

There is an important extrapolation from the preceding argument. Remember the argument used by the materialists in order to posit the necessary condition for the existence of material substance. The primary qualities were independent of mind and, since "Qualities must inhere in a substance," the primary qualities were fundamentally rooted in the material substratum. But consider Berkeley's point. The primary qualities depend upon the secondary qualities. Since the secondary qualities are mind-dependent, so too must the primary qualities be mind-dependent. If the primary qualities are mind-dependent, then there is no need to postulate material substance in one's ontology. Accordingly, material substance is a useless hypothesis. We shall consider Berkeley's worries about material substance in detail later.

At the root of Berkeley's argument against the distinction between the primary and secondary qualities by means of abstraction is the radical empiricist claim that what is *intelligible* must indeed be *imaginable.* In other words, in order for something to be understood, we must be able to picture to ourselves whatever it is that we want to understand. Following this empiricist presupposition, Berkeley discovers that it is impossible to imagine—i.e., to form an image of—a shape without a color. Insofar as it is impossible to imagine this distinction, so too it is impossible to understand this distinctiveness between primary and secondary qualities. That this is opposed to the rationalist account of knowledge will be apparent by recalling Descartes' claim in *Meditation VI*. For Descartes did accept a distinction between imagining and conceiving by the mind. It was because of this distinction that he considered his concept of the chiligon—i.e., the thousand sided figure—as intellectually conceivable but imaginably impossible. Accordingly, the rationalist, in contrast to the empiricist, asserts that the human mind does have a distinct rational ability of conception distinct from the mere reception and association of the data of sense perception. Structurally, this is precisely where the empiricist parts company with the rationalist. Ultimately, this claim is reducible to the fact that a rationalist epistemology readily admits innate ideas whereas a radical empiricist epistemology—in adopting the maxim that nothing is in the intellect which was not first in the senses—argues against the possibility of innate structures of the mind.

Berkeley and Material Substance

If Berkeley is a radical empiricist, then it is rather obvious what his position is regarding the ontological category of material substance. The crux of his argument, however, centers around what might be called the *resemblance pattern*. Berkeley takes Locke seriously when Locke refers to a material substance as an "I know not what." Berkeley counters by claiming that an idea of an "I know not what" is really an idea of *nothing*. Further, if "to be is to be perceived," and if a "nothing" is beyond perception, then how can it "be"? Berkeley's concerns about material substance and the resemblance pattern is a further instantiation of his maxim that "what is intelligible is imaginable." Obviously it is impossible to imagine an "I know not what." On the resemblance pattern, therefore, Berkeley denies any significance to the idea of material substance. That Berkeley's objection is structurally similar to that raised by Stillingfleet and discussed above should be apparent.

In addition, Locke argued that material substance was the ontological groundwork on which the powers of the secondary qualities and the primary qualities themselves ultimately rested. But since, as Berkeley's texts indicate, both primary and secondary qualities depend upon the mind, there is no reason for postulating a strange ontological category called material substance. In other words, Berkeley asserts that material substance can serve no functional hypothesis in an ontology. Therefore, if it serves no useful purpose, then why, Berkeley asks, postulate that category? The gist of Berkeley's claim is that since both primary and secondary qualities depend upon the mind—which is, in essence, subjective idealism—and since any given thing experienced is nothing but a collection of ideas or sensations, these sensations have no need for an ontological category called material substance. However, without material substance, there is no materialism. Hence materialism is false.

If materialism is false, what is a physical object? In Berkeley's ontology, a physical object is nothing more than a collection of sensed qualities—a "bundle of sensations." What Berkeley is focusing our attention on is that, when we perceive a physical object, the ontological analysis of that object is coextensive with an analysis of the perceived sensations. Obviously this is the meaning of Berkeley's maxim: "To be is to be perceived." If this ontological analysis is correct, Berkeley has undercut the need for postulating the category of material substance advocated by Locke and Descartes. Therefore a physical object is nothing more than a bundle of sensations. In the *Principles,* Berkeley provides the following account of an individual object as a "collection of ideas."

1. It is evident to anyone who takes a survey of the *objects* of human knowledge, that they are either ideas (a) actually imprinted on the senses, or else are (b) perceived by attending to the passions and operations of the mind, or lastly (c) ideas formed by help of memory and imagination, either compounding, dividing, or barely representing those originally perceived in the aforesaid ways. By sight I have the ideas of lights and colours, with their several degrees and variations. By touch I perceive hard and soft, heat and cold, motion and resistance, and of all these more and less either as to quantity or degree. Smelling furnishes me with odours, the palate with tastes, and hearing conveys sounds to the mind in all their variety of tone and composition. And as several of these are observed to accompany each other, they come to be marked by one name, and so to be reputed as one thing. Thus, for example, a certain colour, taste, smell, figure, and consistency, having been observed to go together, are accounted one distinct thing, signified by the name *apple.* Other collections of ideas constitute a stone, a tree, a book, and the like sensible things, which, as they are pleasing or disagreeable, excite the passions of love, hatred, joy, grief, and so forth.

2. But, besides all that endless variety of ideas or objects of knowledge, there is likewise something which knows or perceives them, and exercises divers operations, as willing, imagining, remembering, about them (i.e., the ideas). This perceiving, active being is what I call *mind, spirit, soul,* or *myself.* By which words I do not denote any one of my ideas, but a thing entirely distinct from them, wherein they exist, or, which is the same thing, whereby they are perceived—for the existence of an idea consists in being perceived.

3. That neither our thoughts, nor passions, nor ideas formed by the imagination, exist without the mind, is what everybody will allow. And to me it is no less evident that the various sensations or ideas imprinted on the sense, however blended or combined together (that is, whatever objects they compose), cannot exist otherwise than in a mind perceiving them. I think an intuitive knowledge may be obtained of this by anyone that shall attend to what is meant by the term *exist* when applied to sensible things. The table I write on I say exists, that is, I see and feel it. And if I were out of my study I should say it existed—meaning thereby that if I was in my study I might perceive it, or that some other spirit actually does perceive it. There was an odour, that is, it was smelt; there was a sound, that is, it was heard; a colour or figure, and it was perceived by sight or touch. This is all that I can understand by these and the like expressions. For as to what is said of absolute existence of unthinking things without any relation to their being perceived, that is to me perfectly unintelligible. Their *esse* (their existence) is *percipi* (to be perceived), nor is it possible they should have any existence out of the minds or thinking things which perceive them.

4. It is indeed an opinion strangely prevailing among men, that houses, mountains, rivers, and in a word, all sensible objects, have an existence—natural or real —distinct from their being perceived by the understanding. But, with how great an assurance and acquiescence soever this principle may be entertained in the world, yet whoever shall find in his heart to call it in question may, if I am not mistaken, perceive it to involve a manifest contradiction. For, what are the forementioned objects but the things we perceive by sense? And what do we perceive besides our

own ideas or sensations? And is it not plainly repugnant that any one of these, or any combination of them, should exist unperceived?[4]

A physical object for Berkeley, therefore, is nothing but a bundle of sensations. This position will become very important for many later empiricists, especially David Hume.

Berkeley and Common Sense

Throughout his writings, Berkeley makes it clear that he is asserting a common sense view of reality. The materialists, on the other hand, postulated a metaphysical view which is at odds with our ordinary way of looking at physical objects. The materialists must infer a substratum beyond the direct data of experience. Berkeley argues that materialism indeed is contrary to our common sense view of the world.

One immediate reaction to Berkeley's position is to accuse him of putting the cart before the horse. It is Berkeley who is maintaining a completely "uncommon sense" view about reality. For who would deny the existence of matter? Thus subjective idealism certainly seems to be the ridiculous position—not materialism. In fact, Samuel Johnson provided the following "refutation" of Berkeley's idealism:

> After we came out of the church, we stood talking for some time together of Bishop Berkeley's ingenious sophistry to prove the nonexistence of matter, and that everything in the universe is merely ideal. I observed, that though we are satisfied his doctrine is not true, it is impossible to refute it. I never shall forget the alacrity with which Johnson answered, striking his foot with mighty force against a large stone, until he rebounded from it, saying "I refute it thus."

Has Johnson successfully refuted Berkeley's subjective idealism? Once an elucidation of Berkeley's position has been provided, objections like Johnson's are quite common. However, these objections do not get at the heart of Berkeley's ontology. Berkeley indeed provides a common sense position. To understand this, his position must be contrasted with the world view presented by the proponents of the new science. The new science, with its corresponding representative realism consequent from its materialism, asserted that the real world was nothing more than a collection of material particles banging into one another. Our awareness of the ordinary objects of perception—tables, chairs, and beer cans—is an awareness not of the way the world is but rather an *appearance* derived from ultimate reality. Berkeley attacks this "illusory character" of the experienced world. Recall that Descartes faced the same problem. Berkeley, as we have seen, denies the philosophical soundness of representative realism. His gambit centers around that claim that subjective idealism indeed is the common sense view of the world. In other words, what is experienced is what is real. This, in effect, is nothing more than "to be is to be perceived."

It is important to note that the explanation of the external world as provided by contemporary physicists would be in opposition to Berkeley's maxim that "to be is to be perceived." For example, the current explanation of the atom postulates that most of the atom is comprised of empty space. Yet what is felt when banging a fist against an oak table? There is certainly not an impression of emptiness. According to physicists, however, the real world is very empty. Given this view of reality, there is a philosophical tension engendered between the "appearance" of an object—in this case, the hardness of the oak table—and its "reality"—the atomic building blocks which are primarily empty space. Were Berkeley alive today, he would ask some very serious philosophical questions about the physicist's position. As we shall see when we consider the *Second Dialogue*, Berkeley might not deny the existence of all atoms, but he would question the validity of the appearance-reality distinction. Berkeley is suggesting that the philosopher consider the ordinary ways we perceive objects and not the scientific way of perceiving them. In other words, the philosopher first must place his worries with the way humans ordinarily perceive the external world and not with the scientific view of the external world. Berkeley focuses attention upon the philosophical adoption of a common sense view of the external world. This common sense view of philosophy, in effect, rules out the sceptical worries of Descartes as being the fundamental question a philosopher must consider. In the early twentieth century, G.E. Moore, in his celebrated paper, "A Defense of Common Sense," suggested a similar common sense position for determining philosophical questions.

It is necessary that we realize the importance of the appearance-reality distinction in relation to Berkeley's subjective idealism. In *Reality, Knowledge and Value*, Jerome A. Shaffer provides the following interesting remarks about the problem of perception and our knowledge of the external world. Shaffer is also concerned about the problems caused by the physicist's conception of the world.

So far we have been discussing the question of whether anything can be known with certainty. We must now turn to the question, What are we entitled to believe at all, either with certainty or with only some degree of probability, *about the world around us?* Most people believe, at least before they have studied philosophy, that the world around them is for the most part what it seems to be—that physical objects really exist, that they can frequently be known to exist, and that they really have the properties they appear to have. Let us call this the commonsense view of the world, or as it is known in philosophy, "naïve realism."

Naïve realism immediately runs into two sorts of difficulty. Let us call the first the "argument from science." Scientific investigation of the world shows that the nature of physical objects is very different from what it appears to be. Physicists give us reason to think that the stable, enduring, solid, well-defined, colored, tangible objects around us, including our own bodies, are actually vast systems of tiny clusters of energy scattered at relatively great distances from each other, rushing about at enormous speeds, and having few, if any, of the properties that common sense tells us about. The physicists themselves say that they can hardly conceive of the kind of entities that they postulate as the fundamental basis of things. The world as it appears to common sense is a kind of illusion resulting from the peculiar facts about our own nervous systems. To take only one example, the colors that objects seem to us to have result solely from the fact that we are sensitive in a particular way to a very tiny range of electromagnetic radiation and insensitive to the rest. Were we sensitive in different ways or to different waves, as some animals are for example, the whole appearance of the world would be very different to us, and the world of common sense would be quite a different world. Science, then, indicates that the world of common sense is a set of appearances that only accidentally arise from deeper structures, which themselves never appear at all and can at best only be inferred. The real world, if it is known at all, is certainly not the world that appears to us.

We may create further difficulties for the naïve realist in a somewhat different way—a way we referred to in discussing fallibilism as the argument from illusion. Consider the dagger that Macbeth thought he saw before him. It seemed to Macbeth as if he saw a dagger there before him, but since he seemed to see it suspended in midair, he was suspicious of whether it was a real dagger he was seeing or not. Now it is clear that in this case Macbeth thought he saw a dagger, and the reason he thought he saw a dagger was that in terms of the appearances of things, he was presented with the look of a dagger, exactly that look which would have been presented to him if there really had been a dagger there suspended in midair before him. We are therefore forced to distinguish between the appearance-as-if of a dagger and the dagger itself. From the fact that we get an appearance-as-if of a dagger, it is not guaranteed that there is a dagger there. So here again the naïve realist's identification of the appearances of things with the things themselves breaks down. Things are not always what they seem. They might never be what they seem.

Both these arguments make serious difficulties for the naïve realist. He held, you remember, that the world really is just the way it appears to be. But the argument from science and the argument from illusion both force us to admit that at least *sometimes* the appearances of things are quite different from how the things really are and, more important, that what we are aware of in the first instance are the appearances—not the objects themselves. The next natural questions are these, What are the objects themselves if not the appearances? and How are we to know them? [5]

The question Berkeley poses concerns the "relation of inference" from what is experienced directly to what is beyond the data of direct perception. Is this "inference," Berkeley asks, consistent with radical empiricism?

This division between appearance and reality has been reasserted again in the twentieth century by philosophers like Bertrand Russell and Hans Reichenbach. In his *Human Knowledge,* Russell argued that the unobservable entities of physics are inferred from the objects of experience.[6] Russell made his famous distinction between physical space and perceptual space. Events in physical space were unperceived but bore a relation to our perceptions. Obviously, this is a form of representative realism. In a similar manner, Reichenbach distinguished between what he called "concreta" and "illata." Concreta are the direct objects of perception, while illata are the inferred objects of the external world. Reichenbach uses these concepts to distinguish between ". . . the subjective and the objective arrangement of the world." "Our immediate world," Reichenbach suggests, "is, strictly speaking, subjective throughout; it is a substitute world in which we live. The illata have, however, an existence of their own . . . although they are not accessible to direct observation, that is, to immediate existence."[7] Here is another expression of representative realism. Russell and Reichenbach are ascribing significance to language which refers to entities beyond the direct data of sense experience, and Berkeley asks *How?*

In addition, we might look at Berkeley's philosophy as posing a philosophical question about how meaning is to be ascribed to the inferred objects of reality. It is possible, Berkeley suggests, to ascribe meaning to a term *only* when some relevant experience is present to corroborate a meaning with a bit of language. In the *Principles,* Berkeley writes that "it is on this, therefore, that I insist . . .: the absolute existence of unthinking things are *words without a meaning,* or which include a contradiction." Berkeley suggests that both primary and secondary qualities are meaningful insofar as they serve as the direct data of experience. The concept of material substance is meaningless, however, because it is beyond the limits of direct experience. This critique of meaning advocated by Berkeley has strong affinities with the Verification Theory of Meaning championed by the *logical positivists* in the first part of the twentieth century. Following our reading of Berkeley's *Second Dialogue,* we shall consider the structure and development of logical positivism.

In the *Second Dialogue,* Berkeley continues his investigation into the status of ideas. Furthermore, he is concerned about the resemblance problem as far as material substance is concerned. Obviously, since material substance had been characterized as "I know not what," there can be no "objective reality," to use the Cartesian phrase, or "content resemblance" in the mind for material substance. Hylas, however, proposes a different account of material substance which relies on the notion that material substance should be categorized as the *cause* of our ideas. This analysis is structurally similar to the "powers" approach of Locke in regard to the causal apparatus of secondary qualities outside the mind. Philonous responds to this proposal of Hylas by providing an in-depth critique of how cause functions for the materialist. This causal analysis concludes with Berkeley's unique demonstration for the existence of God. The following is from the text of the *Second Dialogue.*

Before reading the selection from the *Second Dialogue,* it will be useful to note the two characters who converse, Hylas and Philonous. Etymologically, the name "Hylas" comes from the Greek term *hyle,* meaning "matter." Hylas is Berkeley's antagonist in the dialogue, arguing for materialism. "Philonous" also has its etymological roots in Greek, coming from two Greek terms: *philos,* meaning "love," and *nous,* meaning "mind" or "truth." Accordingly, Philonous is characterized as the "lover of truth." It should be obvious as to which character is speaking for Berkeley.

SECOND DIALOGUE

George Berkeley

Hylas. I beg your pardon, Philonous, for not meeting you sooner. All this morning my head was so filled with our late conversation that I had not leisure to think of the time of the day, or indeed of anything else.

Philonous. I am glad you were so intent upon it, in hopes if there were any mistakes in your concessions, or fallacies in my reasonings from them, you will now discover them to me.

From George Berkeley, *Three Dialogues between Hylas and Philonous.*

Hyl. I assure you I have done nothing ever since I saw you but search after mistakes and fallacies, and, with that view, have minutely examined the whole series of yesterday's discourse; but all in vain, for the notions it led me into, upon review, appear still more clear and evident; and the more I consider them, the more irresistibly do they force my assent.

Phil. And is not this, think you, a sign that they are genuine, that they proceed from nature and are conformable to right reason? Truth and beauty are in this alike, that the strictest survey sets them off to advantage, while the false luster of error and disguise cannot endure being reviewed or too nearly inspected.

Hyl. I own there is a great deal in what you say. Nor can anyone be more entirely satisfied of the truth of those odd consequences so long as I have in view the reasonings that lead to them. But when these are out of my thoughts, there seems, on the other hand, something so satisfactory, so natural and intelligible in the modern way of explaining things that I profess I know not how to reject it.

Phil. I know not what you mean.

Hyl. I mean the way of accounting for our sensations or ideas.

Phil. How is that?

Hyl. It is supposed the soul makes her residence in some part of the brain, from which the nerves take their rise, and are thence extended to all parts of the body; and that outward objects, by the different impressions they make on the organs of sense, communicate certain vibrative motions to the nerves, and these, being filled with spirits, propagate them to the brain or seat of the soul, which, according to the various impressions or traces thereby made in the brain, is variously affected with ideas.

Phil. And call you this an explication of the manner whereby we are affected with ideas?

Hyl. Why not, Philonous; have you anything to object against it?

Phil. I would first know whether I rightly understand your hypothesis. You make certain traces in the brain to be the causes or occasions of our ideas. Pray tell me whether by the "brain" you mean any sensible thing.

Hyl. What else think you I could mean?

Phil. Sensible things are all immediately perceivable; and those things which are immediately perceivable are ideas, and these exist only in the mind. This much you have, if I mistake not, long since agreed to.

Hyl. I do not deny it.

Phil. The brain therefore you speak of, being a sensible thing, exists only in the mind. Now I would fain know whether you think it reasonable to suppose that one idea or thing existing in the mind occasions all other ideas. And if you think so, pray how do you account for the origin of that primary idea or brain itself?

Hyl. I do not explain the origin of our ideas by that brain which is perceivable to sense, this being itself only a combination of sensible ideas, but by another which I imagine.

Phil. But are not things imagined as truly *in the mind* as things perceived?

Hyl. I must confess they are.

Phil. It comes, therefore, to the same thing; and you have been all this while accounting for ideas by certain motions or impressions of the brain, that is, by some alterations in an idea, whether sensible or imaginable it matters not.

Hyl. I begin to suspect my hypothesis.

Phil. Besides spirits, all that we know or conceive are our own ideas. When, therefore, you say all ideas are occasioned by impressions in the brain, do you conceive this brain or no? If you do, then you talk of ideas imprinted in an idea causing that same idea, which is absurd. If you do not conceive it, you talk unintelligibly, instead of forming a reasonable hypothesis.

Hyl. I now clearly see it was a mere dream. There is nothing in it.

Phil. You need not be much concerned at it, for, after all, this way of explaining things, as you called it, could never have satisfied any reasonable man. What connection is there between a motion in the nerves and the sensations of sound or color in the mind? Or how is it possible these should be the effect of that?

Hyl. But I could never think it had so little in it as now it seems to have.

Phil. Well then, are you at length satisfied that no sensible things have a real existence, and that you are in truth an arrant *skeptic?*

Hyl. It is too plain to be denied.

Phil. Look! are not the fields covered with a delightful verdure? Is there not something in the woods and groves, in the rivers and clear springs, that soothes, that delights, that transports the soul? At the prospect of the wide and deep ocean, or some huge mountain whose top is lost in the clouds, or of an old gloomy forest, are not our minds filled with a pleasing horror? Even in rocks and deserts is there not an agreeable wildness? How sincere a pleasure is it to behold the natural beauties of the earth! To preserve and renew our relish for them, is not the veil of night alternately drawn over her face, and does she not change her dress with the seasons? How aptly are the elements disposed! What variety and use in the meanest productions of nature! What delicacy, what beauty, what contrivance in animal and vegetable bodies! How exquisitely are all things suited, as well to their particular ends as to constitute apposite parts of the whole! And while they mutually aid and support, do they not also set off and illustrate each other? Raise now your thoughts from this ball of earth to all those glorious luminaries that adorn the high arch of heaven. The motion and situation of the planets, are they not admirable for use and order? Were those (miscalled "erratic") globes ever known to stray in their repeated journeys through the pathless void? Do they not measure areas round the sun ever proportioned to the times? So fixed, so immutable are the laws by which the unseen Author of nature actuates the universe. How vivid and radiant is the luster of the fixed stars! How magnificent and rich that negligent profusion with which they appear to be scattered throughout the whole azure vault! Yet, if you take the telescope, it brings into your sight a new host of stars that escape the naked eye. Here they seem contiguous and minute, but to a nearer view, immense orbs of light at various distances, far sunk in the abyss of space. Now you must call imagination to your aid. The feeble narrow sense cannot descry innumerable worlds revolving round the central fires, and in those worlds the energy of an all-perfect Mind displayed in endless forms. But neither sense nor imagination are big enough to comprehend the boundless extent with all its glittering furniture. Though the laboring mind exert and strain each power to its upmost reach, there still stands out ungrasped a surplusage immeasurable. Yet all the vast bodies that compose this mighty frame, how distant and remote soever, are by some secret mechanism, some divine art and force linked in a mutual dependence and intercourse with each other, even with this earth, which was almost slipt from my thoughts and lost in the crowd of worlds. Is not the whole system immense, beautiful, glorious beyond expression and beyond thought! What treatment, then, do those philosophers deserve who deprive these noble and delightful scenes of all reality? How should those principles be entertained that lead us to think all the visible beauty of the creation a false imaginary glare? To be plain, can you expect this skepticism of yours will not be thought extravagantly absurd by all men of sense?

Hyl. Other men may think as they please, but for your part you have nothing to reproach me with. My comfort is you are as much a skeptic as I am.

Phil. There, Hylas, I must beg leave to differ from you.

Hyl. What! Have you all along agreed to the premises, and do you now deny the conclusion and leave me to maintain those paradoxes by myself which you led me into? This surely is not fair.

Phil. I deny that I agreed with you in those notions that led to skepticism. You indeed said the *reality* of sensible things consisted in an *absolute existence* out of the minds of spirits, or distinct from their being perceived. And, pursuant to this notion of reality, you are obliged to deny sensible things any real existence; that is, according to your own definition, you profess yourself a skeptic. But I neither said nor thought the reality of sensible things was to be defined after that manner. To me it is evident, for the reasons you allow of, that sensible things cannot exist otherwise than in a mind or spirit. Whence I conclude, not that they have no real existence, but that, seeing they depend not on my thought and have an existence distinct from being perceived by me, *there must be some other mind wherein they exist.* As sure, therefore, as the sensible world really exists, so sure is there an infinite omnipresent Spirit, who contains and supports it.

Hyl. What! this is no more than I and all Christians hold; nay, and all others, too, who believe there is a God and that He knows and comprehends all things.

Phil. Aye, but here lies the difference. Men commonly believe that all things are known or perceived by God, because they believe the being of a God; whereas I, on the other side, immediately and necessarily conclude the being of a God, because all sensible things must be perceived by Him.

Hyl. But so long as we all believe the same thing, what matter is it how we come by that belief?

Phil. But neither do we agree in the same opinion. For philosophers, though they acknowledge all corporeal beings to be perceived by God, yet they attribute to them an absolute subsistence distinct from their being perceived by any mind whatever, which I do not. Besides, is there no difference between saying, *there is a God, therefore He perceives all things,* and saying, *sensible things do really exist; and if they really exist, they are necessarily perceived by an infinite mind: therefore there is an infinite mind, or God?* This furnishes you with a direct and immediate demonstration, from a most evident principle, of the *being of a God.* Divines and philosophers had proved beyond all controversy, from the beauty and usefulness of the several parts of the creation, that it was the workmanship of God. But that—setting aside all help of astronomy and natural philosophy, all contemplation of the contrivance, order and adjustment of things— an infinite mind should be necessarily inferred from the bare *existence* of the sensible world is an advantage peculiar to them only who have made this easy reflection, that the sensible world is that which we perceive by our several senses; and that nothing is perceived by the senses besides ideas; and that no idea or archetype of an idea can exist otherwise than in a mind. You may now, without any laborious search into the sciences, without any subtlety of reason or tedious length of discourse, oppose and baffle the most strenuous advocate for atheism, those miserable refuges, whether in an external succession of unthinking causes and effects or in a fortunitous concourse of atoms; those wild imaginations of Vanini, Hobbes, and Spinoza: in a word, the whole system of atheism, is it not entirely overthrown by this single reflection on the repugnancy included in supposing the whole or any part, even the most rude and shapeless, of the visible world to exist without a mind? Let any one of those abettors of impiety but look into his own thoughts, and there try if he can conceive how so much as a rock, a desert, a chaos, or confused jumble of atoms, how anything at all, either sensible or imaginable, can exist independent of a mind, and he need go no further to be convinced of his folly. Can anything be fairer than to put a dispute on such an issue and leave it to a man himself to see if he can conceive, even in thought, what he holds to be true in fact, and from a notional to allow it a real existence?

Hyl. It cannot be denied there is something highly serviceable to religion in what you advance. . . .

In the *Second Dialogue,* Berkeley, through Philonous, does two things. First, he responds to the argument proposed by Hylas concerning the causal structure of material substance. Second, he provides a unique proof for the existence of God.

In criticizing Hylas' analysis of the causal structure of material substance, Berkeley focuses attention on the nature of an "efficient cause." An efficient cause is an active agent. Berkeley contrasts this concept with the classical account of material substance, especially as provided by Locke. In the materialist's own system, material substance is inert and passive. Berkeley raises an important philosophical question: How can anything which is passive by definition also be active so that it can serve as an efficient cause? Because a cause denotes an active agent, Berkeley concludes that material substance cannot serve as the cause of our ideas. Accordingly, Berkeley asserts that material substance cannot function as a cause of our ideas. Hence material substance is useless as an ontological category supposedly explaining causation.

Without material substance as a cause of our ideas, what is an adequate causal explanation for the origin of our ideas? Berkeley demands that only an active agent is capable of being a cause. Since matter is essentially passive and only minds are active, a mind is the only ontological category capable of serving as a cause. The mind is an active agent. The mind is the cause of our ideas. The connection with subjective idealism is obvious.

Berkeley next introduces his unique proof for the existence of God. He has already admitted that a cause is a necessary condition for explaining the origin of an idea. Berkeley thus works from a principle of causality as an assumption. Furthermore this cause must be an active agent. Since an idea itself is passive, it cannot be the cause of itself. Mind, however, is an active agent. Thus Berkeley argues that the mind is the cause of ideas—again, an obvious reference to subjective idealism. Berkeley then argues that the human mind is finite; it cannot be the cause of all of its ideas. Berkeley, arguing in a manner similar to Descartes, asserts that an infinite mind is a necessary condition in order to adequately account for all of our ideas. He suggests that the human mind is finite by indicating the common sense observation that we do not have complete control over everything that we perceive. For example, when Ron and Megan open their eyes, they cannot help but see what is in front of them, granting that the conditions of perceptions are normal. The following passages from the *Principles* present a good illustration of this point.

29. But whatever power I may have over my own thoughts, I find the ideas actually perceived by sense have not a like dependence on my will. When in broad daylight, I open my eyes, it is not in my power to choose whether I shall see or not, or to determine what particular objects shall present themselves to my view. And so likewise as to the hearing and other senses. The ideas imprinted on them are not creatures of *my* will. There is therefore some *other* Will of Spirit that produces them.

30. The ideas of sense are more strong, lively, and distinct than those of the imagination. They have likewise a steadiness, order and coherence, and are not excited at random, as those which are the effects of human wills often are, but in a regular train or series—the admirable connection whereof sufficiently testifies the wisdom and benevolence of its Author (God). Now the set rules or established methods, wherein the Mind we depend on excites in us the ideas of sense, are called the *laws of nature*. These we learn by experience, which teaches us that such and such ideas are attended with such and such other ideas, in the ordinary course of things.

33. The ideas imprinted on the senses by the Author of Nature are called *real things*. . . .[8]

Think about the force of the above passages. Berkeley has already philosophically destroyed the concept of material substance as a cause for our ideas. Since the mind, or more properly *a* mind, is necessary for ideas, and since human perceivers are not in complete control of all of their ideas, an infinite mind is needed in order to account for the "regular train or series" of ideas which human perceivers perceive. In Berkeley's system, God functions as a "Super Perceiver." God is the ultimate ground which guarantees the existence, order, and regularity of the physical world. Note that Berkeley explicitly claims that the ideas in the divine mind ground the "laws of nature" for the physical world. Once again, Berkeley proposes that his demonstrations—this time, for God's existence—come from a common sense position. He is convinced that his world does not cease to exist as an ordered and regular whole when he, as a perceiver, is not directly aware of it, e.g., during those times when he is sleeping soundly, is unconscious, and so forth. However, since existence has already been introduced in Berkeley's ontology as "to be perceived," this conviction demands the existence of a Super Perceiver in order to substantiate the common sense conviction that there is an external world really existing independently of our finite perceptions. Berkeley, therefore, does not deny the existence of the real world. Rather, he provides a subtle philosophical critique indicating the ontological insignificance of material substance. In a very real sense, Berkeley's position can be characterized as the refutation of materialism. In contrast to materialism Berkeley introduces God as the author of nature whose ideas ground the laws of nature providing for the order and regularity of the physical world. The following passages from the *Principles* illustrate this point very well.

33. The ideas imprinted on the senses by the Author of nature are called *real things:* and those excited in the imagination being less regular, vivid, and constant, are more properly termed *ideas,* or *images of things,* which they copy and represent. But then our sensations, be they never so vivid and distinct, are nevertheless ideas, that is, they exist in the mind, or are perceived by it, as truly as the ideas of its own framing. The ideas of Sense are allowed to have more reality in them, that is, to be more strong, orderly, and coherent than the creatures of the mind; but this is no argument that they exist without the mind. They are also less dependent on the spirit, or thinking substance which perceives them, in that they are excited by the will of another and more powerful spirit; yet still they are *ideas,* and certainly no idea, whether faint or strong, can exist otherwise than in a mind perceiving it.

34. Before we proceed any farther it is necessary we spend some time in answering objections which may probably be made against the principles we have hitherto laid down. In doing of which, if I seem too prolix to those of quick apprehensions, I desire I may be excused, since all men do not equally apprehend things of this nature, and I am willing to be understood by every one.

First, then, it will be objected that by the foregoing principles all that is real and substantial in nature is banished out of the world, and instead thereof a chimerical scheme of *ideas* takes place. All things that exist exist only in the mind, that is, they are purely notional. What therefore becomes of the sun, moon, and stars? What must we think of houses, rivers, mountains, trees, stones; nay, even of our own bodies? Are all these but so many chimeras and illusions on the fancy? To all which, and whatever else of the same sort may be objected, I answer, that by the principles premised we are not deprived of any one thing in nature. Whatever we see, feel, hear, or any wise conceive or understand, remains as secure as ever, and is as real as ever. There is a *rerum natura,* and the distinction between realities and chimeras retains its full force. This is evident from sect. 29, 30, and 33, where we have shewn what is meant by *real thing,* in opposition to *chimeras* or ideas of our own framing; but then they both equally exist in the mind, and in that sense are alike *ideas.*

35. I do not argue against the existence of any one thing that we can apprehend either by sense or reflection. That the things I see with my eyes and touch with my hands do exist, really exist, I make not the least question. The only thing whose existence we deny is that which *philosophers* call Matter or corporeal substance. And in doing of this there is no damage done to the rest of mankind, who, I dare

say, will never miss it. The Atheist indeed will want the colour of an empty name to support his impiety; and the Philosophers may possibly find they have lost a great handle for trifling and disputation. [But that is all the harm that I can see done.]

36. If any man thinks this detracts from the existence or reality of things, he is very far from understanding what hath been premised in the plainest terms I could think of. Take here an abstract of what has been said:—There are spiritual substances, minds, or human souls, which will or excite ideas in themselves at pleasure; but these are faint, weak, and unsteady in respect of others they perceive by sense—which, being impressed upon them according to certain rules or laws of nature, speak themselves the effects of a mind more powerful and wise than human spirits. These latter are said to have more *reality* in them than the former;—by which is meant that they are more affecting, orderly, and distinct, and that they are not fictions of the mind perceiving them. And in this sense the sun that I see by day is the real sun, and that which I imagine by night is the idea of the former. In the sense here given of *reality*, it is evident that every vegetable, star, mineral, and in general each part of the mundane system, is as much a *real being* by our principles as by any other. Whether others mean anything by the term *reality* different from what I do, I entreat them to look into their own thoughts and see.

37. It will be urged that this much at least is true, to wit, that we take away all corporeal substances. To this my answer is, that if the word *substance* be taken in the vulgar sense—for a combination of sensible qualities, such as extension, solidity, weight, and the like—this we cannot be accused of taking away: but if it be taken in a philosophic sense—for the support of accidents or qualities without the mind—then indeed I acknowledge that we take it away, if one may be said to take away that which never had any existence, not even in the imagination.

38. But after all, say you, it sounds very harsh to say we eat and drink ideas, and are clothed with ideas. I acknowledge it does so—the word *idea* not being used in common discourse to signify the several combinations of sensible qualities which are called *things;* and it is certain that any expression which varies from the familiar use of language will seem harsh and ridiculous. But this doth not concern the truth of the proposition, which in other words is no more than to say, we are fed and clothed with those things which we perceive immediately by our senses. The hardness or softness, the colour, taste, warmth, figure, or suchlike qualities, which combined together constitute the several sorts of victuals and apparel, have been shewn to exist only in the mind that perceives them; and this is all that is meant by calling them *ideas;* which word if it was as ordinarily used as *thing*, would sound no harsher nor more ridiculous than it. I am not for disputing about the propriety, but the truth of the expression. If therefore you agree with me that we eat and drink and are clad with the immediate objects of sense, which cannot exist unperceived or without the mind, I shall readily grant it is more proper or conformable to custom that they should be called things rather than ideas.

39. If it be demanded why I make use of the word *idea*, and do not rather in compliance with custom call them *things;* I answer, I do it for two reasons:—first, because the term *thing*, in contradistinction to *idea*, is generally supposed to denote somewhat existing without the mind; secondly, because *thing* hath a more comprehensive signification than *idea*, including spirit or thinking things as well as ideas. Since therefore the objects of sense exist only in the mind, and are withal thoughtless and inactive, I chose to mark them by the word *idea*, which implies those properties.

40. But, say what we can, some one perhaps may be apt to reply, he will still believe his senses, and never suffer any arguments, how plausible soever, to prevail over the certainty of them. Be it so; assert the evidence of sense as high as you

please, we are willing to do the same. That what I see, hear, and feel doth exist, that is to say, is perceived by me, I no more doubt than I do of my own being. But I do not see how the testimony of sense can be alleged as a proof for the existence of anything which is not perceived by sense. . . .[9]

In order to better understand Berkeley's proof for the existence of God and the role God plays in Berkeley's metaphysics, we should consider the following antinomy that Berkeley proposes. Granting Berkeley's critique of existence— that is, "to be is to be perceived," and its consequence that physical objects are nothing more than "collections of ideas"—Berkeley suggests a disjunction to us. Either (a) we accept the common sense position that physical objects exist in an ordered, regular way even when unperceived by a finite human mind, or (b) we reject the common sense claim and accept the conclusion that physical objects depend upon the mental acts of direct awareness of human perceivers. To accept (b) entails both that the physical objects pop in and out of existence, depending upon whether or not a human perceiver is directly aware of them, and that there is neither order nor regularity in the physical world. To accept (a) demands the placement of a Super Perceiver in one's ontology who is constantly perceiving everything in the physical world. Obviously Berkeley opts for position (a), which he regards as the common sense view. He rejects position (b), which he refers to as radical phenomenalism. Radical phenomenalism asserts that reality is limited to experienced sensations. Berkeley is aware, however, that position (b) is not inconsistent with his "Esse est percipi" maxim. Rather, Berkeley suggests that position (b) is not a common sense position while position (a) is. However, when accepting position (a), one can only do this consistently by also positing the existence of an infinite mind, whom Berkeley refers to as God. God, therefore, provides the regularity and order to the structure of the external world. Without the divine mind, the physical world would be chaotic. Note the similarity with Plato here. Plato postulated the world of the forms in order to account for the regularity of the sensible world. Berkeley does the same thing; but, instead of the forms, Berkeley postulates an infinite mind who acts as a Super Perceiver. Yet both ontologies are used to provide order and regularity for the external world. To summarize, in Berkeley's ontology there is a three-fold division of existents:
1. Ideas, which are passive;
2. Finite spiritual substances, which are active (human minds);
3. Infinite spiritual substance, which is active (God).

Once Berkeley has discussed the nature of mind as an active agent, one may notice that he broadens his base of existential operation by altering his original definition of existence. To exist is now equated with *to perceive*— which includes both finite and infinite minds—and *to be perceived*—which includes all ideas. Therefore existence can be predicated of both active minds and passive ideas. With this analysis, Berkeley has destroyed the position of material substance. In the *First Dialogue*, the thrust of Berkeley's argument is directed against the sceptics and the atheists. Both of these groups, Berkeley suggests, have based their claims upon the concept of material substance. The sceptics permitted material substance to be the cause of knowledge and the atheists permitted material substance to account for the order and regularity of the physical world. In his critique, Berkeley demonstrates the absurdity of postulating material substance. He thus philosophically undercuts the positions of both the sceptics and the atheists. Both positions as far as he is concerned, have the concept of material substance as a necessary condition. Furthermore he suggests that the common sense view is contrary to the adoption of material substance, in that upon analysis material substance is opposed to any common sense position. His analysis, he thinks, demonstrates that subjective idealism is indeed the common sense view of reality. It is the materialists who, with their metaphysical analysis of material substance, have the really uncommon sense view. For Berkeley, nothing could be further from common sense than scepticism and atheism.

The Role of the Super Perceiver in Berkeley's Epistemology

According to Berkeley's epistemology, God's efficacious causality replaces the function of material substance as explained by Locke. In order for a finite mind to have any knowledge, an active efficient cause is needed. Berkeley demonstrates that a Super Perceiver is a necessary condition for human knowledge. A human's awareness of the real world comes from a "divine archetype" in God's mind. In a very real way, human knowledge is received from the divine mind. This accounts for the regularity in the world, the regularity which Berkeley refers to as the fixed order of natural laws in the external world. As we noted earlier, the world for Berkeley is orderly and not chaotic. There is a fixed order in human perception, assuming normal perception conditions. This fixed order in perception, which could also be referred to as the consistency in our perceptions, occurs only because the divine mind is a super regulator. The crux of Berkeley's argument is that ideas are passive. Insofar as matter also is passive, it cannot be the cause of our ideas. An active agent is needed and the ultimate active agent is the infinite divine mind.

The archetype—or grand idea in the divine mind—is a very complex idea. The archetype is the actual ontological foundation for all possible perceptions. In one sense, we might call the archetype the "permanent possibility of sensations." This latter term actually served as the definition of matter proposed by the nineteenth-century empiricist, John Stuart Mill. It seems to characterize quite well the concept of archetype which Berkeley attempts to convey. In other words, when a finite mind has an awareness of a physical object, this awareness is directly caused by means of an archetype. Berkeley refers to the received perception in a human mind as an *ectype*. An ectype is one particular manifestation of a multifaceted archetype. The archetype, it must be remembered, is the grounding of all possible sensations of an individual object. Therefore, when Megan perceives the green apple, her awareness (the ectype) is but one facet of a multifaceted archetype of that particular apple in the divine mind. The archetype, therefore, is a *particular* idea and not a universal idea. There are structural differences between the "form" of Plato and the "archetype" of Berkeley. In other words, the archetype is the foundation for all possible sensations of an *individual, particular* entity—e.g., this particular apple, that telephone pole, or this beer can. Accordingly, there would be an archetype for each individual thing found in the external world. This entails that the divine mind is rather complex, to say the least. This, however, would not bother Berkeley as he must be taken seriously when he considers the infinite character of the divine mind. The following schema might help to illustrate Berkeley's conception of the role of the archetype-ectype distinction in epistemology.

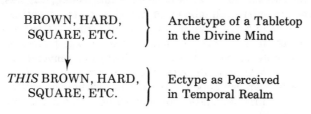

The "brown, hard, square" sensation, which is named a "tabletop," has its foundation in the archetype of the divine mind. To the question, "Does some special entity called a tabletop exist independently of the sensations?" Berkeley responds in the negative. "Tabletop" is just a "name" that finite minds (i.e., human knowers) apply to the bundle of sensations (the ectype) perceived at any one instance. The name has no referent beyond the sensations themselves. This is consistent with Berkeley's claim that a physical object is a bundle of sensations. Remember Berkeley's account of what he meant by an apple. By means of the archetype-ectype distinction, Berkeley believes he is accounting for the regularity of perceptions experienced by a finite mind. It is also Berkeley's philosophical gambit to undercut phenomenalism and its principal consequence, *solipsism*, i.e., the belief that reality is limited to the perceptions of each individual. Furthermore, change in the external world is due to the fixed order of nature established by the archetypes in the divine mind. To use an analogy, Darwin's explanation of evolution by means of "natural selection," given Berkeley's ontology, would take place because throughout the course of time the archetypes were actually directing the process of evolution.

To better understand the function of the archetype-ectype distinction, it is important to realize that the divine mind, as the all perfect Super Perceiver, is continually and constantly aware of every object which exists in the external world. It is as if the divine mind is actually aware of each individual ectype at *every* moment. This is a further instantiation of Berkeley's dictum: "To be is to be perceived." Berkeley argues that the real world does exist. This existence in regard to physical objects is limited to a collection of sensations and not to a metaphysical category called material substance. For Berkeley, the common sense view of the world is based upon regularity. Either there is regularity or there is chaos, and Berkeley opts for regularity. Doing this, he posits the existence of a God to establish the grounds for regularity. This ground for regularity guarantees the common sense view of the world. Later on, David Hume opted for the chaotic view, claiming that there was no sound ontology which could adequately guarantee the ground for regularity in the universe. Berkeley, however, has the divine mind as the Supreme Perceiver, establishing regularity for the universe as a whole.

Bertrand Russell, in "A Free Man's Worship," takes the opposing position regarding order and meaning in the world.

Such, in outline, but even more purposeless, more void of meaning, is the world which Science presents for our belief. Amid such a world, if anywhere, our ideals henceforth must find a home. That man is the product of causes which had no prevision of the end they were achieving; that his origin, his growth, his hopes and fears, his loves and his beliefs, are but the outcome of accidental collocations of atoms; that no fire, no heroism, no intensity of thought and feeling, can preserve an individual beyond the grave; that all labours of the ages, all the devotion, all the inspirations, all the noonday brightness of human genius, are destined to extinction in the vast death of the solar system, and that the whole temple of Man's achievement must inevitably be buried beneath the debris of a universe in ruins— all these things, if not quite beyond dispute, are yet so nearly certain, that no philosophy which rejects them can hope to stand. Only within the scaffolding of these truths, only on the firm foundation of unyielding despair, can the soul's habituation henceforth be safely built.[10]

This position is the exact antithesis of Berkeley's philosophical ontology. Subjective idealism, in the end, was postulated as an ontological position in order to provide meaning and regularity to the external world.

Problems with Berkeley's Philosophy

Some serious philosophical problems result from Berkeley's archetype-ectype account of human knowledge. There are two possible interpretations of this epistemological position, both of which are seriously problematical. This problematical character concerns what constitutes the *object* of knowledge. The first interpretation is that a finite mind (a human knower) *shares* the same kind of content with the content of the archetype in the divine mind. When an ectype is known, the finite mind would be directly aware of one facet of the archetype. The ectype, then, would be one particular facet of the archetype. This interpretation, however, would pose serious theological problems for Berkeley as an Anglican Bishop. In this case, the human mind would be *directly aware* of one aspect of the infinity of the divine mind. Yet this would be contrary to the doctrines of the Judeo-Christian tradition, which assert that the perfect God is unknown. In other words, if an ectype is a sharing of one aspect of an archetype, then the ideas in the divine mind become the object for a human mind. Thus the human mind is directly aware of one aspect of the divine mind; however, this is contrary to the tradition of Judaism and Christianity. Hence, on theological grounds, Berkeley could not have accepted this first interpretation.

The second interpretation is that the human mind, in knowing an ectype, receives a *copy* of that which is in the divine mind as an archetype. However this interpretation is also loaded with problems, but of an epistemological nature this time. This second interpretation leaves Berkeley open to the same kind of objection he himself made against the representative realism of Locke and Descartes. In other words, on this interpretation there would be *two* kinds of objects, two categories of ideas: (a) the archetype, and (b) the ectype.

Given two distinct entities, there needs to be some relation between them, especially since the ectype is a copy of one aspect of the archetype. Yet doesn't this sound like the representative realism Berkeley spent so much time attacking? In other words, on the "copy" interpretation of the archetype-ectype distinction, there would be two different entities. Given this distinctiveness, there must be some relation of similarity between the two since the ectype is supposedly a copy of one aspect of the archetype. In a similar manner, the idea served as a copy of the causal object for the materialists who adopted a representative realist account of perception. As we have seen, the obvious problem is how do we know that the copy—in Berkeley's case, the ectype—indeed resembles the archetype, which is the cause of the ectype? Recall that this is the same problem which confronted the representative realist: How does one know that the idea is a true and veridical copy of the object? Given this second interpretation Berkeley is forced back into the same structural problems with veridical perception faced by the representative realists whom he criticized so strongly on philosophical grounds. If Berkeley accepts this interpretation, then his position is as representative in character as that proposed by Locke.

The upshot of this discussion is that, on either interpretation, the archetype-ectype distinction poses serious philosophical problems for Berkeley's epistemology. If Berkeley accepts the first interpretation, then he is a heretic; if he accepts the second interpretation, then he is a representative realist. Both positions Berkeley would reject. But then how is he to make sense of his archetype-ectype distinction, so crucial to his idealism? Perhaps, in the end, he cannot.

Empiricism and Universals: Nominalism, Conceptualism, and Realism

The *Third Dialogue* is a magnificent example of philosophical dialectic. In it, Berkeley catalogues nearly every possible objection charged against subjective idealism and adeptly responds to these objections. Because of spatial limitations, the *Third Dialogue* is not included here. However we will consider some of the problems Berkeley considered and which have influenced later philosophers, especially the twentieth-century empiricists.

First, we shall consider the issue of abstraction. Berkeley adamantly denies that the mind can abstract any universal characteristics from sensible individuals. Accordingly, there are no universal abstract ideas similar to those considered by the rationalists. Nevertheless, Berkeley is not oblivious to the obvious fact that in ordinary language humans do make use of abstract terms. If there is no such mental process as abstraction, then how is this fact of ordinary language—i.e., the use of general terms—to be explained. Berkeley provides an account of universal ideas and general terms consistent with his empiricism. In denying abstraction, he adamantly affirms that a finite mind can never experience *triangularity, horseness,* or *human nature.* These ideas fail as ideas from the resemblance standpoint. Berkeley admits, however, that the use of universal terms in our language can be explained. Berkeley claims that a human mind can make one particular image of a *"kind of thing"* stand for all the rest of the members of that particular kind. He will pick out one example of a member of a class and designate that member to stand in the place of all of the members of the class or kind in question.

Berkeley's solution to the problem of universals is analogous to the case in Euclidean geometry in which one considers "any given triangle." This given triangle indeed stands for any possible triangle to be discussed within the bounds of Euclidean geometry. Accordingly, the universal idea of triangle, as it were, is a particular instantiation of a triangle which a human mind designates to stand for any other triangle which one will consider. Berkeley applies the same type of argument for "human nature," "horseness," and the rest of the so-called universals. Accordingly, there is no abstract idea in the sense of Cartesian innate ideas but rather a specific idea of an individual member of a class which stands for all the rest of the members of that class or kind. This specific "designated image" is purported to be representative of all the rest of the individuals of that particular class. Consequently, there is no difference *in kind* between a *particular* image and an *abstract* image. In effect, Berkeley denies the need for any type of Platonic universal or Cartesian innate idea.

There is one substantial problem with this epistemological approach, however. We might ask, in virtue of *what* does a perceiver permit one image of, for example, a horse, to stand for all the rest of the members of the class of horses? How is the "commonness" ascertained? Is there some reason why all horses can be compared to the "designated image"? If there is some ground or foundation for the commonness, then Berkeley is right back with some type of universal. In effect, this is a restatement of the old one-many problem which Plato originally faced. For students conversant with the one-many problem and its philosophical ramifications, Berkeley seems rather vulnerable at this point. Moreover, in standing for *all* the members of the class, it seems that the "common image" would tend to become a little blurry to say the least. Take "human nature," for instance. Human beings have many different qualities accidental to their existence, all of which are directly perceived—height, weight, color, and so on. The more extensive the image must be, the less distinct it necessarily becomes. One might legitimately wonder if the designated image solution is really a solution at all. Can the designated image apply to all the members of a class and still have content discernible for the knower? Remember Berkeley's maxim: "What is conceivable must be imaginable." Yet if the designated image is to stand for all the members of a class, will it become so blurry that it cannot be distinctly imagined?

Having considered the problem of universals as treated by three different philosophers—Plato, Descartes, and Berkeley—it will be useful for us to consider some general categories which have been traditionally used by philosophers in discussing the respective positions on universals. There are three generic positions, all of which have become common categories in the history of philosophy. These are exaggerated realism, conceptualism, and nominalism. These categories may be briefly and succinctly described in the following manner:

> *Exaggerated realism:* The universal exists outside of the mind in some state of subsistence. This position is also called Platonism, e.g., Plato and the early Russell.
>
> *Conceptualism:* The universal exists within the structure of the human mind alone, without any reference to an entity in the external world, e.g., Descartes and Leibniz.
>
> *Nominalism:* The universal exists neither in the mind nor in the external world. Universality is nothing more than a characteristic of language, e.g., Berkeley and Hume.

In addition, some philosophers argue for a fourth category, *moderate realism*, which argues that the universal is abstracted from particular instances. This is the position of Aristotle, which we have not yet considered.

It is interesting to note that a similar set of problems confronts the philosopher of mathematics. The following selection from Stephen Barker's *Philosophy of Mathematics* indicates how mathematicians have faced the problems and offered solutions similar to the philosophical positions of exaggerated realism, conceptualism and nominalism. Pay close attention to Barker's distinction between *literalistic* and *nonliteralistic* accounts of number theory.

THE NATURE OF NUMBER THEORY

Stephen F. Barker

. . . The problem of trying to find a literal interpretation of number theory is rather analogous to the problem of 'universals' which preoccupied medieval philosophy. The problem of universals was a problem about the status of properties, such as virtue, squareness, and redness. We perhaps find instances of virtue in the world, but virtue itself seems not to be a thing that is located in space or time; yet we speak of it as though it were something, and we profess to have knowledge of it. Virtue, squareness, redness, and all other such universals appear to be abstract entities; that is, things not located either in space or time. What reality do these universals possess? Their status seems very puzzling and mysterious. If they are intangible, immaterial entities, how then can we have knowledge of them, and how can they be so important in our thinking? Philosophical answers to this medieval problem fell under three headings. Realists maintained that universals were real abstract entities, at least as real as concrete objects, and that the mind has the power to discover and comprehend them by means of rational insight. Conceptualists maintained that though universals are real abstract entities, they do not have any reality in the world apart from our thinking—they are created within the mind. Nominalists maintained that either there are no such things as universals or they are not abstract entities.

As regards number theory, our problem has to do with the reality of the natural numbers (and of sets and ordered pairs) rather than with the reality of properties. But numbers, like properties, appear to be abstract rather than concrete entities—that is, things not located in space or time. This is what makes the medieval question parallel to this one about mathematics. Because the two questions are rather parallel, the answers that modern thinkers have given to the question about numbers can be classified under three headings parallel to the three medieval headings. We may classify as nominalists those who hold that numbers are not abstract entities and that if there is any way of interpreting number theory so as to make it true this must be done by reference to concrete objects. We may classify as conceptualists those who hold that there are numbers and that they are abstract entities, but that they are creations of the mind. And we may classify as realists those who hold without qualm that numbers as abstract entities literally exist independently of our thinking.

Nominalism

Nominalism is the general view that there are no abstract entities, and more specifically it is the view that there are no abstract entities that can be identified as numbers. Is it then possible for a nominalist to hold that there are ways of interpreting number theory so as to make it come out true? Can he maintain that when the mathematics of number appears to be talking about abstract entities it is not really doing so; that it can be interpreted as talking about things the existence of which nominalism can accept? Let us consider some possible nominalistic lines of thought.

Many people, when asked what numbers are, will reply that numbers are ideas in our minds. This line of thought always seems attractive to people confronted with philosophical problems about the existence of something problematic. Suppose that an 'idea' here is understood as being a mental image or some such mental phenomenon in the mind of an individual thinker. An 'idea' of this sort would be something that comes into being at a particular time, lasts for a while, then ceases to exist. It would be definitely located in time, even if not in space, and so would not be an abstract entity in our sense. Thus the view that numbers are ideas of this sort must be classified as a form of nominalism (even though it resembles conceptualism in connecting numbers with the mind).

The suggestion that numbers are ideas in the mind comes very readily to people's lips, but it is not a very satisfactory view. As an attempt to provide an interpretation under which number theory will come out true, this view is defective in several ways. For one thing, number theory holds that there is just one natural number that is zero; yet if numbers were ideas in this sense then there would be as many different numbers that are zero as there are people who have ideas of zero. Also, number theory maintains that every natural number has an immediate successor; but in all probability there are natural numbers (large ones) such that no person has ever formed ideas of their immediate successors. Thus, the view that numbers are ideas entails that, contrary to what number theory claims, there do not exist immediate successors of these large natural numbers. Moreover, number theory cannot be true unless there are infinitely many natural numbers; and it is doubtful, perhaps even senseless, to claim that people possess infinitely many number-ideas in their minds. We must conclude that this line of thought, according to which numbers are ideas, fails to provide any interpretation of number theory under which its axioms and theorems can all come out true.

Another nominalistic line of thought appeals to physical rather than to mental entities. We ordinarily distinguish between numbers and numerals; a numeral is a mark having a certain shape which we think of as being the name of a number. Thus the arabic numeral "5" and the roman numeral "V" are both ordinarily regarded as names for the number five. But suppose we were just to identify numbers with numerals; suppose we say that the numbers are nothing over and above the numerals. This seems to make the numbers into something definite and perceptible; there can be no doubt but that there exist numerals, for we see them. By identifying numbers with numerals it may seem that we rid mathematics of its dependence upon abstract entities.

This nominalistic line of thought is no more satisfactory than the preceding one, however. Under this kind of interpretation the axioms of number theory again do not come out literally true. For example, number theory says that each natural number has exactly one immediate successor; but if numbers were numerals this would not hold true. If by a numeral we mean a particular mark actually written on a piece of paper, on an athlete's uniform, or the like, then there are enormously many numerals for the smaller numbers—but no numerals at all for the very large numbers which no one has ever specifically referred to in writing.

If the numerals won't do, then perhaps the nominalist could just identify each natural number with some particular object in the physical world. Suppose he somehow arranges his interpretation of the primitive terms of number theory so that the symbol "0" is understood as referring to the Peak of Tenerife, "1" as referring to Popocatapetl, "2" as referring to Chacaltaya, and so on. Would something along this line do as a nominalistic interpretation of number theory? No, for infinitely many objects would be required; but there are not that many mountains on earth, nor could we have any assurance that there are that many objects of any kind, even electrons, in the whole universe. We never succeed in observing more than a finite number of objects of any kind; inductive reasoning, based on evidence drawn from our observations, never could establish as probable any conclusion to the effect that there actually exist an infinite number of things of any observable type.

Furthermore, these nominalistic suggestions regarding numbers do not offer any hint as to how the terms "set" and "ordered pair" are to be interpreted nominalistically. A supposed nominalist would not be very consistent if he refused to admit that the natural numbers could be abstract entities, yet did not object to talking about sets of natural numbers (as must be done if we are to define the rationals as sets of ordered pairs of natural numbers). On the face of it, a set (which must be distinguished from its members) appears to be an abstract entity if it is anything at all. It is possible to overlook this if one speaks about a set as an 'aggregate' or a 'collection,' thus making a set of silverware sound like the same thing as a pile of silverware. The pile is indeed a concrete thing located in space and time; it is as concrete as the knives, forks, and spoons that go together to compose it. But the set of silverware cannot be identified with the pile of silverware, for a pile of forty-eight pieces can be identical with a pile of eight place-settings; yet the set of pieces of silverware cannot be identical with the set of place-settings, since these two sets are of different sizes, the former having forty-eight and the latter only eight members. Parallel remarks can be made about ordered pairs.

It seems impossible to avoid the conclusion that number theory cannot be given any thoroughly nominalistic interpretation under which it will come out literally true. The convinced nominalist will have to view the system of number theory as incapable of having any true interpretation. Of course, to say that the axioms and theorems of the mathematics of number are incapable of truth would not necessarily be to deny that they may be useful; false and even senseless talk may sometimes be very helpful in carrying us along through life—in getting bridges built or elections won. For the convinced nominalist, however, the mathematics of number ought not to be regarded as a body of literal knowledge. Some non-nominalists would regard this conclusion as a *reductio ad absurdum* of nominalism.

Conceptualism and the Intuitionists

The view that mathematical objects such as numbers and sets are creatures of the mind, abstract entities brought into being by thinking, is a view that many people have found attractive. It seems to preserve a kind of reality for these entities, while still hard-headedly conceding that they have no independent existence. Moreover, it is a view having a certain charm, for it accords extraordinary dignity to the activity of the mathematician. Indeed, an extreme form of conceptualism would hold that the mind has the power of creating whatever numbers or other mathematical entities it pleases in a perfectly free and omnipotent manner. The mathematician's postulates then could be picturesquely compared to the creative fiats of the Deity: when the mathematician thinks to himself, "Let it be postulated that there are numbers of such-and-such a kind," he thereby brings them into being, his sovereign creative power being like that of an omnipotent Deity who creates out of nothing whatever He wills to be.

It would be too extreme, however, to imagine that the mathematician is entirely free of restrictions in this activity. One cannot compare the mathematician to the creative Deity as described by voluntaristic theologians, who suppose Him to be subject to no restrictions whatsoever (so powerful that He could turn a harlot into a virgin, to use one of the traditional examples). Whatever may or may not hold as regards the Deity, mathematicians at any rate are subject to the requirements of consistency, and cannot bring into being self-contradictions. For example, suppose someone attempts to postulate the existence of an entity answering to the description "A natural number which is the cardinal number of the set of natural numbers." It might at first sight appear that this is a perfectly good description, and that a mathematician could postulate such an entity if he likes. Yet if someone tries to join the assumption that there is such a thing to the normal axioms for the natural numbers, inconsistency results (for if there were a natural number that was the cardinal number of the set of natural numbers, it would have to be both finite and not finite, which is a contradiction). An attempted creative fiat like this would be unsuccessful at bringing its 'object' into being. This instance must serve as a warning that not everyone who imagines himself to have created something has succeeded in doing so. The conceptualist who supposes that thinking can bring numbers into being must at any rate grant that in this game of creation there is a difference between the wish and its execution. Moreover, the principal thinkers who have advocated this conceptualistic view have held that the human mind's creative powers are rather narrowly limited, limited by even more than the requirements of formal logical consistency.

It is the philosopher Kant who was historically the most important representative of a conceptualistic view regarding the mathematics of number. Kant held that the laws of number, like the laws of Euclidean geometry, are both a priori and synthetic. Although Kant did not express his view concerning the philosophy of number in quite as explicit a form as he did his view concerning the philosophy of space, he did say enough to leave his readers with the impression that for him our knowledge of number rests upon an awareness of time as a 'pure form of intuition' and upon awareness by the mind of its own capacity to repeat the act of counting, time after time. This is his explanation of how such synthetic a priori knowledge is possible: in knowing the laws of number the mind is gaining insight only into its own inner workings, not into reality as it is in itself. Of course this is parallel to Kant's view that our synthetic a priori knowledge of Euclidean geometry rests upon awareness of space as a 'form of intuition' and upon the mind's awareness of its own capacity to construct spatial figures in pure imagination. Kant actually says that it is through synthetic a priori insight that we know particular facts about numbers, such as that 5 plus 7 equals 12. This is not very plausible, for particular facts like this, especially ones regarding the larger numbers, surely can and often must be proved. What we might better consider is the view that the basic axioms of number theory should be understood and justified according to Kant's philosophy.

Now, apparently Kant's conception of arithmetic as based on the intuition of counting means that numbers exist if and only if they can be reached by counting; and presumably he would have wanted to say that sets exist if and only if their members can be counted. In consequence, there will be no definitely largest number, since one can always count beyond any number up to which one has counted. But there cannot be any infinite numbers (transfinite numbers) either, since to count infinitely high would be impossible (it would require an infinite length of time, Kant thinks—more than we have available). Similarly, Kant holds that in geometry there is no maximum length of line, for we can imagine extending further any line already drawn; but there cannot be an infinitely long line, as we cannot draw a line that long in imagination (to do so would require infinite time). Thus, both with numbers and with lines, Kant is committed to a doctrine of what is called the *potential* infinite, or of *indefinite* totalities, rather than to the doctrine of the *actual* infinite. Kant's stand is made use of by him elsewhere in his philosophy when he argues that certain unsolvable contradictions (which he calls the antinomies) arise if one argues on the assumption that the spatio-temporal universe could contain any actually infinite totalities. Aristotle, too, had used a somewhat similar notion of the potential infinite in his treatment of philosophical problems, such as Zeno's famous paradoxes of motion.

In recent time a group of mathematicians, among whom the Dutchman Brouwer has been the central figure, have given new currency to a philosophy of mathematics derived from Kant's. Brouwer, like Kant, has maintained that a 'pure intuition' of temporal counting serves as the point of departure for the mathematics of number; and for this reason the name "intuitionism" has been given to the philosophy of this group. For these modern mathematicians, however, intuitionism has not just been a philosophical theory as it was for Kant; for them it has also been a view permeating their actual mathematical work, to such an extent that their judgments about the validity of mathematical arguments have differed from the judgments of other mathematicians who do not accept intuitionism.

Specifically, an argument such as Cantor's argument that there are more real numbers than there are natural numbers is not accepted as valid by intuitionists, although many other mathematicians have regarded it as valid. In carrying out that proof Cantor defined a certain real number (we called it r_0) by saying that in its nonterminating decimal representation its nth digit is to be "5" if the nth digit of r_n is not "5"; otherwise it is to be "6." An intuitionist cannot regard this definition as legitimate, for the definition does not show us how to 'construct' this real number through our pure intuitive activity of counting and calculating. The definition gives us a rule, but to apply the rule and 'create' this real number we would have to complete an infinite number of steps, running through every single digit of the real number; and we have not time for that, the intuitionist holds. Thus he rejects as invalid Cantor's argument that there are more real than natural numbers, and with it he rejects Cantor's whole theory of transfinite numbers.

Cantor's proof is 'non-constructive.' That is, it requires us to envisage the completing of a task involving an infinite number of steps. Now, it might be objected that ordinary reasoning by mathematical induction also seems in a sense to envisage the completing of an infinite number of steps. In ordinary reasoning by mathematical induction, knowing that something holds of zero and that it holds of the successor of each natural number of which it holds, we infer that it holds of all natural numbers. Here, are we entitled to reach the conclusion that whatever-it-is holds for all natural numbers, if we cannot envisage ourselves completing the task of running through all of them? Does the intuitionist reject mathematical induction? The answer is that he need not do so. For our conclusion to the effect that something holds for all the natural numbers is a conclusion that need not be understood as claiming that we have run through the infinite series of natural numbers. Instead, it may be regarded as saying that for any particular natural number you choose, we can count from zero up to it and thus can show that the requirement, whatever it is, holds true of it. Looked at in this way, the reasoning is 'constructive,' since each particular natural number can be reached by running through only a finite number of steps of counting.

From the point of view of intuitionism, we must possess a constructive proof of any mathematical statement about numbers before we are entitled to say that we know the statement is true. If the statement asserts the existence of at least one number of such-and-such a kind, then we must know how to construct, or compute, such a number, using only a finite number of steps. Or if the statement asserts that all numbers are of such-and-such a kind, then for any given number we must be able to demonstrate, using only a finite number of steps, that it is of the given kind. Similarly, before we are entitled to say that we know a statement to be false, we must possess a constructive disproof of it. What about cases in which we so far possess neither a proof nor a disproof of a mathematical statement?

Two well-known examples of mathematical assertions that have neither been proved nor disproved deserve mention. Fermat's so-called 'last theorem' asserts that there do not exist natural numbers which satisfy the equation: $x^n + y^n = z^n$ for n greater than 2. 'Goldbach's conjecture' asserts that every even number can be expressed as the sum of two prime numbers (where a prime number is a number not evenly divisible by any whole number except 1 and itself). Despite a great deal of effort, mathematicians have been unable to find proofs of either of these assertions; nor have they succeeded in disproving them. We have no assurance that they ever will succeed in doing either thing.

Now the intuitionist takes a radical line with regard to examples such as these. The intuitionist believes that numbers are creatures of the mind, and he believes with Kant that whatever the mind creates it must in principle be able to know through and through. He holds that there can be no unknowable (that is, not constructively provable) truth or falsity about numbers. Therefore, he maintains that we have no assurance that Fermat's last theorem and Goldbach's conjecture are either true or false. If they can neither be proved nor disproved, then they are neither true nor false. We cannot prove that they can neither be proved nor disproved (and so possess neither truth nor falsity), but it may well be so, the intuitionist thinks. Intuitionism thus rejects the law of the 'excluded middle'—the principle of traditional logic that every statement is either true or false and that there is no middle possibility. The intuitionist does recognize a middle possibility, and holds that there may well be meaningful statements possessing neither truth nor falsity.[1]

It is clear then, that the intuitionist has a more puritanical standard of logical rigor than had mathematicians such as Cantor. All reasoning acceptable to the former is acceptable to the latter, but (as we saw) some reasoning acceptable to the latter is not acceptable to the former. Now, if Cantor's theory of the transfinite were the only thing in mathematics whose sacrifice was demanded by the intuitionist's scrupulous standards, then perhaps no one would mind very much. We could do without Cantor's theory without feeling any great sense of deprivation. However, there are some important elements of more classical mathematics whose sacrifice the intuitionist's scruples also demand. One important victim would be the theorem in analysis that every bounded set of real numbers has a least upper bound. Intuitionism cannot accept this, because to define the real number that is the least upper bound of a set of real numbers requires a definition that must mention a set to which the thing being defined may belong (such definitions are called 'impredicative' definitions). The intuitionist regards a definition as 'constructing' the entity being defined; but he maintains that a set cannot be regarded as existing unless it has previously been 'constructed' by our deciding what its members are. So he thinks that an impredicative definition cannot succeed in constructing anything, since it presupposes the existence of that which it supposedly is generating. Another important victim of the intuitionist's scruples would be the 'axiom of choice,' which was first stated by the German mathematician Zermelo and shown by him to be an essential assumption in many arguments that have to do with infinite sets. According to the axiom of choice, for any set whose members are sets that are non-empty and mutually exclusive, there exists at least one set having exactly one element in common with each of the sets belonging to the original set. The intuitionist's objection to the axiom of choice is that this set which is declared to exist cannot be 'constructed'; to 'construct' the set we would have to state a rule enabling us, for any given object, to determine, through some finite process of counting or calculating, whether that object belongs to the set. No such rule is available for the kind of set that the axiom of choice declares to exist.

Thus intuitionism, the most influential form of conceptualistic philosophy of number, works considerable havoc upon classical mathematics by rejecting some of its methods of reasoning and some of its axioms. Is the philosophy behind intuitionism attractive enough to make this price seem worth while? Surely not. The whole doctrine that numbers and sets are brought into being by pure intuition of the process of counting is an exceedingly woolly and objectionable doctrine, if taken at all literally. What is this 'pure intuition' supposed to be? What proof is there that the mind can count only at finite speed in 'pure intuition'? Mightn't the mind count infinitely fast in 'pure intuition' and thus 'construct' transfinite numbers? The strangeness of the doctrine is thrown sharply into relief when we realize that it is a consequence of Kant's theory, and presumably of Brouwer's, that the laws of number hold true only of things as the mind intuits (senses) them, not of things as they are in themselves. The view that number is inapplicable to things as they really are in themselves means that things in reality are neither one nor many. This is too close to self-contradiction to be plausible.

The intuitionist's philosophical view about the creation of mathematical entities can of course be separated from his principles of mathematical practice (his rejection of non-constructive arguments, impredicative definitions, and so on). But without the philosophical view, the principles of mathematical practice seem arbitrary and unjustified. Why should one insist upon rejection of certain sorts of mathematical procedures hitherto generally accepted, unless this is done on the basis of some such philosophical doctrine as this?

Realism and the Logistic Thesis

Nominalism and conceptualism both are niggardly and grudging in their attitude towards questions of mathematical existence. The attitude of realism, in contrast, is one of generous amplitude, welcoming a profusion of abstract entities. Unlike the nominalist, the realist has no discriminatory prejudice against abstract entities as such. Unlike the conceptualist, he does not feel that the realm of abstract entities is in any way limited by the mind's poor power to create, for abstract entities exist in and of themselves, not as 'constructed' by the mind. The realist believes that there literally do exist whatever entities the axioms and theorems of number theory seem to speak of. This view about the interpretation of number theory is the most straightforward possible: whenever terms in number theory seem to refer to abstract entities they should be interpreted as doing so, and under such an interpretation the axioms and theorems are true statements.

From the realist's point of view, the task of the mathematician may be compared to a voyage of discovery. The mathematician cannot create or invent the objects of which he speaks, but they are there waiting for him to discover and describe them. As Bertrand Russell put it in one of his early writings:

> All knowledge must be recognition, on pain of being mere delusion; Arithmetic must be discovered in just the same sense in which Columbus discovered the West Indies, and we no more create numbers than he created the Indians . . . Whatever can be thought of has being, and its being is a precondition, not a result, of its being thought of.[2]

From the realist's point of view, there does not seem to be any justification for rejecting non-constructive proofs and impredicative definitions in mathematical reasoning, or for thinking that a statement may be neither true nor false (contrary to the law of excluded middle). If numbers and other mathematical entities are real independently of us, then the conceptualist's scruples all are urged in vain. There is nothing objectionable about non-constructive reasoning: Cantor's proof speaks of a real number whose infinitely long decimal representation we cannot run through, but that is all right, since the reality of the number does not depend on our being able to run through its decimal representation. Cantor has characterized a genuine number, even though we cannot determine specifically what real number it is. Similarly with impredicative definitions: if we view sets as existing in their own right independently of our thinking, then we can feel free in defining an entity to refer to a class that contains it. Moreover, the law of excluded middle need not and must not be denied, for since the natural numbers exist, Fermat's last theorem, for instance, is either true for them or false for them; it must be one or the other, regardless of whether we can ever prove which.

What sort of knowledge will our knowledge of numbers be, according to realism? Here the situation becomes more difficult. The German mathematician Frege, who was the clearest and most forceful proponent of this realistic viewpoint, maintained that our knowledge of number is essentially a matter of a priori rational insight. (Russell, on the whole, agreed.) For Frege, it is a priori knowledge that we attain through use of 'the eye of Reason,' seeing into the timeless structures of numerical reality. Thus, this knowledge is not analytic in the first of the two senses of the word "analytic" that we distinguished before: that is, for Frege, knowledge of numbers is not basically a matter of understanding the meanings of words. When he speaks of Reason being acquainted with mathematical objects, this definitely entails that there is basically more to this kind of mathematical knowledge than understanding of language; it entails that someone might understand the language for numbers as fully as you please, yet if his Reason were clouded so that he failed to apprehend numbers, he would not know the laws of number.

Is Frege's view of our knowledge of number then just a version of the old rationalistic claim that the eye of Reason can gaze into the core of reality? No, not quite. For Frege (joined by Russell a little later) made a very important innovation in the philosophy of number: he held that the laws of number are all analytic. He wrote:

> In arithmetic we are not concerned with objects which we come to know as something alien from without . . . but with objects given directly to our reason and, as its nearest kin, utterly transparent to it.[3]

To the reader accustomed to present-day uses and misuses of the word "analytic" in philosophy, the quotation may sound like a strange way of expressing the view that our knowledge of number is analytic. But Frege employs the word "analytic" only in the second of the two senses that we distinguished. In holding that the laws of number are analytic, Frege is holding nothing more and nothing less than that they are 'reducible' to the laws of logic (when logic is understood broadly). Thus, to say that the laws of number are analytic in this second sense is perfectly compatible with saying that our knowledge of them basically depends upon rational insight. However, it must be the same sort of rational insight as that which gives us knowledge of the laws of logic; and this Frege regards as the very clearest and most direct sort of rational insight.

The doctrine that all the laws of the mathematics of number are derivable from, or can be 'reduced to,' logic alone, has come to be known as 'the logistic thesis.' First stated by Frege, it was later independently formulated by Russell, and in their monumental work, *Principia Mathematica,* Whitehead and Russell undertook to establish the thesis in detail. According to the logistic thesis, the laws of arithmetic and the rest of the mathematics of number are related to those of logic in the same way as the theorems of geometry are related to its axioms. If it is to be shown that this is so, two main things are required: a clear formulation of what the laws of logic are, and a series of definitions of the key terms of number theory which will permit its laws to be deduced from those of logic. It would have been out of the question to derive any part of mathematics from the traditional Aristotelian logic; a much more powerful system of logic than that is required. Frege and Whitehead and Russell contributed in very important ways to working out the laws of this modern and more powerful logic. It is essential to notice that, for their purposes, the terms "set" and "ordered pair" and the laws governing sets and ordered pairs were counted as belonging to logic, rather than to mathematics. (Russell did at one point propose what he called a 'no class' theory, but it was a theory that did without classes—another name for sets—only by using instead the equally or more complicated notions of properties and relations.)

The definitions needed were definitions of all the basic nonlogical terms and symbols of number theory; that includes "zero," "immediate successor," "natural number," and " + " and "x." The procedure of Whitehead and Russell was to define the natural numbers as certain kinds of sets of sets.

Zero is defined as the set of all empty sets; one as the set of all non-empty sets each of which is such that any things belonging to it are identical; two as the set of all sets each having a member distinct from some other member but each being such that any member is identical with one or the other of these; and so on. One such set of sets is said to be the immediate successor of another if and only if, when one member is removed from any set of belonging to the former, then the diminished set belongs to the latter.

Now, the set of natural numbers is a set to which belongs zero and to which belongs every immediate successor of something that belongs. To say this, however, is not to characterize the natural numbers fully, for there are many such sets (e.g., the set of all Frenchmen and natural numbers). What we can say, however, is that all the natural numbers, and they alone, belong to every such set. Thus a natural number can be defined as anything belonging to every set to which zero belongs and to which belongs the immediate successor of anything that belongs. Definitions of what it can mean to add and multiply these natural numbers can also be supplied, and then, with a developed logic which gives laws for sets and ordered pairs (or their equivalents) Peano's axioms and the rest of the laws of number theory can be deduced.

Frege maintained only that the laws of number could be reduced to logic in this manner. Whitehead and Russell had a more ambitious thesis, for they held that all mathematics can be reduced to logic. Geometry would have to be handled through analytic geometry, the points of space being identified with triads of real numbers. Abstract forms of algebra (which do not employ number) could be regarded as deriving from the logic of relations which Whitehead and Russell developed.

It is no accident that the logistic thesis was developed by advocates of realism as a philosophy of number, for these two views go naturally together. To be sure, someone who did not embrace realism might conceivably accept the logistic thesis, or vice versa. It was realism, however, which supplied the motivating intellectual drive behind the work of Frege and Russell, and had they been devotees of nominalism, of the Kantian conceptualism, or of some nonliteralistic philosophy of number, it is less likely that they would have developed the logistic thesis. As it was, they visualized themselves as explorers of a hitherto unknown level of abstract reality, explorers who were able to discover that the vast region of mathematical reality is really only a peninsula of the larger continent of logical reality. It was a bracing and exhilarating way of picturing one's own activity. But like many bright and fresh morning visions, it had begun to fade even before it came clearly into focus. . . .

Formalism

In the preceding chapter we considered literalistic views of the mathematics of number, views which hold that this mathematics possesses its intellectual value because its laws can be interpreted as important truths. Among these views, nominalism seemed incapable of providing any true interpretation, and conceptualism seemed to rest upon a cloudy and unsubstantiated doctrine regarding the mind's supposed creative powers. Realism seemed the least unpromising literalistic view. Yet realism does not stand up well in the light of subsequent developments. If the mathematics of number is the investigation of a field of independently real abstract entities such as sets and numbers, then there ought to be some one true body of laws about these entities. Yet in trying to meet the challenge of the paradoxes, mathematical logicians have developed four basically different kinds of theories, whose laws are by no means entirely in agreement. Each kind of theory is somewhat arbitrary and makeshift, and there seems to be no ground whatever for holding that one of these approaches is truer than the others. The presence of different, partly conflicting theories and the absence of any ground for calling one truer than the others make the realistic philosophy much less tenable than it seemed at first. We cannot feel that we are discovering truths about an independent reality, under these circumstances. Furthermore, Gödel's demonstration of the incompletability of number theory is another blow to the realistic philosophy. If it were an independent reality of sets and numbers that mathematics describes, then one would have expected that the truth about that reality, which would have to be consistent, should allow of being axiomatized completely. A reality the truth about which is necessarily incapable of being described in any complete manner seems a queer and suspect sort of reality—that is, not a reality at all.

Considerations such as these, reinforced also by nominalistic distaste for the doctrine of the reality of sets and numbers and for the doctrine of rational insight, have led many thinkers to the conclusion that the mathematics of number should not be viewed literalistically. Whatever may be the intellectual value of mathematics, their conclusion is that it does not reside in the truth of its descriptions of abstract reality.

We have seen that for the purposes of meta-mathematical study axiomatized mathematical systems can be regarded as formalized. That is, they can be regarded as games with marks, games in which certain strings of marks are derivable from others according to definite rules. Formalism, as a philosophy of mathematics, is the view that mathematical systems should basically be regarded as nothing but formalized systems. The advocate of formalism feels that by regarding mathematical systems just as formalized systems, he escapes a great many confusing and unnecessary questions. What do the laws of number mean? How do we know whether they are true? Do numbers exist? Such questions all evaporate and cannot even be asked, if the view of mathematical systems as nothing but formalized systems is adhered to. The formulas of such a formalized system do not mean anything, they are neither true nor false, they embody no knowledge and no claims about the existence of anything.

However, if we regard mathematics as a game played with meaningless marks, what then is the point of the game? Why is mathematics worth playing? Perhaps some formalists would reply that the game is worth playing and studying just for its own sake, like chess. But that cannot be the full answer, for it does not explain the enormous utility of mathematics for the sciences. How could a game played with meaningless marks be of such value to physics, engineering, and the like? The formalist can give a kind of answer to this without abandoning his view that basically mathematics is to be regarded as a game with meaningless marks. One line of thought for him is that the utility of the system results from the fact that its axioms and transformation rules can be used to derive significant empirical statements from one another. To illustrate the point crudely, the formula "5 X 70 X 90 = 31,500" is a theorem of arithmetic, which is derivable from the axioms according to the definitions and transformation rules. For the formalist, this theorem is just a string of marks, not a statement. The formula can be valuable, however, if we use it as a guide for manipulating empirical statements. The practical value of this formula is that, guided by it, from an empirical statement such as "The farm contains five fields each of seventy acres and needing ninety pounds of fertilizer per acre" we can derive the empirical statement "The farm needs 31,500 pounds of fertilizer." Each of these empirical statements is perfectly meaningful, and need not be thought of as mentioning abstract entities such as numbers. An empirical statement such as "The farm contains five fields" can be regarded as asserting merely that the procedure of counting the fields yields a certain result (pointing successively at each field as one speaks a word, the words "one," "two," "three," "four," "five" suffice); the statement need not be construed as talking about an unobservable abstract entity, the number five.

Now, a formalized system is valuable to science and engineering and agriculture, provided it leads us to make helpful derivations of empirical statements from one another. In order to be reliably helpful, it should never lead us to derive a false empirical statement from a true one. There could of course be a formalized system containing as a theorem the string of marks, "5 X 70 X 90 = 15,300"; but if we allowed that theorem to lead us to derive the empirical statement, "The farm needs 15,300 pounds of fertilizer," from the statement, "The farm contains five fields of seventy acres each needing ninety pounds of fertilizer per acre," then we would be led into agricultural difficulties. A system containing that theorem would not be so easy to apply fruitfully.

The normal arithmetic we use is highly useful because it never does lead us to derive a false empirical statement from a true one. How do we know this? The formalist, who is trying to get away from the (to him) repugnant idea of mathematical 'truth,' cannot reply that we know this because we know that arithmetic is true. If he gives any answer, it can only be that we know this by induction. Past experience shows that our standard arithmetic, when applied as we do apply it, does not lead us to derive false empirical statements from true ones.

Thus the view of the formalist will be that there is no such thing as meaning or truth in mathematical systems; those systems do not contain statements at all, but merely marks. One kind of system is never more 'correct' than another (assuming that both are properly formalized). When organized as formalized systems, the set theory of the intuitionists constitutes a different game with marks than does that of Zermelo or von Neumann, but they are all of them good games. Which shall we play? If one of them turns out in the long run to have applications in science that are more reliable and more fruitful than are the applications of the others, then that is a reason for preferring it. But we do not really have to choose among games; we can play them all, with catholic unconcern. Such would be the view of the formalist.

NOTES

1. For another quite different line of thought that has led some philosophers to reject the law of excluded middle, see Richard Taylor, *Metaphysics*, pp. 66–67, Prentice-Hall Foundations of Philosophy Series.
2. Bertrand Russell, "Is Position in Space and Time Absolute or Relative?" *Mind*, X (1901), 312.
3. Gottlob Frege, *The Foundations of Arithmetic*, trans. J.L. Austin (Oxford: Basil Blackwell & Mott, 1953), p. 115e.

Issues in Berkeley's Philosophy: Mathematics, Images, and Coherence

It is interesting to note that Berkeley offers a formalist account of mathematical truths. Being a consistent empiricist, Berkeley, in denying the existence of either universals or innate ideas, must provide an account of mathematical truths which is radically different from either Plato or Descartes. The critical problem faced by Berkeley, and noted by all the rationalists, is that empirical verification does not pertain to mathematical statements. In other words, there is no empirical methodology which establishes the conditions for justification of mathematical propositions.

Within Berkeley's writings, there is a strong hint of the following formalist account of mathematical propositions. This account was antecedent to the later, more fully developed, formalist positions in the philosophy of mathematics. Berkeley provides the hint that mathematical truths are indeed *stipulative definitions*. A stipulative definition, as the name indicates, is an agreed-upon definition. Such a definition is merely a stipulative use of terminology and, thus, does not depend upon any corresponding entity in the external world to which it must refer in order to be meaningful. In other words, mathematical statements are true only in terms of certain kinds of stipulation. This is the paradigm case for many axiom systems used in contemporary mathematics, especially the non-Euclidean geometries. A certain set of axioms is established by common agreement and then various consequences are derived from these axioms by means of the rules of inference for the system. The truth claims for the entire system, however, depend upon the original stipulated axioms. Accordingly, the mathematical claims do not refer to any existents in the real world.

Albert Einstein summed up the formalist character of contemporary mathematical theories when he wrote that ". . . as far as the laws of mathematics refer to reality, they are not certain; as far as they are certain, they do not refer to reality."

Epistemologically, Berkeley faced a crucial problem in attempting to distinguish an image from reality. If "To be is to be perceived," then does the tabletop depend upon a perceiver in the same way that the "pink elephant" depends upon the mental state of the person under the influence of drugs or alcohol? Berkeley has argued that there is no difference in kind between a veridical image and an illusory image. If so, then are our illusions just as significant as our perceptions of reality? Berkeley answers this objection in the following passages:

30. The ideas of sense are more strong, lively and distinct than those of the imagination. They have likewise a steadiness, order, and coherence, and are not excited at random, as those which are the effects of human wills often are, but in a regular train or series—the admirable connection whereof sufficiently testifies the wisdom and benevolence of its Author. . . .

33. The ideas imprinted on the senses by the Author of nature are called *real things*. And those excited in the imagination being less regular, vivid, and constant, are more properly termed *ideas*, or *images of things*, which they copy and represent. . . .[11]

In these passages, we see that Berkeley argues for the following differences between *ideas* of the imagination and *perceptions* of reality:

A. The image from the imagination, the illusory image, is faint and indistinct. A veridical image, on the other hand, is clear and precise—"strong, lively and distinct. . . ." The vividness of the image is the qualitative way Berkeley distinguishes appearance from reality. Recall, however, that Berkeley's claim here is diametrically opposed to the position of Descartes concerning the very same issue. In *Meditation I*, Descartes originally considered the problem of veridical knowledge because he was unable to distinguish a dream image from a veridical image. Descartes considered that *both* were vivid and lively images. Who is correct? This question probably is resolvable only in terms of research in empirical psychology. Some empirical test must be administered. Neither Descartes' nor Berkeley's philosophizing will offer a conclusive resolution to the matter.

B. Berkeley also uses the criterion of coherence to distinguish appearance from reality. In other words, Berkeley claims that a criterion for distinguishing a dream image from a veridical perception is that the veridical perception "fits in" or "coheres with" the rest of our experience. Certain experiences fit together in an ordered, regular fashion. For instance, if I am dreaming that I am drinking a cold can of Dutch beer on the beautiful sands of Nassau, I can know it is a dream only insofar as it does not fit in with the rest of my experiences. In other words, I realize that in order to travel to Nassau, I must board an airplane for at least a five-hour flight. Yet, on this occasion, I remember going to my bedroom and going to bed for the night. Thus the image of my being in Nassau does not cohere with the rest of my experiences. I do not remember any experiences necessary to get me to the beaches of Nassau. The world of real objects, therefore, is the world of regular, consistent experiences. Ultimately, God experiences the "regularized world." The world fits together in a consistent pattern only because the divine mind always experiences it. Accordingly, "being real" can be denoted in two ways: (1) fitting in with other experiences, and (2) being an idea (archetype) in the mind of God.

We shall end our discussion of Berkeley's philosophy. Berkeley has exerted tremendous influence in English philosophy. We now shall consider two developments of his empiricism: the philosophy of David Hume and the twentieth-century radical empiricism of the logical positivists.

Logical Positivism

A twentieth-century illustration of radical empiricism is logical positivism. This movement in contemporary philosophy had its origins during the 1920s in Vienna. The logical positivists were mainly a group of scientists and mathematicians who were interested in charting a new path for philosophical activity. These scholars were appalled at the then contemporary state of philosophy. At that time, speculative metaphysical studies, greatly influenced by Hegel's absolute idealism, were predominant in western Europe. Pushed to extremes, this Hegelian idealism left little room for the pursuit of scientific thought as characterized by empirical methodology. In opposition to the prevalent speculative metaphysics, the logical positivists sought a method which would, first of all, undercut the idealists, and, secondly, make philosophy more receptive to and compatible with the propositions affirmed by scientists and mathematicians.

Historically, logical positivism was preceded by the philosophy of positivism, whose most celebrated exponent was the French philosopher, Auguste Comte (1798-1857). Comte sought a scientific foundation for speculative thought. Briefly, Comte's position can be schematically outlined as follows. He was very interested in what is presently referred to as the philosophy of history. Comte argued that there were three stages in the process of human development. By human development he referred to the cultural consciousness of human beings in a society rather than the psychological development of each individual. Accordingly, Comte directed his attention to the development of a society's awareness regarding the place of the human being in the cosmos. Comte argued that there was a three-fold process of development. He called these three stages: (1) the Theological Stage, (2) the Metaphysical Stage, and (3) the Positive (Scientific) Stage. In the following passage from his *Cours de philosophie positive*, Comte explicates this three-fold process of development.

THE NATURE AND IMPORTANCE
OF THE POSITIVE PHILOSOPHY

Auguste Comte

The Three Stages of Human Progress. In order to understand the true value and character of the Positive Philosophy, we must take a brief general view of the progressive course of the human mind, regarded as a whole; for no conception can be understood otherwise than through its history.

From the study of the development of human intelligence, in all directions, and through all times, the discovery arises of a great fundamental law, to which it is necessarily subject, and which has a solid foundation of proof, both in the facts of our organization and in our historical experience. The law is this:—that each of our leading conceptions—each branch of our knowledge—passes successively through three different theoretical conditions: the Theological, or fictitious; the Metaphysical, or abstract; and the Scientific, or positive. In other words, the human mind, by its nature, employs in its progress three methods of philosophizing, the character of which is essentially different, and even radically opposed: viz., the theological method, the metaphysical, and the positive. Hence arise three philosophies, or general systems of conceptions on the aggregate of phenomena, each of which excludes the others. The first is the necessary point of departure of the human understanding; and the third is its fixed and definite state. The second is merely a state of transition.

In the theological state, the human mind, seeking the essential nature of beings, the first and final causes (the origin and purpose) of all effects—in short, Absolute knowledge—supposes all phenomena to be produced by the immediate action of supernatural beings.

In the metaphysical state, which is only a modification of the first, the mind supposes, instead of supernatural beings, abstract forces, veritable entities (that is, personified abstractions) inherent in all beings, and capable of producing all phenomena. What is called the explanation of phenomena is, in this stage, a mere reference of each to its proper entity.

In the final, the positive state, the mind has given over the vain search after Absolute notions, the origin and destination of the universe, and the causes of phenomena, and applies itself to the study of their laws—that is, their invariable relations of succession and resemblance. Reasoning and observation, duly combined, are the means of this knowledge. What is now understood when we speak of an explanation of facts is simply the establishment of a connection between single phenomena and some general facts, the number of which continually diminishes with the progress of science.

The Theological system arrived at the highest perfection of which it is capable when it substituted the providential action of a single Being for the varied operations of the numerous divinities which had been before imagined. In the same way, in the last stage of the Metaphysical system, men

Reprinted from Comte's *Cours de philosophie positive,* translated by Harriet Martineau as *The Positive Philosophy of Auguste Comte* (London: Trubner and Co., Ludgate Hill, 1875), pp. 1–3 and 5.

substitute one great entity (Nature) as the cause of all phenomena, instead of the multitude of entities at first supposed. In the same way, again, the ultimate perfection of the Positive system would be (if such perfection could be hoped for) to represent all phenomena as particular aspects of a single general fact—such as Gravitation, for instance.

The importance of the working of this general law will be established hereafter. At present, it must suffice to point out some of the grounds of it.

There is no science which, having attained the positive stage, does not bear marks of having passed through the others. Some time since it was (whatever it might be) composed, as we can now perceive, of metaphysical abstractions; and, further back in the course of time, it took its form from theological conceptions. We shall have only too much occasion to see, as we proceed, that our most advanced sciences still bear very evident marks of the two earlier periods through which they have passed.

The progress of the individual mind is not only an illustration, but an indirect evidence of that of the general mind. The point of departure of the individual and of the race being the same, the phases of the mind of a man correspond to the epochs of the mind of the race. Now, each of us is aware, if he looks back upon his own history, that he was a theologian in his childhood, a metaphysician in his youth, and a natural philosopher in his manhood. All men who are up to their age can verify this for themselves. . . .

The Character of the Positive Philosophy. As we have seen, the first characteristic of the Positive Philosophy is that it regards all phenomena as subjected to invariable natural *Laws.* Our business is,—seeing how vain is any research into what are called *Causes,* whether first or final,—to pursue an accurate discovery of these Laws, with a view to reducing them to the smallest possible number. By speculating upon causes, we could solve no difficulty about origin and purpose. Our real business is to analyse accurately the circumstances of phenomena, and to connect them by the natural relations of succession and resemblance. The best illustration of this is in the case of the doctrine of Gravitation. We say that the general phenomena of the universe are *explained* by it, because it connects under one head the whole immense variety of astronomical facts; exhibiting the constant tendency of atoms toward each other in direct proportion to their masses, and in inverse proportion to the squares of their distance; while the general fact itself is a mere extension of one which is perfectly familiar to us, and which we therefore say that we know;—the weight of bodies on the surface of the earth. As to what weight and attraction are, we have nothing to do with that, for it is not a matter of knowledge at all. Theologians and metaphysicians may imagine and refine about such questions; but positive philosophy rejects them. . . .

From the text of Comte, it is plain that he places great emphasis on the positive stage. The theological stage is characterized by a human interpretation of reality in terms of superstitions and myths. An example might be a snake dance by primitive tribes for the purpose of appeasing the gods. The metaphysical stage is an interpretation of reality using abstractions. Often this entails postulating various entities in order to provide a rational account of the cosmos. An obvious example of the metaphysical stage would be Plato's world of the forms. Comte asserts, however, that human consciousness is now ready to go beyond the absurdities and limitations of metaphysical speculation and, thus, to concentrate on purely scientific inquiries and explanations. Thus emerges the positive stage. This last stage is characterized by the abandonment of metaphysical dogma and the advocation of scientific and factual inquiries employing an empirical methodology. An adequate account of the cosmos must be elucidated in terms of the sheer description of sensory phenomena and sensory phenomena alone. Accordingly, the weight of discovering the true account of the world will be couched in terms of a scientific inquiry rather than through a metaphysical abstraction or by a religious myth. With his accent on the positive stage, Comte lays the groundwork for the advent of the logical positivists in the twentieth century. And logical positivism itself greatly influenced the development of twentieth-century philosophy, especially in English-speaking countries.

The logical positivists, as the term indicates, were influenced by two movements. They adhered to the nineteenth-century positivism of Auguste Comte. In addition, they were greatly impressed with the revolutionary studies made in mathematics and logical theory during the last part of the nineteenth century and the first part of the twentieth century, especially the discovery of non-Euclidean geometry. The logical positivists gathered together in a group, known as the *Vienna Circle*, which sought a new direction for matters philosophical. This new direction would embody Comte's positive stage. This position argued that metaphysics was indeed a meaningless abstraction and thus should be purged from philosophical discussions. The method advocated by the logical positivists was fundamentally linguistic. From their attention to the use of language in the attempt to solve philosophical problems arose the notion of linguistic analysis. This label has become justly famous in contemporary philosophy, although it is not coextensive with logical positivism.

The Verification Theory of Meaning

The logical positivists sought to attain their goal of purging metaphysical abstractions from philosophy by establishing a *criterion of meaning*. Obviously, as users of language, we want to utilize only language which is meaningful and significant. It would be very odd, to say the least, if we wanted to convey meaningless expressions to each other. The logical positivists perceived as their philosophical mission the establishment of a criterion of meaningful language so strong that it would admit as meaningful only those sentences which were also meaningful to mathematics and the physical sciences. At this time it is only fair to admit the following claim. In a very real sense, the logical positivists knew ahead of time the direction they sought for philosophy. Accordingly, what the Verification Theory of Meaning (i.e., their established criterion) did for them was to formulate a means to philosophically justify their claims regarding the abandonment of metaphysics. It is interesting to note that David Hume, in a sense, foreshadowed the logical positivists. While Hume considered ideas, and the logical positivists analyzed sentences, significant similarities exist between the two.

> If we take in our hand any volume—of divinity or school metaphysics, for instance—let us ask, "Does it contain any abstract reasoning concerning quantity or number?" No. "Does it contain any experimental reasoning concerning matters of fact and existence?" No. Commit it then to the flames, for it can contain nothing but sophistry and illusion.[12]

According to Hume, any claims neither mathematical nor empirical deserved nothing better than banishment to the flames. As we shall see, this same program was furthered by the logical positivists. In effect, the twentieth-century logical positivists are direct philosophical descendants of David Hume.

In order to adequately understand the Verification Theory of Meaning, we must return briefly to the German philosopher, Immanuel Kant. It was Kant who formulated the categories of propositions which the logical positivists used. In essence, Kant argued that there were four types of propositions, which can be briefly described as follows:

A Priori: A proposition whose meaning is determined independently of sense experience (e.g., A red rose is red.).

A Posteriori: A proposition whose meaning is determined by a direct appeal to sense experience (e.g., There is a desk in my office.).

Analytic: A proposition whose predicate term is contained within the subject term (e.g., A triangle is a three-sided figure.).

Synthetic: A proposition whose predicate term is not contained within the subject term (e.g., The table is brown.).

By arranging these sentences so that they overlap each other, the following schema can be devised:

	Analytic	Synthetic
A Priori	1	3
A Posteriori	2	4

This combination results in four possibilities for propositions:
1. analytic a priori
2. analytic a posteriori
3. synthetic a priori
4. synthetic a posteriori

The logical positivists will accept only two of the above combinations, numbers one and four (analytic a priori and synthetic a posteriori). Kant argued vigorously for the possibility of synthetic a priori propositions. Most philosophers reject the possibility for analytic a posteriori propositions.

The logical positivists will accept the possibility of analytic a priori propositions insofar as this category admits mathematical definitions. A sentence like "A triangle is a three-sided figure" can be understood without any sense experience. The reason for this a priori characteristic is that the predicate term—"being a three-sided figure"—is exactly what a triangle means. Another example would be "A bachelor is an unmarried person." Being an "unmarried person" is exactly what is meant by the concept of "bachelor." Accordingly, the positivists accepted this category of meaningful propositions because it denotes the type of propositions which are true by definition. The positivists wanted this category especially because it permitted mathematical statements to be significant. Consistent with this position, the positivists argued for a formalist philosophy of mathematics. As we noted above, this theory asserts that mathematical statements are true by definition. In other words, a mathematical proposition is true not because it refers to some quality or characteristic of the real or mental world. Rather, the statement is true because it is so defined. This is consistent with the axiomatic view of mathematical propositions, a view which many contemporary mathematicians adopt. In the study of mathematics many of us have observed this view of mathematical propositions. This is especially true of non-Euclidean geometries.

The logical positivists obviously accept the category of synthetic a posteriori propositions. These propositions are the type which refer to objects which can be empirically verified. Any philosophical position enamoured with the scientific method would want this category of propositions to be significant. An example would be "The table is brown." This is synthetic because the predicate, "brown," is not contained within the concept of what a table is. We might paint the table purple and yet it would still be a table. This is also an a posteriori proposition in that it must be observed through sense knowledge. There is no way to realize that a table is brown from merely considering the concept of table.

The category of synthetic a priori propositions is one which has caused much philosophical controversy since the time of Kant. This category considers propositions which are known independently of sense experience yet possess a predicate which is not contained within the subject term. In Kant's philosophy, the statement, "Every event has a cause," is an example of a synthetic a priori proposition. According to Kant, we know a priori that there is no such thing as an uncaused event. Nevertheless we could analyze the concept of event and not entertain the concept of cause analytically. In other words, cause is not part of the concept of event. There has been much serious philosophical debate over the admissibility of this category. Suffice it to say in an introductory discussion that the logical positivists refused to admit this category into the realm of meaningful discourse. We shall have more to say about this category later.

The final category contains analytic a posteriori propositions. This category would demand that a statement have its predicate contained within its subject, yet be immediately verified through sense experience. Upon consideration, this demand seems linguistically odd. For, if one is aware of a predicate as contained within a subject, then it surely seems superfluous to assert that this sentence must also be made known via sense experience. Put differently, if the subject is contained within the predicate, what else can the statement be except a priori. A mere consideration of the concept itself is sufficient for understanding.

Nevertheless, there is one possible candidate for the analytic a posteriori category. This is Descartes' famous statement, "I think, therefore, I am." (ogito, ergo sum.") Some scholars argue that the "cogito" is a necessarily true statement which is immediately experienced. The "cogito," on this view, is regarded as an immediated intuition. After having read Descartes' *Meditation II* and having our discussion of the necessary conditions for an analytic a posteriori statement, should the "cogito" statement be put in this category?

Briefly, the Verification Theory of Meaning asserted by the logical positivists rendered significant only analytic a priori and synthetic a posteriori propositions. If a proposition fits neither of these categories, then it is meaningless. Under this criterion of meaningful discourse, the statements of both mathematics and the positive sciences become significant. Everything else is meaningless, the logical positivists argued, including classical metaphysics, theology, ethics, and aesthetics. The selection to follow, from A.J. Ayer's *Language, Truth and Logic,* illustrates the concern of the logical positivists to eliminate metaphysics from meaningful discourse and, a fortiori, from legitimate philosophical debate. By means of the verification criterion of meaning, the logical positivists were able to establish their revolution in philosophy. This revolution admits credence only to the claims of science and mathematics. Philosophy functions as the "handmaiden" for the sciences. As one philosopher adeptly put it, "The philosophy of science is philosophy enough!"

THE ELIMINATION OF METAPHYSICS

A.J. Ayer

The traditional disputes of philosophers are, for the most part, as unwarranted as they are unfruitful. The surest way to end them is to establish beyond question what should be the purpose and method of a philosophical enquiry. And this is by no means so difficult a task as the history of philosophy would lead one to suppose. For if there are any questions which science leaves it to philosophy to answer, a straightforward process of elimination must lead to their discovery.

We may begin by criticising the metaphysical thesis that philosophy affords us knowledge of a reality transcending the world of science and common sense. Later on, when we come to define metaphysics and account for its existence, we shall find that it is possible to be a metaphysician without believing in a transcendent reality; for we shall see that many metaphysical utterances are due to the commission of logical errors, rather than to a conscious desire on the part of their authors to go beyond the limits of experience. But it is convenient for us to take the case of those who believe that it is possible to have knowledge of a transcendent reality as a starting-point for our discussion. The arguments which we use to refute them will subsequently be found to apply to the whole of metaphysics.

One way of attacking a metaphysician who claimed to have knowledge of a reality which transcended the phenomenal world would be to enquire

---

From A.J. Ayer, *Language, Truth and Logic* (London: Victor Gollancz, Ltd., 1946), chapter 1, pp. 33–45. Reprinted by permission of Victor Gollancz, Ltd.

from what premises his propositions were deduced. Must he not begin, as other men do, with the evidence of his senses? And if so, what valid process of reasoning can possibly lead him to the conception of a transcendent reality? Surely from empirical premises nothing whatsoever concerning the properties, or even the existence, of anything super-empirical can legitimately be inferred. But this objection would be met by a denial on the part of the metaphysician that his assertions were ultimately based on the evidence of his senses. He would say that he was endowed with a faculty of intellectual intuition which enabled him to know facts that could not be known through sense-experience. And even if it could be shown that he was relying on empirical premises, and that his venture into a non-empirical world was therefore logically unjustified, it would not follow that the assertions which he made concerning this non-empirical world could not be true. For the fact that a conclusion does not follow from its putative premise is not sufficient to show that it is false. Consequently one cannot overthrow a system of transcendent metaphysics merely by criticising the way in which it comes into being. What is required is rather a criticism of the nature of argument which we shall, in fact, pursue. For we shall maintain that no statement which refers to a "reality" transcending the limits of all possible sense-experience can possibly have any literal significance; from which it must follow that the labours of those who have striven to describe such a reality have all been devoted to the production of nonsense.

It may be suggested that this is a proposition which has already been proved by Kant. But although Kant also condemned transcendent meta-physics, he did so on different grounds. For he said that the human under-standing was so constituted that it lost itself in contradictions when it ventured out beyond the limits of possible experience and attempted to deal with things in themselves. And thus he made the impossibility of a transcendent metaphysic not, as we do, a matter of logic, but a matter of fact. He asserted, not that our minds could not conceivably have had the power of penetrating beyond the phenomenal world, but merely that they were in fact devoid of it. And this leads the critic to ask how, if it is possible to know only what lies within the bounds of sense-experience, the author can be justified in asserting that real things do exist beyond, and how can he tell what are the boundaries beyond which the human understanding may not venture, unless he succeeds in passing them himself. As Wittgen-stein says, "in order to draw a limit to thinking, we should have to think both sides of this limit,"[1] a truth to which Bradley gives a special twist in maintaining that the man who is ready to prove that metaphysics is impossible is a brother metaphysician with a rival theory of his own.[2]

Whatever force these objections may have against the Kantian doctrine, they have none whatsoever against the thesis that I am about to set forth. It cannot here be said that the author is himself overstepping the barrier he maintains to be impassable. For the fruitlessness of attempting to tran-scend the limits of possible sense-experience will be deduced, not from a psychological hypothesis concerning the actual constitution of the human mind, but from the rule which determines the literal significance of lan-guage. Our charge against the metaphysician is not that he attempts to employ the understanding in a field where it cannot profitably venture, but that he produces sentences which fail to conform to the conditions under which alone a sentence can be literally significant. Nor are we ourselves obliged to talk nonsense in order to show that all sentences of a certain type are necessarily devoid of literal significance. We need only formulate the criterion which enables us to test whether a sentence expresses a genuine proposition about a matter of fact, and then point out that the sentences under consideration fail to satisfy it. And this we shall now proceed to do. We shall first of all formulate the criterion in somewhat vague terms, and then give the explanations which are necessary to render it precise.

The criterion which we use to test the genuineness of apparent statements of fact is the criterion of verifiability. We say that a sentence is factually significant to any given person, if, and only if, he knows how to verify the proposition which it purports to express—that is, if he knows what observations would lead him, under certain conditions, to accept the proposition as being true, or reject it as being false. If, on the other hand, the putative proposition is of such a character that the assumption of its truth, or falsehood, is consistent with any assumption whatsoever concerning the nature of his future experience, then, as far as he is concerned, it is, if not a tautology, a mere pseudo-proposition. The sentence expressing it may be emotionally significant to him; but it is not literally significant. And with regard to questions the procedure is the same. We enquire in every case what observations would lead us to answer the question, one way or the other; and, if none can be discovered, we must conclude that the sentence under consideration does not, as far as we are concerned, express a genuine question, however strongly its grammatical appearance may suggest that it does.

As the adoption of this procedure is an essential factor in the argument of this book, it needs to be examined in detail.

In the first place, it is necessary to draw a distinction between practical verifiability, and verifiability in principle. Plainly we all understand, in many cases believe, propositions which we have not in fact taken steps to verify. Many of these are propositions which we could verify if we took enough trouble. But there remain a number of significant propositions, concerning matters of fact, which we could not verify even if we chose; simply because we lack the practical means of placing ourselves in the situation where the relevant observations could be made. A simple and familiar example of such a proposition is the proposition that there are mountains on the farther side of the moon.[3] No rocket has yet been invented which would enable me to go and look at the farther side of the moon, so that I am unable to decide the matter by actual observation. But I do know what observations would decide it for me, if, as is theoretically conceivable, I were once in a position to make them. And therefore I say that the proposition is verifiable in principle, if not in practice, and is accordingly significant. On the other hand, such a metaphysical pseudo-proposition as "the Absolute enters into, but is itself incapable of, evolution and progress,"[4] is not even in principle verifiable. For one cannot conceive of an observation which would enable one to determine whether the Absolute did, or did not, enter into evolution and progress. Of course it is possible that the author of such a remark is using English words in a way in which they are not commonly used by English-speaking people, and that he does, in fact, intend to assert something which could be empirically verified. But until he makes us understand how the proposition that he wishes to express would be verified, he fails to communicate anything to us. And if he admits, as I think the author of the remark in question would have admitted, that his words were not intended to express either a tautology or a proposition which was capable, at least in principle, of being verified, then it follows that he has made an utterance which has no literal significance even for himself.

A further distinction which we must make is the distinction between the "strong" and the "weak" sense of the term "verifiable." A proposition is said to be verifiable, in the strong sense of the term, if, and only if, its truth could be conclusively established in experience. But it is verifiable, in the weak sense, if it is possible for experience to render it probable. In which sense are we using the term when we say that a putative proposition is genuine only if it is verifiable?

It seems to me that if we adopt conclusive verifiability as our criterion of significance, as some positivists have proposed,[5] our argument will prove too much. Consider, for example, the case of general propositions of law— such propositions, namely, as "arsenic is poisonous"; "all men are mortal"; "a body tends to expand when it is heated." It is of the very nature of these propositions that their truth cannot be established with certainty by any finite series of observations. But if it is recognised that such general propositions of law are designed to cover an infinite number of cases, then it must be admitted that they cannot, even in principle, be verified conclusively. And then, if we adopt conclusive verifiability as our criterion of significance, we are logically obliged to treat these general propositions of law in the same fashion as we treat the statements of the metaphysician.

In face of this difficulty, some positivists[6] have adopted the heroic course of saying that these general propositions are indeed pieces of nonsense, albeit an essentially important type of nonsense. But here the introduction of the term "important" is simply an attempt to hedge. It serves only to mark the authors' recognition that their view is somewhat too paradoxical, without in any way removing the paradox. Besides, the difficulty is not confined to the case of general propositions of law, though it is there revealed most plainly. It is hardly less obvious in the case of propositions about the remote past. For it must surely be admitted that, however strong the evidence in favour of historical statements may be, their truth can never become more than highly probable. And to maintain that they also constituted an important, or unimportant, type of nonsense, would be unplausible, to say the very least. Indeed, it will be our contention that no proposition, other than a tautology, can possibly be anything more than a probable hypothesis. And if this is correct, the principle that a sentence can be factually significant only if it expresses what is conclusively verifiable is self-stultifying as a criterion of significance. For it leads to the conclusion that it is impossible to make a significant statement of fact at all.

Nor can we accept the suggestion that a sentence should be allowed to be factually significant if, and only if, it expresses something which is definitely confutable by experience.[7] Those who adopt this course assume that, although no finite series of observations is ever sufficient to establish the truth of a hypothesis beyond all possibility of doubt, there are crucial cases in which a single observation, or series of observations, can definitely confute it. But, as we shall show later on, this assumption is false. A hypothesis cannot be conclusively confuted any more than it can be conclusively verified. For when we take the occurrence of certain observations as proof that a given hypothesis is false, we presuppose the existence of certain conditions. And though, in any given case, it may be extremely improbable that this assumption is false, it is not logically impossible. We shall see that there need be no self-contradiction in holding that some of the relevant circumstances are other than we have taken them to be, and consequently that the hypothesis has not really broken down. And if it is not the case that any hypothesis can be definitely confuted, we cannot hold that the genuineness of a proposition depends on the possibility of its definite confutation.

Accordingly, we fall back on the weaker sense of verification. We say that the question that must be asked about any putative statement of fact is not, Would any observations make its truth or falsehood logically certain? but simply, Would any observations be relevant to the determination of its truth or falsehood? And it is only if a negative answer is given to this second question that we conclude that the statement under consideration is nonsensical.

To make our position clearer, we may formulate it in another way. Let us call a proposition which records an actual or possible observation an experimental proposition. Then we may say that it is the mark of a genuine factual proposition, not that it should be equivalent to an experiential proposition, or any finite number of experiential propositions, but simply that some experiential propositions can be deduced from it in conjunction with certain other premises without being deducible from those other premises alone.[8]

This criterion seems liberal enough. In contrast to the principle of conclusive verifiability, it clearly does not deny significance to general propositions or to propositions about the past. Let us see what kinds of assertion it rules out.

A good example of the kind of utterance that is condemned by our criterion as being not even false but nonsensical would be the assertion that the world of sense-experience was altogether unreal. It must, of course, be admitted that our senses do sometimes deceive us. We may, as the result of having certain sensations, expect certain other sensations to be obtainable which are, in fact, not obtainable. But, in all such cases, it is further sense-experience that informs us of the mistakes that arise out of sense-experience. We say that the senses sometimes deceive us, just because the expectations to which our sense-experiences give rise do not always accord with what we subsequently experience. That is, we rely on our senses to substantiate or confute the judgements which are based on our sensations. And therefore the fact that our perceptual judgements are sometimes found to be erroneous has not the slightest tendency to show that the world of sense-experience is unreal. And, indeed, it is plain that no conceivable observation, or series of observations, could have any tendency to show that the world revealed to us by sense-experience was unreal. Consequently, anyone who condemns the sensible world as a world of mere appearance, as opposed to reality, is saying something which, according to our criterion of significance, is literally nonsensical.

An example of a controversy which the application of our criterion obliges us to condemn as fictitious is provided by those who dispute concerning the number of substances that there are in the world. For it is admitted both by monists, who maintain that reality is one substance, and by pluralists, who maintain that reality is many, that it is impossible to imagine any empirical situation which would be relevant to the solution of their dispute. But if we are told that no possible observation could give any probability either to the assertion that reality was one substance or to the assertion that it was many, then we must conclude that neither assertion is significant. We shall see later on that there are genuine logical and empirical questions involved in the dispute between monists and pluralists. But the metaphysical question concerning "substance" is ruled out by our criterion as spurious.

A similar treatment must be accorded to the controversy between realists and idealists, in its metaphysical aspect. A simple illustration, which I have made use of in a similar argument elsewhere,[9] will help to demonstrate this. Let us suppose that a picture is discovered and the suggestion made that it was painted by Goya. There is a definite procedure for dealing with such a question. The experts examine the picture to see in what way it resembles the accredited works of Goya, and to see if it bears any marks which are characteristic of a forgery; they look up contemporary records for evidence of the existence of such a picture, and so on. In the end, they may still disagree, but each one knows what empirical evidence would go to confirm or discredit his opinion. Suppose, now, that these men have studied philosophy, and some of them proceed to maintain that this picture is a set of ideas in the perceiver's mind, or in God's mind, others that it is objectively real. What possible experience could any of them have which would be relevant to the solution of this dispute one way or the other? In the ordinary sense of the term "real," in which it is opposed to "illusory," the reality of the picture is not in doubt. The disputants have satisfied themselves that the picture is real, in this sense, by obtaining a correlated series of sensations of sight and sensations of touch. Is there any similar process by which they could discover whether the picture was real, in the sense in which the term "real" is opposed to "ideal"? Clearly there is none. But, if that is so, the problem is fictitious according to our criterion. This does not mean that the realist-idealist controversy may be dismissed without further ado. For it can legitimately be regarded as a dispute concerning the analysis of existential propositions, and so as involving a logical problem which, as we shall see, can be definitely solved. What we have just shown is that the question at issue between idealists and realists becomes fictitious when, as is often the case, it is given a metaphysical interpretation.

There is no need for us to give further examples of the operation of our criterion of significance. For our object is merely to show that philosophy, as a genuine branch of knowledge, must be distinguished from metaphysics. We are not now concerned with the historical question how much of what has traditionally passed for philosophy is actually metaphysical. We shall, however, point out later on that the majority of the "great philosophers" of the past were not essentially metaphysicians, and thus reassure those who would otherwise be prevented from adopting our criterion by considerations of piety.

As to the validity of the verification principle, in the form in which we have stated it, a demonstration will be given in the course of this book. For it will be shown that all propositions which have factual content are empirical hypotheses; and that the function of an empirical hypothesis is to provide a rule for the anticipation of experience. And this means that every empirical hypothesis must be relevant to some actual, or possible, experience, so that a statement which is not relevant to any experience is not an empirical hypothesis, and accordingly has no factual content. But this is precisely what the principle of verifiability asserts.

It should be mentioned here that the fact that the utterances of the metaphysician are nonsensical does not follow simply from the fact that they are devoid of factual content. It follows from that fact, together with the fact that they are not *a priori* propositions. And in assuming that they are not *a priori* propositions, we are once again anticipating the conclusions of a later chapter in this book. For it will be shown there that *a priori* propositions, which have always been attractive to philosophers on account of their certainty, owe this certainty to the fact that they are tautologies. We may accordingly define a metaphysical sentence as a sentence which purports to express a genuine proposition, but does, in fact, express neither a tautology nor an empirical hypothesis. And as tautologies and empirical hypotheses form the entire class of significant propositions, we are justified in concluding that all metaphysical assertions are nonsensical. Our next task is to show how they come to be made.

The use of the term "substance," to which we have already referred, provides us with a good example of the way in which metaphysics mostly comes to be written. It happens to be the case that we cannot, in our language, refer to the sensible properties of a thing without introducing a word or phrase which appears to stand for the thing itself as opposed to anything which may be said about it. And, as a result of this, those who are infected by the primitive superstition that to every name a single real entity must correspond assume that it is necessary to distinguish logically between the thing itself and any, or all, of its sensible properties. And so they employ the term "substance" to refer to the thing itself. But from the fact that we happen to employ a single word to refer to a thing, and make that word the grammatical subject of the sentences in which we refer to the sensible appearances of the thing, it does not by any means follow that the thing itself is a "simple entity," or that it cannot be defined in terms of the totality of its appearances. It is true that in talking of "its" appearances we appear to distinguish the thing from the appearances, but that is simply an accident of linguistic usage. Logical analysis shows that what makes these "appearances" the "appearances of" the same thing is not their relationship to an entity other than themselves, but their relationship to one another. The metaphysician fails to see this because he is misled by a superficial grammatical feature of his language.

A simpler and clearer instance of the way in which a consideration of grammar leads to metaphysics is the case of the metaphysical concept of Being. The origin of our temptation to raise questions about Being, which no conceivable experience would enable us to answer, lies in the fact that, in our language, sentences which express existential propositions and sentences which express attributive propositions may be of the same grammatical form. For instance, the sentences "Martyrs exist" and "Martyrs suffer" both consist of a noun followed by an intransitive verb, and the fact that they have grammatically the same appearance leads one to assume that they are of the same logical type. It is seen that in the proposition "Martyrs suffer," the members of a certain species are credited with a certain attribute, and it is sometimes assumed that the same thing is true of such a proposition as "Martyrs exist." If this were actually the case, it would, indeed, be as legitimate to speculate about the Being of martyrs as it is to speculate about their suffering. But, as Kant pointed out,[10] existence is not an attribute. For, when we ascribe an attribute to a thing, we covertly assert that it exists: so that if existence were itself an attribute, it would follow that all positive existential propositions were tautologies, and all negative existential propositions self-contradictory; and this is not the case.[11] So that those who raise questions about Being which are based on the assumption that existence is an attribute are guilty of following grammar beyond the boundaries of sense.

A similar mistake has been made in connection with such propositions as "Unicorns are fictitious." Here again the fact that there is a superficial grammatical resemblance between the English sentences "Dogs are faithful" and "Unicorns are fictitious," and between the corresponding sentences in other languages, creates the assumption that they are of the same logical type. Dogs must exist in order to have the property of being faithful, and so it is held that unless unicorns in some way existed they could not have the property of being fictitious. But, as it is plainly self-contradictory to say that fictitious objects exist, the device is adopted of saying that they are real in some non-empirical sense—that they have a mode of real being which is different from the mode of being of existent things. But since there is no way of testing whether an object is real in this sense, as there is for testing whether it is real in the ordinary sense, the assertion that fictitious objects have a special non-empirical mode of real being is devoid of all literal significance. It comes to be made as a result of the assumption that being fictitious is an attribute. And this is a fallacy of the same order as the fallacy of supposing that existence is an attribute, and it can be exposed in the same way.

In general, the postulation of real non-existent entities results from the superstition, just now referred to, that, to every word or phrase that can be the grammatical subject of a sentence, there must somewhere be a real entity corresponding. For as there is no place in the empirical world for many of these "entities," a special non-empirical world is invoked to house them. To this error must be attributed, not only the utterances of a Heidegger, who bases his metaphysics on the assumption that "Nothing" is a name which is used to denote something peculiarly mysterious,[12] but also the prevalence of such problems as those concerning the reality of propositions and universals whose senselessness, though less obvious, is no less complete.

These few examples afford a sufficient indication of the way in which most metaphysical assertions come to be formulated. They show how easy it is to write sentences which are literally nonsensical without seeing that they are nonsensical. And thus we see that the view that a number of the traditional "problems of philosophy" are metaphysical, and consequently fictitious, does not involve any incredible assumptions about the psychology of philosophers.

Among those who recognise that if philosophy is to be accounted a genuine branch of knowledge it must be defined in such a way to distinguish it from metaphysics, it is fashionable to speak of the metaphysician as a kind of misplaced poet. As his statements have no literal meaning, they are not subject to any criteria of truth or falsehood: but they may still serve to express, or arouse, emotion; and thus be subject to ethical or aesthetic standards. And it is suggested that they may have considerable value, as means of moral inspiration, or even as works of art. In this way, an attempt is made to compensate the metaphysician for his extrusion from philosophy.[13]

I am afraid that this compensation is hardly in accordance with his deserts. The view that the metaphysician is to be reckoned among the poets appears to rest on the assumption that both talk nonsense. But this assumption is false. In the vast majority of cases the sentences which are produced by poets do have literal meaning. The difference between the man who uses language scientifically and the man who uses it emotively is not that the one produces sentences which have no sense, but that the one is primarily concerned with the expression of true propositions, the other with the creation of a work of art. Thus, if a work of science contains true and important propositions, its value as a work of science will hardly be diminished by the fact that they are inelegantly expressed. And similarly, a work of art is not necessarily the worse for the fact that all the propositions comprising it are literally false. But to say that many literary works are largely composed of falsehoods, is not to say that they are composed of pseudo-propositions. It is, in fact, very rare for a literary artist to produce sentences which have no literal meaning. And where this does occur, the sentences are carefully chosen for their rhythm and balance. If the author writes nonsense, it is because he considers it most suitable for bringing about the effects for which his writing is designed.

The metaphysician, on the other hand, does not intend to write nonsense. He lapses into it through being deceived by grammar, or through committing errors of reasoning, such as that which leads to the view that the sensible world is unreal. But it is not the mark of a poet simply to make mistakes of this sort. There are some, indeed, who would see in the fact that the metaphysician's utterances are senseless a reason against the view that they have aesthetic value. And, without going so far as this, we may safely say that it does not constitute a reason for it.

It is true, however, that although the greater part of metaphysics is merely the embodiment of humdrum errors, there remain a number of metaphysical passages which are the work of genuine mystical feeling; and they may more plausibly be held to have moral or aesthetic value. But, as far as we are concerned, the distinction between the kind of metaphysics that is produced by a philosopher who has been duped by grammar, and the kind that is produced by a mystic who is trying to express the inexpressible, is of no great importance: what is important to us is to realise that even the utterances of the metaphysician who is attempting to expound a vision are literally senseless; so that henceforth we may pursue our philosophical researches with as little regard for them as for the more inglorious kind of metaphysics which comes from a failure to understand the workings of our language.

NOTES

1. *Tractatus Logico-Philosophicus*, Preface.
2. Bradley, *Appearance and Reality*, 2nd ed., p. I.
3. This example has been used by Professor Schlick to illustrate the same point.
4. A remark taken at random from *Appearance and Reality*, by F.H. Bradley.
5. e.g. M. Schlick, "Positivismus und Realismus," *Erkenntnis*, Vol. 1, 1930. F. Waismann, "Logische Analyse des Warscheinlichkeitsbegriffs," *Erkenntnis*, Vol. I, 1930.
6. e.g., M. Schlick, "Die Kausalitat in der gegenwartigen Physik," *Naturwissenschaft*, Vol. 19, 1931.
7. This has been proposed by Karl Popper in his *Logik der Forschung*.
8. This is an over-simplified statement, which is not literally correct.
9. Vide "Demonstration of the Impossibility of Metaphysics," *Mind*, 1934, p. 339.
10. Vide *The Critique of Pure Reason*, "Transcendental Dialectic," Book II, Chapter iii, section 4.
11. This argument is well stated by John Wisdom, *Interpretation and Analysis*, pp. 62, 63.
12. Vide *Was ist Metaphysik*, by Heidegger: criticised by Rudolf Carnap in his "Uberwindung der Metaphysik durch logische Analyse der Sprache," *Erkenntnis*, Vol. II, 1932.
13. For a discussion of this point, see also C.A. Mace, "Representation and Expression," *Analysis*, Vol. I, No. 3; and "Metaphysics and Emotive Language," *Analysis*, Vol. II, Nos, 1 and 2.

The logical positivists assert the significance only of definitional and descriptive propositions. Anything else is meaningless discourse. A mathematical statement becomes meaningful in that it is "true by definition." The logical positivists suggest that Plato was misguided when he adopted a reference theory of meaning and then concluded, using the analogy of the "divided line," that mathematical propositions must refer to abstract entities in order to be meaningful. To the positivists, mathematical propositions are significant because they are definitions. A definition need not refer because an analytic a priori proposition—which is what a definition really is—has its predicate contained within its subject. That alone suffices for meaning.

Likewise, propositions in the physical sciences are significant because they can be empirically verified. An acid and a base, when combined under proper laboratory conditions, yield a soluble salt and water. One can go to a chemistry lab and *sensibly verify* this fact through an experiment. This is synthetic a posteriori knowledge. Is there a structural similarity between the verification criterion of meaning and Berkeley's principle that "To be is to be perceived"?

Hume and Positivism

David Hume anticipated the verification principle of meaning. Although he discussed the conditions for significant ideas, and not sentences, the similarities are striking.

> All the objects of human reason or inquiry may naturally be divided into two kinds, to wit, *Relations of Ideas,* and *Matters of Fact.* Of the first kind are the sciences of Geometry, Algebra and Arithmetic; and in short, every affirmation which is either intuitively or demonstratively certain. *That the square of the hypothenuse is equal to the square of the two sides,* is a proposition which expresses a relation between these figures. *That three times five is equal to half of thirty* expresses a relation between these numbers. Propositions of this kind are discoverable by the mere operation of thought, without dependence on what is anywhere existent in the universe. Though there never were a circle or triangle in nature, the truths demonstrated by Euclid would forever retain their certainty and evidence.
>
> Matters of fact, which are the second objects of human reason, are not ascertained in the same manner; nor is our evidence of their truth, however great, of a like nature with the foregoing. The contrary of every matter of fact is still possible; because it can never imply a contradiction and is conceived by the mind with the same facility and distinctness, as if ever so conformable to reality. *That the sun will not rise tomorrow* is no less intelligible a proposition, and implies no more contradiction than the affirmation *that it will rise.* We should in vain, therefore, attempt to demonstrate its falsehood. Were it demonstratively false, it would imply a contradiction and could never be distinctly conceived by the mind. . . .
>
> Here, therefore, is a proposition, which not only seems in itself simple and intelligible. But if a proper use were made of it, it might render every dispute equally intelligible, and banish all that jargon, which has so long taken possession of metaphysical reasonings, and drawn disgrace upon them. All ideas, especially abstract ones, are naturally faint and obscure. The mind has but a slender hold of them. They are apt to be confounded with other resembling ideas; and when we have often employed any term, though without a distinct meaning, we are apt to imagine that it has a determinate idea annexed to it. On the contrary, all impressions—i.e., all sensations, either outward or inward—are strong and vivid. The limits between them are more exactly determined: nor is it easy to fall into any error or mistake with regard to them. When we entertain, therefore any suspicion that a philosophical term is employed without any meaning or idea (as is but too frequent), we need but inquire, *From what impression is that supposed idea derived?* And if it be possible to assign any, this will serve to confirm our suspicion. By bringing ideas into so clear a light we may reasonably hope to remove all dispute, which may arise, concerning their nature and reality.[13]

The passage from *Language, Truth and Logic* indicated that the positivists were very much concerned about the status of the verification criterion of meaning itself. In fact, this was one of Ayer's principal concerns. This type of discussion brought out, in many positivists, distinctions regarding different uses of "possibility" and "impossibility." This is germane to a discussion of meaning in that the verification criterion purported to denote the very bounds or limits for the possibility of meaningful discourse. The positivists considered three kinds of impossibility:

1. Logical impossibility

2. Technological impossibility
3. Physical impossibility

Logical impossibility refers to those statements which are totally beyond the limits of empirical verification. For example, "The blue gremlin causes the balloon to rise." It is impossible to ever sensibly verify the existence of a "blue gremlin." Another example would be "God made the heavens and the earth." The logical positivists ask what possible set of empirical circumstances could either confirm or disconfirm either the existence of God or a gremlin. According to them, there are none. Both propositions purport to describe some factual state of affairs. But, the positivists ask, how would one go about empirically verifying either one? Therefore, according to the verification criterion of meaning, propositions of this type are totally beyond the bounds of empirical verification. Obviously all metaphysical propositions fit into this category of meaninglessness.

There are other statements which are impossible to verify, however. Consider the following statements. "There is life on Jupiter," and "The mountains on Mars are made of carbon." Certainly we cannot sensibly verify either one of these propositions at this moment. Yet we could go to a chemistry laboratory and discover that hydrochloric acid and sodium hydroxide yield sodium chloride and water. What is the difference between these two types of descriptive propositions? The positivists argued that the former are examples of statements which are technologically impossible to verify. It is impossible to verify these statements now because of the limits of our present technological capabilities. However sometime in the future we might be able to actually possess the technological expertise and machinery to verify these claims. In other words, it is conceivable that some set of empirical data would count in either confirming or disconfirming the claims about Jupiter and Mars. On the other hand, no matter how technologically advanced a society might become, there is no empirical data which would confirm or disconfirm the existence of Plato's world of the forms.

A statement is physically impossible if it is in violation of a known physical law expressed by the physical sciences. For example: "A body heavier than air will travel upwards in the earth's atmosphere." Obviously this statement is contrary to the law of gravity. How could we ever verify the statement? However, we can verify the opposite claim. We do know that bodies fall in the earth's atmosphere rather than rise. The positivists would argue that, if we can verify the negation of a statement, it indicates that the statement is meaningful. Yet we can empirically verify neither the assertion nor denial of propositions concerning the world of the forms. Metaphysical statements, therefore, are classified in the category of logically impossible statements because they are, in principle, closed to any method of empirical verification.

Problems with Verification

Recall that Ayer discussed both the "strong" and the "weak" senses of verifiability. The strong sense refers to the actual process of empirical verification. Weak verification refers only to *probable* verification. This distinction, as Ayer's passage illustrates, engendered much discussion over the exact status of the verification principle of meaning. Although the totality and complexity of this discussion are beyond the bounds of our introductory discussion, nonetheless we shall consider some of these problems. In fact, the futility the positivists experienced in trying to account for the exact status of the verification principle of meaning led ultimately to the demise of logical positivism. The primary problem concerned the significance of the verification principle itself. On first glance, the verification principle seems to be neither analytic nor synthetic. It certainly is not an object of direct sense experience. But is it merely a definition? Remember that these alone are the conditions for meaningfulness established by the positivists. One possible solution suggested that the verification principle of meaning was itself a "rule" which prescribes how language users should classify meaningful discourse. Some of the positivists argued that it was a "proposal." This solution is problematic, however. If the verification principle of meaning is itself merely a proposal—thus a "stipulative definition,"—then a critic might reasonably ask why we ought to adopt it rather than any other rule of meaning. With his exaggerated theory of reference, Plato might also be regarded as providing a rule of meaning. Thus, if the positivist's criterion is just a proposal, then what grounds for justification did the positivists have for forcing Platonists to amend their ontologies? The exact status of the verification principle of meaning was indeed problematical for the logical positivists.

In his book, *English Philosophy since 1900,* G.J. Warnock elaborates on further problems faced by the logical positivists and the verification principle of meaning:

> . . . (There) arose grave internal difficulties in their (Logical Positivists') position. These all arose out of the problem of defining exactly what was to be meant by "verification." It seems, for example, reasonable to say that, so far as I am concerned, verifying any statement must consist in my having, now or in the future, experiences of the appropriate sort. But from this two odd consequences seem to follow. First, does it not follow, according to the verification principle, that any statement, even a statement which purports to refer to the past, must *really* mean (so far as I am concerned) something about my present or future experience? If verification can occur only now or in the future, can I ever succeed in really *meaning* something about the past? Second, can it really be that any two people ever mean or understand the same thing? Verification for you must occur in your experience, and for me in mine. Hence, what any statement really means must apparently be systematically different for each person who does or might hear or read, speak or write it. How, then do we succeed in communicating with each other? What I mean, others can necessarily not understand. [14]

If Warnock is correct, then what could justify historical knowledge for a positivist? Thus, all past knowledge claims seem to be on dubitable grounds for radical empiricism. Second, does logical positivism entail solipsism? As we will recall, solipsism can be defined as the impossibility of ever having knowledge beyond one's own individual range of awareness. If this is consistent with the verification principle of meaning, could two positivists ever communicate with each other? The problem of linguistic solipsism appears to be directly connected with the strong sense of the verification principle of meaning.

In addition, what is the object of knowledge grasped on a thoroughly empiricist criterion? Remember how Berkeley argued that what we know is nothing more than a bundle of sensations. Roderick Chisholm dwells on the inadequacy of radical empiricism ever to know physical objects in the following passage from his *The Problem of the Criterion.* (Note that *methodist* refers, not to the religious followers of John Wesley, but to an adherent of a radical empiricist *methodology.*)

> Empiricism, then, was a form of what I have called "methodism." The empiricist—like other types of methodist—begins with a criterion and then he uses it to throw out the bad apples. There are two objections, I would say, to empiricism. The first—which applies to every form of methodism (in our present sense of the word)—is that the criterion is very broad and far-reaching and at the same time completely arbitrary. How can one *begin* with a broad generalization? It seems especially odd that the empiricist—who wants to proceed cautiously, step by step, from experience—begins with such a generalization. He leaves us completely in the dark so far as concerns what *reasons* he may have for adopting this particular criterion rather than some other. The second objection applies to empiricism in particular. When we apply the empirical criterion—at least, as it was developed by Hume, as well as by many of those in the nineteenth and twentieth centuries who have called themselves "empiricists"—we seem to throw out, not only the bad apples but the good ones as well, and we are left, in effect, with just a few paring or skins with no meat behind them. Thus Hume virtually conceded that, if you are going to be empiricist, the only matters of fact that you can really know about pertain to the existence of sensations. "Tis vain," he said, "To ask whether there be body." He meant you cannot know whether there are any physical things—whether there are trees, or houses, or bodies, much less whether there are atoms or other such microscopic particles. All you can know is that there are and have been certain sensations. You cannot know whether there is a "you" who experiences those sensations—much less whether there are any other people who experience sensations. And I think, if he had been consistent in his empiricism, he would also have said you cannot really be sure whether there have been any sensations in the past; you can know only that there are certain sensations here and now.[15]

Radical empiricism leaves the philosopher with nothing more than an awareness of a set of directly evident sensations or the memory image of a past awareness. We can assert the veracity of no other empirical statements. In the end, we become sceptics insofar as we know nothing about the nature of the external world, and this is just where Hume directed our radical empiricism. Hume wrote:

> These two propositions are far from being the same: *I have found that such an object has always been attended with such an effect,* and *I foresee, that other objects which are in appearance, similar, will be attended with similar effects.* I shall allow, if you please, that the one proposition may justly be inferred from the other; I know, in fact that it always is inferred. But if you insist that the inference is made by a chain of reasoning, I desire you to produce that reasoning. . . .
>
> When it is asked, *What is the nature of all our reasoning concerning matter of fact?*, the proper answer seems to be, that they are founded on the relation of cause and effect. When again it is asked, *What is the foundation of all our reasonings and conclusions concerning that relation?*, it may be replied in one word, Experience. But if we still carry on sifting humor, and ask, *What is the foundation of all conclusions from experience?*, this implies a new question, which may be of more difficult solution and explication. . . .
>
> I shall content myself . . . with an easy task, and shall pretend only to give a negative answer to the question here proposed. I say then, that, even after we have

experience of the operations of cause and effect, our conclusions from that experience are *not* founded on reasoning, or any process of the understanding. . . .

Here, then, is our natural state of ignorance with regard to the powers and influence of all objects. How is this remedied by experience? It only shows us a number of uniform effects resulting from certain objects, and teaches us that those particular objects, at that particular time, were endowed with such powers and forces. When a new object, endowed with similar sensible qualities, is produced, we expect similar powers and forces, and look for a like effect. From a body of like color and consistency with bread we expect like nourishment and support. But this surely is a step or progress of the mind, which wants to be explained. When a man says, *I have found, in all past instances, such sensible qualities conjoined with such secret powers:* and when he says, *Similar sensible qualities will always be conjoined with similar secret powers,* he is not guilty of a tautology, nor are these propositions in any respect the same. You say that the one proposition is an inference from the other. But you must confess that the inference is not intuitive; neither is it demonstrative: of what nature is it, then? To say it is experimental, is begging the question. For all inferences from experience suppose, as their foundation, that the future will resemble the past, and that similar powers will be conjoined with similar sensible qualities. If there be any suspicion that the course of nature may change, and that the past may be no rule for the future, all experience becomes useless, and can give rise to no inference or conclusion. It is impossible, therefore, that any arguments from experience can prove this resemblance of the past to the future; since all these arguments are founded on the supposition of that resemblance. Let the course of things be allowed hitherto ever so regular; that alone, without some new argument or inference, proves not that, for the future, it will continue so. In vain do you pretend to have learned the nature of bodies from your past experience. Their secret nature, and consequently all their effects and influence, may change, without any change in their sensible qualities. This happens sometimes, and with regard to some objects: why may it not happen always, and with regard to all objects? What logic, what process of argument secures you against this supposition? My practice, you say, refutes my doubts. But you mistake the purport of my question. As an agent, I am quite satisfied in the point; but as a philosopher, who has some share of curiosity, I will not say scepticism, I want to learn the foundation of this inference. No reading, no inquiry has yet been able to remove my difficulty, or give me satisfaction in a matter of such importance. Can I do better than propose the difficulty to the public, even though, perhaps, I have small hopes of obtaining a solution? We shall at least, by this means, be sensible of our ignorance, if we do not augment our knowledge. . . . [16]

Some recent philosophers have been highly critical of Hume's scepticism. Everett J. Nelson, in his presidential address before the American Philosophical Association, argued against this scepticism. Nelson argued for the categories of substance and causality as being necessary presuppositions for any understanding of the world via induction. This was a frontal attack on Hume's scepticism regarding inductive knowledge of matters of fact. These metaphysical presuppositions of causality and substance, Nelson argued, will permit us to indeed have knowledge about the world beyond the immediate data of sensations and memory images. In effect, Nelson was worried about the same problem which forced Berkeley into postulating the Super Perceiver as God. Pay close attention to Nelson's argument for regularity in our experience and the ontological demand for a category beyond immediate sensations in order to account for this regularity in the following.

METAPHYSICAL PRESUPPOSITIONS OF INDUCTION

Everett J. Nelson

Tonight I should like to consider some of the metaphysical presuppositions of induction. Hume taught Kant, and, I wish I could say, all his successors, that the validity of empirical knowledge going beyond immediately given perceptions presupposes objective unities and connections. As a consequence of his not finding these unities or connections in or certified by immediate experience, he affirmed an extreme pluralism and conceded the resulting scepticism. He expressed the problem of induction so well that I cannot do better than to quote him. ". . . all inferences from experience suppose, as their foundation, that the future will resemble the past, and that similar powers will be conjoined with similar qualities. . . . It is impossible . . . that any arguments from experience can prove this resemblance of the past to the future; since all these arguments are founded on the supposition of that resemblance."[1] He held too that the only relation that can support such inferences is a necessary causal connection,[2] and that this necessity which is a constituent of the causal relation is not logical or analytic. It follows then that the foundation of empirical inference, if it have a foundation, is a non-logical causal necessity. I shall argue that causal necessity is synthetic, that it must hold between events in virtue of their properties, and that it is therefore a necessary condition of the soundness of induction. I am not going to try to justify or validate induction, but rather to spell out some of its necessary conditions and in doing so to interrelate certain notions involved in it; e.g., causation, necessity, law, uniformity.

I shall argue accordingly, and following Hume and Kant, that among the necessary conditions of empirical inference is the truth of propositions that assert more than is given in or confirmable by sense experience in so far as empiricism is the doctrine that we may pass with probability from data of experience to what is not part of those data—e.g., propositions about the future from propositions about the present or past—it is a non-empirical doctrine: it presupposes the truth of propositions that are not inferrable from or rendered probable by experience.

I do not deny the usual distinction between deductive and inductive arguments; I do believe however that all valid argument must conform to the canons of demonstrative reasoning. Indeed, as I shall point out, inductive arguments are much more complicated than the usual paradigms of deduction: they involve concepts, principles, and rules we do not find in the latter cases. A proper formulation of an inductive argument will make them and their place in it explicit. It will show that principles going beyond empirical data function as premises or rules, that with them the argument will be deductively valid and without them, invalid and incapable of providing a rational or reasonable ground for accepting the conclusion.

We do indeed in ordinary speech say that employment of induction is rational or reasonable, but this is not because by definition it is rational or reasonable to infer a conclusion that is not implied by the given empirical

Presidential address delivered before the Sixty-Fifth Annual Meeting of the Western Division of the American Philosophical Association in Chicago, Illinois, May 4–6, 1967. Reprinted by permission of the American Philosophical Association and the author.

data, but because we believe that the empirical data of an inductive inference are *reasons* or *evidence* for the conclusion. Even the most confirmed sceptic would not deny that it is rational to infer from *evidence,* but he would ask to be shown that the given data *are* evidence. Hence he may know very well the meaning of being rational and yet question the rationality of inferring, e.g., descriptive propositions about the future from descriptive propositions about the past.

The problem therefore is not whether one is justified in inferring from *evidence,* but whether propositions reporting some data *are* evidence for propositions not implied by them. This problem can not be solved by definition or by appeal to practice—even linguistic practice—but by answering the question whether there is a relation of "evidence for" running from a proposition of certain form, e.g., "This A is B," to a proposition of a different form, "All A are B." And in order to answer this question we must answer two questions: (1) What are the necessary conditions for one proposition to be evidence for another? and (2) Are these conditions satisfied? I shall consider only the first question. Indeed I wish I could answer the second, but that would require a metaphysics which I do not pretend to be able to establish. Accordingly, I shall be concerned only with the first question, What are the necessary conditions of the validity of induction? Justifying induction would of course require establishing the truth of these necessary conditions.

Since the conclusion of an inductive argument goes beyond its empirical premises, we must, as we have said, have principles in virtue of which those premises *are evidence* for the conclusion in the sense that they confer some probability on it and make it reasonable or rational to bet, if the probability is high, that the conclusion is true, and, if the probability is low, that the conclusion is false. One such principle of evidence is what has commonly been called a Principle of Induction.

This principle is then a necessary condition of the validity of inductive arguments. It must be such that it and the empirical data together are sufficient to the probable inference of the conclusion: it must provide the credential in virtue of which empirical data confer probability on the conclusion. Since the basic or primary type of induction is the inference of a universal proposition, the Principle must validate the inference of it. So-called inference of particulars from particulars is no exception to this, for it involves first the inference of a universal and then the application of the universal to further particulars. I shall therefore limit myself to the inference of universal propositions.

But first, since there are two kinds of universal proposition relevant to our discussion, we must distinguish between them. These are lawlike or nomological or, as I shall say nomic, and non-lawlike or as I shall say, accidental, without implying any restriction on the universality asserted. Sentences expressing examples of the first kind are "All crows are black," "All mammals are vertebrates." Sentences expressing examples of the second kind are "All chairs in this room are brown," "All Presidents of the United States are male." Since sentences of the same form are often used to express propositions of different forms, the form of sentence does not, at least in many cases, furnish a reliable clue to the form of proposition it is used to express. Thus the four sentences I just used to express examples have the same form. Since it has been alleged that the form of nomic universals is the same as that of accidental ones, there may after all be no ambiguity of expression to the propositions themselves. There is however one commonly acknowledged difference between nomic and accidental universals, which may help us determine whether they do in fact express intrinsically different propositions; namely, that nomic but not accidental universals support subjunctive and counterfactual conditional propositions. Thus the nomic, "All crows are black," supports the propositions "If this cardinal were a crow, it would be black" and "If Caesar had been a crow, he would have been black." But the accidental, "All chairs in this room are brown" would not support "If the chair outside the door were in this room, it would be brown" or "If the chair Caesar sat on had been in this room, it would have been brown."

What then distinguishes nomic propositions from accidental ones, in virtue of which the former but not the latter support contrary-to-fact conditionals? Two alternative answers have been suggested: (1) Nomic and accidental universals do not differ in their natures or in the relations they assert between their terms, but rather in their relations to certain other propositions; and (2) they do differ in their natures or assertions.

According to the first alternative, both nomic and accidental universals assert just uniformities and, consequently, are not to be distinguished intrinsically. That one universal p is nomic and so supports a subjunctive or counterfactual conditional and that another universal q is accidental and so does not support such a conditional depend not on what p itself asserts or on what q itself asserts, but on a difference in their relations to propositions in a prevailing or accepted theory. Accordingly, a warrant for saying that a given universal proposition is nomic is that it is integrally related to other universal propositions that are elements of a systematically or deductively related set of propositions which are accepted and used in prediction and explanation.

No one doubts that universal propositions constitutive of a theory are significantly related. The question I wish to raise is whether the theory before us provides for these relations and for the supportive power that is alleged to follow from them. My question is this, How can any set of propositions, each of which asserts no more than a constant conjunction and so does not by itself support a counterfactual conditional, confer on some proposition the power to support such a conditional. Since, on the view we are examining, every universal is no more than a statement of a constant conjunction, the theory comprising the members of the set is no more than a truth-function of those members. I repeat my question, If no member of the set by itself entails or supports a counterfactual conditional, how can a truth-function of the members—e.g., a conjunction of them—do so? Manipulate the truth-function as much as you will, nothing but an element or a truth-function of elements put into it will come out of it. The logical alchemy of getting something new—something nontruth-functional—has not been revealed to us. And certainly a counterfactual conditional does assert something new. It asserts more than any statement of constant conjunction or any truth-function of constant conjunctions asserts. If it did not, there would be no point whatever in making support of such a conditional a requisite for a proposition's being a law.

I conclude that this explanation of the distinction between nomic and accidental universals is untenable. It utterly fails to provide for that distinctive character of nomic universals which it itself demands of them, namely, their ability to support counterfactual conditionals, with the result of making laws and lawlike propositions just assertions of constant conjunctions or truth-functions of them. Accordingly, this theory of the nature of law meets in no way the common criticisms of the Humean analysis. I do not depreciate the great importance of pointing out that scientists place systematic demands on candidates for the position of law. But accepting these demands calls for a theory of the nature of law and lawlike propositions, that can make sense of them and can meet them.[3]

The difference between lawlike and non-lawlike propositions remains to be found.

I turn then to the second alternative, namely, that nomic and accidental universals differ in their natures or assertions. My suggestion, which is by no means new, is that a nomic universal does not have the structure that an accidental one has, that it is not a statement of a constant conjunction, and that it asserts something an accidental one does not, namely, a real connection between its terms. Thus the nomic but not the accidental "All A are B" asserts that being an A is sufficient to or necessitates being a B. It is from this assertion of sufficiency or necessitation that a subjunctive or counterfactual conditional proposition follows, Thus, "A is sufficient to B" entails "For any value of x, if x were an A, x would be a B" or "if x had been an A, x would have been a B."

That there is this intrinsic difference between nomic and accidental universals is further supported by a consideration of their contradictories. Thus, the contradictory of the accidental, "All chairs in this room are brown," is "There is at least one chair in this room that is not brown." The contradictory of the nomic, "All crows are black," is not that there is a crow that is not black but simply that there could be one or that being a crow is not sufficient to being black. In general, the contradictory of an accidental universal is the assertion that there is a negative case, whereas the contradictory of a nomic universal asserts only that being a case of the subject is not sufficient to being a case of the predicate. This is even more clearly brought out if, following current logical practice, we translate "All A are B" into "For all x, if x is an A, x is a B." If the proposition expressed by this conditional sentence is accidental, its contradictory is "There is an x such that x is A and x is not B"; whereas if the proposition expressed by it is nomic, its contradictory is "Even if there is an x that is an A, it may not be a B," or "It is possible so far as any relation between A and B is concerned, for there to be an x that is A but not B." Thus the contradictory of "If a student studies, he will pass" is "Even if a student studies, he may not pass." The contradictory simply denies that studying is sufficient to passing; it does not assert that there exists a student who studies but does not pass. I doubt that anyone but a modern logican would assert that the denial of a connection between two kinds of phenomena is the affirmation of the existence of an instance of one of them without an instance of the other.

Accordingly, this difference between the proper contradictories of nomic and accidental propositions corroborates the view that propositions of these types differ intrinsically in what they assert.

I conclude then that lawlike propositions assert real connections and that a necessary condition of there being true lawlike propositions or laws is that there are real connections. Since there is no middle ground between contingency and necessity, these real connections must be necessary connections. Therefore the assertion of a law or lawlike proposition is the assertion of a necessary connection. This far I go along with the rationalists, but only this far, because I have found no convincing argument that the correct or complete analysis of propositions stating natural laws would reveal that they assert logical necessities or that their truth is grounded in relations of logical necessitation. Their positive arguments are quite unconvincing; their negative arguments are essentially objections—sound objections, I believe—to the constant conjunction theory. But from the rejection of the logical theory it does not follow that laws do not assert necessary connections. This would follow only if there were no necessity different from logical necessity.

If I am right in holding that laws and lawlike propositions assert real connections and that these connections are not logical, then there being a non-logical necessity is an indispensable condition of there being laws or true lawlike propositions.

This non-logical necessity must then be synthetic. Accordingly, lawlike propositions assert necessary synthetic connections. Thus the lawlike "All A are B" asserts such a connection going from A to B. Its truth, if it is true, consists in its correspondence to a relation between the properties A and B such that an instance of A is sufficient to or necessitates an instance of B.

What then are these synthetic connections asserted by natural laws, in virtue of which an instance of one property may necessitate an instance of another? They are, as Hume so forcefully told us, causal. Accordingly laws, and nomic propositions in general, assert necessary causal relations or relations derivative from them. I am acutely aware that all of us, having been nurtured in an overwhelmingly empirical tradition, cannot help having qualms when synthetic necessity is mentioned. Nonetheless let us not forget that we accept as necessary many propositions that are not analytic; thus we should not hesitate to assert that a ball cannot be both red and green all over; that, if anything is colored, it is extended; that, if event A happened before B and B before C, then A happened before C. These propositions are not analytic and do not follow from definitions of the key terms in them—red, green, colored, extended, temporal precedence,—for there are no such definitions. We understand these propositions; we do not cavil at unconditionally employing them in argument. We do, I submit, intuit their necessity and that it is grounded in the non-logical concepts involved. This is one reason I am convinced that the expression "synthetic necessity" cannot be dismissed as a meaningless combination of words. I certainly do not however intend to suggest that propositions asserting causal necessities can be known to be true or false intuitively. Nor do I mean to suggest, by analogy with the examples we have used, that the concept of cause can be abstracted from cases of successive events. I know of no convincing argument that it can be; I doubt that it can be; I doubt therefore that it is an empirical concept. But however we got it—whether it is empirical or innate—I do not doubt that we have it. Surely all of us understand perfectly well the assertion that an event A necessitated or was sufficient to event B, that my touching the hot stove was genuinely connected with my being burned and not just coincident with it.

Now if I am correct in holding that laws we infer from experience assert necessary causal connections, we must ask, What is the structure of such inference and what is presupposed by it? The hard core, primary, and primitive evidence for a law is the joint or successive occurrence of one or more instances of properties.

In order to simplify our discussion as much as possible, I shall limit myself to nomic propositions of the form "All A are B" and to instantial evidence for them, namely, instances of AB. I realize that usually when we assert "All A are B" we do not intend to imply that being an A is by itself sufficient to being a B but assume a context of other terms, properties, and relations, such that being A is only one of many causal factors, which, taken together constitute a sufficient condition of being a B. I realize too that in case instances of A and B are contemporaneous we do not intend to imply, when we generalize to "All A are B," that A causally necessitates B, but that "A is a reliable sign of B," because we believe that it is probable that they are jointly caused by interrelated previous events. I shall therefore treat contemporaneous occurrences of A and B, like successive occurrences of them, as evidence for a nomic "All A are B."

Accordingly the inductive problem before us is: What are the necessary conditions of the valid inference of the nomic proposition that "All A are B" from instances of A that are B? These instances of A that are B are presumed to be *evidence* for the conclusion, and in virtue of being evidence for it they are said to render it probable. It has been pointed out again and again that passing from "This A is B," "That A is B," etc., or from "Some A are B," to "All A are B" involves an illicit process. And it has been suggested that this fallacy can be avoided by changing the conclusion from "All A are B" to "On the given data it is probable that 'All A are B,' " which is, if true, logically true. But this suggestion has the consequence that the conclusion, being analytic, is not subject to confirmation or disconfirmation by further instances. With an increase in their number, one logically true conclusion would simply be replaced by another like it, with the consequence of our never arriving at a conclusion significant for empirical knowledge or viable for action, prediction, or belief. The inference of such a conclusion requires a device for dropping the evidence and asserting the conclusion.

In order to provide for conclusions of the type we need and to answer my original question, I suggest that induction by simple enumeration has a structure essentially like or equivalent to the following:

We shall let G stand for the nomic proposition "All A are B." The proposition that all observed A's are B does not by itself imply that G is probable, in any sense of "probable" that would make reasonable the use of G in prediction or action. In other words, the fact *alone* that every A so far observed has been B provides no support for the belief that all A are B. What is needed is a principle implying that if an instance of A is associated with an instance of B, it is probable that they are causally connected in virtue of their properties. Hence in order for an instantial proposition, "This A is B," to be evidence for "All A are B," we need a principle of evidence or what has been commonly called a Principle of Induction. Such a principle must therefore entail that positive instances of G render G probable, viz:

$$PI. \rightarrow .G/A,B \ldots A^nB = a/b.$$

It must provide too for the finite probability values required for the application of the probability calculus, e.g., for a finite probability of G independent of evidential propositions A^iB, and for an increase in the value of a/b as the value of n (the number of positive instances) increases. The Principle must then be a very complicated assertion about the world if it is to warrant the attribution of probability to propositions.

Now, if it be given that the Principle is true, we may by modus ponens infer the probability judgment itself, namely, that G, given the n instances of AB, is probably true to degree a/b.

But the argument does not stop here because this whole judgment containing reference to the evidential data is not the inductive conclusion. That conclusion does not contain the evidence adduced for it. A proposition that a scientist accepts as a law does not refer to the evidence for it. Of course if he is asked why he accepts it he will answer by citing his evidence but he would not incorporate his evidence into it.

We must then go further in order to articulate this detachment of the conclusion from the evidence. In a deductive argument we warrant dropping the premises given as true and asserting the truth of the conclusion implied by them, by a Principle of Deductive Detachment. In induction we seem to employ a corresponding principle, a Principle of Inductive Detachment, in virtue of which we drop the evidential propositions given as true, and proceed to assert that the conclusion itself is probably true. For example, we would pass from " 'On the proposition that the barometer is rapidly falling, it is highly probable that it will soon rain' and 'The barometer is rapidly falling' " to "It is highly probable that it will soon rain." This passage requires the additional premise that the given evidence exhausts the available evidence.

We have used here two different notions of probability: one is relational since essential to it is its reference to evidence; the other is non-relational since it does not refer to evidence. In order to avoid confusing them it might be well to use the word "likely" for the latter notion. Accordingly our second assertion about the weather would be "It is very likely that it will soon rain." The degree of likelihood need not be identical with the degree of probability but rather some function of it, which function would involve other independent variables, one of which would take as values amounts of evidence.

The terminus of the inductive arrangement is that G is likely true. The rationality of accepting G itself as a law or as a guiding principle in action or prediction is simply that it is likely true. It corresponds to the rationality of accepting p as a law or guiding principle in case "p is true" is the terminus of a valid deductive argument.

I hope that the suggestions I have just made concerning the structure of induction by simple enumeration have captured something of its nature, including concepts, principles, and rules that seem to be essential to it.

These suggestions imply that the Principle of Induction functions as a basic premise and that its truth is a necessary condition of the soundness of such inductions. To the question whether or not the Principle is in fact true I have no answer. It raises the metaphysical problem of induction, the solution of which would require insights into the nature of the world, which as I said in the beginning, I do not pretend to have, and which cannot be solved or removed by appeal to the anthropology of belief or usages of language. There is however a preceding question which has been repeatedly raised and which would seem to be amenable to mundane intelligence: namely, Just what must the Principle assert about the formal structure of the world in order that it and the empirical data, taken together, would entail the likelihood of the conclusion? To this question several well-known answers have been proposed; e.g., that nature is uniform, that causation is universal, that independent variety is finite, that there are series of relative frequencies of events having limits. These answers, though each of them suggests something required of the Principle, have been roundly criticized for their imprecision and inadequacy. These criticisms are sound and are supported by the requirements the Principle must satisfy. They justly call for a detailed and technically precise formulation of the structures that any world must embody if inductive inference is to be valid in it. As philosophers we should not be satisfied without an ontology that would give these structures a concrete embodiment by providing a theory involving, for example, space and time, substance, the coexistence and interaction of objects.

Fortunately my purpose tonight does not oblige me to provide the principle of formal structure or to propose an ontology, for it is limited to presenting my reasons for believing that a necessary condition of the validity of inferring what we do inductively infer is the truth of some non-empirical principle that entails that the world or course of events embodies a type of unity that can ground laws and such that instances of them are evidence for them. I have argued that this unity involves necessary causal connections.

I believe that the arguments I have presented are sufficient to show that the uniformity theory of law and of causation is untenable, and a fortiori that a Principle of Induction postulating only the existence of uniformities is inadequate. Still it may be worthwhile to spell out some of the difficulties confronting the uniformity theory, for there is great reluctance to giving it up for a theory which asserts causal necessities that are not given in sensible experience of correlated properties or of successive events, and therefore asserts that there is something that transcends what a phenomenalist, positivist, or strict empiricist would be willing to admit. He may indeed confess that contrary-to-fact conditional propositions and the distinction between nomic and accidental universal propositions threaten the tenability of the uniformity theory; still he believes and hopes that some way may be found to avoid his threat. We have discussed one attempt to avoid it—the view that a nomic proposition differs from an accidental one only in its relation to sets of propositions constituting an accepted theory. This attempt we found unsuccessful.

Nonetheless might it not be sufficient to postulate simply that there are uniformities? This would be a minimum Principle of Induction. It implies only that there are true universal accidental propositions asserting, e.g., that every instance of A is associated with an instance of some property of B. The instances may be the same or distinct particulars. Thus every crow is black or every case of fire is followed by a case of heat. For convenience I shall consider only uniformities expressible by "All A are B"; what I shall say about them will be true mutatis mutandis of assertions of uniformities of other types. I shall raise three considerations about "All A are B": its meaning, its truth, and the evidence for it.

(1) Meaning. I shall assume that, though there might be disagreement on some details of a proposed analysis of this accidental universal, there would be agreement on a core of meaning sufficient for our discussion; namely, on the notion of universality indicated by the quantifier "All," on the fact that "All A are B" implies no singular proposition and is implied by no conjunction of singular propositions, and on the fact that it asserts no more than that every A is associated with a B.

(2) Truth. If "All A are B" is true, what would ground its truth? Needless to say, since it does not assert logical or non-logical real connections, a Coherence Theory of truth cannot be appealed to. We have then no alternative to a Correspondence Theory. Hence the ground of truth of the accidental universal must be something to which it corresponds. To what then would it correspond?

Without committing myself to an ontology of facts, I shall use the language of facts because of its convenience and because it is common to speak of the correspondence of true propositions to facts. We ask then, to what fact would a true statement of uniformity correspond? In the first place, it hardly need be said that we should not allow the fact that there are no dragons to ground the truth of "All dragons are fierce" because (1) it would equally well ground "All dragons are gentle" and (2) science and common sense do not allow the vacuity of a subject class to be sufficient to the truth of laws.

In the second place, if, e.g., "All crows are black" is a true statement of uniformity, the fact to which it corresponds cannot be composed of the finite set of facts having as constituents existing crows, for the generalization is not limited to them. Nor can it correspond to a fact or facts having as constituents past, present, and future crows because most of these crows do not exist: how a fact could have as constituents non-existent entities, I do not understand.

But let us suppose that a god surveys all that was, is, or will be, and finds that every crow that we temporally-bound creatures should say was, is, or will be, is black. Then, since he is aware of all facts, not only those having crows as constituents, he would have before him facts sufficient to ground the statement of uniformity.

The supposition however that there are such facts grounding true accidental universal propositions would cost the Humean empiricist more than he would be happy to pay. He could hardly grant that the theory of time involved has experiential support. And he would find that the population explosion of facts having as constituents what he, you, and I should say are non-existent events and particulars is an ontological inflation not soundly backed by his experiential resources. But for some of us who are not single-heartedly wed to sense experience and the concepts derived from it the price might not be too high if we got for it what we need.

But this, not only we but god would not get. God's knowledge of all true statements of uniformity would not suffice to provide answers to all questions he or even we might ask. He knows, let us say, that every crow that did, does, or will exist is black. But then he asks, or we ask him, Had there existed still another crow, would it have been black? And then he sees that his knowledge provides no answer. Thus, the hypothesis of only sheer uniformities does not provide even for the possibility of answering all questions that we can ask or indeed that we do ask every day. It fails for all questions involving a contrary-to-fact supposition. I hardly need to point out that it equally fails to provide for any non-logical conditionality except in the debased sense of reducing a conditional statement to one of constant conjunction. Thus if god were asked whether being A is a sufficient condition of being B, even in this debased sense, he could answer affirmatively only after inspecting every A that did, does, or will exist.

We turn next to the third consideration, namely, that of evidence for a statement of uniformity. Since on the hypothesis of only uniformities, and therefore of no real connections between properties or events, no instance of AB and no number of them short of all of them, would be evidence for the universal "All A are B," and therefore generalizing would be without foundation. In fact, the assumption that there are only factual uniformities leaves us with a chaos, ontological because everything would be completely independent of everything else, and epistemological because no inferential knowledge beyond the immediately given would be possible. Some philosophers would mitigate this epistemological nihilism by postulating that the independent variety of uniformities in the world is finitely limited or by postulating that series of the relative frequency of events constituting some uniformities approach limits, hoping thereby to make the probability calculus applicable. But adding such postulates to the uniformity theory is disloyal to its empirical commitment. By introducing limitations or prescriptions on existence it abandons what promised to be the great merit of the theory: the assumption of no relations except conjunction.

These considerations demonstrate that the postulate of mere uniformities is a total failure as a Principle of Induction. I must therefore reaffirm that a necessary condition of inductive inference is the holding of necessary conditions and therefore that the category of causal necessitation is a unity of successive events presupposed by the validity of induction.

I have not discussed the conditions necessary for the contemporaneous unity of an object or for what is presupposed by lawlike propositions about it. Time will not permit me properly to consider this unity. I should like nonetheless in a couple of pages to make a few speculative suggestions concerning it, because it is integrally related to the unity of succession. To provide for it the category of causation must be supplemented by other organizing concepts and principles, one of them being a category such as substance. Causation alone, being a relation between successive events, would be consistent with an extreme pluralism of temporal orders and with objects being only collections of unrelated events or instances of properties. Thus you and I at this moment might be just collections of fleeting events, of sensations, feelings, affective tones, images, etc. Also there would be no principle underwriting the distinction between those which are yours and those which are mine or making sense of my saying that *I* now hear my voice and see you. If therefore there are to be objects, e.g., you and I, there must be real bonds between the properties belonging to an object—between the properties that belong to you and between those that belong to me. To provide these bonds is a function of substance. A substance is a particular existent that instantiates not only its compresent properties but also the relations between them. Instantiation of the relations is necessary to their being real bonds and not just extensional functions of the causal relations of which the properties are end terms. Similarly, for an object to persist, each of its successive states must be unified one with another by the instantiation of the causal relations between them. The present and persistent unity we all attribute to objects and certainly to ourselves must be provided for.

The frustration due to the difficulty and maybe the impossibility of conceptually analyzing this complex notion of substantial unity is made a bit less acute by the fact that it is not just fanciful, gratuitous, or hypothetical. For each of us has immediate awareness of one instance of it, namely, ourselves. *What* I am—e.g., the dispositions I have—I infer from experience, but *that* I am one and the same thing that hears my voice and sees you I grasp immediately. Moreover, this immediately intuited unity of the self is not just the unity of an instantaneous slice of experience but rather of a temporal slab of experience. In the specious present, however short it may be, we are aware of the persistence of ourselves and of the unity of our experience of successions. We have then an intuitive basis for making meaningful the unity of objects, including ourselves, and their persistence. And causation as the efficacious determination of the existence and properties of successive events would be provided a temporal span in which one event produces another and in which the future becomes or develops out of the past.

Having then an awareness of the unity of contemporaneous and of successive states, I shall indulge myself in the further speculation that this might afford a clue to the interrelations between objects. It, together with necessary causal connection, would supply the unity those who have held a theory of internal relations have rightly believed is presupposed by the world's being an interrelated system and not just a plurality of independent events. Since the unifying relations would be synthetic, the resulting internality would not entail the unpalatable consequences of the usual theory. Thus it would not entail the coalescence of all objects into one but would allow for the different degrees of relevance of one to others which is attested by experience and presupposed by us in dealing with them; and at the same time it would satisfy necessary conditions of the truth of laws holding between states of different objects and of the inference of them.

If the theory of the presuppositions of induction, which I have presented, is at least in principle sound, the only alternative to scepticism is the acknowledgment that some non-empirical metaphysics is true.

NOTES

1. *An Enquiry Concerning Human Understanding,* Open Court edition, p. 37.
2. *A Treatise of Human Nature,* Selby-Bigge edition, pp. 74–78.
3. It is interesting that proponents of this view usually speak of a law's "supporting" or "warranting" a counterfactual conditional rather than "entailing" one. This may indicate a felt recognition of the logical difficulties I have mentioned and of their having given, instead of a theory resolving them, a factual report of demands practicing scientists seem at times to make.

Verification and Ordinary Language

In addition to the metaphysical and epistemological problems with radical empiricism discussed by Chisholm and Nelson, the Verification Theory of Meaning has problems from a linguistic standpoint. The resulting meaninglessness from a strict adherence of the positivist's criterion produced too broad a category. As we noted, the logical positivists were content to claim that, if a proposition does not pass the verification criterion, it is meaningless. This broad category composing various types of sentences, however, may oversimplify the situation to such a degree that it becomes useless for any serious work in philosophical or linguistic discussions. For example, consider the following list of sentences.

1. The blue gremlin causes the balloon to rise.
2. Jesus Christ ascended into heaven forty days after Easter.
3. Jack is climbing the stairs.
4. Oh ascended Christ, hear our supplications.
5. I wish Jack would climb those stairs.
6. Jack, you climb those stairs right now.

Using the Verification Theory of Meaning, which of the above propositions would be meaningful? Only number three would pass the test. Number six is a command and not a description; therefore, it is not empirically verifiable. Number five is an expression of a wish or aspiration. However, are all propositions above, except number three, to be simply classified as meaningless? Certainly there are finer distinctions and nuances of meaning present in this list than mere description and meaninglessness. Proposition five would be a command. Because a command is not a descriptive statement and, hence, does not pass the verification test, do we want to say that it is meaningless? Proposition two is a paraphrase of a statement found in the Bible. Statement four is a prayer. Statement five is a wish—what the old Latin textbooks called a hortatory subjunctive. To lump all of these propositions together (except number three) in the category of meaningless discourse seems to be a too hasty move for anyone seriously interested in postulating an adequate theory of meaning. G.J. Warnock has made the following observations on this point:

It does not make sense to speak of the verification of commands, prayers, promises, expressions of intention, and so on; these accordingly do not *fail* to be verifiable; and to say of them that they cannot be verified is to make a somewhat trivial
remark which in no way impugns their linguistic respectability, and of course in no
way implies that they are meaningless. The *general* conclusion, then, that non-
satisfaction of the verification principle at once implied the verdict "meaningless"
was always a foolish misunderstanding.[17]

As Warnock notes, the most that the logical positivists can claim is that the
statements of the metaphysician and the theologian are different from the statements of the scientist and the mathematician. To be different certainly does not
entail being meaningless. However the critique of the logical positivists forced
metaphysicians and theologians, and moral philosophers as well, to radically
rethink the conditions for significant discourse in their disciplines. In particular, metaphysical studies have been very chastened by the positivist critique.
Today, however, there is a renewed interest in ontological questions, which
includes the books, *The Metaphysics of Logical Positivism,* by Gustav Berg-
mann and *Individuals: An Essay in Descriptive Metaphysics,* by Peter Strawson. Paul J. Dietl sums up the direction of some contemporary philosophy:

> Some of the most remarkable turns in recent philosophical discussion have been
> the resurrection of issues original readers of *Language, Truth and Logic* would
> have thought forever dead.[18]

However it is also fair to say that metaphysical inquiries, although presently
enjoying a second life, will probably never be the same as before the advent of
the Vienna Circle.

Today logical positivism is dead as a viable philosophical movement. The
difficulties mentioned above, especially the problems encountered in the search
for an adequate analysis of the verification principle itself, hastened the death
notice for a vigorous logical positivism. Too many objections fundamental to
the criterion were raised and went unanswered. In addition, World War II
caused the physical dissolution of the Vienna Circle. However logical
positivism left significant marks in contemporary philosophy, especially in
metaphysics, the philosophy of religion, and, as we shall see later, ethical
theory.

Aristotle's Empiricism

All empiricists in metaphysics and epistemology have not accepted the scepticism of Hume's empiricism. A good example is Aristotle, the student of
Plato. Aristotle argued for the regularity of the external world by means of
what he called *substantial forms.* A form determines an essence, but the essence is never found separated from the individuals. Aristotle also elucidated a
complex epistemology by means of which a knower might abstract the essence
from the individuals. Aristotle indicates this empiricism in the following passage from his *Physics:*

> The natural path of investigation starts from what is more readily knowable and
> more evident to us, and proceeds to that which is more self-evident and intrinsically

more intelligible. . . . It is one thing to be knowable to us humans and another thing to be objectively knowable or intelligible. Accordingly, the method prescribed is this: we should advance from what is clearer and more intelligible to us—even though it be intrinsically less clear and more obscure—and proceed toward that which is intrinsically clearer and more intelligible.

In his logical treatise, *Posterior Analytics,* Aristotle spells out his epistemology. In the following passage, he indicates how the essence—what he refers to as a *nature*—is made known to the human mind.

POSTERIOR ANALYTICS

Aristotle

CHAP. XIX: *Upon the Method and Habit necessary to the ascertainment of Principles.*

Concerning syllogism then and demonstration, what either of them is, and how it is produced, is clear, and at the same time about demonstrative science, for it is the same:[1] but about principles, how they become known, and what is the habit which recognises them, is manifest hence to those who have previously doubted it.

That it is then impossible to have scientific knowledge through demonstration, without a knowledge of first immediate principles, has been elucidated before,[2] still some one may doubt the knowledge of immediate principles, both whether it is the same or not the same, also whether there is a science of each or not, or a science of one, but a different kind (of science) of another, and whether non-inherent habits are ingenerated, or when inherent are latent.[3] If then, indeed, we possess them, it is absurd, for it happens that it (the principle) escapes those who have a more accurate knowledge than demonstration,[4] but if not having them before, we acquire them, how can we know and learn without pre-existent knowledge? for this is impossible, as we said also in the case of demonstration. It is evident then, that they can neither be possessed, nor ingenerated in the ignorant, and in those who have no habit, wherefore it is necessary to possess a certain power, yet not such an one as shall be more excellent according to accuracy than these. Now this appears inherent in all animals, for they have an innate power, which they call sensible perception, but sense being inherent in some animals, a permanency of the sensible object is engendered, but in others it is not engendered. Those, therefore, wherein the sensible object does not remain, either altogether or about those things which do not remain, such have no knowledge without sensible perception, but others when they perceive, retain one certain thing in the soul. Now

Reprinted from O.F. Owen, trans., *The Organon, or Logical Treatises, of Aristotle* (London: Henry G. Bohn, 1853).

since there are many of this kind, a certain difference exists, so that with some, reason is produced from the permanency of such things, but in others it is not. From sense, therefore, as we say, memory is produced, but from repeated remembrance of the same thing, we get experience, for many remembrances in number constitute one experience. From experience, however, or from every universal being at rest in the soul, that one besides the many, which in all of them is one and the same, the principle of art and science arises, if indeed it is conversant with generation, of art, but if with being, of science.[5] Neither, therefore, are definite habits inherent, nor are they produced from other habits more known, but from sensible perception, as when a flight occurs in battle, if one soldier makes a stand, another stands, and then another, until the fight is restored. But the soul has such a state of being, as enables it to suffer this, what, however, we have before said, but not clearly, let us again explain. When one thing without difference abides, there is (then) first, universal in the soul,[6] (for the singular indeed is perceived by sense, but sense is of the universal, as of man, but not of the man Callias.) again, in these it stops, till individuals and universals stop,[7] as such a kind of animal, until animal, and in this again (it stops) after a similar manner. It is manifest then that primary things become necessarily known to us by induction, for thus sensible perception produces the universal. But since, of those habits which are about intellect, by which we ascertain truth, some are always true, but others admit the false, as opinion, and reasoning,[8] but science, and intellect, are always true, and no other kind of knowledge,except intellect, is more accurate than science, but the principles of demonstrations are more known, and all science is connected with reason, there could not be a science of principles: but since nothing can be more true than science except intellect, intellect will belong to principles, and to those who consider from these it is evident also, that as demonstration is not the principle of demonstration, so neither is science the principle of science. If then we have no other true genus (of habit) besides science, intellect will be the principle of science: it will also be the principle (of the knowledge) of the principle, but all this subsists similarly with respect to every thing.

NOTES

1. The methods of explaining demonstration and demonstrative science are identical therefore sometimes, as in this chapter, demonstration is assumed for demonstrative science.

2. Vide book i. ch. 2.We have already noticed the two senses in which $\overset{\text{'}}{\alpha}\mu\epsilon\sigma\sigma$ is used by Aristotle; here it is applied to a proposition not proved by any *higher* middle term; i.e. an axiomatic principle, which constitutes the first premise of a demonstration: cf. An. Post. i. 2. In An. Post. i. 13, it is applied to a premise immediate as to its conclusion. Vide Mansel; Aldrich, p. 104, note.

3. As in infants. Aristotle considered the mind as a piece of blank paper, on which nothing was written but natural inclination $(\tau o\ \pi\epsilon\phi\nu\kappa o\varsigma)$. One difference between disposition $(\delta\iota\alpha\theta\epsilon\sigma\iota\varsigma)$ and habit ($\overset{\text{v}}{\epsilon}\xi\iota\varsigma$), drawn in the Categories and de Anima, (vide marginal references,) consists in considering habit more lasting than disposition, the former applying to the virtues, etc., the latter to heat, cold, health, etc., which last undergo more rapid mutation. The relation between $\delta\acute{\nu}\nu\alpha\mu\iota\varsigma$, $\grave{\epsilon}\nu\acute{\epsilon}o\gamma\epsilon\iota\alpha$, and $\overset{\text{v}}{\epsilon}\xi\iota\varsigma$, given by Aspasius, as quoted by Michelet, is as follows: *Facultas a natura insita jam est potentia quaedam, sed nondum nobis ut loquimur potentia, cujus ex ipso vigore operatio profluat; hanc demum potentiam philosophus habitum vocat.*

4. That is, the thing which is known, or the possession of the principle itself, is concealed from children, who having (suppose) a knowledge of axioms, possess thereby a knowledge more accurate than demonstration. Cf. Waitz.

5. Cf. Trendelenb. c. i. p. 137; Aldrich, Hill, and Mansel upon Induction and Method; Zabarella upon the last; and Whately upon the Province of Reasoning. The "methodus inventionis" can only be a process of inference, for no arrangement of parts is possible before they have been discovered, the discovery of general principles from individual objects of sense, if limited to the inferential process itself, will be induction. The term, however, is sometimes extended so as to include the preliminary accumulation of individuals: in this under sense it will embrace the successive steps given by Aristotle here, of αἴσθησις μνήμη, εμπειοια, επαγωγη. Mansel. Vide also Poetic, ch. xvi.; De Anim. Proem. 167.

6. That is, the first universal notion, or that which remains of those several things which are perceived by the senses, and which do not specifically differ. From first universal notions, another is formed, comprehending those things which the several singulars have in common, until summa genera are arrived at. The universal, of course, is equally and without difference found in many particulars.

7. The universals are so called (ἀμεοη) because they are inherent in singulars, not partially, but wholly, every where totally present with their participants: thus the whole of animal is in one man.

8. Of the powers of the soul, some are irrational and disobedient to reason, as the nutritive, others are capable of being obedient to reason, as anger and desire. But other powers of the soul are rational; and of the rational, some are always true, as intellect and science, others are sometimes true, as opinion andλογισμός, i.e. reasoning about practical and political affairs, and things generable and corruptible, which are in a perpetual flux, and are subject to infinite mutations. For intellect, properly so called, is that power or summit of the soul which energizes about things that possess an invariable sameness of subsistence. Taylor. Vide also Trendelenb. de An. iii. c. 4:6; Biese i. p. 327; Rassow, p. 73. And cf. Eth. Nic. b. i. c. 13, Bohn's ed., where see Browne's note; Poetics, c. 16; Magna Moral. i. 34; and Eudem. vi. et lib. v. c. 3, et seq.

This is a classic philosophical passage illustrating what has become known in the history of philosophy as the Aristotelian doctrine of abstraction. Aristotle suggests that the mind has the innate ability through the repeated sensible experiences of particulars to abstract the universal. Recall Aristotle's words:

> From sense . . . memory is produced, but from repeated remembrance of the same thing, we get experience, for many remembrances in number constitute one experience. From experience, however, or from every universal being at rest in the soul, that one besides the many, which in all of them is one and the same, the principle of art and science arises. . . .

Through many sensible awarenesses of the same kind of event or thing, a memory image is formed out of which emerges experience. Aristotle's use of experience is in the sense of distinguishing a veteran from a rookie in that the former has more "know-how" than the latter. Experience for Aristotle is not limited to mere sense impressions as it was for the British empiricists. The emergence of experience provides the mind with the universal, which, Aristotle suggests, is the basis for art and science. In other words, a conceptual skill is produced when one has experience. The attainment of a universal is explicated in terms of the possession of a skill. For example, when we understand the Pythagorean Theorem, we possess an acquired conceptual skill which enables us to work out the theorem.

The possession of such skills is similar to Ryle's account of "knowing how," which we discussed in chapter 1. Aristotle explicates his theory of universals in terms of the acquisition of conceptual skills. These skills are attained by the process of mental abstraction from the awareness of many particular instances.

Aristotle provides an interesting middle ground theory between the extreme realism of Plato and the excessive nominalism of Hume and the logical positivists. It is by means of the innate structure of the mind that human beings are able to abstract the universal from the many instances of regularity experienced in the external world.

This completes our discussion of empiricism. We have traced the origins and development of empiricism from Locke, Berkeley, and Hume to the twentieth-century logical positivists. We have considered objections to radical empiricism and have observed a middle-ground epistemology as evidenced in the writings of Aristotle. With that, we conclude our investigation into the area of epistemology.

NOTES

1. John Locke, *An Essay Concerning Human Understanding*, Book II, chapter 23, sections 1-4. Locke's essay was first published in 1690.

2. George Berkeley, *Of the Principles of Human Knowledge*, no. 14. This work was first published in 1710.

3. Ibid., no. 10.

4. Ibid., nos, 1, 2, 3, and 4.

5. Copyright © 1971 by Random House, Inc. Reprinted from *Reality, Knowledge and Value: A Basic Introduction to Philosophy*, pp. 35-37, by Jerome Shaffer, by permission of Random House, Inc.

6. Bertrand Russell, *Human Knowledge* (New York: Simon and Shuster, 1948), pp. 229 ff.

7. Hans Reichenbach, *Experience and Prediction* (Chicago: University of Chicago Press, 1938), pp. 212 ff.

8. Berkeley, *Principles*, nos. 29, 30, and 33.

9. Ibid., nos, 33, 34, 35, 36, 37, 38, 39, and 40.

10. From pp. 47-48 in "A Free Man's Worship" in *Mysticism and Logic* by Bertrand Russell. © George Allen & Unwin, Ltd., 1963. By permission of Harper & Row, Publishers, Inc., Barnes & Noble Books.

11. Berkeley, *Principles*, nos. 30 and 33.

12. David Hume, *An Enquiry Concerning Human Understanding*, section 12, part 3. A work first published in 1748.

13. Ibid., section 4, part 1; section 2.

14. G.J. Warnock, *English Philosophy since 1900*, 2nd ed. (Oxford: At the University Press, 1969), p. 38. Copyright © Oxford University Press, 1969. Reprinted by permission of the Oxford University Press.

15. Roderick M. Chisholm, *The Problem of the Criterion* (Milwaukee: Marquette University Press, 1973), pp. 17-18. Reprinted by permission of Marquette University Press.

16. Hume, *Enquiry Concerning Human Understanding*, section 4, parts 1 and 2.

17. Warnock, *English Philosophy*, pp. 36-37. Reprinted by permission of the Oxford University Press.

18. Paul J. Dietl, "On Miracles," *American Philosophical Quarterly* 5 (1968): 130.

five

Philosophy of Religion: Human Encounter with the Divine

In that area of philosophy called the philosophy of religion, which is sometimes referred to as *natural theology, philosophical theology,* or *theodicy,* the principal question concerns the grounds necessary for establishing a philosophical proof for the existence of God. In addition, there are subsidiary questions dealing with the nature of religious experience, the structure of religious knowledge, the nature of miracles, the problem of evil, and the various problems concerned with religious language. Traditionally, however, the problem of the existence of God has been central to the issues considered in this area of philosophical inquiry. Contemporary philosophers of religion have expended much time and effort elucidating questions regarding religious experience and the nature of religious language.

As we begin this inquiry into the philosophy of religion, note that the concept of God as considered in philosophical theology is usually one of a supreme first principle grounding a metaphysical system. Accordingly, the necessity of an implicit or explicit ontological commitment is presupposed in many traditional demonstrations for the existence of God. Obviously, if one has difficulty granting the viability of metaphysics, then, a fortiori, many traditional proofs for God's existence will be dismissed immediately. Whether or not one is presently disposed to accept metaphysical arguments, it is very important from the start to keep in mind the relation between metaphysical systems and many of the traditional demonstrations for the existence of God.

A useful distinction for analyzing proofs for the existence of God is that existing between an a priori and an a posteriori argument. An a priori argument is one whose premises are independent of sense experience. Often this is some version of a "logical" proof for God's existence. Anselm's *ontological argument,* the first proof we shall consider in detail, is an example of an a priori argument. An a posteriori argument, on the other hand, begins with some datum of sense experience. The argument uses this experiential datum as a premise and then proceeds to the establishment of a divine being. There are two types of a posteriori arguments. One type depends upon a metaphysical system. The "Five Ways" of Thomas Aquinas are examples of a posteriori arguments whose structures are intricately connected with a metaphysical system. On the other hand, William Paley's "Argument from Design," while an a posteriori argument, does not so depend upon any presupposed metaphysical theory. The distinction between these two types of a posteriori arguments will become clear as we consider each type in some detail. At this point, however, it is important to know the difference between a priori arguments (those whose premises are independent of sense experience) and a posteriori arguments (those whose premises are dependent upon some datum from sense experience).

The Ontological Argument

Anselm of Canterbury (1033-1109) first formulated the a priori argument which has become known in the philosophical tradition as the ontological argument. Anselm was convinced that he could validly and soundly establish the existence of God—the all-perfect being—from a purely philosophical demonstration. Accordingly, Anselm believed that the conclusion of his demonstration was warranted on rational grounds alone. There was no explicit appeal to religious faith or to religious commitment.

Before we begin to read and analyze Anselm's ontological argument, it will be well to keep the following historical background in mind. Anselm, as did many philosophers of the medieval era, philosophized within the context of the Judeo-Christian tradition. Central to this tradition was the claim of the existence of God as an all-perfect being. God was understood as a being who exemplified the summit of perfection. The writings of the Scriptures, both the Old and the New Testaments, constituted an important literary vehicle of this tradition. These writings were usually referred to as *Revelation*. Reflection upon the content of the Old and the New Testaments became a principal occupation for many medieval philosophers and theologians. The attempt was made, using reason alone, to elucidate the meaning and to understand the entailments of the words found written in the Scriptures. Anselm was very much a part of this tradition. His ontological argument results from his meditations upon the content of revelation. In the Scriptures, Anselm discovers the following passage:

The fool has said in his heart, there is no God! (Psalms 14:1)

Anselm assumes, of course, that since the Scriptures are the written texts of the words of God, they cannot be false. Yet Anselm attempts to discover the deeper meaning of this statement. Why, he wonders, would one be a "fool" if he were an atheist. The brunt of the ontological argument is an attempt to explain why atheism implies foolishness. Anselm assumes that anyone who willingly accepts a self-contradictory statement is being a fool. Classical logicians had argued that the acceptance of a self-contradictory statement is a direct violation of the first principle of reasoning. Following Aristotle, these classical logicians argued that the first principle of reasoning is the principle of noncontradiction. Note the following passage from Aristotle:

For a principle which every one must have who understands anything that is, is not a hypothesis. And that which everyone must know who knows anything, he must already have when he comes to a special study. Evidently then such a principle is the most certain of all; which principle this is, let us proceed to say. It is, that the same attribute cannot at the same time belong and not belong to the same subject and in the same respect. . . . This then is the most certain of all principles, since it answers to the definition given above. For it is impossible for anyone to believe the same thing to be and not to be, as some think Heraclitus says. For what a man says, he does not necessarily believe. And if it is impossible that contrary attributes should belong at the same time to the same subject . . . and if an opinion which contradicts another is contrary to it, obviously it is impossible for the same man at the same time to believe the same thing to be and not to be. For if a man were mistaken on this point he would have contrary opinions at the same time. It is for this reason that all who are carrying out a demonstration reduce it to this as an ultimate belief. For this is naturally the starting point even for all the other axioms (of reason).[1]

Given this tradition, Anselm assumes that by a "fool" the Scriptures must be referring to someone who willingly adopts a self-contradictory proposition. In other words, the person is in direct violation of the principle of noncontradiction, which is the first principle basic to the reasoning process. Obviously the thrust of Anselm's argument will be to show that the proposition, "God exists," is a necessary truth. As we saw in chapter 4, a denial of a necessary truth is a contradiction. An example of an a priori necessary truth would be "A Triangle is a three-sided plane figure." This is obviously the definition of a triangle. The predicate term is contained within the meaning of the subject term. To deny this proposition would be to assert that a triangle is *not* a three-sided plane figure. Of course, if a triangle does not have three intersecting sides, then it cannot be a triangle. Thus the denial of this a priori statement entails a contradiction. Anselm's point is that the statement, "God exists," is also a necessary truth. According to Anselm, a denial of this statement (i.e., "God does not exist") will be as contradictory as the denial of the statement that a triangle has three intersecting sides. How does Anselm do this? Let's read together the following passage from the *Proslogium*, which is the first formulation of Anselm's ontological argument.

And so, Lord, do thou, who dost give understanding to faith, give me, so far as thou knowest it to be profitable, to understand that thou art as we believe; and that thou art that which we believe. And, indeed, we believe that thou art a being than which nothing greater can be conceived. Or is there no such nature, since the fool hath said in his heart, there is no God? (Psalms xiv. 1). But, at any rate, this very fool, when he hears of this being of which I speak—a being than which nothing greater can be conceived—understands what he hears, and what he understands is in his understanding; although he does not understand it to exist.

For, it is one thing for an object to be in the understanding, and another to understand that the object exists. When a painter first conceives of what he will afterwards perform, he has it in his understanding, but he does not yet understand it to be, because he has not yet performed it. But after he has made the painting, he both has it in his understanding, and he understands that it exists, because he has made it.

Hence, even the fool is convinced that something exists in the understanding, at least, than which nothing greater can be conceived. For, when he hears of this, he understands it. And whatever is understood, exists in the understanding. And assuredly that, than which nothing greater can be conceived, cannot exist in the understanding alone. For, suppose it exists in the understanding alone: then it can be conceived to exist in reality; which is greater.

Therefore, if that, than which nothing greater can be conceived, exists in the understanding alone, the very being, than which nothing greater can be conceived, is one, than which a greater can be conceived. But obviously this is impossible. Hence, there is no doubt that there exists a being, than which nothing greater can be conceived, and it exists both in the understanding and in reality.

And it assuredly exists so truly, that it cannot be conceived not to exist. For, it is possible to conceive of a being which cannot be conceived not to exist; and this is greater than one which can be conceived not to exist. Hence, if that, than which nothing greater can be conceived, can be conceived not to exist, it is not that, than which nothing greater can be conceived. But this is an irreconcilable contradiction. There is, then, so truly a being than which nothing greater can be conceived to exist, that it cannot even be conceived not to exist; and this being thou art, O Lord, our God.

So truly, therefore, dost thou exist, O Lord, my God, that thou canst not be conceived not to exist; and rightly. For, if a mind could conceive of a being better than thee, the creature would rise above the Creator; and this is most absurd. And, indeed, whatever else there is, except thee alone, can be conceived not to exist. To thee alone, therefore, it belongs to exist more truly than all other beings, and hence in a higher degree than all others. For, whatever else exists does not exist so truly, and hence in a less degree it belongs to it to exist. Why, then, has the fool said in his heart, there is no God (Psalms xiv. 1), since it is so evident, to a rational mind, that thou dost exist in the highest degree of all? Why, except that he is dull and a fool? [2]

Now let's analyze Anselm's argument for the existence of God. One word of caution at the start, however. Don't dismiss Anselm's procedure too quickly as being a futile exercise in semantics. As historians of philosophy have come to realize, Anselm's argument is much more subtle and intricate than immediately meets the eye.

The focal point of the first formulation of the ontological argument is Anselm's request that we consider the logical ramifications of the meaning of the concept of God. This meaning, Anselm suggests, entails that anyone who understands the meaning of the concept of God, and at the same time asserts the denial of God's existence, becomes involved in a logical contradiction. Just as a denial of a triangle's being three-sided is contradictory, Anselm suggests that the denial of God's existence also is contradictory. Anselm does assume that there is only one correct concept of God. This concept is expressed in terms of an all-perfect being. Anselm would not understand any purported claim for a limited, finite, or material Godhead. That there is a certain cultural dimension to this concept, which was reinforced by the theological heritage of the Middle Ages, will not be denied. At any length, Anselm did understand that the concept of God is commonly understood as an all-perfect being. This notion is still prevalent among religious believers in the Judeo-Christian tradition. Anselm's main point is that the cognitive understanding of the content of an all-perfect being entails the existence of that being.

We can analyze the structure of Anselm's argument in the following way. First of all, Anselm presupposes an important distinction made clear by later philosophers. There are two types of existence: *intentional* and *formal*. This important philosophical distinction was discussed in our treatment of Descartes' philosophy in chapter 3. To briefly reiterate, intentional existence refers to the content of an idea in our mind. This content is expressed by asserting what the idea is *of* or *about*. Formal existence, on the other hand, refers to the real things in the world, or the real thing which the idea is about. For example, an idea of a red table would be an intentional existent. The red table existing in the neighborhood barroom, whether known or unknown at this minute, would be a formally existing thing. Note, however, that formal existents are not coextensive with material existents. A formally existing thing may be either a spiritual being or a material being. This allows God and human souls to be formal existents in Anselm's ontology.

To get at the intentional-formal existence distinction, consider again the above passage from the *Proslogium,* in which Anselm considers the idea in the painter's mind as distinct from the painting itself. Obviously the idea in the mind has an intentional existence and the existential painting outside the mind has a formal existence. This distinction is very important in order to understand adequately the structure of the ontological argument.

Anselm's argument can be stated as follows. The concept of God as the all-perfect being can be expressed as: "An idea of a being none greater than which can be conceived." What else, Anselm suggests, could be the cognitive meaning of an all-perfect being. If Anselm can persuade us to assent to this proposition, then he thinks he's got us committed to the formal existence of God. If we grant that the all-perfect being is one greater than which none can be conceived, then at least we have the idea of an all-perfect being in our minds. Using our philosophical terminology, we have an *intentional* existence of God as an all-perfect being in our minds. Anselm now asks: Can the idea of an all-perfect being be just an intentional existent? He answers *no*. Why, we must ask? Because, Anselm responds, if the idea of the all-perfect being were just in our minds, then it would be possible for there to be a more perfect being. What would this be like? A being that had all of the properties of the all-perfect being, which has intentional existence in our minds, but which also possesses one more property. It exists with formal existence outside of our minds. If this is correct, then Anselm's question is: "Do you really have the idea of an all-perfect being in your mind if you can think of a more perfect being?" This more perfect being would be one which, in addition to all of the properties possessed by the intentional existent of the all-perfect being in our minds, would also possess formal existence outside of the mind. Put differently, Anselm's point is that the concept of the all-perfect being entails that this concept have an external referent outside of the mind. If it lacks such a referent, then it is not the concept of the all-perfect being. In other words, if the concept of the all-perfect being were only in our minds as an intentional existent, then it would not be the all-perfect being; we could always think of a being which was greater or more perfect. Such a being would have formal existence. Thus an all-perfect being which exists only as an intentional existent in someone's mind *cannot* be the all-perfect being. However we started the argument agreeing that the concept of God was best defined as an all-perfect being. Accordingly, Anselm's suggestion is that to deny the formal existence of God, while admitting the existence of God intentionally, is to assert a self-contradiction. This is the gist of Anselm's argument. In a schematic form, the argument can be presented as follows:

God $\underset{df}{=}$ APB (A being greater than which none can be conceived) All-Perfect Being

A. *Intentional Existence*	B. *Formal Existence*
(Content of an idea in the mind)	(A real being outside of the mind)
All-Perfect Being	All-Perfect Being
All Holy	All Holy
All Powerful	All Powerful
All Good, and so forth.	All Good, and so forth.
	+
	Formal Existence

If APB is only in Column A, then it is not the APB. Note that the only difference between column A and column B is that column B represents the APB as a really existing thing. This is indicated by the existential presence of the property of formal existence.

As we can see from this illustration, Anselm's point is that if the idea of the all-perfect being is just in the mind, then it is not an idea of *the* all-perfect being. To deny formal existence to the idea of the all-perfect being is to have a contradiction; the idea of an all-perfect being not existing formally cannot be the idea of the all-perfect being. We started with the cognitive content of the all-perfect being. A nonexistent all-perfect being cannot be the all-perfect being, just as a non-three-sided figure cannot be a triangle. To assert that God does not exist formally is a contradiction. Keep in mind the subtlety of Anselm's point. By asserting that the all-perfect being does not exist, one must have an intentional awareness of such a being. Yet the force of Anselm's proof is that this idea cannot be an intentional existent alone. If it is, then it is not the idea of the all-perfect being. But that very idea of such a being is what we started with. Accordingly, either we accept the formal existence of the all-perfect being or we have contradicted ourselves. Therefore, to claim to understand the cognitive content of the all-perfect being and then to deny formal existence to what is represented by that cognitive content is to affirm a contradiction. This, Anselm suggests, is exactly what anyone does who asserts the proposition, "There is no God." Obviously one must understand that which one asserts not to be. But, Anselm argues, it is impossible to understand the cognitive content of the all-perfect being and to attribute the lack of formal existence to that being. In order to avoid a contradiction, one either admits formal existence for the all-perfect being or admits that the idea which was taken to be that of the all-perfect being really wasn't of such a being after all.

Assuming for the moment that Anselm's argument is both valid and sound, can this argument say anything to the agnostic? Or must its applicability refer only to the atheist? Is there a difference in these two positions which would apply to the force of the ontological argument?

We should have many questions about the structure and validity of Anselm's proof for God's existence. However, before discussing problems with this purported a priori demonstration, let's first consider an objection made to the ontological argument by the monk, Gaunilon, a contemporary of Anselm's.

But that this being must exist, not only in the understanding but also in reality, is thus proved to me:

If it did not so exist, whatever exists in reality would be greater than it. And so the being which has been already proved to exist in my understanding, will not be greater than all other beings.

I still answer: if it should be said that a being which cannot be even conceived in terms of any fact, is in the understanding, I do not deny that this being is, accordingly, in my understanding. But since through this fact it can in no wise attain to real existence also, I do not yet concede to it that existence at all, until some certain proof of it shall be given.

For he who says that this being exists, because otherwise the being which is greater than all will not be greater than all, does not attend strictly enough to what he is saying. For I do not yet say, no, I even deny or doubt that this being is greater than any real object. Nor do I concede to it any other existence than this (if it should be called existence) which it has when the mind, according to a word merely heard, tries to form the image of an object absolutely unknown to it.

How, then, is the veritable existence of that being proved to me from the assumption, by hypothesis, that it is greater than all other beings? For I should still deny this, or doubt your demonstration of it, to this extent, that I should not admit that this being is in my understanding and concept even in the way in which many objects whose real existence is uncertain and doubtful, are in my understanding and concept. For it should be proved first that this being itself really exists somewhere; and then, from the fact that it is greater than all, we shall not hesitate to infer that it also subsists in itself.

For example: it is said that somewhere in the ocean is an island, which, because of the difficulty, or rather the impossibility, of discovering what does not exist, is called the lost island. And they say that this island has an inestimable wealth of all manner of riches and delicacies in greater abundance than is told of the Islands of the Blest; and that having no owner or inhabitant, it is more excellent than all other countries, which are inhabited by mankind, in the abundance with which it is stored.

Now if some one should tell me that there is such an island, I should easily understand his words, in which there is no difficulty. But suppose that he went on to say, as if by a logical inference: "You can no longer doubt that this island which is more excellent than all lands exists somewhere, since you have no doubt that it is in your understanding. And since it is more excellent not to be in the understanding alone, but to exist both in the understanding and in reality, for this reason it must exist. For if it does not exist, any land which really exists will be more excellent than it; and so the island already understood by you to be more excellent will not be more excellent."

If a man should try to prove to me by such reasoning that this island truly exists, and that its existence should no longer be doubted, either I should believe that he was jesting, or I know not which I ought to regard as the greater fool: myself, supposing that I should allow this proof; or him, if he should suppose that he had established with any certainty the existence of this island. For he ought to show first that the hypothetical excellence of this island exists as a real and indubitable fact, and in no wise as any unreal object, or one whose existence is uncertain, in my understanding.[3]

It would be well for a moment if we consider the structure of Gaunilon's objection to Anselm's argument. What is Gaunilon's point? He appears to be using a *reductio ad absurdum* argument in response to the structure of the ontological argument. If Anselm is correct, Gaunilon suggests that he must also accept the valid conclusion regarding the formal existence of an "all-perfect island." Gaunilon asks us to consider the absurdity of such a conclusion. Certainly, Gaunilon suggests, Anselm could have the idea of an all-perfect island in his mind; this would be as an intentional existent. Further, Gaunilon argues, if it is indeed absurd to assert the formal existence of an all-perfect island from the fact that one has an idea of an all-perfect island, so too is it absurd to assert the formal existence of an all-perfect being from the fact that one has a corresponding intentional existent representing the cognitive content of an all-perfect being. In effect, Gaunilon attacks the structure of going from an idea in the mind to an object in the world.

Anselm was not satisfied that Gaunilon had indeed successfully refuted his argument. Like any good philosopher, Anselm responded to Gaunilon with a distinction. Anselm stresses the difference in kind between an all-perfect being and an all-perfect island. This difference concerns the concept of a *necessary being*. In the following text taken from the *Proslogium,* Anselm responds to the objection of Gaunilon. Pay special attention to the stress on the notion of *necessary existence*.

But, you say, it is as if one should suppose an island in the ocean, which surpasses all lands in its fertility, and which, because of the difficulty, or rather the impossibility, of discovering what does not exist, is called a lost island; and should say that there can be no doubt that this island truly exists in reality, for this reason, that one who hears it described easily understands what he hears.

Now I promise confidently that if any man shall devise anything existing either in reality or in concept alone (except that than which a greater cannot be conceived) to which he can adapt the sequence of my reasoning, I will discover that thing, and will give him his lost island, not to be lost again.

But it now appears that this being than which a greater is inconceivable cannot be conceived not to be, because it exists on so assured a ground of truth for otherwise it would not exist at all.

Hence, if any one says that he conceives this being not to exist, I say that at the time when he conceives of this either he conceives of a being than which a greater is inconceivable, or he does not conceive at all. If he does not conceive, he does not conceive of the non-existence of that of which he does not conceive. But if he does conceive, he certainly conceives of a being which cannot be even conceived not to exist. For if it could be conceived not to exist, it could be conceived to have a beginning and an end. But this is impossible.

He, then, who conceives of this being conceives of a being which cannot be even conceived not to exist; but he who conceives of this being does not conceive that it does not exist; else he conceives what is inconceivable. The non-existence, then, of that than which a greater cannot be conceived is inconceivable.[4]

Notice the switch in the structure of Anselm's argument. In this response to Gaunilon's objection, Anselm goes from the concept of an all-perfect being to that of a necessary being. Some new definitions are now in order. There are two types of beings which have formal existence: necessary beings and contingent beings. A necessary being is one that *cannot not exist;* it must exist. Existence is a constitutive property of the essence of a necessary being. Just as having three intersecting sides is a constitutive property necessary to the essence of a triangle, so too is formal existence a constitutive property of a necessary being. On the other hand, a contingent being is one which can either exist or not exist. Existence is extrinsic to the essence of a contingent being. Consequently, since formal existence is not a constitutive part of the essence of a contingent being, such a being can either exist or not exist. Given this distinction, in his response to Gaunilon's objection, Anselm focuses attention on the notion that the all-perfect being is one that cannot be "thought of" as not existing. Since it cannot be thought of as nonexistent, then a constitutive property of its essence must be formal existence. In a similar manner, a triangle cannot be thought of as not having three intersecting sides. However a contingent being can always be thought of as having a beginning and an end. If a beginning and an end can be predicated of any given contingent being, then that being cannot exist essentially.

How does this apply to Gaunilon's objection? Anselm asserts that an island can always be thought of as nonexistent at some point in time. In so far as this is possible, then the island must be a contingent being and not a necessary being. Existence cannot be a constitutive part of an island. God is an all-perfect being only so far as he has existence as a constitutive part of his essence. The necessary being-contingent being distinction is very important in understanding Anselm's response to Gaunilon.

In *Meditation V*, Descartes provides a similar argument concluding to the existence of God as a necessary being. Note the following passage.

> . . . the nature of my mind is such as to compel me to assert to what I clearly conceive while I so conceive it; and I recollect that even when I still strongly adhered to the objects of sense, I reckoned among the number of the most certain truths those I clearly conceived relating to figures, numbers, and other matters that pertain to arithmetic and geometry, and in general to the pure mathematics.
>
> But now if because I can draw from my thought the idea of an object, it follows that all I clearly and distinctly apprehend to pertain to this object, does in truth belong to it, may I not from this derive an argument for the existence of God? It is certain that I no less find the idea of a God in my consciousness, that is the idea of a being supremely perfect, than that of any figure or number whatever: and I know with not less clearness and distinctness that an [actual and] eternal existence pertains to his nature than that all which is demonstrable of any figure or number really belongs to the nature of that figure or number; and, therefore, although all the conclusions of the preceding Meditations were false, the existence of God would pass with me for a truth at least as certain as I ever judged any truth of mathematics to be, although indeed such a doctrine may at first sight appear to contain more sophistry than truth. For, as I have been accustomed in every other matter to distinguish between existence and essence, I easily believe that the existence can be separated from the essence of God, and that thus God may be conceived as not actually existing. But, nevertheless, when I think of it more attentively, it appears that the existence can no more be separated from the essence of God, than the idea of a mountain from that of a valley, or the equality of its three angles to two right angles, from the essence of a [rectilineal] triangle; so that it is not less impossible to conceive a God, that is, a being supremely perfect, to whom existence is awanting, or who is devoid of a certain perfection, than to conceive a mountain without a valley.
>
> But though, in truth, I cannot conceive a God unless as existing, any more than I can a mountain without a valley, yet, just as it does not follow that there is any mountain in the world merely because I conceive a mountain with a valley, so likewise, though I conceive God as existing, it does not seem to follow on that account that God exists; for my thought imposes no necessity on things; and as I may imagine a winged horse, though there be none such, so I could perhaps attribute existence to God, though no God existed. But the cases are not analogous, and a

fallacy lurks under the semblance of this objection: for because I cannot conceive a mountain without a valley, it does not follow that there is any mountain or valley in existence, but simply that the mountain or valley, whether they do or do not exist, are inseparable from each other; whereas, on the other hand, because I cannot conceive God unless as existing, it follows that existence is inseparable from him, and therefore that he really exists: not that this is brought about by my thought, or that it imposes any necessity on things, but, on the contrary, the necessity which lies in the thing itself, that is, the necessity of the existence of God, determines me to think in this way: for it is not in my power to conceive a God without existence, that is, a being supremely perfect, and yet devoid of an absolute perfection, as I am free to imagine a horse with or without wings.

Nor must it be alleged here as an objection, that it is in truth necessary to admit that God exists, after having supposed him to possess all perfections, since existence is one of them, but that my original supposition was not necessary; just as it is not necessary to think that all quadrilateral figures can be inscribed in the circle, since, if I supposed this, I should be constrained to admit that the rhombus, being a figure of four sides, can be therein inscribed, which, however, is manifestly false. This objection is, I say, incompetent; for although it may not be necessary that I shall at any time entertain the notion of Deity, yet each time I happen to think of a first and sovereign being, and to draw, so to speak, the idea of him from the storehouse of the mind, I am necessitated to attribute to him all kinds of perfections, though I may not then enumerate them all, nor think of each of them in particular. And this necessity is sufficient, as soon as I discover that existence is a perfection, to cause me to infer the existence of this first and sovereign being; just as it is not necessary that I should ever imagine any triangle, but whenever I am desirous of considering a rectilineal figure composed of only three angles, it is absolutely necessary to attribute those properties to it from which it is correctly inferred that its three angles are not greater than two right angles, although perhaps I may not then advert to this relation in particular. But when I consider what figures are capable of being inscribed in the circle, it is by no means necessary to hold that all quadrilateral figures are of this number; on the contrary, I cannot even imagine such to be the case, so long as I shall be unwilling to accept in thought aught that I do not clearly and distinctly conceive; and consequently there is a vast difference between false suppositions, as is the one in question, and the true ideas that were born with me, the first and chief of which is the idea of God. For indeed I discern on many grounds that this idea is not factitious depending simply on my thought, but that it is the representation of a true and immutable nature: in the first place because I can conceive no other being, except God, to whose essence existence [necessarily] pertains; in the second, because it is impossible to conceive two or more gods of this kind; and it being supposed that one such God exists, I clearly see that he must have existed from all eternity, and will exist to all eternity; and finally, because I apprehend many other properties in God, none of which I can either diminish or change.[5]

The ontological argument has rekindled much interest among twentieth-century British and American philosophers. Norman Malcolm (1911-   ) has written the following astute analysis of the ontological argument. Not only does Malcolm indicate clearly what he thinks is the structure of the ontological argument, but he also provides consideration and analysis of many classical objections to the ontological argument. It is worthwhile to read closely Malcolm's analysis.

ANSELM'S ONTOLOGICAL ARGUMENTS

Norman Malcolm

I believe that in Anselm's *Proslogion* and *Responsio editoris* there are two different pieces of reasoning which he did not distinguish from one another, and that a good deal of light may be shed on the philosophical problem of "the ontological argument" if we do distinguish them. In Chapter 2 of the *Proslogion*[1] Anselm says that we believe that God is *something a greater than which cannot be conceived.* (The Latin is *aliquid quo nihil maius cogitari possit.* Anselm sometimes uses the alternative expressions *aliquid quo maius nihil cogitari potest, id quo maius cogitari nequit, aliquid quo maius cogitari non valet.*) Even the fool of the Psalm who says in his heart there is no God, when he hears this very thing that Anselm says, namely, "something a greater than which cannot be conceived," understands what he hears, and what he understands is in his understanding though he does not understand that it exists.

Apparently Anselm regards it as tautological to say that whatever is understood is in the understanding (*quidquid intelligitur in intellectu est*): he uses *intelligitur* and *in intellectu est* as interchangeable locutions. The same holds for another formula of his: whatever is thought is in thought (*quidquid cogitatur in cogitatione est*).[2]

Of course many things may exist in the understanding that do not exist in reality; for example, elves. Now, says Anselm, something a greater than which cannot be conceived exists in the understanding. But it cannot exist *only* in the understanding, for to exist in reality is greater. Therefore that thing a greater than which cannot be conceived cannot exist only in the understanding, for then a greater thing could be conceived: namely, one that exists both in the understanding and in reality.[3]

Here I have a question. It is not clear to me whether Anselm means that (a) existence in reality by itself is greater than existence in the understanding, or that (b) existence in reality and existence in the understanding together are greater than existence in the understanding alone. Certainly he accepts (b). But he might also accept (a), as Descartes apparently does in *Meditation III* when he suggests that the mode of being by which a thing is "objectively in the understanding" is *imperfect.*[4] Of course Anselm might accept both (a) and (b). He might hold that in general something is greater if it has both of these "modes of existence" than if it has either one alone, but also that existence in reality is a more perfect mode of existence than existence in the understanding.

In any case, Anselm holds that something is greater if it exists both in the understanding and in reality than if it exists merely in the understanding. An equivalent way of putting this interesting proposition, in a more current terminology, is: something is greater if it is both conceived of and exists than if it is merely conceived of. Anselm's reasoning can be expressed as follows: *id quo maius cogitari nequit* cannot be merely conceived of and not exist, for then it would not be *id quo maius cogitari nequit.* The doctrine that something is greater if it exists in addition to being conceived of, than if it is only conceived of, could be called the doctrine that *existence is a perfection.* Descartes maintained, in so many words, that existence is a perfection,[5] and presumably he was holding Anselm's doctrine, although he does not, in *Meditation V* or elsewhere, argue in the way that Anselm does in *Proslogion 2.*

When Anselm says "And certainly, that than which nothing greater can be conceived cannot exist merely in the understanding. For suppose it exists merely in the understanding, then it can be conceived to exist in reality, which is greater,"[6] he is claiming that if I conceived of a being of great excellence, that being would be *greater* (more excellent, more perfect) if it existed than if it did not exist. His supposition that "it exists merely in the understanding" is the supposition that it is conceived of but does not exist. Anselm repeated this claim in his reply to the criticism of the monk Gaunilo. Speaking of the being a greater than which cannot be conceived, he says:

> I have said that if it exists merely in the understanding it can be conceived to exist in reality, which is greater. Therefore, if it exists merely in the understanding obviously the very being a greater than which cannot be conceived, is one a greater than which can be conceived. What, I ask, can follow better than that? For if it exists merely in the understanding, can it not be conceived to exist in reality? And if it can be so conceived does not he who conceives of this conceive of a thing greater than it, if it does exist merely in the understanding? Can anything follow better than this: that if a being a greater than which cannot be conceived exists merely in the understanding, it is something a greater than which can be conceived? What could be plainer?[7]

He is implying, in the first sentence, that if I conceive of something which does not exist then it is possible for it to exist, and *it will be greater if it exists than if it does not exist.*

The doctrine that existence is a perfection is remarkably queer. It makes sense and is true to say that my future house will be a better one if it is insulated than if it is not insulated; but what could it mean to say that it will be a better house if it exists than if it does not? My future child will be a better man if he is honest than if he is not; but who would understand the saying that he will be a better man if he exists than if he does not? Or who understands the saying that if God exists He is more perfect than if He does not exist? One might say, with some intelligibility, that it would be better (for oneself or for mankind) if God exists than if He does not—but that is a different matter.

A king might desire that his next chancellor should have knowledge, wit, and resolution; but it is ludicrous to add that the king's desire is to have a chancellor who exists. Suppose that two royal councilors, A and B, were asked to draw up separately descriptions of the most perfect chancellor they could conceive, and that the descriptions they produced were identical except that A included existence in his list of attributes of a perfect chancellor and B did not. (I do not mean that B put nonexistence in his list.) One and the same person could satisfy both descriptions. More to the point, any person who satisfied A's description would *necessarily* satisfy B's description and *vice versa!* This is to say that A and B did not produce descriptions that differed in any way but rather one and the same description of necessary and desirable qualities in a chancellor. A only made a show of putting down a desirable quality that B had failed to include.

I believe I am merely restating an observation that Kant made in attacking the notion that "existence" or "being" is a "real predicate." He says:

> By whatever and by however many predicates we may think a thing—even if we completely determine it—we do not make the least addition to the thing when we further declare that this thing *is*. Otherwise, it would not be exactly the same thing that exists, but something more than we had thought in the concept; and we could not, therefore, say that the exact object of my concept exists.[8]

Anselm's ontological proof of *Proslogion 2* is fallacious because it rests on the false doctrine that existence is a perfection (and therefore that "existence" is a "real predicate"). It would be desirable to have a rigorous refutation of the doctrine but I have not been able to provide one. I am compelled to leave the matter at the more or less intuitive level of Kant's observation. In any case, I believe that the doctrine does not belong to Anselm's other formulation of the ontological argument. It is worth noting that Gassendi anticipated Kant's criticism when he said, against Descartes:

> Existence is a perfection neither in God nor in anything else; it is rather that in the absence of which there is no perfection. . . . Hence neither is existence held to exist in a thing in the way that perfections do, nor if the thing lacks existence is it said to be imperfect (or deprived of a perfection), so much as to be nothing.[9]

II

I take up now the consideration of the second ontological proof, which Anselm presents in the very next chapter of the *Proslogion*. (There is no evidence that he thought of himself as offering two different proofs.) Speaking of the being a greater than which cannot be conceived, he says:

> And it so truly exists that it cannot be conceived not to exist. For it is possible to conceive of a being which cannot be conceived not to exist; and this is greater than one which can be conceived not to exist. Hence, if that, than which nothing greater can be conceived, can be conceived not to exist, it is not that than which nothing greater can be conceived. But this is a contradiction. So truly, therefore, is there something than which nothing greater can be conceived, that it cannot even be conceived not to exist.
> And this being thou art, O Lord, our God.[10]

Anselm is saying two things: first, that a being whose nonexistence is logically impossible is "greater" than a being whose nonexistence is logically possible (and therefore that a being a greater than which cannot be conceived must be one whose nonexistence is logically impossible); second, that *God* is a being than which a greater cannot be conceived.

In regard to the second of these assertions, there certainly is *a* use of the word "God," and I think far the more common use, in accordance with which the statements "God is the greatest of all beings," "God is the most perfect being," "God is the supreme being," are *logically* necessary truths, in the same sense that the statement "A square has four sides" is a logically necessary truth. If there is a man named "Jones" who is the tallest man in the world, the statement "Jones is the tallest man in the world" is merely true and is not a logically necessary truth. It is a virtue of Anselm's unusual phrase, "a being greater than which cannot be conceived,"[11] to make it explicit that the sentence "God is the greatest of all beings" expresses a logically necessary truth and not a mere matter of fact such as the one we imagined about Jones.

With regard to Anselm's first assertion (namely, that a being whose nonexistence is logically impossible is greater than a being whose nonexistence is logically possible) perhaps the most puzzling thing about it is the use of the word "greater." It appears to mean exactly the same as "superior," "more excellent," "more perfect." This equivalence by itself is of no help to us, however, since the latter expressions would be equally puzzling here. What is required is some explanation of their use.

We do think of *knowledge,* say, as an excellence, a good thing. If A has more knowledge of algebra than B we express this in common language by saying that A has a *better* knowledge of algebra than B, or that A's knowledge of algebra is *superior* to B's, whereas we should not say that B has a better or superior *ignorance* of algebra than A. We do say "greater ignorance," but here the word "greater" is used purely quantitatively.

Previously I rejected *existence* as a perfection. Anselm is maintaining in the remarks last quoted, not that existence is a perfection, but that *the logical impossibility of nonexistence is a perfection.* In other words, *necessary existence is a perfection.* His first ontological proof uses the principle that a thing is greater if it exists than if it does not exist. His second proof employs the different principle that a thing is greater if it necessarily exists than if it does not necessarily exist.

Some remarks about the notion of *dependence* may help to make this latter principle intelligible. Many things depend for their existence on other things and events. My house was built by a carpenter: its coming into existence was dependent on a certain creative activity. Its continued existence is dependent on many things: that a tree does not crush it, that it is not consumed by fire, and so on. If we reflect on the common meaning of the word "God" (no matter how vague and confused this is), we realize that it is incompatible with this meaning that God's existence should *depend* on anything. Whether we believe in Him or not we must admit that the "almighty and everlasting God" (as several ancient prayers begin), the "Maker of heaven and earth, and of all things visible and invisible" (as is said in the Nicene Creed), cannot be thought of as being brought into existence by anything or as depending for His continued existence on anything. To conceive of anything as dependent upon something else for its existence is to conceive of it as a lesser being than God.

If a housewife has a set of extremely fragile dishes, then as dishes they are *inferior* to those of another set like them in all respects except that they are *not* fragile. Those of the first set are *dependent* for their continued existence on gentle handling; those of the second set are not. There is a definite connection in common language between the notions of dependency and inferiority, and independence and superiority. To say that something which was dependent on nothing whatever was superior to ("greater than") anything that was dependent in any way upon anything is quite in keeping with the everyday use of the terms "superior" and "greater." Correlative with the notions of dependence and independence are the notions of *limited* and *unlimited*. An engine requires fuel and this is a limitation. It is the same thing to say that an engine's operation is *dependent* on as that it is *limited* by its fuel supply. An engine that could accomplish the same work in the same time and was in other respects satisfactory, but did not require fuel, would be a *superior* engine.

God is usually conceived of as an *unlimited* being. He is conceived of as a being who *could not* be limited, that is, as an absolutely unlimited being. This is no less than to conceive of Him as *something a greater than which cannot be conceived.* If God is conceived to be an absolutely unlimited being He must be conceived to be unlimited in regard to His existence as well as His operation. In this conception it will not make sense to say that He depends on anything for coming into or continuing in existence. Nor, as Spinoza observed, will it make sense to say that something could *prevent* Him from existing.[12] Lack of moisture can prevent trees from existing in a certain region of the earth. But it would be contrary to the concept of God as an unlimited being to suppose that anything other than God Himself could prevent Him from existing, and it would be self-contradictory to suppose that He Himself could do it.

Some may be inclined to object that although nothing could prevent God's existence, still it might just *happen* that He did not exist. And if He did exist that too would be by chance. I think, however, that from the supposition that it could happen that God did not exist it would follow that, if He existed, He would have mere duration and not eternity. It would make sense to ask, "How long has He existed?," "Will He still exist next week?," "He was in existence yesterday but how about today?," and so on. It seems absurd to make God the subject of such questions. According to our ordinary conception of Him, He is an eternal being. And eternity does not mean endless duration, as Spinoza noted. To ascribe eternity to something is to exclude as senseless all sentences that imply that it has duration. If a thing has duration then it would be merely a *contingent* fact, if it was a fact, that its duration was endless. The moon could have endless duration but not eternity. If something has endless duration it will *make sense* (although it will be false) to say that it will cease to exist, and it will make sense (although it will be false) to say that something will *cause* it to cease to exist. A being with endless duration is not, therefore, an absolutely unlimited being. That God is conceived to be eternal follows from the fact that He is conceived to be an absolutely unlimited being.

I have been trying to expand the argument of *Proslogion 3*. In *Responsio 1* Anselm adds the following acute point: if you can conceive of a certain thing and this thing does not exist then if it *were* to exist its nonexistence would be *possible.* It follows, I believe, that if the thing were to exist it would depend on other things both for coming into and continuing in existence, and also that it would have duration and not eternity. Therefore it would not be, either in reality or in conception, an unlimited being, *aliquid quo nihil maius cogitari possit.*

Anselm states his argument as follows:

> If it [the thing a greater than which cannot be conceived] can be conceived at all it must exist. For no one who denies or doubts the existence of a being a greater than which is inconceivable, denies or doubts that if it did exist its non-existence, either in reality or in the understanding, would be impossible. For otherwise it would not be a being a greater than which cannot be conceived. But as to whatever can be conceived but does not exist: if it were to exist its non-existence either in reality or in the understanding would be possible. Therefore, if a being a greater than which cannot be conceived, can even be conceived, it must exist.[13]

What Anselm has proved is that the notion of contingent existence or of contingent nonexistence cannot have any application to God. His existence must either be logically necessary or logically impossible. The only intelligible way of rejecting Anselm's claim that God's existence is necessary is to maintain that the concept of God, as a being a greater than which cannot be conceived, is self-contradictory or nonsensical.[14] Supposing that this is false, Anselm is right to deduce God's necessary existence from his characterization of Him as a being a greater than which cannot be conceived.

Let me summarize the proof. If God, a being a greater than which cannot be conceived, does not exist then He cannot *come* into existence. For if He did He would either have been *caused* to come into existence or have *happened* to come into existence, and in either case He would be a limited being, which by our conception of Him He is not. Since He cannot come into existence, if He does not exist His existence is impossible. If He does exist He cannot have come into existence (for the reasons given), nor can He cease to exist, for nothing could cause Him to cease to exist nor could it just happen that He ceased to exist. So if God exists His existence is necessary. Thus God's existence is either impossible or necessary. It can be the former only if the concept of such a being is self-contradictory or in some way logically absurd. Assuming that this is not so, it follows that He necessarily exists.[15]

It may be helpful to express ourselves in the following way: to say, not that *omnipotence* is a property of God, but rather that *necessary omnipotence* is; and to say, not that omniscience is a property of God, but rather that *necessary omniscience* is. We have criteria for determining that a man knows this and that and can do this and that, and for determining that one man has greater knowledge and abilities in a certain subject than another. We could think of various tests to give them. But there is nothing we should wish to describe, seriously and literally, as "testing" God's knowledge and powers. That God is omniscient and omnipotent has not been determined by the application of criteria: rather these are requirements of our conception of Him. They are internal properties of the concept, although they are also rightly said to be properties of God. *Necessary existence* is a property of God in the *same sense* that *necessary omnipotence* and *necessary omniscience* are His properties. And we are not to think that

"God necessarily exists" means that it follows necessarily from something that God exists *contingently.* The a priori proposition "God necessarily exists" entails the proposition "God exists," if and only if the latter also is understood as an a priori proposition: in which case the two propositions are equivalent. In this sense Anselm's proof is a proof of God's existence.

Descartes was somewhat hazy on the question of whether existence is a property of things that exist, but at the same time he saw clearly enough that *necessary existence* is a property of God. Both points are illustrated in his reply to Gassendi's remark, which I quoted above:

> I do not see to what class of reality you wish to assign existence, nor do I see why it may not be said to be a property as well as omnipotence, taking the word property as equivalent to any attribute or anything which can be predicated of a thing, as in the present case it should be by all means regarded. Nay, necessary existence in the case of God is also a true property in the strictest sense of the word, because it belongs to Him and forms part of His essence alone.[16]

Elsewhere he speaks of "the necessity of existence" as being "that crown of perfections without which we cannot comprehend God."[17] He is emphatic on the point that necessary existence applies solely to "an absolute perfect Being."[18]

III

I wish to consider now a part of Kant's criticism of the ontological argument which I believe to be wrong. He says:

> If, in an identical proposition, I reject the predicate while retaining the subject, contradiction results; and I therefore say that the former belongs necessarily to the latter. But if we reject subject and predicate alike, there is no contradiction; for nothing is then left that can be contradicted. To posit a triangle, and yet to reject its three angles, is self-contradictory; but there is no contradiction in rejecting the triangle together with its three angles. The same holds true of the concept of an absolutely necessary being. If its existence is rejected, we reject the thing itself with all its predicates; and no question of contradiction can then arise. There is nothing outside it that would then be contradicted, since the necessity of the thing is not supposed to be derived from anything external; nor is there anything internal that would be contradicted, since in rejecting the thing itself we have at the same time rejected all its internal properties. "God is omnipotent" is a necessary judgment. The omnipotence cannot be rejected if we posit a Deity, that is, an infinite being; for the two concepts are identical. But if we say "There is no God" neither the omnipotence nor any other of its predicates is given; they are one and all rejected together with the subject, and there is therefore not the least contradiction in such a judgment.[19]

To these remarks the reply is that when the concept of God is correctly understood one sees that one cannot "reject the subject." "There is no God" is seen to be a necessarily false statement. Anselm's demonstration proves that the proposition "God exists" has the same a priori footing as the proposition "God is omnipotent."

Many present-day philosophers, in agreement with Kant, declare that existence is not a property and think that this overthrows the ontological argument. Although it is an error to regard existence as a property of things that have contingent existence, it does not follow that it is an error to regard necessary existence as a property of God. A recent writer says, against Anselm, that a proof of God's existence "based on the necessities of thought" is "universally regarded as fallacious: it is not thought possible to build bridges between mere abstractions and concrete existence."[20] But this way of putting the matter obscures the distinction we need to make. Does "concrete existence" mean contingent existence? Then to build bridges between concrete existence and mere abstractions would be like inferring the existence of an island from the concept of a perfect island, which both Anselm and Descartes regarded as absurd. What Anselm did was to give a demonstration that the proposition "God necessarily exists" is entailed by the proposition "God is a being a greater than which cannot be conceived" (which is equivalent to "God is an absolutely unlimited being"). Kant declares that when "I think a being as the supreme reality, without any defect, the question still remains whether it exists or not. . . ."[21]

Another way of criticizing the ontological argument is the following: "Granted that the concept of necessary existence follows from the concept of a being a greater than which cannot be conceived, this amounts to no more than granting the *a priori* truth of the *conditional* proposition, 'If such a being exists then it necessarily exists.' This proposition, however, does not entail the *existence of anything,* and one can deny its antecedent without contradiction." Kant, for example, compares the proposition (or "judgment," as he calls it) "A triangle has three angles" with the proposition "God is a necessary being." He allows that the former is "absolutely necessary" and goes on to say:

> The absolute necessity of the judgment is only a conditional necessity of the thing, or of the predicate in the judgment. The above proposition does not declare that three angles are absolutely necessary, but that, under the condition that there is a triangle (that is, that a triangle is given), three angles will necessarily be found in it.[22]

He is saying, quite correctly, that the proposition about triangles is equivalent to the conditional proposition "If a triangle exists, it has three angles." He then makes the comment that there is no contradiction "in rejecting the triangle together with its three angles." He proceeds to draw the alleged parallel: "The same holds true of the concept of an absolutely necessary being. If its existence is rejected, we reject the thing itself with all its predicates; and no question of contradiction can then arise."[23] The priest, Caterus, made the same objection to Descartes when he said:

> Though it be conceded that an entity of the highest perfection implies its existence by its very name, yet it does not follow that that very existence is anything actual in the real world, but merely that the concept of existence is inseparably united with the concept of highest being. Hence you cannot infer that the existence of God is anything actual, unless you assume that that highest being actually exists; for then it will actually contain all its perfections, together with this perfection of real existence.[24]

I think that Caterus, Kant, and numerous other philosophers have been mistaken in supposing that the proposition "God is a necessary being" (or "God necessarily exists") is equivalent to the conditional proposition "If God exists then He necessarily exists."[25] For how do they want the antecedent clause "*If* God exists" to be understood? Clearly they want it to imply that it is *possible* that God does *not* exist.[26] The whole point of Kant's analysis is to try to show that it is possible to "reject the subject." Let us make this implication explicit in the conditional proposition, so that it reads: "If God exists (and it is possible that He does not) then He necessarily exists." But now it is apparent, I think, that these philosophers have arrived at a self-contradictory position. I do not mean that this conditional proposition, taken alone, is self-contradictory. Their position is self-contradictory in the following way. On the one hand, they agree that the proposition "God necessarily exists" is an a priori truth; Kant implies that it is "absolutely necessary," and Caterus says that God's existence is implied by His very name. On the other hand, they think that it is correct to analyze this proposition in such a way that it will entail the proposition "It is possible that God does not exist." But so far from its being the case that the proposition "God necessarily exists" entails the proposition "It is possible that God does not exist," it is rather the case that they are *incompatible* with one another! Can anything be clearer than the conjunction "God necessarily exists but it is possible that He does not exist" is self-contradictory? Is it not just as plainly self-contradictory as the conjunction "A square necessarily has four sides but it is possible for a square not to have four sides"? In short, this familiar criticism of the ontological argument is self-contradictory, because it accepts *both* of two incompatible propositions.[27]

One conclusion we may draw from our examination of this criticism is that (contrary to Kant) there is a lack of symmetry, in an important respect, between the propositions "A triangle has three angles" and "God has necessary existence," although both are a priori. The former can be expressed in the conditional assertion "If a triangle exists (and it is possible that none does) it has three angles." The latter cannot be expressed in the corresponding conditional assertion without contradiction.

IV

I turn to the question of whether the idea of a being a greater than which cannot be conceived is self-contradictory. Here Leibniz made a contribution to the discussion of the ontological argument. He remarked that the argument of Anselm and Descartes

is not a paralogism, but it is an imperfect demonstration, which assumes something that must still be proved in order to render it mathematically evident; that is, it is tacitly assumed that this idea of the all-great or all-perfect being is possible, and implies no contradiction. And it is already something that by this remark it is proved that, assuming that God is possible, he exists, which is the privilege of divinity alone.[28]

Leibniz undertook to give a proof that God is possible. He defined a *perfection* as a simple, positive quality in the highest degree.[29] He argued that since perfections are *simple* qualities they must be compatible with one another. Therefore the concept of a being possessing all perfections is consistent.

I will not review his argument because I do not find his definition of a perfection intelligible. For one thing, it assumes that certain qualities or attributes are "positive" in their intrinsic nature, and others "negative" or "privative," and I have not been able to clearly understand that. For another thing, it assumes that some qualities are intrinsically simple. I believe that Wittgenstein has shown in the *Investigations* that nothing is *intrinsically* simple, but that whatever has the status of a simple, an indefinable, in one system of concepts, may have the status, of a complex thing, a definable thing, in another system of concepts.

I do not know how to demonstrate that the concept of God—that is, of a being a greater than which cannot be conceived—is not self-contradictory. But I do not think that it is legitimate to demand such a demonstration. I also do not know how to demonstrate that either the concept of a material thing or the concept of *seeing* a material thing is not self-contradictory, and philosophers have argued that both of them are. With respect to any particular reasoning that is offered for holding that the concept of seeing a material thing, for example, is self-contradictory, one may try to show the invalidity of the reasoning and thus free the concept from the charge of being self-contradictory *on that ground.* But I do not understand what it would mean to demonstrate *in general,* and not in respect to any particular reasoning, that the concept is not self-contradictory. So it is with the concept of God. I should think there is no more of a presumption that it is self-contradictory than is the concept of seeing a material thing. Both concepts have a place in the thinking and the lives of human beings.

But even if one allows that Anselm's phrase may be free of self-contradiction, one wants to know how it can have any *meaning* for anyone. Why is it that human beings have even *formed* the concept of an infinite being, a being a greater than which cannot be conceived? This is a legitimate and important question. I am sure there cannot be a deep understanding of that concept without an understanding of the phenomena of human life that give rise to it. To give an account of the latter is beyond my ability. I wish, however, to make one suggestion (which should not be understood as autobiographical).

There is the phenomenon of feeling guilt for something that one has done or thought or felt or for a disposition that one has. One wants to be free of this guilt. But sometimes the guilt is felt to be so great that one is sure that nothing one could do oneself, nor any forgiveness by another human being, would remove it. One feels a guilt that is beyond all measure, a guilt "a greater than which cannot be conceived." Paradoxically, it would seem, one nevertheless has an intense desire to have this incomparable guilt removed. One requires a forgiveness that is beyond all measure, a forgiveness "a greater than which cannot be conceived." Out of such a storm in the soul, I am suggesting, there arises the conception of a forgiving mercy that is limitless, beyond all measure.[30] This is one important feature of the Jewish and Christian conception of God.

I wish to relate this thought to a remark made by Kierkegaard, who was speaking about belief in Christianity but whose remark may have a wider application. He says:

There is only one proof of the truth of Christianity and that, quite rightly, is from the emotions, when the dread of sin and a heavy conscience torture a man into crossing the narrow line between despair bordering upon madness—and Christendom.[31]

One may think it absurd for a human being to feel a guilt of such magnitude, and even more absurd that, if he feels it, he should *desire* its removal. I have nothing to say about that. It may also be absurd for people to fall in love, but they do it. I wish only to say that there *is* that human phenomenon of an unbearably heavy conscience and that it is importantly connected with the genesis of the concept of God, that is, with the formation of the "grammar" of the word "God." I am sure that this concept is related to human experience in other ways. If one had the acuteness and depth to perceive these connections one could grasp the *sense* of the concept. When we encounter this concept as a problem in philosophy, we do not consider the human phenomena that lie behind it. It is not surprising that many philosophers believe that the idea of a necessary being is an arbitrary and absurd construction.

What is the relation of Anselm's ontological argument to religious belief? This is a difficult question. I can imagine an atheist going through the argument, becoming convinced of its validity, acutely defending it against objections, yet remaining an atheist. The only effect it could have on the fool of the Psalm would be that he stopped saying in his heart "There is no God," because he would now realize that this is something he cannot meaningfully say or think. It is hardly to be expected that a demonstrative argument should, in addition, produce in him a living faith. Surely there is a level at which one can view the argument as a piece of logic, following the deductive moves but not being touched religiously? I think so. But even at this level the argument may not be without religious value, for it may help to remove some philosophical scruples that stand in the way of faith. At a deeper level, I suspect that the argument can be thoroughly understood only by one who has a view of that human "form of life" that gives rise to the idea of an infinitely great being, who views it from the *inside* not just from the outside and who has, therefore, at least some inclination to *partake* in that religious form of life. This inclination, in Kierkegaard's words, is "from the emotions." This inclination can hardly be an *effect* of Anselm's argument, but is rather presupposed in the fullest understanding of it. It would be unreasonable to require that the recognition of Anselm's demonstration as valid must produce a conversion.[32]

NOTES

1. I have consulted the Latin text of the *Proslogion,* of *Gaunilonis Pro Insipiente,* and of the *Responsio editoris,* in S. Anselmi, *Opera Omnia,* edited by F.C. Schmitt (Secovii, 1938), Vol. I. With numerous modifications, I have used the English translation by S.N. Deane: *St. Anselm* (La Salle, Ill.: Open Court Publishing Co., 1948).
2. See *Proslogion 1* and *Responsio 2.*
3. Anselm's actual words are: "Et certe id quo maius cogitari nequit, non potest esse in solo intellectu. Si enim vel in solo intellectu est, potest cogitari esse et in re, quod maius est. Si ergo id quo maius cogitari non potest, est in solo intellectu: id ipsum quo maius cogitari non potest, est quo maius cogitari potest. Sed certe hoc esse non potest." *Proslogion 2.*

4. Haldane and Ross, *The Philosophical Works of Descartes,* Vol. I (New York: The Macmillan Company, 1931), 163.

5. *Op. Cit.,* p. 182.

6. *Proslogion 2,* Deane, *St. Anselm,* p. 8.

7. *Responsio 2;* Deane, *St. Anselm,* pp. 157–158.

8. *The Critique of Pure Reason,* tr. by Norman Kemp Smith (New York: The Macmillan Company, 1929), p. 505.

9. Haldane and Ross, *The Philosophical Works of Descartes,* II, 186.

10. *Proslogion 3;* Deane, *St. Anselm,* pp. 8–9.

11. Professor Robert Calhoun has pointed out to me that a similar locution had been used by Augustine. In *De moribus Manichaeorum* (Bk. II, ch. 11, sec. 24), he says that God is a being *quo esse aut cogitari melius nihil possit* (*Patrologiae Patrum Latinorum,* J.P. Migne, ed. [Paris, 1841–1845], Vol. 32; *Augustinus, Vol. 1*).

12. *Ethics,* Part I, prop. 11.

13. *Responsio 1;* Deane, *St. Anselm,* pp. 154-155.

14. Gaunilo attacked Anselm's argument on this very point. He would not concede that a being a greater than which cannot be conceived existed in his understanding (*Gaunilonis Pro Insipiente,* secs. 4 and 5; Deane, *St. Anselm,* pp. 148–150). Anselm's reply is: "I call on your faith and conscience to attest that this is most false" (*Responsio 1;* Deane, *St. Anselm,* p. 154). Gaunilo's faith and conscience will attest that it is false that "God is not a being a greater than which is inconceivable," and false that "He is not understood (*intelligitur*) or conceived (*cogitatur*)" (*ibid.*). Descartes remarks that one would go to "strange extremes" who denied that we understand the words *"that thing which is the most perfect that we can conceive;* for that is what all men call God" (Haldane and Ross, *The Philosophical Works of Descartes,* II, 129).

15. [The following elegant argument occurs in *Responsio 1:* "That than which a greater cannot be conceived cannot be conceived to begin to exist. Whatever can be conceived to exist and does not exist, can be conceived to begin to exist. Therefore, that than which a greater cannot be conceived, cannot be conceived to exist and yet not exist. So if it can be conceived to exist it exists from necessity." (*Nam quo maius cogitari nequit non potest cogitari esse nisi sine initio. Quidquid autem potest cogitari esse et non est, per initium potest cogitari esse. Non ergo quo maius cogitari nequit cogitari potest esse et non est. Si ergo cogitari potest esse, ex necessitate est.*) (Schmitt, *Opera Omnia,* p. 131; Deane, *St. Anselm,* p. 154.)]

16. Haldane and Ross, *The Philosophical Works of Descartes,* II, 228.

17. *Ibid.,* I, 445.

18. E.g., *ibid.,* Principle 15, p. 225.

19. *Op. cit.,* p. 502.

20. J.N. Findlay, "Can God's Existence Be Disproved?" *New Essays in Philosophical Theology,"* A.N. Flew and A. MacIntyre, eds. (New York: The Macmillan Company, 1955), p. 47.

21. *Op. cit.,* pp. 505–506.

22. *Op. cit.,* pp. 501–502.

23. *Ibid.,* p. 502.

24. Haldane and Ross, *The Philosophical Works of Descartes,* II, 7.

25. I have heard it said by more than one person in discussion that Kant's view was that it is really a misuse of language to speak of a "necessary being," on the grounds that necessity is properly predicated only of propositions (judgments) not of *things.* This is not a correct account of Kant. (See his discussion of "The Postulates of Empirical Thought in General," *op. cit.,* pp. 239–256, esp. p. 239 and pp. 247–248.) But if he had held this, as perhaps the above philosophers think he should have, then presumably his view would not have been that the pseudo-proposition "God is a necessary being" is equivalent to the conditional "If God exists then He necessarily exists." Rather his view would have been that the genuine proposition " 'God exists' is necessarily true" is equivalent to the conditional "If God exists then He exists" (*not* "If God exists then He necessarily exists," which would be an illegitimate formulation, on the view imaginatively attributed to Kant).

"If God exists then He exists" is a foolish tautology which says nothing different from the tautology "If a new earth satellite exists then it exists." If "If God exists then He exists" were a correct analysis of " 'God exists' is necessarily true," then "If a new earth satellite exists then it exists" would be a correct analysis of " 'A new earth satellite exists' is necessarily true." If the *analysans* is necessarily true then the *analysandum* must be necessarily true, provided the analysis is correct. If this proposed Kantian analysis of " 'God exists' is necessarily true" were correct, we should be presented with the consequence that not only is it necessarily true that God exists, but also it is necessarily true that a new earth satellite exists, which is absurd.

26. When summarizing Anselm's proof (in Part II, *supra*) I said: "If God exists He necessarily exists." But there I was merely stating an entailment. "If God exists" did not have the implication that it is possible He does not exist. And of course I was not regarding the conditional as *equivalent* to "God necessarily exists."

27. This fallacious criticism of Anselm is implied in the following remarks by Gilson: "To show that the affirmation of necessary existence is analytically implied in the idea of God, would be . . . to show that God is necessary if He exists, but would not prove that He does exist" (E. Gilson, *The Spirit of Medieval Philosophy* [New York: Charles Scribner's Sons, 1940], p. 62).

28. *New Essays Concerning the Human Understanding,* Bk. IV, ch. 10; A.G. Langley, ed. (La Salle, Ill.: Open Court Publishing Company, 1949), p. 504.

29. See *Ibid.,* Appendix X, p. 714.

30. [*Psalm 116:* "The sorrows of death compassed me, and the pains of hell gat hold upon me: I found trouble and sorrow. Then called I upon the name of the Lord; O Lord, I beseech thee, deliver my soul." *Psalm 130:* "Out of the depths have I cried unto thee, O Lord."]

31. *The Journals,* tr. by A. Dru (New York: Oxford University Press, 1938), sec. 926.

32. [Since the appearance of this essay many acute criticisms of it have been published or communicated to me in private correspondence. In *The Philosophical Review,* LXX, No. 1, January 1961, there are the following articles: Raziel Abelson, "Not Necessarily"; R.E. Allen, "The Ontological Argument"; Paul Henle, "Uses of the Ontological Argument"; Gareth B. Matthews, "On Conceivability in Anselm and Malcolm"; Alvin Plantinga, "A Valid Ontological Argument?"; Terence Penelhum, "On the Second Ontological Argument." Some other published articles are: Jan Berg, "An Examination of the Ontological Proof," *Theoria,* XXVII, No. 3 (1961); T.P. Brown, "Professor Malcolm on 'Anselm's Ontological Arguments,' " *Analysis,* October 1961; W.J. Huggett, "The Nonexistence of Ontological Arguments," *The Philosophical Review,* LXXI, No. 3, July 1962; Jerome Shaffer, "Existence, Prediction, and the Ontological Argument," *Mind,* LXXI, No. 283, July 1962. It would be a major undertaking to attempt to reply to all of the criticisms, and I hope that my not doing so will not be construed as a failure to appreciate them. I do not know that it is possible to meet all of the objections; on the other hand, I do not know that it is impossible.]

Jerome Shaffer has provided an interesting analysis concerning a fundamental conceptual blur which proponents of the ontological argument make. In the following section, Shaffer suggests that there are two different functions for a concept—*intension* and *extension*. By focusing on this distinction, Shaffer discusses why the ontological argument fails to achieve that which its proponents claim.

EXISTENCE, PREDICATION, AND THE ONTOLOGICAL ARGUMENT

Jerome Shaffer

. . . What lies at the heart of the puzzle about the Ontological Argument is the fact that our concepts have two quite different aspects, marked by the familiar philosophical distinction of intension and extension. A word like

From Jerome Shaffer, "Existence, Predication, and the Ontological Argument," *Mind* 71, no. 283 (July 1962): 322–25. Reprinted by permission of the publisher.

"horse" has a particular meaning and is logically connected with other words like "animal"; its corresponding concept, the concept of a horse, has a particular content and is connected with other concepts like the concept of an animal. It is this intensional feature of words and their corresponding concepts which makes certain assertions like "A horse is an animal" tautological. But words and concepts are also applicable to things. It turns out to be the case that there have existed, do now exist, and will exist entities such that it is true of each of them that it is a horse, true of each of them that the concept of a horse applies to it. And this fact we may express by saying that the word, "horse" or the concept of a horse has extension. In making assertions about the extension of a concept there are typical forms of expression which we use: ". . . exist", ". . . are non-existent", "There are . . .", "There are no . . .", ". . . are plentiful", ". . . are scarce", ". . . are extinct", ". . . are mythological", ". . . are found in Africa", etc. That such expressions are typically used in assertions about the extension (or lack thereof) of particular concepts is what is correctly brought out in the slogan, " 'Exists' is not a predicate". But the typical use is not the only use. Since any statement, with suitable definition, can be true by virtue of the meanings of the terms, sentences with existential expressions can be used to express tautological statements. The very same sentence which is typically used to make a claim about the extension of the concept may instead be used to make a claim about the intension of the concept. We cannot tell by the form of the expression how the expression is being used. "Particulars exist", when asserted tautologically, is used to make a claim about the *meaning* of the word, "particulars", and therefore cannot be used to make a claim about the extension of the term. Similarly, if someone uses the sentence, "God exists", tautologically, he tells us only that being an existent is a logical requirement for being God. If, on the other hand, someone asserts, "God exists", non-tautologically, then he claims that the term, "God", has extension, applies to some existent. In the case of the Ontological Argument the only valid conclusion is an intensional statement about the meaning of the concept of God. *A fortiori* the conclusion cannot be about whether anything exists to which the concept applies. The *prima facie* plausibility of the Argument comes from the use of a sentence intensionally when the typical use of that sentence is extensional. In this way it conceals the illicit move from an intensional to an extensional statement.

It looked as if the familiar distinction between intension and extension, stood in danger of breaking down in the case of existential tautologies. But we have seen that this is not the case. For even when we have an existential tautology like "Particulars exist" or "God exists", it still remains an open question whether the concept of particulars or the concept of God has application, applies to any existent. What is settled at one level is not settled at another level. It is important to see that we can go on to settle the question at the other level, too, for we can *make* it *a priori* true that the concept has application. For example, let the expression, "the concept of God", mean "a concept which has application and applies to a being such that . . .". Then by definition the concept of God has application; the statement, "The concept of God has application", is now a tautology, given the definition. But nothing is gained by such a manoeuvre. We have given the expression, "the concept of God", a meaning; we have framed a concept, namely the concept of the concept of God, and this concept makes certain statements tautologically true. Yet we can still raise the extensional question, Does this concept refer to any existent? At this level the extensional question would be whether there actually is a concept of God such that this concept has extension, and there is such a concept only if there actually is a God. So making the condition of having application or extension a necessary condition for being a concept of God still leaves open the question, concerning *that* concept, whether it has extension. Nothing has been settled except the meaning of a certain expression.

Why is it that existential assertions cannot be tautological? Because they do not merely tell us what the requirements are for being an *A* but, starting with these requirements, tell us whether anything meets these requirements. Even if it is a conceptual requirement that the thing exist in order to be an instance of the concept, that in no way settles whether the requirement is met. And if we *make* it a tautology that the requirement is met, by framing a concept of a concept, then we are left with the open question whether the newly framed concept has extension. That is what is true in the thesis that no "existential" proposition can be analytic. But we must remember that an "existential" proposition can turn out to be an intensional proposition, and therefore tautological.

Since much of what I have claimed depends upon the legitimacy of the intension-extension distinction, I wish to consider, finally, two threats to this distinction. The first concerns the so-called *intensional object.* When I conceive of an object, think about it, describe it, make a painting of it, long for it, look for it, and expect to find it, it may nevertheless be the case that the object does not exist, that the concept has no extension. But it is tempting to say that there must be something such that I conceive of it, think about it, describe it, etc., tempting to say that the object in some sense exists. And thus it is tempting to say that the mere fact that there is a concept of some object entails that the object in some sense exists. Well, even if one says that, it is obviously not the sense in which the religious usually wish to say that God exists nor the sense in which the atheist wishes to deny that God exists. They disagree about whether anything answers to that concept of an object, not about whether that concept is a concept of an object.

A second, and more troublesome, threat to the intension-extension distinction arises when we try to apply the distinction to certain concepts. We seem quite clear that the concept of a horse does have extension and that the concept of a unicorn does not have extension, and that these are contingent facts. But now suppose we ask whether the concept of a number has extension. If we hold that the concept ultimately has as its extension things in the world, then it still remains a contingent fact that the concept has extension. But suppose we are inclined to say that the concept has extension simply because, as we all know, there are (infinitely) many numbers. Surely it is not a contingent fact that there are (infinitely) many numbers. So if this fact leads us to say that the concept of a number has extension, then it will be a necessary proposition that the concept of a number has extension and, given the concept of a number, we can say *a priori* that the concept applies to (infinitely) many things.

What makes this case puzzling is that we have no idea what would count as establishing that the concept of a number has extension or that it does not have extension. We can investigate whether the concept of a number is a legitimate one, clear and self-consistent; we can note its logical connection with other mathematical concepts; and we can frame propositions which state these connections, even propositions like "There exists a number which is even and prime". But what would count as showing that the concept, over and above its intensional content, has extension as well? Where would one look for traces, signs, evidences, intimations, or testimonies of the existence of numbers? Would we not say of someone who did think such a search sensible that he had misconceived the nature of numbers? Nothing would count as showing that the concept of numbers had extension over and above its intensional content, and this is to say that the notion of extension does not apply here. The most that could be said is that numbers are *in*tensional objects.

The same thing must be said for the existence of God. The most that the Ontological Argument establishes is the intensional object, God, even if this intensional object has the attribute of existence as an intensional feature. To establish that the concept of God has extension requires adducing some additional argument to show that over and above its intensional features, over and above the content of the concept (or the meaning of the word, "God"), the concept of God has extension as well. This additional argument will of necessity have to be an *a posteriori* argument to the effect that certain evidences make it reasonable to think that some actual existent answers to the concept. We are thus led to the result that the Ontological Argument of itself alone cannot show the existence of God, in the sense in which the concept is shown to have extension. And this is just as the religious wish it to be. They do not conceive of God as something whose being expresses itself entirely in the concepts and propositions of a language game. They conceive of Him as something which has effects on the world and can in some way be experienced. Here is a crucial respect in which His status is meant to be different from that of the numbers. The concept of God is a concept which *might* have extension. But some further argument is required to show whether it does or not.

Concepts are like nets. What they catch depends in part upon how we construct them and in part upon what is outside the net. Suppose I produce a net for catching fish one-millionth of an inch long. Of such a net we are entitled to say, "This net catches fish one-millionth of an inch long", and what shows that this statement is true is nothing but the construction of the net. Does the net catch anything? It catches fish one-millionth of an inch long. Still, a question remains. Shall we ever find such fish in our net? For those who hunger for such fish, the existence of the net does not in any way show that what they hunger for shall be given unto them.

The Five Ways of Thomas Aquinas

The a priori argument provided us by Anselm purported to elucidate the ramifications of the concept of God as the all-perfect being. Anselm made absolutely no appeal to any facet from our sense experience of the world. His argument depended exclusively on a serious consideration of the necessary entailments of the meaning of the concept of God as the all-perfect being. Given our earlier distinctions, this refusal to consider any demands from sense experience renders the ontological argument to be a priori in character.

In the tradition of philosophical theology, there have been proofs for the existence of God which start from sense experience. These are the a posteriori proofs. Lucid examples of the a posteriori methodology starting from facets of our sense experience are "The Five Ways" of Thomas Aquinas (1225–1274). Throughout these purported demonstrations, notice that Aquinas begins with some facet of sense experience. This facet serves as the first premise of each argument. Next, by means of a complicated ontological machinery, Aquinas argues that each particular facet of sense experience with which we began the argument cannot be adequately accounted for in a metaphysical system without an ontological postulation of a first principle. This first metaphysical principle is God. As we will see, from the experienced datum of motion, Aquinas concludes to the necessity of a "first mover"; from the experienced datum of causality, Aquinas concludes to the necessity of a "first cause"; and so forth for the remaining three a posteriori arguments for God's existence.

The text of "The Five Ways" is taken from the *Summa Theologiae*. This work, unfinished by Aquinas at his death, has become known, in the tradition of western philosophy, as a masterpiece elucidating a synthesis between Aristotelian philosophy and the Judeo-Christian tradition. As a philosopher, Aquinas was convinced that it was possible to rationally demonstrate the existence of God. Yet he never thought it an easy task. In the *Summa Theologiae*, Aquinas remarks on the difficulty of establishing the existence of God by rational methods alone.

. . . It is necessary for the salvation of humans that there be revelation from God, in addition to the philosophical disciplines investigated by human reason. First, because humans are directed to God as to an end which goes beyond the grasp of human reason. "The eye hath not seen, O God, besides Thee, what things Thou hast prepared for them that wait for Thee. (Isa., lxiv.4) But this end must be first known by human beings who are to direct their thoughts and actions to that end. Therefore, it was necessary for the salvation of human beings that certain propositions which exceed the capacity of human reason should be made known to human beings through divine revelation. Moreover, even in regards to those propositions which human reason can investigate, it was necessary that humans be taught through divine revelation. For the true propositions about God, such as reason can attain through philosophy, would only be known by a few persons, and even then only after a long time and with the accompaniment of many errors. But the whole concept of human salvation, which is in God, depends upon the knowledge of these propositions. Therefore, in order that the salvation of human beings might be more readily and surely attained, it was necessary that they be taught divine propositions through divine revelation. It was necessary, therefore, that in addition to the philosophical disciplines, there should be a "sacred discipline" which is known through divine revelation.

In reading the following account of "The Five Ways," do not be misled by the shortness of the arguments. Each one depends upon a rather sophisticated ontological machinery. In reading each proof, try to grasp the structure of the metaphysical concepts within which Aquinas provides his demonstration.

The Existence of God can be demonstrated in five ways:

The first and more obvious way is the argument from motion. It is certain and evident to our senses that there are some things in the world which are in motion. Now, whatever is in motion is put into motion by another thing. This is so because nothing can be in motion except if it is in potency to that towards which it is in motion. On the other hand, a thing moves inasmuch as it is in act. Motion is nothing other than the reduction of something from potency to act. However, nothing can be reduced from potency to act except by some other thing which is in a state of act. For example, what is actually hot, as fire, makes wood, which is potentially hot, to be actually hot. Hence, the wood undergoes change. It is not possible that the same thing should be at one and the same time in act and in potency in the same respect, but only in different respects. This means that what is actually hot cannot be simultaneously potentially hot. It is simultaneously potentially cold. It is, therefore, impossible that in the same respect and in the same way that a thing should be both mover and thing moved—i.e., that it should move itself. Accordingly, whatever is in motion must be put into motion by another. If that by which it is put in motion be itself put into motion, then this also must have been put into motion by another, and that by another again. This procedure, however, cannot go on into infinity. If that happened, there would be no first mover and, as a consequence, no other mover. This follows because subsequent movers move only because they have been put into motion by the first mover. For example, the staff moves only because it is put in motion by a hand. It is necessary, therefore, that we arrive at a first mover which is put in motion by no other. And this first mover everyone understands to be God.

The second way comes about from an analysis of efficient causes. In the world of sense experience, there is an order of efficient causes. There is no example known nor is such a case possible in which a thing is found to constitute the efficient cause of itself. If it were, it would be prior to itself, which is impossible. In the case of efficient causes, it is not possible to go on to infinity because in every case of efficient causes following in an ordered sequence, the first is the cause of the intermediate cause, and the intermediate is the cause of the ultimate cause, (whether the intermediate cause be one or many). To remove the cause, however, is to remove the effect. Therefore, if there is no first cause in a sequence of efficient causes, there will be neither ultimate nor intermediate causes. However, if in a sequence of efficient causes, it is possible to proceed to an infinity, then there will be no first efficient cause. It follows that there will also be no ultimate effect, nor any intermediate causes working efficiently. But all of this is obviously false. Therefore, it is necessary that a first efficient cause be admitted, to which everyone attributes the name of God.

The third way utilizes the concepts of possibility and necessity. We discover in the world of nature some things that are possible either to be or not to be; these are the things which have been generated and which will corrupt. Given their generation and corruption, it follows that they are possible to be and not to be. However, it is impossible for these things always to exist because that which is possible not to be at some time will not be. Therefore, if everything is possible not to be, then it is possible that there was a time when no things existed. If this were true, then even now there would be no things existing, because whatever does not exist begins to exist only through something which already exists. If follows, therefore, that if at one time nothing existed, it would have been impossible for anything to have begun to exist. As a consequence, even now nothing would be in existence. But this is absurd. Therefore, not everything is merely possible; there must exist something whose existence is necessary. Every necessary thing, however, either has its necessity caused by another thing or not. Yet it is impossible that there be an infinite process in necessary things which have their necessity caused by another thing (This has already been demonstrated in regard to efficient causes). Therefore, we must postulate the existence of some thing which has of itself its own necessity and does not receive it from another. Rather, it causes the property of necessity to others. This thing all humans speak of as God.

The fourth way arises from a consideration of the gradation of perfections found in natural things. Among existing things, some are more and some are less good, true, noble and so forth. The predicates "more" and "less" are said of different things, according as they resemble in their own way something which is the maximum. For example, a thing is said to be "hotter" insofar as it more nearly resembles that which is hottest. Accordingly, there is something which is truest, something best, something noblest, and therefore, something which is the highest being. Those things which are greatest in truth are greatest in being, so Aristotle argues in *The Metaphysics*. The maximum in any genus is the cause of everything in that genus. For example, fire, which is the maximum of heat, is the cause of all hot things. It follows, therefore, that there must be some being which is to all things the cause of their being, goodness, and all the other perfections. This being we call God.

The fifth way comes about from a consideration of the governance of the natural world. We observe that natural things which lack intelligence, nonetheless act for an end. This is evident because they always or in most cases act in the same way so as to obtain the best result. It must be the case that natural things attain their due ends in a designed and not in a fortuitous manner. However, whatever lacks intelligence cannot move toward an end unless it is directed by some other thing which is endowed with knowledge and possesses intelligence. For example, the arrow is shot toward its target under the direction of the archer. It follows, therefore, that some intelligent being exists by whom all natural things are directed to their proper ends. And we call this being God.[6]

Having thoughtfully read each of the five proofs concluding to the existence of God which Aquinas provided in the *Summa Theologiae*, it should be noted that there is a similar a posteriori structure to each of them. We can illustrate this structure in the following way:

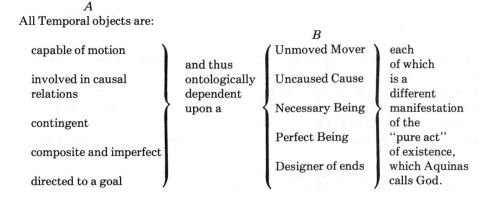

Column A refers to the datum of experience (motion, causality, contingency, imperfection, and purposeful order) from which Aquinas beings each demonstration. This provides the a posteriori character to the Five Ways. Column B refers to the metaphysical principle necessary to provide a complete ontological account of the datum of experience from which each proof began.

Before analyzing in detail the metaphysical presuppositions and implications of the Five Ways of Aquinas, it would be beneficial to read thoughtfully the following important commentary on Aquinas' proofs for the existence of God. It is by F.C. Copleston, an important twentieth-century historian of philosophy.

AQUINAS

F.C. Copleston

. . . Aquinas did not, of course, deny that people can come to know that God exists by other ways than by philosophic reflection. Nor did he ever assert that the belief of most people who accept the proposition that God exists is the result of their having elaborated metaphysical arguments for themselves or of their having thought through the metaphysical arguments developed by others. Nor did he confuse a purely intellectual assent to the conclusion of such a metaphysical argument with a living Christian faith in and love of God. But he did think that reflection on quite familiar features of the world affords ample evidence of God's existence. The reflection itself, sustained and developed at the metaphysical level, is difficult, and he explicitly recognized and acknowledged its difficulty: he certainly did not consider that everyone is capable of sustained metaphysical reflection. At the same time, the empirical facts on which this reflection is based were for him quite familiar facts. In order to see the relation of finite things to the being on which they depend we are not required to pursue scientific research, discovering hitherto unknown empirical facts. Nor does the metaphysician discover God in a manner analogous to the explorer who suddenly comes upon a hitherto unknown island or flower. It is attention and reflection which are required rather than research or exploration.

What, then, are the familiar facts which for Aquinas imply the existence of God? Mention of them can be found in the famous "five ways" of proving God's existence, which are outlined in the *Summa theologica*. . . . In the first way Aquinas begins by saying that "it is certain, and it is clear from sense-experience, that some things in this world are moved." It must be remembered that he, like Aristotle, understands the term "motion" in the broad sense of change, reduction from a state of potentiality to one of act; he does not refer exclusively to local motion. In the second way he starts with the remark that "we find in material things an order of efficient

---

causes." In other words, in our experience of things and of their relations to one another we are aware of efficient causality. Thus while in the first way he begins with the fact that some things are acted upon and changed by other things, the second way is based upon the fact that some things act upon other things, as efficient causes. In the third way he starts by stating that "we find among things some which are capable of existing or not existing, since we find that some things come into being and pass away." In other words, we perceive that some things are corruptible or perishable. In the fourth proof he observes that "we find in things that some are more or less good and true and noble and so on (than others)." Finally in the fifth way he says: "we see that some things which lack knowledge, namely natural bodies, act for an end, which is clear from the fact that they always or in most cases act in the same way, in order to attain what is best."

There is, I think, little difficulty in accepting as empirical facts the starting-points of the first three ways. For nobody really doubts that some things are acted upon and changed or "moved," that some things act on others, and that some things are perishable. Each of us is aware, for example, that he is acted upon and changed, that he sometimes acts as an efficient cause, and that he is perishable. Even if anyone were to cavil at the assertion that he is aware that he himself was born and will die, he knows very well that some other people were born and have died. But the starting-points of the two final arguments may cause some difficulty. The proposition that there are different grades of perfections in things stands in need of a much more thorough analysis than Aquinas accords it in his brief outline of the fourth way. For the schematic outlining of the five proofs was designed, not to satisfy the critical minds of mature philosophers, but as introductory material for "novices" in the study of theology. And in any case Aquinas could naturally take for granted in the thirteenth century ideas which were familiar to his contemporaries and which had not yet been subjected to the radical criticism to which they were later subjected. At the same time there is not very much difficulty in understanding the sort of thing which was meant. We are all accustomed to think and speak as though, for example, there were different degrees of intelligence and intellectual capacity. In order to estimate the different degrees we need, it is true, standards or fixed points of reference; but given these points of reference, we are all accustomed to make statements which imply different grades of perfections. And though these statements stand in need of close analysis, they refer to something which falls within ordinary experience and finds expression in ordinary language. As for the fifth way, the modern reader may find great difficulty in seeing what is meant if he confines his attention to the relevant passage in the Summa theologica. But if he looks at the Summa contra Gentiles (1, 13) he will find Aquinas saying that we see things of different natures co-operating in the production and maintenance of a relatively stable order or system. When Aquinas says that we see purely material things acting for an end, he does not mean to say that they act in a manner analogous to that in which human beings consciously act for definite puposes. Indeed, the point of the argument is that they do not do so. He means the different kinds of things, like fire and water, the behavior of which is determined by their several "forms," co-operate, not consciously but as a matter of fact, in such a way that there is a relatively stable order or system. And here again, though much more would need to be said in a full discussion of the matter, the basic idea is nothing particularly extraordinary nor is it contrary to our ordinary experience and expectations.

It is to be noted also that Aquinas speaks with considerable restraint: he avoids sweeping generalizations. Thus in the first argument he does not say that all material things are "moved" but that we see that some things in this world are moved or changed. In the third argument he does not state that all finite things are contingent but that we are aware that some things come into being and pass away. And in the fifth argument he does not say that there is an invariable world-order or system but that we see natural bodies acting always or in most cases in the same ways. The difficulty, therefore, which may be experienced in regard to Aquinas' proofs of God's existence concerns not so much the empirical facts or alleged empirical facts with which he starts as in seeing that these facts imply God's existence.

Perhaps a word should be said at once about this idea of "implication." As a matter of fact Aquinas does not use the word when talking about the five ways: he speaks of "proof" and of "demonstration." And by "demonstration" he means in this context what he calls *demonstratio quia* (S.T., la, 2, 2), namely a causal proof of God's existence, proceeding from the affirmation of some empirical fact, for example that there are things which change, to the affirmation of a transcendent cause. It is, indeed, his second proof which is strictly the causal argument, in the sense that it deals explicitly with the order of efficient causality; but in every proof the idea of ontological dependence on a transcendent cause appears in some form or other. Aquinas' conviction was that a full understanding of the empirical facts which are selected for consideration in the five ways involves seeing the dependence of these facts on a transcendent cause. The existence of things which change, for instance, is, in his opinion, not self-explanatory: it can be rendered intelligible only if seen as dependent on a transcendent cause, a cause, that is to say, which does not itself belong to the order of changing things.

This may suggest to the modern reader that Aquinas was concerned with causal explanation in the sense that he was concerned with framing an empirical hypothesis to explain certain facts. But he did not regard the proposition affirming God's existence as a causal hypothesis in the sense of being in principle revisable, as a hypothesis, that is to say, which might conceivably have to be revised in the light of fresh empirical data or which might be supplanted by a more economical hypothesis. This point can perhaps be seen most clearly in the case of his third argument, which is based on the fact that there are things which come into being and pass away. In Aquinas' opinion no fresh scientific knowledge about the physical constitution of such things could affect the validity of the argument. He did not look on a "demonstration" of God's existence as an empirical hypothesis in the sense in which the electronic theory, for example, is said to be an empirical hypothesis. It is, of course, open to anyone to say that in his own opinion cosmological arguments in favor of God's existence are in fact analogous to the empirical hypotheses of the sciences and that they have a predictive function; but it does not follow that this interpretation can legitimately be ascribed to Aquinas. We should not be misled by the illustrations which he sometimes offers from contemporary scientific theory. For these are mere illustrations to elucidate a point in terms easily understandable by his readers: they are not meant to indicate that the proofs of God's existence were for him empirical hypotheses in the modern sense of the term.

Does this mean, therefore, that Aquinas regarded the existence of God as being logically entailed by facts such as change or coming into being and passing away? He did not, of course, regard the proposition "there are things which come into being and pass away" as logically entailing the proposition "there is an absolutely necessary or independent being" in the sense that affirmation of the one proposition and denial of the other involves one in a verbal or formal linguistic contradiction. But he thought that metaphysical analysis of what it objectively means to be a thing which comes into being and passes away shows that such a thing must depend existentially on an absolutely necessary being. And he thought that metaphysical analysis of what it objectively means to be a changing thing shows that such a thing depends on a supreme unmoved mover. It follows that for Aquinas one is involved in a contradiction if one affirms the propositions "there are things which come into being and pass away" and "there are things which change" and at the same time denies the propositions "there is an absolutely necessary being" and "there is a supreme unmoved mover." But the contradiction can be made apparent only by means of metaphysical analysis. And the entailment in question is fundamentally an ontological or causal entailment. . . .

. . . After these general remarks I turn to Aquinas' five proofs of the existence of God. In the first proof he argues that "motion" or change means the reduction of a thing from a state of potentiality to one of act, and that a thing cannot be reduced from potentiality to act except under the influence of an agent already in act. In this sense "everything which is moved must be moved by another." He argues finally that in order to avoid an infinite regress in the chain of movers, the existence of a first unmoved mover must be admitted. "And all understand that this is God."

A statement like "all understand that this is God" or "all call this (being) God" occurs at the end of each proof, and I postpone consideration of it for the moment. As for the ruling out of an infinite regress, I shall explain what Aquinas means to reject after outlining the second proof, which is similar in structure to the first.

Whereas in the first proof Aquinas considers things as being acted upon, as being changed or "moved," in the second he considers them as active agents, as efficient causes. He argues that there is a hierarchy of efficient causes, a subordinate cause being dependent on the cause above it in the hierarchy. He then proceeds, after excluding the hypothesis of an infinite regress, to draw the conclusion that there must be a first efficient cause, "which all call God."

Now, it is obviously impossible to discuss these arguments profitably unless they are first understood. And misunderstanding of them is only too easy, since the terms and phrases used are either unfamiliar or liable to be taken in a sense other than the sense intended. In the first place it is essential to understand that in the first argument Aquinas supposes that movement or change is dependent on a "mover" acting here and now, and that in the second argument he supposes that there are efficient causes in the world which even in their causal activity are here and now dependent on the causal activity of other causes. That is why I have spoken of a "hierarchy" rather than of a "series." What he is thinking of can be illustrated in this way. A son is dependent on his father, in the sense that he would not have existed except for the causal activity of his father. But when the son acts for himself, he is not dependent here and now on his father. But he is dependent here and now on other factors. Without the activity of the air, for instance, he could not himself act, and the life-preserving activity of the air is itself dependent here and now on other factors, and they in turn on other factors. I do not say that this illustration is in all respects adequate for the purpose; but it at least illustrates the fact that when Aquinas talks about an "order" of efficient causes he is not thinking of a series stretching back into the past, but of a hierarchy of causes, in which a subordinate member is here and now dependent on the causal activity of a higher member. If I wind up my watch at night, it then proceeds to work without further interference on my part. But the activity of the pen tracing these words on the page is here and now dependent on the activity of my hand, which in turn is here and now dependent on other factors.

The meaning of the rejection of an infinite regress should now be clear. Aquinas is not rejecting the possibility of an infinite series as such. We have already seen that he did not think that anyone had ever succeeded in showing the impossibility of an infinite series of events stretching back into the past. Therefore he does not mean to rule out the possibility of an infinite series of causes and effects, in which a given member depended on the preceding member, say X on Y, but does not, once it exists, depend here and now on the present causal activity of the preceding member. We have to imagine, not a lineal or horizontal series, so to speak, but a vertical hierarchy, in which a lower member depends here and now on the present causal activity of the member above it. It is the latter type of series, if prolonged to infinity, which Aquinas rejects. And he rejects it on the ground that unless there is a "first" member, a mover which is not itself moved or a cause which does not itself depend on the causal activity of a higher cause, it is not possible to explain the "motion" or the causal activity of the lowest member. His point of view is this. Suppress the first unmoved mover and there is no motion or change here and now. Suppress the first efficient cause and there is no causal activity here and now. If therefore we find that some things in the world are changed, there must be a first unmoved mover. And if there are efficient causes in the world, there must be a first efficient, and completely non-dependent cause. The word "first" does not mean first in the temporal order, but supreme or first in the ontological order.

A remark on the word "cause" is here in place. What precisely Aquinas would have said to the David Humes either of the fourteenth century or of the modern era it is obviously impossible to say. But it is clear that he believed in real causal efficacy and real causal relations. He was aware, of course, that causal efficacy is not the object of vision in the sense in which patches of colors are objects of vision; but the human being, he considered, is aware of real causal relations and if we understand "perception" as involving the cooperation of sense and intellect, we can be said to "perceive" causality. And presumably he would have said that the sufficiency of a phenomenalistic interpretation of causality for purposes of physical science proves nothing against the validity of a metaphysical notion of causality. It is obviously possible to dispute whether his analyses of change or "motion" and of efficient causality are valid or invalid and whether there is such a thing as a heirarchy of causes. And our opinion about the validity or invalidity of his arguments for the existence of God will depend very largely on our answers to these questions. But mention of the mathematical infinite series is irrelevant to a discussion of his arguments. And it is this point which I have been trying to make clear.

In the third proof Aquinas starts from the fact that some things come into being and perish, and he concludes from this that it is possible for them to exist or not to exist: they do not exist "necessarily." He then argues that it is impossible for things which are of this kind to exist always; for "that which is capable of not existing, at some time does not exist." If all things were of this kind, at some time there would be nothing. Aquinas is clearly supposing for the sake of argument the hypothesis of infinite time, and his proof is designed to cover this hypothesis. He does not say that infinite time is impossible: what he says is that if time is infinite and if all things are capable of not existing, this potentiality would inevitably be fulfilled in infinite time. There would then be nothing. And if there had ever been nothing, nothing would now exist. For no thing can bring itself into existence. But it is clear as a matter of fact that there are things. Therefore it can never have been true to say that there was literally no thing. Therefore it is impossible that all things should be capable of existing or not existing. There must, then, be some necessary being. But perhaps it is necessary in the sense that it must exist if something else exists; that is to say, its necessity may be hypothetical. We cannot, however, proceed to infinity in the series or hierarchy of necessary beings. If we do so, we do not explain the presence here and now of beings capable of existing or not existing. Therefore we must affirm the existence of a being which is absolutely necessary (*per se necessarium*) and completely independent. "And all call this being *God*."

This argument may appear to be quite unnecessarily complicated and obscure. But it has to be seen in its historical context. As already mentioned, Aquinas designed his argument in such a way as to be independent of the question whether or not the world existed from eternity. He wanted to show that on either hypothesis there must be a necessary being. As for the introduction of hypothetical necessary beings, he wanted to show that even if there are such beings, perhaps within the universe, which are not corruptible in the sense in which a flower is corruptible, there must still be an absolutely independent being. Finally, in regard to terminology, Aquinas uses the common medieval expression "necessary being." He does not actually use the term "contingent being" in the argument and talks instead about "possible" beings; but it comes to the same thing. And though the words "contingent" and "necessary" are now applied to propositions rather than to beings, I have retained Aquinas' mode of speaking. Whether one accepts the argument or not, I do not think that there is any insuperable difficulty in understanding the line of thought.

The fourth argument is admittedly difficult to grasp. Aquinas argues that *there are degrees of perfections in things.* Different kinds of finite things possess different perfections in diverse limited degrees. He then argues not only that if there are different degrees of a perfection like goodness there is a supreme good to which other good things approximate but also that all limited degrees of goodness are caused by the supreme good. And since goodness is a convertible term with being, a thing being good in so far as it has being, the supreme good is the supreme being and the cause of being in all other things. "Therefore there is something which is the cause of the being and goodness and of every perfection in all other things; and this we call *God.*"

Aquinas refers to some remarks of Aristotle in the *Metaphysics;* but this argument puts one in mind at once of Plato's *Symposium* and *Republic.* And the Platonic doctrine of participation seems to be involved. Aquinas was not immediately acquainted with either work, but the Platonic line of thought was familiar to him from other writers. And it has not disappeared from philosophy. Indeed, some of those theists who reject or doubt the validity of the "cosmological" arguments seem to feel a marked attraction for some variety of the fourth way, arguing that in the recognition of objective values we implicitly recognize God as the supreme value. But if the line of thought represented by the fourth way is to mean anything to the average modern reader, it has to be presented in a rather different manner from that in which it is expressed by Aquinas who was able to assume in his readers ideas and points of view which can no longer be presupposed.

Finally, the fifth proof, if we take its statement in the *Summa theologica* together with that in the *Summa contra Gentiles,* can be expressed more or less as follows. *The activity and behaviour of each thing is determined by its form.* But we observe material things of very different types cooperating in such a way as to produce and maintain a relatively stable world-order or system. They achieve an "end," the production and maintenance of a cosmic order. But non-intelligent material things certainly do not co-operate consciously in view of a purpose. If it is said that they co-operate in the realization of an end or purpose, this does not mean that they intend the realization of this order in a manner analogous to that in which a man can act consciously with a view to the achievement of a purpose. Nor, when Aquinas talks about operating "for an end" in this connection, is he thinking of the utility of certain things to the human race. He is not saying, for example, that grass grows to feed the sheep and that sheep exist in order that human beings should have food and clothing. It is of the unconscious co-operation of different kinds of material things in the production and maintenance of a relatively stable cosmic system that he is thinking, not of the benefits accruing to us from our use of certain objects. And his argument is that this co-operation on the part of heterogeneous material things clearly points to the existence of an extrinsic intelligent author of this co-operation, who operates with an end in view. If Aquinas had lived in the days of the evolutionary hypothesis, he would doubtless have argued that this hypothesis supports rather than invalidates the conclusion of the argument.

No one of these arguments was entirely new, as Aquinas himself was very well aware. But he developed them and arranged them to form a coherent whole. I do not mean that he regarded the validity of one particular argument as necessarily depending on the validity of the other four. He doubtless thought that each argument was valid in its own right. But, as I have already remarked, they conform to a certain pattern, and they are mutually complementary in the sense that in each argument things are considered from a different point of view or under a different aspect. They are so many different approaches to God.

In his commentary on "The Five Ways," Copleston posits a fundamental ontological distinction between horizontal and vertical causality. Copleston remarks that this distinction is a necessary condition in order for the machinery of Aquinas' proof to work. Horizontal causality refers to the sequence of events which we observe in the temporal realm. Vertical causality, on the other hand, refers to a type of ontological dependence. It would be well to remember now the discussion concerning ontological dependence which took place in chapter 2, during the consideration of Plato's world of the forms. Ontological dependence refers to the relation the forms have to the individual things found in the external world. To recall from that discussion, if the forms are taken away, then so too will be the individual things of the world. There is a fundamental ontological relationship of dependence between the forms and the individual things. Vertical causality is to be analyzed in the same manner as the relation of ontological dependence in Plato's world of the forms. Aquinas' proofs indicate that there is a property of dependency characteristic of all temporal beings. This dependence can be explained only by the postulation of a first metaphysical principle. This analysis suggests that with the five ways Aquinas provides a proof for the necessity of establishing a foundation for all being. Within this structure, a first metaphysical principle—which he calls God—is established. From motion Aquinas establishes the first mover; from causality, the first cause; from contingency, the necessary being; from imperfection, the all-perfect being; and from order in the universe, the first principle of design.

The First Way

It is now time to examine the structure of some of Aquinas' arguments in detail. Due to limitations of space, we shall consider the First Way and the Third Way. The Second Way is similar in structure to that found in the First and the Third Ways. The Fourth Way is overly complicated in that it is rooted in much neo-Platonism. Hence we shall not consider it in detail here. The Fifth Way, with its emphasis on the evidence of order and design in the universe, is somewhat similar to a proof elucidated by William Paley; we shall consider Paley's proof at length.

The first three ways have a common structure. It is rooted in Aquinas' distinction between act and potency. Briefly, a potency is the ability or capacity an object has to *become* something. In the ontology of Aquinas, the explanation of any "process" can only be in terms of potency and act. For example, a chunk of marble has a potency to become a statue; cold water has the potency to become hot water; an acorn has the potency to become an oak tree; an artist has a potency to produce a painting; and a child has the potency to learn a language. Note that a potency, in Aquinas' philosophy, indicates *any* general disposition a thing possesses which permits it to be changed into something else. An "act," on the other hand, is best illustrated by defining it as the opposite of a potency. An act is the state of completion or perfection that any given object has at a particular moment. For example, the state of cold water as "cold" water; cold water has the "act" of being cold. Other examples of states of actuality would include: the state of the fire as being actually hot; the state of the artist actually here and now painting a picture; the state of the person actually here and now speaking a language. Generally, the completion of a dispositional property is an act. Aquinas discussed the nature of the potency-act distinction in the following way:

> As a receiver is to what it receives, so is a potency to its actuality. And as an actuality is the perfection of what is potential, so being acted upon in this sense implies that a certain perfection of a thing in potency is received from a thing in act. It is the case that only the actual can perfect the potential. Actuality is not, as such, contrary to potency.[7]

In his *Commentary on Aristotle's Physics* (Book III, Lectio 2), Aquinas remarked that ". . . potency and act make up the fundamental division of all reality."

Using these general categories, Aquinas claims that every existing thing is either in act or in potency. As he remarked in the above passage from his *Commentary on Aristotle's Physics*, the most general division of being is found in the act-potency distinction. An entailment of this principle is that it is impossible for any given object to be in potency toward a certain quality and to also possess that quality at the same time. It would be a violation of the principle of contradiction for a thing to be in potency to a property and to possess that property at the same time and in the same respect. Consequently, although act and potency are mutually related to each other, they are nevertheless mutually opposing states. Potency is the capacity and act is the realization of that capacity.

Having examined the nature of the act-potency distinction as it works in Aquinas' ontology, it is time to apply this principle in our explanation and analysis of the First Way. Aquinas defines motion, which we shall regard as any given change or process, as the "act of a thing in potency insofar as it still is in potency." Change, then, is a movement from the state of potency that a thing possesses to the realization or completion of that potency. For example, it is the movement of cold water—which as cold has the potential to be hot—to actually become hot water. By using the categories of potency and act, Aquinas provides an analysis of the facet of *becoming*. According to Aquinas' analysis, every process is the movement from a potency to an act. Let's illustrate this claim in terms of the movement from cold water to hot water:

T_1	T_2	T_3
Water at 35° F.	Water being heated by flame.	Water at 70° F.
Actually 35° F.		Actually 70° F.
Potentially 70° F. (or any degree F. other than 35° F.)		Potentially 35° F. (or any degree F. other than 70° F.)

It is important to note the force of Aquinas' claim here. In order for something to be moved from a state of potency to a corresponding state of actuality, a necessary condition is the existence of some other being which is now in the state of actuality. This other being in the state of actuality causally influences the original thing so its state of potentiality can be reduced to a state of actuality. In the preceding example, what would happen if the fire were not actually fire but a potential fire? In other words, if the Bunsen burner were not in the state of actually heating. Would there be any heat? Of course not. An implication of this example is that a being cannot be both potentially and actually the same quality at the same time. Granting this, for any process of change to occur, it is a necessary condition that there be an additional being which is in a state of actuality and whose state of actuality can initiate the process of transferral from potency to act in the original thing. We may illustrate the force of Aquinas' point in the following way:

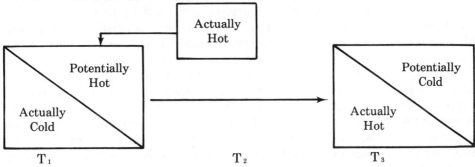

The schematic drawing illustrates the influence of the third being whose state is one of actuality. This factor is important in understanding the structure of Aquinas' First Way.

Given the explanation so far, one crucial question emerges. Is the source of heat always in act or does it also have a potential component as part of its constitution? If it is always in a state of actuality regarding its heating function, then there is no need to search any further for an additional source of explaining the process of heating the water. However, in our example, it is obvious that someone has to turn on the gas and light the Bunsen burner. Accordingly, the same question can be asked about the process in regard to the source of heat actually becoming hot, as was asked about the cold water becoming hot water. If the source of heat is itself a process, then it too demands some external thing "in act" in order to render its state of potency to a corresponding state of actuality. Once we have asked and answered this question, we can ask the very same set of questions about this second source of actuality. This form of questioning forces us into an ontological problem, which can be illustrated in the following way:

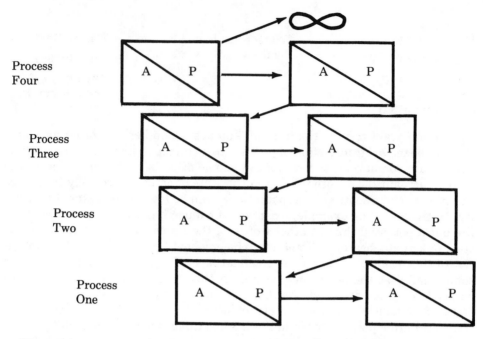

Given this structure, Aquinas then is concerned over the possibility that this series really could progress into infinity. Or must it stop someplace? Is this ontological analysis of process in terms of the potency-act distinction compatible with an infinite series of beings exemplifying various states of potentiality and actuality? The only appropriate place a series of beings having states of potentiality could stop would be at a being that is so constituted that it is always in act. Such a being would lack any state of potentiality whatsoever. Aquinas' response to these questions is that an infinite series of moved movers is impossible. Why is this impossible? Because, Aquinas responds, if there is no origin to the series, then there will be no examples of motion and process now. However there are many examples of motion and process now. Therefore there must be an origin for the series.

We must examine this argument in more detail. There is more to this proof than immediately is obvious. The point Aquinas stresses is that if there were no being which is in a state of complete actuality, then the starting point in the series would be some object which is in potency alone. Refer back to the schematic drawing of the process of moved movers (above). The last entity depicted is one whose state of potentiality is yet to be actualized. But given the force of the potency-act distinction, an entity which is in the state of potentiality cannot be reduced to a state of actuality unless there is a further being which is in a state of actuality. Yet we have already granted that, without a being in a state of actuality, the beginning of the series must be a being only in the state of potentiality. With a beginning point consisting only of a being in a state of potentiality, so Aquinas argues, the series itself can never begin. If the series cannot begin, then there can be no examples of motion and process now. But, to the contrary, there are many examples of such occurrences which can be experienced. So pervasive is this experience that Aquinas maintains that it is an evident fact of everyday experience. The crux of Aquinas' argument is that, in order to provide an adequate explanation of the fact of process in the external world, it is necessary to postulate the existence of a being whose state is such that it lacks any potentiality. This is what Aquinas calls the *unmoved mover*.

We should analyze the concept of an unmoved mover for a moment. An unmoved mover would be a being which is capable of moving something else. Therefore it is in act. But it is also unmoved itself. This means that it is a being which lacks any possible states of potentiality. The unmoved mover, hence, functions as the originating principle in Aquinas' ontology. This being is often referred to as a *pure act*. Obviously this means that it lacks any states of potentiality. It shall be suggested later that a being of pure actuality is best interpreted in terms of the "act of existence."

Given the above analysis, it might be suitable to summarize Aquinas' First Way. The structure of the proof is as follows:

A. We do observe motion and process in the external world. Since this is the starting point of the proof, it is an a posteriori proof. The experience of process—what Aristotle referred to as the experience of "becoming"— is a primitive datum of our experience both of ourselves and of the world around us.

B. Because of the definition of motion or process in terms of a reduction of a potency to its corresponding actuality, some additional being in act is needed as a necessary condition in order to render a change from a state of potentiality to a state of actuality.

C. This succession of moved movers cannot go to infinity. If that were the case, then there would be no present instance of motion or process because we could never go back to the first cause of motion.

D. A first mover itself unmoved is demanded as a necessary condition for explaining motion. Aquinas claims that this is what we call God.

What about the following objection? There is nothing incompatible with an infinite series of moved movers. This is an objection which has been made constantly against the structure of the First Way. It must be noted that Aquinas agreed with the Arabian philosopher, Averroes (1126-1198), in claiming that there was no philosophical demonstration capable of establishing that the temporal world was *not* eternal. In the medieval scheme, eternity implies ontological infinity, which is probably the reason Copleston appeals to the horizontal-vertical causality distinction as a necessary condition in understanding Aquinas' Five Ways. The structure of Aquinas' Five Ways is aligned with vertical causality and not with horizontal causality, and vertical causality is equivalent to the concept of ontological dependence. To interpret Aquinas' proofs only as horizontal dependence would be inconsistent with his explicit affirmation of the impossibility of establishing the noneternity of the temporal world. The horizontal-vertical causality distinction shall be considered at length when we examine the Third Way.

The Third Way

Structurally, the Second Way is similar to the First Way. If we understand what Aquinas attempts to do in analyzing the concept of motion and process in terms of the potency/act distinction, we will readily understand that this basic structure applies equally to the format of his analysis of causality. Before considering the Third Way in detail, the following passage from Etienne Gilson's *The Philosophy of St. Thomas Aquinas* on the act-potency distinction will be helpful in understanding these concepts so central to Aquinas' proofs for the existence of God.

> The principle of the real distinction between *Act and Potency* is one of the most fundamental and far-reaching principles in Thomistic philosophy, having for St. Thomas an even wider application than for Aristotle from whom it emanated. The two notions are complementary and are practically synonymous with "being determined" and "being determinable." In this context "potency" represents "passive potency," as distinct from "active potency" or "faculty." It is a principle or aptitude of receiving or becoming. St. Thomas defines it as "principium per quod alicui competit ut moveatur vel patiatur ab alio" (*Comm. Met.*, V., lect. 14). The realisation of this aptitude or capability is known as "act." As St. Thomas says: "Just as the *action* is the complementary perfection of an active potency, so that which corresponds to the passive potency, as its perfection and completion, is called *act.*" (*Comm. Sent.*, I., dist. XLII., qu. I., art. 1, ad 1^m.)
>
> In God there is no passive capability at all. He is Pure Act, i.e. He has—or more correctly, He *is*—every possible perfection. But in all other beings there is passive potency of some kind. In the pure spirits the distinction must be drawn between their "essence," which has the capability of being, and their "existence," which is the actualisation of that capability. In material beings there is yet a further capability resulting from the nature of matter. This may be the capability of coming to be or of passing away, or that of local movement. The latter is included in the former, though not necessarily vice-versa. Man has both these potencies, but the celestial bodies, the potency of whose matter is completely actualised by their form from the first moment of their existence, have only that of local motion.
>
> In the more detailed application of "potency" and "act," as in the distinction between the soul and its faculties, between the active and the possible intellect, in short, wherever there is a determination of something hitherto undetermined, the general doctrine here given, will serve as a guide. The scope of its application can be seen in the following dictum: *Actus et potentia dividunt ens et quodlibet genus entis.* [Act and potency divide all of being and every genus of being.] [8]

The philosophical structure of the Third Way is similar to that used in the First Way. It depends upon the potency/act distinction. However, in this proof, the concept of "necessary being" is explicitly discussed and analyzed. Insofar as the notion of a necessary being is important in many philosophical proofs for God's existence, it will be well for us to scrutinize carefully the Third Way. Also, it will be helpful to recall our discussion regarding the second formulation of the ontological argument found in the first part of this chapter. Notice that the conclusion reached by both the Third Way and the second formulation of the ontological argument are the same: God is a being who exists necessarily. Yet the starting points for each argument are different. The ontological argument remains an a priori argument, while the Third Way, with its beginning point in our sense experience of the external world, is an a posteriori proof. In many discussions found in natural theology, the Third Way is classified as an example of the cosmological argument. Cosmology has been defined as a philosophical theory referring to the universe as a whole. The Third Way, with its conclusion establishing the indispensability of a being which necessarily exists, affirms something about the nature of the universe. Accordingly, this affirmation and its supporting premises have been termed the *cosmological* argument for the existence of God.

First, some definitions of the crucial concepts utilized in the Third Way are in order. A necessary being is one which *must be*. In other words, it is a being which cannot not be. It is impossible for it not to exist. A contingent being, on the other hand, is a being which either can or cannot be. A contingent being has as a necessary part of its structure the aspect that it did not exist at one time and that it might not exist at some future time. Put differently, a contingent being does not have existence as an essential property. A necessary being, to the contrary, has existence as part of its essence. A constitutive property of a necessary being is existence. With a contingent being, existence is extrinsic to the essence of that being. From this analysis, it follows that the possibility of "corruption,"—which is an Aristotelian term indicating the possibility not to be—is a necessary aspect of any contingent being. Anthony Kenny has provided the following statement concerning the nature of a necessary being, ". . . something is necessary if and only if it is, always will be and always was; and cannot nor could not nor will not be able not to be."[9] Obviously Kenny is stressing the notion of ontological independence in regard to the necessary being. The necessary being is totally independent and depends for its initial existence or continued existence on nothing outside of itself.

There is an important presupposition at work in this proof. Aquinas, following the Aristotelian tradition, accepted the possibility of necessarily existing beings. Contrary to empiricists like Hume and the logical positivists, the concept of necessity is not predicated only of analytic a priori definitions. In other words, within the context of Aristotelian ontology, the concept of necessity is not the exclusive prerogative of analytic propositions. Necessity can significantly be predicated of beings. This is an important presupposition necessary for understanding the structure of the Third Way. Put differently, the important dimension for "necessary" in "necessary being" is not the notion of logical contradiction as espoused by the radical empiricists. Rather it is the concept of causal independence and this is a fundamental metaphysical category—not a logical concept.

The structure of the Third Way is as follows. We observe contingent beings in the world. Everything which we experience in the universe—with the possible exception of an intuition of the "self," if that can be adequately elucidated —can be thought of as coming to be and passing away. This is related to the problem of "becoming" which fascinated Plato so much (recall our discussion in chapter 2). Once again, since this proof depends upon our *experience* of contingency, it is an a posteriori proof.

Given our experience of contingency regarding the things of the world, Aquinas wonders what follows from the assumption that *every* type of existing thing is a contingent being. In other words, what consequences follow from the assertion that everything which exists is contingent. In this discussion, Aquinas asks us to assume an infinite amount of time. If we assume an infinite amount of time, Aquinas affirms that one possibility in this temporal duration is that there will be no contingent beings. If we assume an infinite amount of time, then each one of the infinite number of possibilities can be realized. Assuming that every being which exists is a contingent being, it follows that each of these beings is such that it *might not be* at some time. Aquinas puts these two assumptions together. By assuming an infinite amount of time and assuming that all existing things are contingent, it follows that one of the possibilities in the infinite temporal duration is that none of the contingent beings actually exists. However, if under the assumption of an infinite temporal duration the possibility of nothing existing is realized, then it is impossible for anything now to exist. Of course Aquinas assumes that, from nothing, nothing can come; it is impossible for something to come from nothing. Thus if, in the infinite temporal duration, the stage of nothingness was realized, then it is impossible for any contingent being to exist now. But, Aquinas argues, this is contrary to the evidence from our sense experience of the world. We perceive many contingent beings—maple trees, collie dogs, tulip plants, human beings. Given that contingent beings do exist now and given the fact that if at one time no contingent beings existed, Aquinas suggests that it is a necessary condition, to explain how contingent beings came to be in the first place, that there be a necessary being. This necessary being bestows existence on the whole order of contingent beings. Without the postulation of a necessary being, it would be impossible for any contingent beings to exist. The Third Way is a good example of the horizontal/vertical causality distinction which Copleston described. The necessary being is extrinsic to the level of horizontal causality—which is the order of all contingent beings.

Aquinas next asks about the status of the necessary being. He claims that the only being capable of providing existence to any other being is a being whose essence is existence. Of course, this is how Aquinas defines a necessary being. A constitutive property of the essence of God is existence. Aquinas concludes that, since God is a necessary being, the essence of God is existence. Students of medieval philosophy have been fascinated by this claim. Etienne Gilson attempts to make a connection between the concept of God as a being whose essence is existence and the passage in the Old Testament in which God, in responding to a question from Moses, referred to himself as a being who always exists. The following passage is from Gilson's excellent treatise, *God and Philosophy*.

GOD AND CHRISTIAN PHILOSOPHY

Etienne Gilson

While the Greek philosophers were wondering what place to assign to their gods in a philosophically intelligible world, the Jews had already found the God who was to provide philosophy with an answer to its own question. Not a God imagined by poets or discovered by any thinker as an ultimate answer to his metaphysical problems, but one who had revealed Himself to

From Etienne Gilson, *God and Philosophy* (New Haven: Yale University Press, 1941), pp. 38–43. Reprinted by permission of the publisher.

the Jews, told them His name, and explained to them His nature, in so far at least as His nature can be understood by men.

The first character of the Jewish God was his unicity: "Hear, O Israel: the Lord our God is one Lord."[1] Impossible to achieve a more far-reaching revolution in fewer words or in a simpler way. When Moses made this statement, he was not formulating any metaphysical principle to be later supported by rational justification. Moses was simply speaking as an inspired prophet and defining for the benefit of the Jews what was henceforth to be the sole object of their worship. Yet, essentially religious as it was, this statement contained the seed of a momentous philosophical revolution, in this sense at least, that should any philosopher, speculating at any time about the first principle and cause of the world, hold the Jewish God to be the true God, he would be necessarily driven to identify his supreme philosophical cause with God. In other words, whereas the difficulty was, for a Greek philosopher, to fit a plurality of gods into a reality which he conceived as one, any follower of the Jewish God would know at once that, whatever the nature of reality itself may be said to be, its religious principle must of necessity coincide with its philosophical principle. Each of them being one, they are bound to be the same and to provide men with one and the same explanation of the world.

When the existence of this one true God was proclaimed by Moses to the Jews, they never thought for a moment that their Lord could be some thing. Obviously, their Lord was somebody. Besides, since he was the God of the Jews, they already knew Him; and they knew Him as the Lord God of their fathers, the God of Abraham, the God of Isaac, and the God of Jacob. Time and again, their God had proved to them that He was taking care of His people; their relations with Him had always been personal relations, that is, relations between persons and another person; the only thing they still wanted to know about Him was what to call Him. As a matter of fact, Moses himself did not know the name of the one God; but he knew that the Jews would ask him for it; and instead of engaging upon deep metaphysical meditations to discover the true name of God, he took a typically religious short cut. Moses simply asked God about His name, saying to Him: "Lo, I shall go to the children of Israel, and say to them: The God of your fathers hath sent me to you. If they should say to me: What is His name? What shall I say to them? God said to Moses: I AM WHO AM. He said: Thus shalt thou say to the children of Israel: HE WHO IS, hath sent me to you."[2] Hence the universally known name of the Jewish God— Yahweh, for Yahweh means "He who is."

Here again historians of philosophy find themselves confronted with this to them always unpalatable fact: a nonphilosophical statement which has since become an epoch-making statement in the history of philosophy. The Jewish genius was not a philosophical genius; it was a religious one. Just as the Greeks are our masters in philosophy, the Jews are our masters in religion. So long as the Jews kept their own religious revelation to themselves, nothing happened to philosophy. But owing to the preaching of the Gospel the God of the Jews ceased to be the private God of an elect race and became the universal God of all men. Any Christian convert who was at all familiar with Greek philosophy was then bound to realize the metaphysical import of his new religious belief. His philosophical first principle had to be one with his religious first principle, and since the name of his God was "I am," any Christian philosopher had to posit "I am" as his first principle and supreme cause of all things, even in philosophy. To use our own modern terminology, let us say that a Christian's philosophy is "existential" in its own right.

This point was of such importance that even the earliest Christian thinkers did not fail to see it. When the first educated Greeks became converts to Christianity, the Olympian gods of Homer had already been discredited as mere mythical imaginings through the repeated criticism of the philosophers. But those very philosophers had no less completely discredited themselves by giving to the world the spectacle of their endless contradictions. Even those who were the greatest among them, taken at their very best, had never succeeded in correctly stating what they at least should have held to be the supreme cause of all things. Plato, for instance, had clearly seen that the ultimate philosophical explanation for all that which is should ultimately rest, not within those elements of reality that are always being generated and therefore never really are, but with something which, because it has no generation, truly is, or exists. Now, as has been pointed out by the unknown author of the *Hortatory Address to the Greeks* as early as the third century A.D. what Plato had said was almost exactly what the Christians themselves were saying, "saving only the difference of the article. For Moses said: *He who is,* and Plato: *That which is."* And it is quite true that "either of the expressions seems to apply to the existence of God."[3] If God is "He who is," he also is "that which is," because to be somebody is also to be something. Yet the converse is not true, for to be somebody is much more than to be something.

We are here at the dividing line between Greek thought and Christian thought, that is to say, between Greek philosophy and Christian philosophy. Taken in itself, Christianity was not a philosophy. It was the essentially religious doctrine of the salvation of men through Christ. Christian philosophy arose at the juncture of Greek philosophy and of the Jewish-Christian religious revelation, Greek philosophy providing the technique for a rational explanation of the world, and the Jewish-Christian revelation providing religious beliefs of incalculable philosophical import. What is perhaps the key to the whole history of Christian philosophy and, in so far as modern philosophy bears the mark of Christian thought, to the history of modern philosophy itself, is precisely the fact that, from the second century A.D. on, men have had to use a Greek philosophical technique in order to express ideas that had never entered the head of any Greek philosopher.

NOTES

1. Deuteronomy 6.4.
2. Exodus 3.13–14.
3. *Hortatory Address to the Greeks,* chap. xxii, published among the works of Justin Martyr, in *The Ante-Nicene Fathers* (Buffalo, 1885), I, 272. Cf. E. Gilson, *L'Esprit de la philosophie medievale* (Paris, J. Vrin, 1932), I, 227, n. 7.

A thorough examination of the Fourth and Fifth Ways of Aquinas will not be given. However we shall consider in some detail the argument from design as provided by William Paley. This argument parallels portions of Aquinas' Fifth Way. In fact, both purported proofs are often referred to as *teleological arguments* for the existence of God.

The Cosmological Argument and Metaphysics

Before proceeding to the teleological argument, it would be well for us to reflect on the strengths and weaknesses of the cosmological argument. The fundamental question which arises concerns whether such an ontological explanation is at all possible. From our discussion and analysis of the Third Way, it should be apparent that Aquinas' philosophical theology is intricately connected with his metaphysics. In fact, it is impossible to separate the a posteriori proofs of Aquinas from the presuppositions of his ontology. If one accepts the radical empiricism characteristic of much British empiricism and as exemplified by Hume and the logical positivists, then a fortiori a metaphysical analysis, as elucidated by Aquinas, will be immediately suspect. We must take seriously Hume's criterion of significance regarding philosophical statements. In the *Enquiry,* we find the following passage:

> If we take in our hand any volume—of divinity or school metaphysics, for instance—let us ask: "Does it contain any abstract reasoning concerning quantity or number?" No. "Does it contain any experimental reasoning concerning matters of fact and existence?" No. Commit it then to the flames, for it can contain nothing but sophistry and illusion.[10]

The point which must be affirmed by any proponent of the cosmological argument is that of rescuing metaphysical explanations from the flames to which Hume has committed them. Hume has suggested that it is impossible for metaphysical questions and explanations to be significant. Therefore the possibility of viable ontological explanations must be argued for. Reasons must be given why such an ontological account is both possible and explanatory. W. Norris Clarke has written the following regarding the possibility of raising significant ontological questions about the nature of reality:

> Here, it seems to me, is the truly decisive and fundamental question where two views of (the) nature and range of human intelligence clash head on. Can or cannot the human intelligence raise the radical question about the very existence of the universe as a whole. . . . And if so, is there any legitimate schema or type of explanation which would render meaningful and possible an answer in the theistic sense? Personally, I believe that . . . not only can one *not* prevent someone from reasonably raising the question of the universe as a whole and its sufficient reason or ground, but to raise this question is the necessary . . . fruition of one's intellectual dynamism in depth.[11]

Many philosophers who accept the cogency of the cosmological argument do so because they also accept the demands made by what has traditionally been called the principle of sufficient reason. In other words, given any event, substance, or process, a suitable explanation can be found for it. According to the Third Way, the series of contingent beings is incapable of providing a sufficient explanation for itself. Assuming the principle of sufficient reason as part of human intelligence, philosophers have demanded that adequate explanations be provided. It is in this context that Aquinas offers the Third Way. It is an exemplification of the principle of sufficient reason.

Even if one accepts the possibility of metaphysical explanation, it still remains for Aquinas to convince us that his metaphysical system can indeed demand as a necessary condition the postulation of a first, supreme principle whose essence is existence. This is the pure act of Aquinas' ontology. The pure act is the act of existence. The being whose essence is pure act is such that its essence is constitutively defined as existence. Recall that a constitutive property is a defining property. The point Aquinas asks us to consider is the radical contingent character of every temporal existent. In order to provide an adequate ontological explanation of this contingent character, Aquinas suggests that such radical contingency as a constitutive property demands the postulation of a necessarily existing being. Accordingly, a fruitful way to interpret Aquinas' proofs is to look at each of the five Ways as an attempt to force us to recognize the fundamental contingency of every temporal existent. At its most fundamental level, this contingency is what the potency/act distinction is all about. Any being with a potential aspect is, in that regard, contingent. Insofar as God, as a necessary being, lacks any contingent aspect, so too must he lack any potentiality. This lack of potentiality entails that God be a pure act. A pure act, by definition, is one which lacks any potentialities. In other words, all of its capacities are fully actualized. In the ontology of Aquinas, regarding God as pure act is the significance of the claim that God's essence is constitutively defined as existence.

The radical contingency of finite beings—and this includes every temporal existent—demands as a necessary condition for its ontological explanation the existence of a necessary being whose essence is existence. Thus every contingent being receives its existence, therefore its property of being a "thing," ontologically from the principal act of existence, which is the necessary being. On this theory, therefore, every temporal existent is a *participated existent*. The first being is a necessary being whose essence is existence. It follows from the radical contingency of temporal existents that their essences not have existence as a constitutive property. It is reversed for God as a necessary being. The participated beings receive their existence from the necessary being. We might illustrate this notion in the following way.

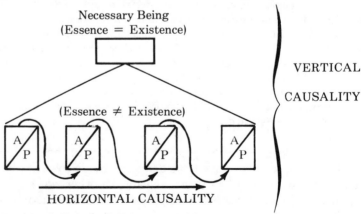

Necessary Being
(Essence = Existence)

VERTICAL

CAUSALITY

(Essence ≠ Existence)

HORIZONTAL CAUSALITY

Assuming the principle of sufficient reason, the necessary being is a necessary condition for providing an ontological explanation of the horizontal series. The things found in the horizontal series are all contingent beings. In effect, the God postulated as the pure act of existence in Aquinas' ontology becomes the *ground of being*. With God as the ground of being, the relation of vertical causality is explained in terms of ontological dependence. At this level, there is a platonic character to the proofs offered by Aquinas. Just as Plato argued that the individuals of the sense world could not be adequately accounted for without postulating the world of the forms, so too is Aquinas arguing that the individual contingent beings found in any temporal series cannot be accounted for without postulating a being whose essence is existence. This is, as we have seen, the necessary being, the being which cannot not be. The fundamental characteristic of Aquinas' Third Way is the notion that a contingent being must receive its existence from the necessary being. In this sense, therefore, the necessary being is the ground of being.

Historians of philosophy have debated over which of Aquinas' five ways is the most important. Some have argued that the Third Way is the most important of the five a posteriori proofs. Certainly the concept of ontological dependence and the horizontal/vertical causality distinction are most clearly exemplified in the Third Way. In the following passage from his book, *Aquinas,* F.C. Copleston discusses the "preeminent importance" of the Third Way, the notion of "existential dependence," and the role of metaphysical explanation in discussing Aquinas' proofs for God's existence.

Does any particular argument possess a special or preeminent importance? Modern Thomists often assert that the third proof, bearing explicitly on the existence of things, is fundamental. But if we look at the two *Summas,* we do not find Aquinas saying this. So far as he gives explicit preference to any particular proof it is to the first, which he declares, somewhat surprisingly, to be the clearest. Presumably he means that "motion" or change is so obvious and familiar that it forms a natural starting-point, though he may also have been influenced by the use which Aristotle made of the argument from motion. In any case it is this argument which he selects for a more elaborate discussion in the *Summa contra Gentiles,* while he does not treat at all of the third way in this work. So it cannot be said that Aquinas gives any special prominence to the third argument. At the same time I must confess that my sympathies are with those Thomists who regard this argument as fundamental and who restate it in other forms. And if it is true to say that Aquinas brought into prominence the existential aspect of metaphysics, it can hardly be said that this procedure is alien to his spirit. All the arguments, indeed, treat of dependence in some form or other. And I think that this idea will be found to be involved in all arguments for the existence of God which are in any real sense *a posteriori.* It seems to me to be involved even in those forms of the moral argument which some theists, who accept the Kantian criticism of the cosmological proofs, substitute for the traditional arguments. But it is the idea of existential dependence which most clearly introduces us to the metaphysical level. And it is the problem arising from the existence of finite and contingent things at all which most clearly points to the existence of a transfinite being. What I mean is this. Some people argue that mystical experience, for example, gives rise to a problem, in the sense that it calls for explanation, and that it is best explained on the hypothesis that this experience involves contact with an existent being, God. But there are others who admit the reality of the problem, namely that mystical experience calls for explanation, but who think that it can be satisfactorily explained without postulating God's existence. Thus whatever one may think of the right solution to the problem it is clear, as a matter of empirical fact, that it is possible to admit the reality of the problem and yet not admit that the solution involves affirming the existence of a transcendent being. But one can hardly admit that the existence of finite being at all constitutes a serious problem and at the same time maintain that the solution can be found anywhere else than in affirming the existence of the transfinite. If one does not wish to embark on the path which leads to the affirmation of transcendent being, however the latter may be described (if it is described at all), one has to deny the reality of the problem, assert that things "just are" and that the existential problem in question is a pseudo-problem. And if one refuses even to sit down at the chess-board and make a move, one cannot, of course, be checkmated. . . . [12]

In discussing the necessary being as an example of a ground of being, it will be helpful if we introduce a selection from the work of the prominent twentieth-century theologian, Paul Tillich. In the following passage from his *Systematic Theology,* Tillich explains what he takes to be three interpretations of the term *God.* Pay close attention to Tillich's analysis of the interpretation of God as the ground of existence.

THREE INTERPRETATIONS OF "GOD"

Paul Tillich

. . . [W]e may distinguish three ways of interpreting the meaning of the term "God." The first one separates God as a being, the highest being, from all other beings, alongside and above which he has his existence. In this position he has brought the universe into being at a certain moment (five thousand or five billion years ago), governs it according to a plan, directs it toward an end, interferes with its ordinary processes in order to overcome resistance and to fulfil his purpose, and will bring it to consummation in a final catastrophe. Within this framework the whole divine-human drama is to be seen. Certainly this is a primitive form of supra-naturalism, but a form which is more decisive for the religious life and its symbolic expression than any theological refinement of this position.

The main argument against it is that it transforms the infinity of God into a finiteness which is merely an extension of the categories of finitude. This is done in respect to space by establishing a supranatural divine world alongside the natural human world; in respect to time by determining a beginning and an end of God's creativity; in respect to causality by making God a cause alongside other causes; in respect to substance by attributing

From Paul Tillich, *Systematic Theology,* vol. 2 (Chicago: University of Chicago Press, 1957), pp. 5–10. Copyright © 1957 by the University of Chicago Press. Reprinted by permission of the publisher.

individual substance to him. Against this kind of supranaturalism the arguments of naturalism are valid and, as such, represent the true concern of religion, the infinity of the infinite, and the inviolability of the created structures of the finite. Theology must accept the antisupranatural criticism of naturalism.

The second way of interpreting the meaning of the term "God" identifies God with the universe, with its essence or with special powers within it. God is the name for the power and meaning of reality. He is not identified with the totality of things. No myth or philosophy has ever asserted such an absurdity. But he is a symbol of the unity, harmony, and power of being; he is the dynamic and creative center of reality. The phrase *deus sive natura,* used by people like Scotus Erigena and Spinoza, does not say that God is identical with nature but that he is identical with the *natura naturans,* the creative nature, the creative ground of all natural objects. In modern naturalism the religious quality of these affirmations has almost disappeared, especially among philosophizing scientists who understand nature in terms of materialism and mechanism. In philosophy proper, in so far as it became positivistic and pragmatistic, such assertions about nature as a whole were required. In so far as a whole philosophy of life involving dynamic processes developed, it again approached the religious forms of naturalism.

The main argument against naturalism in whatever form is that it denies the infinite distance between the whole of finite things and their infinite ground, with the consequence that the term "God" becomes interchangeable with the term "universe" and therefore is semantically superfluous. This semantic situation reveals the failure of naturalism to understand a decisive element in the experience of the holy, namely, the distance between finite man, on the one hand, and the holy in its numerous manifestations, on the other. For this, naturalism cannot account.

The criticism of the supranaturalistic and the naturalistic interpretations of the meaning of "God" calls for a third way which will liberate the discussion from the oscillation between two insufficient and religiously dangerous solutions. Such a third way is not new.

Theologians like Augustine, Thomas, Luther, Zwingli, Calvin, and Schleiermacher have grasped it, although in a restricted form. It agrees with the naturalistic view by asserting that God would not be God if he were not the creative ground of everything that has being, that, in fact, he is the infinite and unconditional power of being or, in the most radical abstraction, that he is being-itself. In this respect God is neither alongside things nor even "above" them; he is nearer to them than they are to themselves. He is their creative ground, here and now, always and everywhere.

Up to this point, the third view could be accepted by some forms of naturalism. But then the ways part. At this point the terms "self-transcendent" and "ecstatic," which I use for the third way of understanding the term "God," become meaningful. The term "self-transcendent" has two elements: "transcending" and "self." God as the ground of being infinitely transcends that of which he is the ground. He stands *against* the world, in so far as the world stands against him, and he stands *for* the world, thereby causing it to stand for him. This mutual freedom from each other and for each other is the only meaningful sense in which the "supra" in "supra-naturalism" can be used. Only in this sense can we speak of "transcendent" with respect to the relation of God and the world. To call God transcendent in this sense does not mean that one must establish a "super-world" of divine objects. It does mean that, within itself, the finite world points beyond itself. In other words, it is self-transcendent.

Now the need for the syllable "self" in "self-transcendent" has also become understandable: the one reality which we encounter is experienced in different dimensions which point to one another. The finitude of the finite points to the infinity of the infinite. It goes beyond itself in order to return to itself in a new dimension. This is what "self-transcendence" means. In terms of immediate experience it is the encounter with the holy, an encounter which has an ecstatic character. The term "ecstatic" in the phrase "ecstatic idea of God" points to the experience of the holy as transcending ordinary experience without removing it. Ecstasy as a state of mind is the exact correlate to self-transcendence as the state of reality. Such an understanding of the idea of God is neither naturalistic nor supranaturalistic. It underlies the whole of the present theological system.

If on the basis of this idea of God, we ask: "What does it mean that God, the ground of everything that is, can stand against the world and for the world?" we must refer to that quality of the world which expresses itself in finite freedom, the quality we experience within ourselves. The traditional discussion between the naturalistic and the supranaturalistic ideas of God uses the prepositions "in" and "above," respectively. Both are taken from the spatial realm and therefore are unable to express the true relation between God and the world—which certainly is not spatial. The self-transcendent idea of God replaces the spatial imagery—at least for theological thought—by the concept of finite freedom. The divine transcendence is identical with the freedom of the created to turn away from the essential unity with the creative ground of its being. Such freedom presupposes two qualities of the created: first, that it is substantially independent of the divine ground; second, that it remains in substantial unity with it. Without the latter unity, the creature would be without the power of being. It is the quality of finite freedom within the created which makes pantheism impossible and not the notion of a highest being alongside the world, whether his relation to the world is described in deistic or theistic terms.

The consequences of the self-transcendent idea of God for concepts like revelation and miracle (which are decisive for the christological problem) have been fully developed in the part entitled "Reason and Revelation." These do not need restatement, but they do show the far-reaching significance of the ecstatic interpretation of the relation between God and the world.

However, there is one problem which has moved into the center of the philosophical interest in religion since the appearance of the first volume. This is the problem of the symbolic knowledge of God. If God as the ground of being infinitely transcends everything that is, two consequences follow: first, whatever one knows about a finite thing one knows about God, because it is rooted in him as its ground; second, anything one knows about a finite thing cannot be applied to God, because he is, as has been said, "quite other" or, as could be said, "ecstatically transcendent." The unity of these two divergent consequences is the analogous or symbolic knowledge of God. A religious symbol uses the material of ordinary experience in speaking of God, but in such a way that the ordinary meaning of the material used is both affirmed and denied. Every religious symbol negates itself in its literal meaning, but it affirms itself in its self-transcending meaning. It is not a sign pointing to something with which it has no inner relationship. It represents the power and meaning of what is symbolized through participation. The symbol participates in the reality which is symbolized. Therefore, one should never say "only a symbol." This is to confuse symbol with sign. Thus it follows that everything religion has to say about God, including his qualities, actions, and manifestations, has a symbolic character and that the meaning of "God" is completely missed if one takes the symbolic language literally.

But, after this has been stated, the question arises (and has arisen in public discussion) as to whether there is a point at which a non-symbolic assertion about God must be made. There is such a point, namely, the statement that everything we say about God is symbolic. Such a statement is an assertion about God which itself is not symbolic. Otherwise we would fall into a circular argument. On the other hand, if we make *one* non-symbolic assertion about God, his ecstatic-transcendent character seems to be endangered. This dialectical difficulty is a mirror of the human situation with respect to the divine ground of being. Although man is actually separated from the infinite, he could not be aware of it if he did not participate in it potentially. This is expressed in the state of being ultimately concerned, a state which is universally human, whatever the content of the concern may be. This is the point at which we must speak non-symbolically about God, but in terms of a quest for him. In the moment, however, in which we describe the character of this point or in which we try to formulate that for which we ask, a combination of symbolic with non-symbolic elements occurs. If we say that God is the infinite, or the unconditional, or being-itself, we speak rationally and ecstatically at the same time. These terms precisely designate the boundary line at which both the symbolic and the non-symbolic coincide. Up to this point every statement is non-symbolic (in the sense of religious symbol). Beyond this point every statement is symbolic (in the sense of religious symbol). The point itself is both non-symbolic and symbolic. This dialectical situation is the conceptual expression of man's existential situation. It is the condition for man's religious existence and for his ability to receive revelation. It is another side of the self-transcendent or ecstatic idea of God, beyond naturalism and supranaturalism.

Hume's Analysis of the Cosmological Argument

In his *Dialogues Concerning Natural Religion,* David Hume objects to the validity of the cosmological argument. He attacks the purported significance of the concept of necessary being. In the following passage from the *Dialogues,* there are three characters participating in the discussion: Demea, Cleanthes, and Philo. Demea argues for the possibility of the cosmological argument;

Cleanthes, in accepting only the argument from design, argues against the notion of the necessary being; and Philo is the quasi-moderator of the discussion who raises the sticky philosophical questions in regard to the positions held by both Demea and Cleanthes. Read the following passage closely in order to clearly grasp Hume's objections to the cosmological argument.

PART IX

But if so many difficulties attend the argument *a posteriori,* said Demea, had we not better adhere to that simple and sublime argument *a priori* which, by offering to us infallible demonstration, cuts off at once all doubt and difficulty? By this argument, too, we may prove the *infinity* of the Divine attributes, which, I am afraid, can never be ascertained with certainty from any other topic. For how can an effect which either is finite or, for aught we know, may be so—how can such an effect, I say, prove an infinite cause? The unity, too, of the Divine Nature it is very difficult, if not absolutely impossible, to deduce merely from contemplating the works of nature; nor will the uniformity alone of the plan, even were it allowed, give us any assurance of that attribute. Whereas the argument *a priori* . . .

You seem to reason, Demea, interposed Cleanthes, as if those advantages and conveniences in the abstract argument were full proofs of its solidity. But it is first proper, in my opinion, to determine what argument of this nature you choose to insist on; and we shall afterwards, from itself, better than from its *useful* consequences, endeavor to determine what value we ought to put upon it.

The argument, replied Demea, which I would insist on is the common one. Whatever exists must have a cause or reason of its existence, it being absolutely impossible for anything to produce itself or be the cause of its own existence. In mounting up, therefore, from effects to causes, we must either go on in tracing an infinite succession, without any ultimate cause at all, or must at last have recourse to some ultimate cause that is *necessarily* existent. Now that the first supposition is absurd may be thus proved. In the infinite chain or succession of causes and effects, each single effect is determined to exist by the power and efficacy of that cause which immediately preceded; but the whole eternal chain or succession, taken together, is not determined or caused by anything, and yet it is evident that it requires a cause or reason, as much as any particular object which begins to exist in time. The question is still reasonable why this particular succession of causes existed from eternity, and not any other succession or no succession at all. If there be no necessarily existent being, any supposition which can be formed is equally possible; nor is there any more absurdity in *nothing's* having existed from eternity than there is in that succession of causes which constitutes the universe. What was it, then, which determined *something* to exist rather than *nothing,* and bestowed being on a particular possibility, exclusive of the rest? *External causes,* there are supposed to be none. *Chance* is a word without a meaning. Was it *nothing?*

From David Hume, *Dialogues Concerning Natural Religion,* a work first published in 1779.

But that can never produce anything. We must, therefore, have recourse to a necessarily existent Being who carries the *reason* of his existence in himself, and who cannot be supposed not to exist, without an express contradiction. There is, consequently, such a Being—that is, there is a Deity.

I shall not leave it to Philo, said Cleanthes, though I know that the starting objections is his chief delight, to point out the weakness of this metaphysical reasoning. It seems to me so obviously ill-grounded, and at the same time of so little consequence to the cause of true piety and religion, that I shall myself venture to show the fallacy of it.

I shall begin with observing that there is an evident absurdity in pretending to demonstrate a matter of fact, or to prove it by any arguments *a priori.* Nothing is demonstrable unless the contrary implies a contradiction. Nothing that is distinctly conceivable implies a contradiction. Whatever we conceive as existent, we can also conceive as non-existent. There is no being, therefore, whose non-existence implies a contradiction. Consequently there is no being whose existence is demonstrable. I propose this argument as entirely decisive, and am willing to rest the whole controversy upon it.

It is pretended that the Deity is a necessarily existent being; and this necessity of his existence is attempted to be explained by asserting that, if we knew his whole essence or nature, we should perceive it to be as impossible for him not to exist, as for twice two not to be four. But it is evident that this can never happen, while our faculties remain the same as at present. It will still be possible for us, at any time, to conceive the non-existence of what we formerly conceived to exist; nor can the mind ever lie under a necessity of supposing any object to remain always in being; in the same manner as we lie under a necessity of always conceiving twice two to be four. The words, therefore, *necessary existence* have no meaning or, which is the same thing, none that is consistent.

But further, why may not the material universe be the necessarily existent Being, according to this pretended explication of necessity? We dare not affirm that we know all the qualities of matter; and, for aught we can determine, it may contain some qualities which, were they known, would make its non-existence appear as great a contradiction as that twice two is five. I find only one argument employed to prove that the material world is not the necessarily existent Being; and this argument is derived from the contingency both of the matter and the form of the world. "Any particle of matter," it is said, "may be *conceived* to be annihilated, and any form may be *conceived* to be altered. Such an annihilation or alteration, therefore, is not impossible."[1] But it seems a great partiality not to perceive that the same argument extends equally to the Deity, so far as we have any conception of him, and that the mind can at least imagine him to be non-existent or his attributes to be altered. It must be some unknown, inconceivable qualities which can make his non-existence appear impossible or his attributes unalterable; and no reason can be assigned why these qualities may not belong to matter. As they are altogether unknown and inconceivable, they can never be proved incompatible with it.

Add to this that in tracing an eternal succession of objects it seems absurd to inquire for a general cause or first author. How can anything that exists from eternity have a cause, since that relation implies a priority in time and a beginning of existence?

In such a chain, too, or succession of objects, each part is caused by that which preceded it, and causes that which succeeds it. Where then is the difficulty? But the *whole,* you say, wants a cause. I answer that the uniting of these parts into a whole, like the uniting of several distinct countries into one kingdom, or several distinct members into one body, is performed merely by an arbitrary act of the mind, and has no influence on the nature of things. Did I show you the particular causes of each individual in a collection of twenty particles of matter, I should think it very unreasonable should you afterwards ask me what was the cause of the whole twenty. This is sufficiently explained in explaining the cause of the parts.

Though the reasonings which you have urged, Cleanthes, may well excuse me, said Philo, from starting any further difficulties, yet I cannot forbear insisting still upon another topic. It is observed by arithmeticians that the products of 9 compose always either 9 or some lesser product of 9 if you add together all the characters of which any of the former products is composed. Thus, of 18, 27, 36, which are products of 9, you make 9 by adding 1 to 8, 2 to 7, 3 to 6. Thus 369 is a product also of 9; and if you add 3, 6, and 9, you make 18, a lesser product of 9.[2] To a superficial observer so wonderful a regularity may be admired as the effect either of chance or design; but a skilful algebraist immediately concludes it to be the work of necessity, and demonstrates that it must forever result from the nature of these numbers. Is it not probable, I ask, that the whole economy of the universe is conducted by a like necessity, though no human algebra can furnish a key which solves the difficulty? And instead of admiring the order of natural beings, may it not happen that, could we penetrate into the intimate nature of bodies, we should clearly see why it was absolutely impossible they could ever admit of any other disposition? So dangerous is it to introduce this idea of necessity into the present question! and so naturally does it afford an inference directly opposite to the religious hypothesis!

But dropping all these abstractions, continued Philo, and confining ourselves to more familiar topics, I shall venture to add an observation that the argument *a priori* has seldom been found very convincing, except to people of a metaphysical head who have accustomed themselves to abstract reasoning, and who, finding from mathematics that the understanding frequently leads to truth through obscurity, and contrary to first appearances, have transferred the same habit of thinking to subjects where it ought not to have place. Other people, even of good sense and the best inclined to religion, feel always some deficiency in such arguments, though they are not perhaps able to explain distinctly where it lies—a certain proof that men ever did and ever will derive their religion from other sources than from this species of reasoning.

NOTES

1. Dr. Clarke.
2. *République des Lettres,* Aut 1685.

Having read Hume's objections to the cosmological argument, how should one respond to them? Did Hume meet the cosmological argument head on? Is his notion of necessity restricted just to logical contradiction? Does this, in effect, beg the question against a proponent of the cosmological argument? Is Hume able to respond to these counter questions? How might one go about responding to Hume? If we think there is some possibility for proving the existence of a divine being by philosophical methods, then we must take Hume's objections seriously. We shall consider the *Dialogues* again when discussing the argument from design. At any length, Hume's critique must be seriously confronted by anyone who wants to forge ahead with significant questions in philosophical theology.

In response to objections similar to those raised by Hume concerning the impossibility of significant discussion regarding a necessary being, F.C. Copleston has made the following remarks:

> . . . (W)hat we call the world is intrinsically unintelligible, apart from the existence of God. You see, I don't believe that the infinity of the series of events—I mean a horizontal series, so to speak—if such an infinity could be proved, would be in the slightest degree relevant to the situation. If you add up chocolates you get chocolates after all and not a sheep. If you add up chocolates to infinity, you presumably get an infinite number of chocolates. So if you add up contingent beings to infinity, you still get contingent beings, not a necessary being. An infinite series of contingent beings will be, to my way of thinking, as unable to cause itself as one contingent being. . . . [13]

In response to the force of the cosmological argument in regard to religious belief in the existence of God, it is interesting to note the words of Blaise Pascal (1623–1662). Pascal suggested that philosophical proofs which purport to establish the existence of God are irrelevant to the religious believer in that the conclusions of such proofs hardly merit the designation of objects of worship. From the perspective of a person committed to religious faith, Pascal thought that God as an object of worship should be expressed as the "God of Abraham, God of Isaac, God of Jacob, not of the philosophers and scholars." In the following passage from *Identity and Difference,* Martin Heidegger, a twentieth-century philosopher, reiterates the thrust of Pascal's point:

> Man can neither pray nor sacrifice to this god. Before the *Causa sui* (the cause itself), a man can neither fall to his knee in awe nor can he play music and dance before this god. The god-less thinking which must abandon the god of philosophy, god as *causa sui,* is thus perhaps closer to the divine god. [14]

The Argument From Design of William Paley

We shall next consider an a posteriori argument for the existence of God which is not intricately connected with a metaphysical system. Early in the nineteenth century, William Paley (1743-1805) provided a much discussed proof from experience, which is a good example of an argument from design. Many students may have heard some variation of this argument before. It appeals to the fact that, since both the universe and all of its individual objects appear to be ordered and designed, this evidence overwhelmingly warrants the assertion of a grand designer. This super designer is the Judeo-Christian God.

In reading Paley's argument, pay special attention to the analogy which he is at great pains to stress. An analogy is an explicit appeal to appropriate similarities between two or more cases. The strength or weakness of Paley's argument will largely depend upon the strength or weakness of the analogy. Note that the designs of a watch and of the human eye are crucial examples in Paley's plea for the recognition of design in the universe.

. . . In crossing a heath, suppose I pitched my foot against a *stone,* and were asked how the stone came to be there, I might possibly answer, that, for anything I knew to the contrary, it had lain there for ever; nor would it, perhaps, be very easy to show the absurdity of this answer. But suppose I found a *watch* upon the ground, and it should be inquired how the watch happened to be in that place, I should hardly think of the answer which I had before given—that, for anything I knew, the watch might have always been there. Yet why should not this answer serve for the watch as well as for the stone? why is it not as admissible in the second case as in the first? For this reason, and for no other, viz., that, when we come to inspect the watch, we perceive (what we could not discover in the stone) that its several parts are framed and put together for a purpose, e.g. that they are so formed and adjusted as to produce motion, and that motion so regulated as to point out the hour of the day; that, if the different parts had been differently shaped from what they are, if a different size from what they are, or placed after any other manner, or in any other order than that in which they are placed, either no motion at all would have been carried on in the machine, or none which could have answered the use that is now served by it. To reckon up a few of the plainest of these parts, and of their offices, all tending to one result:—We see a cylindrical box containing a coiled elastic spring, which, by its endeavor to relax itself, turns round the box. We next observe a flexible chain (artificially wrought for the sake of flexure) communicating the action of the spring from the box to the fusee. We then find a series of wheels, the teeth of which catch in, and apply to, each other, conducting the motion from the fusee to the balance, and from the balance to the pointer, and, at the same time, by the size and shape of those wheels, so regulating that motion as to terminate in causing an index, by an equable and measured progression, to pass over a given space in a given time. We take notice that the wheels are made of brass, in order to keep them from rust; the springs of steel, no other metal being so elastic; that over the face of the watch there is placed a glass, a material employed in no other part of the work, but in the room of which, if there had been any other than a transparent substance, the hour could not be seen without opening the case. This mechanism being observed, (it requires indeed an examination of the instrument, and perhaps some previous knowledge of the sub-

From William Paley, *Natural Theology,* a work first published in 1802.

ject, to perceive and understand it; but being once, as we have said, observed and understood,) the inference, we think, is inevitable, that the watch must have had a maker; that there must have existed, at some time, and at some place or other, an artificer or artificers who formed it for the purpose which we find it actually to answer; who comprehended its construction, and designed its use.

I. Nor would it, I apprehend, weaken the conclusion, that we had never seen a watch made; that we had never known an artist capable of making one; that we were altogether incapable of executing such a piece of workmanship ourselves, or of understanding in what manner it was performed; all this being no more than what is true of some exquisite remains of ancient art, of some lost arts, and, to the generality of mankind, of the more curious productions of modern manufacture. Does one man in a million know how oval frames are turned? Ignorance of this kind exalts our opinion of the unseen and unknown artist's skill, if he be unseen and unknown, but raises no doubt in our minds of the existence and agency of such an artist, at some former time, and in some place or other. Nor can I perceive that it varies at all the inference, whether the question arise concerning a human agent, or concerning an agent of a different species, or an agent possessing, in some respect, a different nature.

II. Neither, secondly, would it invalidate our conclusion, that the watch sometimes went wrong, or that it seldom went exactly right. The purpose of the machinery, the design, and the designer, might be evident, and, in the case supposed, would be evident, in whatever way we accounted for the irregularity of the movement, or whether we could account for it or not. It is not necessary that a machine be perfect, in order to show with what design it was made; still less necessary, where the only question is, whether it were made with any design at all.

III. Nor, thirdly, would it bring any uncertainty into the argument, if there were a few parts of the watch, concerning which we could not discover, or had not yet discovered, in what manner they conduced to the general effect; or even some parts, concerning which we could not ascertain whether they conduced to that effect in any manner whatever. For, as to the first branch of the case, if by the loss, or disorder, or decay of the parts in question, the movement of the watch were found in fact to be stopped, or disturbed, or retarded, no doubt would remain in our minds as to the utility or intention of these parts, although we should be unable to investigate the manner according to which, or the connection by which, the ultimate effect depended upon their action or assistance; and the more complex is the machine, the more likely is this obscurity to arise. Then, as to the second thing supposed, namely, that there were parts which might be spared without prejudice to the movement of the watch, and that he had proved this by experiment, these superfluous parts, even if we were completely assured that they were such, would not vacate the reasoning which we had instituted concerning other parts. The indication of contrivance remained, with respect to them, nearly as it was before.

IV. Nor, fourthly, would any man in his senses think the existence of the watch, with its various machinery, accounted for, by being told that it was one out of possible combinations of material forms; that whatever he had found in the place where he found the watch, must have contained some internal configuration or other; and that this configuration might be the structure now exhibited, viz., of the works of a watch, as well as a different structure.

V. Nor, fifthly, would it yield his inquiry more satisfaction, to be answered, that there existed in things a principle of order, which had disposed the parts of the watch into their present form and situation. He never knew a watch made by the principle of order; nor can he even form to himself an idea of what is meant by a principle of order, distinct from the intelligence of the watchmaker.

VI. Sixthly, he would be surprised to hear that the mechanism of the watch was no proof of contrivance, only a motive to induce the mind to think so:

VII. And not less surprised to be informed, that the watch in his hand was nothing more than the result of the laws of *metallic* nature. It is a perversion of language to assign any law as the efficient, operative cause of anything. A law presupposes an agent; for it is only the mode according to which an agent proceeds; it implies a power; for it is the order according to which that power acts. Without his agent, without this power, which are both distinct from itself, the *law* does nothing, is nothing. The expression, "the law of metallic nature," may sound strange and harsh to a philosophic ear; but it seems quite as justifiable as some others which are more familiar to him such as "the law of vegetable nature," "the law of animal nature," or, indeed, as "the law of nature" in general, when assigned as the cause of phenomena in exclusion of agency and power, or when it is submitted into the place of these.

VIII. Neither, lastly, would our observer be driven out of his conclusion, or from his confidence in its truth, by being told that he knew nothing at all about the matter. He knows enough for his argument: he knows the utility of the end: he knows the subserviency and adaptation of the means to the end. These points being known, his ignorance of other points, his doubts concerning other points, affect not the certainty of his reasoning. The consciousness of knowing little need not beget a distrust of that which he does know. . . .

Every indication of contrivance, every manifestation of design, which existed in the watch, exists in the works of nature; with the difference, on the side of nature, of being greater and more, and that in a degree which exceeds all computation. I mean that the contrivances of nature surpass the contrivances of art, in the complexity, subtilty, and curiosity of the mechanism; and still more, if possible, do they go beyond them in number and variety; yet in a multitude of cases, are not less evidently mechanical, not less evidently contrivances, not less evidently accommodated to their end, or suited to their office, than are the most perfect productions of human ingenuity. . . .

The gist of Paley's argument is not too difficult to follow. However it is important to understand the exact structure of the analogy which Paley has made. He asks us to consider the implication of the recognition of order and design regarding any individual object or set of objects. Just as the watch discovered in the heath—i.e., a barren wasteland—indicated design because of its intricate movements and the interrelations of its many parts, so too does the universe as a whole and many of the individual objects in the universe provide evidence of design because of the orderly arrangement and interrelation of the parts. Paley assumes that the evidence of order and design is evidence enough to assert the existence of a designer. The structure of Paley's analogy is between the order and design in a watch and the order and design in the universe. Just as it is implausible to admit the order and design manifested in the watch, and yet deny that the watch required a designer, so too is it highly implausible to recognize the manifestations of order, design, and purpose in the universe and yet not admit the existence of a designer. We may sketch the structure of Paley's analogy in the following manner:

JUST AS

Watch:	
manifesting evidence	*implies* DESIGNER
of order and design	

SO TOO

Universe:	
manifesting evidence	*implies* DESIGNER
of order and design	

It is important to grasp the point of Paley's argument. We could easily claim, Paley suggests, that the rock discovered in the wasteland (the heath) resulted from the chance occurrence of environmental and atmospheric conditions. For example, the operation of the wind, heat, rain, frost, and so forth could provide a sufficient explanation for the formation of the rock. But, Paley asks, could the watch have occurred under the same chance conditions? Paley asserts an emphatic *no!* It is highly implausible, he suggests, that a watch with all of its ordered parts just fell together in a purposeful way through a chance process. The watch provides even a casual observer with obvious evidence of order, design, and purpose. The watch is a complex mechanism—wheels, cogs, gears, springs, and so forth. Is it plausible, Paley asks, to assume that all this mechanical interrelatedness characteristic of the watch could be sufficiently explained only in terms of a chance occurrence of random events? Paley believes that, in the case of the watch, to assert a chance occurrence as a sufficient explanation is patently absurd. Because any explanation of an object manifesting obvious characteristics of design in terms of a chance occurrence alone is thought to be absurd, Paley concludes that at one time there must have been an intelligent agent who designed and constructed the watch. There is a difference between Paley's argument and the Third Way of Aquinas. Both are a posteriori arguments. Yet the Third Way purported to be a *demonstration* of the existence of a necessary being. The argument from design as given by Paley, on the other hand, suggests the strong *probability* of the existence of a designer. The Third Way is modeled after a demonstration in Euclidean geometry, while the argument from design is a simple argument based upon analogy.

After establishing the connection between the evidence of design in the watch and the need for a designer in order to account for the fact of design, Paley extrapolates his argument from human-made objects to both the universe as a whole and the individual natural objects of the universe—the eye, for instance. He strongly suggests that the natural universe is as complex a mechanism and as intricately designed as any human artifact. Examples of apparent design are obvious: the rotation of the planets in ordered patterns around the sun; the regular succession of day and night; the regularity of the four seasons; the ordered function of the human body and its parts—eye, lungs, heart; and the interrelation of many of these parts with one another—the carbon dioxide/oxygen cycle, for instance. Paley asserts that all of these examples provide manifest evidence of order, design, and purpose. If there is order, design, and purpose in the universe, then someone must have provided these things for the universe. If there is real design, then there must have been a designer. As order and purpose presuppose acting for an end, and as acting for an end implies rational planning, so the designer who instituted order and purpose to the universe must have been a rational being who used intelligence in planning the complex functioning of the interrelated universe.

A principal presupposition Paley has utilized is that order and design entail the existence of a rational designer. Think about this claim for a moment. Does the appearance of design in fact entail the existence of a designer? Furthermore, does the universe as a whole and/or the individual objects found in the universe provide as much evidence for design as Paley suggests? In his critical text on the issues central to philosophical theology, David Hume poses some very hard questions about the nature and structure of the argument from design. Hume's arguments have become the classical critique of any argument extrapolating from the evidence of design in the universe to the existence of a rational designer. Historically, it is true that Hume's *Dialogues Concerning Natural Religion* appeared prior to Paley's form of the argument from design; however Paley seems to have been unaware of Hume's critique. We shall consider in detail some of the forceful objections Hume raised against any form of the argument from design. In addition, we shall spend time examining the problem of evil. The problem of evil is a direct outgrowth of the argument from design. The following selected passages are from Hume's *Dialogues*.

PART V

But to show you still more inconveniences, continued Philo, in your anthropomorphism, please to take a new survey of your principles. *Like effects prove like causes.* This is the experimental argument; and this, you say too, is the sole theological argument. Now it is certain that the liker the

---

From David Hume, *Dialogues Concerning Natural Religion* (1779).

effects are which are seen and the liker the causes which are inferred, the stronger is the argument. Every departure on either side diminishes the probability and renders the experiment less conclusive. You cannot doubt of the principle; neither ought you to reject its consequences.

All the new discoveries in astronomy which prove the immense grandeur and magnificence of the works of nature are so many additional arguments for a Deity, according to the true system of theism; but, according to your hypothesis of experimental theism, they become so many objections, by removing the effect still farther from all resemblance to the effects of human art and contrivance. For if Lucretius, even following the old system of the world, could exclaim:

> Quis regere immensi summam, quis habere profundi
> Indu manu validas potis est moderanter habenas?
> Quis pariter coelos omnes convertere? et omnes
> Ignibus aetheriis terras suffire feraces?
> Omnibus inque locis esse omni tempore praesto?[1]

If Tully [Cicero] esteemed this reasoning so natural as to put it into the mouth of his Epicurean:

> Quibus enim oculis animi intueri potuit vester Plato fabricam illam tanti operis, qua construi a Deo atque aedificari mundum facit? quae molito? quae ferramenta? qui vectes? quae machinae? qui minstri tanti muneris fuerunt? quaemadmodum autem obedire et parere voluntati architecti aer, ignis, aqua, terra potuerunt?[2]

If this argument, I say, had any force in former ages, how much greater must it have at present when the bounds of Nature are so infinitely enlarged and such a magnificent scene is opened to us? It is still more unreasonable to form our idea of so unlimited a cause from our experience of the narrow productions of human design and invention.

The discoveries by microscopes, as they open a new universe in miniature, are still objections, according to you, arguments, according to me. The further we push our researches of this kind, we are still led to infer the universal cause of all to be vastly different from mankind, or from any object of human experience and observation.

And what say you to the discoveries in anatomy, chemistry, botany? . . . These surely are no objections, replied Cleanthes; they only discover new instances of art and contrivance. It is still the image of mind reflected on us from innumerable objects. Add a mind *like the human,* said Philo. I know of no other, replied Cleanthes. And the liker, the better, insisted Philo. To be sure, said Cleanthes.

Now, Cleanthes, said Philo, with an air of alacrity and triumph, mark the consequences. *First,* by this method of reasoning you renounce all claim to infinity in any of the attributes of the Deity. For, as the cause ought to be proportioned to the effect, and the effect, so far as it falls under our cognizance, is not infinite, what pretensions have we, upon your suppositions, to ascribe that attribute to the Divine Being? You will still insist that, by removing him so much from all similarity to human creatures, we give in to the most arbitrary hypothesis, and at the same time weaken all proofs of his existence.

Secondly, you have no reason, on your theory, for ascribing perfection to the Deity, even in his finite capacity, or for supposing him free from every error, mistake, or incoherence, in his undertakings. There are many inexplicable difficulties in the works of nature which, if we allow a perfect author to be proved *a priori,* are easily solved, and become only seeming difficulties from the narrow capacity of man, who cannot trace infinite relations. But according to your method of reasoning, these difficulties become all real, and, perhaps, will be insisted on as new instances of likeness to human art and contrivance. At least, you must acknowledge that it is impossible for us to tell, from our limited views, whether this system contains any great faults or deserves any considerable praise if compared to other possible and even real systems. Could a peasant, if the *Aeneid* were read to him, pronounce that poem to be absolutely faultless, or even assign to it its proper rank among the productions of human wit, he who had never seen any other production?

But were this world ever so perfect a production, it must still remain uncertain whether all the excellences of the work can justly be ascribed to the workman. If we survey a ship, what an exalted idea must we form of the ingenuity of the carpenter who framed so complicated, useful, and beautiful a machine? And what surprise must we feel when we find him a stupid mechanic who imitated others, and copied an art which, through a long succession of ages, after multiplied trials, mistakes, corrections, deliberations, and controversies, had been gradually improving? Many worlds might have been botched and bungled, throughout an eternity, ere this system was struck out; much labor lost, many fruitless trials made, and a slow but continued improvement carried on during infinite ages in the art of world-making. In such subjects, who can determine where the truth, nay, who can conjecture where the probability lies, amidst a great number of hypotheses which may be proposed, and a still greater which may be imagined?

And what shadow of an argument, continued Philo, can you produce from your hypothesis to prove the unity of the Deity? A great number of men join in building a house or ship, in rearing a city, in framing a commonwealth; why may not several deities combine in contriving and framing a world? This is only so much greater similarity to human affairs. By sharing the work among several, we may so much further limit the attributes of each, and get rid of that extensive power and knowledge which must be supposed in one deity, and which, according to you, can only serve to weaken the proof of his existence. And if such foolish, such vicious creatures as man can yet often unite in framing and executing one plan, how much more those deities or demons, whom we may suppose several degrees more perfect!

To multiply causes without necessity is indeed contrary to true philosophy, but this principle applies not to the present case. Were one deity antecedently proved by your theory who were possessed of every attribute requisite to the production of the universe, it would be needless, I own, (though not absurd) to suppose any other deity existent. But while it is still a question whether all these attributes are united in one subject or dispersed among several independent beings, by what phenomena in nature can we pretend to decide the controversy? Where we see a body raised in a scale, we are sure that there is in the opposite scale, however concealed from sight, some counterposing weight equal to it; but it is still allowed to doubt whether that weight be an aggregate of several distinct bodies or one uniform united mass. And if the weight requisite very much exceeds anything which we have ever seen conjoined in any single body, the former supposition becomes still more probable and natural. An intelligent being of such vast power and capacity as is necessary to produce the universe, or, to speak in the language of ancient philosophy, so prodigious an animal exceeds all analogy and even comprehension.

But further, Cleanthes: Men are mortal, and renew their species by generation; and this is common to all living creatures. The two great sexes of male and female, says Milton, animate the world. Why must this circumstance, so universal, so essential, be excluded from those numerous and limited deities? Behold, then, the theogeny of ancient times brought back upon us.

And why not become a perfect anthropomorphite? Why not assert the deity or deities to be corporeal, and to have eyes, a nose, mouth, ears, etc.? Epicurus maintained that no man had ever seen reason but in a human figure; therefore, the gods must have a human figure. And this argument, which is deservedly so much ridiculed by Cicero, becomes, according to you, solid and philsophical.

In a word, Cleanthes, a man who follows your hypothesis is able, perhaps, to assert or conjecture that the universe sometime arose from something like design; but beyond that position he cannot ascertain one single circumstance, and is left afterwards to fix every point of his theology by the utmost license of fancy and hypothesis. This world, for aught he knows, is very faulty and imperfect, compared to a superior standard, and was only the first rude essay of some infant deity who afterwards abandoned it, ashamed of his lame performance; it is the work only of some dependent, inferior deity, and is the object of derision to his superiors; it is the production of old age and dotage in some superannuated deity, and ever since his death has run on at adventures, from the first impulse and active force which it received from him. You justly give signs of horror, Demea, at these strange suppositions; but these, and a thousand more of the same kind, are Cleanthes' suppositions, not mine. From the moment the attributes of the Deity are supposed finite, all these have place. And I cannot, for my part, think that so wild and unsettled a system of theology is, in any respect, preferable to none at all.

These suppositions I absolutely disown, cried Cleanthes: they strike me, however, with no horror, especially when proposed in that rambling way in which they drop from you. On the contrary, they give me pleasure when I see that, by the utmost indulgence of your imagination, you never get rid of the hypothesis of design in the universe, but are obliged at every turn to have recourse to it. To this concession I adhere steadily; and this I regard as a sufficient foundation for religion. . . .

PART VIII

What you ascribe to the fertility of my invention, replied Philo, is entirely owing to the nature of the subject. In subjects adapted to the narrow compass of human reason there is commonly but one determination which carries probability or conviction with it; and to a man of sound judgment all other suppositions but that one appear entirely absurd and chimerical. But in such questions as the present, a hundred contradictory views may preserve a kind of imperfect analogy, and invention has here full scope to exert itself. Without any great effort of thought, I believe that I could, in an instant, propose other systems of cosmogony which would have some faint appearance of truth, though it is a thousand, a million to one if either yours or any one of mine be the true system.

For instance, what if I should revive the old Epicurean hypothesis? This is commonly, and I believe justly, esteemed the most absurd system that has yet been proposed; yet I know not whether, with a few alterations, it might not be brought to bear a faint appearance of probability. Instead of supposing matter infinite, as Epicurus did, let us suppose it finite. A finite number of particles is only susceptible of finite transpositions; and it must happen, in an eternal duration, that every possible order or position must be tried an infinite number of times. This world, therefore, with all its events, even the most minute, has before been produced and destroyed, and will again be produced and destroyed, without any bounds and limitations. No one who has a conception of the powers of infinite, in comparison of finite, will ever scruple this determination.

But this supposes, said Demea, that matter can acquire motion without any voluntary agent or first mover.

And where is the difficulty, replied Philo, of that supposition? Every event, before experience, is equally difficult and incomprehensible; and every event, after experience, is equally easy and intelligible. Motion, in many instances, from gravity, from elasticity, from electricity, begins in matter, without any known voluntary agent; and to suppose always, in these cases, an unknown voluntary agent is mere hypothesis and hypothesis attended with no advantages. The beginning of motion in matter itself is as conceivable *a priori* as its communication from mind and intelligence.

Besides, why may not motion have been propagated by impulse through all eternity, and the same stock of it, or nearly the same, be still upheld in the universe? As much is lost by the composition of motion, as much is gained by its resolution. And whatever the causes are, the fact is certain that matter is and always has been in continual agitation, as far as human experience or tradition reaches. There is not probably, at present, in the whole universe, one particle of matter at absolute rest.

And this very consideration, too, continued Philo, which we have stumbled on in the course of the argument suggests a new hypothesis of cosmogony that is not absolutely absurd and improbable. Is there a system, an order, an economy of things, by which matter can preserve that perpetual agitation which seems essential to it, and yet maintain a constancy in the forms which it produces? There certainly is such an economy, for this is actually the case with the present world. The continual motion of matter, therefore, in less than infinite transpositions, must produce this economy or order, and, by its very nature, that order, when once established, supports itself for many ages if not to eternity. But wherever matter is so poised, arranged, and adjusted, as to continue in perpetual motion, and yet preserve a constancy in the forms, its situation must, of necessity, have all the same appearance of art and contrivance which we observe at present. All the parts of each form must have a relation to each other and to the whole; and the whole itself must have a relation to the other parts of the universe, to the element in which the form subsists, to the materials with which it repairs its waste and decay, and to every other form which is hostile or friendly. A defect in any of these particulars destroys the form, and the matter of which it is composed is again set loose, and is thrown into irregular motions and fermentations till it unite itself to some other regular form. If no such form be prepared to receive it, and if there be a great quantity of this corrupted matter in the universe, the universe itself is entirely disordered, whether it be the feeble embryo of a world in its first beginnings that is thus destroyed or the rotten carcase of one languishing in old age and infirmity. In either case, a chaos ensues till finite though innumerable revolutions produce, at last, some forms whose parts and organs are so adjusted as to support the forms amidst a continued succession of matter.

Suppose (for we shall endeavor to vary the expression) that matter were thrown into any position by a blind, unguided force; it is evident that this first position must, in all probability, be the most confused and most disorderly imaginable, without any resemblance to those works of human contrivance which, along with a symmetry of parts, discover an adjustment of means to ends and a tendency to self-preservation. If the actuating force cease after this operation, matter must remain for ever in disorder and continue an immense chaos, without any proportion or activity. But suppose that the actuating force, whatever it be, still continues in matter, this first position will immediately give place to a second which will likewise, in all probability, be as disorderly as the first, and so on through many successions of changes and revolutions. No particular order or position ever continues a moment unaltered. The original force, still remaining in activity, gives a perpetual restlessness to matter. Every possible situation is produced, and instantly destroyed. If a glimpse or dawn of order appears for a moment, it is instantly hurried away and confounded by that never-ceasing force which actuates every part of matter.

Thus the universe goes on for many ages in a continued succession of chaos and disorder. But is it not possible that it may settle at last, so as not to lose its motion and active force (for that we have supposed inherent in it), yet so as to preserve an uniformity of appearance, amidst the continual motion and fluctuation of its parts? This we find to be the case with the universe at present. Every individual is perpetually changing, and every part of every individual; and yet the whole remains, in appearance, the same. May we not hope for such a position or rather be assured of it from the eternal revolutions of unguided matter; and may not this account for all the appearing wisdom and contrivance which is in the universe? Let us contemplate the subject a little, and we shall find that this adjustment if attained by matter of a seeming stability in the forms, with a real and perpetual revolution or motion of parts, affords a plausible, if not a true, solution of the difficulty.

It is in vain, therefore, to insist upon the uses of the parts in animals or vegetables, and their curious adjustment to each other. I would fain know how an animal could subsist unless its parts were so adjusted? Do we not find that it immediately perishes whenever this adjustment ceases, and that its matter, corrupting, tries some new form? It happens indeed that the parts of the world are so well adjusted that some regular form immediately lays claim to this corrupted matter; and if it were not so, could the world subsist? Must it not dissolve, as well as the animal, and pass through new positions and situations till in great but finite succession it fall, at last, into the present or some such order?

It is well, replied Cleanthes, you told us that this hypothesis was suggested on a sudden, in the course of the argument. Had you had leisure to examine it, you would soon have perceived the insuperable objections to which it is exposed. No form, you say, can subsist unless it possess those powers and organs requisite for its subsistence; some new order or economy must be tried, and so on, without intermission, till at last some order which can support and maintain itself is fallen upon. But according to this hypothesis, whence arise the many conveniences and advantages which men and all animals possess? Two eyes, two ears are not absolutely necessary for the subsistence of the species. Human race might have been propagated and preserved without horses, dogs, cows, sheep, and those innumerable fruits and products which serve to our satisfaction and enjoyment. If no camels had been created for the use of man in the sandy deserts of Africa and Arabia, would the world have been dissolved? If no loadstone had been framed to give that wonderful and useful direction to the needle, would human society and the human kind have been immediately extinguished? Though the maxims of nature be in general very frugal, yet instances of this kind are far from being rare; and any one of them is a sufficient proof of design—and of a benevolent design—which gave rise to the order and arrangement of the universe.

At least, you may safely infer, said Philo, that the foregoing hypothesis is so far incomplete and imperfect, which I shall not scruple to allow. But can we ever reasonably expect greater success in any attempts of this nature? Or can we ever hope to erect a system of cosmogony that will be liable to no exceptions, and will contain no circumstance repugnant to our limited and imperfect experience of the analogy of nature? Your theory itself cannot surely pretend to any such advantage, even though you have run into *anthropomorphism,* the better to preserve a conformity to common experience. Let us once more put it to trial. In all instances which we have ever seen, ideas are copied from real objects, and are ectypal, not archetypal, to express myself in learned terms. You reverse this order and give thought the precedence. In all instances which we have ever seen, thought has no influence upon matter except where that matter is so conjoined with it as to have an equal reciprocal influence upon it. No animal can move immediately anything but the members of its own body; and, indeed, the equality of action and reaction seems to be an universal law of nature; but your theory implies a contradiction to this experience. These instances, with many more which it were easy to collect (particularly the supposition of a mind or system of thought that is eternal or, in other words, an animal ingenerable and immortal)—these instances, I say, may teach all of us sobriety in condemning each other, and let us see that as no system of this kind ought ever to be received from a slight analogy, so neither ought any to be rejected on account of a small incongruity. For that is an inconvenience from which we can justly pronounce no one to be exempted.

All religious systems, it is confessed, are subject to great and insuperable difficulties. Each disputant triumphs in his turn, while he carries on an offensive war, and exposes the absurdities, barbarities, and pernicious tenets of his antagonist. But all of them, on the whole, prepare a complete triumph for the *sceptic,* who tells them that no system ought ever to be embraced with regard to such subjects: for this plain reason that no absurdity ought ever to be assented to with regard to any subject. A total suspense of judgment is here our only reasonable resource. And if every attack, as is commonly observed, and no defence among theologians is successful, how complete must be *his* victory who remains always, with all mankind, on the offensive, and has himself no fixed station or abiding city which he is ever, on any occasion, obliged to defend?

NOTES

1. *De Rerum Natura,* Bk. XI, Chap. 2. "Who can rule the sun, who hold in his hand with controlling force the strong reins, of the immeasurable deep? Who can at once make all the different heavens to roll and warm with ethereal fires all the fruitful earths, or be present in all places at all times?" (Munro's trans.)

2. *De Natura Deorum,* Bk. I, Chap, 8. "For with what eyes of the mind could your Plato see the construction of so vast a work which, according to him, God was putting together and building? What materials, what tools, what bars, what machines, what servants were employed in such gigantic work? How could the air, fire, water, and earth pay obedience and submit to the will of the architect?"

In the passages we have just read from the *Dialogues Concerning Natural Religion,* Hume has stated that in any argument purported to establish the existence of God from the evidence of design in the universe, the fundamental question remains unanswered. Is it possible to distinguish an instance of "authentic" design from an instance of "apparent but not authentic" design? Hume suggests that in an unlimited amount of time, through the random interaction of material atoms, any state of affairs might result. Such a state of affairs, although giving the appearance of design and order, is really nothing more than the product of a chance occurrence. Hume demands that the proponents of the argument from design categorically distinguish between *real* design and *apparent* design. Hume confronts us with the problem of drawing a distinct line between chance happenings and instance of real design. Furthermore Hume affirms that this distinction is indeed quite difficult to make. Hume would probably agree with Darwin's evolutionary theory suggesting that the "survival of the fittest" is a sufficient condition explaining why biological species appear to fit together harmoniously, and that this just happened, without any planning or design.

A rather elementary and unsophisticated example might help here. Suppose one threw a handful of marbles into the air. And suppose, for the sake of argument, that when they fell to the ground, they roughly formed the shape of a star. Now suppose another person entered the room. This new person, from examining the star-shaped arrangement of the marbles, might conclude very quickly that the first person had intentionally placed the marbles in the shape of a star. Yet how is the second person to distinguish, just from his empirical observation of the placement of the marbles, whether or not their arrangement has resulted from explicit, intentional planning or random, chance happening. It would probably be impossible for the person given the evidence at hand to make such a distinction. This is precisely the distinction Hume asks us to consider when confronting the structure of Paley's argument dealing with the purported order, design, and purpose of the universe.

In addition, Hume suggests that the analogy between the universe and a human artifact is quite weak. The analogy based on similarity is supported on rather weak grounds. Hume, somewhat facetiously, suggests that the world could just as easily be compared to a giant vegetable—a pumpkin, perhaps—or to a crustacean or to a spider's web. Hume reminds us that it is precisely this question, in regard to these kinds of objects and events, which must be confronted concerning whether or not they indeed are the results of purposeful design. Think for a moment about an oyster. Open the shell. Does the oyster look designed? Is there any semblance of order, purpose, or design which is immediately evident? Is the oyster more like the rock or the watch, which are the categories Paley originally used. Hume's point is that the oyster indeed may be more like the rock than the watch, and if the universe is more akin to a crustacean than to an intricate machine, so much the worse for Paley's argument. Hume comes to the conclusion that Paley's argument is not strong enough to establish the desired conclusion. Of course, the point of contention which Hume has raised is *not* whether oysters or rocks are actually the results of a designing mind. Rather, the point is, does an oyster provide an objective observer with the *prima facie* evidence of design? It is obvious that an oyster does not exhibit the intricate mechanical complexity normally perceived when we remove the back of a pocket watch. Hume's point strikes at the roots of the argument from design. Is there strong *prima facie* evidence for accepting the claim that there is order, purpose, and design in the universe? Reflecting on this point, Bertrand Russell stated the following:

Such, in outline, but even more purposeless, more void of meaning, is the world which Science presents for our belief. Amid such a world, if anywhere, our ideals henceforward must find a home. That man is the product of causes which had no prevision of the end they were achieving; that his origin, his growth, his hopes and fears, his loves and his beliefs, are but the outcome of accidental collocations of atoms; that no fire, no heroism, no intensity of thought and feeling, can preserve an individual life beyond the grave; that all the labours of the ages, all the devotion, all the inspirations, all the noonday brightness of human genius, are destined to extinction in the vast death of the solar system, and that the whole temple of Man's achievement must inevitably be buried beneath the debris of a universe in ruins—all these things, if not quite beyond dispute, are yet so nearly certain, that no philosophy which rejects them can hope to stand. Only within the scaffolding of these truths, only on the firm foundation of unyielding despair, can the soul's habitation henceforth be safely built. . . .

Brief and powerless is Man's life; on him and all his race the slow, sure doom falls pitiless and dark. Blind to good and evil, reckless of destruction, omnipotent matter rolls on its relentless way; for Man, condemned to-day to lose his dearest, tomorrow himself to pass through the gate of darkness, it remains only to cherish, ere yet the blow falls, the lofty thoughts that ennoble his little day; disdaining the coward terrors of the slave of Fate, to worship at the shrine that his own hands have built; undismayed by the empire of chance, to preserve a mind free from the wanton tyranny that rules his outward life; proudly defiant of the irresistible forces that tolerate, for a moment, his knowledge and his condemnation, to sustain alone, a weary but unyielding Atlas, the world that his own ideals have fashioned despite the trampling march of unconscious power.[15]

Russell's point must be taken seriously. How does one establish the existence of order and purpose in the universe. As we shall see in the chapter on existentialism, the issue regarding the "absurdity" (so common among twentieth-century existentialists) rests on the lack of rational order in the world.

In *Hamlet,* Shakespeare has his listeners ponder the issue of order and design in the world. Consider the following lines:

This most excellent canopy, the air, look you, this brave o'erhanging firmament, this majestical roof fretted with golden fire—why, it appears no other thing to me than a foul and pestilent congregation of vapors. What a piece of work is a man! How noble in reason! . . . And yet, to me, what is this quintessence of dust?[16]

In discussing the merits and weaknesses of the argument from design, we shall now take a different perspective. Let's assume for a moment that the proponents of this argument can successfully refute the preceding objections. Still, can the structure of the argument itself provide us with sufficient proof for the claim that the Judeo-Christian God is an existing reality? Given this perspective, we might raise the following issues:

1. Even if we could infer a designer, this would not have to be an infinitely wise, all-good, and all-powerful deity. From the data used in the argument from design, is the conclusion asserted warranted from the strength of the premises? The basic structure of this argument from analogy is rooted in a cause-effect situation. Paley has requested that we reflect upon certain effects found in the natural world. These empirical effects of order, purpose, and design can be explained only by the postulation of an intelligent designer of the universe. Of course, this designer is purported to be identical with the Judeo-Christian God. Yet, what is the status of the effects that we actually perceive? Are they finite or infinite? Obviously they are finite. Since we are finite beings, our observations are finite in character and the objects perceived in any temporal continuum are finite. Recall our discussion of the concept of *contingency* in regard to Aquinas' Third Way. In the argument from design, however, from finite effects we are asked to assert the existence of an *infinite cause.* Quite obviously, on logical grounds alone, the assertion of an infinite cause of design stretches beyond the data warranted from the cause-effect structure of analogy in the argument. The most we could legitimately conclude by such an argument from analogy is to a *finite* cause. The conclusion of an infinite cause proceeds beyond the strengths of the premises. Of course, we might—like John Stuart Mill—

assert the existence of a limited, finite being as God. Yet this certainly was neither Paley's purpose nor intention in constructing his argument from design. He wanted to provide an a posteriori argument based upon the evidence of design in the universe concluding to the existence of the Judeo-Christian God.

2. From the data presented as evidence in the argument from design, is it legitimate to conclude that there is only one designer? Again, utilizing the cause/effect structure presupposed in the argument, since there are many effects, there might as well be many causes. The data experienced as effects of an intelligent design can tell us nothing about the number of designers. The purported evidence of design is completely compatible with concluding that there were many gods who jointly served as the intelligent planners of the universe. Remember from chapter 2 that there were many gods in Greek mythology. The argument from design cannot legitimately establish the existence of *one* designer.

3. Is the evidence presented by Paley's argument sufficient to conclude that the designer is still around? The data used as premises in the argument from design cannot validly be used to support the claim that the designer is still a living, functioning being. It is here that one can take the "God is dead" movement seriously. It could have been the case that the designer, or designers, after planning the universe, ceased to exist. Just as an architect of a building might cease to exist before the building, which manifests the evidence of his design, is demolished, so too might the designer of the universe cease to exist even though the remnants of design are still visible to present observers. The cathedral of Notre Dame in Paris gives evidence of design. Yet the architects of that massive edifice are no longer alive. These suggestions, of course, are compatible with the deism movement characteristic of many eighteenth- and nineteenth-century theologians. The god of deism, however, is not coextensive with the God of the Judeo-Christian tradition.

4. Similar questions as those raised above can be asked concerning the relation of divine providence, simplicity, omniscience, omnipotence, and the other characteristics attributed to the God of Judaism and Christianity. The argument from design can tell us nothing about whether or not the designer possesses these characteristics. Simply put, these objections point out a severe weakness involved in any attempt to establish the existence of the Judeo-Christian God through an appeal to the evidence of design in the universe. If anything, the argument from design has more significant weaknesses than any of the other arguments we have considered so far. Indeed, it is to the argument from design that Pascal's words ring true—"The God of the philosophers is not the God of Abraham, Isaac, and Jacob."

The Problem of Evil

Despite the force of the preceding objections to the argument from design, there is one telling objection Hume raised which we must consider in some detail. This is usually called the *problem of evil*. It is an extrapolation from the cause/effect structure analyzed above. One effect Hume observed in the world was the evident fact that evil was pervasive. If evil occurs in the world and if it is a type of effect, then how is this facet of the universe to be reconciled with the postulation of an intelligent designer? Following an argument first formulated by the Epicurean philosophers, Hume claims that it is impossible to reconcile the characteristics of an all-powerful and an all-good God with the existence of evil in the world.

It is important that we analyze the basic structure of Hume's argument:

> Assume that two necessary characteristics of God are *all-good* and *all-powerful.* These characteristics have sometimes been presented as omnipotence and supreme benevolence.
>
> Granting this assumption regarding characteristics necessary to God, the following schema can be devised:
>   a. If God is all good, then he would want to alleviate evil.
>   b. If God is all powerful, then he has the ability and capacity to alleviate evil.
>   c. But in fact evil does exist in the world.
>   *Therefore:*
>   d. Either God is able to prevent evil but he is unwilling.
>   e. Or God is willing to prevent evil but he is unable.
>   f. If *d* is correct, then God is a *malevolent* being.
>   g. If *e* is correct, then God is an *impotent* (non-all-powerful) being.
>   *Therefore:*
>   h. If evil exists in the world, it is impossible that there be an existent God having the properties of both all-good and all-powerful.

The force of the argument stresses the purported incompatibility of an all-good/all-powerful God as the designer of the universe with the existence of evil therein; and Hume is convinced that evil exists. In fact, he asserts that it is an all too pervasive datum of our experience.

In the *Dialogues,* Hume painstakingly makes that point. Consider carefully the four categories of evil in the world which Hume explicitly mentions in *Dialogue XI:*
  a. Pains drive animals to action.
  b. The universe is in a state of general chaos.
  c. There is a marked frugality regarding the distribution of natural capacities and powers to animals.
  d. There is evidence of inaccurate workmanship in regard to the fundamental principles of nature.

It is important that we think seriously about the problem of reconciling the existence of evil with the characteristics of an all-good/all-powerful deity. Is it possible to reconcile these items purported to be incompatible? According to Hume's treatise, there is immediate and persuasive evidence that evil not only exists in the world but that it has an almost pervasive dimension.

Throughout the history of philosophy, the problem of evil has been regarded as a very substantial argument against the possibility of the existence of the Judeo-Christian God. However some philosophers and theologians have claimed that the argument, as devised by Epicurus and elaborated by Hume, makes use of some questionable presuppositions. In the history of philosophy, various counter arguments have been proposed which stress alternate accounts of the nature of evil and its relation to a God-centered view of the universe. It would be well for us to consider some of these responses to the problem of evil in more detail.

First, some philosophers, following in the Platonic tradition, have argued that evil is fundamentally an "absence" of a good. On this view, evil is not an existing event, object, or state of affairs. Rather, it is the absence of a due perfection. Thomas Aquinas accepted this view of evil. In the following passage, he presents his analysis of the relation between good and evil:

> An object is called evil insofar as *it lacks a perfection or completion it ought to have.* Accordingly, to lack sight is an evil in human beings. However, it is not an evil in stones.[17]

The analogy Aquinas asserts is that, just as blindness is ontologically the absence of sight and not a positive attribute of reality, so too is evil to be regarded as the absence of a positive perfection. Of course, such a position depends upon the metaphysical postulation of essences. Aquinas' point is that an ontological evil results when a perfection or completion due to an individual classed under an essence is not attained for some reason. In the above passage, sight is a property characteristic of human beings, but certainly not of stones. Many philosophers have not been convinced by this type of argument, primarily because of the almost pervasive evidence of evil in the world. How can so much evil, especially human suffering, be considered a privation or absence of reality? Certainly evil as suffering appears to be an existential facet of human experience. At this point, it is up to philosophers like Aquinas to show that evil can be accounted for as a privation of a due perfection. It seems that so far such an account has been found to be wanting.

Second, some philosophers and theologians have argued that evil is a mere "blessing in disguise." This claim asserts that in the plan of divine economy evil will be used to bring about far greater good than the inconvenience experienced at the present moment. In other words, all the apparent evils in the world will find their places in the framework of the master plan of divine providence. In the *Summa Theologiae*, Thomas Aquinas affirms this position quite explicitly:

> God, nature, and indeed every kind of cause work for the optimum total effect. This total effect regards the completion of each single part, not in isolation but in relation to the entire system. The whole itself, the universe of created beings, is better and more perfect because there are things which can fall short of goodness and which indeed do sometimes fall short without God preventing them. It happens in this way because as Dionysius says, the role of Divine Providence is not to regiment but to respect nature. What may fail should indeed fail some time or other. In addition, as Augustine has said, God is so powerful that he can make good come out even of evil. (*Enchiridion,* xi). Many good things would be omitted if God permitted no evil to exist: fire would not burn unless air were consumed; the lion would not continue to exist unless other animals were killed; just retribution would not be given and long-suffering patience would not be judged praiseworthy except for the iniquity of persecution.[18]

How would Hume respond to the above position? He would probably say, "Why did God provide so much evil to bring about so little good?" What is your thought concerning the pervasive nature of evil Hume claims to exist? Can we justify the appeal to a divine plan in which evil is a necessary condition to bring about further good for the whole?

Finally, the position has been introduced that evil, especially moral evil, is the result of human beings freely choosing to perform actions which have evil consequences. In other words, it is because of free will that evil comes about in the world. Assuming this position, it is an unjustified accusation to blame God for the evil resulting from the exercise of human free choice.

It is possible that this account might explain the existence of evil actions and their consequences, which depend upon the intentional activity of human beings who are capable of free choice. Nevertheless, one might still ask why humans are so strongly inclined to undertake evil actions, given that they have been designed by an all-good deity. In addition, this response in regard to the free will of human beings fails to account for the diversity of the natural evils evident in the world, including earthquakes, tidal waves, famines, and so forth. Can human free will adequately account for these instances of evil? We must say *no.*

Nelson Pike, a contemporary philosopher of religion, has provided the following interesting discussion regarding the limits within which Hume's analysis of the problem of evil is relevant to questions about the existence of God. Pike suggests that the problem of evil as developed by Hume in the *Dialogues Concerning Natural Religion* has limited applicability in regard to the various types of proofs purported to establish the existence of God. It is important to note the structure of Pike's argument establishing this limited applicability. If his suggestions are correct, this severely restricts the pervasive scope and force usually attributed to the problem of evil in dismissing arguments for the existence of God. It is important to pay very close attention to the structure of the argument Pike asserts in his discussion of parts X and XI of Hume's *Dialogues.*

HUME ON EVIL

Nelson Pike

In parts X and XI of the *Dialogues Concerning Natural Religion,* Hume sets forth his views on the traditional theological problem of evil. Hume's remarks on this topic seem to me to contain a rich mixture of insight and oversight. It will be my purpose in this paper to disentangle these contrasting elements of his discussion.[1]

PHILO'S FIRST POSITION

(A) God, according to the traditional Christian view put forward by Cleanthes in the *Dialogues,* is all-powerful, all-knowing, and perfectly good. And it is clear that for Cleanthes, the terms "powerful," "knowing," and "good" apply to God in exactly the same sense in which these terms apply to men. Philo argues as follows. If God is to be all-powerful, all-knowing, and per-

From *The Philosophical Review* 72, no. 2 (1963): 180–97. Reprinted by permission of *The Philosophical Review.*

fectly good (using all key terms in their ordinary sense), then to claim that God exists is to preclude the possibility of admitting that there occur instances of evil; that is, is to preclude the possibility of admitting that there occur instances of suffering, pain, superstition, wickedness, and so forth.[2] The statements, "God exists" and "There occur instances of suffering" are logically incompatible. Of course, no one could deny that there occur instances of suffering. Such a denial would plainly conflict with common experience.[3] Thus it follows from obvious facts that God (having the attributes assigned to Him by Cleanthes) does not exist.

This argument against the existence of God has enjoyed considerable popularity since Hume wrote the *Dialogues.* Concerning the traditional theological problem of evil, F.H. Bradley comments as follows:

> The trouble has come from the idea that the Absolute is a moral person. If you start from that basis, then the relation of evil to the Absolute presents at once an irreducible dilemma. The problem then becomes insoluble, but not because it is obscure or in any way mysterious. To anyone who has the sense and courage to see things as they are, and is resolved not to mystify others or himself, there is really no question to discuss. The dilemma is plainly insoluble because it is based on a clear self-contradiction.[4]

John Stuart Mill,[5] J.E. McTaggart,[6] Antony Flew,[7] H.D. Aiken,[8] J.L. Mackie,[9] C.J. Ducasse,[10] and H.J. McCloskey[11] are but a few of the many others who have echoed Philo's finalistic dismissal of traditional theism after making reference to the logical incompatibility of "God exists" and "There occur instances of suffering." W.T. Stace refers to Hume's discussion of the matter as follows:

> (Assuming that "good" and "powerful" are used in theology as they are used in ordinary discourse), we have to say that Hume was right. The charge has never been answered and never will be. The simultaneous attribution of all-power and all-goodness to the Creator of the whole world is logically incompatible with the existence of evil and pain in the world, for which reason the conception of a finite God, who is not all-powerful . . . has become popular in some quarters.[12]

In the first and second sections of this paper, I shall argue that the argument against the existence of God presented in Part X of the *Dialogues* is quite unconvincing. It is not clear at all that "God exists" and "There occur instances of suffering" are logically incompatible statements.

(B) Moving now to the details of the matter, we may, I think, formulate Philo's first challenge to Cleanthes as follows:

(1) The world contains instances of suffering.
(2) God exists—and is omnipotent and omniscient.
(3) God exists—and is perfectly good.

According to the view advanced by Philo, these three statements constitute an "inconsistent triad." Any two of them might be held together. But if any two of them are endorsed, the third must be denied. Philo argues that to say of God that he is omnipotent and omniscient is to say that he *could* prevent suffering if he wanted to. Unless God could prevent suffering, he would not qualify as both omnipotent and omniscient. But, Philo continues, to say of God that he is perfectly good is to say that God *would* prevent suffering if he could. A being who would not prevent suffering when it was within his power to do so would not qualify as perfectly good. Thus, to affirm propositions (2) and (3) is to affirm the existence of a being who both could prevent suffering if he wanted to and who would prevent suffering if he could. This, of course, is to deny the truth of proposition (1). By similar reasoning, Philo would insist, to affirm (1) and (2) is to deny the truth of (3). And to affirm (1) and (3) is to deny the truth of (2). But, as conceived by Cleanthes, God is both omnipotent-omniscient and perfectly good. Thus, as understood by Cleanthes, "God exists" and "There occur instances of suffering" are logically incompatible statements. Since the latter of these statements is obviously true, the former must be false. Philo reflects: "Nothing can shake the solidarity of this reasoning, so short, so clear (and) so decisive".

It seems to me that this argument is deficient. I do not think it follows from the claim that a being is perfectly good that he would prevent suffering if he could.

Consider this case. A parent forces a child to take a spoonful of bitter medicine. The parent thus brings about an instance of discomfort—suffering. The parent could have refrained from administering the medicine; and he knew that the child would suffer discomfort if he did administer it. Yet, when we are assured that the parent acted in the interest of the child's health and happiness, the fact that he knowingly caused discomfort is not sufficient to remove the parent from the class of perfectly good beings. If the parent fails to fit into this class, it is not because he caused *this* instance of suffering.

Given only that the parent knowingly caused an instance of discomfort, we are tempted to *blame* him for his action—that is, to exclude him from the class of perfectly good beings. But when the full circumstances are known, blame becomes inappropriate. In this case, there is what I shall call a "morally sufficient reason" for the parent's action. To say that there is a morally sufficient reason for his action is simply to say that there is a circumstance or condition which, when known, renders *blame* (though, of course, not *responsibility*) for the action inappropriate. As a general statement, a being who permits (or brings about) an instance of suffering might be perfectly good providing only that there is a morally sufficient reason for his action. Thus, it does not follow from the claim that God is perfectly good that he would prevent suffering if he could. God might fail to prevent suffering or himself bring about suffering, while remaining perfectly good. It is required only that there be a morally sufficient reason for his action.

(C) In the light of these reflections, let us now attempt to put Philo's challenge to Cleanthes in sharper form.

(4) The world contains instances of suffering.

(5) God exists—and is omnipotent, omniscient, and perfectly good.

(6) An omnipotent and omniscient being would have no morally sufficient reason for allowing instances of suffering.

This sequence is logically tight. Suppose (6) and (4) true. If an omnipotent and omniscient being would have no morally sufficient reason for allowing instances of suffering, then, in a world containing such instances, either there would be no omnipotent and omniscient being or that being would be blameworthy. On either of these last alternatives, proposition (5) would be false. Thus, if (6) and (4) are true, (5) must be false. In similar fashion, suppose (6) and (5) true. If an omnipotent and omniscient being would have no morally sufficient reason for allowing suffering, then, if there existed an omnipotent and omniscient being who was also perfectly good, there would occur no suffering. Thus, if (6) and (5) are true, (4) must be false. Lastly, suppose (5) and (4) true. If there existed an omnipotent and omniscient being who was also perfectly good, then if there occurred suffering, the omnipotent and omniscient being (being also perfectly good) would have to have a morally sufficient reason for permitting it. Thus, if (5) and (4) are true, (6) must be false.

Now according to Philo (and all others concerned), proposition (4) is surely true. And proposition (6)—well, what about proposition (6)? At this point, two observations are needed.

First, it would not serve Philo's purpose were he to argue the truth of proposition (6) by enumerating a number of reasons for permitting suffering (which might be assigned to an omnipotent and omniscient being) and then by showing that in each case the reason offered is not a morally sufficient reason (when assigned to an omnipotent and omniscient being). Philo could never claim to have explained all of the possibilities. And at any given point in the argument, Cleanthes could always claim that God's reason for permitting suffering is one which Philo has not yet considered. A retreat to unexamined reasons would remain open to Cleanthes regardless of how complete the list of examined reasons seemed to be.

Second, the position held by Philo in Part X of the *Dialogues* demands that he affirm proposition (6) as a *necessary truth.* If this is not already clear, consider the following inconsistent triad.

(7) All swans are white.
(8) Some swans are not large.
(9) All white things are large.

Suppose (9) true, but not necessarily true. Either (7) or (8) must be false. But the conjunction of (7) and (8) is not contradictory. If the conjunction of (7) and (8) were contradictory, then (9) would be necessary truth. Thus, unless (9) is a necessary truth, the conjunction of (7) and (8) is not contradictory. Note what happens to this antilogism when "colored" is substituted for "large." Now (9) becomes a necessary truth and, correspondingly, (7) and (8) become logically incompatible. The same holds for the inconsistent triad we are now considering. As already discovered, Philo holds that "There are instances of suffering" (proposition 4) and "God exists" (proposition 5) are logically incompatible. But (4) and (5) will be logically incompatible only if (6) is a necessary truth. Thus, if Philo is to argue that (4) and (5) are logically incompatible, he must be prepared to affirm (6) as a necessary truth.

We may now reconstitute Philo's challenge to the position held by Cleanthes.

Proposition (4) is obviously true. No one could deny that there occur instances of suffering. But proposition (6) is a necessary truth. An omnipotent and omniscient being would have no morally sufficient reason for allowing instances of suffering—just as a bachelor would have no wife. Thus, there exists no being who is, at once, omnipotent, omniscient, and perfectly good. Proposition (5) must be false.

(D) This is a formidable challenge to Cleanthes' position. Its strength can best be exposed by reflecting on some of the circumstances or conditions which, in ordinary life, and with respect to ordinary agents, are usually counted as morally sufficient reasons for failing to prevent (or relieve) some given instance of suffering. Let me list five such reasons.

First, consider an agent who lacked physical ability to prevent some instance of suffering. Such an agent could claim to have had a morally sufficient reason for not preventing the instance in question.

Second, consider an agent who lacked knowledge of (or the means of knowing about) a given instance of suffering. Such an agent could claim to have had a morally sufficient reason for not preventing the suffering, even if (on all other counts) he had the ability to prevent it.

Third, consider an agent who knew of an instance of suffering and had the physical ability to prevent it, but did not *realize* that he had this ability. Such an agent could usually claim to have had a morally sufficient reason for not preventing the suffering. Example: if I push the button on the wall, the torment of the man in the next room will cease. I have the physical ability to push the button. I know the man in the next room is in pain. But I do not know that pushing the button will relieve the torment. I do not push the button and thus do not relieve the suffering.

Fourth, consider an agent who had the ability to prevent an instance of suffering, knew of the suffering, knew that he had the ability to prevent it, but did not prevent it because he believed (rightly or wrongly) that to do so would be to fail to effect some future good which would outweigh the negative value of the suffering. Such an agent might well claim to have had a morally sufficient reason for not preventing the suffering. Example: go back to the case of the parent causing discomfort by administering bitter medicine to the child.

Fifth, consider an agent who had the ability to prevent an instance of suffering, knew of the suffering, knew that he had the ability to prevent it, but failed to prevent it because to do so would have involved his preventing a prior good which outweighed the negative value of the suffering. Such an agent might claim to have had a morally sufficient reason for not preventing the suffering. Example: a parent permits a child to eat some birthday cake knowing that his eating the cake will result in the child's feeling slightly ill later in the day. The parent estimates that the child's pleasure of the moment outweighs the discomfort which will result.

Up to this point, Philo would insist, we have not hit on a circumstance or condition which could be used by Cleanthes when constructing a "theodicy," that is, when attempting to identify the morally sufficient reason God has for permitting instances of suffering.

The first three entries on the list are obviously not available. Each makes explicit mention of some lack of knowledge or power on the part of the agent. Nothing more need be said about them.

A theologian might, however, be tempted to use a reason for the fourth type when constructing a theodicy. He might propose that suffering *results in goods* which outweigh the negative value of the suffering. Famine (hunger) leads man to industry and progress. Disease (pain) leads man to knowledge and understanding. Philo suggests that no theodicy of this kind can be successful. An omnipotent and omniscient being could find other means of bringing about the same results. The mere fact that evils give rise to goods cannot serve as a morally sufficient reason for an omnipotent and omniscient being to permit suffering.

A theologian might also be tempted to use reasons of the fifth type when constructing a theodicy. He might propose that instances of suffering *result from goods* which outweigh the negative value of the suffering. That the world is run in accordance with natural law is good. But any such regular operation will result in suffering. That men have the ability to make free choices is good. But free choice will sometimes result in wrong choice and suffering. Philo argues that it is not at all clear that a world run in accordance with natural law is better than one not so regulated. And one might issue a similar challenge with respect to free will. But a more general argument has been offered in the contemporary literature on evil which is exactly analogous to the one suggested by Philo above. According to H.J. McCloskey, an omnipotent and omniscient being could devise a law-governed world which would not include suffering.[13] And according to J.L. Mackie, an omnipotent and omniscient being could create a world containing free agents which would include no suffering or wrong-doing.[14] The import of both of these suggestions is that an omnipotent and omniscient being could create a world containing whatever is good (regularity, free will, and so on) without allowing the suffering which (only factually) results from these goods. The mere fact that suffering results from good cannot serve as a morally sufficient reason for an omnipotent and omniscient being to allow suffering.

Though the above reflections may be far from conclusive, let us grant that, of the morally sufficient reasons so far considered, none could be assigned to an omnipotent and omniscient being. This, of course, is not to say that proposition (6) is true—let alone necessarily true. As mentioned earlier, proposition (6) will not be shown true by an enumerative procedure of the above kind. But consider the matter less rigorously. If none of the reasons so far considered could be assigned to an omnipotent and omniscient being, ought this not to raise a suspicion? Might there not be a principle operating in each of these reasons which guarantees that *no* morally sufficient reason for permitting suffering *could* be assigned to an omnipotent and omniscient being? Such a principle immediately suggests itself. Men are sometimes excused for allowing suffering. But in these cases, men are excused only because they lack the knowledge or power to prevent suffering, or because they lack the knowledge or power to bring about goods (which are causally related to suffering) without also bringing about suffering. In other words, men are excusable only because they are limited. Having a morally sufficient reason for permitting suffering *entails* having some lack of knowledge or power. If this principle is sound (and, indeed, it is initially plausible) then proposition (6) must surely be listed as a necessary truth.

DEMEA'S THEODICY

But the issue is not yet decided. Demea has offered a theodicy which does not fit any of the forms outlined above. And Philo must be willing to consider all proposals if he is to claim "decisiveness" for his argument against Cleanthes.

Demea reasons as follows:

This world is but a point in comparison of the universe; this life but a moment in comparison of eternity. The present evil phenomena, therefore, are rectified in other regions, and in some future period of existence. And the eyes of men, being then opened to larger views of things, see the whole connection of general laws, and trace with adoration, the benevolence and rectitude of the Deity through all mazes and intricacies of his providence.

It might be useful if we had a second statement of this theodicy, one taken from a traditional theological source. In Chapter LXXI of the *Summa Contra Gentiles,* St. Thomas argues as follows:

The good of the whole is of more account than the good of the part. Therefore, it belongs to a prudent governor to overlook a lack of goodness in a part, that there may be an increase of goodness in the whole. Thus, the builder hides the foundation of a house underground, that the whole house may stand firm. Now, if evil were taken away from certain parts of the universe, the perfection of the universe would be much diminished, since its beauty results from the ordered unity of good and evil things, seeing that evil arises from the failure of good, and yet certain goods are occasioned from those very evils through the providence of the governor, even as the silent pause gives sweetness to the chant. Therefore, evil should not be excluded from things by the divine providence.

Neither of these statements seems entirely satisfactory. Demea might be suggesting that the world is good on the whole—that the suffering we discover in our world is, as it were, made up for in other regions of creation. God here appears as the husband who beats his wife on occasion but makes up for it with favors at other times. In St. Thomas' statement, there are unmistakable hints of causal reasoning. Certain goods are "occasioned" by evils, as the foundation of the house permits the house to stand firm. But in both of these statements another theme is at least suggested. Let me state and explain it in my own way without pretense of historical accuracy.

I have a set of ten wooden blocks. There is a T-shaped block, an L-shaped block, an F-shaped block, and so on. No two blocks have the same shape. Let us assign each block a value—say an aesthetic value—making the T-shaped block most valuable and the L-shaped block least valuable. Now the blocks may be fitted together into formations. And let us suppose that the blocks are so shaped that there is one and only one subset of the blocks which will fit together into a square. The L-shaped block is a member of that subset. Further, let us stipulate that any formation of blocks (consisting of two or more blocks fitted together) will have more aesthetic value than any of the blocks taken individually or any subset of the blocks taken as a mere collection. And, as a last assumption, let us say that the square formation has greater aesthetic value than any other logically possible block formation. The L-shaped block is a necessary component of the square formation; that is, the L-shaped block is logically indispensable to the square formation. Thus the L-shaped block is a necessary component of the best of all possible block formations. Hence, the block with the least aesthetic value is logically indispensable to the best of all possible block formations. Without this very block, it would be logically impossible to create the best of all possible block formations.

Working from this model, let us understand Demea's theodicy as follows. Put aside the claim that instances of suffering are *de facto* causes or consequences of greater goods. God, being a perfectly good, omniscient, and omnipotent being, would create the best of all possible worlds. But the best of all possible worlds must contain instances of suffering: they are logically indispensable components. This is why there are instances of suffering in the world which God created.

What shall we say about this theodicy? Philo expresses no opinion on the subject.

Consider this reply to Demea's reasonings. A world containing instances of suffering as necessary components might be the best of all possible worlds. And if a world containing instances of suffering as necessary components were the best of all possible worlds, an omnipotent and omniscient being would have a morally sufficient reason for permitting instances of suffering. But how are we to know that, in fact, instances of suffering are logically indispensable components of the best of all possible worlds? There would appear to be no way of establishing this claim short of assuming that God does in fact exist and then concluding (as did Leibniz) that the world (containing suffering) which he did in fact create is the best of all possible worlds. But, this procedure assumes that God exists. And this latter is precisely the question now at issue.

It seems to me that this reply to Demea's theodicy has considerable merit. First, my hypothetical objector is probably right in suggesting that the only way one could show that the best of all possible worlds must contain instances of suffering would be via the above argument in which the existence of God is assumed. Second, I think my objector is right in allowing that if instances of suffering were logically indispensable components of the best of all possible worlds, this would provide a morally sufficient reason for an omnipotent and omniscient being to permit instances of suffering. And, third, I think that my objector exhibits considerable discretion in not challenging the claim that the best of all possible worlds *might* contain instances of suffering as necessary components. I know of no argument which will show this claim to be true. But on the other hand, I know of no argument which will show this claim to be false. (I shall elaborate this last point directly.)

Thus, as I have said, the above evaluation of the theodicy advanced by Demea seems to have considerable merit. But this evaluation, *if correct,* seems to be sufficient to refute Philo's claim that "God exists" and "There occur instances of suffering" are logically incompatible statements. If instances of suffering were necessary components of the best of all possible worlds, then an omnipotent and omniscient being would have a morally sufficient reason for permitting instances of suffering. Thus, if it is *possible* that instances of suffering are necessary components of the best of all possible worlds, then there *might be* a morally sufficient reason for an omnipotent and omniscient being to permit instances of suffering. Thus if the statement "Instances of suffering are necessary components of the best of all possible worlds" is not contradictory, then proposition (6) is not a necessary truth. And, as we have seen, if proposition (6) is not a necessary truth, then "God exists" and "There occur instances of suffering" are not logically incompatible statements.

What shall we say? Is the statement "Instances of suffering are logically indispensable components of the best of all possible worlds" contradictory? That it is is simply assumed in Philo's first position. But, surely, this is not a trivial assumption. If it is correct, it must be shown to be so; it is not *obviously* correct. And how shall we argue that it is correct? Shall we, for example, assume that any case of suffering contained in any complex of events detracts from the value of the complex? If this principle were analytic, then a world containing an instance of suffering could not be the best of all possible worlds. But G.E. Moore has taught us to be suspicious of any such principle.[15] And John Wisdom has provided a series of counterexamples which tend to show that this very principle is, in fact, not analytic. Example: if I believe (rightly or wrongly) that you are in pain and become unhappy as a result of that belief, the resulting complex would appear to be better by virtue of my unhappiness (suffering) than it would have been had I believed you to be in pain but had not become unhappy (or had become happy) as a result.[16] Philo's argument against the existence of God is not finished. And it is not at all obvious that it is *capable* of effective completion. It is, I submit, far from clear that God and evil could not exist together in the same universe.

PHILO'S SECOND POSITION

At the end of Part X, Philo agrees to "retire" from his first position. He now concedes that "God exists" and "There occur instances of suffering" are not logically incompatible statements. (It is clear from the context that this adjustment in Philo's thinking is made only for purposes of argument and not because Hume senses any inadequacy in Philo's first position.) Most contemporary philosophers think that Hume's major contribution to the literature on evil was made in Part X of the *Dialogues.* But it seems to me that what is of really lasting value in Hume's reflections on this subject is to be found not in Part X, but in the discussion in Part XI which follows Philo's "retirement" from his first position.

(A) Consider, first of all, a theology in which the existence of God is accepted on the basis of what is taken to be a conclusive (a priori) demonstration. (A theology in which the existence of God is taken as an item of faith can be considered here as well.) On this view, that God exists is a settled matter, not subject to review or challenge. It is, as it were, axiomatic to further theological debate. According to Philo, evil in the world presents no special problem for a theology of this sort:

> *Let us allow that, if the goodness of the Deity (I mean a goodness like the human) could be established on any tolerable reasons a priori, these (evil)*

*phenomena, however untoward, would not be sufficient to subvert that prin-
ciple, but might easily, in some unknown manner, be reconcilable to it.*

This point, I think, is essentially correct, but it must be put more firmly.

Recalling the remarks advanced when discussing the inconsistent nature
of propositions (4) through (6) above, a theologian who accepts the existence of God (either as an item of faith or on the basis of an a priori argument) must conclude either that there is some morally sufficient reason for
God's allowing suffering in the world, or that there are no instances of suffering in the world. He will, of course, choose the first alternative. Thus, in
a theology of the sort now under consideration, the theologian begins by
affirming the existence of God and by acknowledging the occurrence of
suffering. It follows *logically* that God has some morally sufficient reason
for allowing instances of suffering. The conclusion is not, as Philo suggests, that there *might be* a morally sufficient reason for evil. The conclusion is, rather, that there *must be* such a reason. It *could* not be otherwise.

What then of the traditional theological problem of evil? Within a theology of the above type, the problem of evil can only be the problem of discovering a *specific* theodicy which is adequate—that is, of discovering
which, if any, of the specific proposals which might be advanced really describes God's morally sufficient reason for allowing instances of suffering.
This problem, of course, is not a major one for the theologian. If the problem of evil is simply the problem of uncovering the specific reason for
evil—given assurance that there is (and must be) some such reason—it can
hardly be counted as a critical problem. Once it is granted that there is
some specific reason for evil, there is a sense in which it is no longer vital
to find it. A theologican of the type we are now considering might never
arrive at a satisfactory theodicy. (Philo's "unknown" reason might remain
forever unknown). He might condemn as erroneous all existing theodicies
and might despair of ever discovering the morally sufficient reason in question. A charge of incompleteness would be the worst that could be leveled
at his world view.

(B) Cleanthes is not, of course, a theologian of the sort just described.
He does not accept the existence of God as an item of faith, nor on the
basis of an a priori argument. In the *Dialogues,* Cleanthes supports his
theological position with an a posteriori argument from design. He argues
that "order" in the universe provides sufficient evidence that the world was
created by an omnipotent, omniscient, and perfectly good being.[17] He proposes the existence of God as a quasi-scientific explanatory hypothesis,
arguing its truth via the claim that it provides an adequate explanation for
observed facts.

Philo has two comments to make regarding the relevance of suffering in
the world for a theology of this kind.

The first is a comment with which Philo is obviously well pleased. It is
offered at the end of Part X and is repeated no less than three times in Part
XI. It is this: even if the existence of God and the occurrence of suffering in
the world are logically compatible, one cannot argue from a world containing suffering to the existence of an omnipotent, omniscient, and perfectly
good creator. This observation, I think all would agree, is correct. Given

only a painting containing vast areas of green, one could not effectively argue that its creator disliked using green. There would be no *logical* conflict in holding that a painter who disliked using green painted a picture containing vast areas of green. But given *only* the picture (and no further information), the hypothesis that its creator disliked using green would be poorly supported indeed.

It is clear that in this first comment Philo has offered a criticism of Cleanthes' *argument* for the existence of God. He explicity says that this complaint is against Cleanthes' *inference* from a world containing instances of suffering to the existence of an omnipotent, omniscient, and perfectly good creator. Philo's second comment, however, is more forceful than this. It is a challenge of the *truth* of Cleanthes' *hypothesis.*

Philo argues as follows:

> Look round this universe. What an immense profusion of beings, animated and organized, sensible and active! You admire this prodigious variety and fecundity. But inspect a little more narrowly these living existences, the only beings worth regarding. How hostile and destructive to each other! How insufficient all of them for their own happiness! . . . There is indeed an opposition of pains and pleasures in the feelings of sensible creatures; but are not all the operations of nature carried on by an opposition of principles, of hot and cold, moist and dry, light and heavy! The true conclusion is that the original Source of all things is entirely indifferent to all these principles, and has no more regard to good above ill than to heat above cold, or to drought above moisture, or to light above heavy.

Philo claims that *there is* an "original Source of all things" and that this source is indifferent with respect to matters of good and evil. He pretends to be inferring this conclusion from observed data. This represents a departure from Philo's much professed skepticism in the *Dialogues.* And, no doubt, many of the criticisms of Cleanthes' position which Philo advanced earlier in the *Dialogues* would apply with equal force to the inference Philo has just offered. But I shall not dwell on this last point. I think the center of Philo's remarks in this passage must be located in their skeptical rather than their metaphysical import. Philo has proposed a hypothesis which is counter to the one offered by Cleanthes. And he claims that his hypothesis is the "true conclusion" to be drawn from the observed data. But the point is not, I think, that Philo's new hypothesis is true, or even probable. The conclusion is, rather, that the hypothesis advanced by Cleanthes is false, or very improbable. When claiming that evil in the world *supports* a hypothesis which is counter to the one offered by Cleanthes, I think Philo simply means to be calling attention to the fact that evil in the world provides *evidence against* Cleanthes' theological position.

Consider the following analogy which, I think, will help expose this point. I am given certain astronomical data. In order to explain the data, I introduce the hypothesis that there exists a planet which has not yet been observed but will be observable at such and such a place in the sky at such and such a time. No other hypothesis seems as good. The anticipated hour arrives and the telescopes are trained on the designated area. No planet appears. Now, either one of two conclusions may be drawn. First, I might conclude that there is no planet there to be seen. This requires either that I reject the original astronomical data or that I admit that what seemed the best explanation of the data is not, in fact, the true explanation. Second, I might conclude that there is a planet there to be seen, but that something in the observational set-up went amiss. Perhaps the equipment was faulty, perhaps there were clouds, and so on. Which conclusion is correct? The answer is not straightforward. I must check both possibilities.

Suppose I find nothing in the observational set-up which is in the least out of order. My equipment is in good working condition, I find no clouds, and so on. To decide to retain the planet hypothesis in the face of the re-calcitrant datum (my failure to observe the planet) is, in part, to decide that there is some circumstance (as yet unknown) which explains the datum *other* than the non-existence of the planet in question. But a decision to retain the planet hypothesis (in the face of my failure to observe the planet and in the absence of an explicit explanation which "squares" this failure with the planet hypothesis) is made correctly *only* when the *evidence for* the planet hypothesis is such as to render its negation less plausible than would be the assumption of a (as yet unknown) circumstance which explains the observational failure. This, I think, is part of the very notion of dealing reasonably with an explanatory hypothesis.

Now Cleanthes has introduced the claim that there exists an omnipotent, omniscient, and perfectly good being as a way of explaining "order" in the world. And Philo, throughout the *Dialogues* (up to and including most of Part XI), has been concerned to show that this procedure provides very little (if any) solid evidence for the existence of God. The inference from the data to the hypothesis is extremely tenuous. Philo is now set for his final thrust at Cleanthes' position. Granting that God and evil are not logically incompatible, the existence of human suffering in the world must still be taken as a recalcitrant datum with respect to Cleanthes' hypothesis. Suffering, as Philo says, is not what we should antecedently expect in a world created by an omnipotent, omniscient, and perfectly good being. Since Cleanthes has offered nothing in the way of an explicit theodicy (that is, an explanation of the recalcitrant datum which would "square" it with his hypothesis) and since the *evidence for* his hypothesis is extremely weak and generally ineffective, there is pretty good reason for thinking that Cleanthes' hypothesis is false.

This, I think, is the skeptical import of Philo's closing remarks in Part XI. On this reading nothing is said about an "original Source of all things" which is indifferent with respect to matters of good and evil. Philo is simply making clear the negative force of the fact of evil in the world for a hypothesis such as the one offered by Cleanthes.

It ought not to go unnoticed that Philo's closing attack on Cleanthes' position has extremely limited application. Evil in the world has central negative importance for theology only when theology is approached as a quasi-scientific subject, as by Cleanthes. That it is seldom approached in this way will be evident to anyone who has studied the history of theology. Within most theological positions, the existence of God is taken as an item of faith or embraced on the basis of an a priori argument. Under these circumstances, where there is nothing to qualify as a "hypothesis" capable of having either negative or positive "evidence," the fact of evil in the world presents no special problem for theology. As Philo himself has suggested, when the existence of God is accepted prior to any rational consideration of the status of evil in the world, the traditional problem of evil reduces to a noncrucial perplexity of relatively minor importance.

NOTES

1. [See p. 339 above.]

2. It is clear that, for Philo, the term "evil" is used simply as a tag for the class containing all instances of suffering, pain and so on. Philo offers no analysis of "evil" nor does his challenge to Cleanthes rest in the least on the particularities of the logic of this term. At one point in Part X, for example, Philo formulates his challenge to Cleanthes without using "evil." Here he speaks only of *misery*. In what is to follow, I shall (following Hume) make little use of "evil." Also, I shall use "suffering" as short for "suffering pain, superstition, wickedness, and so on."

3. Had Philo been dealing with "evil" (defined in some special way) instead of "suffering," this move in the argument might not have been open to him.

4. *Appearance and Reality* (London: Oxford University Press, 1930), p. 174. Italics mine.

5. *Theism* (New York: The Liberal Arts Press, 1957), p. 40. See also *The Utility of Religion* (New York: The Liberal Arts Press, 1957), pp. 73ff.

6. *Some Dogmas of Religion* (London: Edward Arnold, Ltd., 1906), pp. 212f.

7. "Theology and Falsification," in *New Essays in Philosophical Theology*, A. Flew and A. MacIntyre, eds. (New York: The Macmillan Company, 1955), p. 108.

8. "God and Evil: Some Relations Between Faith and Morals," *Ethics*, Vol. LXVIII (1958), p. 77ff.

9. "Evil and Omnipotence," *Mind*, Vol. LXIV (1955).

10. *A Philosophical Scrutiny of Religion* (New York: The Ronald Press Company, 1953), Chap. 16.

11. "God and Evil," *The Philosophical Quarterly*, Vol. X (1960).

12. *Time and Eternity* (Princeton: Princeton University Press, 1952), p. 56.

13. "God and Evil."

14. "Evil and Omnipotence."

15. I refer here to Moore's discussion of "organic unities" in *Principia Ethica* (London: Macmillan & Co., Ltd., 1903), pp. 28ff.

16. "God and Evil," *Mind*, Vol. XLIV (1935), 13f. I have modified Wisdom's example slightly.

17. It is interesting to notice that, in many cases, theologians who have used an argument from design have not attempted to argue that "order" in the world proves the existence of a perfectly moral being. For example, in St. Thomas' "fifth way" and in William Paley's *Natural Theology*, "order" is used to show only that the creator of the world was *intelligent*. There are, however, historical instances of the argument from design being used to prove the goodness as well as the intelligence of a creator. For example, Bishop Berkeley argues this way in the second of the *Dialogues Between Hylas and Philonous*.

Some theologians respond to the problem of evil by claiming that the earth was not created to be a "hedonistic paradise." Even philosophically, one might question Hume's assumption that the fulfillment and total satisfaction of human pleasure-principles should be the *summum bonum* of human existence. Nonetheless, one must provide some philosophical argument to support the anti-Humean claim. It is at this point, however, that philosophers of religion and theologians rely on theological premises, such as the claim that the earth was not created for the satisfaction of human pleasure seeking. Does this presupposition go beyond the reach of philosophical analysis? Furthermore, does this indicate that there are religious claims which exceed the capacity of human reason? More emphatically, does this force the status of religious belief into a type of irrationalism?

This last issue concerning the relation between human reason and religious faith leads us directly into a debate concerning the role of philosophy and philosophical analysis in the discussion of religious questions. This was a hotly debated issue in the Middle Ages, and it continues to excite both philosophers of religion and theologians, especially since the rise of existentialist theology in the late nineteenth century. The following categories, although first formulated before the rise of modern philosophy, are quite helpful in attempting to sort out the different conceptual issues involved in any discussion of the faith/reason problem.

The Faith/Reason Issue

We may spell out three different approaches used to clarify the role of reason in matters of religious belief. Historically, these three approaches were developed by the theologian, Tertullian (165-220), and by the philosopher-theologians, Augustine and Thomas Aquinas.

Tertullian first argued that the philosophical analysis exemplified in the use of reason has no function when matters of religious faith are under consideration. He formulated a classic proposition expressing his firm opinion on these matters: "Credo, quia absurdum est." Roughly translated, this proposition says that "I believe, because the propositions of religious faith are absurd." It is important that in this context we understand the exact meaning of Tertullian's proposition. He certainly did not mean that the propositions of religious faith were ridiculous, stupid, or silly. Quite the contrary, it refers to the fact that the propositions of religious faith are such that they exceed the capacity of human reason to understand them. In other words, every statement found in religious discourse is such that its level of understanding exceeds the capacity of human reason. Given this position, Tertullian excludes from the realm of possibility any use of philosophy to determine the nature and structure of religious propositions. In the end, this position forces all religious propositions into the category of *mystical* statements. Religious propositions and the beliefs held in regard to those propositions have significance only through a blind "leap of faith" on the part of the believer. This view was developed at the time of the Reformation by Martin Luther. A nineteenth-century reformulation of Tertullian's position can be found in the writings of Søren Kierkegaard. Many historians of philosophy regard Kierkegaard as the founder of modern existentialism. In the following chapter, we shall consider Kierkegaard's position in some detail.

Second, Augustine expressed a modified position compared with Tertullian. Augustine's position can be expressed in his classic proposition: "Credo, ut intelligam." This means that Augustine first accepts certain propositions by religious faith, and then he uses the critical powers of reason in order to conceptually elucidate the content of these religious propositions. Augustine realizes that human reason can be a powerful tool for conceptual explanation. It is important for Augustine that the propositions of religious faith be subjected to the scrutiny of philosophical analysis. In this aspect he regards philosophy much as a critical activity. This is similar to C.D. Broad's notion of critical philosophy discussed in chapter 1.

In the area of speculative philosophy, Augustine suggests that his religious faith might serve as a negative guide. As a guide, faith would indicate when his philosophical theories had gone astray. The notion of a "guide" works something like this. Suppose that a demonstration in the philosophy of religion produced a conclusion that was in opposition to a tenet of religious faith. If this happened, Augustine would realize that he indeed had developed an invalid argument. The propositions of religious faith could serve as a "checklist," authenticating the conclusions reached in the speculative pursuits of the philosophy of religion. While not denying the importance of philosophy in the area of religious belief, Augustine subjects it to the authority of religious faith.

The third position regarding the relationship of philosophy to theology was formulated by Thomas Aquinas. Aquinas distinguished three distinct categories of conceptual inquiry:
   A. Natural Philosophy
   B. Natural Theology
   C. Revealed Theology
In the category of natural philosophy, which is what we presently would call the natural and social sciences, Aquinas placed those propositions providing physical explanations of the universe and biological-psychological explanations of the human person. He argued that this category of human knowledge was beyond the bounds of religious faith. He most emphatically assumed that there was no possibility of conflict between scientific knowledge and religious faith. Yet he also argued, with much foresight, that it was indeed a category mistake to force religious commitment into the area of physical and biological accounts of the natural world.

In the category of revealed theology, category C, Aquinas placed theological propositions like the Incarnation, the Resurrection, the Trinity, and the doctrine of grace. These are the uniquely Christian mysteries. Aquinas suggested that it was impossible to clearly and lucidly comprehend the meaning of these propositions by reason alone. In other words, these propositions were beyond the capacity of human reason. Accordingly, any intellectual assent to these propositions was accomplished through religious faith alone.

In the category of natural theology, category B, Aquinas placed what he called the preconditions of religious faith. These are claims about the existence and nature of God, the immortality of the soul, and the notion of divine providence. Aquinas suggested that it was conceptually possible to provide sufficient philosophical demonstrations for these propositions. His model, as we have seen in our discussion of the Five Ways earlier in this chapter, was Euclidean geometry. Just as we can have a rational demonstration of the Pythagorean Theorem, so too can we have a rational demonstration of the existence of God. However, according to Aquinas, such demonstrations were difficult to come by. They required much time and elicited much intellectual energy, were easily subject to philosophical errors, and were attainable only by a few gifted persons. Given these considerations, Aquinas further suggested that the propositions contained in the category of natural theology were also contained in the deposit of religious faith. In other words, Aquinas emphatically argued that there was a moral necessity on God to reveal certain propositions to human beings. This was necessary to God because these propositions were of utmost importance for eternal salvation.

Although we might not accept Aquinas' religious commitments, his conceptual distinctions are quite interesting. He resolves the faith/reason issue by asserting that there are indeed three categories of human knowledge: natural philosophy, natural theology, and revealed theology. Religious faith is excluded from natural philosophy, is absolutely necessary for revealed theology, and can be useful but is not a necessary condition for natural theology. It is because of the category distinctions affirmed by Aquinas that philosophical theology itself became important. Accordingly, Aquinas did permit a justified use of reason which pertained to matters of religious propositions. Most of the interesting work accomplished in the philosophy of religion preceding the twentieth century took place in what Aquinas referred to as natural theology. This is indeed the realm of the metaphysical propositions utilized in discussing the existence and nature of a first cause, a necessary being, and so forth. In this category of natural theology Aquinas clearly had in mind the use of metaphysical demonstrations. From our discussion of the rejection of metaphysics by the logical positivists in chapter 4, it should not be surprising that the confidence expressed by the proponents of a significant natural theology would be subject to serious philosophical attack.

Not only has the area of natural theology been held in disdain by many philosophers and theologians in the twentieth century, but the direction of study in the area of philosophy of religion has been altered significantly. Under the influence of the development of existentialism in the nineteenth century, and with the advent of logical positivism in the twentieth century, the dimension of emphasis changed from a consideration of metaphysical demonstrations to an analysis of the nature and function of religious language. Both the existentialists and the logical positivists argued strongly for the irrelevance of metaphysical demonstrations in regard to the existence and nature of God. The development of much Anglo-American philosophy in the twentieth century has occurred under the rubric of the *Philosophy of Language*. All of these influences—(a) the general linguistic trend of Anglo-American philosophy, (b) the meaningless character attributed to ontological propositions by the logical positivists, and (c) the general disdain for metaphysical speculation common to many nineteenth- and twentieth-century existential theologians—have contributed to the emphasis placed upon questions regarding the nature and function of religious language in contemporary philosophy of religion. This change of emphasis runs counter to the metaphysical demonstrations so common to philosophical theology before the twentieth century. It is fair to say that much effort has been exerted by contemporary philosophers of religion in attempting to elucidate the grounds for significance for religious discourse. The verification criterion of meaning espoused by the logical positivists hovers over the discussions concerning the verifiability—hence, the significance—of religious language. The following passage from Ayer's *Language, Truth and Logic* is a classical statement of the demands made by the verification criterion of meaning on statements common to religious language.

. . . This mention of God brings us to the question of the possibility of religious knowledge. We shall see that this possibility has already been ruled out by our treatment of metaphysics. But, as this is a point of considerable interest, we may be permitted to discuss it at some length.

It is now generally admitted, at any rate by philosophers, that the existence of a being having the attributes which define the god of any non-animistic religion cannot be demonstratively proved. To see that this is so, we have only to ask ourselves what are the premises from which the existence of such a god could be deduced. If the conclusion that a god exists is to be demonstratively certain, then these premises must be certain; for, as the conclusion of a deductive argument is already contained in the premises, any uncertainty there may be about the truth of the premises is necessarily shared by it. But we know that no empirical proposition can ever be anything more than probable. It is only *a priori* propositions that are logically certain. But we cannot deduce the existence of a god from an *a priori* proposition. For we know that the reason why *a priori* propositions are certain is that they are tautologies. And from a set of tautologies nothing but a further tautology can be validly deduced. It follows that there is no possibility of demonstrating the existence of a god.

What is not so generally recognised is that there can be no way of proving that the existence of a god, such as the God of Christianity, is even probable. Yet this also is easily shown. For if the existence of such a god were probable, then the proposition that he existed would be an empirical hypothesis. And in that case it would be possible to deduce from it, and other empirical hypotheses, certain experiential propositions which were not deducible from those other hypotheses alone. But in fact this is not possible. It is sometimes claimed, indeed, that the existence of a certain sort of regularity in nature constitutes sufficient evidence for the existence of a god. But if the sentence "God exists" entails no more than that certain types of phenomena occur in certain sequences, then to assert the existence of a god will be simply equivalent to asserting that there is the requisite regularity in nature; and no religious man would admit that this was all he intended to assert in asserting the existence of a god. He would say that in talking about God, he was talking about a transcendent being who might be known through certain empirical manifestations, but certainly could not be defined in terms of those manifestations. But in that case the term "god" is a metaphysical term. And if "god" is a metaphysical term, then it cannot be even probable that a god exists. For to say that "God exists" is to make a metaphysical utterance which cannot be either true or false. And by the same criterion, no sentence which purports to describe the nature of a transcendent god can possess any literal significance.

It is important not to confuse this view of religious assertions with the view that is adopted by atheists, or agnostics.[1] For it is characteristic of an agnostic to hold that the existence of a god is a possibility in which there is no good reason either to believe or disbelieve; and it is characteristic of an atheist to hold that it is at least probable that no god exists. And our view that all utterances about the nature of God are nonsensical, so far from

From A.J. Ayer, *Language, Truth and Logic* (London: Victor Gollancz, Ltd., 1946), pp. 114–20. Reprinted by permission of Victor Gollancz, Ltd.

being identical with, or even lending any support to, either of these familiar contentions, is actually incompatible with them. For if the assertion that there is a god is nonsensical, then the atheist's assertion that there is no god is equally nonsensical, since it is only a significant proposition that can be significantly contradicted. As for the agnostic, although he refrains from saying either that there is or that there is not a god, he does not deny that the question whether a transcendent god exists is a genuine question. He does not deny that the two sentences "There is a transcendent god" and "There is no transcendent god" express propositions one of which is actually true and the other false. All he says is that we have no means of telling which of them is true, and therefore ought not to commit ourselves to either. But we have seen that the sentences in question do not express propositions at all. And this means that agnosticism also is ruled out.

Thus we offer the theist the same comfort as we gave to the moralist. His assertions cannot possibly be valid, but they cannot be invalid either. As he says nothing at all about the world, he cannot justly be accused of saying anything false, or anything for which he has insufficient grounds. It is only when the theist claims that in asserting the existence of a transcendent god he is expressing a genuine proposition that we are entitled to disagree with him.

It is to be remarked that in cases where deities are identified with natural objects, assertions concerning them may be allowed to be significant. If, for example, a man tells me that the occurrence of thunder is alone both necessary and sufficient to establish the truth of the proposition that Jehovah is angry, I may conclude that, in his usage of words, the sentence "Jehovah is angry" is equivalent to "It is thundering." But in sophisticated religions, though they may be to some extent based on men's awe of natural process which they cannot sufficiently understand, the "person" who is supposed to control the empirical world is not himself located in it; he is held to be superior to the empirical world, and so outside it; and he is endowed with super-empirical attributes. But the notion of a person whose essential attributes are non-empirical is not an intelligible notion at all. We may have a word which is used as if it named this "person," but, unless the sentences in which it occurs express propositions which are empirically verifiable, it cannot be said to symbolize anything. And this is the case with regard to the word "god," in the usage in which it is intended to refer to a transcendent object. The mere existence of the noun is enough to foster the illusion that there is a real, or at any rate a possible entity corresponding to it. It is only when we enquire what God's attributes are that we discover that "God," in this usage, is not a genuine name.

It is common to find belief in a transcendent god conjoined with belief in an after-life. But, in the form which it usually takes, the content of this belief is not a genuine hypothesis. To say that men do not ever die, or that the state of death is merely a state of prolonged insensibility, is indeed to express a significant proposition, though all the available evidence goes to show that it is false. But to say that there is something imperceptible inside a man, which is his soul or his real self, and that it goes on living after he is dead, is to make a metaphysical assertion which has no more factual content that the assertion that there is a transcendent god.

It is worth mentioning that, according to the account which we have given of religious assertions, there is no logical ground for antagonism between religion and natural science. As far as the question of truth or falsehood is concerned, there is no opposition between the natural scientist and the theist who believes in a transcendent god. For since the religious utterances of the theist are not genuine propositions at all, they cannot stand in any logical relation to the propositions of science. Such antagonism as there is between religion and science appears to consist in the fact that science takes away one of the motives which make men religious. For it is acknowledged that one of the ultimate sources of religious feeling lies in the inability of men to determine their own destiny; and science tends to destroy the feeling of awe with which men regard an alien world, by making them believe that they can understand and anticipate the course of natural phenomena, and even to some extent control it. The fact that it has recently become fashionable for physicists themselves to be sympathetic towards religion is a point in favour of this hypothesis. For this sympathy towards religion marks the physicists' own lack of confidence in the validity of their hypotheses, which is a reaction on their part from the anti-religious dogmatism of nineteenth-century scientists, and a natural outcome of the crisis through which physics has just passed.

It is not within the scope of this enquiry to enter more deeply into the causes of religious feeling, or to discuss the probability of the continuance of religious belief. We are concerned only to answer those questions which arise out of our discussion of the possibility of religious knowledge. The point which we wish to establish is that there cannot be any transcendent truths of religion. For the sentences which the theist uses to express such "truths" are not literally significant.

An interesting feature of this conclusion is that it accords with what many theists are accustomed to say themselves. For we are often told that the nature of God is a mystery which transcends the human understanding. But to say that something transcends the human understanding is to say that it is unintelligible. And what is unintelligible cannot significantly be described. Again, we are told that God is not an object of reason but an object of faith. This may be nothing more than an admission that the existence of God must be taken on trust, since it cannot be proved. But it may also be an assertion that God is the object of a purely mystical intuition, and cannot therefore be defined in terms which are intelligible to the reason. And I think there are many theists who would assert this. But if one allows that it is impossible to define God in intelligible terms, then one is allowing that it is impossible for a sentence both to be significant and to be about God. If a mystic admits that the object of his vision is something which cannot be described, then he must also admit that he is bound to talk nonsense when he describes it.

For his part, the mystic may protest that his intuition does reveal truths to him, even though he cannot explain to others what these truths are; and that we who do not possess this faculty of intuition can have no ground for denying that it is a cognitive faculty. For we can hardly maintain a priori that there are no ways of discovering true propositions except those which we ourselves employ. The answer is that we set no limit to the number of ways in which one may come to formulate a true proposition. We do not in any way deny that a synthetic truth may be discovered by purely intuitive methods as well as by the rational method of induction. But we do say that every synthetic proposition, however it may have been arrived at, must be subject to the test of actual experience. We do not deny *a priori* that the mystic is able to discover truths by his own special methods. We wait to hear what are the propositions which embody his discoveries, in order to see whether they are verified or confuted by our empirical observations. But the mystic, so far from producing propositions which are empirically veri- fied, is unable to produce any intelligible propositions at all. And therefore we say that his intuition has not revealed to him any facts. It is no use his saying that he has apprehended facts but is unable to express them. For we know that if he really had acquired any information, he would be able to express it. He would be able to indicate in some way or other how the genuineness of his discovery might be empirically determined. The fact that he cannot reveal what he "knows," or even himself devise an empirical test to validate his "knowledge," shows that his state of mystical intuition is not a genuinely cognitive state. So that in describing his vision the mystic does not give us any information about the external world; he merely gives us indirect information about the condition of his own mind.

These considerations dispose of the argument from religious experience, which many philosophers still regard as a valid argument in favour of the existence of a god. They say that it is logically possible for men to be immediately acquainted with God, as they are immediately acquainted with a sense-content, and that there is no reason why one should be prepared to believe a man when he says that he is seeing a yellow patch, and refuse to believe him when he says that he is seeing God. The answer to this is that if the man who asserts that he is seeing God is merely asserting that he is experiencing a peculiar kind of sense-content, then we do not for a moment deny that his assertion may be true. But, ordinarily, the man who says that he is seeing God is saying not merely that he is experiencing a religious emotion, but also that there exists a transcendent being who is the object of this emotion; just as the man who says that he sees a yellow patch is ordinarily saying not merely that his visual sense-field contains a yellow sense-content, but also that there exists a yellow object to which the sense-content belongs. And it is not irrational to be prepared to believe a man when he asserts the existence of a yellow object, and to refuse to believe him when he asserts the existence of a transcendent god. For whereas the sentence "There exists here a yellow-coloured material thing" expresses a genuine synthetic proposition which could be empirically verified, the sentence "There exists a transcendent god" has, as we have seen, no literal significance.

We conclude, therefore, that the argument from religious experience is altogether fallacious. The fact that people have religious experiences is interesting from the psychological point of view, but it does not in any way imply that there is such a thing as religious knowledge, any more than our having moral experiences implies that there is such a thing as moral knowl- edge. The theist, like the moralist, may believe that his experiences are cognitive experiences, but, unless he can formulate his "knowledge" in propositions that are empirically verifiable, we may be sure that he is deceiving himself. It follows that those philosophers who fill their books with assertions that they intuitively "know" this or that moral or religious "truth" are merely providing material for the psycho-analyst. For no act of intuition can be said to reveal a truth about any matter of fact unless it issues in verifiable propositions. And all such propositions are to be incorporated in the system of empirical propositions which constitutes science.

NOTE

1. This point was suggested to me by Professor H.H. Price.

The influence of Ayer's critique of the significance of religious language has been very great in Anglo-American philosophy. Many contemporary philosophers of religion have looked upon the Verification Theory of Meaning as the single item with which the claims for significant religious discourse must be reconciled.

There are at least two kinds of response which might be made to the charge of meaninglessness for religious language. The first type of response, exemplified in a symposium in which R.M. Hare was a participant,[19] focuses attention on the noncognitive dimension of religious language. The approach abandons the view that religious language is indeed propositional and suggests that new interpretations of religious language are necessary. Hare makes the claim that the suitability of religious language depends upon the notion of a *blik*. A blik is an unverifiable and unfalsifiable interpretation of one's fundamental experiences. Hare illustrates his suggestion with the example of a lunatic student who is convinced that all the teachers at a certain institution are out to murder him. Hare suggests that it would be useless and vain to attempt to allay the lunatic's suspicions by introducing him to the many kind and gentle teachers. Hare's point is that the lunatic does not hold a propositional belief which is open to confirmation or refutation through experimental means alone. The lunatic has, Hare suggests, a blik, albeit an insane one, about teachers. Most of us have a sane blik about teachers. It is *not* the case that we have no blik at all.

Hare extrapolates the notion of a blik to cover the case of religious language. Religious language is not propositional in character and hence not subject to confirmation or nonconfirmation by means of sensible experience alone. Religious belief, accordingly, is characterized in terms of a blik. Hare suggests that we have corresponding bliks in many areas of our experience. His examples are confidence in the structural safety of the steel frame of one's automobile, the assumption that the physical world is stable and not subject to random chance, and the belief in a regular causal system for the external world. At a fundamental level, none of the bliks are subject to direct empirical verification.

The force of Hare's suggestion is to redirect the emphasis of the advocates of the Verification Theory of Meaning and not to dismiss the charge. Religious language, Hare suggests, is nonpropositional and hence not subject to empirical confirmation. One wonders, however, if most religious believers would be content to rest their claims in a totally nonpropositional analysis of religious discourse. If religious language is totally nonpropositional, then how is its noncognitive character distinguished from dreams, wishes, aspirations, prayers, and so forth? If there are no empirical touchstones for religious language, then how is religious belief to be distinguished from a mere illusion? In addition, how are we to distinguish correct from incorrect bliks, a distinction which Hare accepts? Most religious believers affirm that their claims are in reference to the actual structure of the universe. Does the reduction of religious discourse to the character of a blik suit this demand? It seems that it does not.

The second type of response is affirmed by those philosophers of religion who have argued that it is possible to have confirmation of religious language even assuming a strict interpretation of the Verification Theory of Meaning. In his article, "Eschatological Verification," which follows, John Hick develops an interesting response to the charge that religious language is, in principle, irreconcilable with the Verification Theory of Meaning. It is important to realize how seriously philosophers of religion took the charges made by the adherents of strict empiricism that religious language is indeed noncognitive and hence insignificant. Hick suggests that even if a strict interpretation of the Verification Theory of Meaning is correct, there is still ground for significant discourse in the realm of religious language. In effect, Hick bases his analysis on an acceptance of the strongest points affirmed by the logical positivists.

ESCHATOLOGICAL VERIFICATION

John Hick

To ask "Is the existence of God verifiable?" is to pose a question which is too imprecise to be capable of being answered. There are many different concepts of God, and it may be that statements employing some of them are open to verification or falsification while statements employing others of them are not. Again, the notion of verifying is itself by no means perfectly clear and fixed; and it may be that on some views of the nature of verification the existence of God is verifiable whereas on other views it is not.

Instead of seeking to compile a list of the various different concepts of God and the various possible senses of "verify," I wish to argue with regard to one particular concept of deity, namely the Christian concept, that divine existence is in principle verifiable; and as the first stage of this argument I must indicate what I mean by "verifiable."[1]

I

The central core of the concept of verification, I suggest, is the removal of ignorance or uncertainty concerning the truth of some proposition. That *p*

From *Theology Today* 17, no. 1 (April 1960). Reprinted by permission of the author and *Theology Today*.

is verified (whether *p* embodies a theory, hypothesis, prediction, or straightforward assertion) means that something happens which makes it clear that *p* is true. A question is settled so that there is no longer room for rational doubt concerning it. The way in which grounds for rational doubt are excluded varies of course with the subject matter. But this general feature common to all cases of verification is the ascertaining of truth by the removal of grounds for rational doubt. Where such grounds are removed, we rightly speak of verification having taken place.

To characterize verification in this way is to raise the question whether the notion of verification is purely logical or is both logical and psychological. Is the statement that *p* is verified simply the statement that a certain state of affairs exists (or has existed), or is it the statement also that someone is aware that this state of affairs exists (or has existed) and notes that its existence establishes the truth of *p*? A geologist predicts that the earth's surface will be covered with ice in 15 million years time. Suppose that in 15 million years time the earth's surface *is* covered with ice, but that in the meantime the human race has perished, so that no one is left to observe the event or to draw any conclusion concerning the accuracy of the geologist's prediction. Do we now wish to say that his prediction has been verified, or shall we deny that it has been verified on the ground that there is no one left to do the verifying?

The use of "verify" and its cognates is sufficiently various to permit us to speak in either way. But the only sort of verification of theological propositions which is likely to interest us is one in which human beings participate. We may therefore, for our present purpose, treat verification as a logico-psychological rather than as a purely logical concept. I suggest then that "verify" be construed as a verb which has its primary uses in the active voice: I verify, you verify, we verify, they verify or have verified. The impersonal passive, it is verified, now becomes logically secondary. To say that *p* has been verified is to say that (at least) someone has verified it, often with the implication that his or their report to this effect is generally accepted. But it is impossible, on this usage, for *p* to have been verified without someone having verified it. "Verification" is thus primarily the name for an event which takes place in human consciousness.[2] It refers to an experience, the experience of ascertaining that a given proposition or set of propositions is true. To this extent verification is a psychological notion. But of course it is also a logical notion. For needless to say, not *any* experience is rightly called an experience of verifying *p.* Both logical and psychological conditions must be fulfilled in order for verification to have taken place. In this respect, "verify" is like "know." Knowing is an experience which someone has or undergoes, or perhaps a dispositional state in which someone is, and it cannot take place without someone having or undergoing it or being in it; but not by any means every experience which people have, or every dispositional state in which they are, is rightly called knowing.

With regard to this logico-psychological concept of verification, such questions as the following arise. When *A,* but nobody else, has ascertained that *p* is true, can *p* be said to have been verified; or is it required that others also have undergone the same ascertainment? How public, in other words, must verification be? Is it necessary that *p* could in principle be verified by anyone without restriction even though perhaps only A has in fact verified it? If so, what is meant here by "in principle"; does it signify, for example, that p must be verifiable by anyone who performs a certain operation; and does it imply that to do this is within everyone's power?

These questions cannot, I believe, be given any general answer applicable to all instances of the exclusion of rational doubt. The answers must be derived in each case from an investigation of the particular subject matter. It will be the object of subsequent sections of this article to undertake such an investigation in relation to the Christian concept of God.

Verification is often construed as the verification of a prediction. However verification, as the exclusion of grounds for rational doubt, does not necessarily consist in the proving correct of a prediction; a verifying experience does not always need to have been predicted in order to have the effect of excluding rational doubt. But when we are interested in the verifiability of propositions as the criterion for their having factual meaning, the notion of prediction becomes central. If a proposition contains or entails predictions which can be verified or falsified, its character as an assertion (though not of course its character as a true assertion) is thereby guaranteed.

Such predictions may be and often are conditional. For example, statements about the features of the dark side of the moon are rendered meaningful by the conditional predictions which they entail to the effect that if an observer comes to be in such a position in space, he will make such-and-such observations. It would in fact be more accurate to say that the prediction is always conditional, but that sometimes the conditions are so obvious and so likely to be fulfilled in any case that they require no special mention, while sometimes they require for their fulfillment some unusual expedition or operation. A prediction, for example, that the sun will rise within twenty-four hours is intended unconditionally, at least as concerns conditions to be fulfilled by the observer; he is not required by the terms of the prediction to perform any special operation. Even in this case however there is an implied negative condition that he shall not put himself in a situation (such as immuring himself in the depths of a coal mine) from which a sunrise would not be perceptible. Other predictions however are explicitly conditional. In these cases it is true for any particular individual that in order to verify the statement in question he must go through some specified course of action. The prediction is to the effect that if you conduct such an experiment you will obtain such a result; for example, if you go into the next room you will have such-and-such visual experiences, and if you the touch the table which you see you will have such-and-such tactual experiences, and so on. The content of the "if" clause is always determined by the particular subject matter. The logic of "table" determines what you must do to verify statements about tables; the logic of "molecule" determines what you must do to verify statements about molecules; and the logic of "God" determines what you must do to verify statements about God.

In those cases in which the individual who is to verify a proposition must himself first perform some operation, it clearly cannot follow from the circumstances that the proposition is true that everybody has in fact verified it, or that everybody will at some future time verify it. For whether or not any particular person performs the requisite operation is a contingent matter.

II

What is the relation between verification and falsification? We are all familiar today with the phrase, "theology and falsification." Antony Flew[3] and others have raised instead of the question, "What possible experiences would verify 'God exists'?" the matching question "What possible experiences would falsify 'God exists'? What conceivable state of affairs would be incompatible with the existence of God?" In posing the question in this way it was apparently assumed that verification and falsification are symmetrically related, and that the latter is apt to be the more accessible of the two.

In the most common cases, certainly, verification and falsification are symmetrically related. The logically simplest case of verification is provided by the crucial instance. Here it is integral to a given hypothesis that if, in specified circumstances, A occurs, the hypothesis is thereby shown to be true, whereas if B occurs the hypothesis is thereby shown to be false. Verification and falsification are also symmetrically related in the testing of such a proposition as "There is a table in the next room." The verifying experiences in this case are experiences of seeing and touching, predictions of which are entailed by the proposition in question, under the proviso that one goes into the next room; and the absence of such experience in those circumstances serves to falsify the proposition.

But it would be rash to assume, on this basis, that verification and falsification must always be related in this symmetrical fashion. They do not necessarily stand to one another as do the two sides of a coin, so that once the coin is spun it must fall on one side or the other. There are cases in which verification and falsification each correspond to a side on a different coin, so that one can fail to verify without this failure constituting falsification.

Consider, for example, the proposition that "there are three successive sevens in the decimal determination of π." So far as the value of π has been worked out, it does not contain a series of three sevens, but it will always be true that such a series may occur at a point not yet reached in anyone's calculations. Accordingly, the proposition may one day be verified if it is true, but can never be falsified if it is false.

The hypothesis of continued conscious existence after bodily death provides an instance of a different kind of such asymmetry, and one which has a direct bearing upon the theistic problem. This hypothesis has built into it a prediction that one will after the date of one's bodily death have conscious experiences, including the experience of remembering that death. This is a prediction which will be verified in one's own experience if it is true, but which cannot be falsified if it is false. That is to say, it can be false, but *that* it is false can never be a fact which anyone has experientially verified. But this circumstance does not undermine the meaningfulness of the hypothesis, since it is also such that if it be true, it will be known to be true.

It is important to remember that we do not speak of verifying logically necessary truths, but only propositions concerning matters of fact. Accordingly verification is not to be identified with the concept of logical certification or proof. The exclusion of rational doubt concerning some matter of fact is not equivalent to the exclusion of the logical possibility of error or illusion. For truths concerning fact are not logically necessary. Their contrary is never self-contradictory. But at the same time the bare logical possibility of error does not constitute ground for rational doubt as to the veracity of our experience. If it did, no empirical proposition could ever be verified, and indeed the notion of empirical verification would be without use and therefore without sense. What we rightly seek, when we desire the verification of a factual proposition, is not a demonstration of the logical impossibility of the proposition being false (for this would be a self-contradictory demand), but such kind and degree of evidence as suffices, in the type of case in question, to exclude rational doubt.

III

These features of the concept of verification—that verification consists in the exclusion of grounds for rational doubt concerning the truth of some proposition; that this means its exclusion from particular minds; that the nature of the experience which serves to exclude grounds for rational doubt depends upon the particular subject matter; that verification is often related to predictions and that such predictions are often conditional; that verification and falsification may be asymmetrically related; and finally, that the verification of a factual proposition is not equivalent to logical certification—are all relevant to the verification of the central religious claim, "God exists." I wish now to apply these discriminations to the notion of eschatological verification, which has been briefly employed by Ian Crombie in his contribution to *New Essays in Philosophical Theology*,[4] and by myself in *Faith and Knowledge*.[5] This suggestion has on each occasion been greeted with disapproval by both philosophers and theologians. I am, however, still of the opinion that the notion of eschatological verification is sound; and further, that no viable alternative to it has been offered to establish the factual character of theism.

The strength of the notion of eschatological verification is that it is not an *ad hoc* invention but is based upon an actually operative religious concept of God. In the language of Christian faith, the word "God" stands at the center of a system of terms, such as Spirit, grace, Logos, incarnation, Kingdom of God, and many more; and the distinctly Christian conception of God can only be fully grasped in its connection with these related terms.[6] It belongs to a complex of notions which together constitute a picture of the universe in which we live, of man's place therein, of a comprehensive divine purpose interacting with human purposes, and of the general nature of the eventual fulfillment of that divine purpose. This Christian picture of the universe, entailing as it does certain distinctive expectations concerning the future, is a very different picture from any that can be accepted by one who does not believe that the God of the New Testament exists. Further, these differences are such as to show themselves in human experience. The possibility of experiential confirmation is thus built into the Christian concept of God; and the notion of eschatological verification seeks to relate this fact to the problem of theological meaning.

Let me first give a general theological indication of this suggestion, by repeating a parable which I have related elsewhere,[7] and then try to make it more precise and eligible for discussion. Here, first, is the parable.

Two men are travelling together along a road. One of them believes that it leads to a Celestial City, the other that it leads nowhere; but since this is the only road there is, both must travel it. Neither has been this way before, and therefore neither is able to say what they will find around each next corner. During their journey they meet both with moments of refreshment and delight, and with moments of hardship and danger. All the time one of them thinks of his journey as a pilgrimage to the Celestial City and interprets the pleasant parts as encouragements and the obstacles as trials of his purpose and lessons in endurance, prepared by the king of that city and designed to make of him a worthy citizen of the place when at last he arrives there. The other, however, believes none of this and sees their journey as an unavoidable and aimless ramble. Since he has no choice in the matter, he enjoys the good and endures the bad. But for him there is no Celestial City to be reached, no all-encompassing purpose ordaining their journey; only the road itself and the luck of the road in good weather and in bad.

During the course of the journey the issue between them is not an experimental one. They do not entertain different expectations about the coming details of the road, but only about its ultimate destination. And yet when they do turn the last corner it will be apparent that one of them has been right all the time and the other wrong. Thus although the issue between them has not been experimental, it has nevertheless from the start been a real issue. They have not merely felt differently about the road; for one was feeling appropriately and the other inappropriately in relation to the actual state of affairs. Their opposed interpretations of the road constituted genuinely rival assertions, though assertions whose assertion-status has the peculiar characteristic of being guaranteed retrospectively by a future crux.

This parable has of course (like all parables) strict limitations. It is designed to make only one point: that Christian doctrine postulates an ultimate unambiguous state of existence *in patria* as well as our present ambiguous existence *in via*. There is a state of having arrived as well as a state of journeying, an eternal heavenly life as well as an earthly pilgrimage. The alleged future experience of this state cannot, of course, be appealed to as evidence for theism as a present interpretation of our experience; but it does suffice to render the choice between theism and atheism a real and not a merely empty or verbal choice. And although this does not affect the logic of the situation, it should be added that the alternative interpretations are more than theoretical, for they render different practical plans and policies appropriate now.

. . . Let me sketch a very odd possibility (concerning which, however, I wish to emphasize not so much its oddness as its possibility!), and then see how far it can be stretched in the direction of the notion of the resurrection body. In the process of stretching it will become even more odd than it was before; but my aim will be to show that, however odd, it remains within the bounds of the logically possible. This progression will be presented in three pictures, arranged in a self-explanatory order.

First picture: Suppose that at some learned gathering in this country one of the company were suddenly and inexplicably to disappear, and that at the same moment an exact replica of him were suddenly and inexplicably to appear at some comparable meeting in Australia. The person who appears in Australia is exactly similar, as to both bodily and mental characteristics, with the person who disappears in America. There is continuity of memory, complete similarity of bodily features, including even fingerprints, hair and eye coloration and stomach contents, and also of beliefs, habits, and mental propensities. In fact there is everything that would lead us to identify the one who appeared with the one who disappeared, except continuity of occupancy of space. We may suppose, for example, that a deputation of the colleagues of the man who disappeared fly to Australia to interview the replica of him which is reported there, and find that he is in all respects but one exactly as though he had traveled from say, Princeton to Melbourne, by conventional means. The only difference is that he describes how, as he was sitting listening to Dr. Z. reading a paper, on blinking his eye he suddenly found himself sitting in a different room listening to a different paper by an Australian scholar. He asks his colleagues how the meeting had gone after he ceased to be there, and what they had made of his disappearance, and so on. He clearly thinks of himself as the one who was present with them at their meeting in the United States. I suggest that faced with all these circumstances his colleagues would soon, if not immediately, find themselves thinking of him and treating him as the individual who had so inexplicably disappeared from their midst. We should be extending our normal use of "same person" in a way which the postulated facts would both demand and justify if we said that the one who appears in Australia is the same person as the one who disappears in America. The factors inclining us to identify them would far outweigh the factors disinclining us to do this. We should have no reasonable alternative but to extend our usage of "the same person" to cover the strange new case.

Second picture: Now let us suppose that the event in America is not a sudden and inexplicable disappearance, and indeed not a disappearance at all but a sudden death. Only, at the moment when the individual dies, a replica of him as he was at the moment before his death, complete with memory up to that instant, appears in Australia. Even with the corpse on our hands, it would still, I suggest, be an extension of "same person" required and warranted by the postulated facts, to say that the same person who died has been miraculously recreated in Australia. The case would be considerably odder than in the previous picture, because of the existence of the corpse in America contemporaneously with the existence of the living person in Australia. But I submit that, although the oddness of this circumstance may be stated as strongly as you please, and can indeed hardly be overstated, yet it does not exceed the bounds of the logically possible. Once again we must imagine some of the deceased's colleagues going to Australia to interview the person who has suddenly appeared there. He would perfectly remember them and their meeting, be interested in what had happened, and be as amazed and dumbfounded about it as anyone else; and he would perhaps be worried about the possible legal complications if he should return to America to claim his property; and so on. Once again, I believe, they would soon find themselves thinking of him and treating him as the same person as the dead Princetonian. Once again the factors inclining us to say that the one who died and the one who appeared are the same person would outweigh the factors inclining us to say that they are different people. Once again we would have to extend our usage of "the same person" to cover this new case.

Third picture: My third supposal is that the replica, complete with memory, etc., appears, not in Australia, but as a resurrection replica in a different world altogether, a resurrection world inhabited by resurrected persons. This world occupies its own space, distinct from the space with which we are now familiar.[8] That is to say, an object in the resurrected world is not situated at any distance or in any direction from an object in our present world, although each object in either world is spatially related to each other object in the same world.

Mr. X, then, dies. A Mr. X replica, complete with the set of memory traces which Mr. X had at the last moment before his death, comes into existence. It is composed of other material than physical matter, and is located in a resurrection world which does not stand in any spatial relationship with the physical world. Let us leave out of consideration St. Paul's hint that the resurrection body may be as unlike the physical body as is a full grain of wheat from the wheat seed, and consider the simpler picture in which the resurrection body has the same shape as the physical body.[9]

In these circumstances, how does Mr. X know that he has been resurrected or recreated? He remembers dying; or rather he remembers being on what he took to be his death-bed, and becoming progressively weaker until, presumably, he lost consciousness. But how does he know that (to put it Irishly) his "dying" proved fatal; and that he did not, after losing consciousness, begin to recover strength, and has now simply waked up?

The picture is readily enough elaborated to answer this question. Mr. X meets and recognizes a number of relatives and friends and historical personages whom he knows to have died; and from the fact of their presence, and also from their testimony that he has only just now appeared in their world, he is convinced that he has died. Evidences of this kind could mount up to the point at which they are quite as strong as the evidence which, in pictures one and two, convince the individual in question that he has been miraculously translated to Australia. Resurrected persons would be individually no more in doubt about their own identity than we are now, and would be able to identify one another in the same kinds of ways, and with a like degree of assurance, as we do now.

If it be granted that resurrected persons might be able to arrive at a rationally founded conviction that their existence is *post-mortem,* how could they know that the world in which they find themselves is in a different space from that in which their physical bodies were? How could such a one know that he is not in a like situation with the person in picture number two, who dies in America and appears as a full-blooded replica in Australia, leaving his corpse in the U.S.A.—except that now the replica is situated, not in Australia, but on a planet of some other star?

It is of course conceivable that the space of the resurrection world should have properties which are manifestly incompatible with its being a region of physical space. But on the other hand, it is not of the essence of the notion of a resurrection world that its space should have properties different from those of physical space. And supposing it not to have different properties, it is not evident that a resurrected individual could learn from any direct observations that he was not on a planet of some sun which is at so great a distance from our own sun that the stellar scenery visible from it is quite unlike that which we can now see. The grounds that a resurrected person would have for believing that he is in a different space from physical space (supposing there to be no discernible difference in spatial properties) would be the same as the grounds that any of us may have now for believing this concerning resurrected individuals. These grounds are indirect and consist in all those considerations (*e.g.,* Luke 16:26) which lead most of those who consider the question to reject as absurd the possibility of, for example, radio communication or rocket travel between earth and heaven.

V

In the present context my only concern is to claim that this doctrine of the divine creation of bodies, composed of a material other than that of physical matter, which bodies are endowed with sufficient correspondence of characteristics with our present bodies, and sufficient continuity of memory with our present consciousness, for us to speak of the same person being raised up again to life in a new environment, is not self-contradictory. If, then, it cannot be ruled out *ab initio* as meaningless, we may go on to consider whether and how it is related to the possible verification of Christian theism.

So far I have argued that a survival prediction such as is contained in the *corpus* of Christian belief is in principle subject to future verification. But this does not take the argument by any means as far as it must go if it is to succeed. For survival, simply as such, would not serve to verify theism. It would not necessarily be a state of affairs which is manifestly incompatible with the non-existence of God. It might be taken just as a surprising natural fact. The atheist, in his resurrection body, and able to remember his life on earth, might say that the universe has turned out to be more complex, and perhaps more to be approved of, than he had realized. But the mere fact of survival, with a new body in a new environment, would not demonstrate to him that there is a God. It is fully compatible with the notion of survival that the life to come be, so far as the theistic problem is concerned, essentially a continuation of the present life, and religiously no less ambiguous. And in this event, survival after bodily death would not in the least constitute a final verification of theistic faith.

I shall not spend time in trying to draw a picture of a resurrection existence which would merely prolong the religious ambiguity of our present life. The important question, for our purpose, is not whether one can conceive of afterlife experiences which would *not* verify theism (and in point of fact one can fairly easily conceive them), but whether one can conceive of after-life experiences which *would* serve to verify theism.

I think that we can. In trying to do so I shall not appeal to the traditional doctrine, which figures especially in Catholic and mystical theology, of the Beatific Vision of God. The difficulty presented by this doctrine is not so much that of deciding whether there are grounds for believing it, as of deciding what it means. I shall not, however, elaborate this difficulty, but pass directly to the investigation of a different and, as it seems to me, more intelligible possibility. This is the possibility not of a direct vision of God, whatever that might mean, but of a *situation* which points unambiguously to the existence of a loving God. This would be a situation which, so far as its religious significance is concerned, contrasts in a certain important respect with our present situation. Our present situation is one which in some ways seems to confirm and in other ways to contradict the truth of theism. Some events around us suggest the presence of an unseen benevolent intelligence and others suggest that no such intelligence is at work. Our situation is religiously ambiguous. But in order for us to be aware of this fact we must already have some idea, however vague, of what it would be for our situation to be not ambiguous, but on the contrary wholly evidential of God. I therefore want to try to make clearer this presupposed concept of a religiously unambiguous situation.

There are, I suggest, two possible developments of our experience such that, if they occurred in conjunction with one another (whether in this life or in another life to come), they would assure us beyond rational doubt of the reality of God, as conceived in the Christian faith. These are, *first,* an experience of the fulfillment of God's purpose for ourselves, as this has been disclosed in the Christian revelation; in conjunction, *second,* with an experience of communion with God as he has revealed himself in the person of Christ.

The divine purpose for human life, as this is depicted in the New Testament documents, is the bringing of the human person, in society with his fellows, to enjoy a certain valuable quality of personal life, the content of which is given in the character of Christ—which quality of life (*i.e.* life in relationship with God, described in the Fourth Gospel as eternal life) is said to be the proper destiny of human nature and the source of man's final self-fulfillment and happiness. The verification situation with regard to such a fulfillment is asymmetrical. On the one hand, so long as the divine purpose remains unfulfilled, we cannot know that it never will be fulfilled in the future; hence no final falsification is possible of the claim that this fulfillment will occur—unless, of course, the prediction contains a specific time clause which, in Christian teaching, it does not. But on the other hand, if and when the divine purpose *is* fulfilled in our own experience, we must be able to recognize and rejoice in that fulfillment. For the fulfillment would not be for us the promised fulfillment without our own conscious participation in it.

It is important to note that one can say this much without being cognizant in advance of the concrete form which such fulfillment will take. The before-and-after situation is analogous to that of a small child looking forward to adult life and then, having grown to adulthood, looking back upon childhood. The child possesses and can use correctly in various contexts the concept of "being grown-up," although he does not know, concretely, what it is like to be grown-up. But when he reaches adulthood he is nevertheless able to know that he has reached it; he is able to recognize the experience of living a grown-up life even though he did not know in advance just what to expect. For his understanding of adult maturity grows as he himself matures. Something similar may be supposed to happen in the case of the fulfillment of the divine purpose for human life. That fulfillment may be as far removed from our present condition as is mature adulthood from the mind of a little child; nevertheless, we possess already a comparatively vague notion of this final fulfillment, and as we move towards it our concept will itself become more adequate; and if and when we finally reach that fulfillment, the problem of recognizing it will have disappeared in the process.

The other feature that must, I suggest, be present in a state of affairs that would verify theism, is that the fulfillment of God's purpose be apprehended *as* the fulfillment of God's purpose and not simply as a natural state of affairs. To this end it must be accompanied by an experience of communion with God as he has made himself known to men in Christ.

The specifically Christian clause, "as he has made himself known to men in Christ," is essential, for it provides a solution to the problem of recognition in the awareness of God. Several writers have pointed out the logical difficulty involved in any claim to have encountered God.[10] How could one know that it was *God* whom one had encountered? God is described in Christian theology in terms of various absolute qualities, such as omnipotence, omnipresence, perfect goodness, infinite love, etc., which cannot as such be observed by us, as can their finite analogues, limited power, local presence, finite goodness, and human love. One can recognize that a being whom one "encounters" has a given finite degree of power, but how does one recognize that he has *un*limited power? How does one observe that an encountered being is *omni*present? How does one perceive that his goodness and love, which one can perhaps see to exceed any human goodness and love, are actually infinite? Such qualities cannot be given in human experience. One might claim, then, to have encountered a Being whom one presumes, or trusts, or hopes to be God; but one cannot claim to have encountered a Being whom one recognized to be the infinite, almighty, eternal Creator.

This difficulty is met in Christianity by the doctrine of the Incarnation—although this was not among the considerations which led to the formulation of that doctrine. The idea of incarnation provides answers to the two related questions: "How do we know that God has certain absolute qualities which, by their very nature, transcend human experience?" and "How can there be an eschatological verification of theism which is based upon a recognition of the presence of God in his Kingdom?"

In Christianity God is known as "the God and Father of our Lord Jesus Christ."[11] God is the Being about whom Jesus taught; the Being in relation to whom Jesus lived, and into a relationship with whom he brought his disciples; the Being whose *agape* [self-giving love] toward men was seen on earth in the life of Jesus. In short, God is the transcendent Creator who has revealed himself in Christ. Now Jesus' teaching about the Father is a part of that self-disclosure, and it is from this teaching (together with that of the prophets who preceded him) that the Christian knowledge of God's transcendent being is derived. Only God himself knows his own infinite nature; and our human belief about that nature is based upon his self-revelation to men in Christ. As Karl Barth expresses it, "Jesus Christ is the knowability of God."[12] Our beliefs about God's infinite being are not capable of observational verification, being beyond the scope of human experience, but they are susceptible of indirect verification by the removal of rational doubt concerning the authority of Christ. An experience of the reign of the Son in the Kingdom of the Father would confirm that authority, and therewith, indirectly, the validity of Jesus' teaching concerning the character of God in his infinite transcendent nature.

The further question as to how an eschatological experience of the Kingdom of God could be known to be such has already been answered by implication. It is God's union with man in Christ that makes possible man's recognition of the fulfillment of God's purpose for man as being indeed the fulfillment of *God's* purpose for him. The presence of Christ in his Kingdom marks this as being beyond doubt the Kingdom of the God and Father of the Lord Jesus Christ.

It is true that even the experience of the realization of the promised Kingdom of God, with Christ reigning as Lord of the New Aeon, would not constitute a logical certification of his claims nor, accordingly, of the reality of God. But this will not seem remarkable to any philosopher in the empiricist tradition, who knows that it is only a confusion to demand that a factual proposition be an analytic truth. A set of expectations based upon faith in the historic Jesus as the incarnation of God, and in his teaching as being divinely authoritative, could be so fully confirmed in *post-mortem* experience as to leave no grounds for rational doubt as to the validity of that faith.

VI

There remains of course the problem (which falls to the New Testament scholar rather than to the philosopher) whether Christian tradition, and in particular the New Testament, provides a sufficiently authentic "picture" of the mind and character of Christ to make such recognition possible. I cannot here attempt to enter into the vast field of Biblical criticism, and shall confine myself to the logical point, which only emphasizes the importance of the historical question, that a verification of theism made possible by the Incarnation is dependent upon the Christian's having a genuine contact with the person of Christ, even though this is mediated through the life and tradition of the Church.

One further point remains to be considered. When we ask the question, "*To whom* is theism verified?" one is initially inclined to assume that the answer must be, "To everyone." We are inclined to assume that, as in my parable of the journey, the believer must be confirmed in his belief, and the unbeliever converted from his unbelief. But this assumption is neither demanded by the nature of verification nor by any means unequivocably supported by our Christian sources.

We have already noted that a verifiable prediction may be conditional. "There is a table in the next room" entails conditional predictions of the form: if someone goes into the next room he will see, etc. But no one is compelled to go into the next room. Now it may be that the predictions concerning human experience which are entailed by the proposition that God exists are conditional predictions and that no one is compelled to fulfill those conditions. Indeed we stress in much of our theology that the manner of the divine self-disclosure to men is such that our human status as free and responsible beings is respected, and an awareness of God is never forced upon us. It may then be a condition of *post-mortem* verification that we be already in some degree conscious of God by an uncompelled response to his modes of revelation in this world. It may be that such a voluntary consciousness of God is an essential element in the fulfillment of the divine purpose for human nature, so that the verification of theism which consists in an experience of the final fulfillment of that purpose can only be experienced by those who have already entered upon an awareness of God by the religious mode of apperception which we call faith.

If this be so, it has the consequence that only the theistic believer can find the vindication of his belief. This circumstance would not of course set any restriction upon who can become a believer, but it would involve that while theistic faith can be verified—found by one who holds it to be beyond rational doubt—yet it cannot be proved to the nonbeliever. Such an asymmetry would connect with that strand of New Testament teaching which speaks of a division of mankind even in the world to come.

Having noted this possibility I will only express my personal opinion that the logic of the New Testament as a whole, though admittedly not always its explicit content, leads to a belief in ultimate universal salvation. However, my concern here is not to seek to establish the religious facts, but rather to establish that there are such things as religious facts, and in particular that the existence or nonexistence of the God of the New Testament is a matter of fact, and claims as such eventual experiential verification.

NOTES

1. For the considerations that lead Hick to raise this question, see the discussion of logical positivism in chapter 4.

2. This suggestion is closely related to Carnap's insistence that, in contrast to "true," "confirmed" is time-dependent. To say that a statement is confirmed, or verified, is to say that it has been confirmed at a particular time—and, I would add, by a particular person. *See* Rudolf Carnap, "Truth and Confirmation," Feigl and Sellars, *Readings in Philosophical Analysis,* 1949, pp. 119 f.

3. Antony Flew, "Theology and Falsification." On the philosophical antecedents of this change from the notion of verification to that of falsification, *see* Karl R. Popper, *The Logic of Scientific Discovery* (1934; E.T., 1959).

4. *Op. cit.,* p. 126.

5. Ithaca: Cornell University Press and London: Oxford University Press, 1957, pp. 150–62.

6. Its clear recognition of this fact, with regard not only to Christianity but to any religion, is one of the valuable features of Ninian Smart's *Reasons and Faiths* (1958). He remarks, for example, that "the claim that God exists can only be understood by reference to many, if not all, other propositions in the doctrinal scheme from which it is extrapolated" (p. 12).

7. *Faith and Knowledge*, pp. 150f.

8. On this possibility, *see* Anthony Quinton, "Spaces and Times," *Philosophy*, XXXVII, No. 140 (April, 1962).

9. As would seem to be assumed, for example, by Irenaeus (*Adversus Haereses*, Bk. II, Ch. 34, Sec. 1).

10. For example, H.W. Hepburn, *Christianity and Paradox*, 1958, pp. 56f.

11. II Cor. 11:31.

12. *Church Dogmatics*, Vol. II, Pt. I, p. 150.

Contemporary Trends in the Philosophy of Religion

An interesting phenomenon of much recent philosophy of religion is the resurgence of interest in the issues traditionally considered in natural theology. Paul J. Dietl made the following interesting observation:

> Some of the most remarkable turns in recent philosophical discussion have been the resurrection of issues original readers of *Language, Truth and Logic* would have thought forever dead. "Freewill" is no longer considered a pseudoproblem. There is serious controversy concerning the existence of God. Ethics is considered cognitively significant in respectable circles.[20]

Recent work in philosophical theology indicates that natural theology is indeed possible, the verification criterion of meaning notwithstanding. The determined bent of much linguistic philosophy to render religious discourse cognitively meaningless, best expounded in Ayer's *Language, Truth and Logic* and Flew and MacIntyre's *New Essays in Philosophical Theology,* has been discussed above. Students of contemporary linguistic philosophy need not accept the position that the conceptual tools of analytic philosophy entail the negative conclusions of much twentieth-century work in the philosophy of religion. To the contrary, recent work in linguistic philosophy has indicated that "God talk" has certainly not passed into the realm of meaningless discourse demanded by the logical positivists. An excellent set of essays indicating this renewed interest and dimension for philosophical theology is John Donnelly's *Logical Analysis and Contemporary Theism.*[21]

This recent work in philosophical theology indicates two propositions important for students of the contemporary philosophy of language:

A. Analytic philosophy has certainly not paid strict adherence to the verification criterion of meaning and its negative ramifications for ontology, epistemology, and natural theology.

B. Analytic philosophers have not been convinced that the noncognitive conclusion of *Language, Truth and Logic* and *New Essays in Philosophical Theology* is indeed the last word in regard to the question about the significance of statements in religious discourse.

The results of recent discussions by linguistic philosophers indicate that noncognitivism as demanded by the verification criterion of meaning in matters of philosophical theology is not accepted. A consequence of this development is that it is becoming obvious that the tools and methods used in linguistic analysis are not, per se, foreign to theological discussions. In fact, it is fair to state that many investigations found in traditional philosophical theology have been explicitly concerned with what recent philosophers of religion have called conceptual analysis. Accordingly, the methods of linguistic analysis are entirely compatible with work in philosophical theology. These methods are intrinsically neutral. They are merely ways of rigorously "unpacking" very complex philosophical issues. It is fair to say that this was G.E. Moore's principal point when he first distinguished the *truth* of a philosophical proposition from its *analysis*. Therefore the methods of linguistic analysis are quite neutral regarding subject matter.

On the other hand, it cannot be denied that many exponents of linguistic analysis have brought along under the guise of presuppositions much excessive baggage into their conceptual explanations. Too often the presuppositions of Hume's radical empiricism have been accepted as established philosophical presuppositions and principles. Furthermore it is certainly historically true that analytic philosophers of the not too distant past have been caught up in logical empiricism. However logical empiricism and its corollary, "Philosophy of science is philosophy enough," are now quite moribund. Yet linguistic analysis as a method used to seriously confront the basic and fundamental issues of human existence—be these issues ontological, epistemological, metaethical, or religious—has continued very successfully. It is philosophical analysis in this sense which is of invaluable use for natural theology. But this usefulness can be appreciated only if one distinguishes the linguistic method and its many modes of application from the epistemological and ontological presuppositions of logical positivism. Obviously it is a very serious mistake to equate logical positivism with analytic philosophy. To put the matter differently, logical positivism, with its negative ramifications for cognitively significant work in ontology, epistemology, metaethics, and natural theology, is *incidental* to the analytic or linguistic method. Recent work in analytic philosophy clearly demonstrates this claim.

These recent developments have been mentioned, so that beginning students will have an awareness as to the direction some contemporary discussions in philosophical theology have taken. Too often beginning students in philosophy are left with the false impression that all work in philosophical theology ended, if not with Hume, at least with logical positivism. This is not the case. However a complete analysis of this dimension of recent work in the philosophy of religion is beyond the limits imposed on an introductory textbook in philosophical analysis.

NOTES

1. Aristotle, *Metaphysics*, 1005 b 15-35.
2. St. Anselm, *Proslogium*, trans. Sidney Norton Deane (Chicago: Open Court Publishing, 1903), pp. 7-9.
3. Sidney Norton Deane, trans., *Appendix to St. Anselm* (Chicago: Open Court Publishing, 1903), pp. 149-51.
4. Ibid., pp. 158-59.
5. René Descartes, "Meditation V," in John Veitch, trans., *The Method, Meditations and Philosophy of Descartes* (Washington: M. Walter Dunne, 1901).
6. Thomas Aquinas, *Summa Theologiae I*, Q. 2, Art. 3. Translated by Anthony J. Lisska.

7. Thomas Aquinas, *Commentary on Aristotle's On the Soul,* no. 366.

8. Etienne Gilson, *The Philosophy of St. Thomas Aquinas,* trans. E. Bullough (St. Louis and London: B. Herder Book Co., 1939), pp. 78–79. Reprinted by permission of Tan Books and Publishers, Inc.

9. Anthony Kenny, "Necessary Being," *Sophia I* (1962), p. 8.

10. David Hume, *An Enquiry Concerning Human Understanding,* section 12, part 3.

11. W. Norris Clarke, "A Curious Blindspot in the Anglo-American Tradition of Anti-Theistic Argument," *The Monist* 54 (1970): 199.

12. F.C. Copleston, *Aquinas* (London: Penguin Books, Ltd., 1955), pp. 122-24. Copyright © F.C. Copleston, 1955. Reprinted by permission of Penguin Books, Ltd.

13. From a debate between F.C. Copleston and Bertrand Russell, in John Hick, *The Existence of God* (New York: Macmillan Co., 1964), p. 174.

14. Martin Heidegger, *Identity and Difference* (New York: Harper Torchbook, 1974), p. 72.

15. From pp. 47-48 and 56-57 in "A Free Man's Worship" in *Mysticism and Logic* by Bertrand Russell. © George Allen & Unwin, Ltd., 1963. By permission of Harper & Row, Publishers, Inc., Barnes & Noble Books.

16. *Hamlet,* act II, scene 2, lines 310-20.

17. Thomas Aquinas, *Compendium Theologiae,* 114.

18. Thomas Aquinas, *Summa Theologiae,* I, Q. 48, a. 2, ad. 3.

19. R.M. Hare, "A Reply to Flew," in Antony Flew and Alasdair MacIntyre, eds., *New Essays in Philosophical Theology* (New York: Macmillan Co., and London: Student Christian Movement Press, Ltd., 1955). The entire symposium is found on pages 275-95.

20. Paul J. Dietl, "On Miracles," *American Philosophical Quarterly* 5 (1968): 130.

21. John Donnelly, *Logical Analysis and Contemporary Theism* (New York: Fordham University Press, 1972).

Ethics: The Confrontation and Analysis of Moral Phenomena

six

Normative Ethics and Metaethics

In this chapter, we shall begin our discussion and analysis of positions and problems generally treated in that division of philosophy called *ethics* or *moral philosophy*. The content of this chapter consists of discussions and analyses pertaining to the methods and justifications philosophers have proposed in the attempt to come to terms with the uniquely human experience of moral phenomena.

We might say that ethics deals primarily with human actions and human agents. We are concerned with what *grounds warrant* our judgment that such and such actions are right or wrong and that such and such persons—including ourselves—are good or evil persons. Moral philosophers usually attribute the predicates *right* and *wrong* to actions and the predicates *good* and *bad/evil* to persons and events. In our present discussion, this procedure will be followed.

From the start, it is very important to grasp the dimension of ethical arguments and justifications. Ethics, philosophically considered, always stands for more than a merely descriptive account of those judgments and values that people hold. It is also more than what contemporary social scientists often refer to as a "value clarification." Rather, ethical analysis and justification are always attempts to provide "good reasons" for the moral judgments made and values held by individuals. Ethics is much *more* than a clarification of what we might hold about a particular situation. Clarification may indeed be a first step in a meaningful philosophical discussion of moral matters, but ethical analysis must proceed beyond the level of a descriptive account of preferred values.

379

Also note that not every use of the terms *good* and *bad/evil* is a moral use. For instance, we might say that a "TR-6 is a *good* sports car," or "that is a *bad* hammer," and so forth. Obviously this use does not attribute moral value or significance to the car or to the hammer. Accordingly, there is what we might call a nonmoral evaluative use of the terms good and bad/evil. Thus the predicates *right* and *wrong* apply to actions and the predicates *good* and *bad* apply to persons. Both of these classes are evaluative uses of the predicates with moral significance. Nevertheless we must keep in mind that there are also evaluative uses of these terms which do not pertain to moral philosophy. In this chapter we shall discuss in detail only the morally or ethically significant uses of evaluative predicates.

Parenthetically, we should note that an important nonmoral evaluative use of terms like good and bad occurs in the area of aesthetics or art judgments. One correctly speaks of a particular canvas as being a good painting or of a particular performance as being a bad rendition of a play. It is true that there is a value dimension to aesthetics. Nevertheless these dimensions are not ethically significant uses of value terms.

Before discussing individual philosophical positions of moral value in detail, one more distinction commonly acknowledged by contemporary philosophers should be considered. Philosophers usually divide their discussions and analyses of matters of morals into two generic categories: (a) *normative ethics,* and (b) *metaethics.*

Normative ethics is a rational consideration which attempts to justify with good reasons why any given action is called "right" or why any given person is called "good." Simply put, normative ethics provides criteria enabling a human agent to distinguish right from wrong actions and good from evil persons. In principle, the established criteria enable one to correctly and justifiably attribute evaluative predicates to actions and persons. In effect, the criteria established in normative ethics are necessary aids enabling a person to make the important existential choices needed to bring a moral dimension into his or her life. Normative ethics exemplifies what John Dewey had in mind when he argued in *Reconstruction in Philosophy* that the ". . . task of future philosophy is to clarify men's ideas as to the social and moral strifes of their own day . . . (and) . . . its aim is to become so far as is humanly possible an organ for dealing with these conflicts."[1]

Metaethics, on the other hand, goes beyond the material analyzed in normative ethics. Recall that, as we discussed metaphysics in the earlier chapters, the Greek term, *meta,* means "to go beyond." Metaethics, then, is that part of analytic philosophy which asks questions *about* the claims made in normative ethics. Metaethics is primarily an analysis of the "meaning" and "character" of moral terms, a justification of our use of different moral terms, and an analysis of the structure of moral arguments. Therefore metaethics is *about* normative ethics. In metaethics, the philosopher is not interested in providing any set of norms for practical living. Rather, the philosopher who seriously pursues inquiries into metaethics is profoundly interested in the meaning of the terms used in normative ethics and the structure of the argument forms utilized in moral reasoning. For example, does the predicate "goodness" refer to a property or characteristic found in the world? If an affirmative response is provided to this question, then one asks about the status of that property: Is it an empirical fact experienced through the five senses? If not, is it sui-generis and known only by "intuition"? Or is it reducible to some other empirical fact, like pleasure or power or self-fulfillment? Or, on the other hand, do moral properties refer only to the *expression* of a feeling or an emotional reaction experienced in a situation? Or, possibly ethical terms are analyzed in terms of specific uses of language like *commending, exhorting,* or *prescribing.*

In addition to these questions about the use and function of moral language, metaethics also concerns itself with the issues involved in analyzing the structure of moral arguments. For example, is a moral argument similar in structure to deductive arguments in plane geometry? Or does it have a unique formal structure of its own? As we shall see, in affirming the latter position, Aristotle provided us with a unique form of reasoning for moral matters called the *practical syllogism,* as opposed to the *demonstrative* or *speculative syllogism.* Metaethics also treats the function of moral language in argument forms. In other words, can we derive as the conclusion of a moral argument an "ought" statement from premises which are totally descriptive in character? Although we shall not consider these metaethical questions in great detail here, many twentieth-century British and American philosophers have been greatly concerned about the form and structure of moral arguments. Questions like those just considered are discussed in detail in that branch of moral philosophy called metaethics. Indeed, it is an exemplification of Broad's notion of critical philosophy, which we discussed in detail in chapter 1.

We can divide normative ethics into: (a) *teleological theories,* and (b) *deontological theories.* C.D. Broad defined teleological and deontological theories in the following way:

> Teleological theories hold that the rightness or wrongness of an action is always determined by its tendency to produce certain consequences which are intrinsically good or bad.
> Deontological theories hold that there are ethical propositions of the form: "Such and such a kind of action would always be right (or wrong) in such and such circumstances, no matter what its consequences might be." [2]

In principle, a teleological theory—which is derived from the Greek word, *telos,* meaning "end"—asserts that an ethical judgment is based solely on the effects of an action. Accordingly, the entire criterion of a moral act is placed on the side of the effect produced. There is a certain common sense basis for this theory. In facing a moral dilemma, we all have asked ourselves at one time or another: "Should I do this action now? Is it going to hurt anybody?" In this situation, we consider that the effect of the action, i.e., whether or not the action is going to hurt another person, will be our basis for deciding whether or not the action is right and should be performed. Without explicitly realizing it, we are making use of what philosophers refer to as a teleological criterion. Teleological theories can be further divided into two principal categories: (1) *egoist theories,* and (2) *utilitarian theories.*

The basis for this division rests on the scope to which the effects of human actions apply. An ethical egoist asserts that an act is right if and only if the effect of the action benefits the agent. Therefore the sole criterion of the scope of the effect is in terms of the agent himself/herself. A convinced ethical egoist would argue that an action is right only if it affects one's personal well being; one ought to do only that which promotes personal well being. In the history of philosophy, Nietzsche, Epicurus, and Hobbes have usually been classified as ethical egoists. The "Playboy Philosophy" of Hugh Hefner would probably be a contemporary example of ethical egoism.

A utilitarian, on the other hand, asserts that the scope of the action's effects must apply to more than the agent. The type of utilitarian theory depends on the scope admitted, be it family, neighborhood, village, county, country, hemisphere, world, all sentient beings, and so on. A classical example of a normative utilitarian was John Stuart Mill. Mill argued that an action is right if and only if it produces the greatest amount of pleasure for the greatest number of people. We shall consider Mill's utilitarianism in detail later in this chapter.

Note that a teleological theory per se says nothing about which or what type of effect is to be determined as morally relevant. Happiness, pleasure, well-being, power, and so on have been considered as morally relevant by various teleologists. It is up to each teleological theory to justify its interpretation of the exact nature of the end to be sought.

A deontological normative ethical theory, simply put, is one which denies what a teleological theory affirms. The criterion for distinguishing right from wrong actions must be something in addition to merely the effect of the action. Accordingly, an ethical judgment is rendered on grounds other than only the effects produced. Of course, an obvious example of the "other element" would be what we usually refer to as "intention" or "motive." In a deontological theory, the state of mind of the agent or the essential character of the deed are looked upon as important. Emphasis on the importance of motive is sometimes referred to as the *role of conscience.* There are three principal divisions of deontological theories: (a) *deed ethics,* (b) *mixed system,* and (c) *formalism.*

A deed deontology asserts that there are certain actions which are intrinsically right or wrong, no matter what the circumstances. A convinced and committed pacifist would be an example. Such a person would hold that any act of violence, no matter what the circumstances, would be an immoral action. The emphasis is placed upon the action itself rather than the situation or effect of the action.

A mixed deontological theory argues that a moral judgment is justified in terms of consequences and of "something else." This other factor is usually the motive of the agent. Often a mixed deontology will assert that the ground for value judgments is found in the development of the basic needs of human persons. These theories, as espoused by philosophers like Aristotle and Thomas Aquinas and contemporary psychologists like Carl Rogers, are sometimes called "functionalist" normative theories. Insofar as the criterion is something other than the effect of the action alone, a functionalist theory cannot be a teleological theory.

A formalist theory is one in which a moral judgment is justified only in terms of the motive or intention of the agent. For example, Immanuel Kant argued that the moral worth of an action can be determined only if the "respect for the moral law" is intended by the agent. Of course, with any formalist deontological theory, theoretical grounds must be elucidated for distinguishing proper and improper motives. Kant has a very elaborate theory accounting for this distinction. Other philosophers holding the formalist position are the Stoics in antiquity and Peter Abelard in the high Middle Ages. Parenthetically, a formalist position might be extrapolated to include any position which asserts that there are certain rules which are to be followed in an absolute sense.

There are four general aspects which have been used as criteria in justifying moral actions:

1. the end or consequence of the action
2. the action or deed itself
3. the intention of the agent
4. a mixed view incorporating aspects of the above three items.

Like any category system, it is difficult to pigeonhole the positions of various philosophers. Nonetheless the preceding four categories are valuable operational distinctions as we attempt to make sense of the work of philosophers as they have confronted the human experience of moral phenomena.

We shall treat normative ethical theories in some detail. A brief section devoted to the issues of metaethics will follow our discussions of normative theories. Nevertheless the principal emphasis of this chapter will be on normative ethics.

As we begin our discussion of normative theories, it would be well to consider thoroughly the following suggestions made by Kurt Baier in his influential book, *The Moral Point of View*. Baier suggests that a person is acting from the moral point of view only if the following conditions are met: (a) one is not being egoistic, (b) one is acting from principles, (c) one is willing to universalize over the actions, and (d) one considers the good of everyone alike. Many contemporary students of moral philosophy have accepted Baier's characterization of what counts in adopting a moral point of view. As we consider the various positions in normative ethics, it will be important to keep in mind the criteria suggested by Baier determining a unique moral point of view.

The Utilitarianism of John Stuart Mill

The first moral philosopher we shall consider in detail is John Stuart Mill (1806-1873). Mill's utilitarian theory is probably best understood by briefly considering the background within which he philosophized. Mill's father, James Mill, was an early advocate of the *associationist* school of psychology. A collaborator with James Mill was Jeremy Bentham. Bentham was the principal exponent and popularizer of utilitarianism. Bentham argued that the object of morality was to produce the greatest amount of happiness for the greatest number of people in the society. Happiness was defined in terms of a favorable balance of pleasure over pain. Bentham asserted such an argument because he was interested in the utilitarian doctrine through his awareness of the pressing need for reform social legislation in England in the late eighteenth and early nineteenth centuries. Bentham argued that the rationale of the lawmaker in assessing the merits of any proposed piece of legislation should always be determined by the long-term effect on all of the citizens. In accord with this view, the criterion for the enactment of any given law should be its ability to promote happiness for the greatest number of persons living in the social unit. The foil Bentham argued against was the aristocratic claim that laws were somehow innately structured to preserve the interests of the aristocracy. In placing the criterion for a justified law on its beneficial effects for all the citizens and not merely its enhancement of the aristocracy, Bentham believed he could produce the much needed social legislation which would improve the lot of many British subjects in the age of the industrial revolution.

Notice in the following selections that Mill fundamentally accepted the Benthamite doctrines of utilitarianism. Note Mill's definition of utilitarianism in the following passage:

> The creed which accepts as the foundation of morals Utility, or the Greatest Happiness Principle, holds that actions are right in proportion as they tend to promote happiness, wrong as they tend to produce the reverse of happiness. By happiness is intended pleasure, and the absence of pain; by unhappiness, pain and the privation of pleasure. [3]

Mill also accepted a form of *hedonist* utilitarianism. A hedonist is one who places great weight on the experience of pleasure. Mill interpreted happiness as the experience of both intellectual and sensual pleasures.

> . . . pleasure, and freedom from pain, are the only things desirable as ends; and all desirable things are desirable either for the pleasure inherent in themselves, or as means to the promotion of pleasure and the prevention of pain. [4]

Mill describes his normative ethical theory in the following passages. Pay close attention to the teleological character of Mill's position and his dependence upon a fundamentally empiricist methodology.

THE GREATEST HAPPINESS PRINCIPLE

John Stuart Mill

A passing remark is all that needs to be given to the ignorant blunder of supposing that those who stand up for utility as the test of right and wrong, use the term in that restricted and merely colloquial sense in which utility is opposed to pleasure. An apology is due to the philosophical opponents of utilitarianism, for even the momentary appearance of confounding them with anyone capable of so absurd a misconception; which is the more extraordinary, inasmuch as the contrary accusation of referring everything to pleasure, and that too in its grossest form, is another of the common charges against utilitarianism: and, as has been pointedly remarked by an able writer, the same sort of persons, and often the very same persons, denounce the theory "as impracticably dry when the word utility precedes the word pleasure, and as too practicably voluptuous when the word pleasure precedes the word utility." Those who know anything about the matter are aware that every writer, from Epicurus to Bentham, who main-

From *Utilitarianism*, first published in 1863.

tained the theory of utility, meant by it, not something to be contradistinguished from pleasure, but pleasure itself, together with exemption from pain; and instead of opposing the useful to the agreeable or the ornamental, have always declared that the useful means these, among other things. Yet the common herd, including the herd of writers, not only in newspapers and periodicals, but in books of weight and pretension, are perpetually falling into this shallow mistake. Having caught up the word 'utilitarian,' while knowing nothing whatever about it but its sound, they habitually express by it the rejection, or the neglect, of pleasure in some of its forms; of beauty, of ornament, or of amusement. Nor is the term thus ignorantly misapplied solely in disparagement, but occasionally in compliment; as though it implied superiority to frivolity and the mere pleasures of the moment. And this perverted use is the only one in which the word is popularly known, and the one from which the new generation are acquiring their sole notion of its meaning. Those who introduced the word, but who had for many years discontinued it as a distinctive appellation, may well feel themselves called upon to resume it, if by doing so they can hope to contribute anything towards rescuing it from this utter degradation.

The creed which accepts as the foundation of morals Utility, or the Greatest Happiness Principle, holds that actions are right in proportion as they tend to promote happiness, wrong as they tend to produce the reverse of happiness. By 'happiness' is intended pleasure, and the absence of pain; by 'unhappiness,' pain, and the privation of pleasure. To give a clear view of the moral standard set up by the theory, much more requires to be said; in particular, what things it includes in the ideas of pain and pleasure; and to what extent this is left an open question. But these supplementary explanations do not affect the theory of life on which this theory of morality is grounded—namely, that pleasure, and freedom from pain, are the only things desirable as ends; and that all desirable things (which are as numerous in the utilitarian as in any other scheme) are desirable either for the pleasure inherent in themselves, or as means to the promotion of pleasure and the prevention of pain.

Now, such a theory of life excites in many minds, and among them in some of the most estimable in feeling and purpose, inveterate dislike. To suppose that life has (as they express it) no higher end than pleasure—no better and nobler object of desire and pursuit—they designate as utterly mean and groveling; as a doctrine worthy only of swine, to whom the followers of Epicurus were, at a very early period, contemptuously likened; and modern holders of the doctrine are occasionally made the subject of equally polite comparisons by its German, French, and English assailants.

When thus attacked, the Epicureans have always answered that it is not they, but their accusers, who represent human nature in a degrading light; since the accusation supposes human beings to be capable of no pleasures except those of which swine are capable. If this supposition were true, the charge could not be gainsaid, but would then be no longer an imputation: for if the sources of pleasure were precisely the same to human beings and to swine, the rule of life which is good enough for the one would be good enough for the other. The comparison of the Epicurean life to that of beasts is felt as degrading, precisely because a beast's pleasures do not satisfy a human being's conceptions of happiness. Human beings have faculties more elevated than the animal appetites, and when once made conscious of them, do not regard anything as happiness which does not include their gratification. I do not, indeed, consider the Epicureans to have been by any means faultless in drawing out their scheme of consequences from the utilitarian principle. To do this any sufficient manner, many Stoic, as well as Christian elements require to be included. But there is no known Epicurean theory of life which does not assign to the pleasure of the intellect, of the feelings and imagination, and of the moral sentiments, a much higher value as pleasures than to those of mere sensation. It must be admitted, however, that utilitarian writers in general have placed the superiority of mental over bodily pleasures chiefly in the greater permanency, safety, uncostliness, etc., of the former—that is, in their circumstantial advantages rather than in their intrinsic nature. And on all these points utilitarians have fully proved their case; but they might have taken the other, and, as it may be called, higher ground, with entire consistency. It is quite compatible with the principle of utility to recognize the fact, that some *kinds* of pleasure are more desirable and more valuable than others. It would be absurd that while, in estimating all other things, quality is considered as well as quantity, the estimation of pleasures should be supposed to depend on quantity alone.

If I am asked what I mean by difference of quality in pleasures, or what makes one pleasure more valuable than another, merely as a pleasure, except its being greater in amount, there is but one possible answer. Of two pleasures, if there be one to which all or almost all who have experience of both give a decided preference, irrespective of any feeling of moral obligation to prefer it, that is the more desirable pleasure. If one of the two is, by those who are competently acquainted with both, placed so far above the other that they prefer it, even though knowing it to be attended with a greater amount of discontent, and would not resign it for any quantity of the other pleasure which their nature is capable of, we are justified in ascribing to the preferred enjoyment a superiority in quality, so far outweighing quantity as to render it, in comparison, of small account.

Now it is an unquestionable fact that those who are equally acquainted with, and equally capable of appreciating and enjoying, both, do give a most marked preference to the manner of existence which employs their higher faculties. Few human creatures would consent to be changed into any of the lower animals, for a promise of the fullest allowance of a beast's pleasures; no intelligent human being would consent to be a fool, no instructed person would be an ignoramus, no person of feeling and conscience would be selfish and base, even though they should be persuaded that the fool, the dunce, or the rascal is better satisfied with his lot than they are with theirs. They would not resign what they possess more than he, for the most complete satisfaction of all the desires which they have in common with him. If they ever fancy they would, it is only in cases of unhappiness so extreme, that to escape from it they would exchange their lot for almost any other, however undesirable in their own eyes. A being of higher faculties requires more to make him happy, is capable probably of more acute suffering, and certainly accessible to it at more points, than one of an inferior type; but in spite of these liabilities, he can never really wish to sink into what he feels to be a lower grade of existence. We may give what explanation we please of this unwillingness; we may attribute it to pride, a name which is given indiscriminately to some of the most and to some of the least estimable feelings of which mankind are capable; we may refer it to the love of liberty and personal independence, an appeal to which was with the Stoics one of the most effective means for the inculcation of it; to the love of power, or to the love of excitement, both of which do really enter into and contribute to it: but its most appropriate appellation is a sense of dignity, which all human beings possess in one form or other, and in some, though by no means in exact, proportion to their higher faculties, and which is so essential a part of the happiness of those in whom it is strong, that nothing which conflicts with it could be, otherwise than momentarily, an object of desire to them. Whoever supposes that this preference takes place at a sacrifice of happiness—that the superior being, in anything like equal circumstances, is not happier than the inferior—confounds the two very different ideas, of happiness and content. It is indisputable that the being whose capacities of enjoyment are low, has the greatest chance of having them fully satisfied; and a highly-endowed being will always feel that any happiness which he can look for, as the world is constituted, is imperfect. But he can learn to bear its imperfections, if they are at all bearable; and they will not make him envy the being who is indeed unconscious of the imperfections, but only because he feels not at all the good which those imperfections qualify. It is better to be a human being dissatisfied than a pig satisfied; better to be Socrates dissatisfied than a fool satisfied. And if the fool, or the pig, is of a different opinion, it is because they only know their own side of the question. The other party to the comparison knows both sides.

It may be objected, that many who are capable of the higher pleasures, occasionally, under the influence of temptation, post-pone them to the lower. But this is quite compatible with a full appreciation of the intrinsic superiority of the higher. Men often, from infirmity of character, make their election for the nearer good, though they know it to be the less valuable; and this no less when the choice is between two bodily pleasures, than when it is between bodily and mental. They pursue sensual indulgences to the injury of health, though perfectly aware that health is the greater good. It may be further objected, that many who begin with youthful enthusiasm for everything noble, as they advance in years sink into indolence and selfishness. But I do not believe that those who undergo this very common change, voluntarily choose the lower description of pleasures in preference to the higher. I believe that before they devote themselves exclusively to the one, they have already become incapable of the other. Capacity for the nobler feelings is in most natures a very tender plant, easily killed, not only by hostile influences, but by mere want of sustenance; and in the majority of young persons it speedily dies away if the occupations to which their position in life has devoted them, and the society into which it has thrown them, are not favorable to keeping that higher capacity in exercise. Men lose their high aspirations as they lose their intellectual tastes, because they have not time or opportunity for indulging them; and they addict themselves to inferior pleasures, not because they deliberately prefer them, but because they are either the only ones to which they have access, or the only ones which they are any longer capable of enjoying. It may be questioned whether anyone who has remained equally susceptible to both classes of pleasures, ever knowingly and calmly preferred the lower; though many, in all ages, have broken down in an ineffectual attempt to combine both.

From this verdict of the only competent judges, I apprehend there can be no appeal. On a question which is the best worth having of two pleasures, or which of two modes of existence is the most grateful to the feelings, apart from its moral attributes and from its consequences, the judgment of those who are qualified by knowledge of both, or, if they differ, that of the majority among them, must be admitted as final. And there needs be the less hesitation to accept this judgment respecting the quality of pleasures, since there is no other tribunal to be referred to even on the question of quantity. What means are there of determining which is the acutest of two pains, or the intensest of two pleasurable sensations, except the general suffrage of those who are familiar with both? Neither pains nor pleasures are homogeneous, and pain is always heterogeneous with pleasure. What is there to decide whether a particular pleasure is worth purchasing at the cost of a particular pain, except the feelings and judgment of the experienced? When, therefore, those feelings and judgment declare the pleasures derived from the higher faculties to be preferable *in kind*, apart from the question of intensity, to those of which the animal nature, disjoined from the higher faculties, is susceptible, they are entitled on this subject to the same regard.

I have dwelt on this point, as being a necessary part of a perfectly just conception of Utility, or Happiness, considered as the directive rule of human conduct. But it is by no means an indispensable condition to the acceptance of the utilitarian standard; for that standard is not the agent's own greatest happiness, but the greatest amount of happiness altogether; and if it may possibly be doubted whether a noble character is always the happier for its nobleness, there can be no doubt that it makes other people happier, and that the world in general is immensely a gainer by it. Utilitarianism, therefore, could only attain its end by the general cultivation of nobleness of character, even if each individual were only benefited by the nobleness of others, and his own, so far as happiness is concerned, were a sheer deduction from the benefit. But the bare enunciation of such an absurdity as this last, renders refutation superfluous.

According to the Greatest Happiness Principle, as above explained, the ultimate end, with reference to and for the sake of which all other things are desirable (whether we are considering our own good or that of other people), is an existence exempt as far as possible from pain, and as rich as possible in enjoyments, both in point of quantity and quality; the test of quality, and the rule for measuring it against quantity, being the preference felt by those who, in their opportunities of experience, to which must be added their habits of self-consciousness and self-observation, are best furnished with the means of comparison. This, being, according to the utilitarian opinion, the end of human action is necessarily also the standard of morality; which may accordingly be defined, the rules and precepts for human conduct, by the observance of which an existence such as has been described might be, to the greatest extent possible, secured to all mankind; and not to them only, but, so far as the nature of things admits, to the whole sentient creation.

. . . It has already been remarked that questions of ultimate ends do not admit of proof, in the ordinary acceptation of the term. To be incapable of proof by reasoning is common to all first principles, to the first premises of our knowledge, as well as to those of our conduct. But the former, being matters of fact, may be the subject of a direct appeal to the faculties which judge of fact—namely, our senses and our internal consciousness. Can an appeal be made to the same faculties on questions of practical ends? Or by what other faculty is cognizance taken of them?

Questions about ends are, in other words, questions [about] what things are desirable. The utilitarian doctrine is that happiness is desirable, and the only thing desirable, as an end; all other things being only desirable as means to that end. What ought to be required of this doctrine, what conditions is it requisite that the doctrine should fulfill—to make good its claim to be believed?

The only proof capable of being given that an object is visible is that people actually see it. The only proof that a sound is audible is that people hear it; and so of the other sources of our experience. In like manner, I apprehend, the sole evidence it is possible to produce that anything is desirable is that people do actually desire it. If the end which the utilitarian doctrine proposes to itself were not, in theory and in practice, acknowledged to be an end, nothing could ever convince any person that it was so. No reason can be given why the general happiness is desirable, except that each person, so far as he believes it to be attainable, desires his own happiness. This, however, being a fact, we have not only all the proof which the case admits of, but all which it is possible to require, that happiness is a good, that each person's happiness is a good to that person, and the general happiness, therefore, a good to the aggregate of all persons. Happiness has made out its title as *one* of the ends of conduct and, consequently, one of the criteria of morality . . . .

In his account of utilitarianism, Mill is at great pains attempting to persuade the reader that it is not a "swine's ethic." This emphasis results from Mill's great concern that Bentham's utilitarianism not be grossly misunderstood. Note Mill's distinction between *kinds* of pleasure—intellectual and sensual. Mill argues for a *qualitative* difference between the two principal kinds of pleasure. In other words, one kind of pleasure is qualitatively "higher" on the scale of value than the other kind. Some historians of philosophy have argued that Mill's distinction goes beyond the original Benthamite utilitarianism. Bentham appears to assert that pleasures are to be ascertained only insofar as they can be quantitatively measured. Note the following passage from Bentham in which he elucidates the characteristics relevant to the measurement of pleasure. This method has become known as Bentham's *hedonic calculus:*

To a person considered by himself, the value of a pleasure or pain considered by itself, will be greater or less, according to the four following circumstances:

1. Its *intensity.*
2. Its *duration.*
3. Its *certainty* or *uncertainty.*
4. Its *propinquity* or *remoteness.*

These are the circumstances which are to be considered in estimating a pleasure or a pain considered each of them by itself. But when the value of any pleasure or pain is considered for the purpose of estimating the tendency of any act by which it is produced, there are two other circumstances to be taken into account; these are:

5. Its *fecundity,* or the chance it has of being followed by sensations of the same kind: that is, pleasures, if it be a pleasure: pains, if it be a pain.
6. Its *purity,* or the chance it has of not being followed by sensations of the opposite kind: that is, pains, if it be a pleasure; pleasures, if it be a pain.

These last two, however, are in strictness scarcely to be deemed properties of the pleasures or the pain itself; they are not, therefore, in strictness to be deemed properties only of the act, or other event, by which such pleasure or pain has been produced; and accordingly are only to be taken into the account of the tendency of such act or such event. [5]

The six characteristics Bentham notes in the above passage can be translated in quantitative terms alone. Simply put, the more "quantity" a pleasure has, the higher its value. The intrinsic value of pleasure is directly proportionate to the quantified dimension of its occurrence. In order to popularize his hedonic calculus and to give it a more general appeal, Bentham devised the following rhyme:

Intense, long, certain, speedy, fruitful, pure—
Such marks in pleasures and in pains endure.
Such pleasures seek if private be thy end:
If it be public, wide let them extend.
Such pains avoid, whichever be thy view.
If pains must come, let them extend to few.

That Bentham is a thoroughgoing hedonist is well illustrated in the following passage:

Now pleasure is in *itself* a good; nay, even setting aside immunity from pain, the only good: pain is in itself an evil; and indeed without exception, the *only* evil; of else the words good and evil have no meaning. [6]

Further, in the opening words of his *Principles of Morals and Legislation,* Bentham provides a statement unequivocally accepting the tenets of hedonism:

Nature has placed man under the governance of two sovereign masters, *pain* and *pleasure.* It is for them alone to point out what we ought to do, as well as to determine what we shall do. On the one hand, the standards of right and wrong, on the other the chain of causes and effects, are fastened to their throne. They govern us in all that we do, in all we say, in all we think; every effort we can make to throw off our subjections, will serve but to demonstrate and confirm it. The principle of utility recognizes this subjection and assumes it for the foundation of that system the object of which is to rear the fabric of felicity by the hands of reason and law. [7]

Utilitarianism as a Normative Theory

Although a hedonist, John Stuart Mill is quite disturbed at the quantitative reading of Bentham's utilitarianism. Mill asserts that humans are capable of certain pleasures which are beyond the limits of other sentient beings. Of course, Mill is referring to the intellectual pleasures which occur because of the activity of the human understanding. This would include all aspects of the acts of understanding, but especially the aesthetic pleasures of the mind. The mental enjoyment attained from reading poetry is a paradigm case for Mill's view of intellectual pleasure. Mill attained great pleasure from reading the poetry of Wordsworth. In accord with this distinction between "higher" and "lower" pleasures, Mill claims that the sensual pleasures—those associated with satisfying the basic bodily appetites for food, drink, and sex—are common to all the animals. If this is the case, then the notion of human happiness would not be unique. Think for a moment what Mill's claim is about. If his position is true, must Mill have a theory of human nature in order to justify this distinction? And can such a theory of human nature be compatible with Mill's radical empiricism, an empiricism as total as Hume's? As we proceed, we shall see another instance in which Mill's empiricism forces him into a less than adequate solution of a problem.

An important philosophical question remains for Mill. How do we distinguish the higher from the lower pleasures? What criterion indicates which pleasures are qualitatively better? In arguing for this distinction in the above text, Mill appealed to the "competent judges." However, what is a "competent judge"? Mill asserts that it is a person who has experienced both kinds of pleasures and who consistently prefers one kind rather than the other. If a person has a decided preference for one kind of pleasure over another, then the two kinds of pleasure are qualitatively different. To reiterate a brief passage from Mill:

> . . . Of two pleasures, if there be one to which all or almost all who have experience of both give a decided preference irrespective of any feeling of moral obligation to prefer it, that is the more desirable pleasure. [8]

Let's think for a moment about Mill's assertions. Is the general preference of a competent judge sufficient warrant to affirm the qualitative difference Mill ascribes to the higher and lower pleasures? Certainly it is not logically impossible for a group of so-called competent judges to prefer the lower over the higher. Possibly Mill's group of competent judges held the customary nineteenth-century Victorian prejudices. Consider Mill's claim that ". . . It is an unquestionable fact that those who are equally capable of appreciating and enjoying both, do give a most marked preference to the manner of existence which employs their higher faculties." It certainly is not logically impossible for a competent judge to decidedly prefer a lower pleasure. Furthermore, just because a group of purported competent judges affirm either the higher or the lower, does that affirmation alone attribute objective value to either type of pleasure? We should say no. Quite possibly, Mill, bound as he was to the cultural ties and mores of Victorian society, would respond to our question by asserting that it is inconceivable for a proper gentleman or lady to choose the lower pleasures over the higher. But this is certainly not a necessary proposition. On the matter of distinguishing higher from lower pleasures, in rejecting any such distinction, Bentham is far more consistent with his hedonistic utilitarianism than is Mill. On the other hand, could Bentham justify the following propositions from Mill's *Utilitarianism:* "It is better to be a human being dissatisfied than a pig satisfied; better to be Socrates dissatisfied than a fool satisfied"? Are Mill's propositions important for a general theory of value? If so, can Mill justify them in some way other than through the competent judges? Apart from this objection of a possible Victorian bias, is this appeal to the competent judges anything other than a case of majority rule? Is the will of the majority alone sufficient reason to philosophically justify a moral position? Only a moment's reflection should indicate that majority opinion is certainly not equivalent to *morally right.* Because the majority of citizens in the United States in 1800 might have preferred the established practice of slavery does not justify that institution. Think of similar examples illustrating that majority opinion does not necessarily entail morally right propositions.

In considering the problem of distinguishing the higher from the lower pleasures, note that Mill was a radical empiricist following in the footsteps of Locke, Berkeley, and Hume. As we saw in chapter 4, radical empiricism cannot provide an ontological grounding for philosophical claims. Mill's appeal to the competent judges is consistent with his empiricism. As an empiricist, he cannot appeal to any intrinsic essential property in order to ground judgments of value. Insofar as a radical empiricist must rule out any ontological foundation for philosophical distinctions, Mill is forced to appeal to an extrinsic criterion. How might Descartes answer this question? Recall his dualism from chapter 3. Given this dualism of mind and body, Descartes theoretically could argue that the intellectual pleasures are higher in that they belong to the essence of human beings—the rational, spiritual soul. Insofar as the body is not constitutively related to the essence of human nature, any bodily pleasure would not be sufficient to determine human happiness. The historical adequacy of this assertion is not our concern at the moment. Yet Descartes possesses the theoretical machinery necessary to make the distinction between higher and lower pleasures. Mill does not. Thus Mill must opt for something extrinsic to the pleasurable actions themselves, and he uses the decision of the competent judges—those who have experienced both kinds of pleasure and consistently prefer one kind. That such an appeal must be regarded as an inadequate philosophical defense of Mill's distinction should be obvious from our above considerations.

Let us now evaluate utilitarianism as a normative ethical theory. Think through the following objections to any teleological theory with a utilitarian dimension.

1. Is there any viable way to "measure" pleasure? How would one intelligently determine any method to quantitatively measure degrees of pleasure to be distributed over the majority of people? Or, to use Bentham's phrase, how would we construct an adequate "hedonic calculus"? If utilitarianism is to be a viable ethical theory, there must be some method to measure pleasure and to calculate its effects on the majority of people.

2. Utilitarianism, as elucidated by Bentham and Mill, appears to lack any adequate means of distributing pleasure. It would seem that utilitarianism

requires some "principle of distribution"—what we might call *justice*—if there is to be a fair and equitable distribution of pleasure over the majority of persons. And it seems unlikely that a principle of justice itself could be established by the principle of utility alone. If a principle of justice is a necessary condition for a fair utilitarian theory, and if this principle cannot be established by the principle of utility alone, then the addition of such a principle of justice renders the amalgamated theory into a form of mixed deontology. In assessing the demands for a principle of justice, recall the conditions necessary for the adoption of a moral point of view.

There is another way we might look at the problem of distribution. What happens if 100 persons might receive a small degree of pleasure resulting from an action, while ten persons might receive a larger degree of pleasure from its opposite. For the sake of argument, let us assume that we can determine some viable way to measure pleasure. The ten persons each get 100 degrees of pleasure, while the 100 persons each receive ten degrees of pleasure. The total amount of pleasure to be distributed in either case is the same—1,000 degrees. In this hypothetical situation, on what grounds within utilitarianism itself could a moral agent ever arrive at a moral decision? This example points to the distribution problem inherent in any form of straightforward utilitarian theory.

3. If utilitarianism is accepted, then this could justify the majority of a populace hindering and suppressing the human rights of a minority group within the same social unit. For example, what if a majority of persons received happiness provided that a small minority of persons were held in the bondage of slavery? What are the utilitarian arguments which might purport to justify slavery? In a similar vein, Hitler's wanton extermination of the Jewish people and the Roman emperors' persecution of the early Christians could be justified on purported utilitarian grounds. Think for a moment about Hitler's promises of a super Aryan race and the "thousand-year Reich." Then think about the means used by Hitler and his Nazi cohorts to attain that projected goal. Wasn't this a form of utilitarian reasoning? These examples are certainly not to suggest that Mill would have agreed with the heinous crimes perpetrated by Hitler or the Roman emperors. Nonetheless it does force any proponent of utilitarianism into considering the necessity for grounding intrinsic, minimal human rights. Yet can there be an intrinsic, minimal guarantee of human rights in Mill's utilitarianism? Is there any foundation for value beyond the mere accumulation of pleasure for the greatest number of persons? The possibility of suppression of minority groups in pursuit of the happiness of the majority is perhaps the greatest weakness of utilitarianism.

4. Is there any possible way to humanly calculate all the possible consequences of an action? The twentieth-century English philosopher, A.C. Ewing, once remarked that "We cannot possibly foresee all the consequences of any action. For the consequences of an action in the next five minutes will produce other consequences in the following five, and so on forever until the end of time." In response to difficulties of this type, J.J.C. Smart, the Australian philosopher, suggested that the effects of an action relevant in making moral decisions are the ones nearest the action itself. Smart appealed to what he called the "Ripples on the Pond Postulate." To illustrate Smart's point, imagine dropping a small rock into a still pond. The ripples nearest the place at which the rock hits the surface of the water are the biggest. As the ripples pro-

ceed toward the shore and away from the point of impact, they become smaller and smaller. It should be obvious how Smart used this postulate in defense of utilitarianism. The effects nearest the action itself are the ones whose import must be considered in determining the morality of an action. Does the "Ripples on the Pond Postulate" satisfy our demands for a viable means to determine effects relevant for moral decisions?

5. In response to the claims of naturalism espoused by Bentham and Mill, G.E. Moore brought forward the charge that the utilitarians were guilty of what he called the "Naturalistic Fallacy." In elucidating this purported fallacy, Moore used what has become known as the "Open Question Argument." Moore asked if "goodness" is necessarily equivalent to "pleasure." Is one concept totally defined by the other? If the naturalism of the utilitarians is correct, then goodness is defined in terms of pleasure. But, Moore asked, is such a definition legitimate? If the definition is adequate, then the predicate term is contained within the scope of the subject term. Recall our discussion of the analytic-synthetic distinction in chapter 4. Yet Moore asserted that any naturalistic definition of a moral term is always subject to the "Open Question Argument." No matter what the naturalistic content might be, Moore suggested that it is always a viable question to ask, "Well, is that content *good*?" If an adequate definition were given, such a question would be nonsense. Imagine someone asking, "Sure I know what a triangle is—but does it really have three sides?" Of course, this question does not make any sense. Yet, Moore suggested, such a question makes eminent sense in any case of a naturalistic definition of a moral term. If hedonistic naturalism is correct, then goodness is defined in terms of pleasure. But to indicate that such a definition will not hold, Moore remarked that it is always possible and cognitively significant to ask of any pleasure: "Well, is it good?" Insofar as this question is cognitively significant for any naturalistic definition of a moral term, Moore suggested that such naturalistic definitions are subject to the "Open Question Argument." In other words, it is always possible to ask about the moral significance of any naturalistic definition of a moral term. If the naturalistic definition were adequate, then such a question should be logically impossible. However, since the question is indeed cognitively significant, any naturalistic definition cannot be adequate.

Whatever moral properties might turn out to be, it does seem that Moore had a point. We might not wish to call Moore's argument an example of the "naturalistic fallacy." In an important article, William K. Frankena once argued that Moore really indicated a "definist fallacy" rather than a "naturalistic fallacy." In other words, Moore suggested the impossibility of ever *defining* moral properties like goodness, whether or not the definition was in terms of *natural* properties. Whatever the status of Moore's argument regarding the "naturalistic fallacy," any ethical naturalist must wrestle with Moore's objection.

6. Moore raised another objection directly related to Mill's version of utilitarianism. Moore asked about the legitimacy of equating what is *desired* with what is *desirable*. Just because some thing or quality is desired by many persons, does that alone entail the goodness of the desired thing or quality? Is that which is desired equivalent to that which is desirable? Recall that Mill did indeed assert such an equivalence. Moore suggested that Mill blurred two distinct questions. Can we think of examples illustrating Moore's concern?

7. Finally, we might ask, "What is the ultimate justification of the principle of utility?" Henry Sidgwick once argued that it was a self-evident principle. Of course, many philosophers have objected to this claim. If correct, the self-evident nature of the principle of utility is certainly of a different nature than the self-evident character of an analytic a priori definition. Utilitarians have not provided a satisfactory resolution to the question demanding an ultimate justification for the principle of utility itself.

The Formalism of Immanuel Kant

The next normative ethical theory we shall consider in detail is *formalism*. In opposition to a teleological theory, formalism places emphasis on the role of intention or motive in determining right and wrong actions. The moral theory of Immanuel Kant (1724–1804) is probably the best known account of a formalist theory in normative ethics. Kant is very interested in discussing what must count if the ground of morality is *motive* alone. In other words, what kind of theoretical machinery is necessary to establish the role of motive alone as the criterion for making moral judgments. Although rather complicated, the analysis of Kant has been very important and influential in determining the structure and development of much modern moral philosophy. Kant's influence on the development of nineteenth- and twentieth-century philosophy has been so great that one scholar noted that we can philosophize with or against Kant, but we cannot philosophize without him. Another made the following comment:

> Kant can justly be called the father of modern philosophy, for out of him stem nearly all the still current and contending schools of philosophy: Positivism, Pragmatism and Existentialism. [9]

Kant sought to develop an adequate ontological foundation on which to base his moral theory. He argues for the existence and significance of synthetic a priori propositions. Recall our discussion in chapter 4 of the analytic-synthetic distinction. A synthetic a priori proposition is one which is necessarily true but which is not a trivial definition; rather, it says something *about* the world. As we shall see, Kant's moral theory is an explication and analysis of the conditions necessary for an adequate concept of moral obligation. The ultimate foundation will be propositions of a synthetic a priori nature. Kant explicitly asserts that his aim in morals is "to investigate and establish the supreme principle of morality." This principle will be an a priori proposition for Kant. The basis of obligation is not to be sought in the concept of human nature or in the circumstances in which human agents find themselves in the world. Rather, the basis of obligation is an a priori concept of pure reason. Stated differently, there is something about the nature of reason itself which serves as the basis and groundwork for a system of morality. The exact nature of this groundwork for morality will become clear as we proceed in our analysis of Kant's texts.

Throughout his moral theory, Kant wishes to separate the concept of morality and its foundation from both theology and psychology. In the mind of Kant, morality has nothing to do either with what God has commanded or with what humans themselves actually desire. Kant is well aware of the conceptual blur Moor attributed to Mill in confusing the "desired" with the "desirable." By an elaborate theory of the nature of human reason, Kant will establish the separability of these two concepts. Kant was a shrewd observer of human moral agents. He argues that a morality based on religion alone is usually a morality based on fear and not on respect for morality as such. In other words, when morality is intricately connected with a religious system, a moral agent usually acts more from fear of the divine wrath than from respect of or devotion to the principles which determine the moral or religious code of action. Accordingly, Kant wishes to separate morality and its groundwork from any theological system. In this respect, Kant's position has been adopted by most contemporary moral philosophers. Furthermore, Kant argues that human nature itself, with its innate desires or drives, cannot serve as the basis for moral obligation. In this regard, Kant suggests that any psychological theory could not serve as the groundwork for an adequate moral theory. Kant obviously has philosophers like Bentham in mind. Recall the opening passages from *Principles of Morals and Legislation:*

> Nature has placed man under the governance of two sovereign masters, *pain* and *pleasure*. It is for them alone to point out what we ought to do, as well as to determine what we shall do; . . . the standards of right and wrong . . . are fastened to their throne. [10]

Kant categorically rejects this type of argument. A psychological inquiry into the nature of human beings is not sufficient for determining the groundwork of a moral theory. Not only does Kant reject any form of naturalism, but he also rejects any type of teleological theory. As a formalist, his analysis of the criterion for judging moral actions demands more than a mere consideration of effects. The exact role intention plays in this theory will become apparent as we read and discuss Kant's texts.

It is no understatement to say that the philosophical writings of Kant are quite difficult. We will need to read Kant more painstakingly than we normally read philosophical texts. Nevertheless, by attending closely to the structure of Kant's following argument, the effort expended will be rewarded as we begin to grasp the insights of one of the most important moral treatises ever written. The following text is from Kant's *Fundamental Principles of the Metaphysics of Morals.*

TRANSITION FROM THE COMMON RATIONAL KNOWLEDGE OF MORALITY TO THE PHILOSOPHICAL (FIRST SECTION)

Immanuel Kant

Nothing can possibly be conceived in the world, or even out of it, which can be called good without qualification, except a *good will.* Intelligence, wit, judgment, and the other *talents* of the mind, however they may be named,

From Thomas K. Abbott, trans., *Fundamental Principles of the Metaphysics of Morals* (New York and London, 1889). This work was originally published in 1783.

or courage, resolution, perseverance, as qualities of temperament, are undoubtedly good and desirable in many respects; but these gifts of nature may also become extremely bad and mischievous if the will which is to make use of them, and which, therefore, constitutes what is called *character,* is not good. It is the same with the *gifts of fortune.* Power, riches, honor, even health, and the general well-being and contentment with one's condition which is called *happiness,* inspire pride, and often presumption, if there is not a good will to correct the influence of these on the mind, and with this also to rectify the whole principle of acting, and adapt it to its end. The sight of a being who is not adorned with a single feature of a pure and good will, enjoying unbroken prosperity, can never give pleasure to an impartial rational spectator. Thus a good will appears to constitute the indispensable condition even of being worthy of happiness.

There are even some qualities which are of service to this good will itself, and may facilitate its action, yet which have no intrinsic unconditional value, but always presuppose a good will, and this qualifies the esteem that we justly have for them, and does not permit us to regard them as absolutely good. Moderation in the affections and passions, self-control, and calm deliberation are not only good in many respects, but even seem to constitute part of the intrinsic worth of the person; but they are far from deserving to be called good without qualification, although they have been so unconditionally praised by the ancients. For without the principles of a good will, they may become extremely bad; and the coolness of a villain not only makes him far more dangerous, but also directly makes him more abominable in our eyes than he would have been without it.

A good will is good not because of what it performs or effects, not by its aptness for the attainment of some proposed end, but simply by virtue of the volition—that is, it is good in itself, and considered by itself is to be esteemed much higher than all that can be brought about by it in favor of any inclination, nay, even of the sum-total of all inclinations. Even if it should happen that, owing to special disfavor or fortune, or the niggardly provision of a stepmotherly nature, this will should wholly lack power to accomplish its purpose, if with its greatest efforts it should yet achieve nothing, and there should remain only the good will (not, to be sure, a mere wish, but the summoning of all means in our power), then, like a jewel, it would still shine by its own light, as a thing which has its whole value in itself. Its usefulness or fruitlessness can neither add to nor take away anything from this value. It would be, as it were, only the setting to enable us to handle it the more conveniently in common commerce, or to attract to it the attention to those who are not yet connoisseurs, but not to recommend it to true connoisseurs, or to determine its value. . . .

For as reason is not competent to guide the will with certainty in regard to its objects and the satisfaction of all our wants (which it to some extent even multiplies), this being an end to which an implanted instinct would have led with much greater certainty; and since, nevertheless, reason is imparted to us as a practical faculty, that is, as one which is to have influence on the *will,* therefore, admitting that nature generally in the distribution of her capacities has adapted the means to the end, its true destination must be to produce a *will,* not merely good as a *means* to something else, but *good in itself,* for which reason was absolutely necessary. This will then, though not indeed the sole and complete good, must be the supreme good and the condition of every other, even of the desire of happiness. Under these circumstances, there is nothing inconsistent with the wisdom of nature in the fact that the cultivation of reason, which is requisite for the first and unconditional purpose, does in many ways interfere, at least in this life, with the attainment of the second, which is always conditional—namely, happiness. Nay, it may even reduce it to nothing, without nature thereby failing of her purpose. For reason recognizes the establishment of a good will as its highest practical destination, and in attaining this purpose is capable only of a satisfaction of its own proper kind, namely, that from the attainment of an end, which end again is determined by reason only, notwithstanding that this may involve many a disappointment to the ends of inclination.

We have then to develop the notion of a will which deserves to be highly esteemed for itself, and is good without a view to anything further, a notion which exists already in the sound natural understanding, requiring rather to be cleared up than to be taught, and which in estimating the value of our actions, always takes the first place and constitutes the conditions of all the rest. In order to do this, we will take the notion of duty, which includes that of a good will, although implying certain subjective restrictions and hindrances. These, however, far from concealing it or rendering it unrecognizable, rather bring it out by contrast and make it shine forth so much the brighter.

I omit here all actions which are already recognized as inconsistent with duty, although they may be useful for this or that purpose, for with these the question whether they are done *from duty* cannot arise at all, since they even conflict with it. I also set aside those actions which really conform to duty, but to which men have *no* direct *inclination,* performing them because they are impelled thereto by some other inclination. For in this case we can readily distinguish whether the action which agrees with duty is done *from duty* or from a selfish view. It is much harder to make this distinction when the action accords with duty, and the subject has besides a *direct* inclination to it. For example, it is always a matter of duty that a dealer should not overcharge an inexperienced purchaser; and wherever there is much commerce the prudent tradesman does not overcharge, but keeps a fixed price for everyone, so that a child buys of him as well as any other. Men are thus *honestly* served; but this is not enough to make us believe that the tradesman has so acted from duty and from principles of honesty; his own advantage required it; it is out of the question in this case to suppose that he might besides have a direct inclination in favor of the buyers, so that, as it were, from love he should give no advantage to one over another. Accordingly the action was done neither from duty nor from direct inclination, but merely from a selfish view.

On the other hand, it is a duty to maintain one's life; and, in addition, everyone has also a direct inclination to do so. But on this account the often anxious care which most men take for it has no intrinsic worth, and their maxim has no moral import. They preserve their life *as duty requires,* no doubt, but not *because duty requires.* On the other hand, if adversity and hopeless sorrow have completely taken away the relish for life, if the unfortunate one, strong in mind, indignant at his fate rather than desponding or dejected, wishes for death, and yet preserves his life without loving it—not from inclination or fear, but from duty—then his maxim has a moral worth. [The first proposition is that, to have moral worth, an action must be done from duty.] . . .

The second proposition is: That an action done from duty derives its moral worth, *not from the purpose* which is to be attained by it, but from the maxim by which it is determined, and therefore does not depend on the realization of the object of its action, but merely on the *principle of volition* by which the action has taken place, without regard to any object or desire. It is clear from what precedes that the purposes which we may have in view in our actions, or their effects regarded as ends and springs of the will, cannot give to actions any unconditional or moral worth. In what, then, can their worth lie if it is not to consist in the will and in reference to its expected effect? It cannot lie anywhere but in the *principle of the will* without regard to the ends which can be attained by the action. For the will stands between its *a priori* principle, which is formal, and its *a posteriori* spring, which is material, as between two roads, and as it must be determined by something, it follows that it must be determined by the formal principle of volition when an action is done from duty, in which case every material principle has been withdrawn from it.

The third proposition, which is a consequence of the two preceding, I would express thus: *Duty is the necessity of acting from respect for the law.* I may have *inclination* for an object as the effect of my proposed action, but I cannot have *respect* for it just for this reason that it is an effect and not an energy of the will. Similarly, I cannot have respect for inclination, whether my own or another's; I can at most, if my own, approve it; if another's, sometimes even love it, that is, look on it as favorable to my own interest. It is only what is connected with my will as a principle, by no means as an effect—what does not subserve my inclination, but overpowers it, or at least in case of choice excludes it from its calculation—in other words, simply the law itself, which can be an object of respect, and hence a command. Now an action done from duty must wholly exclude the influence of inclination, and with it every object of the will, so that nothing remains which can determine the will except objectively the *law,* and subjectively *pure respect* for this practical law, and consequently the maxim that I should follow this law even to the thwarting of all my inclinations. [*A maxim* is the subjective principle of volition. The objective principle (*i. e.,* that which would also serve subjectively as a practical principle to all rational beings if reason had full power over the faculty of desire) is the practical *law.*]

Thus the moral worth of an action does not lie in the effect expected from it, nor in any principle of action which requires to borrow its motive from this expected effect. For all these effects—agreeableness of one's condition, and even the promotion of the happiness of others—could have been also brought about by other causes, so that for this there would have been no need of the will of a rational being; whereas it is in this alone that the supreme and unconditional good can be found. The preeminent good which we call moral can therefore consist in nothing else than *the conception of law* in itself, *which certainly is only possible in a rational being,* in so far as this conception, and not the expected effect, determines the will. This is a good which is already present in the person who acts accordingly, and we have not to wait for it to appear first in the result.

But what sort of law can that be the conception of which must determine the will, even without paying any regard to the effect expected from it, in order that this will may be called good absolutely and without qualification? As I have deprived the will of every impulse which could arise to it from obedience to any law, there remains nothing but the universal conformity of its actions to law in general, which alone is to serve the will as a principle, that is, I am never to act otherwise than so *that I could also will that my maxim should become a universal law.* Here, now, it is the simple conformity to law in general, without assuming any particular law applicable to certain actions, that serves the will as its principle, and must so serve it if duty is not to be a vain delusion and a chimerical notion. The common reason of men in its practical judgments perfectly coincides with this, and always has in view the principle here suggested. Let the question be, for example: May I when in distress make a promise with the intention not to keep it? I readily distinguish here between the two significations which the question may have: whether it is prudent or whether it is right to make a false promise? The former may undoubtedly often be the case. I see clearly indeed that it is not enough to extricate myself from a present difficulty by means of this subterfuge, but it must be well considered whether there may not hereafter spring from this lie much greater inconvenience than that from which I now free myself, and as, with all my supposed *cunning,* the consequences cannot be so easily foreseen but that credit once lost may be much more injurious to me than any mischief which I seek to avoid at present, it should be considered whether it would not be more *prudent* to act herein according to a universal maxim, and to make it a habit to promise nothing except with the intention of keeping it. But it is soon clear to me that such a maxim will still only be based on the fear of consequences. Now it is a wholly different thing to be truthful from duty, and to be so from apprehension of injurious consequences. In the first case, the very notion of action already implies a law for me; in the second case, I must first look about elsewhere to see what results may be combined with it which would affect myself. For to deviate from the principle of duty is beyond all doubt wicked; but to be unfaithful to my maxim of prudence may often be very advantageous to me, although to abide by it is certainly safer. The shortest way, however, and an unerring one, to discover the answer to this question whether a lying promise is consistent with duty, is to ask myself, Should I be content that my maxim (to extricate myself from difficulty by a false promise) should hold good as a universal law, for myself as well as for others; and should I be able to say to myself, "Every one may make a deceitful promise when he finds himself in a difficulty from which he cannot otherwise extricate himself"? Then I presently become aware that, while I can will the lie, I can by no means will that lying should be a universal law. For with such a law there would be no promises at all, since it would be in vain to allege my intention in regard to my future actions to those who would not believe this allegation, or if they over-hastily did so, would pay me back in my own coin. Hence my maxim, as soon as it should be made a universal law, would necessarily destroy itself.

I do not, therefore, need any far-reaching penetration to discern what I have to do in order that my will may be morally good. Inexperienced in the course of the world, incapable of being prepared for all its contingencies, I only ask myself: Canst thou also will that thy maxim should be a universal law? If not, then it must be rejected, and that not because of a disadvantage accruing from it to myself or even to others, but because it cannot enter as a principle into a possible universal legislation, and reason extorts from me immediate respect for such legislation. I do not indeed as yet *discern* on what this respect is based (this the philosopher may inquire), but at least I understand this—that it is an estimation of the worth which far outweighs all worth of what is recommended by inclination, and that the necessity of acting from *pure* respect for the practical law is what constitutes duty, to which every other motive must give place because it is the condition of a will being good *in itself,* and the worth of such a will is above everything.

Thus, then, without quitting the moral knowledge of common human reason, we have arrived at its principle. And although, no doubt, common men do not conceive it in such an abstract and universal form, yet they always have it really before their eyes and use it as the standard of their decision. Here it would be easy to show how, with this compass in hand, men are well able to distinguish, in every case that occurs, what is good, what bad, conformably to duty or inconsistent with it, if, without in the least teaching them anything new, we only, like Socrates, direct their attention to the principle they themselves employ; and that, therefore, we do not need science and philosophy to know what we should do to be honest and good, yea, even wise and virtuous. . . .

Thus is the *common reason of men* compelled to go out of its sphere and to take a step into the field of a *practical philosophy*, not to satisfy any speculative want (which never occurs to it as long as it is content to be mere sound reason), but even on practical grounds, in order to attain in it information and clear instruction respecting the source of its principle, and the correct determination of it in opposition to the maxims which are based on wants and inclinations, so that it may escape from the perplexity of opposite claims, and not run the risk of losing all genuine moral principles through the equivocation into which it easily falls. Thus, when practical reason cultivates itself, there insensibly arises in it a dialectic which forces it to seek aid in philosophy, just as happens to it in its theoretic use; and in this case, therefore, as well as in the other, it will find rest nowhere but in a thorough critical examination of our reason.

TRANSITION FROM POPULAR MORAL PHILOSOPHY TO THE METAPHYSIC OF MORALS (SECOND SECTION)

. . . The conception of an objective principle, in so far as it is obligatory for a will, is called a command (of reason), and the formula of the command is called an *Imperative.* All imperatives are expressed by the word ought. . . .

They say that something would be good to do or to forbear, but they say it to a will which does not always do a thing because it is conceived to be good to do it. . . .

Now all imperatives command either *hypothetically* or *categorically*. . . . If the action is good only as a means to *something else,* then the imperative is hypothetical; if it is conceived as good *in itself* and consequently as being necessarily the principle of a will which of itself conforms to reason, then it is *categorical.* . . .

Accordingly, the hypothetical imperative only says that the action is good for some purpose, *possible* or *actual.* In the first case it is a Problematical, in the second an Assertorial practical principle [see A and B, below]. The categorical imperative which declares an action to be objectively necessary in itself without reference to any purpose, i.e. without any other end, is valid as an Apodictic practical principle [see C, below]. . . .

[A] All sciences have a practical part, consisting of problems expressing that some end is possible for us, and of imperatives directing how it may be attained. These may, therefore, be called in general imperatives of Skill. Here there is no question whether the end is rational and good, but only what one must do in order to attain it. The precepts for the physician to make his patient thoroughly healthy, and for a poisoner to ensure certain death, are of equal value in this respect, that each serves to effect its purpose perfectly. Since in early youth it cannot be known what ends are likely to occur to us in the course of life, parents seek to have their children taught a *great many things,* and provide for their *skill* in the use of means for all sorts of arbitrary ends, of none of which can they determine whether it may not perhaps hereafter be an object to their pupil, but which it is at all events *possible* that he might aim at; and this anxiety is so great that they commonly neglect to form and correct their judgment on the value of the things which may be chosen as ends.

[B] There is *one* end, however, which may be assumed to be actually such to all rational beings (so far as imperatives apply to them, viz. as dependent beings), and, therefore, one purpose which they not merely *may* have, but which we may with certainty assume that they all actually *have* by a natural necessity, and this is *happiness.* The hypothetical imperative which expresses the practical necessity of an action as means to the advancement of happiness is Assertorial. We are not to present it as necessary for an uncertain and merely possible purpose, but for a purpose which we may presuppose with certainty and *a priori* in every man, because it belongs to his being. Now skill in the choice of means to his own greatest well-being may be called *prudence,* in the narrowest sense. And thus the imperative which refers to the choice of means to one's own happiness, i.e. the precept of prudence, is still always *hypothetical;* the action is not commanded absolutely, but only as a means to another purpose.

[C] Finally, there is an imperative which commands a certain conduct immediately, without having as its condition any other purpose to be attained by it. This imperative is Categorical. It concerns not the matter of the action, or its intended result, but its form and the principle of which it is itself a result; and what is essentially good in it consists in the mental disposition, let the consequence be what it may. This imperative may be called that of Morality. . . .

When I conceive a hypothetical imperative, in general I do not know beforehand what it will contain until I am given the condition. But when I conceive a categorical imperative, I know at once what it contains. For as the imperative contains besides the law only the necessity that the maxims shall conform to this law, while the law contains no conditions restricting it, there remains nothing but the general statement that the maxim of the action should conform to a universal law, and it is this conformity alone that the imperative properly represents as necessary.

[*The Categorical Imperative: first formulation*]. There is therefore but one categorical imperative, namely, this: *Act only on that maxim whereby thou canst at the same time will that it should become a universal law.*

Now if all imperatives of duty can be deduced from this one imperative as from their principle, then, although it should remain undecided whether what is called duty is not merely a vain notion, yet at least we shall be able to show what we understand by it and what this notion means.

Since the universality of the law according to which effects are produced constitutes what is properly called *nature* in the most general sense (as to form), that is the existence of things so far as it is determined by general laws, the imperative of duty may be expressed thus: *Act as if the maxim of thy action were to become by thy will a universal law of nature.*

We will now enumerate a few duties, adopting the usual division of them into duties to ourselves and to others, and into perfect and imperfect duties.

1. A man reduced to despair by a series of misfortunes feels wearied of life, but is still so far in possession of his reason that he can ask himself whether it would not be contrary to his duty to himself to take his own life. Now he inquires whether the maxim of his action could become a universal law of nature. His maxim is: From self-love I adopt it as a principle to shorten my life when its longer duration is likely to bring more evil than satisfaction. It is asked then simply whether this principle founded on self-love can become a universal law of nature. Now we see at once that a system of nature of which it should be a law to destroy life by means of the very feeling whose special nature it is to impel to the improvement of life would contradict itself, and therefore could not exist as a system of nature; hence that maxim cannot possibly exist as a universal law of nature, and consequently would be wholly inconsistent with the supreme principle of all duty.

2. Another finds himself forced by necessity to borrow money. He knows that he will not be able to repay it, but sees also that nothing will be lent to him, unless he promises stoutly to repay it in a definite time. He desires to make this promise, but he has still so much conscience as to ask himself: Is it not unlawful and inconsistent with duty to get out of a difficulty in this way? Suppose, however, that he resolves to do so, then the maxim of his action would be expressed thus: When I think myself in want of money, I will borrow money and promise to repay it, although I know that I never can do so. Now this principle of self-love or of one's own advantage may perhaps be consistent with my whole future welfare; but the question now is, Is it right? I change then the suggestion of self-love into a universal law, and state the question thus: How would it be if my maxim were a universal law? Then I see at once that it could never hold as a universal law of nature, but would necessarily contradict itself. For supposing it to be a

universal law that everyone when he thinks himself in a difficulty should be able to promise whatever he pleases, with the purpose of not keeping his promise, the promise itself would become impossible, as well as the end that one might have in view in it, since no one would consider that anything was promised to him, but would ridicule all such statements as vain pretences.

3. A third finds in himself a talent which with the help of some culture might make him a useful man in many respects. But he finds himself in comfortable circumstances, and prefers to indulge in pleasure rather than to take pains in enlarging and improving his happy natural capacities. He asks, however, whether his maxim of neglect of his natural gifts, besides agreeing with his inclination to indulgence, agrees also with what is called duty. He sees then that a system of nature could indeed subsist with such a universal law although men (like the South Sea islanders) should let their talents rest, and resolve to devote their lives merely to idleness, amusement, and propagation of their species—in a word, to enjoyment; but he cannot possibly *will* that this should be a universal law of nature, or be implanted in us as such by a natural instinct. For, as a rational being, he necessarily wills that his faculties be developed, since they serve him, and have been given him, for all sorts of possible purposes.

4. A fourth, who is in prosperity, while he sees that others have to contend with great wretchedness and that he could help them, thinks: What concern is it of mine? Let everyone be happy as Heaven pleases, or as he can make himself; I will take nothing from him nor even envy him, only I do not wish to contribute anything to his welfare or to his assistance in distress! Now no doubt if such a mode of thinking were a universal law, the human race might very well subsist, and doubtless even better than in a state in which everyone talks of sympathy and good-will, or even takes care occasionally to put it into practice, but, on the other side, also cheats when he can, betrays the rights of men, or otherwise violates them. But although it is possible that a universal law of nature might exist in accordance with that maxim, it is impossible to *will* that such a principle should have the universal validity of a law of nature. For a will which resolved this would contradict itself, inasmuch as many cases might occur in which one would have need of the love and sympathy of others, and in which, by such a law of nature, sprung from his own will, he would deprive himself of all hope of the aid he desires.

These are a few of the many actual duties, or at least what we regard as such, which obviously fall into two classes on the one principle that we have laid down. We must be *able to will* that a maxim of our action should be a universal law. This is the canon of the moral appreciation of the action generally. Some actions are of such a character that their maxim cannot without contradiction be even *conceived* as a universal law of nature, far from it being possible that we should *will* that it *should* be so. In others this intrinsic impossibility is not found, but still it is impossible to *will* that their maxim should be raised to the universality of a law of nature, since such a will would contradict itself. It is easily seen that the former violate strict or rigorous (inflexible) duty; the latter only laxer (meritorious) duty. Thus it has been completely shown by these examples how all duties depend as regards the nature of the obligation (not the object of the action) on the same principle. . . .

Supposing . . . that there were something *whose existence* has *in itself* an absolute worth, something which, being *an end in itself,* could be a source of definite laws, then in this and this alone would lie the source of a possible categorical imperative, *i.e.,* a practical law.

Now I say: man and generally any rational being *exists* as an end in himself, *not merely as a means* to be arbitrarily used by this or that will, but in all his actions, whether they concern himself or other rational beings, must be always regarded at the same time as an end. All objects of the inclinations have only a conditional worth, for if the inclinations and the wants founded on them did not exist, then their object would be without value. But the inclinations themselves being sources of want, are so far from having an absolute worth for which they should be desired, that on the contrary it must be the universal wish of every rational being to be wholly free from them. Thus the worth of any object which is *to be acquired* by our action is always conditional. Beings whose existence depends not on our will but on nature's, have nevertheless, if they are irrational beings, only a relative value as means, and are therefore called *things;* rational beings, on the contrary, are called *persons,* because their very nature points them out as ends in themselves, that is as something which must not be used merely as means, and so far therefore restricts freedom of action (and is an object of respect). These, therefore, are not merely subjective ends whose existence has a worth *for us* as an effect of our action, but *objective ends,* that is things whose existence is an end in itself: an end moreover for which no other can be substituted, which they should subserve *merely* as means, for otherwise nothing whatever would possess *absolute worth;* but if all worth were conditioned and therefore contingent, then there would be no supreme practical principle of reason whatever.

If then there is a supreme practical principle or, in respect of the human will, a categorical imperative, it must be one which, being drawn from the conception of that which is necessarily an end for every one because it is *an end in itself,* constitutes an *objective* principle of will, and can therefore serve as a universal practical law. The foundation of this principle is: *rational nature exists as an end in itself.* Man necessarily conceives his own existence as being so: so far then this is a *subjective* principle of human actions. But every other rational being regards its existence similarly, just on the same rational principle that holds for me: so that it is at the same time an objective principle, from which as a supreme practical law all laws of the will must be capable of being deduced. Accordingly the practical imperative will be as follows: *So act as to treat humanity, whether in thine own person or in that of any other, in every case as an end withal, never as means only.*

. . . The principle: So act in regard to every rational being (thyself and others), that he may always have place in thy maxim as an end in himself, is accordingly essentially identical with this other: Act upon a maxim which, at the same time, involves its own universal validity for every rational being. For that in using means for every end I should limit my maxim by the condition of its holding good as a law for every subject, this comes to the same thing as that the fundamental principle of all maxims of action must be that the subject of all ends, *i.e.,* the rational being himself, be never employed merely as means, but as the supreme condition restricting the use of all means, that is in every case as an end likewise.

. . . We see philosophy brought to a critical position, since it has to be firmly fixed, notwithstanding that it has nothing to support it either in heaven or earth. Here it must show its purity as absolute dictator of its own laws, not the herald of those which are whispered to it by an implanted sense or who knows what tutelary nature. Although these may be better than nothing, yet they can never afford principles dictated by reason, which must have their source wholly *a priori* and thence their commanding authority, expecting everything from the supremacy of the law and the due respect for it, nothing from inclination, or else condemning the man to self-contempt and inward abhorrence.

Thus every empirical element is not only quite incapable of being an aid to the principle of morality, but is even highly prejudicial to the purity of morals, for the proper and inestimable worth of an absolutely good will consists just in this, that the principle of action is free from all influence of contingent grounds, which alone experience can furnish. We cannot too much or too often repeat our warning against this lax and even mean habit of thought which seeks for its principle amongst empirical motives and laws; for human reason in its weariness is glad to rest on this pillow, and in a dream of sweet illusions (in which, instead of Juno, it embraces a cloud) it substitutes for morality a bastard patched up from limbs of various derivation, which looks like anything one chooses to see in it; only not like virtue to one who has once beheld her in her true form.

To behold virtue in her proper form is nothing else but to contemplate morality stripped of all admixture of sensible things and of every spurious ornament of reward or self-love. How much she then eclipses everything else that appears charming to the affections, every one may readily perceive with the least exertion of his reason, if it be not wholly spoiled for abstraction.

An Elucidation of the "Good Will"

Although Kant's analysis is somewhat difficult to understand, by working together we can lucidly unpack the significance and importance of his moral theory. Recall that Kant begins his analysis with the assertion that nothing is good in itself but the *good will.* Using the process of exclusion, Kant considers other concepts which might be suggested as goods in themselves. Kant argues that all such substitutions will fail. Talents or natural gifts cannot be classified as goods in themselves, Kant suggests, because they can easily be misused. A criminal may have an IQ of 155. Insofar as fortune and personal wealth can cause much ill will, neither can they alone be considered as goods in themselves. Yet what about happiness? Mill's utilitarianism asserted unequivocally that the criterion for moral worth was the production of the greatest amount of pleasure for the greatest number of people. Kant suggests that often ostensively evil persons may exhibit the characteristics of happiness, especially if the concept of happiness is closely associated with pleasure; of course, this connection held with the hedonistic naturalism of Bentham and Mill. At times, Kant appears to suggest that a lucid analysis of the concept of happiness is extremely difficult to come by. At other times, there is the hint that Kant accepts the hedonist suggestion that happiness is equivalent to pleasure. Whatever his position, Kant is adamant in affirming that happiness is not the basis for moral worth. But what about the virtues so strongly extolled by certain religious groups—moderation, self-control, and so forth. Kant responds that even a villain could possess these qualities; if this can occur, then virtues such as self-control cannot be the basis for defining morality. The point of Kant's analysis so far is to force us to consider the conceptual difference between useful effects and moral worth. As a proponent of a deontological normative theory of morality, Kant must assert this conceptual difference.

Kant further suggests that if happiness is the end of human activity, and if humans are considered to be "rational animals," then reason is not such a good guide for attaining happiness. Kant argues that instinct rather than reason would be a better guide for attaining the pleasurable fulfillments of human drives. He also realizes that the more a person rationally attempts to attain pleasure, the less pleasure is actually obtained. Joseph Butler (1692-1752) referred to this problem as the *hedonistic paradox*. Simply put, if we seek pleasure as an end in and of itself, we seldom find it. Pleasure, on the other hand, is a resultant property of enjoyed activities. Pleasure accompanies our involvement in various types of activities rather than functioning as an explicit end sought for itself. To seek pleasure alone is never to attain it. Kant agrees with Butler about the appropriateness of the hedonistic paradox. Have you ever experienced this paradox? Think for a moment about what must happen if a pleasant experience is to occur. If we seek pleasure alone, we seldom find it. Throughout his analysis, Kant would accept Aristotle's observation that "to seek utility everywhere is entirely unsuited to persons who are great-souled and free."

We must now begin a conceptual analysis of Kant's notion of the *good will*. Kant explains this concept by carefully "unpacking" what he considers to be foremost in the concept of morality. According to Kant, the primary characteristic of morality is *duty*. Philosophers sometimes have referred to the concept of duty as the "ought situation." The notion of duty brings out the concept of obligation. Kant suggests that the primary difference between a factual situation and a moral situation is the dimension of obligation. This dimension entails that more is required of a moral agent in an ought situation than in a merely factual, descriptive situation. In an ought situation, the agent must command himself/herself to do or avoid doing some specific action. The concept of obligation, therefore, has a "prescriptive" dimension rather than existing merely with a descriptive function. Kant suggests that the conditions necessary for an adequate conceptual analysis of the good will emerge when the concept of duty is subject to careful elucidation. Simply, duty or obligation is the *salient feature* of the moral consciousness. Accordingly, an adequate clarification of moral worth will follow only from a careful analysis of the concept of duty.

In the process of providing a careful interpretation of the concept of duty, Kant stresses three propositions.

PROPOSITION ONE: *For an action to have moral worth, it must be done from duty.* In this discussion, Kant forces us to confront the conceptual difference between having an "inclination" to do an action and having an "obligation" to do an action. The tension between inclination and obligation engulfs Kant's entire treatment of moral philosophy. With this in mind, Kant provides us with the following distinction:

a. An action which *conforms to* or *is in accord with* duty.

b. An action which is done *from* or *for the sake of* duty.

Recall the example Kant used to bring out this distinction. We have a situation in which a shopkeeper does not overcharge or cheat his customers. Yet the mere descriptive facts of this situation do not interest Kant. Rather, he is interested in discovering the motive from which the shopkeeper acted in deciding not to overcharge or cheat his customers. In the situation under discussion, Kant postulates the case in which the shopkeeper does not overcharge or cheat on *prudential* grounds alone. It is bad for his business, so the shopkeeper thinks, if he overcharges or cheats and thus becomes known as a dishonest merchant.

Why does Kant ask that we consider this case? Look again at the above distinction. An action which conforms to duty is one which just *happens* to be in accord with what the moral law dictates. However, the proper motive necessary to establish moral worth is absent. This example provides us with an indication that motive will serve an important function in Kant's complete analysis of actions with moral worth. An action done *from* or *for the sake of duty* is one undertaken only because it is a right action. The action is done because it is right and for that reason alone. In the case of the shopkeeper, the action of being honest was undertaken not because it is a right action but rather because it is good for business not to be dishonest. To reiterate briefly. The shopkeeper could undertake actions of honesty toward his customers for at least two kinds of reasons:

a. on *prudential grounds*—it is not good for business to be dishonest;

b. *for the sake of duty*—because dishonesty is contrary to the demands of the moral law.

With the utilitarian emphasis on only the effects of actions undertaken, could John Stuart Mill have argued for this distinction? Why or why not?

Given the above distinction, note that if an action merely conforms to duty, it is not a wrong action. It is merely an action which lacks moral worth. To possess the characteristic of moral worth, an action must be undertaken solely for the sake of duty. Actions done from instinct, inclination, or undertaken for prudential grounds alone lack the purity of intention demanded for moral worth. Moral worth, according to Kant, is attributed to only those actions which proceed from the motive of respect for the moral law. Further analysis of the characteristics of this intention will occur as we proceed with our analysis of Kant's moral theory. At any length, because of this discussion, there emerge three types of actions in Kant's normative theory:

1. Morally right actions
2. Morally neutral actions
3. Morally wrong actions

So far, Kant has provided us with a criterion enabling us to distinguish between actions which have moral worth (morally right actions) and actions which are morally neutral. Kant has not indicated what counts for an immoral or wrong action.

At this point, it might be worthwhile to briefly discuss Kant's treatment of duty and inclination. Kant often gives the impression that moral worth increases the less one desires or has an inclination to undertake a particular action. It seems that the more we are disinclined to undertake actions which we perceive to be duties yet still perform, the better off we are from a moral perspective. The more we overcome our inclinations and stick to our duty, the more moral worth is attained. One problem with this interpretation is that it runs counter to the notion of an "integrated personality." What if a person has practiced acting for the sake of duty for so long that he or she now desires or is inclined to undertake only those actions which duty prescribes? This would be the blissful state at which desires and duty are united. Kant appears to look askance at such a union. However it certainly seems logically possible for such a union to occur.

PROPOSITION TWO: *An action done from duty acquires moral worth, not from any end produced or achieved, but from the maxim by which the action is determined.* This proposition explicitly indicates the deontological character of Kant's normative ethical theory. The motive—what Kant refers to in proposition two as the "maxim"—is all important in determining the moral worth of the action, while the consequences of the action are completely irrelevant.

At this point, Kant introduces some strange terminology. One type of maxim is called a *subjective principle of volition.* This simply refers to the particular action which an individual agent is inclined to undertake. Consider the three concepts employed in describing the category of subjective principle of volition. "Subjective" refers to one's private motives or inclinations. "Volition" refers to the process of willing or wanting; this is the inclination to undertake a particular course of action. "Principle" is derived from the Latin term, *principium.* This term is best translated as a source or point of origin. In combining all three of these concepts, we have the "source of one's private inclinations." This is Kant's meaning for the subjective principle of volition, otherwise known as a maxim from which a moral agent undertakes a singular action.

An *objective principle of volition* introduces the dimension of "universalizability," which was considered previously in our discussion of the characteristics necessary for the adoption of the moral point of view. An objective principle of volition refers to an action which might be legitimately undertaken in a given set of circumstances by any human agent found in those circumstances. The maxim is no longer limited to individual inclination but is universalized to cover any person who is subject to the given circumstances. The import of proposition two is that an individual maxim—i.e., a private *subjective* principle of volition—must be universalized and become an *objective* principle of volition in order for the action to acquire moral worth and thus be done *for the sake of duty.* Obviously, Kant's discussion of these issues is not self-evidently clear and certainly demands further explication. The most fruitful way to understand Kant's purpose in introducing the objective principle of volition is to proceed to an analysis of proposition three. In so doing, we can arrive at a clearer insight of the objective principle of volition.

PROPOSITION THREE: *Duty is the necessity of acting from respect for the moral law.* Respect for the moral law means that an individual maxim becomes a universal law. It is objective, i.e., applies to all instances which are relevantly similar. It advances beyond the subjective level at which a maxim might be merely a selfish inclination. What is this moral law? To answer this question, Kant provides the first formulation of the categorical imperative. "I am never to act otherwise than so that I could also will that my maxim should become a universal law." A universal law entails that any person may do the same action you are contemplating doing if they find themselves in the same set of relevantly similar circumstances that you find yourself in right now. In other words, if I want to perform a certain action—which means I have a maxim (a subjective principle of volition)—and if I want to determine if that action has moral worth, then I must discover if I am willing to admit that any other persons finding themselves in relevantly similar circumstances could act just as I am now proposing to act.

To illustrate this point, let's take one of Kant's examples: "Should I make a false promise." Imagine a situation in which you must make a false promise. You need one hundred dollars quickly. If you can convince a friend to lend you the money, you may have the money quickly. However you have just accepted a job offer in Australia and plan never to return to your home in this country. You need the one hundred dollars and you promise your friend you'll repay him in one month. Yet you have no intention of every repaying him because you'll be in Australia in two weeks and will probably never see him again. How can you determine if making a false promise is a moral or an immoral action? Kant suggests that you must be willing to *universalize* over your maxim. If your maxim can be successfully universalized, then it will become an objective principle of volition. If this happens, then your action will have moral worth. In the case at hand, you must pass your maxim—your *inclination* to make a false promise—through the test of universalizability. As we shall see, this is what Kant refers to as the test of the categorical imperative.

In the case of making a false promise, is your maxim capable of being universalized? If in the attempt at universalizing, a self-defeating characteristic— what Kant refers to as a contradiction—arises, then the maxim cannot be universalized. The occurrence of a contradiction prevents the maxim from being universalized. Think what would happen if the maxim for making a false promise was universalized. Then everyone could make a false promise anytime the situation seemed convenient. If this happened, the entire practice of "promise-keeping" would fall apart. No one would ever believe another person when he or she attempted to make a false promise. If it was customary for everyone not to keep a promise, would anyone believe another person when a promise was made? Of course not.

But notice how this affects your present situation of needing one hundred dollars. You have an inclination to make a false promise. In order to be successful at making this promise, your friend *must believe* you. A person to whom you are making a promise must believe that you truly intend to fulfill your side of the bargain. In this case, your friend must trust that you will repay him within one month's time, as you stipulated in your promising statement. Accordingly, a person to whom a promise is made must accept in principle the practice of promise-keeping. But we just saw what would happen if your maxim was universalized: the practice of promise-keeping would be destroyed. There would no longer be an accepted practice of promise-keeping because everyone would realize that any promise-making situation is inherently bogus. People would no longer believe a promise-maker. It is at this point that the contradiction arises. When you universalize over your maxim, you destroy the practice of promise-keeping, but you need that very practice in order to carry out your intention in making a false promise. You can't make a false promise if no one will believe you. Therefore making a false promise, when universalized, destroys the very moral practice which is needed in order to make the initial false promise.

Kant's theory affirms that in the case of making a false promise, you cannot universalize over your subjective principle of volition. Insofar as universalizing cannot obtain, then the maxim cannot become an *objective* principle of volition. However, in order for an action to have moral worth, it must be capable of being undertaken from an objective principle of volition. Therefore the inclination to make a false promise can never be an action possessing moral worth because it can never be undertaken from an objective principle of volition. The impossibility of universalizing over the maxim entails that the subjective principle of volition will never attain the status of an objective principle of volition. Thus, unless a maxim can be universalized, it cannot possess the characteristic of moral worth. If an action is to have moral worth, it must be done from a proper intention. This is Kant's formalism. A proper intention is only obtained if one's subjective maxim is capable of being universalized. The impossibility of universalizability entails the impossibility of moral worth. An action will possess moral worth only if it is undertaken from the perspective of a universalized maxim. The process of universalizability is necessary in order for Kant to distinguish between proper and improper intentions.

Hypothetical and Categorical Imperatives

Within the text of *Fundamental Principles of the Metaphysics of Morals,* Kant affirms an important distinction between a *hypothetical* imperative and a *categorical* imperative. A hypothetical imperative is one based upon inclination. An action undertaken from the basis of a hypothetical imperative is always a *means* to some additional goal beyond the action itself. The logical form of a hypothetical imperative is: "If I want to attain X, then I must do Y." For instance, "If I want to learn French, then I must study the vocabulary listings" or "If I want to lose weight, then I must not drink too much beer." In both of these cases, the action undertaken—studying the vocabulary listings or avoiding too much beer drinking—is determined by an end extrinsic to the action itself. In other words, I undertake the activities of studying or avoiding drinking too much beer not on account of these actions in and of themselves. Rather, these actions are undertaken as *means* necessary for the attainment of a further goal. Parenthetically, we should note that Kant would place a teleological theory of ethics into the category of hypothetical imperatives.

A categorical imperative, on the other hand, is done for a reason contained within *itself.* The logical form of the categorical form is: "Do X!" An action is done for itself. It is never undertaken as a means toward the attainment of a further goal. The commanding force of the categorical imperative prescribes that an action be undertaken because of the very nature of the action itself. As we shall see, moral rules are categorical imperatives. Actions of moral worth must be undertaken from the form of the categorical imperative and not from the form of the hypothetical imperative. They must be undertaken for their own sake and not for any extrinsic reason. Think back to the distinction Kant made between an action done *from* or *for the sake of duty* and actions which merely *conform* to duty. An action which only conforms to duty is undertaken from the perspective of a hypothetical imperative. Given this discussion, we should see more clearly why Kant rejected utilitarianism.

It is now time to examine closely the four examples Kant uses in establishing the inherent self-defeating characteristic of immoral actions. Kant suggests that, in the following cases, examples *A* and *B* are contradictions in the *law* while examples *C* and *D* are contradictions in the *will*. Notice the formulation of the categorial imperative that Kant has provided us with: "Act as if the maxim of your action were to become through your will a universal law of nature." This formulation explicitly applies to examples *A* and *B* which follow. Kant asks if the maxim, when universalized, causes a contradiction within the system of nature of which it is a part. In other words, will the universalized principle produce a contradiction within the system itself.

EXAMPLE A: In the case of suicide, Kant argues that a contradiction results within the system itself. Suicide, Kant suggests, is a case of self-love destroying self-love. In this discussion, Kant assumes that the psychological source of all of our actions is a vague principle called "self-love." Second, Kant seems to accept a teleological system of nature. In this case, self-love is ordered to the improvement and fulfillment of a living person's natural capacities. Since self-love is the source of all of our actions, in the case of suicide, this principle— which is directed toward fulfillment and completion—is also the source of destruction. The same principle, self-love, is ordered to complete and destroy at the same time. This is a contradiction within the system of nature. In this case, the system of nature is the structure of the human personality. Schematically, we might outline the contradiction in the following way:

$$\begin{pmatrix} \text{Self-love} \\ \text{to improve} \end{pmatrix} \quad + \quad \begin{pmatrix} \text{Self-love} \\ \text{to destroy} \end{pmatrix} \quad = \quad \begin{matrix} \text{CONTRADICTION} \\ \text{IN NATURE} \end{matrix}$$

EXAMPLE B: We have already discussed in detail the origin of the contradiction in the case of making false promises. The case of promising to repay a debt, yet intending all the while not to repay it, can be illustrated in the following way:

$$\begin{pmatrix} \text{Universalized maxim would} \\ \text{destroy promise-keeping} \end{pmatrix} + \begin{pmatrix} \text{Maxim presupposes} \\ \text{promise-keeping} \end{pmatrix} = \begin{matrix} \text{CONTRADICTION} \\ \text{IN NATURE} \end{matrix}$$

In examples *A* and *B*, there is a contradiction in the very system itself. We will recall that, from working plane geometry in secondary school, a system containing a contradiction will never work. In Kant's moral theory, any action which, when universalized, engenders a contradiction in a system will be immoral. A necessary condition for establishing the immorality of an action is the realization of a contradiction when the maxim from which the action is undertaken is universalized.

The following examples, *C* and *D,* are illustrations of an inability to consistently *will* the maxim when universalized rather than the realization of a contradiction within a system. In these two examples, Kant suggests that, even though the system of nature would not realize a contradiction and thus would be able to continue in existence when the maxim is universalized, nonetheless the will of the moral agent would be inconsistent. Accordingly, the criterion of universalizability for examples C and D is "Can the maxim be *willed consistently*?" rather than "Does a contradiction obtain in a *system of nature*?" An inconsistent will is a sufficient condition for discovering the objective character of an immoral action.

EXAMPLE C: This is the case of the willful neglect of natural gifts and talents. Kant argues that a system of nature might well subsist even though everyone in this particular system neglected the development of their natural talents. Recall that Kant considered the South Sea islanders to be an illustration of a people fitting into this category. Contemporary anthropologists might very well disagree with Kant on this point. Even though there is no contradiction in nature—and Kant believes that the very existence of the South Sea islanders is explicit evidence of this fact—Kant asks about the consistent willing of the maxim to neglect the development of one's talents. Kant appears to suggest that a rational being necessarily wills that his faculties be developed. Otherwise stagnation will result. The contradiction in will might be illustrated in the following manner:

$$\begin{pmatrix} \text{Inclination not to} \\ \text{develop one's} \\ \text{natural talents} \end{pmatrix} \quad + \quad \begin{pmatrix} \text{Rational Beings will} \\ \text{necessarily that} \\ \text{talents be developed} \end{pmatrix} \quad = \quad \begin{array}{l} \text{CONTRADICTION} \\ \text{IN WILL} \end{array}$$

In example C, Kant appears to presuppose that it is a property of a rational being to will to develop his or her natural talents. Yet, because of the freedom of the will, this is not a natural necessity but a moral necessity. That this objection depends upon Kant's unique view of the rational nature of human agents is obvious.

EXAMPLE D: With this case, Kant suggests that one cannot will consistently to ignore others who might be in distress. Kant assumes that a person might indeed need the aid of another at some later time. However, if he universalizes his maxim not to come to the aid of his fellowman, then he excludes from realization the possibility that others will come to aid him if he is in some future state of need. A schematic outline of this example is as follows:

$$\begin{pmatrix} \text{No concern for} \\ \text{others in time} \\ \text{of great need} \end{pmatrix} \quad + \quad \begin{pmatrix} \text{When universalized,} \\ \text{this would apply to} \\ \text{everyone, including} \\ \text{the selfish person} \end{pmatrix} \quad = \quad \begin{array}{l} \text{CONTRADICTION} \\ \text{IN WILL} \end{array}$$

Both sets of examples illustrate the occurrence of a contradiction as a result of universalizing over a maxim. Examples A and B illustrate a necessary condition for rejecting a maxim as being immoral, while examples C and D illustrate a sufficient condition.

It is extremely important that we carefully notice the *objective foundation* Kant has established in order to ascertain the moral worth of actions and, a fortiori, of intentions or motives. Motive or intention does not refer to simply "meaning well" when undertaking actions. The only morally acceptable intention is acting out of "respect for the moral law." Acting out of respect for the moral law obtains only when a moral agent avoids undertaking those actions which, when universalized, bring about a contradiction. And a contradiction may be realized either in the system itself or within the will undertaking the action. These contradictions have an objective character to them. Just as a triangle cannot have four sides in plane geometry, no matter who is considering the problem, so too will an immoral action be objectively contradictory, no matter who is considering the action. With this objective dimension, the contradictions hold for every human being. Therefore the contradictions which arise through immoral actions will obtain universally for every rational agent. In this way, Kant has established an objective groundwork for a moral theory. It is indeed a metaphysics of morals.

Rationality as the Foundation for Morality

An obvious question concerns the relationship between a contradiction and immorality. Kant explicitly affirms this connection. Kant's presuppositions appear to be as follows. Just as the principle of contradiction is that without which we cannot reason, so too is the categorical imperative that without which we cannot have any moral system. Think for a moment what would happen if everyone contradicted themselves all of the time. No one would ever exercise belief in the words of another. Eventually forms of communication would break down. This is why Aristotle argued in his *Metaphysics* that the principle of contradiction is that without which we cannot exercise rationality.

In situations of both communication and morality, a contradiction is self-defeating. As a contradiction in communication defeats communication itself, so too does a contradiction in morality defeat either the system to which it belongs or the consistency of the willing process. Extrapolating from this, Kant urges all of us to apply reason to our moral lives. Consistency, which is the act of being consistent in our reasoning process, is the characterizing feature of a rational life. Kant argues that the application of reason to moral processes results in the command, "Be Rational!" or "Be Consistent!" This is just another translation for the categorical imperative. The ground for the categorical imperative is rationality. Kant regards rationality as an objective end in itself. It is worthwhile in its very nature. Insofar as it is worthwhile in itself, it demands respect and possesses intrinsic dignity. The *good will* is reason exercised in a moral matter. From this discussion we can now understand why Kant initially referred to the good will as the only thing good in itself. It is really the principle of rationality, and this principle alone possesses intrinsic dignity.

It is worthwhile to emphasize Kant's view of human nature. A human being is essentially rational. In defending rationalist ethics, Kant has argued that every immoral action is indeed a contradiction. A contradiction is fundamentally irrational; it strikes at the very root of rationality. It is fruitful in attempting to understand Kant's moral philosophy to extrapolate this account of irrationality into the moral sphere. Consider the following propositions:

    A. A contradiction strikes at the very roots of rationality.
    B. A human being is fundamentally rational.

C. An immoral action lacks moral worth insofar as it is a contradiction.

D. Therefore, an immoral action, because it is a contradiction, strikes at the root of human nature.

Because an immoral action is a contradiction and because human beings are essentially rational, Kant affirms that immorality strikes at the very basis of humanity. An action is immoral for the simple reason that it is an *inhuman* or *nonhuman* action. Insofar as immorality implies a contradiction, to undertake immoral actions is to undertake contradictory actions. This strikes at the very groundwork of our humanity as rational beings. Kant's metaphysical system serves as the ultimate groundwork for his moral theory. Because humans are essentially rational beings and immorality entails irrationality through contradictory actions, in order for us to act in accord with our human nature, we must act morally. In the Kantian system, immorality is fundamentally an exemplification of irrationality.

Kant is to be congratulated for his insistence on the dignity of human beings in an age of scientific revolution. For Kant, the *intrinsic dignity* of all humans is a given. It is fundamentally rooted in rationality. Recall the second formulation of the categorical imperative given above in Kant's text: "So act as to treat humanity always at the same time as an end, and never as a means." Kant stresses this point again in the third formulation of the categorical imperative: "The will of every rational being is a universally legislative will." Kant discusses the "kingdom of ends." This refers to the sought-after time when all human agents will act from the categorical imperative. All humans will treat each other as ends and never as means to obtain further ends. The following maxim has been used to characterize human relationships in the twentieth century: "People treat things as ends and people as means." Kant would find the acceptance of such a principle as morally abhorrent. This dimension of intrinsic human dignity characteristic of Kantian morality is well worth our deepest consideration.

This insight regarding intrinsic dignity is emphasized in Kant's "Treatise on Perpetual Peace." He firmly argues that any monarch who employs soldiers in aggressive wars undertaken for nationalistic interests or kingly avarice is using rational beings as mere means to a further end. In Kant's view, standing armies should be abolished in the course of time. Kant held this position because he considered that the employment of human beings to kill or to be killed necessarily involved a use of them as mere pragmatic instruments in the hands of the rulers of the state. This situation, Kant stresses, is irreconcilable with the basic dignity of human beings founded upon rationality. It would be well for us to consider Kant's message. Two extremely important propositions follow from Kant's treatment of moral philosophy:

1. Human beings are never to be used as a means for some other end.

2. Human beings must be respected and valued as intrinsically worthwhile.

In this regard, Kant's system of normative ethics avoids many of the objections raised against standard forms of utilitarianism. Schematically, we might structure the development and analysis of Kant's moral theory in the following way:

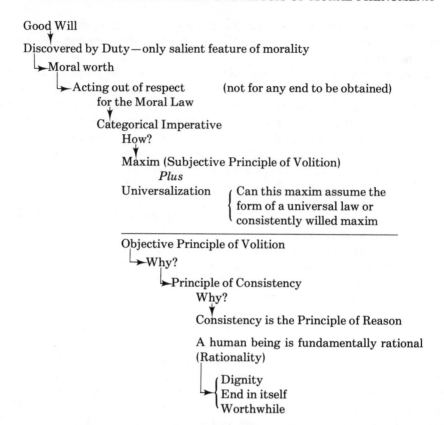

Good Will

Discovered by Duty—only salient feature of morality

↳Moral worth

↳Acting out of respect   (not for any end to be obtained)
for the Moral Law

Categorical Imperative
How?

Maxim (Subjective Principle of Volition)
Plus
Universalization   { Can this maxim assume the
form of a universal law or
consistently willed maxim

Objective Principle of Volition

↳Why?

↳Principle of Consistency
Why?

Consistency is the Principle of Reason

A human being is fundamentally rational
(Rationality)

{ Dignity
↳{ End in itself
{ Worthwhile

Philosophers have suggested the following problems associated with Kant's analysis of the categorical imperative:

The categorical imperative is primarily a *formal* principle. We are told to universalize over our subjective maxims. However Kant's theory tells us very little, if anything, about the content of morally relevant characteristics. Conversely, we are told little about what might count for nonmorally relevant characteristics. Kant might respond by asserting that his intention in writing the *Fundamental Principles of the Metaphysics of Morals* was to elucidate just the formal characteristic necessary to a justified moral theory. The analysis of the categorical imperative does just that. However it is still a legitimate question to seek for the content of morally significant properties. It has been suggested that the definite lack of content in Kant's normative ethical theory is a fundamental weakness with his theory.

In his excellent treatment of the issues in twentieth-century moral philosophy, *Contemporary Moral Philosophy*, G.J. Warnock has made some astute observations about the principle of universalizability as used in R.M. Hare's influential book, *Freedom and Reason*. In the following passage from his book, Warnock is principally interested in Hare's thesis of universalizability. The observations Warnock makes, however, are easily extrapolated to Kant's version of the categorical imperative as discussed above. There are important similarities between Hare's and Kant's accounts of universalizability. Warnock is explicitly interested in the problem of lack of content in regard to the principle of universalizability.

ARGUMENT IN MORALS

G.J. Warnock

We took note, in introducing the prescriptivist amendment to emotivism, that it had at least *prima facie* the considerable advantage of not representing moral discourse and debate as fundamentally non-rational. To guide, we observed, unlike to influence, is essentially to engage in a rational activity; advice, whether accepted or not, may be good or bad, I may have good or bad reasons for offering you the guidance I do. But now we must observe that this advantage turns out to be illusory: prescriptivism too canot find much place for argument.

In Hare's own account of moral reasoning, very great importance is attached to the feature of moral judgment, already mentioned, which he calls 'universalisability'. It is, Hare seems to say—and, as we shall see, not without reason—solely in virtue of this feature that argument, properly so called, is possible in morals; and he is naturally disposed to make quite substantial claims as to what such argument can achieve. Now to say that any proposition in morals is 'universalisable' is, as we briefly noted earlier, to say that one who affirms or accepts that proposition is thereby committed—as a matter of loci—to a certain view of any cases of a certain kind. For me to assert that you ought not to do X in situation Y commits me, as a matter of logic, to the general 'principle' that no one should do things *like X* in situations *like Y*—'like' meaning here 'not relevantly distinguishable from'. Generality of this sort is implicit in all moral judgment.

Now one might think at first sight that, while argument on the basis of this feature is certainly possible, yet such argument could not really achieve very much. For what, on the basis of this feature, can be argued about? What is put in issue? It is plain, I think, that what is put in issue is simply consistency. To appeal, in discussion of some moral judgment that I make, to the feature of universalisability is not to raise the question whether my judgment of the case before me is *right,* but only the question whether it is the same as, or compatible with, the judgments that I make or would make of other cases of the same kind. It is not, indeed, that this matter is unimportant. For people are indeed very commonly prone, from prejudice or bigotry or thoughtlessness, to judge differently cases which are not relevantly different—to make, for example, unjustifiable exceptions in favour of themselves or their friends, and to the detriment of foreigners, or political opponents, persons they dislike, or persons whose existence is inconvenient to them. And in such cases they may indeed be logically obliged—though not necessarily induced—to change or amend their judgments, when the requirement of consistent universalisability is forced upon their attention. Nevertheless, if it appears to you that my judgment of some particular case is morally quite wrong, you may well achieve nothing by appealing to universalisability; for all that may emerge may be that I am

From *Contemporary Moral Philosophy* (London and Basingstoke: Macmillan & Co., 1967), pp. 42–47. Reprinted by permission of Macmillan London and Basingstoke and St. Martin's Press, Inc.

perfectly prepared to make the same (in your view) wrong judgment of any case of this kind. All my standards and principles may seem to you highly objectionable; but, provided that I apply them consistently in every case, they will be quite invulnerable to any argument of this pattern.

But is this point, one may wonder, too abstractly stated? Is the case we envisage really, and not merely theoretically, a possible one? It is easy to say that, in theory, practically any moral judgment, however objectionable, might be consistently 'universalised', and so might stand unscathed against argument founded upon this consideration. But may it not be the case in fact that not many highly objectionable judgments actually would emerge from such scrutiny unscathed? One might think that this would probably be so for the following reason. What is really objectionable, one might think, about many objectionable moral judgments is that one who makes them does so in disregard of, or without giving proper weight to, the wants, or the needs, or the interests, of those concerned (other than himself); he ignores, let us say, or does not properly consider, the fact that the interests of other persons will be gravely damaged by the course of action which he professes morally to approve. But if so—if he is prepared seriously to hold, as a general principle, that such action to the detriment of others' interests is to be morally approved—we can point out that, in virtue of the condition of universalisability, he is committed to approving of the neglect or damage of *his own* interests if and when, as may occur, he is himself in the position of those whose interests will be damaged by the action in this case. If their interests may properly be neglected now, so, when he finds himself in their shoes, may his. But surely only the most irrational of men could want the neglect or frustration of his own interests; and if so, the requirement of universalisability may seem to impose upon any rational man the condition that, in his practical judgments, he *must* pay that regard to the interests of others which, in general, he would want to be paid to his own interests. And it is plain that this would constitute, in practice, a condition of very substantial moral significance and effect.

I think, however, that there is an important equivocation here. It is true—perhaps even necessarily true—that no rational man *wants* the frustration of what he sees as his own interests, or *likes* it when his interests are frustrated. But then what a man wants, or would like, is scarcely the point at issue here: the question is what he would morally approve or find morally objectionable; and that, of course, may not be at all the same thing. If I commend, or adopt as right, some course of action which grossly damages the interests of another, you may point out to me, correctly no doubt, that I would not like it if my own interests were damaged in that way; there is, however, no reason why I should not admit this, and yet still maintain that, if our positions were reversed, that other person would be *right* to damage my interests exactly as I now propose to damage his. The ruthless landlord, for instance, on the point of ejecting his aged, ailing, and needy tenants into the snow, may concede not only that they will greatly dislike this treatment, but that he himself would dislike it no less if he were in their place; nevertheless, he may hold, it is right that they should be ejected, and that he himself should be ejected too, if he were in similar case. That he would not like it, he says, is neither here nor there; the point is that business is business, the economic show must go on. In order, that is, consistently to defend as unobjectionable my neglect of another's interests, I do not have to go to the somewhat unbalanced length of positively wanting my own interests to be neglected, or of somehow not disliking it when they are: all that I am required to do is to concede that neglect of my own interests by others would be unobjectionable. And there is nothing particularly strained or unbalanced about this; it is, for instance, the very essence of the gospel of self-help, of untrammelled competition in the old capitalist style—a gospel which, however morally disagreeable one may find it, has been consistently adopted by very many entirely sane men, and not only by those who have been winners in the jungle war. A man cannot, in effect, by the argument from universalisability, be constrained to attach *much* weight, if any, to the interests of others; for he may be entirely ready to concede that others are not morally required to attach much weight, if any, to his own, however intensely he may dislike it when, in the competitive free-for-all, it happens that he comes out on the losing side. But if this is true, the requirement of universalisability appears, whether in theory or in practice, to set almost no limit to the practical judgments which *can* be consistently made and maintained by sane men; and if so, it does not, as a weapon of moral argument, carry much fire-power.

Why then is Hare inclined to make such large claims for this real, but limited, dialectical weapon? Because (it is not, I think, unfair to say) his doctrine does not allow for genuine argument of any other kind. I asked to give reasons for some moral view I have expressed—that is, on this view, for some 'prescription' that I have issued—I may do one or both of two things: I may adduce certain facts about the case under consideration, or some principle, or principles, of which my presently-expressed view is an instance or application. But my principles, of course, are on this view themselves 'prescriptions' of mine; and such facts as I may adduce about the present case constitute *reasons* for my expressed view of it in so far as I have adopted, i.e. 'prescribed', some principle in accordance with which that view is derivable from those facts. Thus my giving of 'reasons' for my expressed prescription consists, on this view, essentially of my referring to and relying on *further* prescriptions of my own: what are reasons for me, are, for you, not only not necessarily good reasons, but possibly not reasons at all. And thus, what we speak of as argument between two parties emerges essentially as nothing more than the articulation by each of his own position. For you to say that my view is *wrong* is to say only that your position excludes that view; for me to 'argue' that my view is *right* is to show only that my position includes it. And there is nothing else, on this view, that argument can do; for there are no 'reasons' that either party can appeal to independently of, and so genuinely in support of, his own pre-scriptions. In this way it must inevitably appear to Hare that *real* argument can address itself only to the question of consistency; for so long as a man prescribes consistently, then on this view he has (since he has provided himself with) all the 'reasons' that any of his particular pronouncements may require; and if I have 'reasons' for views that differ from his, he need claim only that my reasons are not reasons for him.

It is, I believe, often not really noticed how surprising (at least) Hare's view of this question is. Most of us, no doubt, would agree readily enough that in moral matters we have to make up our own minds; we ourselves must decide on, embrace, commit ourselves to our moral standpoint. Further, we are probably ready enough to agree that moral discourse seems little susceptible of demonstrative argument; we have seldom much hope, in moral controversy, of confronting an opponent with a cogent proof of our views. Now it may seem that Hare is saying no more than this; but he is saying much more. For he is saying, not only that it is for us to decide what our moral opinions are, but also that it is for us to decide what to take as grounds for or against any moral opinion. We are not only, as it were, free to decide on the evidence, but also free to decide what evidence is. I do not, it seems, decide that flogging is wrong because I *am* against cruelty; rather, I decide that flogging is wrong because I *decide to be* against cruelty. And what, if I did make that decision, would be my ground for making it? That I am opposed to the deliberate infliction of pain? No—rather that I *decide to be* opposed to it. And so on. Now there are people, I think, whose moral views do seem to be formed and defended in this way—who, as one might say, not only make up their own minds, but also make up their own evidence; who pick and choose not only on the question what is right or wrong, but also on the question what are even to be admitted as relevant considerations. But such a person, surely, is not so much a model as a menace; not an exemplar of moral reasoning, but a total abstainer from any serious concern with reason. And if this really were a general feature of the human predicament, then to find cogent arguments in morals would not merely be difficult; it would be as hopeless as trying to play a competitive game in which each competitor was making up his own rules as he went along. All this is a matter to which we shall return in due course.

Simple maxims, when universalized, might indeed become too rigorous. Kant appears to adopt a form of rule deontology. Certain moral rules are derived by means of the categorical imperative. These moral rules hold for every moral agent. We have observed what Kant said about never making false promises. This can be extrapolated to the case of never telling lies. But what if one had to tell a lie in order to save a life? We might refer to this case as one of "life-saving lies." To expand our maxim, the subjective principle of volition could be enlarged to include as a relevant characteristic the situation of needing to lie in order to save a life. If this can occur, however, when do we draw the line as to what stops the process of expansion? Some philosophers, especially followers of situationalist ethics and some existentialists, have asserted that every moral situation is, in itself, unique. Given this fundamental uniqueness of every moral situation, it is impossible to derive a maxim which is capable of universalization. Combining this uniqueness of moral situations with the expandability of maxims, one might argue that in order to discover an adequate maxim for each moral situation, the maxim would be expanded so much to cover the relevant properties that it would be impossible to ever engage in the process of universalization. At root issue here is the charge that moral situations are indeed unique. If this uniqueness holds, then it would be impossible to universalize over any maxims. Is a moral situation so unique that it is logically impossible that a rule or set of rules might apply to the situation? The contemporary British philosopher, R.M. Hare, has the following to say regarding the purported uniqueness of all moral situations:

> If some British admirers of the Existentialists were to be followed, we should all be like the latter person; we should say to ourselves that people, and the situations in which they find themselves, are unique, and that therefore we must approach every new situation with a completely open mind and do our moral thinking about it *ab initio*. This is an absurd prescription, only made plausible by concentrating our attention, by means of novels and short stories, on moral situations of extreme complexity, which really do require a lot of consideration. It is important to realize that there are moral problems of this kind; but if *all* moral questions were treated like this, not only should we never get around to considering more than the first few that we happened to encounter, but any kind of moral development or learning from experience would be quite impossible. What the wiser among us do is to think deeply about the crucial moral questions, especially those that face us in our own lives; but when we have arrived at an answer to a particular problem, to crystallize it into not too specific or detailed form, so that its salient features may stand out and serve us again in a like situation without need for *so much* thought. We may then have time to think about *other* problems, and shall not continually be finding ourselves at a loss about what we ought to do.[11]

Kant would probably agree with Hare's response to those holding that all moral situations are indeed unique. The question we must ask ourselves is: Are there relevant similarities to moral situations which would make possible the development of moral rules by a process of universalization? The exact nature of a moral rule and its relation to particular circumstances will be discussed more in detail as we proceed into our consideration of Aristotle's *Nicomachean Ethics*.

One of the most influential of contemporary Kantian scholars, H.J. Paton, has written the following account in defense of what he takes to be some common misinterpretations of the *Fundamental Principles of the Metaphysics of Morals*. Paton suggests that Kant's formalism, legalism, and disregard of consequences are not sufficient grounds for rejecting his moral system. Pay close attention to Paton's defense of Kant. Does Paton satisfy our demands for making Kant's moral system indeed workable? The following passage has been taken from Paton's commentary on Kant's ethical theory entitled *The Categorical Imperative*.

SOME COMMON MISINTERPRETATIONS OF KANT

H.J. Paton

CRITICISMS

It may be thought that Kant's doctrine is paradoxical, and that we have somehow been tricked by the subtlety and complexity of the argument. We began with a good will 'shining like a jewel for its own sake.' We end with a merely formal maxim, a mysterious reverence for empty law as such, a

From H.J. Paton, *The Categorical Imperative* (London: Hutchinson Publishing Group, Ltd., 1947), pp. 74–77. Reprinted by permission of Hutchinson Publishing Group, Ltd.

vague principle of law-abidingness, and an unworkable test of universality for the maxims of our actions. All this formalism and legalism may leave us cold. Furthermore, it may be said, we have been argued gradually into a manifestly ludicrous view, the view that in determining our duty no account whatever is to be taken of the results sought or attained by our action.

These criticisms can be answered only by a re-examination of our previous argument and indeed of Kant's argument as a whole, but we may attempt to make brief comments on some of the points raised.

KANT'S FORMALISM

On the theoretical side there is little justification for complaining of Kant's formalism. We ought not to expect an abstract philosophical analysis of moral goodness to arouse the same warm emotion as may be aroused by the spectacle of a good man or a good action; nor is it the business of a moral philosopher to 'emotionalise the district'—to quote the phrase used by a disappointed American visitor to one of Professor Cook Wilson's lectures. Kant's terminology may be technical, but it was familiar in his time, if not in ours. It is well adapted to the expression of his meaning; nor is it on acquaintance more rebarbative than that of many modern philosophers.

It is hard to see why we should blame a philosopher for being too formal in dealing with the form of anything, even the form of morality. We do not blame Mr. Bertrand Russell because his logic is too formal, though some people may wish that he would write another kind of logic as well. Why should we complain that Kant's ethics is too formal, especially as he *has* written another kind of ethics, his *Metaphysics of Morals,* not to mention his *Lectures?* In the *Groundwork* Kant, as he says, is dealing with the supreme principle of morality: he is dealing with the *a priori* part of ethics in abstraction and considering the form of moral action apart from the matter. When Kant sets before himself a programme of this kind he is in the habit of sticking to it. It is hard to see why he should be blamed for keeping to his subject and excluding irrelevancies. It is still harder to see why he should be charged with forgetting that moral action has a matter as well as a form, an empirical as well as an *a priori* element, and an object as well as a supreme principle. Kant does not forget. He expects his readers to remember.

KANT'S LEGALISM

It may be replied that this answer does not really meet the criticism, which is concerned more with the formalism or legalism of his moral attitude than with his method of exposition. No doubt, it may be said, good men of a certain type may take a pride in obeying the law for the sake of law, and in controlling inclinations from the standpoint of a detached and unmoved reason; but it is a great mistake to identify such a type with the moral life at its best.

It is true that a man's philosophy, and especially his moral philosophy, takes a certain colour from his own individual moral attitude. This applies to Kant as to any one else, and may help to explain certain idiosyncrasies of emphasis and perspective; but I do not think it vitiates his analysis, and it certainly does not excuse us from meeting his arguments. Kant himself was a gentle and humane man with a passion for freedom and a hatred of intolerance: there is no evidence whatever to suggest that he was either cold or domineering or ascetic. I have tried to expose, in the course of my discussion, some of the misconceptions on which this charge of legalism is based; but there is one special point which must be added in the present connexion.

The main ground for charging Kant with legalism is the belief that he bids us perform our moral actions for the sake of a vague abstraction called the law, and thereby forbids us to perform moral actions for their own sake. Since this view is completely opposed to Kant's doctrine, and yet may easily be read into his language, I will try to make his position clear.

According to Kant every action aims at a result or end or object. In non-moral behavior we perform the action because we desire the object; we then have what Kant calls a 'pathological' interest in the object, and our interest in the action is *mediate*—that is, it depends on our interest in the object. In moral behaviour we perform the action because the action, aiming as it does at certain results, is an embodiment of the moral law; but it must not be supposed that the action is then willed only as a means to an empty abstraction called 'the law'. On the contrary, we take an *immediate* interest in the action itself 'when the universal validity of its maxim is a sufficient determining ground of the will'.[1] One of Kant's strongest convictions is that we take an *immediate* interest in moral actions. This is the reason why on his view actions done out of immediate inclinations, such as sympathy and benevolence, are more difficult to distinguish from moral actions than are actions done from self-interest, where there is no immediate inclination to the action. This immediate moral interest is indeed another name for 'reverence',[2] which we may feel for actions, and still more for persons, in whom the law is embodied.

I do not believe that there need be any real inconsistency in Kant about this: he is entitled to say both that we take an immediate interest in a moral action and that we do the action for the sake of the law. The category of means and end is inadequate to action, and grossly inadequate to moral action. The law is not for Kant an end to which the action is a means: it is the form or principle of the action itself. Although it is the condition of the action's goodness, it is nevertheless an element in the action itself.[3]

THE IGNORING OF CONSEQUENCES

Nothing, I suppose, will ever get rid of the illusion that for Kant a good man must take no account of consequences—in some sense which means that a good man must be a perfect fool. This interpretation rests on the ambiguities of language.[4] There is a sense in which the good man will take no account of consequences in deciding what he ought to do. He will not *begin* with the consequences and say that because an action will have certain consequences which he desires, therefore he will regard the action as his duty. He knows that it may be his duty not to produce results which he may greatly desire. Kant is right in saying that the expected consequences cannot be the *determining ground* of an action if it is to have moral worth. Nevertheless the good man begins with the *maxim* of a proposed action and asks himself whether the maxim can be willed as a universal law; and the maxim is always of the form 'if I am in certain circumstances, I will perform an action likely to have certain consequences'. How could we propose to steal or to kill or to act at all, if we ignored the fact that an action has consequences? Nevertheless we must not judge the action to be right or wrong according as we like or dislike the consequences. The test is whether the maxim of such an action is compatible with the nature of a universal law which is to hold for others as well as for myself. A good man aims at consequences because of the law: he does not obey the law merely because of the consequences.

Such is the simple and obvious truth so often caricatured. If Kant had said merely that we must not allow our desires for particular consequences to determine our judgment of what our duty is, he would have avoided a great deal of misunderstanding.

THE SOUNDNESS OF KANT'S DOCTRINE

One of the great merits of Kant's doctrine is the sharp distinction which he makes between the *a priori* and the empirical, between duty and inclination. Since he wrote, there is no longer any excuse for the muddled thinking which confuses *my* good with *the* good and consciously or unconsciously substitutes for the moral motive mere desire for our own personal happiness either in this world or the next. A veiled and unconscious hedonism is as corrupting as it is confused. The primary aim of a good man is not to satisfy his own inclinations, however generous, but to obey a law which is the same for all, and only so does he cease to be self-centered and become moral. There is no more fundamental difference than that between a life of prudence or self-love and one of moral goodness.

We cannot give a general description of moral action by reference to its objects, both because the objects of moral action vary indefinitely and because they may be produced by action which is not moral. Moral action must be described, not by its objects, but by its motive or principle or maxim; and this principle or maxim, for the same reasons as before, cannot *merely* be one of producing certain objects. The only possibility is that it should be a maxim of obeying a law which is the same for all: in Kant's language, it must be a formal maxim.

A man who is guided by the formal maxim of morality must not be conceived as acting in a vacuum. In the light of this maxim he selects and controls his ordinary maxims of self-love and inclination. In this way, he resembles the prudent man, who selects and controls his maxims of inclination in the light of the maxim of self-love. The behavior of the prudent man is familiar to us all, though we do not describe it in Kant's language; and it too is the work of practical reason. The work of reason in moral action is not very much more difficult to conceive than the work of reason in prudential action.

I will add one more point in anticipation of what is to follow. One of the reasons why Kant ascribes absolute value to a good will is that in obeying law for its own sake a good man is raised above the stream of events which we call nature: he is no longer at the mercy of his own natural instincts and desires. A good man is free in so far as he obeys the formal law which is the product of his rational will instead of being pulled about by desire, and it is this freedom which arouses Kant's veneration. Whatever be our judgment of this, we do well to note that Kant's view of the formal character of the moral law is necessary to his doctrine of freedom. So far his philosophy has at least the merit of being consistent.

NOTES

1. *Groundword* (*Fundamental Principles*), 460 n. (= 122 n.). See also 413 n. (= 38 n.).
2. *Gr.*, 401 n. (= 17n.).
3. Compare Chart I §7, at the end. What Kant says about the highest good—in *K.p.V.*, 109–10 = 244–5 (= 196–7)—applies to any action or object. I will summarise and simplify. If our volition is determined by the thought of an action or object independently of the law, then our action is not moral. The moral law is the only determining ground of the pure will. But *it goes without saying* (*Es versteht sich von selbst*) that if the moral law is *included* in the concept of such an action or object as its supreme condition, then the concept of such an action or object and of its realisation by our will is *at the same time* the determining ground of the pure will.
4. It is, however, also encouraged by a tendency in Kant to exaggerate the generally sound principle that in many cases remoter consequences ought to be ignored.

With Paton's commentary, we conclude our discussion of Kant's theory of moral obligation. It is a total formalism and completely deontological in character. Kant's formalism is easily contrasted with Mill's teleological theory.

The Naturalism of Aristotle

The next position in normative ethics that we shall consider in detail is the naturalism of Aristotle. Aristotle's moral theory is often referred to as one of *eudaimonia.* This is the Greek term for "well being." The general thrust of the theory is that moral virtue, and consequently the foundation for moral value, is to be found in the development of human capacities and potentialities. This is indeed a form of naturalism because Aristotle's theory of human nature asserts that all human beings are similar in relevant natural characteristics. Aristotle grounds his theory of value on the proper development and functioning of these natural characteristics. From the start, it is important to note that Aristotle's position is one of dynamism. The dimension of developmental process will play an important role in Aristotle's analysis of the foundation of moral value. Aristotle considered that human beings are essentially constituted in such a way that certain activities follow from their fundamental nature. It is in the development of these activities that human well being is derived. Aristotle shares the common Greek notion of virtue as *arete,* meaning "excellence." Arete is translated in Aristotle's system as *eudaimonia;* in other words, excellence refers to well being. The attainment of well being is the ground of moral virtue. As we will note in reading Aristotle's texts, well being is interpreted as happiness.

In the history of philosophy, Aristotle's *Nicomachean Ethics* is recognized as one of the most important accounts explicating the cluster of issues central to moral philosophy. The following passages are taken from Books One, Two, and Ten of the *Nicomachean Ethics.*

NICOMACHEAN ETHICS

Aristotle

. . . Every art and every inquiry, and similarly every action and pursuit, is thought to aim at some good; and for this reason the good has rightly been declared to be that at which all things aim. But a certain difference is found among ends; some are activities, others are products apart from the activities that produce them. Where there are ends apart from the actions, it is the nature of the products to be better than the activities. Now, as there are many actions, arts, and sciences, their ends also are many; the end of the medical art is health, that of shipbuilding a vessel, that of strategy victory, that of economics wealth. But where such arts fall under a single capacity— as bridle-making and the other arts concerned with the equipment of horses fall under the art of riding, and this and every military action under strategy, in the same way other arts fall under yet others—in all of these the ends of the master arts are to be preferred to all the subordinate ends; for it is for the sake of the former that the latter are pursued. It makes no difference whether the activities themselves are the ends of the actions, or something else apart from the activities, as in the case of the sciences just mentioned.

If, then, there is some end of the things we do, which we desire for its own sake (everything else being desired for the sake of this), and if we do not choose everything for the sake of something else (for at that rate the process would go on to infinity, so that our desire would be empty and vain), clearly this must be the good and the chief good. Will not the knowledge of it, then, have a great influence on life? Shall we not, like archers who have a mark to aim at, be more likely to hit upon what is right? If so, we must try, in outline at least to determine what it is, and of which of the sciences or capacities it is the object. It would seem to belong to the most authoritative art and that which is most truly the master art. And politics appears to be of this nature; for it is this that ordains which of the sciences should be studied in a state, and which each class of citizens should learn and up to what point they should learn them; and we see even the most highly esteemed of capacities to fall under this, e.g. strategy, economics, rhetoric; now, since politics uses the rest of the sciences, and since, again, it legislates as to what we are to do and what we are to abstain from, the end of this science must include those of the others, so that this end must be the good of man. For even if the end is the same for a single man and for a state, that of the state seems at all events something greater and more complete whether to attain or to preserve; though it is worth while to attain the end merely for one man, it is finer and more godlike to attain it for a nation or for city-states. . . .

Our discussion will be adequate if it has as much clearness as the subject-matter admits of, for precision is not to be sought for alike in all dis-

From Aristotle, "Nicomachean Ethics," in W.D. Ross, trans. and ed., *The Oxford Translation of Aristotle,* vol. 9 (Oxford: At the University Press, 1925). Reprinted by permission of the Oxford University Press.

cussions, any more than in all the products of the crafts. Now fine and just actions, which political science investigates, admit of much variety and fluctuation of opinion, so that they may be thought to exist only by convention, and not by nature. And goods also give rise to a similar fluctuation because they bring harm to many people; for before now men have been undone by reason of their wealth, and others by reason of their courage. We must be content, then, in speaking of such subjects and with such premises to indicate the truth roughly and in outline, and in speaking about things which are only for the most part true and with premises of the same kind to reach conclusions that are no better. In the same spirit, therefore, should each type of statement be *received;* for it is the mark of an educated man to look for precision in each class of things just so far as the nature of the subject admits; it is evidently equally foolish to accept probable reasoning from a mathematician and to demand from a rhetorician scientific proofs.

Now each man judges well the things he knows, and of these he is a good judge. And so the man who has been educated in a subject is a good judge of that subject, and the man who has received an all-round education is a good judge in general. Hence a young man is not a proper hearer of lectures on political science; for he is inexperienced in the actions that occur in life, but its discussions start from these and are about these; and, further, since he tends to follow his passions, his study will be vain and unprofitable, because the end aimed at is not knowledge but action. And it makes no difference whether he is young in years or youthful in character; the defect does not depend on time, but on his living, and pursuing each successive object, as passion directs. For to such persons, as to the incontinent, knowledge brings no profit; but to those who desire and act in accordance with a rational principle knowledge about such matters will be of great benefit. . . .

Let us resume our inquiry and state, in view of the fact that all knowledge and every pursuit aims at some good, what it is that we say political science aims at and what is the highest of all goods achievable by action. Verbally there is very general agreement; for both the general run of men and people of superior refinement say that it is happiness, and identify living well and doing well with being happy; but with regard to what happiness is they differ, and the many do not give the same account as the wise. For the former think it is some plain and obvious thing, like pleasure, wealth, or honour; they differ, however, from one another—and often even the same man identifies it with different things, with health when he is ill, with wealth when he is poor; but conscious of their ignorance, they admire those who proclaim some great ideal that is above their comprehension. Now some thought [*e.g.,* Plato] that apart from these many goods there is another which is self-subsistent and causes the goodness of all these as well. To examine all the opinions that have been held were perhaps somewhat fruitless; enough to examine those that are most prevalent or that seem to be arguable. . . .

Let us again return to the good we are seeking, and ask what it can be. It seems different in different actions and arts; it is different in medicine, in strategy, and in the other arts likewise. What then is the good of each?

Surely that for whose sake everything else is done. In medicine this is health, in strategy victory, in architecture a house, in any other sphere something else, and in every action and pursuit the end; for it is the sake of this that all men do whatever else they do. Therefore, if there is an end for all that we do, this will be the good achievable by action, and if there are more than one, these will be the goods achievable by action.

So the argument has by a different course reached the same point; but we must try to state this even more clearly. Since there are evidently more than one end, and we choose some of these (e.g. wealth, flutes, and in general instruments) for the sake of something else, clearly not all ends are final ends; but the chief good is evidently something final. Therefore, if there is only one final end, this will be what we are seeking, and if there are more than one end, the most final of these will be what we are seeking. Now we call that which is in itself worthy of pursuit more final than that which is worthy of pursuit for the sake of something else, and that which is never desirable for the sake of something else more final than the things that are desirable both in themselves and for the sake of that other thing, and therefore we call final without qualification that which is always desirable in itself and never for the sake of something else.

Now such a thing happiness, above all else, is held to be; for this we choose always for itself and never for the sake of something else, but honour, pleasure, reason, and every virtue we choose indeed for themselves (for if nothing resulted from them we should still choose each of them), but we choose them also for the sake of happiness, judging that by means of them we shall be happy. Happiness, on the other hand, no one chooses for the sake of these, nor, in general, for anything other than itself.

From the point of view of self-sufficiency the same result seems to follow; for the final good is thought to be self-sufficient. Now by self-sufficient we do not mean that which is sufficient for a man by himself, for one who lives a solitary life, but also for parents, children, wife, and in general for his friends and fellow citizens, since man is born for citizenship. But some limit must be set to this; for if we extend our requirement to ancestors and descendants and friends' friends we are in for an infinite series. Let us examine this question, however, on another occasion; the self-sufficient we now define as that which when isolated makes life desirable and lacking in nothing; and such we think happiness to be; and further we think it most desirable of all things, without being counted as one good thing among others—if it were so counted it would clearly be made more desirable by the addition of even the least of goods; for that which is added becomes an excess of goods, and of goods the greater is always more desirable. Happiness, then, is something final and self-sufficient, and is the end of action.

Presumably, however, to say that happiness is the chief good seems a platitude, and a clearer account of what it is is still desired. This might perhaps be given, if we could first ascertain the function of man. For just as for a flute-player, a sculptor, or any artist, and, in general, for all things that have a function or activity, the good and the 'well' is thought to reside in the function, so would it seem to be for man, if he has a function. Have the carpenter, then, and the tanner certain functions or activities, and has man none? Is he born without a function? Or as eye, hand, foot, and in general each of the parts evidently has a function, may one lay it down that man similarly has a function apart from all these? What then can this be? Life seems to be common even to plants, but we are seeking what is peculiar to man. Let us exclude, therefore, the life of nutrition and growth. Next there would be a life of perception, but *it* also seems to be common even to the horse, the ox, and every animal. There remains, then, an active life of the element that has a rational principle; of this, one part has such a principle in the sense of being obedient to one, the other in the sense of possessing one and exercising thought. And, as 'life of the rational element' also has two meanings, we must state that life in the sense of activity is what we mean; for this seems to be the more proper sense of the term. Now if the function of man is an activity of soul which follows or implies a rational principle, and if we say 'a so-and-so' and 'a good so-and-so' have a function which is the same in kind, e.g. a lyre-player and a good lyre-player, and so without qualification in all cases, eminence in respect of goodness being added to the name of the function (for the function of a lyre-player is to play the lyre, and that of a good lyre-player is to do so well): if this is the case [and we state the function of man to be a certain kind of life, and this to be an activity or actions of the soul implying a rational principle, and the function of a good man to be the good and noble performance of these, and if any action is well performed when it is performed in accordance with the appropriate excellence: if this is the case,] human good turns out to be activity of soul in accordance with virtue, and if there are more than one virtue, in accordance with the best and most complete.

But we must add 'in a complete life.' For one swallow does not make a summer, nor does one day; and so too one day, or a short time, does not make a man blessed and happy. . . . [Also, a happy person] needs the external goods as well; for it is impossible, or not easy, to do noble acts without the proper equipment. In many actions we use friends and riches and political power as instruments; and there are some things the lack of which takes the lustre from happiness, as good birth, goodly children, beauty; for the man who is very ugly in appearance or ill-born or solitary and childless is not very likely to be happy, and perhaps a man would be still less likely if he had thoroughly bad children or friends or had lost good children or friends by death. . . .

Since happiness is an activity of soul in accordance with perfect virtue, we must consider the nature of virtue; for perhaps we shall thus see better the nature of happiness. The true student of politics, too, is thought to have studied virtue above all things; for he wishes to make his fellow citizens good and obedient to the laws. As an example of this we have the lawgivers of the Cretans and the Spartans, and any others of the kind that there may have been. And if this inquiry belongs to political science, clearly the pursuit of it will be in accordance with our original plan. But clearly the virtue we must study is human virtue; for the good we were seeking was human good and the happiness human happiness. By human virtue we mean not that of the body but that of the soul; and happiness also we call an activity of the soul. But if this is so, clearly the student of politics must know somehow the facts about soul, as the man who is to heal the eyes or the body as a whole must know about the eyes or the body; and all the more since politics is more prized and better than medicine; but even among doctors the best educated spend much labour on acquiring knowledge of the body. The student of politics, then, must study the soul, and must study it with these objects in view, and do so just to the extent which is sufficient for the questions we are discussing; for further precision is perhaps something more laborious than our purposes require.

Some things are said about it, adequately enough, even in the discussions outside our school, and we must use these; e.g. that one element in the soul is irrational and one has a rational principle. Whether these are separated as the parts of the body or of anything divisible are, or are distinct by definition but by nature inseparable, like convex and concave in the circumference of a circle, does not affect the present question.

Of the irrational element one division seems to be widely distributed, and vegetative in its nature, I mean that which causes nutrition and growth; for it is this kind of power of the soul that one must assign to all nurslings and to embryos, and this same power to full-grown creatures; this is more reasonable than to assign some different power to them. Now the excellence of this seems to be common to all species and not specifically human . . . let us leave the nutritive faculty alone, since it has by its nature no share in human excellence.

There seems to be also another irrational element in the soul—one which in a sense, however, shares in a rational principle. For we praise the rational principle of the continent man and of the incontinent, and the part of their soul that has such a principle, since it urges them aright and towards the best objects; but there is found in them also another element naturally opposed to the rational principle, which fights against and resists that principle. For exactly as paralyzed limbs when we intend to move them to the right turn on the contrary to the left, so is it with the soul; the impulses of incontinent people move in contrary directions. But while in the body we see that which moves astray, in the soul we do not. No doubt, however, we must none the less suppose that in the soul too there is something contrary to the rational principle, resisting and opposing it. In what sense it is distinct from the other elements does not concern us. Now even this seems to have a share in a rational principle, as we said; at any rate in the continent man it obeys the rational principle—and presumably in the temperate and brave man it is still more obedient; for in him it speaks, on all matters, with the same voice as the rational principle.

Therefore the irrational element also appears to be twofold. For the vegetative element in no way shares in a rational principle, but the appetitive, and in general the desiring element in a sense shares in it, in so far as it listens to and obeys it; this is the sense in which we speak of 'taking account' of one's father or one's friends, not that in which we speak of 'accounting' for a mathematical property. That the irrational element is in some sense persuaded by a rational principle is indicated also by the giving of advice and by all reproof and exhortation. And if this element also must be said to have a rational principle, that which has a rational principle (as well as that which has not) will be twofold, one subdivision having it in the strict sense and in itself, and the other having a tendency to obey as one does one's father.

Virtue too is distinguished into kinds in accordance with this difference; for we say that some of the virtues are intellectual and others moral, philosophic wisdom and understanding and practical wisdom being intellectual, liberality and temperance moral. For in speaking about a man's character we do not say that he is wise or has understanding but that he is good-tempered or temperate; yet we praise the wise man also with respect to his state of mind; and of states of mind we call those which merit praise virtues.

BOOK II

Virtue, then, being of two kinds, intellectual and moral, intellectual virtue in the main owes both its birth and its growth to teaching (for which reason it requires experience and time), while moral virtue comes about as a result of habit, whence also its name *ethike* is one that is formed by a slight variation from the word *ethos* (habit). From this it is also plain that none of the moral virtues arises in us by nature; for nothing that exists by nature can form a habit contrary to its nature. For instance the stone which by nature moves downwards cannot be habituated to move upwards, not even if one tries to train it by throwing it up ten thousand times; nor can fire be habituated to move downwards, nor can anything else that by nature behaves in one way be trained to behave in another. Neither by nature, then, nor contrary to nature do the virtues arise in us; rather we are adapted by nature to receive them, and are made perfect by habit.

Again, of all the things that come to us by nature we first acquire the potentiality and later exhibit the activity (this is plain in the case of the senses; for it was not by often seeing or often hearing that we got these senses, but on the contrary we had them before we used them, and did not come to have them by using them); but the virtues we get by first exercising them, as also happens in the case of the arts as well. For the things we have to learn before we can do them, we learn by doing them, e.g. men become builders by building and lyre-players by playing the lyre; so too we become just by doing just acts, temperate by doing temperate acts, brave by doing brave acts. . . .

We must, however, not only describe [moral] virtue as a state of character, but also say what sort of state it is. We may remark, then, that every virtue or excellence brings into good condition the thing of which it is the excellence and makes the work of that thing be done well; e.g. the excellence of the eye makes both the eye and its work good; for it is by the excellence of the eye that we see well. Similarly the excellence of the horse makes a horse both good in itself and good at running and at carrying its rider and at awaiting the attack of the enemy. Therefore, if this is true in every case, the virtue of man also will be the state of character which makes a man good and which makes him do his own work well.

How this is to happen we have stated already, but it will be made plain also by the following consideration of the specific nature of virtue. In everything that is continuous and divisible it is possible to take more, less, or an equal amount, and that either in terms of the thing itself or relatively to us;

and the equal is an intermediate between excess and defect. By the intermediate in the object I mean that which is equidistant from each of the extremes, which is one and the same for all men; by the intermediate relatively to us that which is neither too much nor too little—and this is not one, nor the same for all. For instance, if ten is many and two is few, six is the intermediate, taken in terms of the object; for it exceeds and is exceeded by an equal amount; this is intermediate according to arithmetical proportion. But the intermediate relatively to us is not to be taken so; if ten pounds are too much for a particular person to eat and two too little, it does not follow that the trainer will order six pounds; for this also is perhaps too much for the person who is to take it, or too little—too little for Milo, too much for the beginner in athletic exercises. The same is true of running and wrestling. Thus a master of any art avoids excess and defect, but seeks the intermediate and chooses this—the intermediate not in the object but relatively to us. . . .

. . . Virtue, then, is a state of character concerned with choice, lying in a mean, i.e. the mean relative to us, this being determined by a rational principle, and by that principle by which the man of practical wisdom would determine it. Now it is a mean between two vices, that which depends on excess and that which depends on defect; and again it is a mean because the vices respectively fall short of or exceed what is right in both passions and actions, while virtue both finds and chooses that which is intermediate. Hence in respect of its substance and the definition which states its essence virtue is a mean, with regard to what is best and right an extreme.

But not every action nor every passion admits of a mean; for some have names that already imply badness, e.g. spite, shamelessness, envy, and in the case of actions adultery, theft, murder; for all of these and suchlike things imply by their names that they are themselves bad, and not the excesses or deficiencies of them. It is not possible, then, ever to be right with regard to them; one must always be wrong. Nor does goodness or badness with regard to such things depend on committing adultery with the right woman, at the right time, and in the right way, but simply to do any of them is to go wrong. It would be equally absurd, then, to expect that in unjust, cowardly, and voluptuous action there should be a mean, an excess, and a deficiency; for at that rate there would be a mean of excess and of deficiency, an excess of excess, and a deficiency of deficiency. But as there is no excess and deficiency of temperance and courage because what is intermediate is in a sense an extreme, so too of the actions we have mentioned there is no mean nor any excess and deficiency, but however they are done they are wrong; for in general there is neither a mean of excess and deficiency, nor excess and deficiency of a mean.

We must, however, not only make this general statement, but also apply it to the individual facts. For among statements about conduct those which are general apply more widely, but those which are particular are more genuine, since conduct has to do with individual cases, and our statements must harmonize with the facts in these cases. We may take these cases from our table. With regard to feelings of fear and confidence courage is the mean; of the people who exceed, he who exceeds in fearlessness has no name (many of the states have no name), while the man who exceeds in confidence is rash, and he who exceeds in fear and falls short in confidence is a coward. With regard to pleasures and pains—not all of them, and not so much with regard to the pains—the mean is temperance, the excess self-indulgence. Persons deficient with regard to the pleasures are not often found; hence such persons also have received no name. But let us call them 'insensible.'

With regard to giving and taking of money the mean is liberality, the excess and the defect prodigality and meanness. In these actions people exceed and fall short in contrary ways; the prodigal exceeds in spending and falls short in taking, while the mean man exceeds in taking and falls short in spending. . . . With regard to money there are also other dispositions—a mean, magnificence (for the magnificent man differs from the liberal man; the former deals with large sums, the latter with small ones), an excess, tastelessness and vulgarity, and a deficiency, niggardliness . . .

With regard to honour and dishonour the mean is proper pride, the excess is known as a sort of 'empty vanity,' and the deficiency is undue humility; and as we said liberality was related to magnificence, differing from it by dealing with small sums, so there is a state similarly related to proper pride, being concerned with small honours while that is concerned with great. For it is possible to desire honour as one ought, and more than one ought, and less, and the man who exceeds in his desires is called ambitious, the man who falls short unambitious, while the intermediate person has no name. The dispositions also are nameless, except that that of the ambitious man is called ambition. Hence the people who are at the extremes lay claim to the middle place; and we ourselves sometimes call the intermediate person ambitious and sometimes unambitious, and sometimes praise the ambitious man and sometimes the unambitious. The reason of our doing this will be stated in what follows; but now let us speak of the remaining states according to the method which has been indicated.

With regard to anger also there is an excess, a deficiency, and a mean. Although they can scarcely be said to have names, yet since we call the intermediate person good-tempered let us call the mean good temper; of the persons at the extremes let the one who exceeds be called irascible, and his vice irascibility, and the man who falls short an inirascible sort of person, and the deficiency inirascibility. . . .

BOOK X

If happiness is activity in accordance with virtue, it is reasonable that it should be in accordance with the highest virtue; and this will be that of the best thing in us. Whether it be reason or something else that is this element which is thought to be our natural ruler and guide and to take thought of things noble and divine, whether it be itself also divine or only the most divine element in us, the activity of this in accordance with its proper virtue will be perfect happiness. That this activity is contemplative we have already said.

Now this would seem to be in agreement both with what we said before and with the truth. For, firstly, this activity is the best (since not only is reason the best thing in us, but the objects of reason are the best of knowable objects); and, secondly, it is the most continuous, since we can contemplate truth more continuously than we can *do* anything. And we think happiness has pleasure mingled with it, but the activity of philosophic wisdom is admittedly the pleasantest of virtuous activities; at all events the pursuit of it is thought to offer pleasures marvellous for their purity and their enduringness, and it is to be expected that those who know will pass their time more pleasantly than those who inquire. And the self-sufficiency that is spoken of must belong most to the contemplative activity. For while a philosopher, as well as a just man or one possessing any other virtue, needs the necessaries of life, when they are sufficiently equipped with things of that sort the just man needs people towards whom and with whom he shall act justly, and the temperate man, the brave man, and each of the others is in the same case, but the philosopher, even when by himself, can contemplate truth, and the better the wiser he is; he can perhaps do so better if he has fellow-workers, but still he is the most self-sufficient. And this activity alone would seem to be loved for its own sake; for nothing arises from it apart from the contemplating, while from practical activities we gain more or less apart from the action. And happiness is thought to depend on leisure; for we are busy that we may have leisure, and make war that we may live in peace. Now the activity of the practical virtues is exhibited in political or military affairs, but the actions concerned with these seem to be unleisurely. Warlike actions are completely so (for no one chooses to be at war, or provokes war, for the sake of being at war; any one would seem absolutely murderous if he were to make enemies of his friends in order to bring about battle and slaughter); but the action of the statesman is also unleisurely, and—apart from the political action itself—aims at despotic power and honours, or at all events happiness, for him and his fellow citizens—a happiness different from political action, and evidently sought as being different. So if among virtuous actions political and military actions are distinguished by nobility and greatness, and these are unleisurely and aim at an end and are not desirable for their sake, but the activity of reason, which is contemplative, seems both to be superior in serious worth and to aim at no end beyond itself, and to have its pleasure proper to itself (and this augments the activity), and the self-sufficiency, leisureliness, unweariedness (so far as this is possible for man), and all the other attributes ascribed to the supremely happy man are evidently those connected with this activity, it follows that this will be the complete happiness of man, if it be allowed a complete term of life (for none of the attributes of happiness is *in*complete).

But such a life would be too high for man; for it is not in so far as he is man that he will live so, but in so far as something divine is present in him; and by so much as this is superior to our composite nature is its activity superior to that which is the exercise of the other kind of virtue. If reason is divine, then, in comparison with man, the life according to it is divine in comparison with human life. But we must not follow those who advise us, being men, to think of human things, and, being mortal, of mortal things, but must, so far as we can, make ourselves immortal, and strain every nerve to live in accordance with the best thing in us; for even if it be small in bulk, much more does it in power and worth surpass everything. This would seem, too, to be each man himself, since it is the authoritative and better part of him. It would be strange, then, if he were to choose not the life of his self but that of something else. And what we said before will apply now; that which is proper to each thing is by nature best and most pleasant for each thing; for man, therefore, the life according to reason is best and pleasantest, since reason more than anything else *is* man. This life therefore is also the happiest.

Let's examine in some detail the passages we have just read from Aristotle's *Nicomachean Ethics.* Aristotle accepts a "function" concept of morality. Moral virtue will be analyzed in terms of the "function" of human beings. This function position is intricately connected with the concept of eudaimonia, expressed earlier. The ground for human value is found in the proper function of human beings. In an important sense, Aristotle developed the Socratic insights into virtue. The notion of virtue is connected to both knowledge and to the proper perfection of human beings. Yet Aristotle will not appeal to Plato's world of the forms in order to ground the proper function of human beings.

The following principle underlies Aristotle's account of moral virtue: If some X has a distinct and unique function, then the ultimate perfection—the *arete* or excellence—of that X will depend upon the exercise and developmental activity of that specific function. Virtue is thus defined as the acquired habits which enable us to function well. The ontological ground for moral virtue is in the "functioning well" of human beings, and this concept of functioning well depends upon a cogent analysis of human nature. It is the properties common to human nature from which Aristotle's naturalism will develop. As we shall see as we proceed in this section of our inquiry into normative ethics, the concept of functioning well as a human person will be developed by natural law ethical theorists and by some twentieth-century psychologists, especially Carl Rogers.

This concept of function must be examined more critically. Aristotle suggests that the "rational" capacity is the unique ontological property distinguishing human beings from the rest of the objects found in the natural realm. The functioning well of human beings will be in accord with the perfection of the rational part of human nature. Aristotle suggests that, although the "living functions" and the "sensitive functions" are necessary in order to attain human well being, neither is sufficient to account for it alone. Human virtue and happiness require the development of some aspect of reason. A virtuous person must develop the rational dimension along with the other two dimensions, the living and the sensitive. This will become more clear as we proceed.

Aristotle indicates that all rational activity is directed toward an end. When we act rationally, we act for a purpose. Aristotle's suggestion in Book I of the *Nicomachean Ethics* is that there is an ultimate end for human actions. This means that Aristotle believes that there is one ultimate cause or reason for every action we undertake. Recall from the text that Aristotle refers to this ultimate end as "happiness." He defined happiness as "an activity of human beings in accord with reason." The end of human activity to be obtained is happiness or well being. The means for attaining this end of well being is virtue.

Virtuous activities are those which proceed from our acquired habits, directing our actions toward our developmental perfection. Obviously the Greek notion of excellence is hovering over Aristotle's analysis.

Yet how does this concept of function elucidated by Aristotle provide content to a moral theory? What is the relationship between happiness and the make-up of human nature? What is the "rational capacity" and how is it ulitized? What is the "end" of human nature? These are important questions pertinent to the Aristotelian account of moral value. The medieval philosopher, Thomas Aquinas, adopted much of Aristotle's ethical naturalism. The following exhibits some interesting insights toward understanding these Aristotelian concepts.

. . . the percepts of natural law are related to practical reason in the same manner that the fundamental principles of demonstrations are related to speculative (theoretical) reason. Both are sets of self-evident principles.

A principle is called "self-evident" in two senses. In one way, objectively and in another way as relative to us as knowers. A proposition is "objectively self-evident" if its predicate is contained within the concept of the subject. However, if someone does not know the concept (intelligibility) of the subject, such a proposition will not be self-evident. For example, the proposition, "Humans are rational" when taken in itself is self-evident, because to say "human" is to say "rational". Nonetheless, if a person does not know the conceptual significance of "human," this proposition would not be self-evident to that person. Therefore, as Boethius argues in his DE HEBDOMADIBUS, there are certain axioms or propositions which are generally self-evident to everyone. In this category are propositions whose terms every person understands. For example, "every whole is greater than its parts," and "two things equal to a third are equal to one another." However, there are some propositions which are self-evident only to those who are educated and who thus understand the meaning of the terms of such propositions. For example, if one understands that angels are incorporeal, then it is self-evident that angels do not occupy a place by filling it up. However, this is not evident to those who are uneducated and thus who do not understand this point.

Among those propositions which fall within the possibility of everyone's grasp, there is a certain order of precedence. What fundamentally falls within one's mental grasp is "being." The understanding of being is included in everything that a person grasps intellectually. Therefore, the first and fundamental indemonstrable principle is the principle of contradiction: "To affirm and simultaneously to deny is excluded." This first principle is founded upon the intelligibility of being and non-being. And as Aristotle argues in the METAPHYSICS, all other principles are based upon this first fundamental principle.

Now, just as "being" is the first thing to fall within the intellectual grasp of the mind, so "good" is the first thing to fall within the grasp of the practical reason. Practical reason is reason directed toward a work. Every active principle acts on account of an end, and the end includes in its concept the intelligibility of good.

It follows, therefore, that the first principle of practical reason is founded upon the intelligibility of good; that is, "Good is what each thing tends toward." The first principle of practical reason—the primary precept of the law—can be formulated in the following manner: "GOOD IS TO BE DONE AND PURSUED AND EVIL IS TO BE AVOIDED." All the rest of the precepts of the natural law are based upon this principle. Hence, under precepts of the natural law come all those actions which are to be done and those actions which are to be avoided, which actions practical reason grasps naturally as uniquely human goods or their opposites.

Insofar as good has the intelligibility of end and evil has the intelligibility of contrary to end, it follows that reason grasps naturally as goods (accordingly, as things to be pursued by work, and their opposites as evils and thus things to be avoided) all of the objects which follow from the natural inclinations central to the concept of human nature.

First, there is in human beings an inclination based upon the aspect of human nature which is shared with all living things; this is that everything according to its own nature tends to preserve its own being. In accord with this inclination or natural tendency, those things (actions, events, processes) by which human life is preserved and by which threats to human life are met fall under the natural law. Second, there are in human beings inclinations towards more restricted goods which are based upon the fact that human nature has common properties with other animals. In accord with this inclination, those things are said to be in agreement with the natural law (which nature teaches all animals) among which are the sexual union of male and female, the care of children, and so forth. Third, there is in human beings an inclination to those goods based upon the rational properties of human nature. These goods are uniquely related to human beings. For example, human beings have a natural inclination to know the true propositions about God and concerning those necessities required for living in a human society. In accord with this inclination arise elements of the natural law. For example, human beings should avoid ignorance and should not offend those persons among whom he or she must live in social units, and so on.[12]

In this passage from Aquinas, the nature of morality is analyzed from an Aristotelian perspective. Note the distinction Aquinas draws in regard to reason. There are two aspects to the reasoning process: *speculative reasoning* and *practical reasoning*. Speculative reasoning is used when we arrive at a conclusion of theoretical truth by means of a philosophical argument. Aquinas' paradigm for speculative reasoning would be Euclidean geometry. Practical reasoning, on the other hand, is not directed toward knowing a truth but rather toward undertaking an action. Since morality is concerned with right actions to be undertaken, practical reasoning will be utilized in moral philosophy.

Aquinas further indicates that both aspects of the reasoning process have their own unique first principles. Following Aristotle's insight, Aquinas argues that it is impossible to not have first principles in any inquiry. To not reach a first principle is to be caught in an infinite regress. Accordingly, it is impossible to have a demonstration for each principle in an inquiry. Again following Aristotle, Aquinas argues that the first principles of each type of reasoning are grasped by intuition. The first principle of speculative reasoning is the *Principle of Contradiction*. Note that Aquinas does not offer a demonstration for this principle. In Euclidean geometry, we begin with unproven postulates; an appeal to intuition has been made. So too with the first principles of speculative reasoning, Aquinas appeals to one's intuition. Simply put, without the principle of contradiction, we would not be able to reason at all. Think about what would happen if one would contradict himself all of the time. Would we be able to communicate with each other? Of course not. What would we ever be able to believe? This is, obviously, very similar to Kant's reason for showing the self-defeating character of the universalized practice of making false promises. In the same manner of intuition, Aquinas postulates the first principle of practical reasoning, "Good is to be done and evil avoided." Notice how Aquinas defines the good, "Good is defined in terms of an end." Thus an end, per se, is a good.

Now connect this with the concept of functioning well for which Aristotle argued previously. The end of human nature, therefore, is functioning well. The end based upon the metaphysical view of a human person is the good, by definition. Notice how interconnected these positions are. Before continuing this analysis of Aquinas' natural law ethic, it will be helpful for us to read the following contemporary commentary on Aquinas' position.

THE TRADITIONAL CONCEPT OF NATURAL LAW: AN INTERPRETATION

Columba Ryan, O.P.

I do not however propose to set out in any formal manner the teaching of Aquinas. Rather, I shall take him as a kind of guide and mentor in proposing what will be a personal statement of the concept of natural law that may be at once faithful to the role it plays in the tradition on this matter, and of relevance to the issues in which it is today customarily invoked in moral teaching. That it is a matter of some importance to understand the concept can hardly be gainsaid when one hears it so constantly invoked in arguments about contraception, nuclear warfare, religious freedom and so forth. And quite apart from these applications, the concept has been given renewed attention as the result of the need to have some theory which will justify the rejection of unjust legislation. It may seem to many, and as I think rightly, that without an appeal to something like natural law, such proceedings as the Nuremberg trial have no rational basis. The importance of the theory of natural law is that it affords the possibility of rebellion; it provides a court of appeal, and without it there is no court of appeal beyond the edicts of men.

It is true that, merely because one law within a given legal system may be criticized by reference to other laws within the system, it cannot be argued that there must be some criterion outside the whole system whereby the totality of the laws may be criticized. This would involve the logical fallacy that because all the laws can be referred to some criterion, there is one criterion for all laws. But what I should wish to say is that the very possibility of any law being referred to any criterion, even within a legal system, implies that there is, within the legal system, a structure which makes possible critical scrutiny. Or, more simply, the calling in question of the obligatory character of any given law raises the whole problem of the obligatory character of law, and this obligatory character within a legal system constitutes the kernel of the concept of natural law.

Permission for excerpt from "The Traditional Concept of Natural Law: An Interpretation," by Columba Ryan, O.P., found in *Light on the Natural Law*, edited by Illtud Evans, O.P., Baltimore: Helicon Press, Inc., 1965.

This leads to an observation of some importance. The fact that we use the word "law" in speaking both of natural law and positive law may easily lead us to suppose that such "laws" are in every respect the same sort of thing, laws standing side by side. The temptation then is to look for a natural law which functions in the same way as positive law (to look for a kind of written code "in the heavens" or "in men's hearts" and so on), and upon finding that there is no such thing, and that, by comparison with positive laws, the natural law is vague and the subject of endless disagreement, to conclude that it simply does not exist. But this would be a simple mistake, the result of a systematically misleading expression. For in fact to speak of both the natural law and positive law as "laws" is to do the same kind of thing as to speak of tables and chairs as objects or beings or things, and to speak of God likewise. If this leads us to think of God as one more thing alongside of and beyond things like tables and chairs, we are being systematically misled by the expression "object" or "being" or "thing." This is a "category mistake." Instead we should understand that God is interior to, and the very ground of possibility, of every "thing" that is. Likewise, in speaking of natural law as "law" we should think of it not as lying alongside of, and somehow superior to, all other laws, but as that which is at the heart of, and constitutes the possibility, indeed the obligatory character, of every other law. In other words when we are speaking of natural law, we are in the field of ethics or morality rather than in that of legality in a narrow sense.

It is important to have made this observation for it goes some way to meeting the objection commonly made that natural law is so vague and so much the matter of endless controversy as to be useless in the practical business of reaching legal decisions or agreement on disputed points. The assumption from which this objection springs is that natural law is to fulfill the functions of positive law, only "more so" or in a higher order of justice; it is the objection of practical lawyers concerned with getting things settled. But in fact this is not the function of natural law as such; for though the natural law may be embodied in directives of a more or less general kind, as we shall see, the point of describing such directives as belonging to natural law is not so much to call attention to their content as to the moral character of their obligatory force. The theory of natural law is a theory of what makes laws laws, not an easy substitute for making laws, for legislating. . . .

By way of beginning, at last, a more constructive account, I shall use an extremely crude analogy, but one that, because of its simplicity, may do more than a more sophisticated account to make its point.

Manufactured products, whether simple or more complicated, are as often as not accompanied, when they are bought, by the maker's instructions or rules of how to use them. These rules are not arbitrary fiats of the manufacturer which might be entirely different from what they are. They tell the buyer how to get the best out of the product; if it is used in such and such a way, it will last, and perform its function well; if used in some other way, it will be broken, or give indifferent service.

What the manufacturer is doing is to tell the buyer what he knows of the nature of his product. Admittedly, we have here to do with an artifact, and the maker's knowledge is based on his having designed the product for a purpose. But his rules do not reflect this knowledge alone; they are to some extent based also on the knowledge he has of the materials used—they will stand up to certain usages while to others they will not.

There is some sense in which the rules listed by the maker are not simply written on his paper list of instructions. They reflect what may be said to be built into the products. In this sense they are the "rules" or "laws" of its very make-up; the "rules" of its nature. Nor is it even necessary that a list of instructions should be provided. It would theoretically be possible for the buyer to examine the thing, take it to pieces and reassemble it, and arrive at the same set of rules; he would then have read them off the product itself.

All this provides an analogy, though only a partial one, to natural law. Instead of manufacturers' products, we have to do with human beings. There could, theoretically, be issued with every human baby rules for his proper "use"—describing the way he is to be used to get the best out of him, to see that, as a human being, he finds proper fulfilment. But in fact, of course, no list of rules is issued. It is left for men to discover for themselves the "rules" built into their nature as human beings, to discover how to use themselves if they are to get the best out of themselves and find their proper human fulfilment. And by natural law is meant not these "rules" as built into them (my use throughout of inverted commas has been intentional, to call attention to the fact that such "rules" are scarcely properly so called) but these "rules" as recognized by men on reflection upon what it is to be human and to find human fulfilment.

Here it is important to insist that "to be human" must be understood in the total human context. Arguments for something's being in accordance with or against the natural law often enough appear to forget this. One example may illustrate this point. What Dr. Rock cites as "a typical statement of the conventional Catholic position" runs as follows: "The reason why the artificial practice of birth control is immoral is written into the very nature of the sexual organs and the marital act itself. The sex organs were made by God to reproduce the human race. Only when husband and wife unite naturally is the union of sperm possible. Therefore the primary purpose of the marital act is the conception of human life." Apart from a good many things wrong with this argument as it stands, and the fact that if it proves anything it proves too much for it would be equally applicable to birth control applied to animals, the whole approach appears to me wrong. For it seems to suppose that by a simple inspection of physical organs, rules can be reached for human behaviour. But man is not simply a complex of organs. "Human beings define themselves in relation to the world, and in relation to those around them." To discover what it is to be human and to achieve properly human fulfilment, account must be taken of man not simply as a biological object, not even simply biologically (which would introduce a whole consideration of his ecology), but in the specifically human dimension in which he enters into communication with others at a human level. That is "natural" to man which constitutes him not merely in isolation, but in relation to the whole world-for-man which he creates around him (the highly artificial world of civilization), and in relation to other persons who stand not simply as objects but as other subjects around him. This is a point to which we shall have occasion later to return. It needs here to be made very forcefully because of the frequency with which it is overlooked in natural law arguments.

When we insisted earlier that the natural law is not to be taken as referring to the "rules" built in to a man's make-up, but to his recognition of these "rules", we touched, in fact, upon the difference between the natural law and what may be called "the laws of nature" (if we may use the later expression in a rather restricted sense). We may say that the "rules" built into the make-up of things—whether of inanimate objects, plants, animals, human beings—constitute in each the "law" of their nature. But only in man, with his capacity to reflect upon and know himself, can there be any question of natural law, the recognition for himself of how he is to act; and only in his case, with his freedom of action, can there be a responsible following or deviation from the "rules" of his nature (and even this only to a limited extent).

Human Nature as a Set of Dispositional Properties

Having read the texts of Aristotle, Aquinas, and the commentary by Ryan, it is now time to clarify in detail the normative ethics based upon Aristotelian eudaimonism. Recall the analogy Ryan suggested between a manufactured product and human nature. If we want the manufactured product to function well, then we must follow the instruction manual. However attempting to determine the instructions for human nature is a different question. Such determination will come, the Aristotelians tell us, from a conceptual analysis of human nature itself. In principle, this detailed analysis depends upon input from psychology, anthropology, sociology, biology, and so forth. A human being can be defined, some contemporary Aristotelians suggest, in terms of a "set of dispositional properties." A dispositional property is an ability, capacity, or potency to carry out some process. For example, a china cup has the dispositional property to hold hot coffee, while a wax paper cup lacks this capacity. An acorn has a dispositional property to grow into an oak tree, while a pebble does not. A dispositional property is a built-in ability of an object to progress or develop in a certain manner given other external circumstances and conditions. If a human being is to be defined in terms of a set of dispositional properties, the important question concerns determining what these properties are.

The Aristotelians suggest a three-fold generic division of dispositional properties: (a) *living* dispositions, (b) *sensitive* dispositions, and (c) *rational* dispositions. One might refer to these dispositional properties as innate drives. In *The Concept of Law,* H.L.A. Hart has referred to some of these dispositions as "natural necessities." Contemporary social scientists have spoken of this concept in terms of "basic needs." Whatever the terminology used to describe these dispositional properties, it is important to realize that these properties provide the dynamic basis for defining human nature. It is from these dispositions that the Aristotelians will derive the set of fundamental human rights. In turn, obligations are derived from the rights. Rights and obligations are regarded as correlative concepts. According to this Aristotelian scheme, a human right is a basic and radical possession of each individual human being. The foundation for these rights is the very constitution of human nature. If human nature is altered essentially, the basic set of dispositional properties will be altered. Accordingly, a change could result in the fundamental set of human rights. The point to be emphasized is that human rights are innately based upon the concept of human nature. They are not bestowed by a government, dictator, president, or any other external influence. Rights belong to human beings because of what human beings innately are. It is through the concept of dispositional property that an adequate conceptual account of the content of human nature can be made. A partial listing of the basic dispositional properties constituting human nature and the derived rights and obligations is provided in the following schema.

DISPOSITIONAL PROPERTIES	HUMAN RIGHT	OBLIGATION
A. *Living Dispositions or inclinations:*		
1. To continue in existence	To life	Killing is to be avoided.
2. Nutrition and growth	To basic necessities of life.	Minimal necessities are to be available for everyone.
B. *Sensitive Dispositions or inclinations:*		
1. To have Sense Experiences	To integrity of bodily faculties.	Protect self and others from physical harm.
2. To Care for Offspring	To care for one's own offspring without external influence.	Provide adquate direction and care for child development.
C. *Rational Dispositions or inclinations:*		
1. To Understand (Innate curiosity)	To know the truth.	Lying is to be avoided.
2. To live together in social communities	To live in a just society.	Justice is to be promoted.

This is merely a brief, limited sketch of some of the dispositional properties which define the content of human nature. There are many more. However it should provide students with a degree of conceptual clarity about the theoretical machinery necessary for an Aristotelian naturalistic moral theory. Each disposition determines a fundamental human right. According to this scheme, because we possess a disposition to continue in existence, we have a natural right to that state of continued existence. In order to justify the inclusion of a disposition to continue in existence within the set of constitutive dispositional properties defining human nature, an Aristotelian naturalist will appeal to empirical facts gained from biological studies. For example, each of us probably has observed what happens when an ordinary house plant is placed on the kitchen window sill. The plant grows outward toward the sunlight. This is necessary in order for photosynthesis to occur and maintain the plant's living state. Likewise, when an infection occurs in an animal body, the organism, through its innate drives, tends to isolate and ward off the infection. Information gained from the observation of living things serves as the basis for a discussion about the innate disposition to continue to exist.

Our discussion has centered on very basic and quite general dispositional properties. The Aristotelian naturalist, however, makes an explicit appeal to empirical evidence in order to establish the content dimension of the dispositional properties. It is only through such an empirical investigation that an adequate concept of human dispositions can be derived.

Virtue as the Mean Between Extremes

But how does this position contribute to the process of making moral decisions? An adequate response to this question requires an analysis of Aristotle's doctrine of "the mean." Aristotle strongly suggests that every conclusion in practical or moral reasoning is dependent upon the particular situations in which the human agent finds himself or herself. While it is true that the set of natural dispositional properties and their corresponding fulfillment through activities establish the foundations for moral laws, the exact fulfillment of a dispositional property through an activity depends very much upon the circumstances attendant to the particular situation. The natural moral law demands that the moral rules themselves, which are natural rights based upon the set of defining dispositional properties, have a degree of certainty. As long as human beings have the unique set of dispositional properties which comprise human nature, the fundamental human rights will have an ontological foundation. However the situation determines the precise following and development of the dispositional property. In the *Nicomachean Ethics*, Aristotle suggests that a virtuous action is a mean between two extremes. In every situation involving a human action, an excess or defect of the action might be undertaken. The mean between the extremes of excess and defect establishes the middle ground for virtuous actions. This middle ground between the two extremes is the grounding for actions of excellence. Recall that the Greek notion of virtue is one of excellence. Aristotle's suggestion is that true excellence or functioning well will be obtained only if a human agent chooses to follow the mean action and avoid the extremes of excess or defect. The concept of moderation follows from the analysis of the mean. The following diagram illustrates Aristotle's account of the mean found in every situation involving human action.

Conditions holding for any human action — Defect — Mean (Virtue) — Excess

It is important to realize that Aristotle does not intend that there be one precise midpoint for every human action-situation which each human agent must follow in order to attain excellence when undertaking actions. Aristotle provides us with the example of eating. In this example, the mean is not a mathematical proportion. For the sake of argument, let us suppose that in order to promote and maintain adequate health everyone must eat and drink at least two pounds of food and liquid daily. Let us suppose also that eating and drinking eight pounds of food and beverage every day would quickly result in obesity with all the accompanying dangers to health. In our hypothetical example, therefore, eating and drinking less than two pounds of food and drink would be an action of *defect,* while eating and drinking more than eight pounds would be an action of *excess.*

In our hypothetical example, the mathematical *mean* is five pounds. From this, does it follow that every person must eat five pounds and only five pounds in order to survive? A little common sense reflection will immediately indicate that the mathematical mean could not possibly be followed by every individual. For the sake of argument, let us consider two persons: a 90-pound librarian and a 270-pound professional football tackle. Would each of these person require the same amount of food in order to survive well and maintain a state of sufficient health? Of course not. This is why Aristotle affirms that the moral mean cannot be equated with the mathematical mean. The demands of the particular individual and the unique situations in which moral agents find themselves are equally important in determining the moral mean. The librarian might function well physically with only two and three-quarter pounds of sustenance a day while the pro-football tackle at the training table might need over seven pounds. Even though five pounds of food and drink is the mathematical mean, it cannot be the moral mean. Functioning well physically, which is a necessary condition for obtaining eudaimonia, requires something more than merely following the mathematical mean. It is because of this that both Aristotle and Aquinas strongly suggest that the circumstances surrounding the situation and the demands of the individual are equally important in determining the mean for the action to be undertaken.

We will now consider a specific moral virtue. Consider the situation of facing danger. Courage is the virtue exercised in situations of danger, and, as in all human actions, there is the possibility of defect and excess. The defect would be *cowardice* while the excess would be *foolhardiness.* Schematically, we have the following illustration:

Situation of
Facing Danger

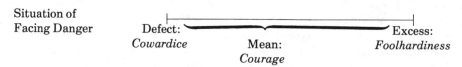

Defect: Excess:
Cowardice   Mean: *Foolhardiness*
                  Courage

In order to be virtuous, must each person have the same degree of courage? Keeping in mind our discussion of the food example, try to determine what Aristotle's response will be.

Once again we can use the example of the 90-pound librarian and the 270-pound pro-football tackle. Let us suppose that a person was being mugged in broad daylight on a major city street. Furthermore, let us suppose that the mugger was an ordinary person of average height and weight, was not a black-belt karate expert, did not have a gun, and so forth. If virtuous actions—in this case, courage—are the mean actions between the extremes of defect and excess, how is the mean determined for each individual? The defect would be an action of cowardice. While observing the mugging, suppose both the librarian and the football tackle turned their backs, walked away in fear, and did nothing to help.

This would be an example of cowardice, or at least apathy. However is the same action of courage required from both the librarian and the football tackle? Of course not. It might be a justified act of courage for the librarian to run to a telephone as fast as he could and call for emergency assistance. If the pro-football tackle only ran for a phone, we might justifiably have asked more from him. In these circumstances, an act of courage for him would be to subdue the mugger and thwart the attack. This assumes that the football tackle could do this without undo harm to himself. This example illustrates the importance of situational circumstances and the demands of the agent in Aristotelian ethics. The action to be undertaken in a particular situation is determined by the mean relative to the condition of the agent. Nonetheless the content of the dispositional properties from which the actions spring remains constant; this content determines the function of human nature. It is upon this content that Aristotelian naturalism is based. For Aristotelians, therefore, the content, situation, and individual are all equally important. In addition, one must have an intention to perform well and attain eudaimonia. All of these factors render Aristotelian ethics an example of a mixed deontological system of normative ethics. The following examples are taken from Aristotle's *Nicomachean Ethics* and elucidate other virtues.

HUMAN SITUATION	DEFECT	MEAN	EXCESS

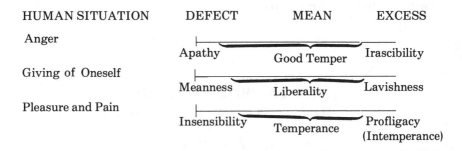

Think of concrete examples illustrating each of these virtues and vices, as elucidated in Aristotelian moral theory. Always keep in mind Aristotle's position: virtue is the mean while vice is either a defect or an excess of a human action.

The Aristotelian position is one of naturalism. Some philosophers have argued that such a naturalism cannot adequately account for the status of obligatory statements. In other words, how does one legitimately derive an obligatory statement from a set of statements describing natural dispositions? While it is true that Aristotle was not as sophisticated in regard to the is-ought dichotomy as the contemporary followers of Hume and Kant, nonetheless one can suggest a possible solution for Aristotle to this objection. In our discussion of Kant, recall that what counted for an immoral action was what struck at the roots of our very humanity. As we are essentially rational beings, and since, according to Kant, an immoral action is a contradiction and thus inherently irrational, it is wrong to undertake immoral actions because such an undertaking renders us nonhuman. Aristotle can utilize the same theme. Not to seek eudaimonia and thus fail to attain a state of functioning well is to strike at the very roots of what we are as human beings. Not to function well is to be

nonhuman. At this level Aristotle's naturalism and Kant's categorical imperative have the same obligatory character. To be immoral, both philosophers
maintain, is to be inhuman.

Any essentialist position must satisfy the demand that a set of dispositional
properties constituting human nature is indeed capable of being known. It is
possible that all Aristotle needs is what contemporary psychologists have
referred to as a "relative constancy" regarding the set of dispositional properties. As long as the constancy can be determined in most cases, Aristotle has
enough material from which to base his moral theory.

A serious problem, however, concerns the ordering of the dispositional
properties among themselves. Does one set of properties have priority over the
other two? Or do all three generic sets maintain an equal balance? Following
Plato, Aristotle suggests that the rational dimension takes priority. It is difficult to understand exactly what this means. Does it follow then that a human
being could have a good reason to commit suicide? In this instance, one might
have a good reason to frustrate the living disposition. Aristotle would probably
not accept this, yet it is difficult to see how he would argue against it.

The contemporary psychologist, Carl Rogers, has strongly suggested that
there be an organismic base for value theory. The naturalism expressed by
Rogers has interesting similarities to that espoused by Aristotle and Aquinas
as we will note in the following article.

THE VALUING PROCESS
IN THE MATURE PERSON

Carl R. Rogers

There is a great deal of concern today with the problem of values. Youth, in
almost every country, is deeply uncertain of its value orientation; the values
associated with various religions have lost much of their influence;
sophisticated individuals in every culture seem unsure and troubled as to
the goals they hold in esteem. The reasons are not far to seek. The world
culture, in all its aspects, seems increasingly scientific and relativistic, and
the rigid, absolute views on values which comes to us from the past appear
anachronistic. Even more important, perhaps, is the fact that the modern
individual is assailed from every angle by divergent and contradictory value
claims. It is no longer possible, as it was in the not too distant historical
past, to settle comfortably into the value system of one's forebears or one's
life without ever examining the nature and the assumptions of that system.

In this situation it is not surprising that value orientations from the past
appear to be in a state of disintegration or collapse. Men question whether
there are, or can be, any universal values. It is often felt that we may have
lost, in our modern world, all possibility of any general or cross-cultural
basis for values. One natural result of this uncertainty and confusion is that

From the *Journal of Abnormal and Social Psychology* 68, no. 2 (1964): 160–67. Copyright
1964 by the American Psychological Association. Reprinted by permission.

there is an increasing concern about, interest in, and a searching for, a sound or meaningful value approach which can hold its own in today's world.

I share this general concern. As with other issues the general problem faced by the culture is painfully and specifically evident in the cultural microcosm which is called the therapeutic relationship, which is my sphere of experience.

As a consequence of this experience I should like to attempt a modest theoretical approach to this whole problem. I have observed changes in the approach to values as the individual grows from infancy to adulthood. I observe further changes when, if he is fortunate, he continues to grow toward true psychological maturity. Many of these observations grow out of my experience as therapist, where I have had the mind stretching opportunity of seeing the ways in which individuals move toward a richer life. From these observations I believe I see some directional threads emerging which might offer a new concept of the valuing process, more tenable in the modern world. I have made a beginning by presenting some of these ideas partially in previous writings; I would like now to voice them more clearly and more fully.

SOME DEFINITIONS

Charles Morris has made some useful distinctions in regard to values. There are "operative values," which are the behaviors of organisms in which they show preference for one object or objective rather than another. The lowly earthworm, selecting the smooth arm of a **Y** maze rather than the arm which is paved with sandpaper, is giving an indication of an operative value.

There are also "conceived values," the preference of an individual for a symbolized object. "Honesty is the best policy" is such a conceived value.

There is also the term "objective value," to refer to what is objectively preferable, whether or not it is sensed or conceived of as desirable. I will be concerned primarily with operative or conceptualized values.

INFANT'S WAY OF VALUING

Let me first speak about the infant. The living human being has, at the outset, a clear approach to values. We can infer from studying his behavior that he prefers those experiences which maintain, enhance, or actualize his organism, and rejects those which do not serve this end. Watch him for a bit:

Hunger is negatively valued. His expression of this often comes through loud and clear.

Food is positively valued. But when he is satisfied, food is negatively valued, and the same milk he responded to so eagerly is now spit out, or the breast which seemed so satisfying is now rejected as he turns his head away from the nipple with an amusing facial expression of disgust and revulsion.

He values security, and the holding and caressing which seem to communicate security.

He values new experience for its own sake, and we observe this is his obvious pleasure in discovering his toes, in his searching movements, in his endless curiosity.

He shows a clear negative valuing of pain, bitter tastes, sudden loud sounds.

All of this is commonplace, but let us look at these facts in terms of what they tell us about the infant's approach to values. It is first of all a flexible, changing, valuing *process,* not a fixed system. He likes food and dislikes the same food. He values security and rest, and rejects it for new experience. What is going on seems best described as an organismic valuing process, in which each element, each moment of what he is experiencing is somehow weighed, and selected or rejected, depending on whether, at that moment, it tends to actualize the organism or not. This complicated weighing of experience is clearly an organismic, not a conscious or symbolic function. These are operative, not conceived values. But this process can nonetheless deal with complex value problems. I would remind you of the experiment in which young infants had spread in front of them a score or more of dishes of natural (that is, unflavored) foods. Over a period of time they clearly tended to value the foods which enhanced their own survival, growth, and development. If for a time a child gorged himself on starches, this would soon be balanced by a protein "binge." If at times he chose a diet deficient in some vitamin, he would later seek out foods rich in this very vitamin. The physiological wisdom of his body guided his behavioral movements, resulting in what we might think of as objectively sound value choices.

Another aspect of the infant's approach to values is that the source or locus of the evaluating process is clearly within himself. Unlike many of us, he *knows* what he likes and dislikes, and the origin of these value choices lies strictly within himself. He is the center of the valuing process, the evidence for his choices being supplied by his own senses. He is not at this point influenced by what his parents think he should prefer, or by what the church says, or by the opinion of the latest "expert" in the field, or by the persuasive talents of an advertising firm. It is from within his own experiencing that his organism is saying in nonverbal terms, "This is good for me." "That is bad for me." "I like this." "I strongly dislike that." He would laugh at our concern over values, if he could understand it.

CHANGE IN THE VALUING PROCESS

What happens to this efficient, soundly based valuing process? By what sequence of events do we exchange it for the more rigid, uncertain, inefficient approach to values which characterizes most of us as adults? Let me try to state briefly one of the major ways in which I think this happens.

The infant needs love, wants it, tends to behave in ways which will bring a repetition of this wanted experience. But this brings complications. He pulls baby sister's hair, and finds it satisfying to hear her wails and protests. He then hears that he is "a naughty, bad boy," and this may be reinforced by a slap on the hand. He is cut off from affection. As this experience is repeated, and many, many others like it, he gradually learns that what "feels good" is often "bad" in the eyes of significant others. Then the next step occurs, in which he comes to take the same attitude toward himself which these others have taken. Now, as he pulls his sister's hair, he solemnly intones, "Bad, bad boy." He is introjecting the value judgment of another, taking it in as his own. To that degree he loses touch with his own organismic valuing process. He has deserted the wisdom of his organism, giving up the locus of evaluation, and is trying to behave in terms of values set by another, in order to hold love.

Or take another example at an older level. A boy senses, though perhaps not consciously, that he is more loved and prized by his parents when he thinks of being a doctor than when he thinks of being an artist. Gradually he introjects the values attached to being a doctor. He comes to want, above all, to be a doctor. Then in college he is baffled by the fact that he repeatedly fails in chemistry, which is absolutely necessary to becoming a physician, in spite of the fact that the guidance counselor assures him he has the ability to pass the course. Only in counseling interviews does he begin to realize how completely he has lost touch with his organismic reactions, how out of touch he is with his own valuing process.

Perhaps these illustrations will indicate that in an attempt to gain or hold love, approval, esteem, the individual relinquishes the locus of evaluation which was his in infancy, and places it in others. He learns to have a basic *dis*trust for his own experiencing as a guide to his behavior. He learns from others a large number of conceived values, and adopts them as his own, even though they may be widely discrepant from what he is experiencing.

SOME INTROJECTED PATTERNS

It is in this fashion, I believe, that most of us accumulate the introjected value patterns by which we live. In the fantastically complex culture of today, the patterns we introject as desirable or undesirable come from a variety of sources and are often highly contradictory. Let me list a few of the introjections which are commonly held.

Sexual desires and behaviors are mostly bad. The sources of this construct are many—parents, church, teachers.

Disobedience is bad. Here parents and teachers combine with the military to emphasize this concept. To obey is good. To obey without question is even better.

Making money is the highest good. The sources of this conceived value are too numerous to mention.

Learning an accumulation of scholarly facts is highly desirable. Education is the source.

Communism is utterly bad. Here the government is a major source.

To love thy neighbor is the highest good. This concept comes from the church, perhaps from the parents.

Cooperation and teamwork are preferable to acting alone. Here companions are an important source.

Cheating is clever and desirable. The peer group again is the origin.

Coca-Colas, chewing gum, electric refrigerators, and automobiles are all utterly desirable. From Jamaica to Japan, from Copenhagen to Kowloon, the "Coca-Cola culture" has come to be regarded as the acme of desirability.

This is a small and diversified sample of the myriads of conceived values which individuals often introject, and hold as their own, without ever having considered their inner organismic reactions to these patterns and objects.

COMMON CHARACTERISTICS OF ADULT VALUING

I believe it will be clear from the foregoing that the usual adult—I feel I am speaking for most of us—has an approach to values which has these characteristics:

The majority of his values are introjected from other individuals or groups significant to him, but are regarded by him as his own.

The source or locus of evaluation on most matters lies outside of himself.

The criterion by which his values are set is the degree to which they will cause him to be loved, accepted, or esteemed.

These conceived preferences are either not related at all, or not clearly related, to his own process of experiencing.

Often there is a wide and unrecognized discrepancy between the evidence supplied by his own experience, and these conceived values.

Because these conceptions are not open to testing in experience, he must hold them in a rigid and unchanging fashion. The alternative would be a collapse of his values. Hence his values are "right."

Because they are untestable, there is no ready way of solving contradictions. If he has taken in from the community the conception that money is the *summum bonum* and from the church the conception that love of one's neighbor is the highest value, he has no way of discovering which has more value for *him.* Hence a common aspect of modern life is living with absolutely contradictory values. We calmly discuss the possibility of dropping a hydrogen bomb on Russia, but find tears in our eyes when we see headlines about the suffering of one small child.

Because he has relinquished the locus of evaluation to others, and has lost touch with his own valuing process, he feels profoundly insecure and easily threatened in his values. If some of these conceptions were destroyed, what would take their place? This threatening possibility makes him hold his value conceptions more rigidly or more confusedly, or both.

FUNDAMENTAL DISCREPANCY

I believe that this picture of the individual, with values mostly introjected, held as fixed concepts, rarely examined or tested, is the picture of most of us. By taking over the conceptions of others as our own, we lose contact with the potential wisdom of our own functioning, and lose confidence in ourselves. Since these value constructs are often sharply at variance with what is going on in our own experiencing, we have in a very basic way divorced ourselves from ourselves, and this accounts for much of modern strain and insecurity. This fundamental discrepancy between the individual's concept and what he is actually experiencing between the intellectual structure of his values and the valuing process going on unrecognized within—this is part of the fundamental estrangement of modern man from himself.

RESTORING CONTACT WITH EXPERIENCE

Some individuals are fortunate in going beyond the picture I have just given, developing further in the direction of psychological maturity. We see this happen in psychotherapy where we endeavor to provide a climate favorable to the growth of the person. We also see it happen in life, whenever life provides a therapeutic climate for the individual. Let me concentrate on this further maturing of a value approach as I have seen it in therapy.

As the client senses and realizes that he is prized as a person he can slowly begin to value the different aspects of himself. Most importantly, he can begin, with much difficulty at first, to sense and to feel what is going on within him, what he is feeling, what he is experiencing, how he is reacting. He uses his experiencing as a direct referent to which he can turn in forming accurate conceptualizations and as a guide to his behavior. Gendlin (1961, 1962) has elaborated the way in which this occurs. As his experiencing becomes more and more open to him, as he is able to live more freely in the process of his feelings, then significant changes begin to occur in his approach to values. It begins to assume many of the characteristics it had in infancy.

INTROJECTED VALUES IN RELATION TO EXPERIENCING

Perhaps I can indicate this by reviewing a few of the brief examples of introjected values which I have given, and suggesting what happens to them as the individual comes closer to what is going on within him.

> The individual in therapy looks back and realizes. "But I *enjoyed* pulling my sister's hair—and that doesn't make me a bad person."
>
> The student failing chemistry realizes, as he gets close to his own experiencing, "I don't like chemistry; I don't value being a doctor, even though my parents do; and I am not a failure for having these feelings."
>
> The adult recognizes that sexual desires and behavior may be richly satisfying and permanently enriching in their consequences, or shallow and temporary and less than satisfying. He goes by his own experiencing, which does not always coincide with social norms.
>
> He recognizes freely that this communist book or person expresses attitudes and goals which he shares as well as ideas and values which he does not share.
>
> He realizes that at times he experiences cooperation as meaningful and valuable to him, and that at other times he wishes to be alone and act alone.

VALUING IN THE MATURE PERSON

The valuing process which seems to develop in this more mature person is in some ways very much like that in the infant, and in some ways quite different. It is fluid, flexible, based on this particular moment, and the degree to which this moment is experienced as enhancing and actualizing. Values are not held rigidly, but are continually changing. The painting which last year seemed meaningful now appears uninteresting, the way of working with individuals which was formerly experienced as good now seems inadequate, the belief which then seemed true is now experienced as only partly true, or perhaps false.

Another characteristic of the way this person values experience is that it is highly differentiated, or as the semanticists would say, extensional. The examples in the preceding section indicate that what were previously rather solid monolithic introjected values now become differentiated, tied to a particular time and experience.

Another characteristic of the mature individual's approach is that the locus of evaluation is again established firmly within the person. It is his own experience which provides the value information or feedback. This does not mean that he is not open to all the evidence he can obtain from other sources. But it means that this is taken for what it is—outside evidence—and is not as significant as his own reactions. Thus he may be told by a friend that a new book is very disappointing. He reads two unfavorable reviews of the book. Thus his tentative hypothesis is that he will not value the book. Yet if he reads the book his valuing will be based upon the reactions it stirs in *him,* not on what he has been told by others.

There is also involved in this valuing process a letting oneself down into the immediacy of what one is experiencing, endeavoring to sense and to clarify all its complex meanings. I think of a client who, toward the close of therapy, when puzzled about an issue, would put his head in his hands and say, "Now what *is* it that I'm feeling? I want to get next to it. I want to learn what it is." Then he would wait, quietly and patiently, trying to listen to himself, until he could discern the exact flavor of the feelings he was experiencing. He, like others, was trying to get close to himself.

In getting close to what is going on within himself, the process is much more complex than it is in the infant. In the mature person it has much more scope and sweep. For there is involved in the present moment of experiencing the memory traces of all the relevant learnings from the past. This moment has not only its immediate sensory impact, but it has meaning growing out of similar experiences in the past. It has both the new and the old in it. So when I experience a painting or a person, my experiencing contains within it the learnings I have accumulated from past meetings with paintings or persons, as well as the new impact of this particular encounter. Likewise the moment of experiencing contains, for the mature adult, hypotheses about consequences. "It is not pleasant to express forthrightly my negative feelings to this person, but past experience indicates that in a continuing relationship it will be helpful in the long run." Past and future are both in this moment and enter into the valuing.

I find that in the person I am speaking of (and here again we see a similarity to the infant), the criterion of the valuing process is the degree to which the object of the experience actualizes the individual himself. Does it make him a richer, more complete, more fully developed person? This may sound as though it were a selfish or unsocial criterion, but it does not prove to be so, since deep and helpful relationships with others are experienced as actualizing.

Like the infant, too, the psychologically mature adult trusts and uses the wisdom of his organism, with the difference that he is able to do so knowingly. He realizes that if he can trust all of himself, his feelings and his intuitions may be wiser than his mind, that as a total person he can be more sensitive and accurate than his thoughts alone. Hence he is not afraid to say, "I feel that this experience [or this thing, or this direction] is good. Later I will probably know *why* I feel it is good." He trusts the totality of himself, having moved toward becoming what Lancelot Whyte regards as "the unitary man."

It should be evident from what I have been saying that this valuing process in the mature individual is not an easy or simple thing. The process is complex, the choices often very perplexing and difficult, and there is no guarantee that the choice which is made will in fact prove to be self-actualizing. But because whatever evidence exists is available to the individual, and because he is open to his experiencing, errors are correctable. If this chosen course of action is not self-enhancing this will be sensed and he can make an adjustment or revision. He thrives on a maximum feedback interchange, and thus, like the gyroscopic compass on a ship, can continually correct his course toward his true goal of self-fulfillment.

SOME PROPOSITIONS REGARDING THE VALUING PROCESS

Let me sharpen the meaning of what I have been saying by stating two propositions which contain the essential elements of this viewpoint. While it may not be possible to devise empirical tests of each proposition in its entirety, yet each is to some degree capable of being tested through the methods of psychological science. I would also state that though the following propositions are stated firmly in order to give them clarity, I am actually advancing them as decidedly tentative hypotheses.

Hypothesis I. There is an organismic base for an organized valuing process within the human individual.

It is hypothesized that this base is something the human being shares with the rest of the animate world. It is part of the functioning life process of any healthy organism. It is the capacity for receiving feedback information which enables the organism continually to adjust its behavior and reactions so as to achieve the maximum possible self-enhancement.

Hypothesis II. This valuing process in the human being is effective in achieving self-enhancement to the degree that the individual is open to the experiencing which is going on within himself.

I have tried to give two examples of individuals who are close to their own experiencing: the tiny infant who has not yet learned to deny in his awareness the processes going on within; and the psychologically mature person who has relearned the advantages of this open state.

There is a corollary to this second proposition which might be put in the following terms. One way of assisting the individual to move toward openness to experience is through a relationship in which he is prized as a separate person, in which the experiencing going on within him is empathically understood and valued, and in which he is given the freedom to experience his own feelings and those of others without being threatened in doing so.

This corollary obviously grows out of therapeutic experience. It is a brief statement of the essential qualities in the therapeutic relationship. There are already some empirical studies, of which the one by Barrett-Lennard is a good example, which give support to such a statement.

PROPOSITIONS REGARDING THE OUTCOMES OF THE VALUING PROCESS

I come now to the nub of any theory of values or valuing. What are its consequences? I should like to move into this new ground by stating bluntly two propositions as to the qualities of behavior which emerge from this valuing process. I shall then give some of the evidence from my experience as a therapist in support of these propositions.

Hypothesis III. In persons who are moving toward greater openness to their experiencing, there is an organismic commonality of value directions.

Hypothesis IV. These common value directions are of such kinds as to enhance the development of the individual himself, of others in his community, and to make for the survival and evolution of his species.

It has been a striking fact of my experience that in therapy, where individuals are valued, where there is greater freedom to feel and to be, certain value directions seem to emerge. These are not chaotic directions but instead exhibit a surprising commonality. This commonality is not dependent on the personality of the therapist, for I have seen these trends emerge in the clients of therapists sharply different in personality. This commonality does not seem to be due to the influences of any one culture, for I have found evidence of these directions in cultures as divergent as those of the United States, Holland, France, and Japan. I like to think that this commonality of value directions is due to the fact that we all belong to the same species—that just as a human infant tends, individually, to select a diet similar to that selected by other human infants, so a client in therapy tends, individually, to choose value directions similar to those chosen by other clients. As a species there may be certain elements of experience which tend to make for inner development and which would be chosen by all individuals if they were genuinely free to choose.

Let me indicate a few of these value directions as I see them in my clients as they move in the direction of personal growth and maturity.

> They tend to move away from facades. Pretense, defensiveness, putting up a front, tend to be negatively valued.
> They tend to move away from "oughts." The compelling feeling of "I ought to do or be thus and so" is negatively valued. The client moves away from being what he "ought to be," no matter who has set that imperative.
> They tend to move away from meeting the expectations of others. Pleasing others, as a goal in itself, is negatively valued.
> Being real is positively valued. The client tends to move toward being himself, being his real feelings, being what he is. This seems to be a very deep preference.
> Self-direction is positively valued. The client discovers an increasing pride and confidence in making his own choices, guiding his own life.
> One's self, one's own feelings come to be positively valued. From a point where he looks upon himself with contempt and despair, the client comes to value himself and his reactions as being of worth.
> Being a process is positively valued. From desiring some fixed goal, clients come to prefer the excitement of being a process of potentialities being born.
> Sensitivity to others and acceptance of others is positively valued. The client comes to appreciate others for what they are, just as he has come to appreciate himself for what he is.
> Deep relationships are positively valued. To achieve a close, intimate, real, fully communicative relationship with another person seems to meet a deep need in every individual, and is very highly valued.
> Perhaps more than all else, the client comes to value an openness to all of his inner and outer experience. To be open to and sensitive to his own *inner* reactions and feelings, the reactions and feelings of others, and the realities of the objective world—this is a direction which he clearly prefers. This openness becomes the client's most valued resource.

These then are some of the preferred directions which I have observed in individuals moving toward maturity. Though I am sure that the list I have given is inadequate and perhaps to some degree inaccurate, it holds for me exciting possibilities. Let me try to explain why.

I find it significant that when individuals are prized as persons, the values they select do not run the full gamut of possibilities. I do not find, in such a climate of freedom, that one person comes to value fraud and murder and thievery, while another values a life of self-sacrifice, and another values only money. Instead there seems to be a deep and underlying thread of commonality. I believe that when the human being is inwardly free to choose whatever he deeply values, he tends to value those objects, experiences, and goals which make for his own survival, growth, and development, and for the survival and development of others. I hypothesize that it is *characteristic* of the human organism to prefer such actualizing and socialized goals when he is exposed to a growth promoting climate.

A corollary of what I have been saying is that in *any* culture, given a climate of respect and freedom in which he is valued as a person, the mature individual would tend to choose and prefer these same value directions. This is a significant hypothesis which could be tested. It means that though the individual of whom I am speaking would not have a consistent or even a stable system of conceived values, the valuing process within him would lead to emerging value directions which would be constant across cultures and across time.

Another implication I see is that individuals who exhibit the fluid valuing process I have tried to describe, whose value directions are generally those I have listed, would be highly effective in the ongoing process of human evolution. If the human species is to survive at all on this globe, the human being must become more readily adaptive to new problems and situations, must be able to select that which is valuable for development and survival out of new and complex situations, must be accurate in his appreciation of reality if he is to make such selections. The psychologically mature person as I have described him has, I believe, the qualities which would cause him to value those experiences which would make for the survival and enhancement of the human race. He would be a worthy participant and guide in the process of human evolution.

Finally, it appears that we have returned to the issue of universality of values, but by a different route. Instead of universal values "out there," or a universal value system imposed by some group—philosophers, rulers, priests, or psychologists—we have the possibility of universal human value directions *emerging* from the experiencing of the human organism. Evidence from therapy indicates that both personal and social values emerge as natural, and experienced, when the individual is close to his own organismic valuing process. The suggestion is that though modern man no longer trusts religion or science or philosophy nor any system of beliefs to *give* him values, he may find an organismic valuing base within himself which, if he can learn again to be in touch with it, will prove to be an organized, adaptive, and social approach to the perplexing value issues which face all of us.

In Rogers' account, the naturalistic basis for value theory is explicitly maintained. He suggests that a viable naturalism must be grounded in the experience of the human organism. There is an apparent conceptual similarity between Rogers' account and the functional concept elucidated by Aristotle. Recall the "organismic commonality" which Rogers asserts as part of his system. Organismic commonality appears to suggest that all human beings function essentially the same way. This seems like a return to the concept of a "human nature" with a set of "basic needs" or "natural necessities." Rogers also rejects entirely any set of values which is not derived from an organismic base. He refers to such an occurrence as the acceptance of "introjected values." Aristotelians too would resoundingly avoid introjected values. The goal of the value theory as proposed by Rogers is the "fully functioning person." Note again the Aristotelian theme in Rogers' analysis. As self-actualization and functioning well are important to the determination of value in Rogers' theory, so too is eudaimonia central to Aristotle's account of moral philosophy. Rogers and Aristotle appear to have elucidated conceptually similar theories of ethical naturalism. Granting the similarities, where might lie serious differences?

The following selection by Lawrence Kohlberg indicates the results of his research into the psychological dimension of moral development. It is interesting to note what Kohlberg refers to as the "culturally universal invariant sequence of stages of moral judgment." Kohlberg strongly suggests that each of us, no matter what our cultural differences, proceeds in similar ways in the process of moral development. In reading Kohlberg's account of the six stages, recall the Kantian discussion of universalizability.

THE CLAIM TO MORAL ADEQUACY OF A HIGHEST STAGE OF MORAL JUDGMENT

Lawrence Kohlberg

I. REVIEW OF PSYCHOLOGICAL THEORY

Over a period of almost twenty years of empirical research, my colleagues and I have rather firmly established a culturally universal invariant sequence of stages of moral judgment; these stages are grossly summarized in Table 1:

Table 1. Definition of Moral Stages

I. Preconventional level

At this level the child is responsive to cultural rules and labels of good and bad, right or wrong, but interprets these labels either in terms of the physical or the hedonistic consequences of action (punishment, reward, exchange of favors) or in terms of the physical power of those who enunciate the rules and labels. The level is divided into the following two stages:

From *The Journal of Philosophy* 70, no. 18 (Oct. 25, 1973): pp. 630–33. Reprinted by permission of the author and *The Journal of Philosophy*.

Stage 1: *The punishment-and-obedience orientation.* The physical consequences of action determine its goodness or badness regardless of the human meaning or value of these consequences. Avoidance of punishment and unquestioning deference to power are valued in their own right, not in terms of respect for an underlying moral order supported by punishment and authority (the latter being stage 4).

Stage 2: *The instrumental-relativist orientation.* Right action consists of that which instrumentally satisfies one's own needs and occasionally the needs of others. Human relations are viewed in terms like those of the market place. Elements of fairness, of reciprocity, and of equal sharing are present, but they are always interpreted in a physical pragmatic way. Reciprocity is a matter of "you scratch my back and I'll scratch yours," not of loyalty, gratitude, or justice.

II. Conventional level

At this level, maintaining the expectations of the individual's family, group, or nation is perceived as valuable in its own right, regardless of immediate and obvious consequences. The attitude is not only one of *conformity* to personal expectations and social order, but of loyalty to it, of actively *maintaining,* supporting, and justifying the order, and of identifying with the persons or group involved in it. At this level, there are the following two stages:

Stage 3: *The interpersonal concordance or "good boy—nice girl" orientation.* Good behavior is that which pleases or helps others and is approved by them. There is much conformity to stereotypical images of what is majority or "natural" behavior. Behavior is frequently judged by intention—"he means well" becomes important for the first time. One earns approval by being "nice."

Stage 4: *The "law and order" orientation.* There is orientation toward authority, fixed rules, and the maintenance of the social order. Right behavior consists of doing one's duty, showing respect for authority, and maintaining the given social order for its own sake.

III. Postconventional, autonomous, or principled level

At this level, there is a clear effort to define moral values and principles that have validity and application apart from the authority of the groups or persons holding these principles and apart from the individual's own identification with these groups. This level again has two stages:

Stage 5: *The social-contract legalistic orientation,* generally with utilitarian overtones. Right action tends to be defined in terms of general individual rights, and standards which have been critically examined and agreed upon by the whole society. There is a clear awareness of the relativism of personal values and opinions and a corresponding emphasis upon procedural rules for reaching consensus. Aside from what is constitutionally and democratically agreed upon, the right is a matter of personal "values" and "opinion." The result is an emphasis upon the "legal point of view," but with an emphasis upon the possibility of changing law in terms of rational considerations of social utility (rather than freezing it in terms of stage 4 "law and order"). Outside the legal realm, free agreement and contract is the binding element of obligation. This is the "official" morality of the American government and constitution.

Stage 6: *The universal-ethical-principle orientation.* Right is defined by the decision of conscience in control with self-chosen *ethical prin-*

ciples appealing to logical comprehensiveness, universality, and consistency. These principles are abstract and ethical (the Golden Rule, the categorical imperative); they are not concrete moral rules like the Ten Commandments. At heart, these are universal principles of *justice,* of the *reciprocity* and *equality* of human *rights,* and of respect for the dignity of human beings as *individual persons* ("From Is to Ought," pp. 164/5).

As Table 1 indicates, the last stage, stage 6, has a distinctively Kantian ring, centering moral judgment on concepts of obligation as these are defined by principles of respect for persons and of justice. In part, this corresponds to an initial "formalist" or "structuralist" bias of both our moral and our psychological theory. Our psychological theory of morality derives largely from Piaget,[1] who claims that both logic and morality develop through stages and that each stage is a structure, which formally considered, is in better equilibrium than its predecessor. It assumes, that is, that each new (logical or moral) stage is a new structure which includes elements of earlier structures but transforms them in such a way as to represent a more stable and extensive equilibrium. Our theory assumes that new moral structures presuppose new logical structures, i.e., that a new logical stage (or substage) is a necessary but not sufficient condition for a new moral stage. It assumes, however, that moral judgments (or moral equilibrium) involves two related processes or conditions absent in the logical domain. First, moral judgments involve role-taking, taking the point of view of others conceived as *subjects* and coordinating those points of view, whereas logic involves only coordinating points of view upon objects. Second, equilibrated moral judgments involve principles of justice or fairness. A moral situation in disequilibrium is one in which there are unresolved conflicting claims. A resolution of the situation is one in which each is "given his due" according to some principle of justice that can be recognized as fair by all the conflicting parties involved. These "equilibration" assumptions of our psychological theory are naturally allied to the formalistic tradition in philosophic ethics from Kant to Rawls. This isomorphism of psychological and normative theory generates the claim that a psychologically more advanced stage of moral judgment is more morally adequate, by moral-philosophic criteria. The isomorphism assumption is a two-way street. While moral philosophical criteria of adequacy of moral judgment help define a standard of psychological adequacy or advance, the study of psychological advance feeds back and clarifies these criteria. Our psychological theory as to why individuals move from one stage to the next is grounded on a moral-philosophical theory which specifies that the later stage is morally better or more adequate than the earlier stage. Our psychological theory claims that individuals prefer the highest stage of reasoning they comprehend, a claim supported by research. This claim of our psychological theory derives from a philosophical claim that a later stage is "objectively" preferable or more adequate by certain *moral* criteria. This philosophic claim, however, would for us be thrown into question if the facts of moral advance were inconsistent with its psychological implications.

Our assumption of isomorphism implies first the assumption of continuity between the context of discovery of moral viewpoints (studied by the psychology of moral development) and the context of justification of moral viewpoints (studied by formal moral philosophy). This implies that the philosopher's *justification* of a higher stage of moral reasoning maps into the psychologist's *explanation* of movement to that stage, and vice versa. The isomorphism assumption is plausible if one believes that the developing human being and the moral philosopher are engaged in fundamentally the same moral task.

NOTE

1. Jean Piaget, *The Moral Judgment of the Child* (Glencoe, Ill.: Free Press, 1948; first edition, 1932).

Metaethics

Having discussed three theories of normative ethics in some detail, it would be well for us now to consider briefly a principal issue treated in metaethics. Metaethics, as a separate branch of ethics, is primarily a twentieth-century contribution to moral philosophy. The following discussions in metaethics will concentrate on one principle issue, namely, the nature of moral terms and the function of moral language.

In discussions of moral language in metaethics, a primary question concerns the nature of reference in regard to moral terms. Do moral terms refer to an objective reality in the external world? If so, what is it? If there is no objective reference, then how do we account for the significance of moral terms? There are two generic responses to these questions: (a) cognitive theories, and (b) noncognitive theories. A cognitive theory asserts that there is some type of objective referent for moral terms. A noncognitive theory asserts that there is no referent for moral terms. We may further divide cognitive theories into two areas: (a) naturalism, and (b) intuitionism, or as it is sometimes called, absolutism.

Ethical naturalism asserts that ethical terms refer to some "natural," empirical property found in the external world. In the history of philosophy, Jeremy Bentham and John Stuart Mill are considered principal exponents of ethical naturalism. Recall from our discussion of Mill's utilitarianism that goodness was defined in terms of pleasure. Given Mill's naturalism, in order to discover what is good, we must discover what is pleasurable. Pleasure, according to a utilitarian naturalist, is a natural, empirically verifiable property. In theory, these natural properties were quantifiably measurable by some scientific, synthetic process. Recall our discussion above of Bentham's hedonic calculus.

In our consideration of Mill's utilitarianism, G.E. Moore charged that any form of ethical naturalism committed what he called "the naturalistic fallacy." The force of Moore's argument was directed at the purported fallacy inherent in any attempt to define goodness in terms of natural properties. Moore's question, directed at the naturalist, was "Does goodness really mean the same thing as pleasure?" According to Moore, any natural property could be substituted for pleasure. This is Moore's famous *open question argument*. Moore suggested that, no matter what natural property was used in defining goodness, one could still significantly ask the following question: "Well, is that natural property good?" Insofar as it is always cognitively significant to ask the open question about any purported naturalist definition of goodness, Moore concluded that any such definition was conceptually inadequate. Moore also concluded that there was no one natural property which could be legitimately identified with goodness. Therefore it is, in principle, logically impossible to define goodness in terms of any natural property.

In response to the weakness brought on by the naturalistic fallacy and inherent in any form of ethical naturalism, Moore responded by determining his own cognitive moral theory. In contemporary discussions of metaethics, Moore's theory is usually referred to as *intuitionism*. However, in *Language, Truth and Logic*, A.J. Ayer termed it *absolutism*. The basic claim of Moore's intuitionism is that the moral property of goodness, although it indeed does have an objective foundation in the external world, does not refer nor is reducible to any individual or set of natural properties. Rather, there is a unique type of nonnatural property which serves as the referent for "goodness" in moral language. Goodness, therefore, is a sui-generis property. In order to know this unique nonnatural property, Moore argued for the significance of direct intuition. A moral agent can directly intuit this sui-generis property of goodness. Insofar as goodness is an ontological feature of the world, Moore's intuitionism is a form of cognitivism. There is an objective referent for the term goodness as used in moral language. Yet the sui-generis property is never equivalent to an individual or set of natural properties. Prompted by the demands of the naturalistic fallacy, Moore's intuitionism asserts that goodness is not exhausted by any natural properties. Yet Moore thought he could circumvent the problems of naturalism and still have an objective foundation for moral judgments. This objective status was obtained by the move to nonnatural properties. The following discusses Moore's analysis regarding the indefinable nature of goodness:

> "Good," then, if we mean by it the quality which we assert to belong to a thing, when we say that the thing is good, is incapable of any definition, in the most important sense of that word.
>   . . . If I am asked "What is good?" my answer is that good is good, and that is the end of the matter. Or if I am asked "How is good to be defined?" my answer is that it cannot be defined, and that is all I have to say about it. [13]

In this way, Moore argued for the indefinability of good. Good as a nonnatural property is known in a self-evident manner through intuition.

Of course, there are very serious problems with Moore's account of intuitionism. First of all, we need to ask about the ontological status of the nonnatural property. Moore affirms that this property cannot be detected by any normal techniques of experience, observation, or investigation. Moore emphasizes that these nonnatural properties are nonempirical, but he has little to say about their positive status. Second, does one need a special epistemological faculty in order to encounter this unique ontological property? For example, do we have a special faculty of moral intuition? Moore seems to respond negatively; yet he is disturbingly silent when asked to account for the epistemological awareness of the sui-generis property of good. Third, can there be any possibility of moral disagreement and argumentation assuming the directly evident character of Moore's position? What if a person tries as hard as he or she possibly can to "intuit" the nonnatural property, yet just can't quite grasp it. The intuitionist can only respond, "Well, keep on trying; you'll eventually get it!" Furthermore, can the intuitionist ever be certain that intuitionism itself is correct? With Moore's intuitionism, the method of verification is totally private. This private nature eliminates any public verification. In effect, the only method of verification common to intuitionism is the intuition itself. But an intuition is private to a single knower. Accordingly, a serious form of ethical privatism results from intuitionism. In an a priori fashion, intuitionism rules out the possibility of significant moral disagreement.

In his *Contemporary Moral Philosophy*, G.J. Warnock noted that as a theory intuitionism ". . . seems deliberately, almost perversely, to answer no questions, to throw no light on any problem."[14] Warnock goes on to suggest that while insisting that there is indeed a crucial difference between ethical statements and descriptive statements, intuitionism ". . . amounts in practice to a refusal to discuss what the difference is."[15] This lack of precision and the absence of explanatory power characteristic of intuitionism brought forward the charge that maybe there were no such referents for ethical terms. With this charge came the advent of noncognitive theories of metaethics. Basically, a noncognitivist affirms that ethical terms do not have any objective foundation whatsoever. Upon analysis, ethical language depends solely upon the subjective responses of the agent.

The least complex type of noncognitive theory was that proposed by A.J. Ayer in *Language, Truth and Logic*. Ayer's noncognitivism is usually referred to as *emotivism*. As a noncognitivist theory of moral language, emotivism was an attempt to reconcile the demands of moral language with the verification theory of meaning of the logical positivists. Recalling our discussion of logical positivism in chapter 4, Ayer's *Language, Truth and Logic* became the English manifesto of logical positivism. Using the verification theory of meaning, the logical positivists established as the criterion for meaning the categories of analytic a priori statements and synthetic a posteriori statements. Since moral language fitted into neither category, the early positivists were puzzled about what to do with it. Given the importance of moral language in the area of human conduct, the positivists did not wish to consign it to the realm of meaningless discourse. In addition to meaning attributed to matters of logic and matters of fact, the logical positivists discussed what came to be known as "emotive meaning." Some of the logical positivists suggested that ethical language means merely the "expression" of an emotion. Of course, the emotions expressed were those experienced when confronting a moral situation. "*X* is good" literally means something like "Yea *X*!"; "*Y* is evil" means something like "Boo *Y*!" There is no referent in the objective world for moral language. As cheering for our favorite football team is an expression of a favorable emotion, so too is moral language a linguistic convention for the expression of those emotions felt in moral situations.

By means of the naturalistic fallacy, Moore had argued that naturalism was inadequate. Yet Moore's response to naturalism, evidenced through his intuitionism, possessed an exclusive nonverificatory characteristic. The logical positivists moved the analysis even farther. Perhaps, they suggested, not only is there no naturalistic equivalent for moral language, but possibly there is also no objective referent. In matters of moral discourse, there is no objective referent to be found. Moral terms are linguistic conventions used for the actual expression of our sentiments when confronting moral situations. The following passage from Ayer's *Language, Truth and Logic* is a classic statement of emotivism, as elucidated by the early adherents to logical positivism.

CRITIQUE OF ETHICS

A.J. Ayer

There is still one objection to be met before we can claim to have justified our view that all synthetic propositions are empirical hypotheses. This objection is based on the common supposition that our speculative knowledge is of two distinct kinds—that which relates to questions of empirical fact, and that which relates to questions of value. It will be said that "statements of value" are genuine synthetic propositions, but that they cannot with any show of justice be represented as hypotheses, which are used to predict the course of our sensations; and, accordingly, that the existence of ethics and aesthetics as branches of speculative knowledge presents an insuperable objection to our radical empiricist thesis.

In face of this objection, it is our business to give an account of "judgements of value" which is both satisfactory in itself and consistent with our general empiricist principles. We shall set ourselves to show that in so far as statements of value are significant, they are ordinary "scientific" statements; and that in so far as they are not scientific, they are not in the literal sense significant, but are simply expressions of emotion which can be neither true nor false. In maintaining this view, we may confine ourselves for the present to the case of ethical statements. What is said about them will be found to apply, *mutatis mutandis,* to the case of aesthetic statements also.[1]

The ordinary system of ethics, as elaborated in the works of ethical philosophers, is very far from being a homogeneous whole. Not only is it apt to contain pieces of metaphysics, and analyses of non-ethical concepts: its actual ethical contents are themselves of very different kinds. We may divide them, indeed, into four main classes. There are, first of all, propositions which express definitions of ethical terms, or judgements about the legitimacy or possibility of certain definitions. Secondly, there are propositions describing the phenomena of moral experience, and their causes. Thirdly, there are exhortations to moral virtue. And, lastly, there

---

From A.J. Ayer, *Language, Truth and Logic* (London: Victor Gollancz, Ltd., 1946), pp. 102–14. Reprinted by permission of the publisher.

are actual ethical judgements. It is unfortunately the case that the distinction between these four classes, plain as it is, is commonly ignored by ethical philosophers; with the result that it is often very difficult to tell from their works what it is that they are seeking to discover or prove.

In fact, it is easy to see that only the first of our four classes, namely that which comprises the propositions relating to the definitions of ethical terms, can be said to constitute ethical philosophy. The propositions which describe the phenomena of moral experience, and their causes, must be assigned to the science of psychology, or sociology. The exhortations to moral virtue are not propositions at all, but ejaculations or commands which are designed to provoke the reader to action of a certain sort. Accordingly, they do not belong to any branch of philosophy or science. As for the expressions of ethical judgements, we have not yet determined how they should be classified. But inasmuch as they are certainly neither definitions nor comments upon definitions, nor quotations, we may say decisively that they do not belong to ethical philosophy. A strictly philosophical treatise on ethics should therefore make no ethical pronouncements. But it should, by giving an analysis of ethical terms, show what is the category to which all such pronouncements belong. And this is what we are now about to do.

A question which is often discussed by ethical philosophers is whether it is possible to find definitions which would reduce all ethical terms to one or two fundamental terms. But this question, though it undeniably belongs to ethical philosophy, is not relevant to our present enquiry. We are not now concerned to discover which term, within the sphere of ethical terms, is to be taken as fundamental; whether, for example, "good" can be defined in terms of "right" or "right" in terms of "good," or both in terms of "value." What we are interested in is the possibility of reducing the whole sphere of ethical terms to non-ethical terms. We are enquiring whether statements of ethical value can be translated into statements of empirical fact.

That they can be so translated is the contention of those ethical philosophers who are commonly called subjectivists, and of those who are known as utilitarians. For the utilitarian defines the rightness of actions, and the goodness of ends, in terms of the pleasure, or happiness, or satisfaction, to which they give rise; the subjectivist, in terms of the feelings of approval which a certain person, or group of people, has towards them. Each of these types of definition makes moral judgements into a sub-class of psychological or sociological judgements; and for this reason they are very attractive to us. For, if either was correct, it would follow that ethical assertions were not generically different from the factual assertions which are ordinarily contrasted with them; and the account which we have already given of empirical hypotheses would apply to them also.

Nevertheless we shall not adopt either a subjectivist or a utilitarian analysis of ethical terms. We reject the subjectivist view that to call an action right, or a thing good, is to say that it is generally approved of, because it is not self-contradictory to assert that some actions which are generally approved of are not right, or that some things which are generally approved of are not good. And we reject the alternative subjectivist view that a man who asserts that a certain action is right, or that a certain thing is good, is saying that he himself approves of it, on the ground that a man who confessed that he sometimes approved of what was bad or wrong would not be contradicting himself. And a similar argument is fatal to utilitarianism. We cannot agree that to call an action right is to say that of all the actions possible in the circumstances it would cause, or be likely to cause, the greatest happiness, or the greatest balance of pleasure over pain, or the greatest balance of satisfied over unsatisfied desire, because we find that it is not self-contradictory to say that it is sometimes wrong to perform the action which would actually or probably cause the greatest happiness, or the greatest balance of pleasure over pain, or of satisfied over unsatisfied desire. And since it is not self-contradictory to say that some pleasant things are not good, or that some bad things are desired, it cannot be the case that the sentence "x is good" is equivalent to "x is pleasant," or to "x is desired." And to every other variant of utilitarianism with which I am acquainted the same objection can be made. And therefore we should, I think, conclude that the validity of ethical judgements is not determined by the felicific tendencies of actions, any more than by the nature of people's feelings; but that it must be regarded as "absolute" or "intrinsic," and not empirically calculable.

If we say this, we are not, of course, denying that it is possible to invent a language in which all ethical symbols are definable in non-ethical terms, or even that it is desirable to invent such a language and adopt it in place of our own; what we are denying is that the suggested reduction of ethical to non-ethical statements is consistent with the conventions of our actual language. That is, we reject utilitarianism and subjectivism, not as pro- posals to replace our existing ethical notions by new ones, but as analyses of our existing ethical notions. Our contention is simply that, in our lan- guage, sentences which contain normative ethical symbols are not equiva- lent to sentences which express psychological propositions, or indeed empirical propositions of any kind.

It is advisable here to make it plain that it is only normative ethical symbols, and not descriptive ethical symbols, that are held by us to be indefinable in factual terms. There is a danger of confusing these two types of symbols, because they are commonly constituted by signs of the same sensible form. Thus a complex sign of the form "x is wrong" may constitute a sentence which expresses a moral judgement concerning a certain type of conduct, or it may constitute a sentence which states that a certain type of conduct is repugnant to the moral sense of a particular society. In the latter case, the symbol "wrong" is a descriptive ethical symbol, and the sentence in which it occurs expresses an ordinary sociological proposition; in the former case, the symbol "wrong" is a normative ethical symbol, and the sentence in which it occurs does not, we maintain, express an empirical proposition at all. It is only with normative ethics that we are at present concerned; so that whenever ethical symbols are used in the course of this argument without qualification, they are always to be in- terpreted as symbols of the normative type.

In admitting that normative ethical concepts are irreducible to empirical concepts, we seem to be leaving the way clear for the "absolutist" view of ethics—that is, the view that statements of value are not controlled by observation, as ordinary empirical propositions are, but only by a mysterious "intellectual intuition." A feature of this theory, which is seldom recognized by its advocates, is that it makes statements of value unverifiable. For it is notorious that what seems intuitively certain to one person may seem doubtful, or even false, to another. So that unless it is possible to provide some criterion by which one may decide between conflicting intuitions, a mere appeal to intuition is worthless as a test of a proposition's validity. But in the case of moral judgements, no such criterion can be given. Some moralists claim to settle the matter by saying that they "know" that their own moral judgements are correct. But such an assertion is of purely psychological interest, and has not the slightest tendency to prove the validity of any moral judgement. For dissentient moralists may equally well "know" that their ethical views are correct. And, as far as subjective certainty goes, there will be nothing to choose between them. When such differences of opinion arise in connection with an ordinary empirical proposition, one may attempt to resolve them by referring to, or actually carrying out, some relevant empirical test. But with regard to ethical statements, there is, on the "absolutist" or "intuitionist" theory, no relevant empirical test. We are therefore justified in saying that on this theory ethical statements are held to be unverifiable. They are, of course, also held to be genuine synthetic propositions.

Considering the use which we have made of the principle that a synthetic proposition is significant only if it is empirically verifiable, it is clear that the acceptance of an "absolutist" theory of ethics would undermine the whole of our main argument. And as we have already rejected the "naturalistic" theories which are commonly supposed to provide the only alternative to "absolutism" in ethics, we seem to have reached a difficult position. We shall meet the difficulty by showing that the correct treatment of ethical statements is afforded by a third theory, which is wholly compatible with our radical empiricism.

We begin by admitting that the fundamental ethical concepts are unanalysable, inasmuch as there is no criterion by which one can test the validity of the judgements in which they occur. So far we are in agreement with the absolutists. But, unlike the absolutists, we are able to give an explanation of this fact about ethical concepts. We say that the reason why they are unanalysable is that they are mere pseudo-concepts. The presence of an ethical symbol in a proposition adds nothing to its factual content. Thus if I say to someone, "You acted wrongly in stealing that money," I am not stating anything more than if I had simply said, "You stole that money." In adding that this action is wrong I am not making any further statement about it. I am simply evincing my moral disapproval of it. It is as if I had said, "You stole that money," in a peculiar tone of horror, or written it with the addition of some special exclamation marks. The tone, or the exclamation marks, adds nothing to the literal meaning of the sentence. It merely serves to show that the expression of it is attended by certain feelings in the speaker.

If now I generalise my previous statement and say, "Stealing money is wrong," I produce a sentence which has no factual meaning—that is, expresses no proposition which can be either true or false. It is as if I had written "Stealing money!!"—where the shape and thickness of the exclamation marks show, by a suitable convention, that a special sort of moral disapproval is the feeling which is being expressed. It is clear that there is nothing said here which can be true or false. Another man may disagree with me about the wrongness of stealing, in the sense that he may not have the same feelings about stealing as I have, and he may quarrel with me on account of my moral sentiments. But he cannot, strictly speaking, contradict me. For in saying that a certain type of action is right or wrong, I am not making any factual statement, not even a statement about my own state of mind. I am merely expressing certain moral sentiments. And the man who is ostensibly contradicting me is merely expressing his moral sentiments. So that there is plainly no sense in asking which of us is in the right. For neither of us is asserting a genuine proposition.

What we have just been saying about the symbol "wrong" applies to all normative ethical symbols. Sometimes they occur in sentences which record ordinary empirical facts besides expressing ethical feeling about those facts: sometimes they occur in sentences which simply express ethical feeling about a certain type of action, or situation, without making any statement of fact. But in every case in which one would commonly be said to be making an ethical judgement, the function of the relevant ethical word is purely "emotive." It is used to express feeling about certain objects, but not to make any assertion about them.

It is worth mentioning that ethical terms do not serve only to express feeling. They are calculated also to arouse feeling, and so to stimulate action. Indeed some of them are used in such a way as to give the sentences in which they occur the effect of commands. Thus the sentence "It is your duty to tell the truth" may be regarded both as the expression of a certain sort of ethical feeling about truthfulness and as the expression of the command "Tell the truth." The sentence "You ought to tell the truth" also involves the command "Tell the truth," but here the tone of the command is less emphatic. In the sentence "It is good to tell the truth" the command has become little more than a suggestion. And thus the "meaning" of the word "good," in its ethical usage, is differentiated from that of the word "duty" or the word "ought." In fact we may define the meaning of the various ethical words in terms both of the different feelings they are ordinarily taken to express, and also the different responses which they are calculated to provoke.

We can now see why it is impossible to find a criterion for determining the validity of ethical judgements. It is not because they have an "absolute" validity which is mysteriously independent of ordinary sense-experience, but because they have no objective validity whatsoever. If a sentence makes no statement at all, there is obviously no sense in asking whether what it says is true or false. And we have seen that sentences which simply express moral judgements do not say anything. They are pure expressions of feeling and as such do not come under the category of truth and falsehood. They are unverifiable for the same reason as a cry of pain or a word of command is unverifiable—because they do not express genuine propositions.

Thus, although our theory of ethics might fairly be said to be radically subjectivist, it differs in a very important respect from the orthodox subjectivist theory. For the orthodox subjectivist does not deny, as we do, that the sentences of a moralizer express genuine propositions. All he denies is that they express propositions of a unique non-empirical character. His own view is that they express propositions about the speaker's feelings. If this were so, ethical judgements clearly would be capable of being true or false. They would be true if the speaker had the relevant feelings, and false if he had not. And this is a matter which is, in principle, empirically verifiable. Furthermore they could be significantly contradicted. For if I say, "Tolerance is a virtue," and someone answers, "You don't approve of it," he would, on the ordinary subjectivist theory, be contradicting me. On our theory, he would not be contradicting me, because, in saying that tolerance was a virtue, I should not be making any statement about my own feelings or about anything else. I should simply be evincing my feelings, which is not at all the same thing as saying that I have them.

The distinction between the expression of feeling and the assertion of feeling is complicated by the fact that the assertion that one has a certain feeling often accompanies the expression of that feeling, and is then, indeed, a factor in the expression of that feeling. Thus I may simultaneously express boredom and say that I am bored, and in that case my utterance of the words, "I am bored," is one of the circumstances which make it true to say that I am expressing or evincing boredom. But I can express boredom without actually saying that I am bored. I can express it by my tone and gestures, while making a statement about something wholly unconnected with it, or by an ejaculation, or without uttering any words at all. So that even if the assertion that one has a certain feeling always involves the expression of that feeling, the expression of a feeling assuredly does not always involve the assertion that one has it. And this is the important point to grasp in considering the distinction between our theory and the ordinary subjectivist theory. For whereas the subjectivist holds that ethical statements actually assert the existence of certain feelings, we hold that ethical statements are expressions and excitants of feeling which do not necessarily involve any assertions.

We have already remarked that the main objection to the ordinary subjectivist theory is that the validity of ethical judgements is not determined by the nature of their author's feelings. And this is an objection which our theory escapes. For it does not imply that the existence of any feelings is a necessary and sufficient condition of the validity of an ethical judgement. It implies, on the contrary, that ethical judgements have no validity.

There is, however, a celebrated argument against subjectivist theories which our theory does not escape. It has been pointed out by Moore that if ethical statements were simply statements about the speaker's feelings, it would be impossible to argue about questions of value.[2] To take a typical example: if a man said that thrift was a virtue, and another replied that it was a vice, they would not, on this theory, be disputing with one another.

One would be saying that he approved of thrift, and the other that *he* didn't; and there is no reason why both these statements should not be true. Now Moore held it to be obvious that we do dispute about questions of value, and accordingly concluded that the particular form of subjectivism which he was discussing was false.

It is plain that the conclusion that it is impossible to dispute about questions of value follows from our theory also. For as we hold that such sentences as "Thrift is a virtue" and "Thrift is a vice" do not express propositions at all, we clearly cannot hold that they express incompatible propositions. We must therefore admit that if Moore's argument really refutes the ordinary subjectivist theory, it also refutes ours. But, in fact, we deny that it does refute even the ordinary subjectivist theory. For we hold that one really never does dispute about questions of value.

This may seem, at first sight, to be a very paradoxical assertion. For we certainly do engage in disputes which are ordinarily regarded as disputes about questions of value. But, in all such cases, we find, if we consider the matter closely, that the dispute is not really about a question of value, but about a question of fact. When someone disagrees with us about the moral value of a certain action or type of action, we do admittedly resort to argument in order to win him over to our way of thinking. But we do not attempt to show by our arguments that he has the "wrong" ethical feeling towards a situation whose nature he has correctly apprehended. What we attempt to show is that he is mistaken about the facts of the case. We argue that he has misconceived the agent's motive: or that he has misjudged the effects of the action, or its probable effects in view of the agent's knowledge; or that he has failed to take into account the special circumstances in which the agent was placed. Or else we employ more general arguments about the effects which actions of a certain type tend to produce, or the qualities which are usually manifested in their performance. We do this in the hope that we have only to get our opponent to agree with us about the nature of the empirical facts for him to adopt the same moral attitude towards them as we do. And as the people with whom we argue have generally received the same moral education as ourselves, and live in the same social order, our expectation is usually justified. But if our opponent happens to have undergone a different process of moral "conditioning" from ourselves, so that, even when he acknowledges all the facts, he still disagrees with us about the moral value of the actions under discussion, then we abandon the attempt to convince him by argument. We say that it is impossible to argue with him because he has a distorted or undeveloped moral sense; which signifies merely that he employs a different set of values from our own. We feel that our own system of values is superior, and therefore speak in such derogatory terms of his. But we cannot bring forward any arguments to show that our system is superior. For our judgement that it is so is itself a judgement of value, and accordingly outside the scope of argument. It is because argument fails us when we come to deal with pure questions of value, as distinct from questions of fact, that we finally resort to mere abuse.

In short, we find that argument is possible on moral questions only if some system of values is presupposed. If our opponent concurs with us in expressing moral disapproval of all actions of a given type *t*, then we may get him to condemn a particular action A, by bringing forward arguments to show that A is of type *t*. For the question whether A does or does not belong to that type is a plain question of fact. Given that a man has certain moral principles, we argue that he must, in order to be consistent, react morally to certain things in a certain way. What we do not and cannot argue about is the validity of these moral principles. We merely praise or condemn them in the light of our own feelings.

If anyone doubts the accuracy of this account of moral disputes, let him try to construct even an imaginary argument on a question of value which does not reduce itself to an argument about a question of logic or about an empirical matter of fact. I am confident that he will not succeed in producing a single example. And if that is the case, he must allow that its involving the impossibility of purely ethical arguments is not, as Moore thought, a ground of objection to our theory, but rather a point in favour of it.

Having upheld our theory against the only criticism which appeared to threaten it, we may now use it to define the nature of all ethical enquiries. We find that ethical philosophy consists simply in saying that ethical concepts are pseudo-concepts and therefore unanalysable. The further task of describing the different feelings that the different ethical terms are used to express, and the different reactions that they customarily provoke, is a task for the psychologist. There cannot be such a thing as ethical science, if by ethical science one means the elaboration of a "true" system of morals. For we have seen that, as ethical judgements are mere expressions of feeling, there can be no way of determining the validity of any ethical system, and, indeed, no sense in asking whether any such system is true. All that one may legitimately enquire in this connection is, What are the moral habits of a given person or group of people, and what causes them to have precisely those habits and feelings? And this enquiry falls wholly within the scope of the existing social sciences.

It appears, then, that ethics, as a branch of knowledge, is nothing more than a department of psychology and sociology. And in case anyone thinks that we are overlooking the existence of casuistry, we may remark that casuistry is not a science, but is a purely analytical investigation of the structure of a given moral system. In other words, it is an exercise in formal logic.

When one comes to pursue the psychological enquiries which constitute ethical science, one is immediately enabled to account for the Kantian and hedonistic theories of morals. For one finds that one of the chief causes of moral behaviour is fear, both conscious and unconscious, of a god's displeasure, and fear of the enmity of society. And this, indeed, is the reason why moral precepts present themselves to some people as "categorical" commands. And one finds, also, that the moral code of a society is partly determined by the beliefs of that society concerning the conditions of its own happiness—or, in other words, that a society tends to encourage or discourage a given type of conduct by the use of moral sanctions according as it appears to promote or detract from the contentment of the society as a whole. And this is the reason why altruism is recommended in most moral codes and egotism condemned. It is from the observation of this connection between morality and happiness that hedonistic or eudaemonistic theories of morals ultimately spring, just as the moral theory of Kant is based on the fact, previously explained, that moral precepts have for some people the force of inexorable commands. As each of these theories ignores the fact which lies at the root of the other, both may be criticized as being one-sided; but this is not the main objection to either of them. Their essential defect is that they treat propositions which refer to the causes and attributes of our ethical feelings as if they were definitions of ethical concepts. And thus they fail to recognise that ethical concepts are pseudo-concepts and consequently indefinable.

As we have already said, our conclusions about the nature of ethics apply to aesthetics also. Aesthetic terms are used in exactly the same way as ethical terms. Such aesthetic words as "beautiful" and "hideous" are employed, as ethical words are employed, not to make statements of fact, but simply to express certain feelings and evoke a certain response. It follows, as in ethics, that there is no sense in attributing objective validity to aesthetic judgements, and no possibility of arguing about questions of value in aesthetics, but only about questions of fact. A scientific treatment of aesthetics would show us what in general were the causes of aesthetic feeling, why various societies produced and admired the works of art they did, why taste varies as it does within a given society, and so forth. And these are ordinary psychological or sociological questions. They have, of course, little or nothing to do with aesthetic criticism as we understand it. But that is because the purpose of aesthetic criticism is not so much to give knowledge as to communicate emotion. The critic, by calling attention to certain features of the work under review, and expressing his own feelings about them, endeavours to make us share his attitude towards the work as a whole. The only relevant propositions that he formulates are propositions describing the nature of the work. And these are plain records of fact. We conclude, therefore, that there is nothing in aesthetics, any more than there is in ethics, to justify the view that it embodies a unique type of knowledge.

It should now be clear that the only information which we can legitimately derive from the study of our aesthetic and moral experiences is information about our own mental and physical make-up. We take note of these experiences as providing data for our psychological and sociological generalisations. And this is the only way in which they serve to increase our knowledge. It follows that any attempt to make our use of ethical and aesthetic concepts the basis of a metaphysical theory concerning the existence of a world of values, as distinct from the world of facts, involves a false analysis of these concepts. Our own analysis has shown that the phenomena of moral experience cannot fairly be used to support any rationalist or metaphysical doctrine whatsoever. In particular, they cannot, as Kant hoped, be used to establish the existence of a transcendent god.

NOTES

1. The argument that follows should be read in conjunction with the Introduction, pp. 20–2 [of Ayer, *Language, Truth and Logic*].
2. cf. *Philosophical Studies*, "The Nature of Moral Philosophy."

Emotivism and Irrationalism

There have been many variations of noncognitive theories. Ayer argued that moral statements are nothing more than expressions of emotions. Rudolph Carnap once argued that ethical judgments are commands. In his *Ethics and Language,* C.L. Stevenson proposed that the function of moral language was to express the speaker's attitude as well as to evoke similar attitudes in others. Yet throughout these emotivist positions, there is an excessive nonrational character. This nonrational character is clearly indicated in the following sentence from an early linguistic philospher, W.H.F. Barnes; Barnes claimed that "value judgments in their origin are not strictly judgments at all. . . . They are exclamations expressive of approval." [16] Morals are not a matter for argument. The emphasis placed on emotional feeling could hardly avoid charges involving the nonrational character of emotivism. Yet is moral discussion nothing more than an expression of feelings? Certainly all of us have experienced situations where our feelings went counter to our moral principles. This nonrational characteristic of moral language as evidenced in the writings of the early positivists has caused much critical thinking among contemporary moral philosophers.

In his book, *The Place of Reason in Ethics,* Stephen Toulmin adroitly criticizes emotivism. Consider carefully the following passage in which Toulmin refers to the irrationalism of noncognitivism as its fatal weakness.

> What we want to know is in which of these (noncognitivist) discussions the arguments presented were *worthy* of acceptance, and the reasons given *good* reasons; in which of them persuasion was achieved at least in part by valid reasoning, and in which agreement was obtained by means of *mere* persuasion—fine rhetoric unsupported by valid arguments or good reasons. And it is over the criteria (or rather the complete lack of criteria) given for the validity of ethical arguments that the most telling objection to this (and any) subjective (or noncognitivist) theory arise. [17]

R.M. Hare has written two influential monographs dealing with noncognitivism, *The Language of Morals* and *Freedom and Reason.* Hare suggested that the function of "good" is "to commend." Hare refers to this function as the *evaluative meaning* of good. The evaluative meaning always remains the same, while the descriptive meaning of the things to which "good" is applied can change. A sports car and a knife are "good" for different reasons. Yet, Hare suggests, every evaluative use of good has the commending function in common; the primary function of "good" is "to commend." Hare further suggests that ". . . when we commend . . . anything, it is always in order, at least indirectly, to guide choices, our own or other people's. . . ." [18] With the distinction between descriptive meaning and evaluative meaning, Hare attempts to provide a role for reasoning once again in moral discourse. Hare's position has become known as *prescriptivism.* We might show the gradual progression from naturalism to intuitionism to emotivism in the following manner:

A.   Naturalism evoked serious problems with its attempt to account for the one property in nature which was equivalent to goodness.

B.   Intuitionism followed directly from the pitfalls of naturalistic utilitarianism. Moore argued that if the naturalistic fallacy is correct, then the thrust of naturalism is fundamentally misguided. Possibly, the intuitionists suggested, there is a nonnatural property existing in some fashion within the ontological structure of the world. This nonnatural property would be known by a direct intuition. The intuitionist, therefore, salvaged the objective foundation for moral language common to naturalism. Yet the price paid proved insurmountable as it became impossible to verify the nonnatural property. This lack of verification led directly to emotivism.

C. Emotivism followed on the coattails of the Verification Theory of Meaning into the mainstream of twentieth-century linguistic philosophy. Given the tenets of the Verification Theory of Meaning, Moore's nonnatural ontological properties would become meaningless discourse. The same was true of any ontological theory. Moore's analysis of nonnatural properties was certainly ontological in character. Accepting the nonnaturalism of Moore, the positivists nevertheless denied the objective reference for moral terms. Moral terms and their corresponding judgments were nothing more than the expression of emotional responses, the evoking of attitudes, the uttering of commands, or the prescribing of advice.

Schematically, we might outline this development of metaethical theories in the following way:

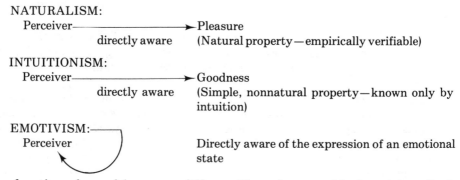

NATURALISM:
    Perceiver————————————▶Pleasure
                directly aware   (Natural property—empirically verifiable)

INTUITIONISM:
    Perceiver————————————▶Goodness
                directly aware   (Simple, nonnatural property—known only by
                                   intuition)

EMOTIVISM:
    Perceiver   Directly aware of the expression of an emotional
                                  state

The function of moral language differs with each metaethical position. Such questions have puzzled the minds of many twentieth-century moral philosophers.

This discussion of metaethics concludes our treatment of issues in moral philosophy. We have discussed a teleological theory as evidenced in the writings of John Stuart Mill, a formalist theory as found in Immanuel Kant, and a mixed theory as promoted by Aristotle and Carl Rogers. These are very important issues, ones which must be confronted if we are to attain the "examined life" about which Socrates said so much.

NOTES

1. John Dewey, *Reconstruction in Philosophy* (New York: Henry Holt, 1920), p. 26.
2. C.D. Broad, *Five Types of Ethical Theory* (New York: Harcourt, Brace and World, 1934), p. 207.
3. John Stuart Mill, *Utilitarianism,* first published in 1863.
4. Ibid.
5. Jeremy Bentham, *Introduction to the Principles of Morals and Legislation* (New York: Hafner Press, 1948), pp. 29–30. Reprinted by permission of Hafner Press, a division of Macmillan Publishing Co., Inc.
6. Ibid., p. 102.

7. Ibid., pp. 1-2.

8. Mill, *Utilitarianism.*

9. William Barrett, *Irrational Man* (Garden City, N.Y.: Doubleday, 1958), p. 162.

10. Bentham, *Principles of Morals and Legislation*, pp. 1-2.

11. R.M. Hare, *Freedom and Reason* (Oxford: At the University Press, 1963), pp. 41-42. Copyright © Oxford University Press, 1963. Reprinted by permission of the Oxford University Press.

12. Thomas Aquinas, *Summa Theologiae*, I-II, Q. 94, Art. 2. Translated by Anthony J. Lisska.

13. G.E. Moore, *Principia Ethica* (Cambridge: At the University Press, 1903), pp. 9 and 6.

14. G.J. Warnock, *Contemporary Moral Philosophy* (New York: St. Martin's Press, 1967), pp. 12-13.

15. Ibid., p. 13.

16. W.H.F. Barnes, "A Suggestion about Value," *Analysis* I (1934): 45.

17. Stephen Toulmin, *An Examination of the Place of Reason in Ethics* (Cambridge: At the University Press, 1970), p. 38.

18. R.M. Hare, *The Language of Morals* (New York: Oxford University Press, 1952), p. 127.

seven

Existentialism and Phenomenology: The Confrontation with the Human Condition

Existentialism and the Tradition of Western Philosophy

In the nineteenth and twentieth centuries, a branch of philosophy has developed which some historians of philosophy take to be a total reaction to and rejection of the classical ways of doing philosophy. This branch is called *existentialism,* and the cluster of philosophers adopting this mode of philosophizing are existentialists. Probably some students have already read the plays or novels of two of the more famous French existentialists of the twentieth century, Jean-Paul Sartre (1905-   ) and Albert Camus (1913-1960). Through the literary genre, Sartre and Camus have popularized many of the themes and concerns central to existentialism. In this chapter, we shall consider together some of the general themes of existentialism, trace its origin in the nineteenth-century writings of Soren Kierkegaard (1813-1855), elucidate the themes found in some of the twentieth-century existentialists, and attempt a critical evaluation of existentialism as a response to classical philosophy. We shall also briefly consider the origin and development of phenomenology. Phenomenology and existentialism are considered to be the two principal contributions of recent continental philosophy to Western thought.

Before discussing the individual existentialists, we should treat some general themes of this contemporary movement in philosophy. In one sense, existentialism is not so much a complete philosophical system in itself as it is a label or term applied to widely different revolts against traditional ways of doing philosophy. The existentialists exhibit a marked dissatisfaction with the traditional modes of engaging in the activity of philosophy. Many existentialists regard traditional philosophy as being superficial and removed from the issues and concerns central to human life. Traditional philosophy has been all too academic, so the existentialists charge; yet they go even further. They refuse to belong to any school of philosophy. Moreover, there is the explicit affirmation by some existentialists that it is impossible to ever attempt an adequate philosophical synthesis. Insofar as much traditional philosophy has been regarded as system building, the existentialists repudiate this tendency. Walter Kaufman, a contemporary commentator on existentialism, once noted that the beginning student might readily conclude that the only thing all existentialists have in common is a "marked aversion for each other." In fact, most of the philosophers clustered under the rubric of "existentialist" have repudiated that very label.

Generally, we might say that the existentialists, in rejecting traditional modes of philosophical activity, are rejecting what might be called *essentialism*. In other words, they argue that traditional philosophy, in searching for the essential properties of things and events, has overlooked the importance of the individual. Existentialism is in stark contrast to Platonism. Recall our discussion of Plato in chapter 2. In Plato's epistemology and ontology, the individuals and the awareness of individuals were relegated to secondary importance. It was the intellectual knowledge attained by directly grasping the world of forms which counted for authentic knowledge and human fulfillment. The world of individuals existing in the space-time realm was the world of mere "becoming." An awareness of the world of becoming was mere opinion. Given the Platonic ontology, the individuals existing in the space-time realm were secondary in importance to the transcendental world of the forms. In Platonism, stress was placed on attaining knowledge of the essential properties found in the world of the forms. Accordingly, the existing individuals lost metaphysical importance. Human excellence, in Platonism, was attained by knowing the forms, not by knowing individuals.

It is this Platonic detachment from the individual as found in existing situations which bothers the existentialists. They want philosophers to replace the emphasis on the human condition. This emphasis will preclude any movement away from the existential world in order to attain metaphysical solace in the transcendental world of the forms. In opposition to the essentialism of traditional philosophy, the existentialists will place great value on "existing" as an individual in particular situations. This will pertain to the epistemology, metaphysics, and ethics of existentialism. Existentialists argue that traditional philosophy, especially the search for essential properties, has tended to dehumanize individuals. As Kierkegaard will argue, *the* category for existentialism is the individual.

Søren Kierkegaard

Most historians of philosophy acknowledge that the nineteenth-century Danish philosopher, Søren Kierkegaard, is the father of what has come to be known as existentialism. Admittedly, some of the themes expressed in existentialism are to be found in the writings of earlier philosophers, especially Pascal, Descartes, and Augustine. In fact, Kierkegaard himself had a profound and abiding respect for Socrates. Nevertheless it is with Kierkegaard that we find the seeds of what later developed as existentialism in Western Europe.

Kierkegaard was more interested in theological issues than in traditional philosophical problems. Yet he expressed a concern for the human condition and inaugurated a vocabulary which later was assimilated by the twentieth-century existentialists.

Perhaps the best way to understand the mode of Kierkegaard's philosophizing is to consider that against which he reacted. Kierkegaard believed that the propositions expressed in the systematic philosophy of G.W.F. Hegel were detrimental to understanding the human condition. Hegel argued that there are three different ways of approaching reality: (1) through art, (2) through religion, and (3) through philosophy. Hegel asserted that, by means of art, human beings captured reality through differing material embodiments. Possibly an example of abstract art would be fruitful here. An abstract painting is not supposed to bear a one-to-one correspondence with reality. Nonetheless, through the mastery of the artist, it captures some facet of reality. Picasso's classic painting "Guernica," graphically depicts the horrors of war. Yet it is certainly much different than a television newsreel of a battle scene. Thus, since art does not depict reality precisely, Hegel deemed it insufficient.

Second, Hegel argued that the propositions of religion also attempt to express the human encounter with reality. Yet this is done, so Hegel argued, by means of faith, and through the use of myths and stories. The six-day account of creation in the Bible's first book, Genesis, is a good example of Hegel's use of religious propositions. Here too a message about that which is real is purported; yet it is not a completely real account in that it contains elements of myth. Hence, according to Hegel, religion too was an inadequate way of approaching and understanding reality.

Hegel believed it was only through the use of philosophical concepts that one could really understand the structure of reality. This was the only way to attain true knowledge. Philosophy goes beyond the mythological propositions expressed in religious language to directly confront the "real." In the Hegelian synthesis, this was done through pure concepts. Although we cannot explain the entire Hegelian synthesis here, it is important to grasp certain aspects of that position. As a maxim, Hegel accepted that reality must conform to the dictates of reason. And it was through a complicated and sophisticated development of concepts that Hegel attempted to encompass all of that which is real. His is truly a form of "absolute idealism." For our purposes, it is important to note that Hegel argued that the propositions expressing the concepts of philosophy are superior to those used in the myths and stories of religious language. If one is really to understand reality, then one must step beyond the limits of religion and discover the truth expressed in the pure concepts of philosophy. Philosophy was indeed superior to religion. It was this purported superiority of philosophy over religion and the objective aspect of philosophical understanding against which Kierkegaard reacted.

We might say that Kierkegaard developed his existentialist philosophy as a possible resolution to a problem he faced. This problem can be expressed succinctly as: "How to be a Christian in Christendom." This was a problem because of two reasons: (1) Hegelian philosophy, and (2) Christendom, which meant for Kierkegaard the Danish state church.

Hegelian philosophy, as we have just seen, asserted the superiority of philosophical speculation over the statements found in religion. This accent upon philosophical speculation, which led to "objectivity" in understanding the real, demanded a personal detachment from the understanding process. The subjective elements in understanding were to be suppressed so that the sheer contemplation demanded for objective understanding might be attained. Hegelian philosophy, therefore, fostered a spirit of speculation. This is what Kierkegaard often refers to as *objectivity*. In the existentialist jargon, objectivity will become a term of opprobrium.

By Christendom, Kierkegaard meant the nineteenth-century Danish state religion. This was a form of Lutheranism practiced by the citizens of Denmark. An established church, which is granted a certain status and privilege by the political institutions of a country, has many drawbacks. The one Kierkegaard noticed most is that being a Christian—i.e., being a member of the state church—had become a matter-of-fact, routine event in the life of every Danish citizen. Being a Christian was as automatic as being a citizen of Denmark. The effect of the state religion was to make it very easy to be a Christian. Kierkegaard recoiled in anguish at this situation. The effect of Christendom on Christianity was to deny the difficult dimension demanded by a commitment to the Christian way of life. In many of his works, Kierkegaard expressly evokes his intention of making such matters difficult. The point to keep in mind is that Kierkegaard believed that it had become too easy to become and remain a Christian.

In his work, *Point of View*, Kierkegaard makes the following observation about the state of Christianity in Denmark.

> Everyone with some capacity for observation, who seriously considers what is called Christendom, or the conditions in a so-called Christian country, must be assailed by profound misgivings. What does it mean that all these thousands and thousands call themselves Christians as a matter of course? These many, many men, of whom the greater part, so far as one can judge, live in categories quite foreign to Christianity! . . . People who perhaps never enter a Church, never think of God, never mention His name except in oaths! People upon whom it has never dawned that they might have any obligation to God. . . . Yet all these people . . . are called Christians, call themselves Christians, are recognized as Christians by the State, are buried as Christians by the Church, are certified as Christians for all eternity. . . .[1]

In his *Attack on Christendom*, Kierkegaard reiterates his theme that Christianity in Christendom is indeed an illusion.

> The thought of Christianity was to want to change everything. The result of the Christianity of "Christendom" is that everything, absolutely everything, has remained as it was, only everything has assumed the name of "Christian"—and so (musicians strike up the tune) we live a life of paganism. . . . rather we live a pagan life . . . by the help of the thought that the whole thing is Christian.[2]

Kierkegaard regarded this state of affairs as a "frightful illusion, a tremendous confusion" concerning the authentic nature of Christianity. Thus he sought to remedy this terrible situation, and this meant for him ". . . neither more nor less than proposing to reintroduce Christianity into Christendom." This reintroduction stressed living the Christian doctrines subjectively. This concept of subjectivity greatly influenced twentieth-century existentialism.

It is important to reflect for a minute on the above discussion. Kierkegaard's fundamental problem was how to be a Christian within the context of nineteenth-century Denmark. This was a problem because of the general acceptance of Hegelian philosophy and the entrenchment of the state religion. Hegelian philosophy espoused the primary importance of objective contemplation and the state religion fostered a spirit of routine Christianity. In response to Hegelian philosophy, Kierkegaard will emphasize what he takes to be the reflection of the individual on his state of existence. In response to the entrenched state Lutheranism, Kierkegaard will emphasize the importance of living the doctrines of Christianity. And this state religion, fostering an attitude of non-involvement, is exactly what he thinks has happened. The problem was compounded, however, because many of the ministers of Danish Lutheranism were trained in Hegelian philosophy. In accord with this training, these ministers were placing great emphasis on the importance of detached contemplation and the subservience of religion to philosophy. Both Hegelian philosophy and Christendom fostered what Kierkegaard called objectivity. This tendency, he argued, must be countered in order to bring about a renewal in the lives of the Danish Christians.

In response to the objectivity asserted by the Hegelians, Kierkegaard will emphasize subjectivity. Subjectivity will become a classic concept expressed in the writings of many existentialists. In terms of Christianity, Kierkegaard asserts that the problem of objectivity is an inquiry into the *truth* or truth conditions of the propositions expressed in religious systems. Belief is then regarded as "propositional." In other words, religious belief is concerned with the truth conditions of propositions. This is objectivity in religion, and Kierkegaard will emphasize subjectivity. This is best expressed as the relationship of the individual to Christianity. Conventionally speaking, we might say that this is a case of "believing-in" rather than "belief." This is subjective in that it expressedly refers to the state of the consciousness of the individual. The individual is to be aware of his or her state as a Christian and attempt to implement daily the difficult demands of that doctrine. This is where commitment enters into the picture. Commitment is a state of believing-in rather than a state of belief. There is an active involvement. In response to the objectivity of both Hegelianism and Christendom, Kierkegaard places great accent on individual awareness of the Christian doctrine in one's life, together with the expressed demand to live the doctrine. The individual's personal existential relationship to the Christian doctrine is crucially important for Kierkegaard's response to the malaise in nineteenth-century Christendom. Subjectivity, he urges, is the "appropriation and assimilation" of the content of Christianity in the believer's life. To avoid this dimension is not to deserve the accolade of "Christian." In fact, in one of his works, Kierkegaard defines existentialism in the following way: ". . . to live existentially expressing and existentially probing the depths of what one calls his view of life." The following passages express quite well the general themes central to Kierkegaard's existentialism.

 . . . Every human being must be assumed in essential possession of what essentially belongs to being a man. The task of the subjective thinker is to transform

himself into an instrument that clearly and definitely expresses in existence whatever is essentially human. To rely on a differential trait in this connection is a misunderstanding, for to have a little more brain and the like is insignificant. That
our age has forsaken the individuals in order to take refuge in the collective idea,
has its natural explanation in an aesthetic despair which has not yet found the
ethical. Men have perceived that it avails nothing to be ever so distinguished an
individual man, since no difference avails anything. A new difference has consequently been hit upon: the difference of being born in the nineteenth century.
Everyone tries to determine his bit of existence in relation to the age as quickly
as possible and so consoles himself. But it avails nothing, being only a higher and
more glittering illusion. And just as there have lived fools in ancient times, as well
as in every generation, who have confounded themselves, in the vanity of their
delusion, with one or another distinguished man, pretending to be this or that individual, so the peculiarity of our age is that the fools are not even content to confuse
themselves with some great man, but identify themselves with the age, with the
century, with the contemporary generation, with humanity at large. To wish to
live as a particular human being (which is what everyone undoubtedly is), relying
upon a difference, is the weakness of cowardice; to will to live as a particular
human being (which everyone undoubtedly is) in the same sense as is open to every
other human being, is the ethical victory over life and all its illusions. And this
victory is perhaps the hardest of all to win in the theocentric nineteenth century.[3]

While abstract thought seeks to understand the concrete abstractly, the subjective thinker has conversely to understand the abstract concretely. Abstract
thought turns from concrete men to consider man in general; the subjective thinker
seeks to understand the abstract determination of being human in terms of this
particular existing human being.

To understand oneself in existence was the Greek principle. However little content the doctrine of a Greek philosopher sometimes represented, the philosopher
had nevertheless one advantage: he was never comical. I am well aware that if
someone were nowadays to live like a Greek philosopher, existentially expressing
and existentially probing the depths of what he must call his view of life, he would be
regarded as a lunatic. Let it be so. But for an honored philosopher to be extremely
profound and ingenious, to the point of never remembering, although he specu-
lates upon existential problems like Christianity, to ask himself who in all the world
his speculation concerns, much less to think that it concerns himself: that I find to
be ridiculous.[4]

. . . My principal thought was that in our age, because of the great increase of
knowledge, we had forgotten what it means to *exist*, and what *inwardness* signifies, and that the misunderstanding between speculative philosophy and Christianity was explicable on that ground. I now resolved to go back as far as possible,
in order not to reach the religious mode of existence too soon, to say nothing of the
specifically Christian mode of religious existence, in order not to leave difficulties
unexplored behind me. If men had forgotten what it means to exist religiously,
they had doubtless also forgotten what it means to exist as human beings; this
must therefore be set forth. But above all it must not be done in a dogmatizing
manner, for then the misunderstanding would instantly take the explanatory effort
to itself in a new misunderstanding, as if existing consisted in getting to know
something about this or that. If communicated in the form of knowledge, the recipient is led to adopt the misunderstanding that it is knowledge he is to receive, and
then we are again in the sphere of knowledge. Only one who has some conception
of the enduring capacity of a misunderstanding to assimilate even the most strenuous effort of explanation and still remain the same misunderstanding, will be able

to appreciate the difficulties of an authorship where every word must be watched, and every sentence pass through the process of a double reflection.[5]

From the speculative standpoint, Christianity is viewed as an historical phenomenon. The problem of its truth therefore becomes the problem of so interpenetrating it with thought, that Christianity at last reveals itself as the eternal truth.

The speculative approach to the problem is characterized by one excellent trait: it has no presuppositions. It proceeds from nothing, it assumes nothing as given, it begs no postulates. Here then we may be sure of avoiding such presuppositions as were met with in the preceding.

And yet, something is after all assumed: Christianity is assumed as given. Alas and alack! philosophy is altogether too polite. How strange is the way of the world! Once it was at the risk of his life that a man dared to profess himself a Christian; now it is to make oneself suspect to venture to doubt that one is a Christian. Especially when this doubt does not mean that the individual launches a violent attack against Christianity with a view to abolishing it; for in that case it would perhaps be admitted that there was something in it. But if a man were to say quite simply and unassumingly, that he was concerned for himself, lest perhaps he had no right to call himself a Christian, he would indeed not suffer persecution or be put to death, but he would be smothered in angry glances, and people would say: "How tiresome to make such a fuss about nothing at all; why can't he behave like the rest of us, who are all Christians? It is just as it is with F.F., who refuses to wear a hat on his head like others, but insists on dressing differently." And if he happened to be married, his wife would say to him: "Dear husband of mine, how can you get such notions into your head? How can you doubt that you are a Christian? Are you not a Dane, and does not the geography say that the Lutheran form of the Christian religion is the ruling religion in Denmark? For you are surely not a Jew, nor are you a Mohammedan; what then can you be if not a Christian? It is a thousand years since paganism was driven out of Denmark, so I know you are not a pagan. Do you not perform your duties at the office like a conscientious civil servant; are you not a good citizen of a Christian nation, a Lutheran Christian state? So then of course you must be a Christian."[6]

. . . The speculative philosopher, unless he is as objective as the wife of our new civil servant, proposes to contemplate Christianity from the philosophical standpoint. It is a matter of indifference to him whether anyone accepts it or not; such anxieties are left to theologues and laymen—and also surely to those who really are Christians, and who are by no means indifferent as to whether they are Christians or not. The philosopher contemplates Christianity for the sake of interpenetrating it with his speculative thought; aye, with his genuinely speculative thought. But suppose this whole proceeding were a chimera, a sheer impossibility; suppose that Christianity is subjectivity, an inner transformation, an actualization of inwardness, and that only two kinds of people can know anything about it: those who with an infinite passionate interest in an eternal happiness base this their happiness upon their believing relationship to Christianity, and those who with an opposite passion, but in passion, reject it—the happy and the unhappy lovers. Suppose that an objective indifference can therefore learn nothing at all. . . .[7]

. . . Now if Christianity is essentially something objective, it is necessary for the observer to be objective. But if Christianity is essentially subjective, it is a mistake for the observer to be objective. In every case where the object of knowledge is the very inwardness of the subjectivity of the individual, it is necessary for the knower to be in a corresponding condition. But the utmost tension of human subjectivity finds its expression in the infinite passionate interest in an eternal happiness. Even in the case of earthly love it is a necessary requirement for a would-be observer, that he should know the inwardness of love. But here the interest is not so great as it is in the case of an eternal happiness, because all love is affected by illusion, and hence has a quasi-objective aspect, which makes it possible to speak of something like an experience at second-hand. But when love is interpenetrated with a God-relationship, this imperfection of illusion disappears, together with the remaining semblance of objectivity; and now it holds true that one not in this condition can gain nothing by all his efforts to observe. In the infinite passionate interest for his eternal happiness, the subject is in a state of the utmost tension, in the very extremity of subjectivity, not indeed where there is no object, which is the imperfect and undialectical distinction, but where God is negatively present in the subject; whose mode of subjectivity becomes, by virtue of this interest, the form for an eternal happiness.[8]

. . . If the speculative philosopher is at the same time a believer, as is also af- firmed, he must long ago have perceived that philosophy can never acquire the same significance for him as faith. It is precisely as a believer that he is infinitely interested in his eternal happiness, and it is in faith that he is assured of it. (It should be noted that this assurance is the sort of assurance that can be had in faith, i.e. not an assurance once for all, but a daily acquisition of the sure faith through the infinite personal passionate interest.) And he does not base his eternal happi- ness upon his philosophical speculations. Rather, he associates circumspectly with philosophy, let it lure him away from the certainty of faith (which has in every moment the infinite dialectic of uncertainty present with it) so as to rest in an indif- ferent objective knowledge. This is the simple dialectical analysis of the situation. If, therefore, he says that he bases his eternal happiness on his speculation, he con- tradicts himself and becomes comical, because philosophy in its objectivity is wholly indifferent to his and my and your eternal happiness. An eternal happiness inheres precisely in the recessive self-feeling of the subject, acquired through his utmost exertion. And besides contradicting himself, such a philosopher lies, with respect to his pretensions to be a believer.[9]

. . . Christianity does not lend itself to objective observation, precisely because it proposes to intensify subjectivity to the utmost; and when the subject has thus put himself in the right attitude, he cannot attach his eternal happiness to speculative philosophy.

This contradiction between the subject who is in passion infinitely interested, and philosophical speculation viewed as something that might assist him, I shall permit myself to illustrate by means of an image from the sensible world. In sawing wood it is important not to press down too hard on the saw; the lighter the pressure exerted by the sawyer, the better the saw operates. If a man were to press down with all his strength, he would no longer be able to saw at all. In the same way it is necessary for the philosopher to make himself objectively light; but everyone who is in passion infinitely interested in his eternal happiness makes himself subjec- tively as heavy as possible. Precisely for this reason he prevents himself from speculating. Now if Christianity requires this interest in the individual subject (which is the assumption, since this is the point on which the problem turns), it is easy to see that he cannot find what he seeks in speculation. This can also be ex- pressed by saying that speculative philosophy does not permit the problem to arise at all; and it follows that all its pretense of answering the problem constitutes only a mystification.[10]

. . . It is impossible to exist without passion, unless we understand the word "exist" in the loose sense of a so-called existence. Every Greek thinker was there- fore essentially a passionate thinker. I have often reflected how one might bring a man into a state of passion. I have thought in this connection that if I could get him seated on a horse and the horse made to take fright and gallop wildly, or better still, for the sake of bringing the passion out, if I could take a man who wanted to arrive at a certain place as quickly as possible, and hence already had some passion, and could set him astride a horse that can scarcely walk—and yet this is what existence is like if one is to become consciously aware of it. Or if a driver were otherwise not especially inclined toward passion, if someone hitched a team of horses to a wagon for him, one of them a Pegasus and the other a worn-out jade, and told him to drive—I think one might succeed. And it is just this that it means to exist, if one is to become conscious of it. Eternity is the winged horse, infinitely fast, and time is a worn-out jade; the existing individual is the driver. That is to say, he is such a driver when his mode of existence is not an existence loosely so called; for then he is no driver, but a drunken peasant who lies asleep in the wagon and lets the horses take care of themselves. To be sure, he also drives and is a driver; and so there are perhaps many who—also exist.[11]

The difficulty that inheres in existence, with which the existing individual is confronted, is one that never really comes to expression in the language of abstract thought, much less receives an explanation. Because abstract thought is *sub specie aeterni* it ignores the concrete and the temporal, the existential process, the predicament of the existing individual arising from his being a synthesis of the temporal and the eternal situated in existence.* Now if we assume that abstract thought is the highest manifestation of human activity, it follows that philosophy and the philosophers proudly desert existence, leaving the rest of us to face the worst. And something else, too, follows for the abstract thinker himself, namely, that since he is an existing individual he must in one way or another be suffering from absentmindedness.

The abstract problem of reality (if it is permissible to treat this problem abstractly, the particular and the accidental being constituents of the real, and directly opposed to abstraction) is not nearly so difficult a problem as it is to raise and to answer the question of what it means that this definite something is a reality. This definite something is just what abstract thought abstracts from. But the difficulty lies in bringing this definite something and the ideality of thought together, by penetrating the concrete particularity with thought. Abstract thought cannot even take cognizance of this contradiction, since the very process of abstraction prevents the contradiction from arising.

This questionable character of abstract thought becomes apparent especially in connection with all existential problems, where abstract thought gets rid of the difficulty by leaving it out, and then proceeds to boast of having explained everything. It explains immortality in general, and all goes quite smoothly, in that immortality is identified with eternity, with the eternity which is essentially the medium of all thought. But whether an existing individual human being is immortal, which is the difficulty, abstract thought does not trouble to inquire. It is disinterested; but the difficulty inherent in existence constitutes the interest of the existing individual, who is infinitely interested in existing. Abstract thought thus helps me with respect to my immortality by first annihilating me as a particular existing individual and then making me immortal, about as when the doctor in Holberg killed the patient with his medicine—but also expelled the fever. Such an abstract thinker, one who neglects to take into account the relationship between his abstract thought and his own existence as an individual, not careful to clarify this relationship to himself, makes a comical impression upon the mind even if he is ever so distinguished, because he is in process of ceasing to be a human being. While a genuine human being, as a synthesis of the finite and the infinite, finds his reality in holding these two factors together, infinitely interested in existing—such an abstract thinker is a duplex being: a fantastic creature who moves in the pure being of abstract thought, and on the other hand, a sometimes pitiful professorial figure which the former deposits, about as when one sets down a walking stick. When one reads the story of such a thinker's life (for his writings are perhaps excellent), one trembles to think of what it means to be a man.† If a lacemaker were to produce ever so beautiful laces, it nevertheless makes one sad to contemplate such a poor stunted creature. And so it is a comical sight to see a thinker who in spite of all pretensions, personally existed like a nincompoop; who did indeed marry, but without knowing love or its power, and whose marriage must therefore have been as impersonal as his thought; whose personal life was devoid of pathos or pathological struggles, concerned only with the question of which university offered the best livelihood. Such an anomaly one would think impossible in the case of a thinker, to be met with only in the external world and its wretchedness, where one human being is the slave of another, and it is impossible to admire the laces without shedding tears for the lacemakers. But one would suppose that a thinker lived the richest human life—so at least it was in Greece.

It is different with the abstract thinker who without having understood himself, or the relationship that abstract thought bears to existence, simply follows the promptings of his talent or is made by training to become something of this sort. I am very well aware that one tends to admire an artistic career where the artist simply pursues his talent without at all making himself clear over what it means to be a human being, and that our admiration tends to forget the person of the artist over his artistry. But I also know that such a life has its tragedy in being a differential type of existence not personally reflected in the ethical; and I know that in Greece, at least, a thinker was not a stunted, crippled creature who produced works of art, but was himself a work of art in his existence. One would suppose that being a thinker was the last thing in the world to constitute a differential trait with respect to being human. If it is the case that an abstract thinker is devoid of a sensitiveness for the comical, this circumstance is in itself a proof that while his thought may be the product of a distinguished talent, it is not the thought of one who has in any eminent sense existed as a human being. We are told that thought is the highest stage of human life, that it includes everything else as subordinated to itself; and at the same time no objection is urged against the thinker failing to exist essentially *qua* human being, but only as a differential talent. That the pronouncement made concerning thought fails to be reduplicated in the concept of the thinker, that the thinker's existence contradicts his thought, shows that we are here dealing merely with professions. It is professed that thought is higher than feeling and imagination, and this is professed by a thinker who lacks pathos and passion. Thought is higher than irony and humor—this is professed by a thinker who is wholly lacking in a sense for the comical. How comical! Just as the whole enterprise of abstract thought in dealing with Christianity and with existential problems is an essay in the comical, so the so-called pure thought is in general a psychological curiosity, a remarkable species of combining and construing in a fantastic medium, the medium of pure being. The facile deification of this pure thought as the highest stage in life shows that the thinker who does it has never existed *qua* human being. It is evidence among other things that he has never willed in any eminent sense of the word; I do not mean willing in the sense of exploit, but from the standpoint of inwardness.

*That Hegel in his *Logic* nevertheless permits himself to utilize a consciousness that is only too well informed about the concrete, and what it is that the professor needs next in spite of the necessary transition, is of course a fault, which Trendelenburg has very effectively called to our attention. To cite an example from the field of the subject immediately before us, how is the transition effected by which *die Existenz* becomes a plurality of existences? *"Die Existenz ist die unmittelbare Einheit der Reflexion-in-sich und der Reflexion-in-anders. Sie* *ist daher* (?) *die unbestimmte Menge von Existierenden.* " How does the purely abstract determination of existence come to be split up in this manner?

†And when you read in his writings that thought and being are one, it is impossible not to think, in view of his own life and mode of existence, that the being which is thus identical with thought can scarcely be the being of a man. [12]

. . . Christianity is not a doctrine* but an existential communication expressing an existential contradiction. If Christianity were a doctrine it would *eo ipso* not be an opposite to speculative thought, but rather a phase within it. Christianity has to do with existence, with the act of existing; but existence and existing constitute precisely the opposite of speculation. The Eleatic doctrine, for example, is not relevant to existing but to speculation, and it is therefore proper to assign to it a place within speculative thought. Precisely because Christianity is not a doctrine it exhibits the principle, as was noted above, that there is a tremendous difference between knowing what Christianity is and being a Christian. In connection with a doctrine such a distinction is unthinkable, because a doctrine is not relevant to existing. It is not my fault that the age in which we live has reversed the relationship, and transformed Christianity into a philosophical doctrine that asks to be understood, and turned *being* a Christian into a triviality.

*Now if only I might escape the fate of having a facile thinker explain to a reading public how stupid my entire book is, as is more than sufficiently evident from my willingness to be responsible for such an assertion as that Christianity is not a doctrine. Let us try to understand one another. Surely it is one thing for something to be a philosophical doctrine which desires to be intellectually grasped and speculatively understood, and quite another thing to be a doctrine that proposes to be realized in existence. If the question of understanding is to be raised in connection with a doctrine of the latter sort, this must consist in understanding that the task is to exist in it, in understanding the difficulty of existing in it, and what a tremendous essential task such a doctrine posits for the learner. At a time when it has come to be generally assumed in connection with such a doctrine (an existential communication) that it is very easy to be what the doctrine requires, but very hard to understand this doctrine speculatively, one may be in harmony with the doctrine (the existential communication) when he seeks to show how difficult it is existentially to submit to the doctrine. In the case of such a doctrine, it is contrariwise a misunderstanding to speculate upon it. Christianity is a doctrine of this kind. To speculate upon it is a misunderstanding, and the farther one goes in this direction the greater is the misunderstanding. When one finally reaches the stage of not only speculating about it, but of understanding it speculatively, one has reached the highest pitch of misunderstanding. This stage is reached in the mediation of Christianity and speculation, and hence it is quite correct to say that modern speculation is the most extreme possible misunderstanding of Christianity. This being the case, and when it is furthermore admitted that the nineteenth century is so dreadfully speculative, it is to be apprehended that the word "doctrine" will at once be interpreted to mean a philosophical doctrine which demands to be understood, and ought to be understood. To avoid this danger I have chosen to call Christianity an existential communication, in order definitely to indicate its heterogeneity with speculation. [13]

But in order to avoid confusion, it is at once necessary to recall that our treatment of the problem does not raise the question of the truth of Christianity. It merely deals with the question of the individual's relationship to Christianity. It has nothing whatever to do with the systematic zeal of the personally indifferent individual to arrange the truths of Christianity in paragraphs; it deals with the concern of the infinitely interested individual for his own relationship to such a doctrine. To put it as simply as possible, using myself by way of illustration: I, Johannes Climacus, born in this city and now thirty years old, a common ordinary human being like most people, assume that there awaits me a highest good, an eternal happiness, in the same sense that such a good awaits a servant-girl or a professor. I have heard that Christianity proposes itself as a condition for the acquirement of this good, and now I ask how I may establish a proper relationship to this doctrine. "What extraordinary presumption," I seem to hear a thinker say, "what egotistical vanity to dare lay so much stress upon one's own petty self in this theocentric age, in the speculatively significant nineteenth century, which is entirely immersed in the great problems of universal history." I shudder at the reproof; and if I had not already hardened myself against a number of fearful things, I would no doubt slink quietly away, like a dog with his tail between his legs. But my conscience is quite clear in this matter; it is not I who have become so presumptuous of my own accord, but it is Christianity itself which compels me to ask the question in this manner. It puts quite an extraordinary emphasis upon my own petty self, and upon every other self however petty, in that it proposes to endow each self with an eternal happiness, provided a proper relationship is established.

Without having understood Christianity, since I merely present the problem, I have still understood enough to apprehend that it proposes to bestow an eternal happiness upon the individual man, thus presuming an infinite interest in his eternal happiness as *conditio sine qua non;* an interest by virtue of which the individual hates father and mother, and thus doubtless also snaps his fingers at speculative systems and outlines of universal history. Although I am only an outsider, I have at least understood so much, that the only unpardonable offense against the majesty of Christianity is for the individual to take his relationship to it for granted, treating it as a matter of course. However unassuming it may seem to permit oneself this kind of a relationship to Christianity, Christianity judges it as insolence. I must therefore respectfully decline the assistance of all the theocentric helpers and helpers' helpers, in so far as they propose to help me into Christianity on such a basis. Then I rather prefer to remain where I am, with my infinite interest, with the problem, with the possibility.

It is not entirely impossible that one who is infinitely interested in his eternal happiness may sometime come into possession of it. But it is surely quite impossible for one who has lost a sensibility for it (and this can scarcely be anything else than the infinite interest), ever to enjoy an eternal happiness. If the sense for it is once lost, it may perhaps be impossible to recover it. The foolish virgins had lost the infinite passion of expectation. And so their lamps were extinguished. Then came the cry: The bridegroom cometh. Thereupon they run to the market-place to buy new oil for themselves, hoping to begin all over again, letting bygones be bygones. And so it was, to be sure, everything was forgotten. The door was shut against them, and they were left outside; when they knocked for admittance, the bridegroom said: "I do not know you." This was no mere quip in which the bridegroom indulged, but the sober truth; for they had made themselves strangers, in the spiritual sense of the word, through having lost the infinite passion.

The objective problem consists of an inquiry into the truth of Christianity. The subjection problem concerns the relationship of the individual to Christianity. To put it quite simply: How may I, Johannes Climacus, participate in the happiness promised by Christianity? The problem concerns myself alone; partly because, if it is properly posed, it will concern everyone else in the same manner; and partly because all the others already have faith as something given, as a triviality of little value, or as a triviality which amounts to something only when tricked out with a few proofs. So that the posing of the problem cannot be regarded as presumption on my part, but only as a special kind of madness.

In order to make my problem clear I shall first present the objective problem, and show how this is dealt with. In this manner the historical will receive its just due. Then I shall proceed to present the subjective problem. This is at bottom more than the promised sequel, which proposed to invest the problem in its historical costume; since the historical costume is given merely by citing the one word: Christianity. The first part of what follows is then the promised sequel; the second part is a new attempt of the same general tenor as the *Fragments,* a new approach to the problem of that piece. [14]

An Analysis of Subjectivity

The theme of subjectivity continually occurs in the writings of Kierkegaard. Although it is rather difficult to define the complete significance of this concept in Kierkegaard's philosophy, there are certain traits proper to the concept which we can identify. The following five propositions help unpack the significance of subjectivity for Kierkegaard.

1. *Subjectivity is the appropriation and assimilation of Christianity.* As we have seen, Kierkegaard reacted violently to the demands for objective speculation as espoused by the Hegelians. Speculation meant for him the discovery of objective truths without any passion or human involvement—there was a total *lack* of personal interest. But Christianity is (according to Kierkegaard) fundamentally a way of life. The doctrines expressed in Christianity were to be inculcated in one's daily life. They were not propositions to be contemplated in an abstract manner.

2. *Subjectivity is the agent's (thinker's) constant awareness that he or she is an existing individual.* Kierkegaard strongly urges that we not lose or ignore the concrete in favor of the abstract. Life is a process and not something fixed. This demands a persistent striving. To strive toward the perfection demanded by the doctrines of Christianity requires that the individual be aware of how he or she is living and how well the incorporation of the Christian message has been made into one's lifestyle.

3. *Subjectivity is the Moral.* The gist of morality is to put our convictions into practice. Virtue, contrary to Socrates' teaching, is not knowledge alone. There is an important action component. To speculate without acting is not to be engaged with the moral. Simply put, the ethical is a "doing," not a "thinking." Therefore action and commitment are important aspects of subjectivity.

4. *Subjectivity is decision, choice, and passion.* In order to live an ethical life, one must form moral decisions; the moral dimension of our lives demands that we choose between alternatives. Insofar as ethical choices affect our well being as human agents and our view of ourselves in the state called the human condition, one cannot make ethical choices without becoming emotionally involved. This is what Kierkegaard refers to as passion. An ethical decision requires that our whole being become involved. This is emotional involvement, passionate choice, and commitment. Insofar as subjectivity is connected with the moral, subjectivity demands that decisions be made. For one cannot engage in an ethical life without making moral decisions. This further reinforces the action dimension of existentialism.

5. *Subjectivity is despair, fear, and trembling.* This proposition follows from the above. If one is emotionally involved in making moral decisions—i.e., if the decisions strike at the very foundation of our being human—then how can one be in such a state without experiencing fear and despair? What guarantee do we have that we will have made the correct decision? All of us are very painfully aware that moral decision making does not possess the same degree of certainty as mathematical theorems. Thus moral decision making involves risk. There is no guarantee of success. In effect, Kierkegaard argues that any existential choice demands risk taking on the part of the individual. Insofar as risk is a necessary condition of moral decision making, so too is fear and trembling. For who can stand in the face of a genuine risk situation and not experience fear and

trembling? To not have experienced fear and trembling in making moral decisions, Kierkegaard suggests, is not to have been in an existentially demanding
moral situation.

In the analysis of subjectivity, remember the easy-going nature of the Danish citizens of Christendom. Insofar as Christianity was routine and ordinary,
there was absolutely no risk to the situation. Yet Kierkegaard argues that a
true adherent to the Christian message must necessarily become a subjective
individual, and subjectivity is not an easy aspect of the human condition. Subjectivity brings about the difficult aspects involved with living the Christian
doctrine, which Kierkegaard wanted to emphasize. Subjectivity is a necessary
condition of living a genuine Christian life.

Schematically, we might compare the Hegelian system with Kierkegaard's
response:

HEGEL	KIERKEGAARD
Abstract	Concrete
Universal	Singular
Speculative	Practical
Metaphysical	Moral
The Idea (Concept)	The Individual
Therefore, *Objectivity*	Therefore, *Subjectivity*

The Three Stages

Kierkegaard postulated three stages which he believes every authentic Christian must go through in attaining the perfection demanded by the Christian
message. In the following passages, Kierkegaard elucidates the structure of
these stages and the properties appropriate to each stage. Pay close attention
to the accompanying human qualities—despair, anguish, and dread—because
these same concepts will occur again in the writings of the twentieth-century
French existentialists.

. . . There are three stages: an aesthetic, an ethical, and a religious. But these
are not distinguished abstractly, as the immediate, the mediate and the synthesis
of the two, but rather concretely, in existential determinations, as enjoyment-
perdition; action-victory; suffering. But in spite of this triple division the book is
nevertheless an either-or. The ethical and the religious stages have in fact an essential relationship to one another. The difficulty with *Either-Or* is that it was rounded
out to a conclusion ethically, as was shown above. In the *Stages* this is clarified,
and the religious is thus assigned to its proper place.

The aesthetic and the ethical stages are again brought forward, in a certain sense
as recapitulation, but then again as something new. It would also be a poor testimony to existential inwardness if every such stage were not capable of a renewal
in the presentation, though it may be venturesome to reject the apparent
assistance of externals in calling attention to the difference, as by choosing new
names, and the like. The ethicist again concentrates on marriage as the most
dialectically complex of the revelations that reality affords. Nevertheless he brings
forward a new aspect, and emphasizes particularly the category of time and its

significance, as the medium for the beauty that increases with age; while from the aesthetic point of view, time and existence in time is more or less a regress.

On account of the triple division, the existential situation as between the stages has been subjected to a rearrangement. In *Either-Or* the aesthetic standpoint is represented by means of an existential possibility, while the ethicist is existing. Now the aesthetic is existential; the ethicist is militant, fighting *ancipito proelio* against the aesthetic, over which he again readily gains the victory, not by means of the seductive gifts of the intellect, but with ethical passion and pathos; he seeks also to defend himself against the religious. In rounding out his position as an ethicist, he does his utmost to defend himself against the decisive form of a higher standpoint. That he should thus defend himself is quite in order, since he is not a standpoint but an existing individual. It is a fundamental confusion in recent philosophy to mistake the abstract consideration of a standpoint with existence, so that when a man has knowledge of this or that standpoint he supposes himself to exist in it; every existing individuality must precisely as existing be more or less one-sided. From the abstract point of view there is no decisive conflict between the standpoints, because abstraction precisely removes that in which the decision inheres: *the existing subject*. But in spite of this consideration, the immanent transition of speculative philosophy is still a chimera, an illusion, as if it were possible for the one standpoint necessarily to determine itself into the other; for the category of transition is itself a breach of immanence, a *leap*.

The aestheticist in *Either-Or* was an existential possibility, a young, richly gifted, partly hopeful human being, experimenting with himself and with life; one "with whom it was impossible to grow angry, because the evil that was in him, like the conceptions of evil in the Middle Ages, had something of the childlike in it"; he was not really an actuality, but "a possibility of everything": thus the aestheticist so to speak walked about in the Judge's living room.* The Judge's relation to him was one of open-hearted geniality; he was ethically sure of himself and essentially admonitory, like a somewhat older and more mature person in relation to a younger man, whose talents, whose intellectual superiority he in a manner recognizes, though unconditionally having the ascendancy over him through sureness, experience, and inwardness in living. In the *Stages* the aesthetic receives a more pronounced existential character; and hence there comes to revelation latently, in the presentation itself, the fact that an aesthetic existence, even when a milder light falls upon it, is perdition. But it is not a foreign standpoint that makes this clear, as when the Judge admonishes a young man whose life is not in the deepest sense yet decided. It is too late to admonish a decisively aesthetic existence; to assume to warn Victor Eremita, Constantine Constantius, The Fashion Tailor, or a Johannes the Seducer is to make oneself ridiculous, and to produce an effect quite as comical as a situation I once experienced: a man in an instant of danger catches up a little stick from a child—to beat a huge bandit who had forced his way into the room. Though myself sharing in the danger I was involuntarily moved to laughter, because it looked as if the man were beating clothes. The relationship between the Judge and the aesthetic in *Either-Or* made it natural and psychologically correct for the Judge to admonish. However, even in that work there was no decision in the finite sense (see the Preface), so that the reader could say: "Well, that settles it." A reader who needs the reassurance of a warning lecture in order to see that a standpoint is erroneous, or needs an unfortunate consequence, like madness, suicide, poverty and the like, does not really see anything, but only imagines that he sees; and when an author conducts himself in that manner he only shows that he writes in a womanish fashion for childish readers.† Take such a figure as Johannes the Seducer. Whoever needs that he should become mad or shoot himself in order to be enabled to see that his standpoint is perdition, does not see it, notwithstanding, but merely imagines it. Whoever understands it, understands it the instant the Seducer opens his mouth to speak; he hears in every word the perdition and the condemnation. The reader who needs an outer infliction of punishment merely exposes himself to be made a fool of, for an author can take a very decent man and have him become mad, and then such a reader will believe that it was an illegitimate standpoint.

The aesthetic stage is represented by "In vino veritas." Those who make their appearance here are indeed aestheticists, but are by no means ignorant of the ethical. Hence they are not merely delineated, but speak for themselves as persons fully qualified to give an account of their mode of existence. In our age it is believed that knowledge settles everything, and that if a man only acquires a knowledge of the truth, the more briefly and the more quickly the better, he is helped. But to exist and to know are two very different things.

The Young Man comes closest to being merely a possibility, and therefore he is still a hopeful case. He is essentially melancholy of thought. Constantine Constantius is case-hardened understanding. Victor Eremita is sympathetic irony. The Fashion Tailor is demoniac despair in passion. Johannes the Seducer is perdition in cold blood, a "marked" individuality in whom life is extinct. All are consistent to the point of despair.

Just as the second part of *Either-Or* answers and corrects every misdirection in the first part, so one will here find an explanation in what the ethicist has to say, only that he expresses himself essentially, and nowhere takes direct cognizance of what according to the plan of the work he cannot be supposed to know. It is thus left to the reader himself to put two and two together, if he so desires; but nothing is done to minister to a reader's indolence. To be sure, it is just this that readers want; they want to read books in the royal fashion in which a king reads a petition, where a marginal outline relieves him from the petitioner's prolixity. In relation to the pseudonymous authors this expectation is doubtless a misunderstanding from the side of the reader; from the impression I have of them I do not know that they seek any sort of favors from the lofty majority-majesty of the reading public. That would also seem to me a very strange thing to do. I have always conceived of an author as a man who knows something more, or knows the same thing otherwise, than the reader; that is the reason he is an author, and otherwise he has no reason to be one. But it has never occurred to me to think of the author as a supplicant, a beggar knocking at the door of the reading public, a peddler who with the aid of a devil of a ready tongue and a little fancy gold stuff on the cover, which quite catches the eyes of the daughters in the family, succeeds in foisting his books upon them.

Johannes the Seducer ends with the proposition that *woman is only the moment.* This is in its generality the essential aesthetic principle, namely, that the moment is everything, and in so far again essentially nothing; just as the sophistic proposition that everything is true means that nothing is true. The significance attached to time is in general decisive for every standpoint up to that of the paradox, which paradoxically accentuates time. In the same degree that time is accentuated, in the same degree we go forward from the aesthetic, the metaphysical, to the ethical, the religious, and the Christian-religious.

Where Johannes the Seducer ends, there the Judge begins: that *woman's beauty increases with the years.* Here time is accentuated ethically, but not otherwise than that a retirement out of existence into the eternal, by way of recollection, is still possible.

The aesthetic stage is very briefly indicated, and it is presumably in order to lay the accent quite emphatically upon the religious that the author has called the first part *A Recollection.* By pressing the aesthetic back, the ethical and particularly the religious are brought to the front.

As far as the detailed content is concerned, I shall not further pursue it. Its significance, if it has any, will consist in the existential inwardness with which the various stages are exhibited to the intuition, in passion, irony, pathos, humor, and dialectics. This sort of thing will of course have no interest for *Docents*. It is perhaps not unthinkable that a *Docent* might finally carry his politeness so far as to say *en passant*, in an intermediary proposition, in a remark affixed to a paragraph of the System: "This author represents inwardness." In this way the author and an uninformed circle of readers have been told all about it. Passion, pathos, irony, dialectics, humor, enthusiasm, and so forth—these are things that *Docents* view as something subordinate, as something everybody has. When therefore it is said of an author that he represents inwardness, everything has been said by means of this brief word that everybody can say, and much more indeed than the author himself has said. Everybody now knows what to think about it, and every *Docent* could have produced everything in this genre, but has left it to reduced subjects. Whether everyone really does know concretely what inwardness is, and would be able in the capacity of an author to produce something in that direction, I shall not attempt to decide. Of everyone who is silent, I am prepared to assume that this is the case; but the *Docents* are not silent.

Still, as I have said, I have nothing to do with the content of the book. My thesis was that subjectivity, inwardness, is the truth. This principle was for me decisive with respect to the problem of Christianity, and the same consideration has led me to pursue a certain tendency in the pseudonymous books, which to the very last have honestly abstained from doctrination. Particularly I thought I ought to take cognizance of the last of these books, because it was published after my *Fragments*, recalling the earlier publications by means of a free reproduction, and determining the religious stage through humor as *confinium*.

*Even the "Diary of the Seducer" was only a terrible possibility, which the aestheticist had in his fumbling mode of existence evoked, precisely because he had to try himself in everything, though without really having been anything.

†Here I would recall something to which *Frater Taciturnus* has called attention. The Hegelian philosophy culminates in the proposition that the outward is the inward and the inward is the outward. With this Hegel virtually finishes. But this principle is essentially an aesthetic-metaphysical one, and in this way the Hegelian philosophy is happily finished, or it is fraudulently finished by lumping everything (including the ethical and the religious) indiscriminately in the aesthetic-metaphysical. Even the ethical posits opposition of a sort between the inward and the outward, inasmuch as it regards the outward as neutral. Outwardness, as the material of action, is neutral, for what the ethical accentuates is the purpose, and it is simply immoral to be concerned about the result; outwardness proves nothing at all ethically; outward victory proves nothing at all ethically, for ethically question is raised only about the inward; outward punishment is of little significance, and the ethical, so far from requiring with aesthetic fussiness the visibility of punishment, says proudly, "I shall punish sure enough, i.e. inwardly; and it is simply immoral to rate outward punishment as of any account in comparison with inward."—The religious posits decisively an opposition between the outward and the inward, posits it decisively as opposition, and therein lies suffering as an existence-category for the religious life, but therein lies also the inner infinity of inwardness inwardly directed. If our age had not the distinction of simply ignoring the duty of existing, it would be inconceivable that such wisdom as the Hegelian could be regarded as the highest, as maybe it is for aesthetic contemplators, but not either for ethical or for religious existers.[15]

. . . *Either-Or*, whose very title is suggestive, exhibits the existential relationship between the aesthetic and the ethical in existing individualities. This is for me the book's indirect polemic against speculative philosophy, which is indifferent to the existential. The fact that there is no result and no finite decision, is an indirect expression for the truth as inwardness, and thus perhaps a polemic against the truth as knowledge. The preface itself says something about it, but not didactically, for then I could know with certainty, but in the merry form of jest and hypothesis. The fact that there is no author is a means of keeping the reader at a distance.

The first of the Diapsalmata posits a rift in existence, in the form of a poet's suffering, in such a way as this might have persisted in a poet-existence, which "B" uses against "A." The last sentence in the entire work is as follows: Only the truth which *edifies* is truth *for you*. This is an essential predicate relating to the truth as inwardness; its decisive characterization as edifying *for you*, i.e. for the subject, constitutes its essential difference from all objective knowledge, in that the subjectivity itself becomes the mark of the truth.

The *first* part represents an existential possibility which cannot win through to existence, a melancholy that needs to be ethically worked up. Melancholy is its essential character, and this is so deep, that though autopathic it deceptively occupies itself with the sufferings of others (Shadowgraphs), and for the rest deceives by concealing itself under the cloak of pleasure, rationality, demoralization; the deception and the concealment being at one and the same time its strength and its weakness, its strength in imagination and its weakness in winning through to existence. It is an imagination-existence in aesthetic passion, and therefore paradoxical, colliding with time; it is in its maximum despair; it is therefore not existence; but an existential possibility tending towards existence, and brought so close to it that you feel how every moment is wasted as long as it has not yet come to a decision. But the existential possibility in the existing "A" refuses to become aware of this, and keeps existence away by the most subtle of all deceptions, by thinking; he has thought everything possible, and yet he has not existed at all. The consequence of this is that only the Diapsalmata are pure lyrical effusions; the rest has abundant thought-content, which may easily deceive, as if having thought about something were identical with existing. Had a poet planned the work, he would scarcely have thought about this, and would perhaps by the work itself have set the old misunderstanding on its feet again. The relation is not to be conceived as that between an immature and a mature thought, but between not existing and existing. "A" is therefore a developed thinker, he is far superior to "B" as a dialectician, he has been endowed with all the seductive gifts of soul and understanding; thereby it becomes clearer by what characteristic it is that "B" differs from him.

The *second* part represents an ethical individual existing by virtue of the ethical. It is also the second part which brings the first part into the open; for "A" would again have conceived of the possibility of being an author, actually have realized the writing, and then let it lie. The ethicist has *despaired* (the first part *was* despair); in this despair he has *chosen himself;* in and by this choice he *reveals himself* ("the expression which sharply differentiates between the ethical and the aesthetic is this: it is every man's duty to reveal himself"—the first part was concealment); he is a husband ("A" was familiar with every possibility within the erotic sphere, and yet not actually in love, for then he would instantly, in a way, have been in course of consolidating himself), and concentrates himself, precisely in opposition to the concealment of the aesthetic, upon marriage as the deepest form of life's revelation, by which *time* is taken into the service of the ethically existing individual, and the possibility of *gaining a history* becomes the ethical victory of continuity over concealment, melancholy, illusory passion, and despair. Through phantom-like images of the mist, through the distractions of an abundant thought-content, whose elaboration, if it has any value, is absolutely the merit of the author, we win through to an entirely individual human being, existing in the strength of the ethical. This then constitutes the change of scene; or rather, now the scene is there: instead of a world of possibilities, glowing with imagination and dialectically organized, we have an individual—and only the truth which edifies is truth for you; that is, the truth is inwardness, but please to note, existential inwardness, here qualified as ethical.

And so this brush is over. The merit of the book, if it has any, is not my concern. If it has any merit, this will essentially consist in not giving any result, but in transforming everything into inwardness: in the first part, an imaginative inwardness which evokes the possibilities with intensified passion, with sufficient dialectical power to transform all into nothing in despair; in the second part, an ethical pathos, which with a quiet incorruptible, and yet infinite passion embraces the modest ethical task, and edified thereby stands self-revealed before God and man. [16]

. . . But a trial is a transitional phase (compare for its dialectic *Repetition*), the individual who has undergone such a trial returns to an existence in the ethical, though retaining an everlasting impression of its fearfulness, an impression of greater inwardness than that in which the experienced person is reminded by his gray hairs of the moment of fear and peril in which his hair turned gray. The teleological suspension of the ethical must be given a more distinctively religious expression. The ethical will then be present every moment with its infinite requirement, but the individual is not capable of realizing this requirement. This impotence of the individual must not be understood as the imperfection of a persistent striving toward the attainment of an ideal; for in that case no suspension is posited; just as an official is not suspended from his office if he performs its duties only moderately well. The suspension in question consists in the individual's finding himself in a state precisely the opposite of that which the ethical requires, so that far from being able to begin, each moment he remains in this state he is more and more prevented from beginning. He is not related to the task as possibility to actuality, but as impossibility. Thus the individual is suspended from the requirements of the ethical in the most terrible manner, being in the suspension heterogeneous with the ethical, which nevertheless has an infinite claim upon him; each moment it requires itself of the individual, and each moment it thereby only more definitely determines the heterogeneity as heterogeneity. Abraham was not heterogeneous with the ethical in his temptation, the temptation in which God tempts a man, as the story in Genesis says of Abraham; he was quite completely capable of realizing it, but was prevented by something higher, which through accentuating itself *absolutely* transformed the voice of duty into a temptation. As soon as this something higher sets the tempted individual free, all is again in order, though the fearful memory that this could happen, even if only for the tenth of a second, still remains. For the length of time the suspension lasts is less important, the decisive thing is that it is there. But these things nobody thinks about; the sermon uses the category of a "trial" quite unceremoniously (the ethical being the temptation); though this is a category which absolutely confuses the ethical, and in general all immediately direct human thought. But it is as if it were nothing—and doubtless that is what it is.

Now the situation is different. Duty is the absolute, its requirement an absolute requirement, and yet the individual is prevented from realizing it; aye, in a desperate ironical manner he is as if set free (in the same sense that the Scriptures speak of being set free from the law of God) through having become heterogeneous with it; and the more profoundly its requirement is made known to him, the clearer becomes his fearful freedom. The terrible emancipation from the requirement of realizing the ethical, the heterogeneity of the individual with the ethical, this suspension from the ethical, is *Sin*, considered as the state in which a human being is.

Sin is a decisive expression for the religious mode of existence. As long as sin is not yet posited, the suspension from the ethical becomes a transitory phase which again vanishes, or remains outside life as something altogether irregular. But sin is the decisive expression for the religious mode of existence; it is not a moment within something else, within another order of things, but is itself the beginning of the religious order of things. In none of the pseudonymous books had sin been brought to the attention. It is indeed true that the ethicist in *Either-Or* had given the ethical category of choosing oneself a religious color by accompanying the act of despair with an act of repentance, repenting himself out of continuity with the race; but this was an emasculation which presumably had its ground in the plan of keeping the work within ethical categories—quite in accordance with my wishes, in order, namely, that each phase might be made clear by itself. The edifying reflection at the close of *Either-Or*, "that over against God we are always in the wrong," constitutes no determination of sin as a fundamental condition, but is merely the discrepancy of the finite and the infinite brought to rest in an enthusiastic reconciliation in the infinite. It is the last enthusiastic cry in which the finite spirit appeals to God, within the sphere of freedom: "I cannot understand Thee, but still I will love Thee, Thou art always right; even if it seemed to me as if Thou didst not love me, I will nevertheless love Thee." Hence it was that the theme was so worded: the edification that lies in the thought, etc.; the edifying is not sought in the annulment of the misunderstanding, but in the enthusiastic endurance of it, and in this final act of courage as if bringing about its annulment. In *Fear and Trembling* sin was used incidentally to illuminate the nature of Abraham's ethical suspension, but not further.

So the matter stood when there was published a book, *The Concept of Dread*, described as a simple indicational psychological inquiry, tending toward the dogmatic problem of original sin. Just as *Either-Or* had made sure that the teleological suspension should not be mistaken for aesthetic secrecy, so the three pseudonymous books had together made sure that sin, when it came to be brought forward, should not be mistaken for this or that weakness and imperfection; sorrow over it not be confounded with sighs and tears and blubbering over ourselves and this vale of tears; the suffering involved in it not confounded with a *quodlibet*. Sin is decisive for an entire existential sphere, the religious taken in the strictest sense. Precisely because in our age knowledge is much too abundant, it is a very easy matter to mix everything up together in a confusion of tongues, where aestheticists use the most decisive Christian terminology in the spirit of genial wit, and clergymen use it as an official formulary independent of content.

But if it is the misfortune of our age that it has too much knowledge, that it has forgotten what it means to exist, and what inwardness signifies, then it was of importance not to apprehend sin in abstract terms, in which indeed it cannot be apprehended at all, or at least decisively, because it has an essential relationship to existence. In so far it was a good thing that the book was a psychological inquiry, which itself explains that sin has no place in the system, presumably like immortality, faith, the paradox, and other similar concepts having an essential relationship to existence, from which the systematic thought abstracts. The term "dread" does not suggest paragraph-importance, but rather existential inwardness. Just as fear and trembling represent the state of mind of the individual while under teleological suspension, so dread represents his state of mind in the desperate emancipation from the task of realizing the ethical. The inwardness of sin, as dread in the existing individual, is the greatest possible and most painful possible distance from the truth, when truth is subjectivity.[17]

In elucidating his themes regarding existentialism, Kierkegaard suggests that human beings develop through a three-stage evolution, each stage progressing toward a greater degree of acceptance of the human condition. These three stages are: (1) aesthetic, (2) ethical, and (3) religious.

The Aesthetic Stage.   This stage is more or less the "natural stage" of human beings. Kierkegaard suggests that this is the stage in which all of us find ourselves before we make any attempt to understand the depths of the human condition. He also refers to this stage of human development as the *Don Juan* stage. It is characterized by a total lack of commitment. There is no "taking a stand" on any issue whatsoever. Without taking a stand, any human being fails to assume any degree of responsibility and, accordingly, has no fixed direction in his or her life. On this level, a human person is a "nothing." There is already a hint of where Kierkegaard is taking us. A human being makes his or her essence—i.e., determines the degree of humanity—by affirming commitments. Without making any commitments, a human being is a nothing. This theme will occur repeatedly in the writings of the existentialists. The person found in the aesthetic stage has no human self—there is a "scattering of the soul." This kind of person wants to taste everything but never desires to commit himself/herself to any thing, person, or event. Kierkegaard once remarked that this stage was characterized by the "rotation method." There was a continually changing emphasis by the person from one thing to another without ever making a commitment. Lest this stage be misunderstood, Kierkegaard is not only referring to matters of the senses. There can also be an intellectual Don Juan. Faust, the medieval philosopher who sold his soul to the devil in exchange for knowledge and power, is Kierkegaard's example of an intellectual Don Juan. Kierkegaard suggests that a person could just as easily remain uncommitted to a set of ideas and continually float from one theory to the next as remain uncommitted to persons. Accordingly, the notion of absolute commitment characterizes the aesthetic stage. The intellectual Don Juan is a brilliant mind who remains uncommitted.

Kierkegaard suggests that the aesthetic stage is so constructed that almost no one could remain in it unless he or she was tremendously interested in being a bore. Since, in this stage, the human being is a nothing, it ultimately results in despair and melancholy. The person who finds his or her life to be a terrible bore cannot help but slip into the state of despair and melancholy. The aesthetic stage forces the human agent to make a commitment. Again, the subjectivity of existentialism rises to the surface. A person transcends the state of boredom and melancholy by subjectively committing himself/herself to an ethical system.

The Ethical Stage.   The move from the aesthetic stage to the ethical stage is accomplished by a sublimation or commitment to a universal principle of law or morality. A person who subordinates himself/herself to a moral code is no longer one standing outside the human condition. Rather, this person is one who has taken on the task of leading a moral life, and this demands commitment. For example, a person might become committed to a utilitarian moral system and conscientiously attempt to guide his or her every action by means of the principle of utility; or become a Kantian and be committed to the principle of universality; or rigorously accept the Ten Commandments and attempt to lead a life in accord with this moral code. The point is that the person has indeed transcended the limits of the aesthetic stage by affirming a commitment to a moral system. In seeking a way beyond the despair of the aesthetic stage, the person affirming the demands of the ethical stage believes that this is enough to foster human perfection and human completion. In other words, the commitment to the moral code is regarded as a sufficient condition for moral perfection and human happiness.

Yet Kierkegaard suggests that the moral law in itself is insufficient to produce complete human satisfaction. The moral law, Kierkegaard suggests, places demands on humans which they can never satisfy. Any system of morality places the demand of moral perfection on each individual human agent, but human agents can never reach that level of moral rectitude. Kierkegaard expresses this point by suggesting that a moral system places an infinite demand on a finite being. The demands of moral perfection are beyond the capabilities of human beings. Simply put, Kierkegaard suggests that there is a strain of imperfection built into every human being. This is similar to what Aristotle called moral weakness. The Jewish and Christian religious traditions refer to this as the pains of original sin. No matter how one might describe this state, the focal point is that human beings cannot ever attain the limits of perfection demanded by any moral system. Kierkegaard is stressing a point which each of us has felt. No matter how strongly we may be committed to a moral code, there are times when we do not live up to the demands of that code. We give in to temptation. This facet of moral weakness in human nature is what each human being becomes aware of when he or she is in the ethical stage. Kierkegaard at times talks of this as the state of human *creatureliness*. This signifies that humans as moral beings are dependent upon something other than their own powers for moral perfection. Insofar as we are dependent, it is impossible for us to attain complete and total moral perfection. Kierkegaard thus sees the moral law, by its very nature and character, as making an impossible demand on the very existence of human beings. The human condition is such that it is impossible for us to reach the moral perfection demanded by a rational moral code.

The realization of this inherent weakness in human nature results, Kierkegaard suggests, in a state of *anguish*. Remember what prompted a human being to enter the ethical stage; it was the state of boredom experienced from the aesthetic stage. Thus the commitment affirmed in adopting a moral position is seen as being an impossible task. The ethical stage, in affirming the necessity of commitment, is a move toward defining the individual. Nonetheless, it also is a hindrance to such a definition. Thus more is needed, and this is the prelude for the religious stage.

The Religious Stage.   Kierkegaard suggests that persons grasp their imperfection and transcend the imperfection experienced in the ethical stage by making a *leap of faith* to the divine realm. This is the affirmation of the "spirit" beyond the demands of the moral law. In this stage, a human affirms the essence of the human condition, and that is one of imperfection. The person accepts his/her state of dependence—the state of "creatureliness." This acceptance of dependence demands a leap of faith to that "being" upon which we depend. In Kierkegaard's system, this is the God of Christianity. The passage from the ethical to the religious stage demands a choice, and the choice is into an incomprehensible objective reality. The leap of faith must be taken seriously and literally. In the religious stage, reason is a kind of madness, and all wisdom of a rational nature is seen as foolishness. The faith of the religious stage is beyond the rational. It is *absurd*.

The leap of faith to a divine being, for Kierkegaard, is a transcendence of all rationality. Reason is transcended completely. The religious stage is characterized by the leap of faith, and this leap is irrational. This is why Kierkegaard refers to it as the absurd. The absurd does not mean ridiculous, crazy, or stupid. It does mean that it is beyond the possibility of reason to understand. The absolute character of commitment and perfect trust is manifested here. One has trust by believing in the person of God, not by a rational demonstration. Hence the religious stage is one of complete subjectivity. It is not one of accepting the propositions of theology, but rather a start of *believing in* the personhood of God.

The religious stage is characterized by an absolute commitment and a perfect act of trust. We affirm our inherent imperfection and corresponding incapacity to attain moral perfection on our own. We trust in God to help us out. Yet since this perfect trust is irrational and beyond reason, there is the characteristic of dread. This is the religious stage of fear and trembling. Kierkegaard suggests that no human being could possibly stand in the religious stage without the experience of fear and trembling. Notice the direct attack on the Christians of Christendom for whom Christianity was nothing more than carrying out external liturgical events. There was no existential shock in being a Christian. Yet Kierkegaard suggests that without the experience of dread one has not experienced the demands of the religious stage.

Why the emphasis on dread? Kierkegaard's favorite example might shed some light here. Kierkegaard often uses the biblical patriarch, Abraham, as the "knight of faith." Abraham's situation in responding to the commands of God placed him into direct conflict between the demands of the ethical and the demands of the religious. Recall for a moment the biblical account of Abraham and Isaac. Isaac was Abraham's son by Sara. Sara was quite old when Isaac was born; in fact, Sara had given up hope of ever bearing children. When Isaac was a young man, God commanded Abraham to take Isaac onto a mountain and offer him to God as a sacrifice. Notice the conflict which erupts in this situation. This conflict, Kierkegaard suggests, is so overwhelming that no person could be in Abraham's position and not feel deep existential dread.

Abraham, as a father, had the highest obligation to his children. Since Isaac was his only son by Sara, this bond would be even stronger. Furthermore, Abraham observed the Ten Commandments, one of which is an explicit prohibition against killing another human person. Nonetheless, God commanded Abraham to sacrifice Isaac. Because of his commitment to God, Abraham had to view the sacrifice of Isaac in a different dimension. The religious situation demanded this acceptance, but how could Abraham be in this situation without feeling dread? Not only was he asked to sacrifice his beloved son, but he experienced this tension between the demands of his ethical system—the Ten Commandments—and the demands expressed to him directly by God. How can one be in this stage without experiencing fear and trembling? Here we have a paradox between sacrifice and murder. The faith of Abraham as witnessed in the religious stage begins only where reason leaves off. The religious stage, which is part of the human condition because of the limitations of the ethical stage, contains the experiences of dread, fear, and trembling. Kierkegaard is suggesting that the human existence, when viewed existentially, is not easy. And the demands of commitment represent the only way of bringing about a human response to the human condition.

Notice how this system elucidated by Kierkegaard is in direct response to Hegel. Hegel suggested that the religious state of awareness—the propositions affirmed by religious believers—was capable of being understood in the philosophical stage through sheer concepts. Kierkegaard, to the contrary, suggests that the elements of religion are indeed beyond the capability of reason. Not only that, the dimension emphasized by faith is one of acceptance or commitment, not one of rational belief and understanding. It is subjective rather than objective. The subject matter of the religious stage is absurd—it transcends the competency of reason. Hegel was mistaken in subsuming religion to philosophy. For, as Kierkegaard believes, the subjective demands of the religious stage begin where reason stops. The subjective dimension of religious faith is absurd. Kierkegaard remarks that "faith is a passion."

The concept of the absurd is probably best applied to the uniquely religious mysteries of Christianity. Claims like the Trinity, the doctrine of Grace, the Incarnation, and so forth are regarded as being beyond the capability of religious understanding. Kierkegaard remarks that the understanding of such propositions is indeed impossible. They transcend the limits of human reason. Rather than being understood, they are propositions to which one makes a commitment; one commits himself/herself to a religious way of life. This is totally beyond the competency of human reason, and this commitment, as illustrated by Kierkegaard's example of Abraham, is one demanding dread. It is not easy to be a Christian, and through the three stages Kierkegaard has kept his promise of making difficulties for the Danish Christians.

Jean-Paul Sartre

The writings of Kierkegaard had little direct influence on the philosophical and theological community outside of Denmark until the early part of the twentieth century. At that time, a German translation was made. Due to this translation, following World War I a great interest in Kierkegaardian themes developed at several German universities, especially Heidelberg and Freiburg. Karl Jaspers and Martin Heidegger, among others, used various themes found in the writings of Kierkegaard to develop their own distinctive philosophical positions. From the German universities the interest in existentialist ideas spread to France; the name of Jean-Paul Sartre is the one linked by most American students with French existentialism.

Jean-Paul Sartre (1905-   ) has had an illustrious literary and philosophical career. As the author of novels and a gifted playwright, Sartre has successfully used the literary genre to convey his existentialist themes. Although he has written uniquely philosophical works—some of which, such as his monumental *Being and Nothingness,* have genuinely influenced the philosophic community—Sartre is best known (among American students) for his plays and novels.

In order to better grasp the underlying significance of Sartre's literary works, it is helpful to understand the philosophical framework within which Sartre writes. It is fruitful to look at Sartre as a philosopher who denies any ultimate significance to the Platonic model of explanation. Remember that in chapter 2 we discussed Plato's world view in some detail. Plato's position argued that the transcendental world of the forms provided ultimate meaning and significance for the world. As appropriated by the early Jewish and Christian theologians, Plato's world of the forms became identified with the divine archetypes in the mind of God. Accordingly, it was because of these divine archetypes, after which the world was patterned, that the world exhibited rationality. Sartre fundamentally denies any coherence or significance to this pattern.

Let's examine this Platonic pattern a bit more. If we do not see the significance of the Platonic scheme of interpretation, many of Sartre's themes will not make sense. Sartre claims that the fundamental principle of existentialist thought is that "Existence precedes essence." The converse of this proposition, one which Sartre argues is dependent upon the Platonic scheme, is that "Essence precedes existence." This latter proposition means that there is a pattern or blueprint after which individuals are copied. The design is ontologically prior to the exemplification of the individuals under the design. Obviously, design functions here as essence. Thus, if the proposition that "Essence precedes existence" is true, this entails that the essence of an individual has ontological precedence over the individual. This is exactly what Plato's world of the forms accomplishes. Schematically, we might illustrate this point in the following way:

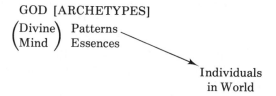

GOD [ARCHETYPES]
(Divine Mind) Patterns Essences
Individuals
in World

If this Platonic world view is correct, then indeed there is a basis for order in the world and for an objective foundation for a moral theory. Recall that, for Plato, virtue was equivalent to knowledge. Knowledge occurred only when the human mind was in direct contact with the world of the forms. Insofar as Sartre regards this Platonic pattern exemplified by Judaism and Christianity as insufficient, he strenuously argues that the proposition, "Essence precedes existence," is false as applicable to human beings. Human beings exist first. Then they make their own essence by the actions and commitments they undertake. Accordingly, for Sartre, there is no such ontological category as human essence. Sartre argues that since the view of God was abandoned by the philosophic atheism of the eighteenth century, it is philosophically inconsistent to adhere to a view of human essence. Hence the proposition that "Existence precedes essence" is true for human beings. As Sartre will suggest, the whole thrust of existentialism is nothing more than an attempt to draw the full implications from a consistently atheistic position.

The following selection is from Sartre's famous work, *Existentialism*. It is a very good introductory account of the basic themes found in Sartre's existential philosophy.

EXISTENTIALISM

Jean-Paul Sartre

. . . What is meant by the term *existentialism?*

Most people who use the word would be rather embarrassed if they had to explain it, since, now that the word is all the rage, even the work of a musician or painter is being called existentialist. A gossip columnist in *Clartés* signs himself *The Existentialist,* so that by this time the word has been so stretched and has taken on so broad a meaning, that it no longer means anything at all. It seems that for want of an advance-guard doctrine analogous to surrealism, the kind of people who are eager for scandal and flurry turn to this philosophy which in other respects does not at all serve their purposes in this sphere.

Actually, it is the least scandalous, the most austere of doctrines. It is intended strictly for specialists and philosophers. Yet it can be defined easily. What complicates matters is that there are two kinds of existentialist; first, those who are Christian, among whom I would include Jaspers and Gabriel Marcel, both Catholic; and on the other hand the atheistic existentialists, among whom I class Heidegger, and then the French existentialists and myself. What they have in common is that they think that existence precedes essence, or, if you prefer, that subjectivity must be the starting point.

Just what does that mean? Let us consider some object that is manufactured, for example, a book or a paper-cutter: here is an object which has been made by an artisan whose inspiration came from a concept. He referred to the concept of what a paper-cutter is and likewise to a known method of production, which is part of the concept, something which is, by and large, a routine. Thus, the paper-cutter is at once an object produced in a certain way and, on the other hand, one having a specific use; and one can not postulate a man who produces a paper-cutter but does not know what it is used for. Therefore, let us say that, for the paper-cutter, essence—that is, the ensemble of both the production routines and the properties which enable it to be both produced and defined—precedes existence. Thus, the presence of the paper-cutter or book in front of me is determined. Therefore, we have here a technical view of the world whereby it can be said that production precedes existence.

When we conceive God as the Creator, He is generally thought of as a superior sort of artisan. Whatever doctrine we may be considering, whether one like that of Descartes or that of Leibnitz, we always grant that will more or less follows understanding or, at the very least, accompanies it, and that when God creates He knows exactly what He is creating. Thus, the concept of man in the mind of God is comparable to the concept of paper-cutter in the mind of the manufacturer, and, following certain techniques and a conception, God produces man, just as the artisan, following a definition and a technique, makes a paper-cutter. Thus, the individual man is the realization of a certain concept in the divine intelligence.

In the eighteenth century, the atheism of the *philosophes* discarded the idea of God, but not so much for the notion that essence precedes exis-

From Jean-Paul Sartre, *Existentialism,* translated by Bernard Frechtman (New York: Philosophical Library, 1947). Reprinted by permission of the Philosophical Library and Methuen & Co., Ltd.

tence. To a certain extent, this idea is found everywhere; we find it in Diderot, in Voltaire, and even in Kant. Man has a human nature; this human nature, which is the concept of the human, is found in all men, which means that each man is a particular example of a universal concept, man. In Kant, the result of this universality is that the wild-man, the natural man, as well as the bourgeois, are circumscribed by the same definition and have the same basic qualities. Thus, here too the essence of man precedes the historical existence that we find in nature.

Atheistic existentialism, which I represent, is more coherent. It states that if God does not exist, there is at least one being in whom existence precedes essence, a being who exists before he can be defined by any concept, and that this being is man, or, as Heidegger says, human reality. What is meant here by saying that existence precedes essence? It means that, first of all, man exists, turns up, appears on the scene, and, only afterwards, defines himself. If man, as the existentialist conceives him, is indefinable, it is because at first he is nothing. Only afterward will he be something, and he himself will have made what he will be. Thus, there is no human nature, since there is no God to conceive it. Not only is man what he conceives himself to be, but he is also only what he wills himself to be after his thrust toward existence.

Man is nothing else but what he makes of himself. Such is the first principle of existentialism. It is also what is called subjectivity, the name we are labeled with when charges are brought against us. But what do we mean by this, if not that man has a greater dignity than a stone or table? For we mean that man first exists, that is, that man first of all is the being who hurls himself toward a future and who is conscious of imagining himself as being in the future. Man is at the start of a plan which is aware of itself, rather than a patch of moss, a piece of garbage, or a cauliflower; nothing exists prior to this plan; there is nothing in heaven; man will be what he will have planned to be. Not what he will want to be. Because by the word "will" we generally mean a conscious decision, which is subsequent to what we have already made of ourselves. I may want to belong to a political party, write a book, get married; but all that is only a manifestation of an earlier, more spontaneous choice that is called "will." But if existence really does precede essence, man is responsible for what he is. Thus, existentialism's first move is to make every man aware of what he is and to make the full responsibility of his existence rest on him. And when we say that a man is responsible for himself, we do not only mean that he is responsible for his own individuality, but that he is responsible for all men. . . .

. . . When we say that man chooses his own self, we mean that every one of us does likewise; but we also mean by that that in making this choice he also chooses all men. In fact, in creating the man that we want to be, there is not a single one of our acts which does not at the same time create an image of man as we think he ought to be. To choose to be this or that is to affirm at the same time the value of what we choose, because we can never choose evil. We always choose the good, and nothing can be good for us without being good for all.

If, on the other hand, existence precedes essence, and if we grant that we exist and fashion our image at one and the same time, the image is valid for everybody and for our whole age. Thus, our responsibility is much greater than we might have supposed, because it involves all mankind. If I am a workingman and choose a join a Christian trade-union rather than be a communist, and if by being a member I want to show that the best thing for man is resignation, that the kingdom of man is not of this world, I am not only involving my own case—I want to be resigned for everyone. As a result, my action has involved all humanity. To take a more individual matter, if I want to marry, to have children; even if this marriage depends solely on my own circumstances or passion or wish, I am involving all humanity in monogamy and not merely myself. Therefore, I am responsible for myself and for everyone else. I am creating a certain image of man of my own choosing. In choosing myself, I choose man.

This helps us understand what the actual content is of such rather grandiloquent words as anguish, forlornness, despair. As you will see, it's all quite simple.

First, what is meant by anguish? The existentialists say at once that man is anguish. What that means is this: the man who involves himself and who realizes that he is not only the person he chooses to be, but also a law-maker who is, at the same time, choosing all mankind as well as himself, can not help escape the feeling of his total and deep responsibility. Of course, there are many people who are not anxious; but we claim that they are hiding their anxiety, that they are fleeing from it. Certainly, many people believe that when they do something, they themselves are the only ones involved, and when someone says to them. "What if everyone acted that way?" they shrug their shoulders and answer, "Everyone doesn't act that way." But really, one should always ask himself, "What would happen if everybody looked at things that way?" There is no escaping this disturbing thought except by a kind of double-dealing. A man who lies and makes excuses for himself by saying "not everybody does that," is someone with an uneasy conscience, because the act of lying implies that a universal value is conferred upon the lie.

Anguish is evident even when it conceals itself. This is the anguish that Kierkegaard called the anguish of Abraham. You know the story: an angel has ordered Abraham to sacrifice his son; if it really were an angel who has come and said, "You are Abraham, you shall sacrifice your son," everything would be all right. But everyone might first wonder, "Is it really an angel, and am I really Abraham? What proof do I have?"

There was a madwoman who had hallucinations; someone used to speak to her on the telephone and give her orders. Her doctor asked her, "Who is it who talks to you?" She answered, "He says it's God." What proof did she really have that it was God? If an angel comes to me, what proof is there that it's an angel? And if I hear voices, what proof is there that they come from heaven and not from hell, or from the subconscious, or a pathological condition? What proves that they are addressed to me? What proof is there that I have been appointed to impose my choice and my conception of man on humanity? I'll never find any proof or sign to convince me of that. If a voice addresses me, it is always for me to decide that this is the angel's voice; if I consider that such an act is a good one, it is I who will choose to say that it is good rather than bad.

Now, I'm not being singled out as an Abraham, and yet at every moment I'm obliged to perform exemplary acts. For every man, everything happens as if all mankind had its eyes fixed on him and were guiding itself by what he does. And every man ought to say to himself, "Am I really the kind of man who has the right to act in such a way that humanity might guide itself by my actions?" And if he does not say that to himself, he is masking his anguish.

There is no question here of the kind of anguish which would lead to quietism, to inaction. It is a matter of a simple sort of anguish that anybody who has had responsibilities is familiar with. For example, when a military officer takes the responsibility for an attack and sends a certain number of men to death, he chooses to do so, and in the main he alone makes the choice. Doubtless, orders come from above, but they are too broad; he interprets them, and on this interpretation depend the lives of ten or fourteen or twenty men. In making a decision he can not help having a certain anguish. All leaders know this anguish. That doesn't keep them from acting; on the contrary, it is the very condition of their action. For it implies that they envisage a number of possibilities, and when they choose one, they realize that it has value only because it is chosen. We shall see that this kind of anguish, which is the kind that existentialism describes, is explained, in addition, by a direct responsibility to the other men whom it involves. It is not a curtain separating us from action, but is part of action itself.

When we speak of forlornness, a term Heidegger was fond of, we mean only that God does not exist and that we have to face all the consequences of this. The existentialist is strongly opposed to a certain kind of secular ethics which would like to abolish God with the least possible expense. About 1880, some French teachers tried to set up a secular ethics which went something like this: God is a useless and costly hypothesis; we are discarding it; but, meanwhile, in order for there to be an ethics, a society, a civilization, it is essential that certain values be taken seriously and that they be considered as having an *a priori* existence. It must be obligatory, *a priori,* to be honest, not to lie, not to beat your wife, to have children, etc., etc. So we're going to try a little device which will make it possible to show that values exist all the same, inscribed in a heaven of ideas, though otherwise God does not exist. In other words—and this, I believe, is the tendency of everything called reformism in France—nothing will be changed if God does not exist. We shall find ourselves with the same norms of honesty, progress, and humanism, and we shall have made of God an outdated hypothesis which will peacefully die off by itself.

The existentialist, on the contrary, thinks it very distressing that God does not exist, because all possibility of finding values in a heaven of ideas disappears along with Him; there can no longer be an *a priori* Good, since there is no infinite and perfect consciousness to think it. Nowhere is it written that the Good exists, that we must be honest, that we must not lie; because the fact is we are on a plane where there are only men. Dostoievsky said, "If God didn't exist, everything would be possible." That is the very starting point of existentialism. Indeed, everything is permissible if God does not exist, and as a result man is forlorn, because neither within him nor without does he find anything to cling to. He can't start making excuses for himself.

If existence really does precede essence, there is no explaining things away by reference to a fixed and given human nature. In other words, there is no determinism, man is free, man is freedom. On the other hand, if God does not exist, we find no values or commands to turn to which legitimize our conduct. So, in the bright realm of values, we have no excuse behind us, nor justification before us. We are alone, with no excuses.

That is the idea I shall try to convey when I say that man is condemned to be free. Condemned, because he did not create himself, yet, in other respects is free; because, once thrown into the world, he is responsible for everything he does. The existentialist does not believe in the power of passion. He will never agree that a sweeping passion is a ravaging torrent which fatally leads a man to certain acts and is therefore an excuse. He thinks that man is responsible for his passion.

The existentialist does not think that man is going to help himself by finding in the world some omen by which to orient himself. Because he thinks that man will interpret the omen to suit himself. Therefore, he thinks that man, with no support and no aid, is condemned every moment to invent man. Ponge, in a very fine article, has said, "Man is the future of man." That's exactly it. But if it is taken to mean that this future is recorded in heaven, that God sees it, then it is false, because it would really no longer be a future. If it is taken to mean that, whatever a man may be, there is a future to be forged, a virgin future before him, then this remark is sound. But then we are forlorn.

To give you an example which will enable you to understand forlornness better, I shall cite the case of one of my students who came to see me under the following circumstances: his father was on bad terms with his mother, and, moreover, was inclined to be a collaborationist; his older brother had been killed in the German offensive of 1940, and the young man, with somewhat immature but generous feelings, wanted to avenge him. His mother lived alone with him, very much upset by the half-treason of her husband and the death of her older son; the boy was her only consolation.

The boy was faced with the choice of leaving for England and joining the Free French Forces—that is, leaving his mother behind—or remaining with his mother and helping her to carry on. He was fully aware that the woman lived only for him and that his going-off—and perhaps his death—would plunge her into despair. He was also aware that every act that he did for his mother's sake was a sure thing, in the sense that it was helping her to carry on, whereas every effort he made toward going off and fighting was an uncertain move which might run aground and prove completely useless; for example, on his way to England he might, while passing through Spain, be detained indefinitely in a Spanish camp; he might reach England or Algiers and be stuck in an office at a desk job. As a result, he was faced with two very different kinds of action: one, concrete, immediate, but concerning only one individual; the other concerned an incomparably vaster group, a national collectivity, but for that very reason was dubious, and might be interrupted en route. And, at the same time, he was wavering between two kinds of ethics. On the one hand, an ethics of sympathy, of personal devotion; on the other, a broader ethics, but one whose efficacy was more dubious. He had to choose between the two.

Who could help him choose? Christian doctrine? No. Christian doctrine says, "Be charitable, love your neighbor, take the more rugged path, etc.,

etc." But which is the more rugged path? Whom should he love as a brother? The fighting man or his mother? Which does the greater good, the vague act of fighting in a group, or the concrete one of helping a particular human being to go on living? Who can decide *a priori*? Nobody. No book of ethics can tell him. The Kantian ethics says, "Never treat any person as a means, but as an end." Very well, if I stay with my mother, I'll treat her as an end and not as a means; but by virtue of this very fact, I'm running the risk of treating the people around me who are fighting, as means; and, conversely, if I go to join those who are fighting, I'll be treating them as an end, and, by doing that, I run the risk of treating my mother as a means.

If values are vague, and if they are always too broad for the concrete and specific case that we are considering, the only thing left for us is to trust our instincts. That's what this young man tried to do; and when I saw him, he said, "In the end, feeling is what counts. I ought to choose whichever pushes me in one direction. If I feel that I love my mother enough to sacrifice everything else for her—my desire for vengeance, for action, for adventure—then I'll stay with her. If, on the contrary, I feel that my love for my mother isn't enough, I'll leave."

But how is the value of a feeling determined? What gives his feeling for his mother value? Precisely the fact that he remained with her. I may say that I like so-and-so well enough to sacrifice a certain amount of money for him, but I may say so only if I've done it. I may say "I love my mother well enough to remain with her" if I have remained with her. The only way to determine the value of this affection is, precisely, to perform an act which confirms and defines it. But, since I require this affection to justify my act, I find myself caught in a vicious circle. . . .

. . . Forlornness implies that we ourselves choose our being. Forlornness and anguish go together.

As for despair, the term has a very simple meaning. It means that we shall confine ourselves to reckoning only with what depends upon our will, or on the ensemble of probabilities which make our action possible. When we want something, we always have to reckon with probabilities. I may be counting on the arrival of a friend. The friend is coming by rail or streetcar; this supposes that the train will arrive on schedule, or that the streetcar will not jump the track. I am left in the realm of possibility; but possibilities are to be reckoned with only to the point where my action comports with the ensemble of these possibilities, and no further. The moment the possibilities I am considering are not rigorously involved by my action, I ought to disengage myself from them, because no God, no scheme, can adapt the world and its possibilities to my will. When Descartes said, "Conquer yourself rather than the world," he meant essentially the same thing. . . .

Actually, things will be as man will have decided they are to be. Does that mean that I should abandon myself to quietism? No. First, I should involve myself; then, act on the old saw, "Nothing ventured, nothing gained." Nor does it mean that I shouldn't belong to a party, but rather that I shall have no illusions and shall do what I can. For example, suppose I ask myself, "Will socialization, as such, ever come about?" I know nothing about it. All I know is that I'm going to do everything in my power to bring it about.

Beyond that, I can't count on anything. Quietism is the attitude of people who say, "Let others do what I can't do." The doctrine I am presenting is the very opposite of quietism, since it declares. "There is no reality except in action." Moreover, it goes further, since it adds, "Man is nothing else than his plan; he exists only to the extent that he fulfills himself; he is therefore nothing else than the ensemble of his acts, nothing else than his life." . . .

. . . You see that it can not be taken for a philosophy of quietism, since it defines man in terms of action; nor for a pessimistic description of man—there is no doctrine more optimistic, since man's destiny is within himself; nor for an attempt to discourage man from acting, since it tells him that the only hope is in his acting and that action is the only thing that enables a man to live. Consequently, we are dealing here with an ethics of action and involvement.

Nevertheless, on the basis of a few notions like these, we are still charged with immuring man in his private subjectivity. There again we're very much misunderstood. Subjectivity of the individual is indeed our point of departure, and this for strictly philosophic reasons. Not because we are bourgeois, but because we want a doctrine based on truth and not a lot of fine theories, full of hope but with no real basis. There can be no other truth to take off from than this: *I think; therefore, I exist.* There we have the absolute truth of consciousness becoming aware of itself. Every theory which takes man out of the moment in which he becomes aware of himself is, at its very beginning, a theory which confounds truth, for outside the Cartesian *cogito,* all views are only probable, and a doctrine of probability which is not bound to a truth dissolves into thin air. In order to describe the probable, you must have a firm hold on the true. Therefore, before there can be any truth whatsoever, there must be an absolute truth; and this one is simple and easily arrived at; it's on everyone's doorstep; it's a matter of grasping it directly.

Secondly, this theory is the only one which gives man dignity, the only one which does not reduce him to an object. The effect of all materialism is to treat all men, including the one philosophizing, as objects, that is, as an ensemble of determined reactions in no way distinguished from the ensemble of qualities and phenomena which constitute a table or a chair or a stone. We definitely wish to establish the human realm as an ensemble of values distinct from the material realm. But the subjectivity that we have thus arrived at, and which we have claimed to be truth, is not a strictly individual subjectivity, for we have demonstrated that one discovers in the *cogito* not only himself, but others as well. . . .

And before going any further, let it be said at once that we are not dealing here with an aesthetic ethics, because our opponents are so dishonest that they even accuse us of that. The example I've chosen is a comparison only.

Having said that, may I ask whether anyone has ever accused an artist who has painted a picture of not having drawn his inspiration from rules set up *a priori?* Has anyone ever asked, "What painting ought he to make?" It is clearly understood that there is no definite painting to be made, that the artist is engaged in the making of his painting, and that the painting to be made is precisely the painting he will have made. It is clearly understood that there are no *a priori* aesthetic values, but that there are values which appear subsequently in the coherence of the painting, in the correspondence between what the artist intended and the result. Nobody can tell what the painting of tomorrow will be like. Painting can be judged only after it has once been made. What connection does that have with ethics? We are in the same creative situation. We never say that a work of art is arbitrary. When we speak of a canvas of Picasso, we never say that it is arbitrary; we understand quite well that he was making himself what he is at the very time he was painting, that the ensemble of his work is embodied in his life.

The same holds on the ethical plane. What art and ethics have in common is that we have creation and invention in both cases. We can not decide *a priori* what there is to be done. I think that I pointed that out quite sufficiently when I mentioned the case of the student who came to see me, and who might have applied to all the ethical systems, *Kantian* or otherwise, without getting any sort of guidance. He was obliged to devise his law himself. Never let it be said by us that this man—who, taking affection, individual action, and kind-heartedness toward a specific person as his ethical first principle, chooses to remain with his mother, or who, preferring to make a sacrifice, chooses to go to England—has made an arbitrary choice. Man makes himself. He isn't ready made at the start. In choosing his ethics, he makes himself, and force of circumstances is such that he can not abstain from choosing one. We define man only in relationship to involvement. It is therefore absurd to charge us with arbitrariness of choice. . . .

. . . but if I've discarded God the Father, there has to be someone to invent values. You've got to take things as they are. Moreover, to say that we invent values means nothing else but this: life has no meaning *a priori*. Before you come alive, life is nothing; it's up to you to give it a meaning, and value is nothing else but the meaning that you choose. In that way, you see, there is a possibility of creating a human community. . . .

Existentialism is nothing else than an attempt to draw all the consequences of a coherent atheistic position. It isn't trying to plunge man into despair at all. But if one calls every attitude of unbelief despair, like the Christians, then the word is not being used in its original sense. Existentialism isn't so atheistic that it wears itself out showing that God doesn't exist. Rather, it declares that even if God did exist, that would change nothing. There you've got our point of view. Not that we believe that God exists, but we think that the problem of His existence is not the issue. In this sense existentialism is optimistic, a doctrine of action, and it is plain dishonesty for Christians to make no distinction between their own despair and ours and then to call us despairing.

Let's examine in detail the claims Sartre suggests as basic to his existential-ist philosophy. In order to help us come to terms with existentialism, we shall look at Sartre's position through five propositions. These propositions are central to Sartre's view on existentialism.

1. *Existence precedes essence.*   Sartre suggests that this proposition is funda-mental to existentialist philosophy. He assumes that there is no God. With the denial of God, Sartre claims that it follows that there is no exemplar for human beings. In other words, there is no ideal or model after which human beings have been patterned. This is in contrast to various human artifacts. Sartre gives the example of the penknife, for which the opposite holds true. The pen-knife had a blueprint before it was produced at the knife factory. Hence its "essence" preceded its existence. This essence, or blueprint, for the penknife is determined before a penknife is actually made. But, Sartre argues, the only being capable of determining the essence for human beings would be God. However, if there is no God, there cannot be a predetermined essence for human beings. Because there is no God, Sartre argues that there can be no exemplar for humans. Consequently, human beings must make their own essences; each person must determine his/her own definition. Human beings must determine what they shall be. They have no predetermined essence. This is the signifi-cance of Sartre's proposition that, in the case of human beings, "Existence precedes essence."

2. *Human beings make themselves—human beings are their actions.*   Sartre suggests that at first a human being is "nothing." With no predetermined essence, there is no nature or set of constitutive properties which define human nature. This is quite similar to Kierkegaard's aesthetic stage. At first, a human being has no commitments or undertakings. The human essence is determined only insofar as commitments are undertaken. Sartre suggests that, at the beginning, every human being is turned towards the future—human beings are that which they will make themselves to be. Hence a human being *is* his or her own actions. In fact, Sartre claims that "There is no reality except in action."

Sartre's famous distinction between *en-soi* and *pour-soi* is important here. An en-soi is translated as a "being-in-itself," while a pour-soi is a "being-for-itself." Human beings are examples of pour-soi, while nonhumans are en-soi. A pour-soi is characterized by intentional consciousness. Recall that, in chapter 4 while discussing Descartes' epistemology, an analysis of intentionality was provided. Intentionality is the ontological property which distinguishes knowers from nonknowers. A knower is a being capable of getting beyond itself through the process of knowing. It can "tend toward" the object to be known. It can "get beyond itself" through the process of knowing. An en-soi, on the other hand, lacks this property of intentional consciousness. It is "locked up" in itself. Without the property of intentionality, it cannot get beyond itself as a pour-soi can. The Cartesian distinction between human beings characterized by "extension" is a rough analogy between pour-soi and en-soi.

Sartre's analysis of pour-soi in terms of intentionality is not just in terms of knowing, however. Sartre is concerned about "freedom." A human being is essentially a free being, and as a pour-soi, is open to the future. Each human is fundamentally a choosing being. The content of a pour-soi, thus, comes from the actions which are undertaken. A pour-soi is open to choice. Consequently, a human person as a pour-soi is a nothing until actions are undertaken. Without acting, a human being remains a nothing; however a human being cannot avoid acting forever. Each person must act. Even to choose not to choose is a choice. Because we are pour-soi at a fundamental level we are choosing beings. This choosing nature, however, does not provide any content to our nature. The content comes only from the actions which are undertaken. Sartre's proposition that "there is no reality except in action" should be clearer now.

3. *The consequences of choice are anguish, abandonment, and despair.* As we have just seen, Sartre has argued that because we are fundamentally pour-soi it is necessary that we make choices. However, because we have no predetermined essence, which might indicate what moral choices are to be made, and because there is no God, who could prescribe choices for us, it follows that we must act on our own. Given this existential condition in which human beings find themselves, Sartre argues that the attitudinal properties of anguish, abandonment, and despair necessarily follow each commitment. Let's examine each of these characteristics in more detail.

a. *Anguish.* Sartre talks about the "anguish of responsibility." He suggests that each person, in choosing, chooses for everyone. In effect, each person becomes the legislature for the whole human race. Insofar as, in choosing, every choice becomes the image for everyone else, what else, Sartre asks, are we to feel but a tremendous sense of the anguish associated with responsibility.

It is difficult to ascertain exactly what Sartre proposes here. Some philosophers have suggested that he is suggesting a form of the Kantian categorical imperative. In other words, Kant's thesis of universalizability is similar to what Sartre suggests by asserting that in choosing we choose for all. At any length, we have the utmost responsibility for our choices. Sartre totally rejects any type of Freudian psychology which renders human beings unresponsible for their actions because of the influence of the subconscious. After all, Sartre strongly affirms that we are essentially free beings.

The significance here is the notion that, without any absolute values, one person could look upon another's choice as an example of that which is to be done. Thus our individual choices, insofar as they might become models for others, hold us responsible for the choices of others. Hence the anguish of responsibility.

It is extremely difficult to ferret out the precise significance of Sartre's proposal regarding the anguish of responsibility. However he strongly asserts that we as individuals must assume full responsibility for the choices we make.

b. *Forlornment.* Since there is no God to prescribe what right actions are to be undertaken, nor can we reliably follow the actions of others, how else are we to feel but totally abandoned in our search for assistance regarding choices to be made. Since we are fundamentally pour-soi, it follows that we must act. Nonetheless, there are no guidelines for us to follow. Sartre affirms that since God does not exist, it is necessary for twentieth-century human beings to draw the consequence of his absence. This means that there is no longer any a priori good or a supreme principle of morality. Sartre takes Dostoevsky's maxim seriously: "If God is dead, then everything is permitted." If everything is permitted, there are no guidelines from which human beings might justify their choices. As human beings we are abandoned because we cannot find anything to depend upon either within or outside of ourselves. Forlornment or abandonment, Sartre suggests, is a central experience confronted in the human situation.

A consequence of forlornment or abandonment is that we as human beings are "condemned to be free." We are condemned since there is no specific content to human nature; obviously, this is opposed to the Aristotelian and Kantian themes discusssed in the last chapter. It is almost as if Sartre wished there were moral models from which to choose. But since there are none, we must recognize that fact and face it. Hence we must realize that we are radically condemned to freedom.

Accordingly, Sartre believes that it is fundamentally disingenuous to hold onto any form of morality which depends upon the postulation of a unique human nature. Sartre asserts that, in fact, many philosophers have done this, and it is essential to dismiss any view of human nature or human essence. The only way in which human essence could possibly be philosophically significant is for there to be a God. With no God, there can be no human essence. God functions in Sartre's philosophy as an "essence giver." With no God, there can be no essence. This is a fundamental assumption of Sartre's philosophy.

It might be interesting philosophically to consider how Aristotle might respond to Sartre on this point. Certainly Aristotle held for a view of human nature. Even though there is a "first mover" in Aristotle's ontology, nonetheless this first mover has no role in determining the content of a human essence. Nonetheless, in his *Metaphysics* and *Nicomachean Ethics,* Aristotle explicitly argues for the existence of natural kinds. Recall from the preceding chapter that Aristotle bases his "functional" view of normative ethics upon the dispositional properties which comprise a human nature. Aristotle's "first mover," however, has nothing to do with determining the content of a human nature. It seems that the only view of essence which Sartre understands is the Platonic position. Quite possibly, the proposition that "Existence precedes essence" only dismisses the Platonic view of essence and leaves untouched the Aristotelian position. This is a suggestion that the student might want to pursue further.

c. *Despair.* Sartre suggests that in each situation demanding a choice there is a multitude of possibilities beyond our control. We have no way to successfully predict the outcome of our undertakings. Risk is centrally involved with every choice. The actuality of every event is uncertain. Every choice is a rejection of other possibilities. In choosing one person to marry, we eliminate others; in choosing one college to attend, we eliminate others. Without any guidelines upon which to make a commitment, we necessarily act without hope, and this absence of hope is despair. There is an essential risk-taking involved in any choice. Insofar as we have no guarantee that our choice is indeed correct, the element of despair comes into our condition. Sartre argues that because we must choose, we eventually fall into despair, and he wants us to realize that experiencing despair is crucial toward understanding the human condition.

4. *Human beings must undertake commitments and actions.* Because every human being is a pour-soi and experiences the pressures of life, by necessity we must make choices. As Sartre says, "There is no reality except in action." We

human beings make ourselves, and we make ourselves by the choice of our moralities—i.e., the commitments we undertake.

5. *Existentialism is nothing else but an attempt to draw the full conclusions from a consistently atheistic position.*   Sartre argues that we human beings of the twentieth century must face the fact that there is no God. We must take full responsibility for determining our actions. This responsibility must not fail or be diminished by assuming guidelines based upon a spurious notion of human nature. As Sartre has said: "If I have excluded God the father, there must be someone to invent values." By determining the type of lives we want to live, that someone is each one of us. As a pour-soi we must choose. Yet we must not forsake this task because of the psychological difficulties encountered, e.g., anguish, abandonment, and despair.

Sartre claims that the existentialism he postulates has the following consequences:

a. The heart and center of existentialism is the absolute character of the free commitment. By undertaking commitments and actions, every human being develops his or her own being in realizing a type of humanity.

b. There is no difference between a free being and an absolute being. Our freedom is absolute. This follows from his account of human beings as pour-soi. The human nature as a pour-soi is totally "diaphanous." The structure and content come to it only through the actions and commitments undertaken.

c. Given his view of the human condition, Sartre argues that the life of each one of us is nothing until it is lived, but it is ours to make sense of. The value of life is totally dependent upon the sense that each of us chooses. Again the absolute character of the free commitment is fundamentally important for Sartre's existentialism.

This is indeed a philosophy of action. We must have engagements, make commitments, and undertake actions, which constitutes having a morality. This is indeed an interpretation of "subjectivity" as ennunciated by Kierkegaard. Notice the similarity between the concepts of Sartre and Kierkegaard. Yet there is a radically different context. Kierkegaard the theist versus Sartre the atheist. Given this similarity of structure yet radically different perspectives leads many critics to strongly suggest that existentialism fundamentally lacks any substantive content. It is merely a methodology in which one engages and an attitude which one takes. We shall pursue this point—the lack of content—when evaluating twentieth-century existentialism.

A contemporary philosopher, Alvin Plantinga, has argued strongly that Sartre's philosophy actually constitutes no morality at all. The following is an excerpt from Plantinga's article entitled "An Existentialist's Ethics." Pay close attention to Plantinga's criticisms of Sartre's position.

AN EXISTENTIALIST'S ETHICS

Alvin Plantinga

ABSOLUTE FREEDOM AND MORALITY

Sartre's moral philosophy follows from his doctrine of absolute freedom. In this section I shall indicate the implication for ethics Sartre draws from this doctrine, and then try to show that it is inconsistent with any kind of morality, Sartre's ethical doctrines center about the notions of responsibility and anguish.

1. He holds that the doctrine of absolute freedom implies absolute responsibility. "But if existence really does precede essence, man is responsible for what he is. Thus existentialism's first move is to make every man aware of what he is and to make the full responsibility of his existence rest on him" (*Existentialism,* p. 19). Since we constitute ourselves, since we choose our own essences, whatever we are is the result of our own choice. Hence we are responsible for what we are. If I am a failure, it is only because I have chosen to fail; there is no one and nothing to blame but myself. But our responsibility extends considerably further than this. I am responsible, says Sartre, not only for myself, but for all mankind. "In fact, in creating the man that we want to be, there is not a single one of our acts which does not at the same time create an image of man as we think he ought to be. To choose to be this or that is to affirm at the same time the value of what we choose, because we can never choose evil. We always choose the good, and nothing can be good for us without being good for all" (*Existentialism,* p. 20). In choosing myself, I choose man; hence I am a kind of universal legislator: "The man who involves himself and who realizes that he is not only the person he chooses to be but also the law maker who is, at the same time, choosing all mankind as well as himself cannot help escape the feeling of his total and deep responsibility" (*Existentialism,* p. 24). A man who acts must always ask himself "Am I really the kind of man who has the right to act in such a way that humanity might guide itself by my actions?" (loc cit.).

I am responsible for whatever I am, and, in addition, in choosing myself I act as a universal legislator who sets up standards for the whole of mankind. But even this is not the extent of my responsibility. As the for-itself, I am the being by whom nothing, and therefore truth, comes into the world. We have noted that in-itself apart from man is a pure undifferentiated whole, a Parmenidean plenum in which there are no distinctions and about which, therefore, nothing can be said. Whatever actual structure the world has is a result of the free activity of the for-itself. A passage from *La Nausée* will make clear Sartre's view of the for-itself as it is apart from the negating activity of human reality:

> And then all of a sudden, there it is, clear as day: existence had suddenly unveiled itself. It had lost the harmless look of an abstract category: it was the very paste of things, this root was kneaded into existence. Or rather the root,

From *The Review of Metaphysics* 12, no. 2 (December 1958): 245–50. Reprinted by permission of *The Review of Metaphysics.*

the park gates, the bench, the sparse grass, all that had vanished: the diversity of things, their individuality was only an appearance, a veneer. This veneer had melted, leaving soft, monstrous masses, all in disorder—naked, in a frightful obscene nakedness.[1]

Structureless and without form, the in-itself is like Aristotle's prime matter. And therefore, says Sartre, I *choose* my world. For I give to it whatever characteristics it actually has. I constitute it as a world characterized by the law and structure it exhibits. And I do this as a free individual. This is what distinguishes Sartre from any kind of Kantianism: for Sartre, the structures imposed by the for-itself upon the in-itself do not flow from any kind of inner necessity, nor are they given in the nature of reason. I freely choose them; I could have chosen others.[2] Thus:

The essential consequence of our earlier remarks is that man being concerned to be free carries the weight of the whole world on his shoulders; he is responsible for the world and for himself as a way of being. We are taking the word "responsibility" in its ordinary sense as "consciousness of being the incontestable author of an event or of an object." In this sense the responsibility of the for-itself is overwhelming, since he is the one by whom it happens that there is a world; since he is also the one who makes himself be, then whatever may be the situation in which he finds himself, the for-itself must wholly assume this situation with its peculiar coefficient of adversity, even though it be insupportable. He must assume the situation with the proud consciousness of being the author of it, for the very worst disadvantages or the worst threats which can endanger my person have meaning only in and through my project; and it is on the grounds of the engagement which I am that they appear. It is therefore senseless to think of complaining since nothing foreign has decided what we feel, what we live, or what we are (BN 554).

The point of this passage is clear: man is absolutely and totally responsible since he is absolutely and totally free. In his choice he defines himself, he defines the other, and he constitutes the world, not by creating it or giving it being, but by giving it whatever limitation, differentiation, form, and meaning that it has.

2. The result of this fearful responsibility is anguish. Man is anguished because he *alone* must choose, and because he *must* choose. He is anguished also because he has no guarantee that he will not, at some future date, choose a different essence for himself and therefore cease to be as *this* man. Anguish appears when we realize that there is nothing between us and our lives; when we realize that we are entirely free and therefore utterly responsible. In *The Reprieve* Mathieu contemplates the fact that the coming war has completely cut him off from his past. " 'I am free,' he said suddenly. And his joy changed, on the spot, to a crushing sense of anguish."[3] Anguish is the way our freedom reveals itself to consciousness. It is the consciousness that nothing separates me from any possibility whatever (BN 32). We cannot escape anguish. We may try—to try to escape anguish [is] to adopt the attitude of "bad faith" (BN 43), but such an attempt is doomed to failure, for we *are* anguish just as we are freedom. Even in bad faith we do not escape anguish, for in order to try to escape it, conceal it from ourselves, we must already know it (BN 45).

Such is Sartre's doctrine of the responsibility and anguish following from our absolute freedom. This doctrine seems to take crucial moral notions very seriously. But in the last analysis the doctrine of absolute freedom undercuts the very possibility of morality. Sartre's responsibility and anguish are a delusion. Every choice, he tells us, is unconditioned and completely contingent; there is nothing to which it can appeal, and it is therefore "absurd." "It is absurd in this sense; that the choice is that by which all foundations, all reasons come into being, that by which the very notion of the absurd receives a meaning. It is absurd as being beyond all reasons" (BN 479). Every choice defines both value and rationality. But if that is so, then it is impossible to make a wrong choice. As we have seen, and as Sartre constantly repeats, my choice defines value; prior to my choice there is no right or wrong. But then my choice, in defining the right, can never be mistaken. *Whatever* I choose is right by definition. Sartre is surreptitiously holding on to the meaning of responsibility appropriate to a world in which there are objective values which I may decide to realize or to reject. But if there is no value exterior to choice, then this notion of responsibility is no longer appropriate or even meaningful. If every action, every decision, constitutes a moral Weltanschauung, then there is no possibility of guilt, and no point to anguish. I am then a being whose every decision constitutes the moral standard and who by definition cannot commit a wrong.

For Sartre, *every* action, *every* choice, is necessarily right. But morality presupposes that there is a something morally at stake when I choose or act; there is the possibility of right and wrong, better or worse. For Sartre these distinctions disappear; the notion of a wrong action is for him analytically impossible. And if every actual action is right by definition, there can be no distinction between right and wrong. If the notions of *Action* and *Choice* analytically entail that the action or choice in question is right, then to say that "X is a right action" is to say no more than "X is an action." This doctrine makes negative moral judgments impossible and positive ones otiose.

And thereby the notions of responsibility and anguish lose their point. Sartre tells us of a military commander who has decided to send men on a mission that may cost them their lives. The man is anguished. But why should he be? If we think of the preservation of human life as a value prior to any choice on our part, we can understand his anguish—he is forced to choose a positive disvalue. But if his very choice constitutes value, then no matter what he chooses, he will be right. Why then be anguished?

Sartre is not unaware of the difficulty and makes an attempt to reply to it. In *Being and Nothingness* he tries to show that, appearances to the contrary, his doctrine does not mean that action and choice are merely arbitrary and capricious. His doctrine there is that every action and every choice is an expression of a more fundamental, aboriginal choice—the choice by which we define our being (BN 464). And therefore a man's actions can be guided by reference to this fundamental and original choice. But the difficulty with this, as an answer to the charge that any choice is morally arbitrary, is that it is *logically* impossible, in Sartre's system, for anyone to contradict his fundamental choice. He is, of course, completely free to make a choice inconsistent with the aboriginal choice he has been expressing; but in so doing he simply makes a new aboriginal choice (BN 464–465). If my moral standards are defined by my fundamental choice, and if in acting inconsistently with these standards I am simply making another fundamental choice, then any action or choice is morally correct by definition. Therefore this reply to the objection I have raised seems to miss the mark completely.[4]

In *Existentialism,* he gives a different answer to this kind of objection. There he tells us that certain choices are dishonest, based upon manifest errors, and constitute a rejection of freedom. The man who denies his freedom is taking refuge in "bad faith." But it is man's nature to desire freedom; we *are* freedom. Therefore to try to escape freedom is to be either a "coward or a stinker" (*Existentialism,* p. 51). But this is obviously an inadequate answer. For if man desires freedom by his very nature,[5] how can anyone fail to desire it? If the basis of the obligation to desire freedom and to accept it is that as a matter of fact we *do* desire it, then anyone who refuses to desire it has by that very fact destroyed the basis for his obligation to desire it.

The conclusion seems to be that Sartre's theory of freedom is quite inconsistent with morality. Any choice is as good as any other; there is no possibility of making a moral mistake. And that is fatal to morality. An absolute freedom, like a thorough-going determinism undercuts the very possibility of morality.

NOTES

1. (English title: The Diary of Antoine Roquentin), tr. Lloyd Alexander (London, 1948), pp. 170–171.
2. This might be the "existential psychoanalytic" explanation of radical insanity. The psychotic has simply given a different structure to his world.
3. Op. cit., p. 352.
4. As a matter of fact, there is in Sartre's philosophy no reason why a person could not oscillate between several different projects or initial choices—this might be the "existential psychoanalytic" explanation of multiple personality.
5. Insofar as Sartre is saying that man *must* desire freedom *by his very nature,* he seems to be contradicting the doctrine of absolute freedom and the doctrine that existence precedes essence.

Albert Camus

Another famous twentieth-century French existentialist is Albert Camus (1913-1960). Born in Algeria, Camus was a highly regarded literary figure of the mid-twentieth century. As a recipient of the Nobel Prize for literature in 1957, his writings exerted a profound influence toward the recognition of existentialism in the United States. While probably more famous for his novels and plays, nonetheless Camus' essays, especially *The Myth of Sisyphus* (*Le Mythe de Sisyphe*) and *The Rebel* (*L'homme Revolte*), have been widely read outside the philosophical community. Although active as a playwright in his native

Algiers, Camus' literary fame began with the publication of his widely read novel, *The Stranger (L'etranger)*. During the Nazi occupation of France during World War II, Camus was very active in the resistance movement. In the decade after World War II, Camus' essays, novels, and plays established him as a member of the first rank of European writers. He also was involved in political activity with Sartre following the war. In fact, during the post-war period, Sartre and Camus were associated popularly as the leading figures in the existentialist movement. Following the publication of *The Rebel*, a controversy developed between Sartre and Camus, which eventually caused an ideological separation. Camus' last major work was a novel, *The Fall (La Chute)*. He died in a tragic accident in 1960. His sudden death stunned the literary world. Upon hearing of Camus' tragic accident, Francois Mauriac remarked that his death was ". . . one of the greatest losses that could have affected French letters at the present time." Although he had an almost worshipful following among younger European intellectuals, his elders in the literary world also held him in high regard. Mauriac noted that "a whole generation became aware of itself and of its problems through Camus."

Many powerful forces helped shape the direction of Camus' existentialism. Born in poverty in Algeria, Camus experienced the injustice which accompanies being a poor native in a colonial country. During World War II, the savagery of the Nazi occupation of France, as well as the counterattacks of the French resistance movement, provided him with a deepening sense of the absurdity of the human condition. Camus' philosophy was an attempt to confront these diverse experiences in a way which said something significant about the human condition. He once summed up the thrust of his work with the following remark: "In the darkest depths of nihilism, I have sought only for the means of transcending it."

In this chapter, we shall emphasize Camus' early philosophy as expressed in *The Myth of Sisyphus*. We shall also briefly consider some of the themes which emerged in Camus' later writings, especially *The Rebel*. For those readers already conversant with some of Camus' work, it is interesting to point out that *The Myth of Sisyphus* provides the philosophical underpinning for *The Stranger*, while *The Rebel* provides the underpinning for *The Plague*.

During the early stages of his philosophical development, Camus regarded the human condition as one in which human beings are lonely figures adrift in a meaningless world. Human existence was regarded as an absolute vacuum, devoid of significance. *The Myth of Sisyphus*, which best elucidates the theme of meaninglessness and absurdity, is indeed a collection of bleak essays. In fact, the subtitle of this work is *An Essay on the Absurd*. In these existential descriptions of the human condition, the passage through life was compared to the pointless labor of the mythological character, Sisyphus. Sisyphus had been condemned for all eternity to roll a great boulder up a hill only to have it roll down again, this same pointless activity continuing forever. Camus' novel, *The Stranger*, is the literary manifestation of the philosophical themes expressed in *The Myth of Sisyphus*. *The Stranger* is the desolate tale of a French Algerian who, the day after his mother dies, spends his time watching a comedy film, beginning an affair with a young woman, and murdering another person. As he is about to be executed for the murder he has committed, he remarks, "How could I fail to see that nothing (in a human's life) was more important than an execution . . . and that it was even, in a way, the only really interesting thing for a man." The utter absurdity of human existence is vividly portrayed in Camus' early works. The following passage taken from *The Myth of Sisyphus* describes the role of Sisyphus and his part in transcending human absurdity.

The gods had condemned Sispyhus to ceaselessly rolling a rock to the top of a mountain, whence the stone would fall back of its own weight. They had thought with some reason that there is no more dreadful punishment than futile and hopeless labor.

If one believes Homer, Sisyphus was the wisest and most prudent of mortals. According to another tradition, however, he was disposed to practice the profession of highwayman. I see no contradiction in this. Opinions differ as to the reasons why he became the futile laborer of the underworld. To begin with, he is accused of a certain levity in regard to the gods. He stole their secrets. Aegina, the daughter of Aesopus, was carried off by Jupiter. The father was shocked by that disappearance and complained to Sisyphus. He, who knew of the abduction, offered to tell about it on condition that Aesopus would give water to the citadel of Corinth. To the celestial thunderbolts he preferred the benediction of water. He was punished for this in the underworld. Homer tells us also that Sisyphus had put Death in chains. Pluto could not endure the sight of his deserted, silent empire. He dispatched the god of war, who liberated Death from the hands of her conqueror.

It is said also that Sisyphus, being near to death, rashly wanted to test his wife's love. He ordered her to cast his unburied body into the middle of the public square. Sisyphus woke up in the underworld. And there, annoyed by an obedience so contrary to human love, he obtained from Pluto permission to return to earth in order to chastise his wife. But when he had seen again the face of this world, enjoyed water and sun, warm stones and the sea, he no longer wanted to go back to the infernal darkness. Recalls, signs of anger, warnings were of no avail. Many years more he lived facing the curve of the gulf, the sparkling sea, and the smiles of earth. A decree of the gods was necessary. Mercury came and seized the impudent man by the collar and, snatching him from his joys, led him forcibly back to the underworld, where his rock was ready for him.

You have already grasped that Sisyphus is the absurd hero. He *is*, as much through his passions as through his torture. His scorn of the gods, his hatred of death, and his passion for life won him that unspeakable penalty in which the whole being is exerted toward accomplishing nothing. This is the price that must be paid for the passions of this earth. Nothing is told us about Sisyphus in the underworld. Myths are made for the imagination to breathe life into them. As for this myth, one sees merely the whole effort of a body straining to raise the huge stone, to roll it and push it up a slope a hundred times over; one sees the face screwed up, the cheek tight against the stone, the shoulder bracing the clay-covered mass, the foot wedging it, the fresh start with arms outstretched, the wholly human security of two earth-clotted hands. At the very end of his long effort measured by skyless space and time without depth, the purpose is achieved. Then Sisyphus watches the stone rush down in a few moments toward that lower world whence he will have to push it up again toward the summit. He goes back down to the plain.

It is during that return, that pause, that Sisyphus interests me. A face that toils so close to stones is already stone itself! I see that man going back down with a heavy yet measured step toward the torment of which he will never know the end. That hour like a breathing-space which returns as surely as his suffering, that is the hour of consciousness. At each of those moments when he leaves the heights and gradually sinks toward the lairs of the gods, he is superior to his fate. He is stronger than his rock.

If this myth is tragic, that is because its hero is conscious. Where would his torture be, indeed, if at every step the hope of succeeding upheld him? The work-man of today works every day in his life at the same tasks, and this fate is no less absurd. But it is tragic only at the rare moments when it becomes conscious. Sisy-phus, proletarian of the gods, powerless and rebellious, knows the whole extent of his wretched condition: it is what he thinks of during his descent. The lucidity that was to constitute his torture at the same time crowns his victory. There is no fate that cannot be surmounted by scorn.

If the descent is thus sometimes performed in sorrow, it can also take place in joy. This word is not too much. Again I fancy Sisyphus returning toward his rock, and the sorrow was in the beginning. When the images of earth cling too tightly to memory, when the call of happiness becomes too insistent, it happens that melancholy rises in man's heart: this is the rock's victory, this is the rock itself. The boundless grief is too heavy to bear. These are our nights of Gethsem-ane. But crushing truths perish from being acknowledged. Thus, Oedipus at the outset obeys his fate without knowing it. But from the moment he knows, his tragedy begins. Yet at the same moment, blind and desperate, he realizes that the only bond linking him to the world is the cool hand of a girl. Then a tremendous remark rings out: "Despite so many ordeals, my advanced age and the nobility of my soul make me conclude that all is well." Sophocles' Oedipus, like Dostoevsky's Kirilov, thus gives the recipe for the absurd victory. Ancient wisdom confirms modern heroism.

One does not discover the absurd without being tempted to write a manual of happiness. "What! by such narrow ways—?" There is but one world, however. Happiness and the absurd are two sons of the same earth. They are inseparable. It would be a mistake to say that happiness necessarily springs from the absurd discovery. It happens as well that the feeling of the absurd springs from happi-ness. "I conclude that all is well," says Oedipus, and that remark is sacred. It echoes in the wild and limited universe of man. It teaches that all is not, has not been, exhausted. It drives out of this world a god who had come into it with dis-satisfaction and a preference for futile sufferings. It makes of fate a human matter, which must be settled among men.

All Sisyphus' silent joy is contained therein. His fate belongs to him. His rock is his thing. Likewise, the absurd man, when he contemplates his torment, silences all the idols. In the universe suddenly restored to its silence, the myriad wonder-ing little voices of the earth rise up. Unconscious, secret calls, invitations from all the faces, they are the necessary reverse and price of victory. There is no sun without shadow, and it is essential to know the night. The absurd man says yes and his effort will henceforth be unceasing. If there is a personal fate, there is no higher destiny, or at least there is but one which he concludes is inevitable and despicable. For the rest, he knows himself to be the master of his days. At that subtle moment when man glances backward over his life, Sisyphus returning toward his rock, in that slight pivoting he contemplates that series of unrelated actions which becomes his fate, created by him, combined under his memory's eye and soon sealed by his death. Thus, convinced of the wholly human origin of all that is human, a blind man eager to see who knows that the night has no end, he is still on the go. The rock is still rolling.

I leave Sisyphus at the foot of the mountain! One always finds one's burden again. But Sisyphus teaches the higher fidelity that negates the gods and raises rocks. He too concludes that all is well. Thus universe henceforth without a master seems to him neither sterile nor futile. Each atom of that stone, each mineral flake of that night-filled mountain, in itself forms a world. The struggle itself toward the heights is enough to fill a man's heart. One must imagine Sisyphus happy.[18]

In the preceding passage Camus compares our existential condition with the plight of Sisyphus. Like Sartre, Camus has a fundamental message which concerns the rejection of the Platonic scheme of explanation. In regard to human beings, Camus also would accept the proposition that "Existence precedes essence," together with all its Sartrean implications. In fact, as a graduate student, Camus wrote his dissertation on themes expressed by the third-century Neo-Platonist, Plotinus. Camus' existentialism can best be understood against the background of Neo-Platonism. Plotinus claimed that there was an ultimate metaphysical principle that he called the *One*, which provided meaning, purpose, and order to the world. In some respects, the One is analogous to the "form of the good" expounded in Plato's *Republic* or to "God" as described in Judeo-Christian theology. This first metaphysical principle serves as a foundation, establishing the final appeal for understanding and the ultimate norm for moral prescription.

Like Sartre, Camus claims that if there is no One or God, then any ultimate explanation for either the cosmos as a whole or for individual human beings found in that cosmos is radically absent. With no ultimate principle, Camus asserts that there cannot be any meaning or significance to the whole. Without meaning, the cosmos is absurd. Again, like Sartre, Camus seems to suggest that insofar as there is no essence giver, there is no sense to be made of human essence. Furthermore it is only through the notion of essence coming from God or some other metaphysical principle of order that any sense can be made of purpose or meaning in the cosmos. Camus argues emphatically that there is no possibility for the discovery of any ultimate explanation of reality. Indeed, we are limited to grasping singular propositions about the universe, such as offering descriptions of isolated events, objects, and processes. However, it is impossible ever to discover a complete and total explanation of reality such as postulated by Plato, the Neo-Platonists, the Hegelians, or the Judeo-Christian theologians. The following passage from *The Myth of Sisyphus* illustrates the futility of ever discovering an all-encompassing rational explanation for the cosmos.

At the final stage you teach me that this wonderous and multicolored universe can be reduced . . . to the electron. All this is good and I wait for you to continue. But you tell me of an invisible planetary system in which electrons gravitate around a nucleus. You explain this world to me with animage. I realize then that you have been reduced to poetry: I shall never know.[19]

Camus' thesis asserts that although there are individual propositions about the universe which are true, there is no general proposition capable of explaining the origin and purpose of the cosmos. There is no explanation of the whole. Given the impossibility of ever discovering a total explanation, Camus claims that this engenders the experience of absurdity. The world is unexplainable and we are isolated individuals in that meaningless world.

Camus further elucidates the concept of absurdity in regard to the human condition by emphasizing the role of chance and the ever-present dominance of death. Chance occurrences play a pervasive role in our lives. Often they are the determining factors for various events central to our existence. Furthermore, the finality of death awaits each of us. With chance and death such continual prospects, how can we live but an utterly desolate existence. Our life, our hopes, our aspirations can be snuffed out in an arbitrary instant—like, for example, the tragic automobile accident in which Camus was killed. Camus, however, will attempt to provide a means for transcending this absurdity. He will emphasize living every moment to the fullest by engaging in as many actions as possible. This will become clear as we proceed.

In *The Myth of Sisyphus,* Camus speaks of two senses of absurdity:

1. The world is absurd as an object of awareness. This means that there is no ultimate explanation which can be discovered. It is not that it is difficult to discover such an explanation; rather, it is impossible to find any explanation because no such explanation exists.

2. Absurdity also describes the relation between the human mind and the absurd world. Camus suggests that it is absurd that human beings should continue attempting to discover understanding in the cosmos, which lacks any such understanding. It is absurd to try to accomplish that which cannot be done. This second sense of absurdity comes about from the meeting of the universe and the human mind. The human mind desires an ultimate explanation, but the universe can provide no such answer. Our continual search to understand that which is, in principle, incomprehensible is the second sense of absurdity. We seek to discover significance from the universe and the universe is silent. In an ultimate sense there is nothing comprehensible about the universe. Thus our constant attempt to comprehend that which is incomprehensible is absurd. Note the following passage from *The Myth of Sisyphus:*

> I said that the world is absurd, but I was too hasty. The world in itself is not reasonable, that is all that can be said. But what is absurd is the confrontation of this irrational and the wild longing for clarity whose call echoes in the human heart. The absurd depends as much on man as on the world. [20]

Given such absurdity of the universe, one may wonder why he or she should continue living. If there is no meaning to our lives, why not end it all through suicide? Camus realizes the pressing nature of this question. In fact, he argues that the first and most important philosophical question concerns the confrontation of suicide. In the following extended passage from *The Myth of Sisyphus,* Camus describes both the dimension of suicide as the fundamental philosophical question, as well as providing the means for human beings to transcend the possibility of suicide. Camus will suggest an "ethic of quantity." He places great emphasis on the number of our experiences and the gusto with which we live our lives. We must rebel against the absurdity by not giving in to it. As with Sisyphus—who Camus suggested must be regarded as happy—we too must not surrender to the absurdity but confront it directly through revolt. We must live the ethic of quantity.

ABSURDITY AND SUICIDE

There is but one truly serious philosophical problem, and that is suicide. Judging whether life is or is not worth living amounts to answering the fundamental question of philosophy. All the rest—whether or not the world has three dimensions, whether the mind has nine or twelve categories—comes afterwards. These are games; one must first answer. And if it is true, as Nietzsche claims, that a philosopher, to deserve our respect, must preach by example, you can appreciate the importance of that reply, for it will precede the definitive act. These are facts the heart can feel; yet they call for careful study before they become clear to the intellect.

If I ask myself how to judge that this question is more urgent that that, I reply that one judges by the actions it entails. I have never seen anyone die for the ontological argument. Galileo, who held a scientific truth of great importance, abjured it with the greatest ease as soon as it endangered his life. In a certain sense, he did right.[1] That truth was not worth the stake. Whether the earth or the sun revolves around the other is a matter of profound indifference. To tell the truth, it is a futile question. On the other hand, I see many people die because they judge that life is not worth living. I see others paradoxically getting killed for the ideas or illusions that give them a reason for living (what is called a reason for living is also an excellent reason for dying). I therefore conclude that the meaning of life is the most urgent of questions. How to answer it? On all essential problems (I mean thereby those that run the risk of leading to death or those that intensify the passion of living) there are probably but two methods of thought: the method of La Palisse and the method of Don Quixote. Solely the balance between evidence and lyricism can allow us to achieve simultaneously emotion and lucidity. In a subject at once so humble and so heavy with emotion, the learned and classical dialectic must yield, one can see, to a more modest attitude of mind deriving at one and the same time from common sense and understanding.

Suicide has never been dealt with except as a social phenomenon. On the contrary, we are concerned here, at the outset, with the relationship between individual thought and suicide. An act like this is prepared within the silence of the heart, as is a great work of art. The man himself is ignorant of it. One evening he pulls the trigger or jumps. Of an apartment-building manager who had killed himself I was told that he had lost his daughter five years before, that he had changed greatly since, and that that experience had "undermined" him. A more exact word cannot be imagined. Beginning to think is beginning to be undermined. Society has but little connection with such beginnings. The worm is in man's heart. That is where it must be sought. One must follow and understand this fatal game that leads from lucidity in the face of existence to flight from light.

There are many causes for a suicide, and generally the most obvious ones were not the most powerful. Rarely is suicide committed (yet the hypothesis is not excluded) through reflection. What sets off the crisis is almost always unverifiable. Newspapers often speak of "personal sorrows" or of "incurable illness." These explanations are plausible. But one would have to know whether a friend of the desperate man had not that very day addressed him indifferently. He is the guilty one. For that is enough to precipitate all the rancors and all the boredom still in suspension.[2]

But if it is hard to fix the precise instant, the subtle step when the mind opted for death, it is easier to deduce from the act itself the consequences it implies. In a sense, and as in melodrama, killing yourself amounts to confessing. It is confessing that life is too much for you or that you do not understand it. Let's not go too far in such analogies, however, but rather return to everyday words. It is merely confessing that that "is not worth the trouble." Living, naturally, is never easy. You continue making the gestures commanded by existence for many reasons, the first of which is habit. Dying voluntarily implies that you have recognized, even instinctively, the ridiculous character of that habit, the absence of any profound reason for living, the insane character of that daily agitation, and the uselessness of suffering.

What, then, is that incalculable feeling that deprives the mind of the sleep necessary to life? A world that can be explained even with bad reasons is a familiar world. But, on the other hand, in a universe suddenly divested of illusions and lights, man feels an alien, a stranger. His exile is without remedy since he is deprived of the memory of a lost home or the hope of a promised land. This divorce between man and his life, the actor and his setting, is properly the feeling of absurdity. All healthy men having thought of their own suicide, it can be seen, without further explanation, that there is a direct connection between this feeling and the longing for death.

The subject of this essay is precisely this relationship between the absurd and the suicide, the exact degree to which suicide is a solution to the absurd. The principle can be established that for a man who does not cheat, what he believes to be true must determine his action. Belief in the absurdity of existence must then dictate his conduct. It is legitimate to wonder, clearly and without false pathos, whether a conclusion of this importance requires forsaking as rapidly as possible an incomprehensible condition. I am speaking, of course, of men inclined to be in harmony with themselves.

Stated clearly, this problem may seem both simple and insoluble. But it is wrongly assumed that simple questions involve answers that are no less simple and that evidence implies evidence. A priori and reversing the terms of the problem, just as one does or does not kill oneself, it seems that there are but two philosophical solutions, either yes or no. This would be too easy. But allowance must be made for those who, without concluding, continue questioning. Here I am only slightly indulging in irony: this is the majority. I notice also that those who answer "no" act as if they thought "yes." As a matter of fact, if I accept the Nietzschean criterion, they think "yes" in one way or another. On the other hand, it often happens that those who commit suicide were assured of the meaning of life. These contradictions are constant. It may even be said that they have never been so keen as on this point where, on the contrary, logic seems so desirable. It is a commonplace to compare philosophical theories and the behavior of those who profess them. But it must be said that of the thinkers who refused a meaning to life none except Kirilov who belongs to literature, Peregrinos who is born of legend,[3] and Jule Lequier who belongs to hypothesis, admitted his logic to the point of refusing that life. Schopenhauer is often cited, as a fit subject for laughter, because he praised suicide while seated at a well-set table. This is no subject for joking. That way of not taking the tragic seriously is not so grievous, but it helps to judge a man.

In the face of such contradictions and obscurities must we conclude that there is no relationship between the opinion one has about life and the act one commits to leave it? Let us not exaggerate in this direction. In a man's attachment to life there is something stronger than all the ills in the world. The body's judgment is as good as the mind's, and the body shrinks from annihilation. We get into the habit of living before acquiring the habit of thinking. In that race which daily hastens us toward death, the body maintains its irreparable lead. In short, the essence of that contradiction lies in what I shall call the act of eluding because it is both less and more than diversion in the Pascalian sense. Eluding is the invariable game. The typical act of eluding, the fatal evasion that constitutes the third theme of this essay, is hope. Hope of another life one must "deserve" or trickery of those who live not for life itself but for some great idea that will transcend it, refine it, give it a meaning, and betray it.

Thus everything contributes to spreading confusion. Hitherto, and it has not been wasted effort, people have played on words and pretended to believe that refusing to grant a meaning to life necessarily leads to declaring that it is not worth living. In truth, there is no necessary common measure between these two judgments. One merely has to refuse to be misled by the confusions, divorces, and inconsistencies previously pointed out. One must brush everything aside and go straight to the real problem. One kills oneself because life is not worth living, that is certainly a truth—yet an unfruitful one because it is a truism. But does that insult to existence, that flat denial in which it is plunged come from the fact that it has no meaning? Does its absurdity require one to escape it through hope or suicide—this is what must be clarified, hunted down, and elucidated while brushing aside all the rest. Does the Absurd dictate death? This problem must be given priority over others, outside all methods of thought and all exercises of the disinterested mind. Shades of meaning, contradictions, the psychology that an "objective" mind can always introduce into all problems have no place in this pursuit and this passion. It calls simply for an unjust—in other words, logical—thought. That is not easy. It is always easy to be logical. It is almost impossible to be logical to the bitter end. Men who die by their own hand consequently follow to its conclusion their emotional inclination. Reflection on suicide gives me an opportunity to raise the only problem to interest me: is there a logic to the point of death? I cannot know unless I pursue, without reckless passion, in the sole light of evidence, the reasoning of which I am here suggesting the source. This is what I call an absurd reasoning. Many have begun it. I do not yet know whether or not they kept to it.

When Karl Jaspers, revealing the impossibility of constituting the world as a unity, exclaims: "This limitation leads me to myself, where I can no longer withdraw behind an objective point of view that I am merely representing, where neither I myself nor the existence of others can any longer become an object for me," he is evoking after many others those waterless deserts where thought reaches its confines. After many others, yes indeed, but how eager they were to get out of them! At that last crossroad where thought hesitates, many men have arrived and even some of the humblest. They then abdicated what was most precious to them, their life. Others, princes of the mind, abdicated likewise, but they initiated the suicide of their thought in its purest revolt. The real effort is to stay there, rather, in so far as that is possible, and to examine closely the odd vegetation of those distant regions. Tenacity and acumen are privileged spectators of this inhuman show in which absurdity, hope, and death carry on their dialogue. The mind can then analyze the figures of that elementary yet subtle dance before illustrating them and reliving them itself. . . .

ABSURD FREEDOM

Now the main thing is done, I hold certain facts from which I cannot separate. What I know, what is certain, what I cannot deny, what I cannot reject—this is what counts. I can negate everything of that part of me that lives on vague nostalgias, except this desire for unity, this longing to solve, this need for clarity and cohesion. I can refute everything in this world surrounding me that offends or enraptures me, except this chaos, this sovereign chance and this divine equivalence which springs from anarchy. I don't know whether this world has a meaning that transcends it. But I know that I do not know that meaning and that it is impossible for me just now to know it. What can a meaning outside my condition mean to me? I can understand only in human terms. What I touch, what resists me—that is what I understand. And these two certainties—my appetite for the absolute and for unity and the impossibility of reducing this world to a rational and reasonable principle—I also know that I cannot reconcile them. What other truth can I admit without lying, without bringing in a hope I lack and which means nothing within the limits of my condition?

If I were a tree among trees, a cat among animals, this life would have a meaning, or rather this problem would not arise, for I should belong to this world. I should *be* this world to which I am now opposed by my whole consciousness and my whole insistence upon familiarity. This ridiculous reason is what sets me in opposition to all creation. I cannot cross it out with a stroke of the pen. What I believe to be true I must therefore preserve. What seems to me so obvious, even against me, I must support. And what constitutes the basis of that conflict, of that break between the world and my mind, but the awareness of it? If therefore I want to preserve it, I can through a constant awareness, ever revived, ever alert. This is what, for the moment, I must remember. At this moment the absurd, so obvious and yet so hard to win, returns to a man's life and finds its home there. At this moment, too, the mind can leave the arid, dried-up path of lucid effort. That path now emerges in daily life. It encounters the world of the anonymous impersonal pronoun "one," but henceforth man enters in with his revolt and his lucidity. He has forgotten how to hope. This hell of the present is his Kingdom at last. All problems recover their sharp edge. Abstract evidence retreats before the poetry of forms and colors. Spiritual conflicts become embodied and return to the abject and magnificent shelter of man's heart. None of them is settled. But all are transfigured. Is one going to die, escape by the leap, rebuild a mansion of ideas and forms to one's own scale? Is one, on the contrary, going to take up the heart-rending and marvelous wager of the absurd? Let's make a final effort in this regard and draw all our conclusions. The body, affection, creation, action, human nobility will then resume their places in this mad world. At last man will again find there the wine of the absurd and the bread of indifference on which he feeds his greatness.

Let us insist again on the method: it is a matter of persisting. At a certain point on his path the absurd man is tempted. History is not lacking in either religions or prophets, even without gods. He is asked to leap. All he can reply is that he doesn't fully understand, that it is not obvious. Indeed, he does not want to do anything but what he fully understands. He is assured that this is the sin of pride, but he does not understand the notion of sin; that perhaps hell is in store, but he has not enough imagination to visualize that strange future; that he is losing immortal life, but that seems to him an idle consideration. An attempt is made to get him to admit his guilt. He feels innocent. To tell the truth, that is all he feels—his irreparable innocence. This is what allows him everything. Hence, what he demands of himself is to live *solely* with what he knows, to accommodate himself to what is, and to bring in nothing that is not certain. He is told that nothing is. But this at least is a certainty. And it is with this that he is concerned: he wants to find out if it is possible to live *without appeal*.

Now I can broach the notion of suicide. It has already been felt what solution might be given. At this point the problem is reversed. It was previously a question of finding out whether or not life had to have a meaning to be lived. It now becomes clear, on the contrary, that it will be lived all the better if it has no meaning. Living an experience, a particular fate, is accepting it fully. Now, no one will live this fate, knowing it to be absurd, unless he does everything to keep before him that absurd brought to light by consciousness. Negating one of the terms of the opposition on which he lives amounts to escaping it. To abolish conscious revolt is to elude the problem. The theme of permanent revolution is thus carried into individual experience. Living is keeping the absurd alive. Keeping it alive is, above all, contemplating it. Unlike Eurydice, the absurd dies only when we turn away from it. One of the only coherent philosophical positions is thus revolt. It is a constant confrontation between man and his own obscurity. It is an insistence upon an impossible transparency. It challenges the world anew every second. Just as danger provided man the unique opportunity of seizing awareness, so metaphysical revolt extends awareness to the whole of experience. It is that constant presence of man in his own eyes. It is not aspiration, for it is devoid of hope. That revolt is the certainty of a crushing fate, without the resignation that ought to accompany it.

This is where it is seen to what a degree absurd experience is remote from suicide. It may be thought that suicide follows revolt—but wrongly. For it does not represent the logical outcome of revolt. It is just the contrary by the consent it presupposes. Suicide, like the leap, is acceptance at its extreme. Everything is over and man returns to his essential history. His future, his unique and dreadful future—he sees and rushes toward it. In its way, suicide settles the absurd. It engulfs the absurd in the same death. But I know that in order to keep alive, the absurd cannot be settled. It escapes suicide to the extent that it is simultaneously awareness and rejection of death. It is, at the extreme limit of the condemned man's last thought, that shoelace that despite everything he sees a few yards away, on the very brink of his dizzying fall. The contrary of suicide, in fact, is the man condemned to death.

That revolt gives life its value. Spread out over the whole length of a life, it restores its majesty to that life. To a man devoid of blinders, there is no finer sight than that of the intelligence at grips with a reality that transcends it. The sight of human pride is unequaled. No disparagement is of any use. That discipline that the mind imposes on itself, that will conjured up out of nothing, that face-to-face struggle have something exceptional about them. To impoverish that reality who inhumanity constitutes man's majesty is tantamount to impoverishing man himself. I understand then why the doctrines that explain everything to me also debilitate me at the same time. They relieve me of the weight of my own life, and yet I must carry it alone. At this juncture, I cannot conceive that a skeptical metaphysics can be joined to an ethics of renunciation.

Consciousness and revolt, these rejections are the contrary of renunciation. Everything that is indomitable and passionate in a human heart quickens them, on the contrary, with its own life. It is essential to die unreconciled and not of one's own free will. Suicide is a repudiation. The absurd man can only drain everything to the bitter end, and deplete himself. The absurd is his extreme tension, which he maintains constantly by solitary effort, for he knows that in that consciousness and in that day-to-day revolt he gives proof of his only truth, which is defiance. This is a first consequence.

If I remain in that prearranged position which consists in drawing all the conclusions (and nothing else) involved in a newly discovered notion, I am faced with a second paradox. In order to remain faithful to that method, I have nothing to do with the problem of metaphysical liberty. Knowing whether or not man is free doesn't interest me. I can experience only my own freedom. As to it, I can have no general notions, but merely a few clear insights. The problem of "freedom as such" has no meaning. For it is linked in quite a different way with the problem of God. Knowing whether or not man is free involves knowing whether he can have a master. The absurdity peculiar to this problem comes from the fact that the very notion that makes the problem of freedom possible also takes away all its meaning. For in the presence of God there is less a problem of freedom than a problem of evil. You know the alternative: either we are not free and God the all-powerful is responsible for evil. Or we are free and responsible but God is not all-powerful. All the scholastic subtleties have neither added anything to nor subtracted anything from the acuteness of this paradox.

This is why I cannot get lost in the glorification or the mere definition of a notion which eludes me and loses its meaning as soon as it goes beyond the frame of reference of my individual experience. I cannot understand what kind of freedom would be given me by a higher being. I have lost the sense of hierarchy. The only conception of freedom I can have is that of the prisoner or the individual in the midst of the State. The only one I know is freedom of thought and action. Now if the absurd cancels all my chances of eternal freedom, it restores and magnifies, on the other hand, my freedom of action. That privation of hope and future means an increase in man's availability.

Before encountering the absurd, the everyday man lives with aims, a concern for the future or for justification (with regard to whom or what is not the question). He weighs his chances, he counts on "someday," his retirement or the labor of his sons. He still thinks that something in his life can be directed. In truth, he acts as if he were free, even if all the facts make a point of contradicting that liberty. But after the absurd, everything is upset. That idea that "I am," my way of acting as if everything has a meaning (even if, on occasion, I have said that nothing has)—all that is given the lie in vertiginous fashion by the absurdity of a possible death. Thinking of the future, establishing aims for oneself, having preferences—all this presupposes a belief in freedom, even if one occasionally ascertains that one doesn't feel it. But at that moment I am well aware that that higher liberty, that freedom *to be,* which alone can serve as basis for a truth, does not exist. Death is there as the only reality. After death the chips are down. I am not even free, either, to perpetuate myself, but a slave, and, above all, a slave without hope of an eternal revolution, without recourse to contempt. And who without a revolution and without contempt can remain a slave? What freedom can exist in the fullest sense without assurance of eternity?

But at the same time the absurd man realizes that hitherto he was bound to that postulate of freedom on the illusion of which he was living. In a certain sense, that hampered him. To the extent to which he imagined a purpose to his life, he adapted himself to the demands of a purpose to be achieved and became the slave of his liberty. Thus I could not act otherwise than as the father (or the engineer or the leader of a nation, or the post-office sub-clerk) that I am preparing to be. I think I can choose to be that rather than something else. I think so unconsciously, to be sure. But at the same time I strengthen my postulate with the beliefs of those around me, with the presumptions of my human environment (others are so sure of being free, and that cheerful mood is so contagious!). However far one may remain from any presumption, moral or social, one is partly influenced by them and even, for the best among them (there are good and bad presumptions), one adapts one's life to them. Thus the absurd man realizes that he was not really free. To speak clearly, to the extent to which I hope, to which I worry about a truth that might be individual to me, about a way of being or creating, to the extent to which I arrange my life and prove thereby that I accept its having a meaning, I create for myself barriers between which I confine my life. I do like so many bureaucrats of the mind and heart who only fill me with disgust and whose only vice, I now see clearly, is to take man's freedom seriously.

The absurd enlightens me on this point: there is no future. Henceforth this is the reason for my inner freedom. I shall use two comparisons here.

Mystics, to begin with, find freedom in giving themselves. By losing themselves in their god, by accepting his rules, they become secretly free. In spontaneously accepted slavery they recover a deeper independence. But what does that freedom mean? It may be said, above all, that they *feel* free with regard to themselves, and not so much free as liberated. Likewise, completely turned toward death (taken here as the most obvious absurdity), the absurd man feels released from everything outside that passionate attention crystallizing in him. He enjoys a freedom with regard to common rules. It can be seen at this point that the initial themes of existential philosophy keep their entire value. The return to consciousness, the escape from everyday sleep represent the first steps of absurd freedom. But it is existential *preaching* that is alluded to, and with it that spiritual leap which basically escapes consciousness. In the same way (this is my second comparison) the slaves of antiquity did not belong to themselves. But they knew that freedom which consists in not feeling responsible.[4] Death, too, has patrician hands which, while crushing, also liberate.

Losing oneself in that bottomless certainty, feeling henceforth sufficiently remote from one's own life to increase it and take a broad view of it—this involves the principle of a liberation. Such new independence has a definite time limit, like any freedom of action. It does not write a check on eternity. But it takes the place of the illusions of *freedom,* which all stopped with death. The divine availability of the condemned man before whom the prison doors open in a certain early dawn, that unbelievable disinterestedness with regard to everything except for the pure flame of life— it is clear that death and the absurd are here the principles of the only reasonable freedom: that which a human heart can experience and live. This is a second consequence. The absurd man thus catches sight of a burning and frigid, transparent and limited universe in which nothing is possible but everything is given, and beyond which all is collapse and nothingness. He can then decide to accept such a universe and draw from it his strength, his refusal to hope, and the unyielding evidence of a life without consolation.

But what does life mean in such a universe? Nothing else for the moment but indifference to the future and a desire to use up everything that is given. Belief in the meaning of life always implies a scale of values, a choice, our preferences. Belief in the absurd, according to our definitions, teaches the contrary. But this is worth examining.

Knowing whether or not one can live *without appeal* is all that interests me. I do not want to get out of my depth. This aspect of life being given me, can I adapt myself to it? Now, faced with this particular concern, belief in the absurd is tantamount to substituting the quantity of experiences for the quality. If I convince myself that this life has no other aspect than that of the absurd, if I feel that its whole equilibrium depends on that perpetual opposition between my conscious revolt and the darkness in which it struggles, if I admit that my freedom has no meaning except in relation to its limited fate, then I must say that what counts is not the best living but the most living. It is not up to me to wonder if this is vulgar or revolting, elegant or deplorable. Once and for all, value judgments are discarded here in favor of factual judgments. I have merely to draw the conclusions from what I can see and to risk nothing that is hypothetical. Supposing that living in this way were not honorable, then true propriety would command me to be dishonorable.

The most living; in the broadest sense, that rule means nothing. It calls for definition. It seems to begin with the fact that the notion of quantity has not been sufficiently explored. For it can account for a large scale of human experience. A man's rule of conduct and his scale of values have no meaning except through the quantity and variety of experiences he has been in a position to accumulate. Now, the conditions of modern life impose on the majority of men the same quantity of experiences and consequently the same profound experience. To be sure there must also be taken into consideration the individual's spontaneous contribution, the "given" element in him. But I cannot judge of that, and let me repeat that my rule here is to get along with the immediate evidence. I see, then, that the individual character of a common code of ethics lies not so much in the ideal importance of its basic principles as in the norm of an experience that it is possible to measure. To stretch a point somewhat, the Greeks had the code of their leisure just as we have the code of our eight-hour day. But already many men among the most tragic cause us to foresee that a longer experience changes this table of values. They make us imagine that adventurer of the everyday who through mere quantity of experiences would break all records (I am purposely using this sports expression) and would thus win his own code of ethics.[5] Yet let's avoid romanticism and just ask ourselves what such an attitude may mean to a man with his mind made up to take up his bet and to observe strictly what he takes to be the rules of the game.

Breaking all the records is first and foremost being faced with the world as often as possible. How can that be done without contradictions and without playing on words? For on the one hand the absurd teaches that all experiences are unimportant, and on the other it urges toward the greatest quantity of experiences. How, then, can one fail to do as so many of those men I was speaking of earlier—choose the form of life that brings us the most possible of that human matter, thereby introducing a scale of values that on the other hand one claims to reject?

But again it is the absurd and its contradictory life that teaches us. For the mistake is thinking that that quantity of experiences depends solely on us. Here we have to be oversimple. To two men living the same number of years, the world always provides the same sum of experiences. It is up to us to be conscious of them. Being aware of one's life, one's revolt, one's freedom, and to the maximum, is living, and to the maximum. Where lucidity dominates, the scale of values becomes useless. Let's be even more simple. Let us say that the sole obstacle, the sole deficiency to be made good, is constituted by premature death. Thus it is that no depth, no emotion, no passion, and no sacrifice could render equal in the eyes of the absurd man (even if he wished it so) a conscious life of forty years and lucidity spread over sixty years.[6] Madness and death are his irreparables. Man does not choose. The absurd and the extra life it involves *therefore do not depend on man's will,* but on its contrary, which is death.[7] Weighing words carefully, it is altogether a question of luck. One just has to be able to consent to this. There will never be any substitute for twenty years of life and experience.

By what is an odd inconsistency in such an alert race, the Greeks claimed that those who died young were beloved of the gods. And that is true only if you are willing to believe that entering the ridiculous world of the gods is forever losing the purest of joys, which is feeling, and feeling on this earth. The present and the succession of presents before a constantly conscious soul is the ideal of the absurd man. But the word "ideal" rings false in this connection. It is not even his vocation, but merely the third consequence of his reasoning. Having started from an anguished awareness of the inhuman, the meditation on the absurd returns at the end of its itinerary to the very heart of the passionate flames of human revolt. [8]

Thus I draw from the absurd three consequences, which are my revolt, my freedom, and my passion. By the mere activity of consciousness I transform into a rule of life what was an invitation to death—and I refuse suicide. I know, to be sure, the dull resonance that vibrates throughout these days. Yet I have but a word to say: that it is necessary. When Nietzsche writes: "It clearly seems that the chief thing in heaven and on earth is to *obey* at length and in a single direction: in the long run there results something for which it is worth the trouble of living on this earth as, for example, virtue, art, music, the dance, reason, the mind—something that transfigures, something delicate, mad, or divine," he elucidates the rule of a really distinguished code of ethics. But he also points the way of the absurd man. Obeying the flame is both the easiest and the hardest thing to do. However, it is good for man to judge himself occasionally. He is alone in being able to do so.

"Prayer," says Alain, "is when night descends over thought." "But the mind must meet the night," reply the mystics and the existentials. Yes, indeed, but not that night that is born under closed eyelids and through the mere will of man—dark, impenetrable night that the mind calls up in order to plunge into it. If it must encounter a night, let it be rather that of despair, which remains lucid—polar night, vigil of the mind, whence will arise perhaps that white and virginal brightness which outlines every object in the light of the intelligence. At that degree, equivalence encounters passionate understanding. Then it is no longer even a question of judging the existential leap. It resumes its place amid the age-old fresco of human attitudes. For the spectator, if he is conscious, that leap is still absurd. In so far as it thinks it solves the paradox, it reinstates it intact. On this score, it is stirring. On this score, everything resumes its place and the absurd world is reborn in all its splendor and diversity.

But it is bad to stop, hard to be satisfied with a single way of seeing, to go without contradiction, perhaps the most subtle of all spiritual forces. The preceding merely defines a way of thinking. But the point is to live. . . .

NOTES

1. From the point of view of the relative value of truth. On the other hand, from the point of view of virile behavior, this scholar's fragility may well make us smile.

2. Let us not miss this opportunity to point out the relative character of this essay. Suicide may indeed be related to much more honorable considerations—for example, the political suicides of protest, as they were called, during the Chinese revolution.

3. I have heard of an emulator of Peregrinos, a post-war writer who, after having finished his first book, committed suicide to attract attention to his work. Attention was in fact attracted, but the book was judged no good.

4. I am concerned here with a factual comparison, not with an apology of humility. The absurd man is the contrary of the reconciled man.

5. Quantity sometimes constitutes quality. If I can believe the latest restatements of scientific theory, all matter is constituted by centers of energy. Their greater or lesser quantity makes its specificity more or less remarkable. A billion ions and one ion differ not only in quantity but also in quality. It is easy to find an analogy in human experience.

6. Same reflection on a notion as different as the idea of eternal nothingness. It neither adds anything to nor subtracts anything from reality. In psychological experience of nothingness, it is by the consideration of what will happen in two thousand years that our own nothingness truly takes on meaning. In one of its aspects, eternal nothingness is made up precisely of the sum of lives to come which will not be ours.

7. The will is only the agent here: it tends to maintain consciousness. It provides a discipline of life, and that is appreciable.

8. What matters is coherence. We start out here from acceptance of the world. But Oriental thought teaches that one can indulge in the same effort of logic by choosing *against* the world. That is just as legitimate and gives this essay its perspectives and its limits. But when the negation of the world is pursued just as rigorously, one often achieves (in certain Vedantic schools) similar results regarding, for instance, the indifference of works. In a book of great importance, *Le Choix*, Jean Grenier establishes in this way a veritable "philosophy of indifference."

In this selection we have seen Camus wrestle with the problem of suicide and the response of revolt, which the lucid individual must make to the absurd world. The theme of subjectivity as elucidated by Kierkegaard can be observed in the qualities of *lucidity* and *consciousness* enunciated by Camus. The existential individual is one who, while realizing the ultimate absurdity of the world, does not succumb to that absurdity. Rather, the existential individual responds to the absurd by means of *revolt*. This "defiant person" is the one responding to the absurdity of the cosmos. Camus suggests that this attitude of revolt is what provides life with its value. This attitude produces an awareness of freedom. There is no absolute scale of values, no objective foundation for moral prescriptions. What counts for living existentially is not objectively following a code but unconsciously engaging in the most amount of living possible. Camus emphasizes this point, which has come to be known as the *Ethic of Quantity*, when he states emphatically that "I say what counts is not the best living but the most living."

Camus' concept of the "most living" means that the truly existential person is aware of the absurd situation, aware of one's revolt, aware of one's freedom. This awareness, furthermore, must be developed to the maximum degree possible. To be existentially authentic, we must be supremely conscious of each experience. This leads to the concept of the Ethic of Quantity. The greatest number of actions consciously experienced leads to authenticity. Once again, we can see the theme of Kierkegaard's subjectivity being illustrated in Camus. In effect, all experiences are indifferent. Revolt, freedom, and consciousness are the characteristics of the lucid individual. Being lucid entails a consciousness of the present moment. To place hope on the future, be it the realization of the classless society or the beatitude of the afterlife, is to deny radically the lucidity demanded of the existential individual. A fiercely intense consciousness and keen awareness of the actions undertaken in the present moment are necessary for lucidity. With the emphasis on the present, the authentic individual can have no illusions either about the rationality of the cosmos or the hope of a better future. The lucid person is one who is thoroughly convinced that living existentially is not a matter of explaining but rather a matter of experiencing. Once again, the theme of subjectivity is paramount.

Does Camus provide us in the twentieth century with a workable guide for realizing human fulfillment? Will the "Ethic of the Absurd" satisfy our demands for a viable morality? Can Camus justify his claims? The following article, "Albert Camus and the Ethic of Absurdity," by Herbert Hochberg, provides us with an interesting elucidation of Camus' arguments and the significance of his propositions in the general scheme of existentialist thought. Hochberg traces the background material of Neo-Platonism, examines Camus' analysis of the absurd in *The Myth of Sisyphus,* and discusses the themes expressed in *The Rebel.*

ALBERT CAMUS AND THE ETHIC OF ABSURDITY [1]

Herbert Hochberg

Albert Camus sought, in *The Myth of Sisyphus,* to establish the absurdity of the human condition. [2] There and in *The Rebel* he further sought to derive an ethic from that condition—the ethic of the absurd man. Here we shall see that in the second task he failed completely, while, in the first, partial success is purchased at the price of triviality and, even so, rests on paradoxical ambiguities in his notion of "absurdity."

To grasp Camus's notion of the absurd, one must juxtapose it against a background of the philosophical ideas of the Greek Neo-Platonist, Plotinus. Plotinus envisioned the world as a "chain of Being." That is, he conceived of reality as a hierarchical arrangement of different sorts of entities culminating in the *One* or *Absolute.* Embracing the eternal and unchanging Platonic ideas, or essences, as a pattern for "explaining" or "accounting for" the varied and changing world of ordinary experience. Plotinus felt that the Platonic forms themselves required an explanation. He did so primarily from one of the most basic and pervasive motives that has entranced philosophers from the days of the Greeks to the present—the idea that diversity has to be explained in terms of some ultimate unity. For, where distinctions remain, the monist feels that the relationships among the diverse things require explanation. The search for an explanation, on this pattern, can only come to rest in some all-embracing unity, which, allowing of no distinctions within itself, somehow accounts for all the diversity that there is and, in turn, requires no explanation. It is, in its way,

From *Ethics* 75, no. 2 (January 1965): 87–102. Reprinted by permission of the author and the University of Chicago Press.

the old idea of the one and the many. Plato sought to account for the many particulars of a certain kind in terms of the universal form in which they all participated. But, for Plotinus, the Platonic forms, being many, could not then be the ultimate source of explanation and, hence of reality. The ultimate sources of explanation and reality coalesce, since to explain a thing is to account for its being in terms of some other entity. Thus the explanatory order reflects the "chain of Being." The ultimate level of explanation and source of reality could then only be some absolute unity. Being the source of the Platonic forms, the One was not, in turn, a form or idea itself. Since the ideas or forms also functioned as the objects and means of rational thought, the One was held to be incapable of being rationally comprehended. Another line of reasoning led to the same conclusion. Rational thought, for Plotinus, inescapably involved two dualisms: that of knower and known and that of subject and predicate. First, in thought there was the distinction between the knower and the object of knowledge and, second, judgments involved ascribing a predicate to a subject. Rational thought, involving such dualisms, was thus held to be incapable of comprehending *absolute unity*. The comprehension of the One must then go beyond the rational thought and beyond all dualisms. Platonic rationalism, pushed to this extreme, lapses or, perhaps, leaps into mysticism. In the mystic experience the One is finally reached and grasped. But the diversity characteristic of reason and ordinary experience must be avoided, hence the soul, in experiencing and comprehending the Absolute, becomes "one with the One." The mystic finally escapes diversity and gains comprehension by being absorbed into the Absolute.

By providing the ultimate explanation for, and source of, all things, the One constitutes the productive cause of all else. The pattern of Plotinus thus provides a dividend, for not only does the soul fulfil its desire to comprehend in the obliterating mystical experience, but it attains the very source and cause of its existence. In reaching the One, it joins the highest link in the chain of being and, consequently, achieves salvation. Starting out to explain the ordinary world, one thus ends by discovering its insignificance and the need to flee from it to something higher. The Absolute provides a haven as well as an explanation. By so doing, it gives man an end or destiny, union with it, as well as an ethic. One's life is to be lived so as to prepare for salvation. This is a union not only with the ultimate source of reality but with the absolute good, for the One, as man's final end, is the ultimate source of value. The "chain of being" is simultaneously a "chain of value," and something is good insofar as it is real. If one then asks how evil can come from the ultimate source of all, which is the absolute good, one is told that evil is simply the absence of goodness or reality and, as such, is non-being. The further one gets from the Absolute, the lower one sinks on the chain of being and of value. Since the ordinary world is the lowest link, to flee it is to flee from a lesser state of being and of value to the highest of both—to the true, the good, and the beautiful.

One can see, on the basis of the preceding sketch of Plotinus' view, some of the things that would appeal to Christians eager to find a metaphysical defense for their faith. However, there are pitfalls. One is the so-called problem of evil. Unlike Augustine, some may feel that there is still a puzzle in reconciling the absolute goodness of God with the evils of the world. The contrast seems, if we may anticipate, "absurd." A second problem is found in the deterministic element of Plotinus' world view. The Absolute is not modeled on a mind confronted with choices about which it exercises its free will. The things of this world are explained by the Absolute's being their necessary ground or condition. Hence all flows from it as rigorously as theorems from axioms in deductive systems. Orthodox Christianity obviously cannot make its peace with such a theme. In part the issue erupted in the Middle Ages in the scholastic attempts to reconcile a personal God's "knowledge" of all with man's freedom to create the future. For, some wondered, in what sense does man freely create what God knew he would do? These problems are not confined to Christians. They will bother anyone simultaneously intoxicated with the Plotinian pattern, man's freedom, and evil. Camus is such a one. Around these themes he attempts to construct an ethic.

The Myth of Sisyphus is purportedly an examination of the absurdity of man's condition and an attempt to provide a rationale for not committing suicide in the face of that absurdity. What does Camus mean by "absurdity"? Actually, he means several things, and, as we shall see, his arguments depend on these different senses. But, basically, he simply means that there is no Plotinian absolute—no ultimate unity, divine or secular, which explains all.[3] Camus thinks in terms of absurdity since he accepts Plotinus' pattern but rejects its culmination in the One. That is, he holds to the idea that explanation and understanding of the things of this world are to be had if and only if there is such an absolute, and yet he rejects it. Camus opts for "all or nothing" since, as he sometimes puts it, "to understand is, above all, to unify." The lack of such an ultimate unifying principle or entity forces us to accept the fact that all is absurd. This is Camus's thesis. Unfortunately, he obscures the simplicity of his route to the absurd by rehearsing some bad and irrelevant arguments from various philosophical sources, which supposedly show the impossibility of any knowledge.[4] But he need not have bothered with these feathery buttresses. Once he has accepted the Absolute, after accepting the theme that such an ultimate unity is a necessary ground for comprehending the things of the world, it follows, in his terms, that the world is incomprehensible and, consequently, absurd.

One may wonder why Camus, after adopting the monist's pattern, rejects the Absolute, and suffers from a "nostalgia for unity." There are several reasons, none original.

First, Camus notes the paradoxical nature of the Plotinian solution—its culmination in a mystical irrationalism, and he is not one to accept the verbal solution that this irrationalism culminates in something "above" reason rather than below it. For Camus, as for many before him, to accept the Absolute is to relinquish the search for an explanation, since one explains things in terms of something that is rationally incomprehensible. In short, while Camus requires that an explanation culminate in absolute unity, he also requires that an explanation be rationally comprehended and meaningful in terms of ordinary experience.[5] Here he is irretrievably caught between two themes. The criterion of unity requires the Absolute; the criterion of rational comprehension rejects it. Camus's incompatible criteria for what may constitute an explanation of the things of the world lead him to conclude that there can be no explanation and no comprehension. Actually the paradox stems from a deeper incompatibility that Camus accepts. I spoke above of "meaningful in terms of ordinary experience." "Empiricism" is an ambiguous term. But one theme that may be associated with this viewpoint is the contention that there is no extraordinary experience, whether it be mystical union with the Absolute or the intuitive grasp of certain eternal truths, that is philosophically significant. To the empiricist those who claim to experience the Absolute require analysis of a non-philosophical variety. In one way or another empiricists have suggested that what is comprehensible must be found so in terms of ordinary experience. In keeping with this they have tended to formulate criteria of meaning and have held as meaningless attempts to explain the realm of ordinary experience in terms of something which transcends that realm. Camus is such an empiricist. For him, in one sense of the trio of terms "meaningful," "comprehensible," and "rational," only things of this world can fall under them. Yet, to give a meaning to, a rationale for, or comprehension of the things of this world is, on the Plotinian pattern, to do so in terms of something beyond this world—some absolute unity. Accepting this, Camus is also a monist. Thus the Absolute, or God, is required to give a meaning to this world and yet is, at the same time, meaningless, since it is not of this world. In one sense of the term, the world is "meaningless" because there is no absolute; in another sense, there is no absolute, since any such "thing" would be "meaningless" in not being of this world. Camus's combination of empiricism and the Plotinian pattern leads him to the view that all is meaningless and absurd—the things of this world and whatever transcends this world.[6]

Closely intertwined with this first point is a second. One motive of an advocate of a transcendent absolute is the desire to give a point or purpose and, consequently, a value to the world and life. Yet, in doing so, he automatically deprecates the world of ordinary experiences in virtue of its insignificance when compared to its source. In giving a "value" to the world and life one *minimizes* the "values" of both. Since this world is the only one Camus comprehends and its joys and values the only ones he grasps, he can only be satisfied with giving the world, somehow, an *intrinsic value.* Doing this necessitates the rejection of a transcendent absolute. But in such rejection one foregoes giving the world value in the sense of purpose or meaning. Thus the world will have to be, ultimately, with value and meaning and without value and meaning. This will be the contradiction of the absurd condition that Camus will face in *The Rebel.*[7] But, again, the paradox depends on different senses of the same term and is thus no paradox. What is involved, as we shall see, is Camus's failure to provide the intrinsic value he seeks.

Third, Camus rejects the transcendent One in that it provides a cue for the entrance of the Christian God. He rejects God, in part, due to the problem of evil.[8] He cannot see any reconciliation between the existence of God and the existence of unwarranted suffering. In short, reason cannot comprehend how God can exist in the face of such evil. Since there is such evil, God cannot then exist. The paradox here is in requiring a rational explanation for there being a God with certain qualities and a world containing evil. Since, for Camus, this situation allows of no such explanation, it is absurd; but here the absurdity is a ground for the rejection of God. The point is that God, taken as an explanation, leads one to absurdity and, hence, cannot constitute an explanation. Nor is Camus one to accept the piety, be it that of priest or commissar, that all is for the best in the end. Such sentiments, to him, may be used to justify anything while really only covering up the absence of any justification. For the ultimate appeal is then to a mystique of faith and not to reason or experience. He is not tempted to trade future glories for present miseries. To buttress this sentiment he goes back to one of his uses of "meaning." He comprehends what he experiences. Future heavens, beyond the pale of experience, are incomprehensible. Thus to act in their name is incomprehensible or irrational, while to be rational is to act in terms of what one comprehends, the joys and experiences of this world. As we shall see, the absurd man is, ultimately, the rational man.

A fourth reason for rejecting the Absolute is based on the deterministic element it contains. Camus sees the Absolute as a threat to man's freedom. "Freedom," linked to "spontaneity," is opposed to what is *explainable.* Recall, for a moment, the discussions one hears time and again centering around purported proofs that there cannot be, in principle, scientific explanations of human behavior. In a sense the behavior scientist has replaced God in our current variations of the scholastic perplexity. But whereas God was above attacks on the logical limitations of his knowledge, the behavior scientists are not granted such divine immunity. Camus deals with the issue in its original form; he denies the Absolute to assert his freedom.[9]

For these reasons Camus denies the Absolute, hence God, and "establishes" the "absurdity" of the world. Following this he attempts to work out what some call the logic of the absurd, using, I take it, absurdist logic. The program is simple enough. He asserts, in Cartesian fashion, that he knows two things for certain—his own existence and the world's. Starting with what he knows for certain, his systematic construction begins. But, as we have seen, man cannot grasp rationally an explanation of his and the world's existence. This is, as we saw, one meaning of the absurd condition: the lack of explanation. But, as Camus uses the term, he finds it absurd that there is no explanation while one is craved. In this latter sense he speaks of the absurdity arising from the confrontation of man and the world, while belonging to neither alone.[10] He speaks this way for several reasons.

First, many contemporary writers, particularly on the Continent, are entranced by the notion of "contradiction." Historically, the absurd or irrational has been linked with the contradictory. In a loose sense of this term we may speak of a contradiction involved in craving for the impossible, in our "nostalgia for the Absolute." Hence, this situation is absurd. Second, speaking in this way permits Camus to juxtapose man to the rest of the world. This emphasizes his place, his difference, and his importance. Man becomes the creator of the absurd condition. When we recall that ever since Descartes, the problem of man's role in a physical universe has bothered commentators on the human condition, we can understand the need Camus feels for giving him a unique place. The destruction of the Absolute gives man his freedom, the absurd condition guarantees him a unique and independent role. Note that this role is due, in part, to the existence of his rational faculty, his seeking to comprehend rationally what is incomprehensible. In traditional fashion man's reason is what ultimately distinguishes him. As Camus sometimes puts it, man is the only creature that seeks a meaning for things. Third, this juxtaposition presents us with the feel of a tense dialectical situation. Camus has an affinity for the confrontation of opposites, be they "contradictions" or conflicts. We shall see how this permeates his view and how he makes use of the theme of "conflict" in his ethic. It is almost as if, having destroyed the Absolute as a sort of final cause to draw men to it, one requires an inherent tension to get things moving. One may here note that Camus, like many continental thinkers, while critical of Hegelian philosophy is impregnated with Hegelian patterns of thought. Fourth, and basically, he has to put the matter in terms of a juxtaposition of man and the universe to get his solution to the problem he raised: to show that life is worth living and that metaphysical suicide is to be rejected. This now follows from the absurd situation which arises out of the polarity between man and the universe— between man's desire to know and the world's silence. Having rejected the Absolute, Camus takes the absurd condition as a fact. It follows from the two previously stated facts of one's existence and the world's existence, plus, as we saw, a healthy dose of Greek metaphysics. If man removes himself, he destroys the situation and hence the absurd condition. Since the absurd condition is taken as a fact, one who destroys himself denies this fact. But he who denies a fact puts himself in opposition to what is, to, in short, the truth. To oppose the truth, recognizing it to be true, is to contradict oneself. Recognizing a truth, one ought to preserve it, rather than deny it. It follows that one ought not to commit metaphysical suicide in the face of the meaningless universe. In sum and in substance this is the argument of *The Myth of Sisyphus.*[11] One hopes that it is not the sole barrier holding some from suicide, for it commits a twofold blunder. First, there is the unfortunate play on the notion of preserving or, alternatively, denying a truth or a fact. Need one do more than point out that it is quite one thing to deny that some one has a wart by stating that it is not so; it is quite another thing to "deny" that fact by removing the wart. Of course, in Camus's case one removes the disease by removing the patient, but the point is still the same. Second, Camus has leaped from the factual premise that the juxtaposition of man and the universe is absurd, to the evaluative conclusion that this state ought to be preserved. As we noted, his play on the term "preserve" provides the verbal bridge. For this transition we have no justification. Without such justification, Camus has not, in the least way, made his point. He has simply begged the question. To produce such a justification would obviously involve the construction of an ethic. But it is precisely on this point that Camus builds his ethical view. Hence all that follows leans on a hollow argument. His lack of coherence may be explained by the fact that, having denied a transcendent source of value, he must, if he is to have an ethic at all, anchor his values somehow in the world of ordinary experience. Values must come about from the factual condition of the world as it is. This being so, one might be led to think that values must "emerge" from facts, and what is more natural than to have one's values emerge from what is for Camus one of the most fundamental facts of all—man's absurd condition?

Whatever explains his logical lapses, they remain with us. Hence, unlike some who find his logic impeccable and his premise about the absurd unfortunate, I find his logic quite inadequate while his premise, given the Plotinian framework, quite understandable. If by the world being absurd all one means to assert is that there is no Plotinian absolute or Christian God, many will accept Camus's thesis; but then, it has been said before and doesn't say very much.

Be that as it may, on the basis of the concept of the absurd and some absurd logic, Camus has repudiated metaphysical suicide. He has done so by discovering an absolute value through "reasoning" about the absurd condition. The value is life, since the preservation of life is necessary to maintain the absurd polarity between man and the world. Camus has denied a transcendent source of value and yet seems to have found a basic value, one created by man. This fact even further enhances man's place in the universe as the creator of values. With this value Camus will attempt to construct an ethic and repudiate nihilism, which is an ever present threat to him. We can see why nihilism is such a threat. Recall that adherents of the Absolute tend to minimize the ordinary world of change, becoming, and decay—the stage of ordinary living and experience. Camus repudiates any attempt to minimize the ordinary world and the pleasures of the senses. He has then a further ground for rejecting the Absolute. In rejecting any transcendent absolute, he is left with this world and this life. These, as we saw, become the sole possible sources of value. Since there is no external standard, one may be tempted to hold that differences of value can only arise from quantitative differences in this world—from the amount of it, in the form of experience or living, that one partakes of. In this way one can be led to hold that a life with more experiences is preferable to one with less. Thus an "ethic of quantity" may arise from holding this life to be an absolute value. Indeed, in *The Myth of Sisyphus* Camus is taken with such a view, but it obviously contains the seed of nihilism—a potential justification for a future Marquis de Sade.[12]

Camus is also led to assert the absolute value of life by his well-known preoccupation with death. In death he finds, paradoxically, a satisfaction for "nostalgia for unity." Death in its way "unifies" all men, and, in so doing, furnishes an "absolute." Unlike the One, it is not an end we seek, but one we seek to avoid. Yet we cannot do so. The conflict of fact and desire thus breaks out once again. We seek to understand the world and cannot; we seek to avoid death and cannot. Just as the first conflict led him to speak of absurdity, so does the second. Death becomes a further sense of the absurd. However, like the absolutes of Plotinus and Christianity it provides us with a source of value. The point here is to oppose the new absolute or absurd, not join it. In seeking to avoid it and to oppose it unconditionally, we create an absolute rule: Do not kill. Again life becomes an absolute value, and the drama of man is viewed as a struggle against death. Note that in struggling against the absurd, in the form of death, we preserve the absurd, in the form of the polarity between man and the world. But in speaking of death as an enemy to be opposed, Camus can introduce a further notion—that of rebellion, for rebellion needs an antagonist. The absurd, in the earlier senses, does not provide it explicitly enough; death does. It also provides as we saw, an ultimate unity that Camus always seeks, so deep is the Plotinian pattern imbedded in his thought. That men die becomes an ultimate sad fact beyond which we cannot go. This fact is also taken to be absurd in that it is inexplicable. But there is a further air of paradox about all this. Death is absurd on three counts: the conflict of our desire for immortality with our mortality, the inexplicability of it, and its denying or negating the only meaningful existence we know. Alternatively, death would not be absurd if we were immortal, if there was a point to it, and if this was not the only meaningful existence. In short, death would not be absurd if we introduce God and subservient immortal souls. But, paradoxically, it is also absurd on other grounds with God. For, recall, Camus is struck by the problem of evil, and he views death as an absolute evil. God, responsible for death, is both an abomination and a contradiction. Thus, death is absurd if God exists, and absurdity results with or without God. Death destroys God, and, in a sense, takes his place in Camus's scheme of things as an absolute opponent. It is almost as if Camus rejects God as a source of value but finds such a source in man's opposition to the devil, as absolute evil. With a transcendent God or One, we face a deterministic framework and loss of freedom. Death, too, seems to be a limit on our most basic freedom—to exist. But, Camus also sees it as a liberator.[13] Not only does it free us from a transcendent absolute, but it frees us in smaller ways. For just as we lose our freedom with a transcendent absolute that defines our purpose, we tend to lose it by thinking in terms of the future. We propose roles for ourselves and hence limit our freedom by living within these roles, be they those of bank teller, professor, or what have you. Realizing, through death, that there is no future, we may reject these roles and be free.[14] So the realization of death brings us freedom. In one sense Camus simply speaks nonsense and here makes contact with the "existentialist" of left-bank café society and the "authentic man" of recent literature. But in another sense, he is merely advocating the life of his "lucid" or "absurd" man. This will be elaborated in a moment. Death, in addition to being a "liberator," finally provides us with an absolute unity that is not transcendent. For, in a sense, death is part of the world of ordinary experience. We have found a unity which, in this sense, we can comprehend. But, as we saw, being inexplicable it is still absurd. Hence, even the unity we find does not provide us with comprehension but again demonstrates the lack of such. Yet through it we gain freedom. Thus Camus has another fundamental value. In destroying the Absolute we become free, and this fact too must be "preserved." We have, then, two values, life and freedom, while death is an absolute opponent. However, we face the threat of nihilism through an ethic of quantity. This threat must be removed and the two values integrated. In short, all the grounds Camus uses for asserting the absolute value of life must be coherently put together. The intellectual glue is provided by his notions of *lucidity* and *limitation.*

Recall the three basic grounds. The first was the necessity for preserving the truth of the absurd condition. It can lead us to look at Camus as a lonely but courageous bearer of the burden of life—as one who does one's duty solely by living—in short, as Sisyphus. The second was the upholding of the joys of sensual life in the face of their deprecation by a transcendent absolute. Here one can look at Camus as a sort of happy pagan, shuttling between beach, bedroom, and bar, decrying moral codes, and rhapsodizing about the quantity and variety of experience. Finally in the third, we find the rebel, the resolute opponent of death. In him some see the ground of a social ethic finally propounded in Camus's later work. We shall deal with that shortly. First, let us see how all these themes are put together.

We have seen how the absurd condition may be said to arise from man's consciousness. Once it is produced one may then recognize it or not. He who does is lucid. Thus, once again, as with the Greeks, we have a distinction between men on the basis of knowledge. Except the knowledge here is of the absurd condition, not of Platonic forms or mystical absolutes. But then this has become the ultimate fact concerning man's relation to the world. The lucid man then knows the ultimate truth. Moreover, his knowledge is rational, having been arrived at by reason and in terms of this world. The lucid man further recognizes that he must preserve the absurd condition. In this way he comes to advocate the absolute value of life. In recognizing the absurd condition, he rejects all transcendent values and notes that this life is all we have. He will enjoy it to the full, but with limits. For in recognizing the absolute value of life and the absolute opposition of death, the lucid man recognizes these *in general.* He has found the absolute value of all life, not just of his; and he opposes death in all its forms, not just his own death. In maintaining life to be an absolute value, the lucid man maintains the equality of all lives, with respect to the right to live. The lucid man will not kill himself or another, since the maintaining of the absurd condition weighs equally against suicide and murder. This imposes a limitation on the enjoyment of life and avoids the nihilism implicit in the ethic of quantity. Likewise, one's freedom is limited by the absolute value of life. Hence, this second value, freedom, is subordinate to the first, life. Even so, it, in turn, provides a further limitation on the way one lives one's life. The lucid man does not interfere with the "legitimate" freedom of others. Thus the lucid man becomes the moral man, and out of absurdity emerges morality. But, within the limits so imposed, the lucid man will reap the sensual fruits of this life. This is the point of the "freedom" the absurd man finds in death and the rejection of "roles." All this is implicit in *The Myth of Sisyphus,* though the preoccupation with freedom and the rebellion against death are explicitly the themes of *The Rebel.* But nowhere does Camus overcome the basic defects we noted earlier. This, in its way, is the whole story. We have seen how it stands on weak ground. What we shall see next is how, aside from its inadequate origins, it collapses of its own weight.

In the early pages of *The Rebel* Camus states two things. First, he holds that there seems to be a contradiction in his "absurdist" view, for he has introduced the value of life after claiming that there are no values. Second, he holds that murder and suicide are linked together in the absurdist position.[15] We have already seen that this second point is implicit in *The Myth of Sisyphus* and that there is really no contradiction in his "absurdist" view, since what he denies is a *transcendent* source of value. *The Rebel* is devoted to showing how a value, and hence an ethic, arises from the absurdist position. But this too adds nothing to *The Myth of Sisyphus*. There is, however, an elaboration of his ethical view in *The Rebel* and an attempt to reconcile the possible conflicts that may arise due to his holding life and freedom to be basic values.

The Rebel is dominated by Camus's opposition to nihilism, of which he sees two kinds. One is the nihilism of "all is permitted," the rejection of all moral standards; the other is the nihilism of absolutists who permit all means in the name of some absolute end.[16] Together, these two forms of nihilism pose a dilemma that must be avoided. The absolute value of life serves as a reply to the second form of nihilism as well as the first. For the basic crime of nihilists of the second kind is the subversion of human life to some other-worldly goal—other-worldly either in the sense of not of this world or of it but in some utopian future. In the name of such goals nihilists do not hesitate to murder and in this way deny the absolute value of life. In so doing they align themselves with man's eternal enemy—death. To rebel against death, as the lucid man does, is thus to reject these tyrannies, be they of church or state. And, in so doing, the lucid man becomes the rebel.

Camus considers rebellion to contain essentially the commitment to the struggle against death, by limiting it.[17] The revolt against death is, in fact, the archetype for all rebellion. Thus nihilists of either kind cannot be rebels. Much of the argument of *The Rebel* is devoted to this point. In establishing this betrayal of rebellion in history Camus feels he has established the intellectual impotency of nihilism. His ethic of rebellion furnishes him with a basis of criticism for all forms of nihilism. But it is tailored for the denunciation of injustice rather than the propounding of justice. One may, as Camus does, criticize all who seek to subvert human life and freedom to other ends, for, on Camus's view, this constitutes injustice. Thus the rebellion against death becomes the model for the denunciation of injustice and is the dominant motif of *The Rebel.* One can see why Camus's ethic must be one of opposition and condemnation from the very structure of his position. To specify some long-range program as embodying justice aside from the values of life and freedom would involve either other standards of value or at least a proposal as to what, in the long run, would be the closest realization of these two values. In the first case one clearly has the possibility of subjecting the values of life and freedom to these other standards. In the second case, the same thing may happen, since such programs for the realization of values tend to subvert the values themselves. In short any utopian program contains the seeds of nihilism since it leads us to the acceptance of an absolute other than life and hence, ultimately, to tyranny. Yet Camus feels he must say something more specific about the "good society." This leads him to the role of the artist.

In speaking of the artist Camus almost portrays a utopian community where all are artists. His pattern is simple. Recall that the absolute value of life involves the equality of all lives. If one then notes with Marx that political equality depends on one's role in the social and economic hierarchy, one may, with Camus, hold that true equality will involve men working at tasks to which we attach equal dignity. Since we must have plumbers as well as painters, Camus's solution lies in turning the plumber into an artist. Being an artist, he will take pride in his work and achieve equality with all other artists. Thus art or craftsmanship, rather than the dictatorship of the proletariat, becomes the great equalizer and hope for the future.[18] There are other reasons for Camus's intoxication with the role of the artist. The artist is a creator. As such he is the embodiment of the absurd condition on three counts. First, creation is opposed to destruction and hence "death." Second, the artist rebels against and "makes over" reality just as the rebel rejects his condition. Moreover, both the artist and the rebel reject existing reality in the name of some unifying principle. Third, the absurd condition, recall, is maintained by a tense opposition between man and the world. The problem of the artist is also one of maintaining such a tense opposition—between form and matter. A work of art is, in effect, a model of the absurd condition, and the artist the absurd man par excellence.[19] In creation the artist, like man as the creator of values, replaces God. Perhaps this too enhances the role of the artist for Camus. Be that as it may, from Camus's conception of the artist it is obvious how an aesthetic can emerge that may condemn, however unprecisely, the art of social realism on the one hand and highly abstract art on the other. This, of course, fits with Camus's rejection of the different forms of nihilism pervasive in the political societies these forms of art represent. Perhaps from the inherent "dialectical" tensions a new art and a new society may be thought to emerge. If so, the Hegelian strain in his thought would offer Camus a hope for the future.

But Camus does not, in the end, offer any utopia, for all utopias tend to become tyrannies. Also he sees in the prevalence of evil and death signs of the imperfection of man. Our task must be the more mundane one of limiting hell rather than trying to attain heaven. Man's condition is perpetually one of injustice and death which all men face. This condition, in its way, insures the rejection of all absolutes. For if injustice were thought to be conquerable, we would face an ideal in whose name all might be permissible—the condition of absolute justice. Thus the perpetual state of injustice guarantees the inadequacy of any utopia. Simultaneously, it guarantees the perpetual timeliness of Camus's ethic of rebellion. For man's opponents are always with him and man's rebellion always relevant.[20] Our common struggle need never cease and this struggle, in turn, reflects a further "unity" in the face of death. This struggle also provides Camus with a rhetorical device. He puts the philosophical questioner of his ethic in the position of playing intellectual games while, so to speak, the nihilists are at the door. Times of conflict are not compatible with intellectual searching into one's basic values. One declares them and struggles for them. Camus makes dramatic use of this persuasive device in *The Rebel.* At times he seems to hold that values are things one cannot, ultimately, reason about. Yet he often attempts not only to reason about them but to "prove" them.

In *The Rebel* Camus offers what seems to be a further argument for his "ethic of rebellion." It is perhaps on the basis of this particular argument that some see in his work the basis of a "new" social ethic. He argues that one rebels in the name of universal properties inherent in men. Thus rebellion is based on something common to men and not on egotistical grounds. He concludes that one rebels in the name of all men, or universally. The rebel even includes his master in this "natural unity" in whose name he rebels. Camus sees the fact that rebels give up their lives to struggle for rights as evidence that they hold these rights to be more important than their lives. These rights or values thus "transcend" the individual and are common to all. This shows, to Camus, that man rebels in the name of a universal "human nature" or essence which all men share.[21] Thus the value of the rebel, life, is anchored in the essence of man. Here, Camus's reasoning rests on a twofold confusion and is patently circular. Universals, or properties, are sometimes said to "transcend" the individuals that have them in that they "belong" to more than one particular thing and their existence is independent of any one particular exemplification. Values may be said to "transcend" an individual in that (*a*) he is willing to die for them; (*b*) other individuals may subscribe to these values; (*c*) they provide a standard by which one judges actions, rather than arising out of one's actions. But subscribing to values and holding that they "transcend" individuals in senses (*a*), (*b*), and (*c*) does not imply that there is a universal "human nature," something permanent in man that "transcends" any given man in the sense that a universal property "transcends" any exemplification of it. That both universals, as philosophers have thought of them, and values are spoken of as "transcending" individuals provides *part* of the bridge whereby Camus proceeds from the premise that one rebels for values to the conclusion that there is a universal human nature. The remaining part is supplied by the term "universal." A "universal" in the sense of a *common property* need not be "universal" in that it applies to all things. To be trite, the property of being a man applies to all men but that of being tall only to some. Yet both are "universals" in the sense of common properties. Camus thinks that because one rebels in the name of common properties, or universals, one rebels *universally*, in the name of all men. One might think, however, that a slave could rebel in the name of properties that only some men have in common or in the name of "transcendent" values that do not require him to rebel for "all men." Part of Camus's rejection of this line is explained by the confusions about "transcend" and "universal." But the link between "universal" as a property and "universal" in application involves another, circular thread. Camus holds that to rebel against the condition of slavery is to assert that *no one* ought to suffer the indignities of slavery. Since the slave rebels for all men, he rebels in the name of his master as well. Thus he cannot, consistently, either kill or enslave his master. So Camus's argument runs from (*a*) rebellion in the name of a transcendent value to (*b*) rebellion in the name of a "universal" or "essence" to (*c*) rebellion in the name of all instances of that universal to (*d*) rebellion in the name of all men, since that universal is common or "essential" to all men. But the contention that *no one* ought to suffer the indignities of slavery or be murdered can mean *at least* two things. First, one can take it in some ideal sense to the effect that a world without such indignities would be a better world, other things "being equal." Second, one can mean that, no matter what the consequences or the context, no man must be enslaved or murdered. Taking the first sense, the rebel might justify political murder as a necessary step for "progress." If so, Camus's case would not have been made, and, moreover, this is just what he wishes to avoid as a form of nihilism and absolutism. Taking the second sense, Camus patently begs the question. For the rebel then simply and explicitly adheres to the assertion that lives may not be taken. Thus the discussion of *The Rebel* does not take us beyond the "argument" of *The Myth of Sisyphus.* That is why for Camus to rebel is to rebel against the condition of man, that is, death and absurdity. This being so, Camus believes he has shown that the rebel cannot kill. Aside from the circularity, all this is comprehensible if we recall Camus's preoccupation with nihilism. Consider the three propositions: (*a*) life is the only absolute value; (*b*) all lives are of equal value; (*c*) one may not take a life. Camus takes (*b*) and (*c*) to follow from and "explicate" (*a*). Thus from the absolute value of life, he argues that one cannot kill at all. For, the ambiguity of adhering to life as the only absolute value may still allow one to hold that a life may be taken if such a course of action leads to less loss of life "on the whole." And if one does this, he is on the verge of an ethic of quantity, of absolutism, and of nihilism since, again, in the name of saving life in the "long run," all may be permitted. This is why, in *The Rebel,* Camus thinks in terms of an unrelenting and absolute opposition to death. Consequently, the rebel, the embodiment of Camus's ethic, cannot kill. To avoid any danger of absolutism in the name of some positive "good" or value, the absolute value becomes opposition to death; hence the rebel's ethic is one of ceaseless opposition, rebellion, and conflict.

Put in this way it is clear how the "equality of all lives," with respect to being killed, follows from the absolute opposition to death. It is also clear that, again, no argument has been offered in support of the "ethic" of the rebel. What further becomes clear, in the context and terms of Camus's own work, is the inadequacy inherent in the simplicity of his biblical stricture. This we see when he considers the possible justification of political murder in his concept of the "just assassin." Before discussing that concept it is interesting to note that in appealing to "human nature" to anchor his ethic, Camus seems to desert one of the basic themes of *The Myth of Sisyphus.* For he offers a variant of those views which hold objective values to be grounded in the very nature of man. And, insofar as one speaks of such values as deriving from man's essence and that essence "transcending" man, one is led to hold that such values have a transcendent source. Man's values, then, in some sense, come from his essence rather than arise out of his existential condition. One cannot help but wonder if this traditional pattern appeals to Camus as providing an anchor and an objective ground for the values which are created in rebellion. But one can also see why he might feel that he has not abandoned his earlier view. For the rebel's value, the rejection of death, is "created" by man's "absurd" confrontation of the world and his "metaphysical" rebellion. Thus man, not God, is the source of man's values. Perhaps Camus would even feel that, in holding both that there is a human essence which is presupposed by the rebel's value and that this value emerges from man's existential condition, he has reconciled any conflict between "essence" and "existence." It may be relevant to recall the mixing of the two senses of "universal" we noticed earlier. For one sense has to do with essence; the other with instances, or existences, of such essence. Whatever the relevance of such "metaphysical" intrusions, man's existential condition, involving death, murder, and slavery, is unjust. Man opposes it, or rebels against it, by asserting his essence or value—by opposing death. But sometimes in our unjust condition we will be faced with choosing between murder and slavery—between our two values of life and freedom. What choice are we to make? Camus is not a pacifist. Nor can he avoid the problem. To assassinate for the cause of freedom is to reject the absolute value of life, that is, the absolute opposition to death. The assassin contradicts the ultimate value of the rebel and betrays rebellion, even though he does so in the name of another value—freedom. Yet to avoid doing so in some cases is to perpetuate slavery. This too must not be allowed. Camus thus faces a dilemma. His solution is disarmingly simple, novel, and incoherent. He introduces the notion of the "just assassin."[22] The assassin murders and contradicts the value of life. Contradictions must be removed. The way out is for the assassin to "remove" the contradiction by killing himself. Here we come full circle. On the basis of the absolute value of life Camus has rejected suicide, capital punishment, and murder. He ends by acquiescing in certain cases to all three, for the suicide of the just assassin is suicide in the form of self-imposed capital punishment.[23] Obviously all this is a way of saying that the just assassin's act is both right and wrong. It is right in that it can be done, in the cause of freedom; it is wrong in that it must be punished for implementing death. Usually when principles conflict, we reconcile them either by altering one or recognizing an order of precedence. This can "remove" the conflict. Camus in recognizing a "just assassin" acknowledges a breach with the absolute value of life. But he must cling to that value or his whole intellectual edifice crumbles. Hence he sees the conflict as existing not in his principles but in the life of the assassin. The suicide of the assassin removes the contradiction and enables Camus to keep his conflicting principles intact until the next embodiment of their conflict.[24] It, in turn, will be removed in the same way. By this act of intellectual juggling Camus both acknowledges and denies that life is an absolute value.

Camus's notion of the "just assassin" is, in some ways, symbolic of his thought. Recognizing that murder and expediency can become institutionalized and yet that freedom may require one to kill, the "just assassin" serves freedom and avoids, in his suicide, the institutionalization of murder. He pays for his principles with his life.[25] This embodies, as so much of Camus's work does, a noble thought. Yet it is symptomatic of a desperately inadequate consideration of, and proposed solution to, the problems of ethics.

This combination of nobility without lucidity is what seems so disturbing about Camus. But then something he wrote might serve as a commentary on his thought.

> Even if the novel describes only nostalgia, despair, frustration, it still creates a form of salvation. To talk of despair is to conquer it. Despairing literature is a contradiction in terms.[26]

Camus consistently wrote of man's absurd condition. Perhaps in this way he sought to conquer it. Indeed, it may be true that just to talk of despair and our absurd condition is to conquer it—psychologically. But to "conquer" it in another sense, as Camus sought to do, a bit more is required.

NOTES

1. This paper was first read to the Philosophy Club at Indiana University in 1962 and later delivered at the University of Göteborg in 1963.

2. Notes are to the Vintage editions of *The Myth of Sisyphus*, trans. Justin O'Brien (New York: Vintage Books, 1959), hereinafter referred to as *MOS;* and *The Rebel*, trans. Anthony Bower (New York: Vintage Books, 1958), hereinafter *R*.

3. *MOS*, pp. 13–16, 20, 27, 33–39.

4. *MOS*, pp. 13–14.

5. *MOS*, pp. 32, 34, 38, 42.

6. By a meaning criterion, either explicit or implicit, a consistent *empiricist* would avoid Camus's dilemma by rejecting both "the Absolute" and the sense of "explanation" that an Absolute provides as meaningless notions. Hence any Plotinian scheme would be rejected. It is no accident that the empirically oriented Thomists resort to a doctrine of "analogy" to speak of God or refer to him in terms of his effects.

7. *R*, p. 8.

8. *MOS*, p. 42. It would also be relevant to recall *The Plague*.

9. There are suggestions of this in *MOS*, p. 16, where Camus links "universal reason" with "determinism," and again on p. 41, where he touches on the classical problem of free will and holds that the very notion that makes the problem possible (that of God as a transcendent master) also makes it meaningless. Preoccupied with the question of evil, Camus chooses to see the "paradox" of God in terms of the problem of evil. Nevertheless, in proceeding (*MOS*, p. 42), by his empiricism, to declare that "the only conception of freedom I can have is that of the prisoner or the individual in the midst of the State," he rejects the traditional problem of free will as meaningless; for it involves a "notion which eludes me and loses its meaning as soon as it goes beyond the frame of reference of my individual experience." This also serves to reject any suggestion of a "deeper freedom" granted by God. The theme is taken up again in *R* where Camus holds that absolute justice destroys freedom (p. 288) and in a footnote writes: "Jean Grenier lays the foundation for an argument that can be summed up thus: absolute freedom is the destruction of all value; absolute value suppresses all freedom. Likewise Palante: 'If there is a single and universal truth, freedom has no reason for existing."

10. *MOS*, pp. 22–23, 16.

11. *MOS*, pp. 23–24, 38–41; and *R*, p. 6.

12. *MOS*, pp. 45–46.

13. *MOS*, pp. 43–44.

14. *MOS*, p. 43.

15. *R*, pp. 6–8.

16. *R*, pp. 57–60, 102–4.

17. *R*, pp. 100–101.

18. *R*, pp. 273–74.

19. *R*, pp. 257–58, 270–76. Camus apparently makes use of the traditional dichotomy of "art and science" in his thesis of the absurd condition. *Explanation* is impossible, but art can both describe the world in its diversity as well as create new experiences. Thus art, rather than *rationalist* science and philosophy, is more "in tune" with "the absurd." In fact science and philosophy must merge with art in describing and creating, since neither can,

ultimately, explain anything. Hence the traditional and "arbitrary" opposition between art, on the one hand, and science and philosophy, on the other, is "overcome" (MOS, pp. 70–74).

20. R, pp. 286–92, 303. Also, Camus believes that a notion of absolute justice or value (aside from that of life) is inconsistent with freedom (see n. 7 above). Thus just as Camus has his version of original sin by holding to the perpetual injustice of man's condition, he also adheres, in his way, to the idea that injustice and evil are necessary conditions for human freedom.

21. R, pp. 15–17, 281.

22. R, pp. 282–86.

23. Strictly speaking Camus has rejected only "philosophical" or "metaphysical" suicide, i.e., suicide based on the realization that the human condition is absurd. Thus no formal contradiction is involved. However, his rejection of philosophical suicide and his advocacy of the assassin's suicide both stem from his "discovery" of the absurdity of life. (In this paper I have not gone into any question of the legitimacy of suicide in other contexts, and, if Camus approved of suicide in some cases, what complications this would involve him in regarding the absolute value of "life." Such points would take us out of the context of MOS and R.)

24. Perhaps Camus does not see the conflict as imbedded in his principles as they, as such, are "abstractions." Thus a contradiction or conflict only arises in an actual or existential situation. A contradiction then only arises in the person of one who embraces conflicting principles—in the rebel who murders. The rebel's suicide removes the actual or existential, as opposed to abstract, contradiction. One who thinks, like Camus, of essence and existential conditions may have something vaguely like this in mind.

25. Camus is much taken by the nobility of sacrifice. In fact he sometimes seems to value the sacrifice of one's life for one's fellows almost as much as he values life itself. This is understandable in that sacrifice signifies (a) a "unity" with one's fellow men, and (b) submission to a "value" over and above one's own life. For Camus, as we have seen, both (a) and (b), in different senses, inject "meaning" into a meaningless universe. Sacrifice, so to speak, is the test of the absurd man's commitment.

26. R, p. 263.

Some scholars argue that the horrors of the Nazi occupation of France caused Camus to modify his Ethic of Quantity. Following the war, Camus desperately sought for a framework within which to postulate a groundwork for human solidarity. In the following passage from his *Existentialism*, Vincent Martin stresses the change Camus underwent from the Ethic of Quantity found in *The Myth of Sisyphus* and *The Stranger*, to the themes of human solidarity found in *The Rebel* and *The Plague*.

The Camus described thus far might have gone along with his philosophy in peace and quiet but the invasion of France by the Nazis showed its basic inadequacy. If one admits the principles and the conclusions of Camus, then he has no right to protest against the ruthless tactics of the Nazis. If morality is only man-made, then it is left to each individual to make his own standards; if men are innocent in the meaning of Camus, namely, that there is no right and wrong but only consistency; if men are innocent in the sense that there are only responsible agents but no guilty ones, then one would be forced to admit that Hitler with his concentration camps and his gas chambers was just as right as anyone else. If one is entirely captivated by the nihilism of Nietzsche's doctrine, why should one feel outraged when Hitler makes that nihilism more existential by putting it into practice?

Hence World War II brought certain changes in the thought of Camus, for it made him reexamine some of his basic tenets. As a member of the French Resistance, and as a human being outraged by the inhumanity of the Nazis, and later on by the same brutality of the Communists, Camus realized that the individualism of his earlier writings could never explain the sacrifice, the nobility, the purpose which he saw among the men fighting the Nazi terror. And so the moral thought of Camus became more social, more universal, less nihilistic.

We still have absurdity; we still begin with the denial of God; we still have rebellion. But we now ask, why should we not commit suicide; why should we rebel? Because we understand that life is good. But if life is good for me, it is also good for others. I find now a human worth, a human dignity; I see now that there is a nature common to all men; that this human nature has value which must be recognized by me and by all other men. It is no longer a sense of man rebelling by himself and for himself; there is now an awareness of human solidarity; there is now a return to Greek thought with its insistence upon the objectivity and universality of natures, especially human nature. Man is now not so solitary for Camus as he had been in his earlier works, for there is now a sharper appreciation of the comradeship, the union among men. Since my own life is a good which I should not surrender by suicide, so the life of the other is a good which I should not destroy by murder.

With his new sense of human nature and human solidarity Camus insists that freedom is not absolute but only relative, for it must respect the rights of the other. Just as this individual has freedom, so does the other individual have freedom, and my freedom must respect his.

Moderation is the word now used by Camus; my freedom must be relative; my desire for justice must be temperate; my violence against those who would destroy me and other men must be moderate. For a sense of absolute freedom can come to mean a ruthless freedom: that one man is dictator and the rest his slaves. A sense of absolute justice can mean an intolerant efficiency: that all must be destroyed who stand in the way of that absolute justice; and this means tyranny. This is a relative world, a world of relative knowledge and relative goods; and therefore man's rebellion must be moderate. Man has for too long been under the domination of German Ideology, says Camus; he needs a return to the moderation of the Greeks.

Would this new awareness of the universality of human nature have led Camus further along the thought of the ancient Greeks, Plato and Aristotle, so that like them he would have recognized that the world is a thing of order, purpose, and beauty which points to an intelligent cause, namely, God? Who can say, for in January, 1960, death cut him down in a tragic auto accident.[21]

Summary of Existentialist Themes

Now that we have discussed in some detail the existential thought of Kierkegaard, Sartre, and Camus, it is time to reflect briefly on the meaning of existentialism. As stated at the beginning, it is next to impossible to define categorically the nature and scope of existentialism. Nonetheless, certain common themes do emerge when we confront the existentialist writers. We might list these common themes in the following way:

1. Existentialism means an absorbing interest and concern with the human condition. The existentialists have an intensely passionate awareness of the demands brought about by human living, especially human decision making. This is highlighted by the analysis of subjectivity given by Kierkegaard.

2. Existentialists emphasize the role of commitment in human undertakings. Their concern with human existence entails that our lives must be full lives,

committed lives, lives full of choices and decisions. We make our very being through the choices we undertake. For the existentialists, the philosophy of human existence is philosophy enough.

3. The demand for commitment implies that consciousness plays a decisive role in matters of human existence. We must be *subjective* beings, thoroughly conscious of the nature of our actions and commitments. The emphasis on subjectivity tends to downplay objective inquiries. At times, some of the existentialists appear to profess a total lack of interest in traditional objective inquiries, especially inquiries depending upon the application of scientific methodology.

4. There is strong emphasis on individuality. Among many existentialists, each person is indeed an island. The whole thrust of existentialist language is directed toward subjectivity and consciousness. Subjectivity is fiercely individualistic.

5. Each of the three existentialists we have considered place emphasis on the role of the *absurd*. Of course, as we have discovered, there are vast differences between the absurd of Kierkegaard and the absurd of Sartre and Camus. Kierkegaard is a theist and Sartre and Camus are atheists. Nonetheless, in all three cases, there is the firm insistence that a rational comprehension of ultimate meaning is impossible.

6. Because of the lack of ultimate significance to either the cosmos or to our place in the cosmos, the qualities of *dread* and *anxiety* play important roles in existentialist thought. In fundamental matters demanding choices and commitments, there is no ontological foundation or objective value system which might serve as a basis for moral prescriptions. Nonetheless we must choose. The demands placed upon human beings because of the necessity of making commitments produce intense feelings of anguish and dread. The existentialists emphasize the centrality of these attitudinal qualities for our very human existence. These attitudes are not to be hidden or run away from; they are to be confronted as central to living an authentic human life.

Among all else, the existentialists have focused attention on the demands of being human. Traditional philosophy, they argue, has been too abstract, too universal, too removed from the demands of human existence. The emphasis on *subjectivity, commitment,* and *involvement* give significance to what authentic human existence is all about. With the examination and clarification of these attitudinal qualities, the existentialists believe that they have helped provide significance to the process of living. The analysis of the human condition, they argue, is the sum and substance of what philosophy ought to be.

Phenomenology

In addition to the themes of existentialism expressed in the writings of Sartre and Camus, there is another dimension to contemporary European philosophy called phenomenology. This branch of philosophy was briefly mentioned in chapter 1.

The advocates of phenomenology are very interested in probing the function of consciousness. Edmund Husserl (1859-1938) is usually considered the father of this branch of continental philosophy. However, Husserl remarked that it was Franz Brentano (1838-1907) who "earned the epoch-making advantage of

making phenomenology possible . . . (in that) he presented to the modern era
the idea of Intentionality. . . ." We observed in chapter 3 that the notion of
intentionality is the characteristic which distinguishes knowers from nonknowers. In his "Psychologie vom Empirischen Standpunkte," Brentano discussed the characteristic of mental phenomena and related his discussion to
psychological treatises written in the middle ages.

> Every mental phenomenon is characterized by what the Scholastics of the
> middle ages called the intentional (or mental) inexistence of an object, and what
> we, although with not entirely unambiguous terms, would call the reference to a
> content, a direction towards an object. . . .[22]

Every mental act is characterized by the direction toward the object known.

The following selection from Quentin Lauer's *The Triumph of Subjectivity*
provides an interesting and illuminating account of what is meant by phenomenology. Lauer discusses various historical positions in philosophy which
help the reader to place phenomenology in the context of Western philosophy.
Students in psychology will profit from this selection in that many psychologists who consider themselves nonbehaviorists are usually called phenomenologists. That Lauer, and a fortiori Husserl, has a more restricted meaning for his
philosophical use of phenomenology than what is normally expressed by non-
behaviorist psychologists will be apparent in the selection. Although phenomenology as a philosophical position and methodology is neither widely
accepted nor practiced by Anglo-American philosophers, it is important that
American students confront this important continental contribution to philosophy. In addition, themes like intentionality are widely discussed by both
phenomenologists and analytic philosophers. Hence there is ground here for a
common discussion.

WHAT IS PHENOMENOLOGY?

Quentin Lauer

With the passage of time it becomes more and more difficult to determine
what the words "phenomenology" and "phenomenological" are supposed
to mean in the contexts in which they are used. Like the terms "existentialism" and "existential" it has become fashionable to designate thereby
some sort of profound, recondite, and very up-to-date approach to philosophy or science, without it being entirely clear in what sense the terms are
being applied. There is a sense, of course, in which this vague use is justified, since every attempt to get away from speculative constructionism and
to limit oneself to the data which are presented in consciousness—

describing rather than explaining them—is to that extent phenomenological, at least in method. Still, the sort of vagueness which goes with modishness leads to confusion and makes for a terminology almost empty of meaning. In recent years, for example, phenomenology has in some minds become so intimately bound up with existentialism that the two terms are used almost indiscriminately, despite significant differences in the attitudes represented by the two titles. The reason for this may be that the thought of Jean-Paul Sartre, which is both phenomenological and existential, is taken as typical. Many thinkers, such as Martin Heidegger and Gabriel Marcel, who consider their own approach to philosophy as phenomenological, have expressly indicated their desire not to be identified with the direction represented by Sartre. Others, such as Jean Hering or Dietrich von Hildebrand, would see no sense in referring to their thought as in any way "existential."

In whatever context the term phenomenology is used, however, it refers back to the distinction introduced by Kant between the *phenomenon* or appearance of reality in consciousness, and the *noumenon,* or being of reality in itself. Kant himself did not develop a phenomenology as such, but since his *Critique of Pure Reason* recognizes scientific knowledge only of *phenomena* and not at all of *noumena,* his critique can be considered a sort of phenomenology. According to this position whatever is known is phenomenon, precisely because to be known means to appear to consciousness in a special way, so that what does not in any way appear is not known—at least not by speculative reason. Still, according to Kant, it is possible to *think* what is not *known,* and this we think of as a "thing-in-itself" or *noumenon,* of which the *phenomenon* is the known aspect. This sort of phenomenology, which will restrict scientific knowledge to appearances, is directed both against the rationalism of Descartes, which seeks a rational knowledge of all reality, and against the phenomenism of Hume, which will accept no scientific knowledge at all except that of mathematics. Kant insists that there can be true scientific knowledge which is not mathematical, but he denies that there can be such a knowledge in metaphysics.

The first philosopher to characterize his own approach to philosophy as phenomenology was Hegel. Like Kant he contended that phenomena are all we have to go on, but unlike Kant he was convinced that they afforded a sufficient basis for a universal science of being. He saw no need of even thinking of an unknown thing-in-itself. Phenomena, according to Hegel, reveal all that is to be revealed—not simply in themselves but through the medium of the dialectical process, which is the necessary process of human thought. Beginning with the simplest form of consciousness, which is immediate sense perception, he brings us through consciousness of self (in a series of dialectics which reveal the social and historical nature of knowledge) to reason, wherein reality is reduced to unity, ultimately to that of the Absolute Idea, Absolute Spirit, which *is* all reality. To be *fully* conscious of self is to be fully conscious of all reality, since the ultimate self is all reality. In all this Hegel sees no departure from the original phenomenon, since the dialectical process constitutes an unbreakable chain which has never lost contact with the first experience.

With the positivism of Ernst Mach and of the Vienna Circle, which drew its inspiration from Mach, we find another kind of phenomenology, which is not ordinarily characterized as such. In spirit these men were closer to Kant than they were to Hegel, since they preferred Kant's rejection of metaphysics (at least from the point of view of speculative reason) to Hegel's affirmation of it. They would ask no questions at all with regard to reality, convinced as they were that to such questions there were no answers; they were simply satisfied with describing consciousness, the data of which are susceptible only of description, not of explanation. And in this description they found no grounds for affirming a reality, whether it be the "substance" of Spinoza or the "thing-in-itself" of Kant. An approach so exclusively descriptive as this is obviously completely non-metaphysical. Unfortunately, however, many particular positivist interpretations have a tendency not only to eliminate reality as an object of scientific inquiry but to reject any reality whatever, a position which in its negative way is just as metaphysical as its opposite. When Freud in his clinical work confines himself to a pure description of the behaviors he has observed, his approach, too, can be called phenomenological, at least to the extent that any description of what is observed will always be phenomenological.[1] It is, of course, problematical just how successful one can be in completely avoiding any metaphysics whatever—unless one confines oneself to a pure analysis of meaning, which is what the logical positivists of the Vienna Circle do. This results in a sort of mathematics of language, which is probably more purely descriptive than even the most completely conscious phenomenology.

When the term "phenomenology" is used today it usually refers to the philosophy of Edmund Husserl or of someone of those who have drawn their inspiration from him. From the beginning of his philosophical career, Husserl was opposed to what he called the "dualism" of Kant, the "constructionism" of Hegel, and the "naturalism" or "psychologism" of the positivists. He agrees with them in asserting that only phenomena are *given,* but he will claim that *in* them is given the very *essence* of that which is. Here there is no concern with reality as existing, since existence is at best contingent and as such can add to reality nothing which would be the object of scientific knowledge. If one has described phenomena, one has described all that can be described, but in the very constant elements of that description is revealed the *essence* of what is described. Such a description can say nothing regarding the existence of what is described, but the phenomenological "intuition" in which the description terminates tells us *what* its object *necessarily* is. To know this is to have an "essential" and hence a "scientific" knowledge of being. Contemporary phenomenologists usually follow the development elaborated by Husserl—at least in its methodological aspects—though many of them have rejected the idealistic and metaphysical implications of Husserl's own position. They consider as phenomenology's distinctive mark its capacity to reveal essences, not its refusal to come to terms with "existing" reality. Unlike the investigations of Husserl, those of his followers range over a very wide field, so that there is scarcely an aspect of philosophy or of science which has not been investigated phenomenologically. To mention but a few: we find that Heidegger, Jaspers, Sartre, Marcel, and Conrad-Martius are developing the phenomenological method in its ontological implications; Pfänder, Geiger, Merleau-Ponty, Ricoeur, and Binswanger apply it to psychology; Scheler,

Von Hildebrand, and Hartmann have developed a phenomenological ethics and general theory of values; Otto, Hering, and Van der Leeuw have studied religion in the same way; while in esthetics Simmel, Ingarden, Malraux, Duffrenne, and Lipps have been conspicuously successful. Among these same authors we find contributions to epistemological, sociological, linguistic, and logical developments. All are in one way or another concerned with the *essences* of the concepts employed in these disciplines.

Though there is a certain unity of purpose discernible in all these efforts, still there is a certain disadvantage in speaking of the phenomenological method or of phenomenology, without further qualification. The disadvantage is twofold. First of all, the genius of Kant has been so influential that one almost inevitably thinks of phenomena in terms of the Kantian dichotomy of *phenomenon* and *noumenon,* thus giving rise to the opinion that a phenomenology must either be a phenomenism *à la* Hume, which simply refuses to go beyond sensible appearances, or else an introductory stage to a sort of noumenology, which would be some kind of modified Scholasticism, wherein the being which is sought would be something "behind" the phenomenon. The second disadvantage is that, even where the distinction between phenomenology and phenomenism is recognized, there is a tendency to group all phenomenologists together, without attention to the really great differences between the phenomenologies of Scheler, Husserl, Marcel, and Heidegger—to mention a few. It is true, of course, that Husserl provided the impetus for what might loosely be termed "the phenomenological movement," but in so doing he evolved a philosophy which is peculiarly his own, in which no one of his disciples followed him to the limit. Still, if we are to understand what phenomenology means as a contemporary philosophical attitude, we must first understand what it meant in the mind of its founder, Edmund Husserl.

The problem of reconciling reality and thought about reality is as old as philosophy—we might say, as old as thought itself. The problem is complicated by the obvious fact that we cannot know reality independently of consciousness, and we cannot know consciousness independently of reality—to do so would be to meet the one and the other in isolation, which is an impossibility. We meet consciousness only as consciousness of something; and we meet reality only as a reality of which we are conscious. It seems reasonable to assume that the normal individual will, without reflection, see a certain duality in his experiences of the world about him: in them there is a world which he experiences, and which he assumes to be independently of himself pretty much as he experiences it; and there is also the experience wherein he grasps this world, which he assumes to be distinct from the world. It is also reasonable to assume that he has never been able to analyze his experiences to such an extent that he can isolate— the way one does in analyzing water into hydrogen and oxygen (if even that is possible)—the "elements" which belong to the "independent" world of reality and those which have been contributed by the very act of experiencing this reality. Finally, it seems reasonable to assume that he will not be too much concerned.

The philosopher, however, is committed to penetrating this mystery— for mystery it is—and to coming up with some sort of consistent reconciliation of the two worlds, if he is to continue plying his trade. In a certain sense, the history of philosophy is the record of a series of attempts to make this reconciliation. The problem as it faces us, and as it has faced philosophers from the beginning of philosophizing—apart from the accuracy of the original judgment which the "normal" individual makes— offers a limited number of approaches to a solution. One can approach it from the side of the reality of which we are conscious, from that of the consciousness we have of reality, or from the point of view of a contact between the two. Despite the limited number of approaches, however, there seems to be no limit to the explanations which have been and will continue to be attempted.

The phenomenologist is no exception in this almost universal quest for a solution.[2] Whatever may be his particular position, he seeks to reduce the problem to its simplest terms and *in* them, rather than *from* them, to find a solution, or at least, the approach to a solution. According to the phenomenologist, if there is a solution at all, it must be contained in the *data* of the problem—although, of course, there is a disagreement as to what the data are. The point of agreement, however—and this is what makes each a phenomenologist—is that only phenomena are *given* and that therefore, if an answer is to be found, it must be sought in phenomena. There will be a disagreement as to just what are to be considered as phenomena and as to what can be discovered in them, but there will be agreement that we cannot enlist the aid of the non-phenomenal in seeking our solution. As Maurice Merleau-Ponty, one of the most coherent of the phenomenologists, has expressed it, "Phenomenology is an inventory of consciousness as of that wherein a universe resides."[3] If we are to know what anything is—and this the phenomenologist will do—we must examine the consciousness we have of it; if this does not give us an answer, nothing will.

The consciousness with which the phenomenologist is here concerned, is not consciousness as a psychic function, in the way it is, for example, to the experimental psychologist. He is concerned with consciousness as a kind of being which things exercise, the only kind of being directly available to the investigator. Thus, for him, consciousness is best expressed by the German word *Bewusstsein,* which means the kind of being an object of knowledge has in being known. This is not necessarily an identification of being and being-known, but it is an assertion that the only key we have to being is in examining its being-known. Now, even a superficial examination of any act of consciousness will reveal two inescapable facts: (1) it cannot be isolated from other acts of consciousness, but belongs to a whole life of consciousness, is conditioned by all the dispositions of which a subject is capable, is prepared for and colored by the whole series of conscious acts which have preceded it; (2) it is never completely arbitrary, in the sense of being conditioned only subjectively; it is what it is because it is consciousness of this or that object, which, precisely as an object, is in some sense independent of the individual act wherein it is grasped; there is some similarity between the experiences of one subject and another when faced with a similar situation, no matter what the previous experiences of the two may have been.

The attempts to reduce the problem to its simplest terms, however, is not so simple after all. If the only approach we have is through consciousness, and if every act of consciousness is a complex of insepara-ble elements, some objective and some subjective, the analysis of con-sciousness which will reveal to us the very meaning of being is a complex affair. The phenomenologist, however, is convinced that this analysis can be made and that in making it he can return to the very origin of conscious-ness, distinguishing what is pure consciousness from all the accretions which custom, prejudice, assumption, and tradition have built around it. When he has uncovered consciousness in this pure form, he is convinced that he will have arrived at an understanding of the only being which can have significance for him.

In speaking thus of phenomenology we have admittedly come to treat exclusively of the kind of phenomenology advocated by Edmund Husserl and by those who follow him more or less closely. In this sense phenomen-ology is both a method and a philosophy. As a method it outlines the steps which must be taken in order to arrive at the pure phenomenon, wherein is revealed the very essence not only of appearances but also of that which appears.[4] As a philosophy it claims to give necessary, essential knowledge of that which is,[5] since contingent existence cannot change what reason has recognized as the very essence of its object.[6] In the course of its inves-tigations, therefore, it discovers (or claims to discover) that the quasi infin-ity of objects which go to make up an experienced world can be described in terms of the consciousness wherein they are experienced. Phenomen-ology is conceived as a return to "things," as opposed to illusions, verbal-isms, or mental constructions, precisely because a "thing" *is* the direct object of consciousness in its purified form. The color "red" is no less a thing than is a horse, since each has an "essence" which is entirely inde-pendent of any concrete, contingent existence it may have. It is sufficient that the experience of red can be as clearly distinguished from the experi-ence of green as can the experience of horse from that of man. The dispute as to whether colors are "primary" or "secondary" qualities is entirely with-out significance; each color has an essence which can be grasped in con-sciousness, precisely because the essence of any color is contained in the experience of that color. The fact that the content of this experience is an essence is manifest from the fact that it can be clearly distinguished from whatever is essentially something else.[7] In this sense an imaginary object has its distinct *essence* just as truly as does a "real" object. Whether an object is *real* or *fictitious* can be determined by an analysis of the act of which it is object.

All this, however, would be without significance if it were not aimed at discovering "objective" essences, which are what they are not only inde-pendently of contingent existence but also independently of any arbitrary meaning which a subject *wants* to give them. Though it is of the essence of an object to be related to a subject, the phenomenologist will deny that "things" act upon subjects in such a way as to engender this relation or that subjects simply "produce" objects. He will insist that by investigating pure consciousness he can discover a relationship which is truly objective, in the sense that its validity is not derived from the conscious act wherein the relationship resides, and is necessary, in the sense that it could not be otherwise, no matter who the subject grasping the object may be. Husserl's own phenomenological investigations were, it is true, chiefly logical, epistemological, and to a certain extent ontological. Still, phenomenology even as he conceived it is at its persuasive best in the realm of values.

Realistic systems of philosophy have always found the question of moral, religious, esthetic, and social values a particularly difficult hurdle to clear since the subjective elements in all value judgments are too obvious to be ignored. One can, of course, explain evaluations in terms of the objective values which are being judged, and then describe objective values in terms of their relationship to an evaluating subject; but this sort of thing looks suspiciously like going around in a circle. It is perhaps for this reason that there were no consistent attempts to evolve theories of value, until the days when idealism was enjoying widespread triumph. Idealistic theories, however, have always run the risk of becoming so subjective that the very concept of value loses any communicable significance. Husserl himself was not particularly successful—we might even say that he was eminently unsuccessful—in coming to terms with the complicated problems of value,[8] but his theories, particularly in their ontological aspects, inspired others to look for a world of values which are *what* they are independently of any particular or general judgments regarding them. According to Scheler, Hartmann, Von Hildebrand, and others such values are to be *discovered in* things and not to be *imposed on* things by an observing—and evaluating—subject. And the techniques for discovering them are to be the phenomenological techniques of objective analysis and description, resulting in an *"intuition"* of value essences (essential values).

It is not our purpose in this study to examine all (or even some) of the theories which can in one way or another be called phenomenological. It is rather to examine more in detail the theoretical bases for phenomenology as such, as conceived and elaborated by Husserl. From this, it is hoped, we shall be able to understand the idea which Husserl held out of avoiding in philosophical investigations the Scylla of uncritical objectivism and the Charybdis of arbitrary subjectivism. Husserl himself, it is true, does not seem to have seen or at least formulated clearly, the possibility of a dialectical interplay of subjective and objective elements in all thought about being, but he did see the necessity of lessening the gap between the subjective and the objective, and even, if necessary, of refusing entirely to recognize its existence. He also faced the necessity of approaching the problem with the only instruments at his disposal, with the instruments clearly contained in consciousness itself. His insistence on remaining completely and purely rational[9] throughout the process made it impossible for him to enjoy fully the riches which his digging had uncovered; but his is still the merit of having uncovered them.[10]

NOTES

1. Martin Heidegger, *Sein and Zeit* (7th ed.; Tubingen: Niemeyer, 1953) p. 35, says that the expression "descriptive phenomenology" is tautological—the two terms are inseparable.
2. We say "almost universal" because the positivist *claims*, at least, to be utterly unconcerned with the *what* of reality or of consciousness. His only objection to any "explanation" which may be given should be that he cannot understand what the explanation means, which is fair enough, if he remains there.
3. *La structure du comportement* (3rd ed.; Paris: Presses Universitaires de France, 1953), p. 215.

4. According to Husserl, there is no essence other than that discoverable in appearances.

5. "Phenomenology, which will be nothing less than a theory of essence contained in pure intuition," from *Ideen I*, edited by Walter Biemel on the basis of the author's own marginal notations to the 1922 edition (The Hague: Martinus Nijhoff, 1950), 154. "With regard to phenomenology, it wants to be a *descriptive* theory of essences," *ibid.*, p. 171. Among the followers of Husserl there is considerable divergence of emphasis, some stressing the *description* of phenomena, others stressing the discovery of *essences* in phenomena. As is so frequently the case, the differences seem to be traceable to the predispositions which each has brought with him in his approach to phenomenology.

For a complete Bibliography of significant Husserliana, consult the author's *La phénoménologie de Husserl* (Paris: Presses Universitaires de France, 1954).

6. If there is any difference at all between phenomenon and reality, it cannot be other than accidental, since the essence of that which is remains absolutely identical. "Immanent being, then, is undoubtedly absolute being, in the sense that, in principle, *nulla 're' indiget ad existendum*," *ibid.*, p. 115; cf. *Nachwort zu meinen Ideen* (Halle: Niemeyer, 1930) p. 14.

7. Moritz Schlick has objected that phenomenology has labored hard to produce some very inconsequential distinctions, which distinctions are ultimately nothing more than the distinctions one chooses to assign to terms: cf. "Is there a Factual *a Priori?*", *Readings in Philosophical Analysis,* ed. Feigl and Sellars (New York: Appleton-Century-Crofts, 1949) pp. 277–85. There is, it is true, in the works of the phenomenologists a suspicion that the distinctions they make are derived from convictions which antecede the use of the phenomenological method.

8. In a sort of diary, Husserl recounted, in September, 1916, his decision to pursue theoretical truth as a value in preference to other values in life. Neither here nor anywhere else, however, does he justify the objectivity of the value judgment itself. Cf. "Philosophie als strenge Wissenschaft," *Logos,* I (1911), 289–341, 338.

9. "This aim or principle of the greatest possible rationality we recognize as the loftiest aim of the rational sciences," *Logische Untersuchungen,* I (4th ed.; Halle: Niemeyer, 1928), 216.

10. Husserl was convinced that the groundwork of this sort of rationality had to be firmly laid before any further advances could be made. For this reason his whole work takes on an extremely programmatic character; he saw his own function as that of assuring the possibility of advancing on solid ground.

This concludes our discussion of continental philosophy. We have discussed the origins of continental philosophy in the writings of Søren Kierkegaard and his contribution to the development of the concept of subjectivity, which is central to much continental philosophy. We have observed the development of two existentialists, Sartre and Camus, and have seen the structure of phenomenology in Lauer's account. Although not widely known by American philosophers, nonetheless it is important that the beginning students in philosophy become aware of the continental contributions to the development of Western philosophy.

NOTES

1. Søren Kierkegaard, *Point of View,* translated by Walter Lowrie (London: Oxford University Press, 1939), pp. 22–23.

2. Søren Kierkegaard, *Attack upon Christendom,* translated by Walter Lowrie (Boston: Beacon Press, 1956), p. 164.

3. Søren Kierkegaard, *Concluding Unscientific Postscript,* translated by David Swenson and Walter Lowrie (copyright ©1941, 1969, by Princeton University Press; Princeton Paperback,

1968), pp. 318-19. Reprinted by permission of Princeton University Press and the American Scandinavian Foundation.

4. Ibid., p. 315.

5. Ibid., p. 223.

6. Ibid., p. 49.

7. Ibid., p. 51.

8. Ibid., pp. 51-52.

9. Ibid., pp. 53-54.

10. Ibid., p. 55.

11. Ibid., p. 276.

12. Ibid., pp. 267-69.

13. Ibid., p. 339.

14. Ibid., pp. 18-20.

15. Ibid., pp. 261-66.

16. Ibid., pp. 226-28.

17. Ibid., pp. 238-40.

18. Copyright ©1955 by Alfred A. Knopf, Inc. Reprinted from *The Myth of Sisyphus and Other Essays,* by Albert Camus, translated by Justin O'Brien, by permission of Alfred A. Knopf, Inc.

19. Ibid., p. 19.

20. Ibid., p. 21.

21. Vincent M. Martin, *Existentialism* (Washington, D.C.: The Thomist Press, 1962), pp. 38-40. Reprinted by permission of the publisher.

22. Franz Brentano, "Psychologie vom Empirischen Standpunkte," in Robert C. Solomon, *Phenomenology and Existentialism* (New York: Harper and Row, 1972), p. 187.

Index